George Washington Slept Here

"George Washington" (James W. Gallagher) signing autographs at the thirty-fourth annual recreation of the crossing of the Delaware, Washington Crossing, Pennsylvania, Christmas, 1986

George Washington Slept Here

Colonial Revivals and American Culture 1876–1986

Karal Ann Marling

HARVARD UNIVERSITY PRESS   Cambridge, Massachusetts, and London, England   1988

Library of Congress Cataloging-in-Publication Data

Marling, Karal Ann.
  George Washington slept here : colonial revivals and American
culture, 1876–1986 / Karal Ann Marling.
      p.   cm.
  Bibliography: p.
  Includes index.
  ISBN 0-674-34951-2 (alk. paper)
  1. Washington, George, 1732–1799—Influence. 2. United States—
Popular culture. 3. Washington, George, 1732–1799—Anniversaries,
etc. I. Title.
E312.17.M3 1988   87-33026
973.9—dc19   CIP

This book about the Father of His Country

is dedicated with love to

Raymond Marling,

the father of the author

Preface

This book traces the incidence of George Washington imagery in the popular culture from 1876—when the Philadelphia Centennial Exposition replaced the Civil War Washington, a wishful symbol of national unity, with a more complex figure who both endorsed a century of material progress and expressed reservations about the price paid for it—to a cold afternoon in the 1980s when Ronald Reagan dragged Washington into his inaugural festivities as a mark of his adherence to a never-to-be-defined credo of traditional American values.

I have pursued Washington on his errant journey through a panoply of media. These include paintings, often high-cultural productions brought down to earth by the uses to which reproductions are put; mid-cult items, such as Washington profiles and silhouettes once deemed suitable for hanging in a tasteful domestic setting but now generally snickered at; and pure schlock, like a Washington luncheon plate, for which even those who can do without the superior connotations of the word "kitsch" are hard pressed to find a better term. In all but the most rarefied of historical and art historical circles, using visual evidence from every point on the spectrum of aesthetic quality is a commonplace today, and sources once considered subliterary are also gaining a toehold in the canon.

But in addition to magazine fiction, the odd historical romance, and an old silent movie in which a Revolutionary War–era father and son solemnly drape a picture of Washington with a flag and swear mute allegiance to it, in addition to portraits and statues and other more or less familiar kinds of material culture, I have also been concerned here with cultural products whose usefulness has not been universally conceded. Society balls, pageants, parade floats, the programs of civic ceremonies and patriotic exercises, and various kinds of displays of historic relics are all means through which ideas about George Washington and his world were variously created, transformed, transmitted, and understood; it is also interesting that, at any given moment in time, the most important hero is apt to be attached to whichever medium is itself the hottest.

In the late 1920s, when Washington trivia amounted to another of the crazes of the day—like miniature golf, green pepper-eating, or flagpole-sitting—public opinion polls almost always featured his solemn self, competing with Jesus Christ and Henry Ford for the title of the most significant human being in history, or ranked with "the Babe" as every kid's favorite personality. An unofficial presidential preference poll of Connecticut fifth-, sixth-, seventh-, and eighth-graders reported by the *New Yorker* in 1984, when he was coming back after a long dry spell, and the verdicts of juvenile juries were treated as sheer whimsy, put Washington in seventh place behind Reagan, Mondale, and a flock of other would-be candidates for the White House.

Inclusion in the polls was a mark of special honor in the 1920s, however, just as being the subject of a float, back at the turn of the century, conferred unique distinction. Both were mass media par excellence. The former helped everybody to be as up-to-the-minute in viewpoint as everybody else in an age of radios, phones, and teletype machines; the latter, on the eve of the advent of the silver screen, was the closest thing to a motion picture screened for thousands simultaneously in the teeming streets of the city.

So the sequence of paradigm dramas through which I trace the vicissitudes of Washington's image and influence is itself a commentary on the workings of mass culture. And even when Washington is, at some few junctures in this narrative, not quite uppermost in the thoughts of his countrymen, he is nonetheless apt to be the darling of decorators' manuals, historical belles-lettres for the genteel, or Americanization campaigns directed at unruly immigrants. The history of Washington mass culture thus intersects in meaningful ways with notions of class, ethnicity, sexual stereotypes, and social distinctions based on birth, wealth, and good taste.

However fascinating or boring one may find George Washington of Virginia, the sheer ubiquity of his persona makes him an excellent figure through which to trace out the workings of the media, the changing content of public discourse, and the private preoccupations of American society in the modern era. If Washington is not always at the top of the polls or in the deepest recesses of swelling patriot hearts, he is close to the seats of power during every one of those hundred-odd years. The more modern we become, in fact, the more desperately we cling to our Washingtons, to our old-fashioned heroes, to an imagined colonial past, to the good old days when patriots stood firm on their pedestals.

A word about the genesis of this book, a book about George Washington and much more: the details of his physical appearance, his on-again-off-again sex life, his birthplace, his childhood, his relics, and his heroic significance to the citizens of the country of which he has long been known as the official father. In response to an invitation from Kenneth Ames to say something cogent about the colonial revival at the 1981 Winterthur Museum Conference, I tried to explain the iconography of Grant Wood's several neocolonial paintings of the 1930s and thus came upon the official, multivolume report of the United States George Washington Bicentennial Commission. That agency had, in 1932, sponsored a celebration of the two hundredth anniversary of the birth of our first president and had performed its duty with such gusto as to leave almost no aspect of American daily life untouched by Washingtoniana.

And lest the man in the street question such written evidence, my rounds of the flea markets of the Upper Midwest turned up bag after box of cast-off treasures from that long-ago celebration. There were George Washington plates, plaques, and paper dolls; bookmarks, bookends, and bad novels; plaster carnival prizes, pot-metal clock ornaments, respectable bronzes, deplorable silver-plated spoons; coasters, razors, pocket knives, all manner of calendars, and framed devotional prints; and a spattering of choice Martha Washington artifacts, too.

Paul Holmer, Jeff Tordoff, and I came home from assorted shopping-mall parking lots and antique "shoppes" Sunday after Sunday loaded down with the stuff. By the time the conference was safely over, we were hooked. There were more Georges out there for the having than the Washington worshipers of '32 had ever dreamt of: metal hatchets marked "1889," Washington booklets issued free to customers by various corporations in the 1920s, even fragile bits and pieces saved from visits to the great Philadelphia Centennial Exposition of 1876. It all suggested that the national penchant for living on terms of intimacy with the person of George Washington was of somewhat longer duration than my Winterthur lecture had admitted.

At first, I thought that the nature of heroism was the key to Washington's persistence, and, with detours through Carlyle, Nietzsche, and Joseph Campbell, I worked my way back to Beowulf, by no means the greatest of the supermen to whom genealogists of the nineteenth century had traced the ancestry of the general. By the 1920s, when the so-called debunkers unwittingly revived the rich body of Washington legend, that mythology was a part of the common culture. If nobody really believed the cherry tree story—or put much stock in fearless honesty, for that matter—the broad outlines of the tale and the rest of Parson Weems's engaging fantasies were as familiar to Americans as baseball, cherry pie, Lucky Lindy, or Silent Cal, all of which, in fact, seemed to have borrowed snippets of the meaning imputed to them from the Washington cycle.

Or had the Washington of the 1920s been remade in the image of Babe Ruth? Divagations on the creation of heroes in the works of

Daniel Boorstin, Warren Susman, Sidney Hook, Norman Mailer, and Tom Wolfe did not resolve the chicken-and-egg problem to my satisfaction but did make me doubt anew that any all-purpose theory would cover the astonishing variety of reasons for people's desire to purchase and use Lindbergh lamps, JFK-in-heaven-with-Martin-and-Bobby tapestries, and George Washington ashtrays.

By this time, with Washington loot spilling out of the closets and more arriving daily from solicitous friends, I knew that my inquiry would have to move beyond the Depression years—beyond "my" period, that is. But some tentative conclusions were mandated by the curve plotting the incidence of souvenirs, speeches, magazine articles, movies, cartoons, ads, sober histories, and other samples of Washingtoniana in the fifty-year period centered on the 1930s. Much to my surprise, for instance, the 1932 bicentennial did not represent a peak in national interest in the Pater Patriae. Instead, it was a kind of hillock on a high plateau of enthusiasm that stretched backward into the mists of the turn of the century but fell off sharply, in the opposite direction, after 1939, when an inflated statue of Washington lurked near the futuristic Trylon and Perisphere on the grounds of the New York World's Fair. As a meaningful and potent symbol, *that* George Washington, I thought I was prepared to argue, had "died" just before World War II. The hitherto ever-popular Washington of myth and legend was, of course, a casualty of the baby boom and a postwar technology with no further need for the stoic hero of Valley Forge.

If the end of the story looked easy, the beginning promised to be impossible. With the encouragement of Jules Prown and Lillian Miller, however, I applied to Winterthur for a grant that would give me access to the museum's superb library of books bearing on American material culture of the eighteenth and nineteenth centuries, books that themselves, in many cases, dated to the period of Henry Francis du Pont's collecting career, and thus promised, I thought, to disclose just why the early twentieth century treasured the memory of Washington and the furnishings of his day. As the Louise Crowninshield Fellow, I had the pleasure of spending the spring of 1985, including a gloriously stormy Washington's Birthday, holed up with the Winterthur collection and with the group of people most likely to challenge hasty conclusions about the death or birth of culture heroes.

Ken Ames guided me to trade catalogues full of George Washington highboys, and dated the undatable. Ian Quimby told me to read Alice Morse Earle and thus set me on the trail of an influential group of fin de siècle lady-antiquarians who also retailed Washington love stories. I came home so intrigued with the Washington revival launched at the 1876 Philadelphia fair that the permutations and convolutions of the Washington symbol in the twentieth century, the erstwhile focus of this book, seemed for the moment both obvious and a little meager.

But in the meantime Bob Gambone, Tracy Smith, and Kate Roberts, my graduate research assistants, and a variety of friends, and friends of friends, fascinated by Washington—Anedith Nash, John Jenson, Marilyn McGriff, Sue Beckham, Colleen Sheehy, Tim Garvey, Sidney and Ada Simon, John and Claire Steyaert, Marion Nelson, Joe Bensen, Rob Silberman, Tom Trow, Ken Ellison, Pat Hemmis, and Jim Gearity come to mind, and lots of clippings and pictures were left in my mailbox by anonymous well-wishers—had swollen the collection of modern material to such proportions that it became necessary to write about it or move out.

What American history means, exactly how it signifies, and why it counts have been the questions implicit in all my writing, and this book on Washington is no exception. Michael Kammen, Warren Susman, and Gene Wise wrote the texts that helped me to frame those queries; Professor Kammen has also been a tireless correspondent whose fat envelopes over the past several years have bulged with bibliographic references, pictures of George in various of his manifestations, and words of gentle encouragement. Along with Lillian Miller and Jim Dennis, he also read my manuscript during its evolution and offered sound advice. To be sure, the defects in the finished product reflect my stubbornness, not the quality of their counsel.

I have mentioned above some of the others whose acts of kindness and comradeship made my task easier. Melinda Ward, of the Walker Art Center; Walter Leedy, of Cleveland State University; Helen Cooper, of the Yale Art Gallery; Frank Bergon and Tom McHugh, of Vassar College; and Kate Johnson, of the Minneapolis Institute of Arts, all gave me the opportunity to lecture on aspects of my Washington research. That in turn brought in more anonymous parcels and provided the stimulus for vigorous and richly deserved criticism at early stages in the project.

Camera at the ready, Joe Bensen scouted America's vacationlands on my behalf in search of touristic Washingtoniana. Eric Mortenson took pictures of the three-dimensional objects and even provided a pick-up and delivery service for the improbable artifacts that he photographed with respect and sensitivity; a generous research grant from the Graduate School of the University of Minnesota paid for most of his work. The university also allowed me the sabbatical leave during which some of the research and all of the writing were completed.

Sue and Phil Kendall provided room and board in Philadelphia as I was en route to Winterthur, where Michele Bogart, one of my "roommates" at the Golf Cottage, and Kate Hutchins, our frequent lunch companion, dispensed good cheer on dark days. At one particularly low ebb, Peter Murphy and Colleen Sheehy baked a terrific cake in the shape of Washington; eating George with relish, as we did almost before the frosting had set, gave me the strength to get on with it.

And Lindsay Waters, my good friend and editor at Harvard University Press, kept me at it through several years of attempting to find easier things to do. He helped me try, in the pages that follow, to be as honest as George Washington is supposed to have been.

Contents

George Washington Slept Here

Two Prayers in the Snow

1

Colonial Culture in the 1980s

Washington as a Secular Icon

The attendant ceremonies were preempted by cold weather and snow, but Ronald Reagan's second inaugural address, as it was reported in the papers and the weekly magazines, was full of vintage Washingtoniana matched to the political season and the temperatures in the nation's capital. Reagan opened his speech with the image of President-elect Washington resting his right hand on the Bible for the first solemn oath of office, and concluded with a heart-rending picture of General Washington falling "to his knees in the hard snow of Valley Forge" to pray.[1]

The first incident was true enough. In 1889, at New York City's ceremonial recreation of the oath-taking, the same Bible was laid reverently upon a blue plush cushion atop a "richly carved ebony table" that once belonged to Chancellor Livingston (he administered the oath on April 30, 1789), and the whole ensemble of relics was placed by the elbow of President Harrison, who, seated in "an ancient-looking mahogany chair—the very one in which Washington sat a century ago"—presided over the event from a platform built at the corner of Wall and Nassau Streets. The intersection was the actual site of Washington's inauguration, a hallowed spot now marked by a gigantic bronze statue of the first president that loomed over his successor, the antique chair, the old table, the velvet cushion, and the precious Bible (Figure 1.1).[2] Borrowed from St. John's Masonic Lodge No. 1 in 1889, the Bible had been hastily borrowed in 1789, too, when none could be found within the precincts of Federal Hall, and according to tradition, Washington had bent over the open book at the conclusion of the phrase "So—help—me—God!" and kissed the holy pages.[3]

1.1
The Inaugural Masonic Bible, upon which George Washington took the oath of office at Federal Hall, New York, April 30, 1789

So began the American nation, in a seemly gesture of piety—or so the fortieth president, a man with a large political debt to fundamentalist preachers, strongly suggested at the outset of his address. But if Reagan's sentimental and self-serving word-picture of George Washington with his hand on the Scriptures was essentially accurate, his closing portrait of the general kneeling on the cold, hard ground of Valley Forge, entreating heaven to protect the Continental Army and bless the United States to come, was purest fancy. The fiction, to be sure, was widespread. It even had the semiofficial sanction of the U.S. Postal Service, whose much-beloved Christmas stamp for 1977 honored the bicentennial of the sojourn at Valley Forge with a treacly likeness of the praying patriot, his head bowed, his three-cornered hat discarded in a snowbank, an adaptation of the Washington's Birthday cover of the *Saturday Evening Post* for 1935, designed by J. C. Leyendecker, better known as the inventor of the "Arrow Collar Man" (Figures 1.2, 1.3).[4]

1.2
Christmas stamp designed by Steven Dohanos, 1977

Nor was the Christmas design for 1977 the first postal tribute to the prayer in the snow that never happened: the red two-cent stamp issued in 1928 to commemorate the 150th anniversary of Washington's winter encampment fleshed out the story with a wealth of convincing detail (Figure 1.4).[5] Washington at prayer, deep in the snowy woods in this version, was the centerpiece of a tiny composition that also included, at his left hand, the general's horse, with its head lowered in dumb solemnity, and a clump of ragged rebels huddled around a campfire. At his right, a house appeared in the distance along with a shadowy figure, apparently spying on Washington's private devotions. The onlooker hidden in the bushes, the house, the horse, and the rest all came from a famous 1866 print by John McRae (Figure 1.5), after a once-famous picture by Henry Brueckner—a picture so well known in Reagan's youth that writers of the 1920s and 1930s had merely to allude to it in passing as "the Brueckner."[6]

Never mind that the clear-eyed, no-nonsense debunkers of the day thought "the idea of this two-fisted man going about bellowing in the woods . . . grotesque."[7] Never mind that the meticulous *New York Times,* in the special rotogravure section published in 1932 in honor of the bicentennial of Washington's birth, took care to caption its reproduction of the work, "The Prayer at Valley Forge . . . the Legendary Incident in the Winter of 1777–78."[8] Despite cavils and caveats, "the Brueckner" fostered unquestioning belief in the incident depicted. The soldiers and the horse were the homely stuff of real life; as for the fellow peering through the branches at the spectacle, he was an eyewitness to history whose act of observation guaranteed the authenticity of the pictorial document. He was Isaac Potts and, so the story went, he was a Tory (or a pacifist) and a practicing Quaker—a man, in other words, with no apparent reason to tell lies favorable to the character of Washington.

1.3
J. C. Leyendecker, Washington's Birthday cover for the *Saturday Evening Post*, 1935

One Isaac Potts had indeed rented to Washington the stone farm-house that served as his headquarters at Valley Forge and as the background of the painting/print/stamp. Physical evidence of Potts's existence was provided by the building, "saved" in 1879 by a committee of ladies known as the Centennial Association of Valley Forge, formed in the flush of patriotic fervor attendant upon the great Philadelphia Centennial Exposition of 1876.[9] When the National Society of Daughters of the American Revolution (DAR) was founded in 1890, the same ladies joined en masse, bringing their shrine and the elaborate cycle of myth it supported into fresh national prominence.[10]

If Isaac Potts was a genuine historical character whose house and the roomfuls of period furniture installed therein by the DAR both attested to his corporeal reality, his glimpse of the praying Washington was a fiction promulgated by the infamous Parson Weems, inventor of the "I cannot tell a lie" fable of little George and the cherry tree.[11] The prayer-in-the-snow story first appeared in an article Weems wrote for *The Federalist* in 1804 and proved so arresting that the author incorporated the incident into the eighth edition of his perennially popular *Life of George Washington, with Curious Anecdotes Equally Honorable to Himself and Exemplary to His Young Countrymen.*[12]

"In the winter of '77," he wrote, in a once-upon-a-time tone,

while Washington . . . lay encamped at Valley Forge, a certain good old FRIEND, of the respectable family and name of Potts, if I mistake not, had occasion to pass through the woods near headquarters. Treading his way along in the

1.4
Commemorative stamp issued in honor of the Valley Forge Sesquicentennial, 1928

1.5
John McRae, *The Prayer at Valley Forge*, 1866, engraving after a painting by Henry Brueckner

1.6
Lambert Sachs, *General Washington at Prayer at Valley Forge*, 1854

venerable grove, suddenly he heard the sound of a human voice. . . . As he approached the spot with a cautious step, whom should he behold, in a dark natural bower of ancient oaks, but the commander in chief of the American armies on his knees at prayer! Motionless with surprise, friend Potts continued on the place till the general, having ended his devotions, arose; and, with a countenance of angel[ic] serenity, retired to headquarters.[13]

As Mason Weems tells the story, the "FRIEND" scurries home and tells his wife, Sarah, that now, at last, he can support the Revolutionary War: "Thee knows that I always thought the sword and the gospel utterly inconsistent; and that no man could be a soldier and a christian at the same time. But George Washington has this day convinced me of my mistake." Then he sees a prophetic vision in which heaven answers the prayers of the worthy general. "If George Washington be not a man of God, I am greatly deceived," Weems makes Potts exclaim, "and still more shall I be deceived if God do not, through him, work out a great salvation for America."[14]

Old Bishop Meade, the Virginia historian who knew Weems well enough to call him one of "nature's oddities" (and whose consuming interest in matters pertaining to Washington led him to install the "hind seat" of the great man's English coach in his study "in the form of a sofa"), was openly skeptical of most of the edifying tales manufactured by his clerical comrade. But because he, too, was eager to promote certain moral causes by associating them somehow with the first president, the bishop wanted Washington to have said those chilly prayers. "It is firmly believed," Meade wrote in 1857, "that when in crowded lodgings at Valley Forge, where every thing was unfavorable to private devotions, his frequent visits to a neighboring wood were for this purpose."[15] That tacit endorsement of the prayer-in-the-snow incident, coming as it did from a respected clergyman, contributed to a resurgence of interest in the theme and so to the genesis of "the Brueckner."

Before the Civil War, Washington's prayer was most often treated as an edifying parable for children, a staple of herobiographies for the young, Sunday school tracts, and schoolbooks: the 1832 centennial of Washington's birth inspired a flood of such literature aimed at the juvenile market.[16] Adult versions of the scenario were identified, somewhat reluctantly, as myth. George Lippard's 1847 story of Washington tempted in the snowy woods, like Christ in the desert, by Sir William Howe—the satanic Howe offers his American foe a prominent place in the British peerage if he will betray the rebel cause—is derived from Weems, for instance, down to the detail of the Tory eyewitness concealed in the brush. But Lippard's book was titled *Washington and His Generals; or, Legends of the Revolution* and attributed the more fantastic and far-fetched incidents presented to a body of "tradition," without absolute claims of authenticity.[17]

The concordance between his Washington story and the biblical account of the prayer of Jesus in Gethsemane was noted by Lippard and gave early illustrators of the theme suitable compositional prototypes. An 1854 painting by Lambert Sachs, *General Washington at Prayer at Valley Forge,* for example, shows the great leader with one knee bent and one arm outstretched to the Father in a gesture of supplication: Washington is a new Christ in the Garden of America, a lush, leafy place, a kind of snowless Eden (Figure 1.6).[18] With the deepening of sectional conflict and acrimony toward midcentury, however, Washington became an important symbol of union, the prayerful, anxious father of a nation indivisible: the mythical aspects of his life, and most especially of those key points in his biography when nationhood seemed to hang in the balance, became persuasive fact.

In Benson Lossing's widely read *Pictorial Field-Book of the Revolution* of 1859, insubstantial legend hardened into the matter-of-fact declaration that Washington, motivated by "one holy sentiment—*love of country,*" prayed for his country-to-be in its hour of crisis and was observed doing so.[19] Accordingly, to the image of that Potts-like observer who testified to the veracity of the incident, graphic renderings of the scene conceived during the Civil War era added such gritty historical detail as snowbanks, leafless trees, shivering Continentals, and Washington's faithful horse. "The Brueckner," as well as later redactions of the prayer-in-the-snow motif by such artists as Alonzo Chappel and Charles Currier, were propaganda pieces, arguing first for the preservation and then for the restoration of the United States of America that George Washington and God had called into being in the cold, white-clad woods of Valley Forge (Figures 1.7, 1.8).

In 1880 the relationship between the praying episode and contemporary events was revealed without apology in an article published by Wesley Bradshaw in the *National Tribune* and reprinted frequently thereafter. "You have doubtless heard the story of Washington's going to the thicket to pray," says the ninety-nine-year-old Anthony Sherman, who purportedly gave his testimony to Bradshaw on the steps of Independence Hall on the Fourth of July, 1859; "I want to tell you an incident of Washington's life—one which no one alive knows of except myself; and which, if you live, you will before long see verified." With that preamble, the old man launched into a graphic description of "General Washington's vision," the result of an angelic visitation to the snows of Valley Forge. As Washington prayed, a celestial being appeared before him and, addressing him as "Son of the Republic," disclosed the future of America—the settlement of the continent, from Atlantic to Pacific; the Civil War; and finally an awful invasion by foreign foes, repulsed by divine intervention on behalf of a nation in which every "child of the Republic" has learned to live, like Washington, "for his God, his land, and his Union."[20]

1.7
Alonzo Chappel, *George Washington Praying at Valley Forge*

1.8.
Charles Currier lithograph, *Washington at Prayer*

Old Mr. Sherman, a living link with the heroic past, maintained that he had heard about the vision from the lips of Washington himself. Like Isaac Potts, then, he became a guarantor of history. But since the Sherman story and the Weems account neatly reinforced each other, the paradoxical effect of this fresh piece of firsthand evidence was to diminish the role of the eyewitness. If the story of Washington's open-air piety was unquestionably true in its broad outlines, it could be presented without those subsidiary vignettes of earnest observers lurking in bushes. The historical narrative of Washington's prayer at Valley Forge could become a sacred icon instead, a holy card of American civil religion.

One of the pillars of that half-secular, quasi-official form of dilute Protestantism sometimes called civil religion was the Young Men's Christian Association. The YMCA's West Side branch on New York's West Fifty-seventh Street found itself, in 1907, at the eye of a storm of controversy over the first modern version of the prayer in the snow to dispense with scraps of true-to-life genre and portraits of onlookers vouching for the truthfulness of the image. At issue was a massive bronze plaque entitled *Washington at Prayer at Valley Forge*, by J. E. Kelly, a sculptor best known for the reliefs of Molly Pitcher and other episodes from Revolutionary history on the grandiose monument to the Battle of Monmouth in Freehold, New Jersey.[21] The YMCA plaque in New York was similar in style, noteworthy for a realism so extreme that reporters for the local papers could count the stitches in the three vertical ribs on the backs of Washington's kid gloves (Figure 1.9).[22]

Kelly also prided himself on his historical realism: he had conducted "researches [on the prayer] among the less well-known narratives of the Valley Forge encampment of 1777–78, and was fully convinced of its historic basis and authenticity on all points."[23] Because he believed in the reality of the incident, the sculptor found it easy to jettison the traditional iconography, which included the Potts figure witnessing and responding to the scene on behalf of the viewer: the viewer is Kelly's eyewitness to the severely restricted repertory of details that signify an event at once miraculous and self-evidently true. The horse, the hat, the trees, and the kneeling figure with the true-to-life gloves tell it all.

The iconographic purge also suggests, of course, that the story had grown famous and familiar—that most people needed a minimum of clues to identify the scene and grasp its import. So Kelly could dispense with the rigid frontal view of Washington's head derived from Gilbert Stuart's famous portrait and used by most of his predecessors to facilitate recognition of the hero. Because he could risk a profile view (modeled on the famous Houdon bust at Mount Vernon), Kelly's is the first praying Washington to kneel weightily and humbly on both knees, without the tortuous convolutions needed to combine a frontal

1.9
James E. Kelly, *Washington at Prayer at Valley Forge*, 1904; from a photolithograph framed for commercial distribution, ca. 1932–1942

rendering of the face with some suggestion of spatial recession in the legs. Washington's prayerful pose was as real as the prayer itself, as real as the ribs on the backs of his gloves.

Installed in a corridor of the Y on November 26, 1904, in the spirit of Thanksgiving Day exercises, Kelly's bas-relief was commissioned by John J. Clancy, a patriotic real estate man (he was a member of New York's Washington Colonial Guards and Lafayette Post No. 140 of the GAR—Grand Army of the Republic) with an office on Broadway, near Fifty-eighth Street.[24] Because the plaque had been well received, its proud sponsor decided to present a replica of *George Washington at Prayer at Valley Forge* to the Sub-Treasury, that most hallowed of all federal buildings, built on the site of Washington's inauguration. Clancy wanted to affix his donation to the base of the easternmost granite column along the Wall Street façade during a gala Washington's Birthday celebration orchestrated by himself. First, however, the Treasury Department balked. The duplicate was duly inscribed—"Presented by the Lafayette Post, Feb. 22, 1907, in behalf of the donor, J. J. Clancy"—but according to Assistant Treasurer Hamilton Fish, "the name of no living man could adorn the front of the Sub-Treasury." As Valentine's Day approached, therefore, the offending legend was excised. Then, suddenly, another rule came to light that excluded replicas of original artworks from Treasury Department facilities. Days before the scheduled unveiling, President Theodore Roosevelt, drawn into the controversy by his local connections, was forced to uphold the ban.

Meanwhile, Clancy and his friends sat around the Seventy-first Regiment Armory scratching their heads. "I'll tell you what we'll do with it," said one. "We'll go down to Mount Vernon next summer and put it on the base of the flagstaff there." But it was Clancy himself who saved the day. "If they won't let us put up a replica, I'll get them an original," he declared, swapping plaques with the YMCA.[25] And the show on the front stoop of the Sub-Treasury went on as scheduled, at noon on the twenty-second of February, with the J. E. Kelly original wreathed in roses; one "stalwart, grizzled patriot in a Guard's uniform of buff and blue" standing at attention; "the blare of bugles and . . . the clatter of drum sticks" on the frosty air; and "a great trooping swarm of young cherry tree unbelievers from the public schools, waving American flags and cheering."[26]

Like the ceremony, the plaque was a great success. It was the delight of the sculptor's later years to see facsimiles installed in churches, colleges, schools, and historical societies, and to autograph copies of the several prints depicting his most famous work.[27] A postcard version, still sold today, recounts Potts's prophecy of victory and bears this caption: "Lest We Forget—the Value of Prayer." The association between prayer and warfare, between prayer and national crisis, between God and nationalism, accounts for the revival of the image during the Depression, when postcard reproductions of Kelly's relief, flanked by Old Glory, were cased in red-white-and-blue frames for distribution to loyal customers of Midwestern feed lots and hardware stores, and J. C. Leyendecker designed his prayer-in-the-snow cover for the *Saturday Evening Post.*[28]

By luck, unerring instinct for the pungent political metaphor, or good market research, Ronald Reagan had, in telling his Washington story during the snowy winter of 1985, seized upon one of the most potent yet malleable symbols in the collective consciousness of the nation. He had summoned up the Washington of Valley Forge, the prayerful warrior, the unifier, the protective father of us all, the omniscient elder, as old as America and wise beyond his years (Figure 1.10). Reagan's inaugural parable, to be sure, was about himself; the president pointedly did not invoke the little prig with the hatchet, the ardent swain of old Virginia, the hot-tempered, hot-blooded soldier, or the aristocratic Excellency bowing to guests at his wife's Friday levees. And by choosing the particular Washington he did, Reagan invited his countrymen to reflect upon the kinship between the oldest and the newest acts in the great American drama, both introduced by tableaux vivants of strong, paternal men, one in the knee breeches of 1778, one in the thermal long johns of 1985, come to a snowy Armageddon to do battle for the Lord. Colonial history shaped the present or, at the very least, helped us to understand it. Perhaps the past was really a kind of story, like the story of Washington's prayer in the snow, a story every generation rewrote anew to account for its choices, its heroes—a story told to rehearse the unfolding chapters of its own autobiography.

1.10
Prayer Room window, adjacent to the rotunda, U.S. Capitol, 1955

Gilbert Stuart's Portrait of Washington

The colonial historian Michael Kammen argues that, in different ways and for different reasons, American novelists, artists, poets, editorial writers, and politicians have consistently de-Revolutionized the Revolution Washington led.[29] But as the social historian Warren Susman once suggested, historical periods and figures also have a kind of perverse half-life of their own.[30] In 1985, Ronald Reagan expected the public at large to grasp his allusions to Washington; he even counted on a degree of mass familiarity with the Washington symbols cast up by the sporadic colonial revivals of the nineteenth and twentieth centuries. Connectedness to an American heritage, whether real or imaginary, was desirable and feasible in 1985. In 1965 or 1915 or 1895, that enterprise was accorded a different value, and the terms of the dialectic between now and long ago were different, too.[31] At selected moments in the ongoing life of his countrymen, Lincoln, in his guise as the Common Man or the Western Rail-Splitter or the Great Emancipator, might be preferred to the stately Washington by the speechwriters. Furniture manufacturers might copy the ornate chairs of the Louis XIV period rather than the rectilinear Hepplewhite sideboard in the family dining room at Mount Vernon. Painters might abjure history altogether and depict a future world of abstract form and pure color instead.[32]

In 1985, colonial history and Washington *did* mean something, especially when a popular president summoned up his memory in a voice warmed and softened by emotion. The speaker vouched for the veracity of the images he summoned up. Likewise, in 1880, a report that Washington had prophesied the Civil War on the basis of a heaven-sent vision made an appeal to the skeptical on the basis of the origin of the tale. It was attributed to old Mr. Sherman, who swore, on the steps of Independence Hall, that he had heard it from the lips of Washington himself. And as a cultural idol, George Washington clearly counted for more when the memory of the living man still persisted among eyewitnesses to colonial history. The panicky sense that Washington and his era were about to slip away into nothingness was strongest at midcentury. Sherman's testimony on Washington's vision was solicited in 1859. In 1864 the Reverend Elias Brewster Hillard published *The Last Men of the Revolution,* a compilation of biographies and photographs of the survivors of Washington's army, accompanied by interviews with the few remaining worthies.

This spate of interest in the maunderings of aged Continentals also coincided with the upheaval of the Civil War—the second revolution—and with a wave of nostalgia for an idealized Old Republic in the ancient days of the nation's forefathers.[33] Their war, unlike the later one, seemed unambiguously noble, heroic, and "right." Their vanishing world seemed simpler, purer, better somehow. His was, Hillard saw with painful clarity, "the last generation that will be connected by living links with the great period in which our national independence was achieved. . . . Our own are the last eyes that will look on men who looked on Washington; our ears the last that will hear the living voices of those who heard his words."[34]

In a preelectronic age, far less inclined than our own to believe in what cannot be seen and touched, the role of the eyewitness to a rapidly receding past was crucial in holding fast to the substance of that firsthand experience. By his questions Hillard sought, with disappointing results, to visualize the palpable forms of the Founding Fathers at second hand, through the rheumy eyes of the last of the pensioners. "Was [George Washington] as fine a looking man as he is reported to have been?" he asked the venerable Samuel Downing of Edinburgh, New York. "Oh!" exclaimed that patriarch, lifting up both hands, "but you never got a smile out of him. He was a nice man. We loved him. They'd sell their lives for him."[35]

1.11
Gilbert Stuart, *George Washington* (the Athenaeum Portrait), 1796

1.12
Carl H. Schmolze, *Washington Sitting for His Portrait to Gilbert Stuart,* 1858

As a cogent account of the physiognomy of Washington, Downing's reply was vague, but its value did not lie in details. Insofar as he had already entered the chilly pantheon of marble heroes, Washington had grown awesome, remote, and unreal to a Civil War generation that needed a convincing symbol of unity regained and bucolic peace restored. In the creation of such a symbol—and the many illustrators of Parson Weems's prayer-in-the-snow fable grasped the fact instinctively—the mere existence of the observing eyewitness was as important as any testimony he might give: Potts and his ilk, regardless of the content of their recollections, made Washington and the events of *his* bygone generation real. However watery and dimmed by the years, eyes that once saw Washington in the flesh brought the heroic age very close to an unheroic present.

So when Hillard asked the old veterans if Washington was "as fine a looking man" as the writers said, he was not really soliciting a word-portrait of lips, blue eyes, and fabled false teeth; the writers could and did conjure up their stories about Washington's looks out of the merest gossamer nothings. What Hillard really wanted was assurance that a flesh-and-blood Washington had existed, and that the flawed, flesh-and-blood mortals of his own time could aspire to emulate his deeds.

The Civil War directed attention to the corporeal Washington, a solid, human being in imminent danger of dissolving into myth. Between the great centennial celebration of 1876 and the turn of the century, a generation of materialists, moved to belief by what they could see and hold in their hands, became increasingly concerned with the physical particulars of that famous person. Americans who verified the reality of the Civil War from Mathew Brady's photographs, and the plausibility of Hillard's transcripts from his photographs of the aged Revolutionary veterans, began to ask strange new questions about the Father of His Country. What did Washington look like? *Really* look like? Gilbert Stuart's daughter was induced to speak to the issue in *Scribner's*; collectors of rare Washington engravings denigrated one another's prize pieces in the public prints; and whole turgid books were written on the subject.[36]

The point had been moot at least since 1823, when John Neal, in his novel *Randolph,* declared that "if George Washington should appear on earth, just as he sat to Stuart, I am sure that he would be treated as an imposter, when compared with Stuart's likeness of him, unless he produced his credentials."[37] Gilbert Stuart's portrait with the unfinished background, the so-called Athenaeum Portrait of 1796, had by midcentury become not only iconic but irksome to such commentators as Nathaniel Hawthorne, who thought the prunes-and-prisms likeness trotted out whenever an image of the hero was required had made Washington into an inhuman wraith, a disembodied portrait head (Figure 1.11). "Did any body ever see Washington nude?" he asked, with a fine rhetorical flourish, in 1853. "It is inconceivable. He had no nakedness, but I imagine he was born with his clothes on, and his hair powdered, and made a stately bow on his first appearance in the world."[38] And Thackeray, who had collected Washington pictures in the course of research for his popular historical novel *The Virginians,* is said to have shown a copy of the Stuart portrait to his friends with this remark: "Look at him. Does he not look as if he had just said a good, stupid thing?"[39]

The wealth of disparaging comment on the Stuart portrait hints at its ubiquity and, in a backhanded way, helps to account for the several nineteenth-century history paintings showing Stuart painting Washington in his Germantown studio.[40] The definitive treatment of this confrontation came in 1858, with Carl H. Schmolze's *Washington Sitting for His Portrait to Gilbert Stuart,* in which Washington, rigidly facing toward the painter's left in canonical Athenaeum fashion, seems too uncomfortable to be diverted by Martha, Nelly Custis, and an army officer—probably Henry Knox—while Stuart, seated at his easel on the opposite edge of the picture, discusses his plans with Washington's companions (Figure 1.12).[41] The painting is a complex statement. As Mark Thistlethwaite has demonstrated, it argues for the preeminence of the American artist as a recorder of native history; the homage to Stuart, that is, implicitly criticizes a recent decision of Congress to commission foreign-born artists—including Emanuel Leutze, of *Washington Crossing the Delaware* fame—to complete a cycle of historical murals in the U.S. Capitol building.[42]

It is also, of course, an acknowledgment of the almost mythic status of Stuart's potent icon, and another expression of the desperate veneration for Washington, author and symbol of national identity, widespread in the years preceding the Civil War. But the treatment of the subject, with its wealth of genre detail and the assembled cast of witnesses to Stuart's act of observation, stresses above all else the documentary reliability of the Athenaeum Portrait and the homey intimacy of the occasion.

The bloodless icon is both verified and humanized in Schmolze's canvas and in J. L. G. Ferris's even more cozy *Painter and President* (subtitled "Gilbert Stuart Painting the Athenaeum Portrait of Washington"), a work created, it appears, between 1916 and 1920 but little appreciated until the observances of the 1932 bicentennial of Washington's birth landed the picture on giveaway calendars and in the color supplement pages of popular magazines (Figure 1.13).[43] Schmolze and Ferris were both Philadelphians, with a natural interest in the history of their city. To paint such histories, to pay tribute to a predecessor's greatest commission, was a respectable artistic undertaking in the 1850s, when Schmolze was looking into the details of Stuart's sittings.

1.13
Bicentennial commemorative calendar for 1932, manufactured by Brown and Bigelow of St. Paul, and featuring J. L. G. Ferris's *Painter and President*

To do so after the turn of the century, when musty history painting had yielded to incipient modernism, was another matter. Jean Leon Gerome Ferris, who trained under Bouguereau and was named for M. J. L. Gérôme, was, like them, an old-fashioned academician. From 1900 until his death thirty years later, as academic art completed its fall from favor, Ferris worked ceaselessly on what came to be known as the Archive of '76—seventy-six enormous historical machines, all copyrighted, a substantial number of which depicted Washington and his contemporaries. This amazing body of work was exhibited first in the chamber in Independence Hall where Washington was inaugurated in 1793, and later in Congress Hall, before passing into the public domain and the collection of the Smithsonian's division of history, just in time for the bicentennial year.[44]

In the 1920s and 1930s, at the height of the vogue for buying "colonial"-style living room suites from Grand Rapids and mounting George and Martha Washington pageants to mark patriotic observances, Ferris's eye for the telling detail served him well. Schmolze had imagined the Stuart atelier as a dim place, with a few dusty busts in the corner, enlivened mainly by the pleated trim on the ladies' sober gowns. But the studio according to Ferris is a place not unlike the living room of one of his viewers: the turnings on Stuart's gateleg table, the gilded curves of his looking glass, his mismatched chairs (one Cromwellian, the other Philadelphia Chippendale), are period "antiques," lovingly treated and positioned for easy recognition. The costumes are bright, attractive, and arranged so that the sorts of satin slippers, bonnets, fans, eyeglasses, and buckles most often displayed as relics of the Revolutionary era are clearly visible.

At least part of the pleasure the painting brings is the joy of figuring out from personal experience the import of the persons and objects depicted. Just as the viewer is invited to compare a lacy shawl or a green glass bottle with photographs of similar artifacts in the current issue of the *Saturday Evening Post* and with the colonial reproductions advertised in its pages, so too Ferris implicates his audience in the painting by including two views of Washington: the Athenaeum Portrait on the easel before Gilbert Stuart, and the real live Washington, facing in the opposite direction to catch a glimpse of his likeness.[45] It was the viewer himself—or, more likely, judging from the cluttered domesticity of Ferris's work, the viewer *her*self—who recognized the real Washington in this uncanonical, eyes-right guise. The viewer thus became a modern-day Isaac (or Sarah) Potts, a living eyewitness to history.

During the 1932 celebration and, indeed, throughout most of the half-century before it, Stuart's portrait was known to most Americans in one of two forms. Currency was the principal vehicle of transmission. Stuart's Washington was the face on the dollar bill, from the day

1.14
"The little red stamp," with Stuart's portrait of George Washington; part of the 1932 bicentennial commemorative issue of twelve portrait stamps

the government began issuing paper money in the 1860s. In 1923, without ado or explanation, the image was suddenly reversed: thereafter the banknote Washington, like the seated model in Ferris's painting, always faced to the observer's right.[46] The change troubled no one. Besides, the Stuart was properly aligned on the little red stamp that moved the bulk of the nation's personal mail (Figure 1.14). Since the 1880s, a Washington portrait printed in red had identified the stamp used for mailing a letter first class. The 1903 series, for instance, had featured an adaptation of the Athenaeum Portrait matrixed in a shield of stars and stripes. The special twelve-stamp set issued for the bicentennial allowed the postal patron to compare the two-cent Stuart—in red, of course—with lesser-known representations by Charles Willson Peale, Saint-Memin, Trumbull, and Houdon.[47]

And the official United States George Washington Bicentennial Commission recirculated, as an exercise for third- and fourth-grade classes, a well-known Sam Walter Foss poem called "I'm the Little Red Stamp," which called for little boys to dress up in sandwich boards made of colored manila paper and to act out a remarkably pugnacious rhymed playlet in tribute to the Washington icon:

> I'm the little red stamp with George Washington's picture;
> And I go wherever I may,
> To any spot in George Washington's land;
> And I go by the shortest way.
> And the guns of wrath would clear my path,
> A thousand guns at need,
> Of the hands that should dare to block my course,
> Or slacken my onward speed.
>
> Stand back! Hands off Uncle Sam's mail!
> Stand back there! Back! I say;
> For the little red stamp with George Washington's picture
> Must have the right of way.[48]

Washington by the Hearth with Betsy Ross

The mass production of George Washington images was, it can be argued, part of a steadily mounting tendency to domesticate him. In the late nineteenth century, pictures of Gilbert Stuart painting Washington in a familial setting were given added substance and resonance by the creation of Betsy Ross, a heroine who allowed some of Washington's charisma to be transferred to women and their home-centered work for the national good. The Betsy Ross myth and the whole spectrum of Washington-related activities for children (planned by women educators) contrived to create a more personable, even lovable, hero. Thus teachers' manuals of the 1932 bicentennial period are crammed with ideas for instilling patriotism in the young through the celebration of elaborate rites based on the colorful canon of Washington apocrypha. When small boys were not disguised as postage stamps or crossing let's-pretend rivers muffled in tablecloths, pedagogues liked to see them in little knee breeches, swinging tinfoil hatchets at cardboard cherry trees and declaiming verses on the theme of truthfulness (Figure 1.15).[49] But what to do with the little girls in the meantime was something of a problem, given the lack of exciting moments from later colonial history in which females figured prominently.

One ingenious authoress equipped seven girls with little hatchets of their own; as the lead characters in "What Should Have Happened" brandished their weapons, however, they denounced George Washington for his act of juvenile vandalism against the cherry tree and declared that had *they* been on the spot, they would have chopped some firewood instead, and made dried-apple pies for dinner.[50] Another instructress reminded young ladies in verse that when they wore colonial costumes, they also put on certain grown-up responsibilities:

> Yet take care, children, that you wear,
>   Not only clothes of ancient days,
> But manners of those gracious dames,
>   Who won all by their gentle ways. . . .

1.15
John McRae, *"Father, I Can Not Tell a Lie; I Cut the Tree,"* 1867 engraving after a painting by G. G. White

> This hand which holds a painted fan
> > Must work, that tired hands may rest;
> Since Martha Washington, you know,
> > Could spin and weave at want's request.[51]

Worthy sentiments, those, to be sure, but a bit dull, considering that the boys got to tell lies and stand up in rowboats! The compensation, perhaps, came in the sheer fun of playing dress-up in cotton-wool wigs and stiff panniers, even if the ladies-in-training, once bedecked in their colonial finery, did little but pantomime a "colonial dames' tea party" or assume comely, Martha Washington attitudes on the fringes of all-male theatricals (Figure 1.16).

By the 1950s, when I went to grammar school, George Washington playlets were a thing of the past: anything that involved liberating little hoodlums from their desks, to wreak God knows what havoc on their surroundings, was interdicted at all times. Costumes were out, too, because some families lacked the wherewithal to supply them. February 22 was still a major school holiday, however, on a par with Halloween and Valentine's Day, the other fixed dates on the festival calendar that were celebrated in the classroom with special treats and decorations.[52] But the usual complement of witches and hearts was no match for the sheer quantity of commemorative stuff turned out by deskbound student labor in honor of Washington's Birthday.

I remember owning a holiday stencil book during those years, much prized by teachers and classmates alike for its wealth of Washington profiles, five-pointed stars, cherry boughs, and, of course, hatchets; to this day, I can, should the occasion arise, produce a creditable facsimile of one of the principal February motifs—three brilliant red cherries, dangling from a clump of leaves—in two or three dimensions and in almost any of the accepted grade-school media, including papier-mâché and cookie dough. Most years, in fact, my mother and I made Washington's Birthday sugar cookies for the whole class with one of those hatchet-shaped cookie cutters with the green wooden handles that used to come in every decent set, along with a Christmas bell and star, a Valentine heart, and a half-moon for Halloween (Figure 1.17). Good Americans ate hatchet cookies in school in Washington's honor, and when they got home, they always had cherry pie for dessert.

All my memories of Washington's Birthday center on the preparation of those ritual foods and the crêpe- and construction-paper accessories that went with them. As for the Weemsian story of the six-year-old George owning up to the awful deed—"I can't tell a lie, Pa, you know I can't tell a lie; I cut it with my hatchet"—I must have learned it by a kind of osmosis, for it never figured in our annual February routine.[53] I must have come by it somehow, because I do recall thinking it highly improper of a substitute teacher, one year, to try to arrogate Washington hatchets to Abe Lincoln, on the grounds that the

1.16
Mother-and-daughter pageant costumes with panniers, designed for circulation by the United States George Washington Bicentennial Commission, 1932

1.17
George Washington hatchet cookie cutters (tinned steel), ca. 1935–1950

1.18
J. L. G. Ferris, *The Making of the Flag by Betsy Ross*

1.19
H. W. Pierce, *A New England Kitchen, a Hundred Years Ago*, drawing made at the Philadelphia Centennial Exposition, 1876

Rail-Splitter had used an axe and those two implements looked pretty much the same. But the cherry tree story did not recall the antics of any of the six-year-old boys of my acquaintance; its connotations were almost wholly feminine and domestic. Washington was a creature of pies and piecrusts, cookies in the oven, paper doilies carefully cut apart to form the lace at his throat, feats of amazing skill with crayons and paste and scissors—things that girls were good at.

The story of Mistress Ross, the seamstress who purportedly made the Stars and Stripes for George Washington, was a singular exception to the rule that consigned little girls to minor roles in the holiday pageantry. For that reason alone, a large number of Betsy Ross tableaux and drills appeared in handbooks for teachers, although sometimes, unaccountably, girls were barred even from set-pieces honoring this unique "founding mother." Such was the case with a recitation called "The Making of 'Old Glory,'" in which eight boys, lined up across the front of the stage, produce from behind their backs at the proper moments the various patriotic devices associated with the flag—the stars, the bars, the three colors, and so forth. Betsy Ross is represented by a picture of her house and by a large white "card bearing the name 'Betsy Ross' in plain letters [because] there is no authentic picture of this noted woman."[54]

If her physical appearance was in doubt in the 1930s, her traditional accouterments were not. *Washington and Betsy Ross: A Dramatic Action in Two Scenes,* adapted by the folklorist and pageant-master Percy MacKaye from his famous Washington "ballad-play" of 1918, and much reprinted thereafter for school use, contains the best-known attribute of all: the square of white cloth clever Betsy folds and snips with a single cut when Washington wants five-pointed stars on the American flag (Figure 1.18).[55] The star symbolizes the occupations appropriate to the virtuous woman—Betsy wields her sewing scissors in her nation's service and not the cannon primed by Molly Pitcher, a far less popular heroine in consequence of her questionable seizure of masculine implements—and also the nimble wits and fingers that, exercised in their proper, domestic sphere, can put the strongest male to shame.

In pictures of Betsy Ross, her sewing gear is always prominently displayed, her workbasket a badge of honor. Most representations show a spinning wheel as well, lest the point remain in doubt, and a capacious hearth, a fireplace that, after 1876 and the functioning "New England Kitchen" of "Ye Olden Time" displayed at the Philadelphia Centennial, came to stand for the colonial period in general and for the cozy, housewifely warmth and charm with which Americans of the waning nineteenth century were pleased to endow the gracious homes of their colonial forebears (Figure 1.19).[56] The ideal colonial hearth also needed a man of the house and a lady with some active claim to the respect of history, and history promptly supplied a George

1.20
Charles H. Weisgerber, *Birth of Our Nation's Flag*, lithograph after the painting shown at the 1893 Columbian Exposition

Washington to stand on one side of the toasty fire of patriotic memory and a Betsy Ross to sit sweetly on the other.

Because she came to light for the first time in 1870 in a paper presented by her grandson, William J. Canby, and because her house—the "Flag House" now—at 239 Arch Street in Philadelphia was available for inspection as a historic site, the legend of Betsy Ross was given an enormous boost by the Centennial Exposition.[57] And parts of the story were plausible. Documents vouched for the existence of one Elizabeth Ross, a much-married seamstress resident in Arch Street. On or about June 1, 1776, when she was supposed to have made the flag under the personal supervision of General Washington, she had recently been widowed; George Ross, the uncle of her late husband, John, was a known associate of Washington's and, along with Robert Morris, was always placed at the scene as a witness, a kind of domesticated Potts.[58]

The thread linking Betsy Ross, seamstress of Arch Street, with the flag was a slender one, however, a filament of hearsay and must-have-beens supplied by Canby and his brother in the form of facile suppositions about the date and place at which the familiar banner was "invented," the relationship between the design and the Washington coat of arms (it too featured five-pointed stars), and depositions from ancient needlewomen once employed in the Ross establishment who dutifully recited Betsy's recollections of embroidering the ruffles on the general's shirts before he ever came to her with his tricolored bundle of yardgoods.[59]

For a variety of reasons, including the publicity generated by the centennial of 1876, the new tradition took hold. Preble, for example, in the revised edition of his *History of the Flag of the United States of America* published in 1880, accepts Canby's account of his grandmother with the flag spread across her lap as definitive, although he chastises a certain Colonel J. Franklin Reigart for circulating a pamphlet containing a spurious portrait of Betsy at her work, actually taken from the photograph of a Quaker lady still living in Lancaster.[60] That fake Betsy Ross artifacts existed at all is proof of the appeal of the story: like the cherry tree and the dollar-thrown-across-the-Rappahannock stories, like his desperate prayer in an hour of need, like his ability to have "slept" almost everywhere, the story of Washington's homespun collaboration with the seamstress of Arch Street fills a specific human need to achieve a measure of material intimacy with important figures and great events of the past.[61]

Visiting the Flag House enhanced the feeling that it was almost possible to step back into history and to mingle with the likes of Washington on terms of easy familiarity. The narrow "Building in which the First American Flag was Made"—in 1870 the shop of Franke the tailor—became a full-fledged tourist attraction as soon as Canby's

1.21
Commercially framed, ready-to-hang
chromolithograph of Betsy Ross, ca.
1890–1900

revelations were broadcast, and then became, in short order, the
"Birthplace of the Flag" Tavern, with a large sign bearing a likeness
of Mrs. Ross's handiwork. But interest waned after the centennial, and
although the spirit revived a bit in 1882, with the bicentennial of the
city of Philadelphia, the sagging structure was finally marked for
demolition in 1892.

What saved the Flag House and the legend it enshrined was a
copyrighted painting executed by Charles H. Weisgerber (Figure 1.20).
Entitled *Birth of Our Nation's Flag,* the work included Washington,
George Ross, Morris, the flag, the workbasket, a slice of the spinning
wheel, and the big hearth, as well as a "portrait" of Betsy Ross created
by making a composite of the features of those of her daughters whose
likenesses had survived.[62] Shown at the Columbian Exposition in
Chicago in 1893 and chromolithographed shortly thereafter, Weisgerber's recreation of the legendary scene provided an appealing bit of
historical genre for the contemporary American home, invoking as it
did "the cult of true womanhood," ensconced in a setting that was
the last word in interior decor. Copies, adaptations, and variations
sometimes improved upon the original by adding a touch of sentiment,
as in the print (Figure 1.21) showing two chubby children, the girl
clinging to Betsy's maternal skirts (the boy is the drummer from
Archibald Willard's *Spirit of '76*).

All the images, authentic or pirated, stimulated a fresh, national
enthusiasm for observances in honor of the flag and for measures to
honor its Philadelphia creator: in 1893, Flag Day was celebrated for
the first time, with ceremonies on Arch Street, and five years later the

American Flag House and Betsy Ross Memorial Association, with a roster of sponsors that included such prominent figures as the Honorable John Wanamaker, began to sell ten-cent subscriptions to the drive to save the house. Every subscriber got a certificate designed by Weisgerber, with a copy of his Betsy Ross picture on it, and by the time the campaign closed with the purchase and restoration of the property in 1905, a million certificates had been distributed to enthusiasts, it was said, in every state and territory.[63]

If the prayer-in-the-snow tale provided a parable of great value at specific historical moments, it also supplied certain traits lacking in other accounts of the hero's life and times. The tears that streamed down his face, in some children's versions of the story, made the adult Washington—a cool, marmoreal eminence at best—more accessible to boys and girls who cried when they skinned their knees and knelt with folded hands by their cots to say their bedtime prayers.[64] In the company of the praying George Washington, Betsy Ross filled other lacunae in the cycle of colonial myth. She provided the feminine element sorely lacking in an all-male creation myth of the American Revolution, for instance. She answered the need for a decorous Revolutionary heroine whose exploits would not prove too heroic for emulation by properly brought-up little girls. And she did have exploits, or one exploit, at least, to her credit.

Unlike Martha Washington, who lacked a defined role in the stirring events of her era, Mistress Ross, if her descendants were to be believed, had done something of consequence for the cause; hence her popularity as a character in the schoolroom pageants mounted in the years between the World Wars. But her persistent pictorial association with children—children entirely devoid of narrative connection to the story of the flag—supplied maternal overtones to complement the lonely isolation of Washington, the childless Father of His Country. With her capacious lap filled with the American flag, Betsy chastely sufficed as the symbolic "Mother of Her Country," a vivid character still familiar today to a generation of high school and college students hard-pressed to cite the century in which the Revolution occurred.[65]

Washington Today

Some myths persist, against all odds, and even pageantry is not quite dead. On the afternoon of Christmas Day, 150 or so uniformed "soldiers" still meet annually on the banks of the Delaware River, in Pennsylvania's Washington Crossing Historic Park, to recreate that fateful day in 1776 by rowing across the stream in "authentic reproductions of the boats" used in Washington's surprise attack on Trenton. The dramatis personae are a select and hardly representative few, however. In 1984 the late John B. Kelly, Jr., of Philadelphia, brother

1.22
The Seventh Annual Washington Crossing Assembly at the Union League of Philadelphia, November 1984; John B. Kelly, Jr., is the figure at the center, dressed up like George Washington

of the late Princess Grace of Monaco, portrayed Washington.[66] He practiced for the big day by wearing his costume and wig to the Washington Crossing Assembly, a charity ball mounted in November by the Union League to raise money for a scholarship program and attended by flocks of socially prominent Kellys and Biddles (Figure 1.22).[67] With the signal exception of high society, in whose ranks conservatism and the demands of charitable socializing combine to ensure that a century-old tradition of dressing up in costume to simulate make-believe history will not peter out, playing at Betsy Ross and George Washington is a thing of the past. Although the powdered hair and the short pants made the past vivid in a way that no other kind of experience could duplicate, most of us nowadays assign such pageantry to our school days, or to our parents', long ago. The doers of the 1930s, snipping five-pointed stars out of scraps of old bedsheets, have become the watchers of today, in a world of onlookers whose participation in their own edification and entertainment consists largely of changing the channel. Television's heroes are of the here and now; on the tube, Ronald Reagan's nice-guy demeanor counts for just as much as his verbal invocation of George Washington at prayer.

When Washington did become the unlikely hero of a dramatic miniseries, buoyed up by President Reagan's televised state visits to Colonial Williamsburg and the residual effects of the 250th anniversary of his birth, he was of interest chiefly for his stilted, unconsummated, and wholly uncontemporary affair with Jaclyn Smith, sultry star of *Charlie's Angels,* first of the sexually provocative shows known in the trade as jiggle programming.[68] That three-day, prime-time George Washington epic, sponsored by General Motors and broadcast by CBS in the spring of 1984 (there was an abbreviated sequel in 1986), was a fluke that, despite some critical success, aroused little public enthusiasm.[69] Washington was too stiff, too remote from the electronic present, in his powdered hair and knee breeches, to match the sizzle brought to her part by his costar.

Although he has failed to register as a personality, however, Washington enjoys a curious and persistent popularity as an icon of the networks. His televised portrait is ubiquitous. The TV Washington is the face on the dollar bill that serves as the logo for economic coverage on the nightly news, a shorthand symbol for runaway inflation, the farm crisis, an unfavorable balance of payments, new taxes, and "money matters" in general (Figure 1.23).[70] His is the face that advertises big February sales in department stores and used-car lots (Figure 1.24). A vague, chiefly fiscal presence, the presiding deity of postindustrial capitalism, the Father of Sound Monetary Policy, Washington seems to stand for the dollar he adorns—a dollar to be saved at sales or spent on bargain plane tickets and cut-rate T-shirts (Figures 1.25, 1.26).

1.23
George Washington is the patron saint of the anchorman Peter Jennings in the segment called "Money Matters" on the ABC evening news.

"Historicism makes a comeback—" reads a glossy ad for Williamsburg-reproduction furniture in the *New Yorker* in the year of Reagan's prayer-in-the-snow inaugural; "Was it ever away?"[71] Perhaps not. Washington and his colonial epoch have acquired a new relevance in the 1980s, for a variety of reasons. The resurgence of political conservatism has surely helped, along with the incumbent president's relish for historical yarns embellished by colorful props that would have done Betsy Ross's parlor proud. The "yuppie" quest for the soundest value per dollar spent on "quality" household appointments has filled the best stores with Chippendale sofas and with sterling snuffboxes destined to perch on piecrust tables. A certain anti-egalitarian revival of interest in the rites of high society according to "Miss Manners" can also be observed, a relish for the formal, courtly etiquette perfected at Williamsburg in Washington's time.

Given these fresh ripples on the tide of the colonial revival, the question posed by the ad in the *New Yorker* is a rhetorical one. The past is still venerated, and historicism has never really been away. Neither has George Washington. He's been with us, in an intimate and a particularly concrete fashion, ever since the morning of May 10, 1876, when the good "general's shorts"—the buff-colored knee breeches he actually wore at Annapolis, in 1783, for the ceremonial resignation of his commission—went on display in a glass case in the U.S. Government Building at the Philadelphia Centennial Exposition, to mark the hundredth birthday of his country.[72]

1.24
Ad for Donaldson's department store,
Minneapolis, December 11, 1983

![Visit your father. WASHINGTON D.C. Travel poster showing George Washington's face.](REPUBLIC AIRLINES)

1.25
Travel poster, ca. 1980, designed by
Scott Baker for Republic Airlines

1.26
T-shirt, ca. 1984–85, worn by students at
George Washington University

Knee breeches are real; stories and pictures, however vivid, remain abstractions, symbols for things that could be touched once, for words once spoken and feelings that stung the heart. And the memories embedded in such symbols are not without their force. The oral and the pictorial traditions from which Ronald Reagan drew his image of an America forever governed by constitutional order acting in harmony with the divine will were well established in the nineteenth century. That collective American memory was also grounded in the figure of George Washington: it was *he* who prayed in the bitter cold of Valley Forge, and taught a nation to do so; it was *he* who became president by law and solemn oath, not force of arms, with his hand upon a borrowed Bible.

In the waning twentieth century, the relationship between person and principle is not quite so absolute. On one level, the 1985 inaugural speech fostered a sense of community between an aging president and his contemporaries, Americans who had grown up in the 1920s and 1930s when Washington pageants and old-fashioned moral lessons drawn from history books were still in vogue. Among his listeners were at least some who, like a friend of mine, had heard an old man interviewed on the radio back when he and Ronald Reagan were kids. The man on the radio told about meeting an aged party when he was just a child himself, and *that* old fellow had actually seen George Washington in the flesh. But the words of Reagan's speech meant something else to listeners who had never heard about George Washington from an old man's lips and never wore knee breeches and a woolly wig to school. To those members of his audience for whom the prayer-in-the-snow incident was a brand-new piece of information, the Reagan inaugural promoted communality on different grounds: it created the same vague sense of grandfatherly warmth that clings to any story told by an elder about the days gone by. Washington and Washingtoniana were all but incidental to the pull of history itself, to the imagined security of a realm forever immune to the awful vagaries of change. George Washington was not, strictly speaking, essential to his own biography on that chilly day in 1985 when Ronald Reagan invoked his name.

The process that allows history to be separated from its heroes can be observed in operation in Philadelphia in 1876, when the George Washington introduced to fairgoers by way of the very pants he wore all but vanished behind a barrier constructed of his own possessions. His buff nether-garments adorned a display of Revolutionary War relics arranged so as to suggest preparations for that most down-to-earth of human activities—the evening meal. Paradoxically, however, the quest for a new intimacy with George Washington based on tangible, material remains resulted in a fascination with those artifacts so consuming that Americans all but devoured their own past in an orgy of centennial bean-and-gingerbread suppers and Martha Washington teas.

Teatime at Valley Forge

2

The Philadelphia Centennial Exposition
of 1876

The Cult of Domesticity

The author of a guidebook to the Philadelphia Centennial Exposition of 1876 probably didn't mean to be irreverent when he complained that "the cases containing General Washington's shorts . . . might have been advantageously devoted" to the collection of rare fossils from the headwaters of the Missouri, shoehorned instead into leftover crannies in the official U.S. government display (Figure 2.1). Geological research promised to increase the mineral wealth of the nation, he reasoned. The practical benefits of meditating on the relics of the past were almost nil.

The centennial was a suitable occasion for looking back "at the road" traversed over the past century, but the vista mainly served to show fairgoers how lucky they were to live in the prosperous, modern present: "They pause to contemplate [America's] gloomy beginning, the perilous precipices along which it wound, and the sudden quagmires that often interrupted it, all now softened by distance and the consciousness of success."[1] Those bad old days were over now. So why not leave the general's historic clothes to molder in their dusty reliquary at the Patent Office?

Although the organizers of the Philadelphia fair were more interested in the Corliss Engine and patented devices for crushing fossil rock than they were in the nation's colonial heritage, the juxtaposition between the preindustrial past, represented by Washington's all-too-human buff breeches, and the patented byproducts of American mechanical know-how ranged about those ancient garments fascinated some fair-watchers.[2] Washington's military clothes, along with his campaign tent, his field gear, and assorted household items from Mount Vernon had gradually found their way into federal custody over the years, with the bulk of the material coming from George Washing-

2.1
One of several popular illustrations of the "Washington Relics" displayed by the Patent Office at the Philadelphia Centennial Exposition of 1876

ton Parke Custis of Arlington, the general's adopted grandson, the "Child of Mount Vernon, . . . the last human link with the Father of His Country."[3] A garrulous eccentric who painted amateur pictures of the battles of the Revolution and dabbled in historical drama on the same theme, Custis used the tent as a marquee for Fourth of July picnics and May sheep-shearings on the green lawns of his Potomac estate. He was even known to dress up in his grandpa's Annapolis uniform once in a while.[4] But during the decade preceding the Civil War—Arlington, in the meantime, became Robert E. Lee's house—the Custis collection, safe from further desecrations, fetched up in the newish sandstone building on F Street in Washington that housed the U.S. Patent Office.

Visitors filed past in great numbers, more every year. Somehow, it was the sight of Washington's clothes that touched them and drew them back. The historian Benson Lossing made the pilgrimage to F Street in 1870 and headed straight for the great soldier's personal effects, garments he had once inspected at Arlington. He sketched the Annapolis uniform, the blue coat flattened out, lining side down, the waistcoat and breeches arranged alongside it. Without the wearer inside, clothes always look small and forlorn, and in the text beneath his drawing Lossing captured that note of vulnerability. He also hinted at the sense of intimacy with the hero fostered by the impress of that once-living heart and hand upon the fragile fabric:

It was on Christmas eve, 1783, that Washington, a private citizen, arrived at Mount Vernon, and laid aside forever the military clothes which he had worn perhaps through more than half the campaigns of the war just ended. Around them clustered many interesting associations, and they were preserved with care during the remaining sixteen years of his life. And they are still preserved, in a condition almost as perfect as when the illustrious owner hung them in his wardrobe for the last time. They are in a glass case, with other mementoes of the FATHER OF HIS COUNTRY, in the great model hall of the Patent Office at Washington city. The coat is made of deep blue cloth, faced with a yellow called buff, with large plain gilt buttons. The waistcoast and breeches are made of the same kind of buff cloth as the facings of the coat.[5]

There was no arcane reason why Washington's wardrobe came to be exhibited in the company of clever devices for pitting cherries. The Model Hall of the Patent Office had been chosen for the safekeeping of the Washington artifacts, and the Declaration of Independence as well, because the building was supposed to be fireproof. With the approach of the centennial year, however, as a commentator for *Harper's Weekly* was quick to observe, the makeshift balance between patents and pilgrims, between technology and history, began to shift slowly toward Washington's shorts.

The Patent Office, it seems, had decided to represent itself to the world in Philadelphia by recreating, within the confines of the Gov-

ernment Building, its curious mixture of old relics and up-to-date resourcefulness:

The Centennial occasion, which has made so much stir all over the country, has also made a flutter among these invaluable relics, which were very naturally considered as a central point of attraction, around which the more legitimate exhibits of the Patent-office in the Government Building might cluster.

Without disparagement to the machines and tools which form the collection of Patent-office models . . . the heart embraces the personal, and bounds in sympathy and interest as we see, and perhaps handle, the sword, cane, compass, clothing, of

"the first, the last, the best;
THE CINCINNATUS of the West."[6]

Although few, if any, visitors to the Centennial Exposition were actually given the opportunity to touch the relics, the "personal" interest Washington's possessions held for many was enhanced by the manner in which they were displayed. Woodcuts illustrating the contents of the principal case suggest that the artifacts were arranged to simulate a camp scene during the Revolutionary War (Figure 2.2).[7] The folding cot was spread with Washington's own blankets and covered with a pair of counterpanes worked by Martha. The portable table was laid for tea with his salt- and butter-boxes, his casters, his tinned plates.

Behind the bed, off to the side of the table, near his sword and pistols, "in a somewhat natural position on a chair, [were] the regimentals worn by General Washington when he resigned his commission at Annapolis." The uniform, rumpled and stretched into an almost-human simulacrum of the living Washington, brought the

American past back to life in a visceral way. It was almost as if the general were really present in Philadelphia in 1876—almost as if the world of 1776 had come back into being for a moment, in the casual litter of coverlets, breeches, and plates.[8]

Today, scholars usually trace a radical new mode of exhibiting relics back to 1907, to the Essex Institute in Salem, Massachusetts. There in the kitchen, parlor, and bedroom set up on the second floor, George Francis Dow is said to have invented the "period room," a display of antiquities so arranged as to recreate the environment of everyday life and to foster the delightful illusion that the onlooker has just wandered back, accidentally, in time. Dow is said to have borrowed the idea, in turn, from an outdoor exhibit of old houses at the Nordiska Museum in Sweden.[9] But long before Dow learned about the Nordiska Museum, ordinary visitors to the Philadelphia fair were being captivated by a series of tableaux consisting of lifelike, life-size figures, attired in real clothes and representing typical episodes in the life of the contemporary Scandinavian peasantry—the happy arrival of a new baby, the tragic death of an infant, the elk hunt.[10] These ethnographic set-pieces made up the Swedish division of the international section. Much remarked upon in guidebooks for their immediacy and their power to engage the emotions of the viewer, the Swedish tableaux differed from the Washington-in-camp scene mounted by the Patent Office only in degree. Without the help of stuffed dummies or plaster heads with wigs of human hair, George Washington still contrived to sit upon the chair behind his narrow bed and dine with his phantom comrades. Why, his breeches even crumpled as he bent his knee!

In some souls the merest glimpse of Washington's haberdashery inspired a flutter of patriotic fervor. "There is certainly no exhibit in the entire exposition," chirped the earnest reporter for *Frank Leslie's Illustrated Weekly* before passing on to an in-depth analysis of hydraulic pumps and the Eureka Wheat-Cleaner, "which is so calculated to rouse our feelings of national pride and to thrill our hearts with memories of the days of '76 as is this one."[11] The managers of the Pennsylvania pavilion, bewailing the fact that their state had kept its "specimens of ancient fabrics and handiwork; ancestral relics; Indian curiosities; and quaint old records and manuscripts" away from the fairgrounds for fear of fire, lauded the federal government for taking a risk "even with the sacred relics of the Father of his Country, which . . . constituted one of the finest characteristics of that excellent exhibit." In no other way, except by firsthand observation of tangible things from the nation's past, "could . . . the wonderful advancement and prosperity" of Pennsylvania and the nation at large "have been so fitly illustrated."[12]

To many visitors to the cases in the Patent Office section, then, the past was of interest chiefly because it was so remote and strange, because its old-fashioned artifacts gave visible proof of just how wondrous the modern present really was.[13] But those who peered through the glass at Washington's quaint costumes and accouterments sometimes caught sight of a reflection of themselves, or someone not very different—of a historical figure who seemed almost contemporary. The author of *The Illustrated History of the Centennial Exhibition* stood before the case and solemnly enumerated every andiron, mirror, and fork. "Every cord, every button and tent-pin was in its place," he observed, "for [Washington] was careful of little things."[14] And because his fussiness was manifest in his fitted knife cases and his carefully preserved breeches, a very human Washington—he was "careful of little things" and, presumably, put on his breeches one leg at a time—emerged from one's encounter with his relics, a Washington not wholly unlike the journalist or the wide-eyed tourist who stood on the other side of the glass, looking in at an evening meal during the campaign of 1776, just after the general took command of his army beneath the venerable Cambridge Elm, or a frugal teatime in the snow of Valley Forge.

Indeed, the descriptive label affixed to the exhibit by its custodians seemed specially calculated to bridge the century that yawned between Washington and the fairgoer of 1876—or so William Dean Howells maintained, with a show of mock horror, in his report to the *Atlantic Monthly*:

There are . . . people of culture in this region who would sign a petition asking the government to change the language of the placard on the clothes of the Father of His Country, which now reads, "Coat, Vest, and Pants of George Washington," whereas it is his honored waistcoat which is meant, and his buckskin breeches: pantaloons were then unknown, and "pants" were undreamt-of. . . . This placard is a real drawback to one's enjoyment of the clothes, which are so familiarly like, from pictures, that one is startled not to find Washington's face looking out of the coat-collar. The government had been well advised in putting on view these and other personal relics, like his camp-bed, his table furniture, his sword, his pistols, and so forth. . . . In the satisfaction of thus drawing nearer to the past in the realization of . . . historic lives, one's passion for historic wardrobes mounts.[15]

However anachronistic, calling Washington's "pants" by their nineteenth-century name both reflected and encouraged an easy familiarity with the past. That elision blurred the distinction between 1776 and 1876, making Washington into a plausibly ordinary kind of person and contradicting the present-mindedness of guidebook sages who found the detritus of 1776 useful only as a foil to their celebration of technological progress. Ordinary people were invited to respond to the relics on a very functional, physical level as they might respond to their own pants and household gear. And if the reactions of the host of fictional "folks" concocted to represent the common wisdom are to be trusted, the Washington display accomplished its goal.

2.3
Souvenir Centennial Exposition plaque, with gilt-silver medallion and a facsimile of Washington's signature, 1876

2.4
Fragment of a textile machine-printed in red and black in honor of the Centennial Exposition of 1876

"Josiah Allen's wife," better known as just plain "Samantha," toured the Centennial, exclaiming in her thick, country dialect over everything she saw. "Has George Washington got any clothes here to the Sentinal?" she asks at the very end of her stay, in the course of a discussion of "relicks" of the True Cross reportedly for sale in the amusement zone. On hearing about the Patent Office display, she rushes over to the Government Building, battling crowds all the way:

But though I see everything on my way and more too seeminly, I didn't seem to sense anything as it should be sensed, till I stood before them relicks; and then, oh! what feelings I did feel as I see that coat and vest that George had buttoned up so many times over true patriotism, truthfulness, and honor. When I see the bed he had slept on, the little round table he had eat on, the wooden bottomed chair he had sot down on, the belluses he had blowed the fire with in cold storms and discouragements. . . . Why, they all rousted up my mind so, that I told Josiah I must see Independence Hall before I slept, or I wouldn't answer for the consequences. I was fearfully rousted up in my mind, as much so as if my emotions had been all stirred up with that little hatchet that G. W. couldn't tell a lie with.[16]

If, on the warrant of his perfectly commonplace buttons and buttonholes, Samantha could call him George, then old Mr. Pettingill, the so-called Centennial Liar, could make up stories about Washington the henpecked husband after a peep at his horse-drawn coach: "I saw the carriage George Washington rode in, and three queens and a jack that he shoved under the seat when he sat outside of the church playing draw-poker, and Mrs. Washington lighted in on him earlier than he expected from a short sermon, and I saw a handful of his hair that Mrs. Washington took out of his head that identical Sabbath morning."[17] Locks of light brown hair said to be from the head of George Washington did indeed surface from time to time, as the old ladies who were the daughters of the Revolutionary veterans willed their cedar chests to their favorite nieces and nephews in the 1860s and 1870s. "It's my earnest request," read the testimonial sealed away with one such keepsake, "[that] this may be preserved to succeeding generations. . . . The hair is of his own head. This will increase its value with time."[18]

In the centennial year, first-class relics of Washington circulated privately, by and large, as familial tokens, marks of a special distinction conferred by the most intimate, first-person contact with the person of Washington. But the line between humbug and historical authenticity was admittedly thin. In the 1830s Barnum had rung up the curtain on his remarkable career by exhibiting Joice Heth, a black woman who claimed to be 161 years old, the slave of Washington's father and nursemaid to "dear little George," on whose person she was the first "to put clothes."[19] The hoax was legendary; the humorist Walter F. Brown alluded to it in his book of cartoons on the centennial celebration, which contained a "Portrait of Gen. Washington's Nurse, Aged 105," and the author's prediction that at least a dozen competing mammies would turn up at the great exposition.[20] Yet despite that reasonable inference, official records disclose no influx of imposters into Philadelphia.

The buyer, nonetheless, had ample cause to beware when contemplating the purchase of one of the many relics adorned with Washington's likeness and offered for sale to the Samanthas and the Mr. Pettingills in attendance to commemorate their moment of proximity to the chief Founding Father's personal effects. The many gewgaws offered for sale on the fairgrounds promised to prolong the immediacy of that experience by giving the pilgrim possession of an artifact stamped with the look of instant antiquity. The hallmark of historical authenticity on a Centennial Exposition souvenir often consisted of a facsimile of Washington's signature worked into the design. A plaque of stamped metal therefore attests to its own documentary value by the old-fashioned signature just below the olive branch that further identifies Washington the statesman, the man of peace, a man whose military uniforms and camp gear contrive to exude a cozy domesticity in keeping with the fair's overall emphasis on the avid but pacific pursuit of prosperity (Figure 2.3).

Centennial handkerchiefs printed while-you-wait with Washington profiles, machine-woven bookmarks of silk with the Athenaeum portrait prominently displayed, textiles of all kinds, and silver-plated belt buckles with inset tintypes of George and Martha were among the most popular and inexpensive mementos of 1876 (Figure 2.4).[21] The iconography of these items emphasized the man—the beloved face, the fellow with the big, looping signature, the husband, the human being—not the president or the general. But motifs stressing the human Washington also adorned objects of personal use, objects that reinforced the impression of a ready, everyday familiarity between the eighteenth-century icon and his modern, nineteenth-century idolaters. The decision to put Washington's portrait on a paperweight, a bitters bottle, a flatiron trivet, or a glass plate can be charged to a defect of taste, a want of decorum (Figures 2.5, 2.6). But the purchase of such an object can also be understood as an assertion of the easy kinship between the hero and the owner of a "First in the Hearts of His Countrymen" bread plate, with handles bearing the fair dates (available in a choice of clear or frosted models).

Between that class of objects really owned and touched by George Washington and the bric-a-brac merely graced with his likeness falls another loose category of relics. This third group of artifacts, associated with Washington and '76 by the most tenuous of links, was given a place of honor in the exposition for reasons that provide fresh insight into the historical sensibilities of the period. In the Women's Pavilion, hard by the remarkable *Sleeping Iolanthe* carved in fresh butter by

2.5
Centennial trivet for a flatiron

2.6
Centennial bitters bottle

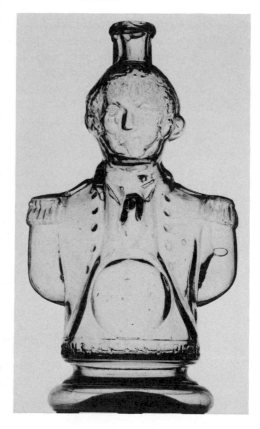

Mrs. Caroline Brooks of Arkansas, was "a bouquet of wax flowers . . . made by the great-granddaughters of the author of the Declaration of Independence, who, in the midst of the rejoicings of the Centennial," remarked one commentator, "were left to make an almost hopeless struggle with poverty."[22]

Wax flowers of no intrinsic interest basked in whatever light their distant associations with Washington's generation provided. They were curiosities, on a par with the unremarkable mittens assigned space in the Women's Building because they had been knit "at the age of one hundred years and four months" by Mrs. Abigail F. Lovering of Oxford, Maine. But in among "the hats of common grass" gathered and woven by another old woman from the Midwest and the patented crumb-receivers and griddle-greasers contributed by somewhat younger entrepreneurial females, the Board of Lady Managers also installed an item sent for exhibition by Mrs. E. E. Boynton of Evanston, Illinois. Mrs. Boynton was not a relative of Jefferson's. She was not famous, destitute, or, apparently, skilled in knitting mittens or sculpting foodstuffs. Her contribution to the Centennial Exposition consisted, in its entirety, of a "tea kettle, one hundred years old," lent for the duration.[23]

Generic 1876 trophies, like the hundred-year-old tea kettle, were much in evidence: what was old was curious and worthy of close inspection. More fascinating were objects fabricated from ancient materials bearing rich historical associations. Hence the attention paid to Item #300 in the official government catalogue of the fair, a suite of "chamber furniture of wood from Independence Square" manufactured by the firm of George J. Henkel of Philadelphia.[24] The chairs and tables, it was said, were done "in the style of 1776." And they were "made from the wood of an old maple tree that grew in Independence Square, and was over two hundred years old, having been planted around 1650 and cut down in 1875."[25]

2.7
Nelson, Matter and Company exhibit for the Philadelphia Centennial as shown on a trade card

American Architect dismissed the claim of authenticity, calling the Henkel suite "one of the eccentricities of the Exhibition": "It showed how little can be done in the way of imitation by one who does not understand the true spirit of what he is imitating. This was nothing less than a caricature of the substantial surroundings which our ancestors possessed. The fact that it was made from an old maple-tree which grew in Independence Square could not lend sufficient sentiment to the subject to redeem it from this charge."[26] But like the public at large, most other visitors to the furniture galleries were confused about the precise configuration of shapes to be expected from a Chippendale or a Tudor piece, and even shakier on the proper nomenclature for old chairs. One otherwise reliable handbook to the exposition, for instance, praised for fidelity to the period the firm of Schasty & Co., makers of fine furniture, because they had showed "some Rococco sets in reproduction of the fashion of the Revolution."[27]

The Henkel and the Schasty suites probably survive somewhere in the environs of Philadelphia, although given their uncolonial appearance, they may never be identified as "the" exhibits. What run-of-the-mill manufacturers and their clients meant by "the style of 1776" can be deduced, however, from examination of other specimens of historic furniture made for the Philadelphia Centennial and preserved in pictures or in ornate reality. The prizewinning bedroom set shown by Nelson, Matter and Company of Grand Rapids, Michigan, and lovingly illustrated on a trade card thereafter, aimed for a colonial flavor by cramming a large statue of George Washington into a Gothic niche let into the headboard, just above the sleeper's pillow (Figure 2.7). Otherwise, the massive bedstead and dressing case are sixteenth-century in character, or "Renaissance" as the nineteenth century interpreted it, with supplemental garniture from the age of the cathedrals and the days of '76.[28]

That same Renaissance mode imparted an eclectic vigor to the so-called Washington Elm Chair shown at the Centennial Exposition by Colonel Charles H. Clarke of Milwaukee as an act of piety. Clarke was not a furnituremaker. As a young man living in Cambridge in 1857, he had come into possession (after a violent thunderstorm) of a limb of the old tree under which Washington had taken command of his army in 1775. Clarke left the cumbersome relic behind when he moved to Wisconsin. But when the fair was announced he sent for his wood, brought together two designers, a woodworker, a carver, an upholsterer, and a lady to embroider the likeness of the standing Washington, and commissioned a chair to send back east to Philadelphia, along with a number of "canes and ornamental goblets, urns, vases, etc." made from the leftover scraps (Figure 2.8).[29]

2.8
Centennial chair with portrait of George Washington embroidered by Mrs. Kavanaugh; the chair itself was made from a limb of the Cambridge Elm and exhibited by Charles H. Clarke of Milwaukee

2.9
The Massachusetts state building at the
Centennial Exposition; it typifies the
"colonial" style of 1876

2.10
"Antiquing": a photograph posed by Mary
Northend to illustrate this novel activity

The relentless domesticity with which Washington and his era were presented at the Centennial Exposition suggests that conventional political and military history were matters of indifference to fairgoers and exhibitors alike. The historic Cambridge Elm became a comfy chair for the fireside—or a chair, at any rate—and any number of choice objets d'art for the parlor whatnot, rather than becoming a chest to hold the Constitution, a lectern for Congress, a beam in Milwaukee City Hall, or a timber in the official state building of Massachusetts. The daily life of Washington—the household minutiae of breeches and pepper shakers—held a deep and abiding fascination that spilled over into *any* old hundred-year-old tea kettle and turned venerable trees from historical places into bits of interior décor.

The Massachusetts pavilion at the fair, although it lacked the magic that might have been imparted by fragments of the Cambridge Elm, was, in fact, "a cottage, a quaint affair modeled after the homes of the past" (Figure 2.9).[30] As such, its half-timbered turret, its shingles, clapboards, arched doorway, and ample porches helped to flesh out the prevailing vision of a domestic past of great, nostalgic charm. The style of the pavilion designed by Clarence Luce was called "colonial," even though admiring descriptions of what "colonial" signified disclose an architectural muddle to which touches of the Pilgrim or Revolutionary eras adhere with difficulty. "Massachusetts brought before the world, as her State Building, a specimen of Colonial architecture, quaint-looking, derived partly from the English and partly from the French, and it attracted considerable attention," recalled one analyst. But the structure was really most noteworthy, he hastened to admit, because "this was one of the few State buildings which adopted as their model the style of houses common to Colonial times."[31]

"Colonial" really meant homelike:

Somewhat sombre in appearance, quaint and old-fashioned in style, the addition of the central cupola seems to be all that would distinguish the building of the Bay State from one of those practical, comfortable houses which are still to be met with in the neighborhood of Cape Cod and in other parts of Massachusetts. . . . It is in the style of the colonial times. The front has an overhanging roof, and in the gable is a square oriel window for the second story, whilst beneath is an old-fashioned porch. . . . On each side of the front is a one-story structure analogous to the New England kitchen or the "keeping room."[32]

Colonial meant cozy—a cozy home with a big kitchen, a broad chimneypiece, and ancestral relics strewn about in quaint profusion. In that last detail, colonialism betrayed the fine hand of the nascent collector (Figure 2.10). The Ladies' Centennial Committee of Salem, Massachusetts, had assembled a cache of ancient treasures in the rooms of the Essex Institute in the months prior to the opening of the great fair, to raise money in support of the state effort. Their exhibition of "Rare Colonial, Provincial and Revolutionary Relics" included a "wine-glass used by Gen. Washington while in Salem, 1789"; the baby clothes of Judge Curwen, who tried the Salem witches; and an Elizabethan cupboard "stored away for the past fifty years in a barn." Press notices of the Salem show attributed the survival of these rarities either to the pride of the descendants of the settlers "or the mania of some 'collector.'" Judging by the quotation marks, the collector was a new breed in 1876, but one to which the planners of certain of the New England displays pandered shamelessly with nooks-and-cranniesful of curious heirlooms.[33]

The Connecticut Cottage at the Philadelphia Exposition was another neocolonial paradise for the collector, crammed with "ancient furniture, clock, tile, settee, etc., etc.," etc.[34] Built after a picturesque and somewhat fanciful watercolor reminiscence of a Connecticut saltbox by Donald G. Mitchell, the headquarters of the Land of Steady Habits was universally recognized as "an old-style dwelling," albeit one "improved and beautified to some degree by the porches and piazzas," decorative half-timbering everywhere, and a four-foot overhang at the front.[35] The wayward exterior was, nonetheless, "intended to represent a colonial homestead of a century ago." That feat was perhaps more readily accomplished in the paneled interior, a dim, murky, and thoroughly domestic environment that exuded the essence of home from an ample colonial hearth, "an old-fashioned fireplace opposite the front door," bedecked with tasteful symbols of distaff virtue, pioneer simplicity, and sturdy yeoman grit (Figure 2.11).[36]

Over the pine mantelpiece, "stained to give the dark look of age," hung a portrait of Israel Putnam, Connecticut's Revolutionary hero; his stout old musket—the one he used to kill the famous wolf in Pomfret—was mounted beneath the painting: "The fire-place, with its great brass andirons and fender, its tiles of painted china representing Connecticut wild-flowers and scenes in Putnam's life, presented a very attractive picture. On the right of it stood a small flax-wheel, dark and glossy with time. [Nearby was] the old silver . . . after the Elder Brewster pattern."[37]

According to the Connecticut Board of Centennial Managers, the spinning wheel and the silverware (a plated tea service from the Meriden Britannia Company said to be an exact copy of Elder Brewster's "May-Flower" set) were calculated touches, intended to remind the visitor "of a century before, as he rested his tired limbs on a heavy wooden settle, made in 1769." Nearly every object arranged in the hearthside tableau had a similar historic interest. Among them was a little table lent by John H. Most of Old Saybrook, one of a number of articles, some for sale as souvenirs of colonial Connecticut, all made from fragments of the venerable Charter Oak.[38]

2.11
Interior of the Connecticut building, 1876 fair

Designated by persistent tradition as the place where the liberal colonial charter had been hidden away in 1687, the oak tree gradually became the centerpiece of a cult of sorts. People with pretensions to proper ancestry had their portraits painted beside it, views of the lot in Hartford on which it stood sold briskly, and, after the 1830s and the sesquicentennial of the supposed concealment of the document, "every leaf, twig, acorn, and branch" that fell from the oak was whisked away, thus initiating a spirited trade in Charter Oak relics.[39] Mr. Most was the unofficial high priest of the cult, cabinetmaker to the historian who owned the tree, and heir to a substantial chunk of the wood carefully divided up after the mighty oak, weakened by weather and the depredations of small boys with matches, was finally toppled by a storm in the summer of 1856.

In the Main Building at the Centennial Exposition, alongside the Henkel chamber suite made from a maple in Independence Square, Most exhibited "furniture made from wood of the 'Charter Oak,'" including a piano finished in 1857 and valued at $2,500, a duplicate of one sold as a historical keepsake at the great New York Sanitary Fair held during the Civil War.[40] There were smaller items, too:

a bureau, $1,200; . . . five canes, $25 each; six napkin rings, $30; four card-cases, $10 each; four whist counters, $5 each. . . . In the Connecticut Cottage was exhibited a wooden ham, weight nine pounds . . . ; a rustic mantel ornament enclosing a representation of the old oak . . . and most interesting of all, a banner of navy blue cloth, upon which appeared, in letters formed of Charter Oak wood, the names of all the Governors of Connecticut from 1776 to 1876. . . . A happy suggestion that nutmegs made of Charter Oak would be esteemed, not only as relics, but as humorous proofs of the truth of the story that wooden nutmegs are really produced by the enterprising Yankees of Connecticut, was seconded by Mr. Most, who made a large number, and sold them readily at fifty and twenty-five cents each.[41]

With the exception, perhaps, of the "old oaken bucket" and well-box (it was a fake—dry, of course, and three feet deep) just outside the door of the cottage, of "Old Put.'s" portrait ("There, dew look at that there splendid picter of Gineral Washington!" cried one old lady), and of his magnet (against which hundreds rubbed the blades of their pocket knives or packages of needles, to give them special powers), the most popular features of Connecticut's showing at the Centennial were the fragments of the Charter Oak. Although visitors were "inclined to be rather quizzical on the subject of the authenticity of the Charter Oak relics," they bought them freely enough: John Most quickly ran out of his fifty-cent "nutmegs," such marvels of verisimilitude that attendants were sometimes able to palm off the genuine article on the unwary as specimens of his handiwork (Figure 2.12).[42]

2.12
A wooden nutmeg, made by John H. Most from the Charter Oak and sold at the Connecticut Cottage in 1876

2.13
Interior of the New England Kitchen
attraction at the fair

Ranked next in shoppers' favor to Most's relics—did they burn "Charter Oak fire-wood," too? wondered visitors—was a photographic souvenir, a stereopticon view of the interior of the Connecticut Cottage with the fireplace, the spinning wheel, the silverware, and the wooden ham dangling off to one side. The popularity of this icon of homeyness was matched only by public enthusiasm for the capacious working hearth at which the twenty-odd costumed ladies of the Old New England Log-House and Kitchen (also known as the New England Farmer's Home and Modern Kitchen) prepared and served "a boiled dinner, beans, brown bread and old-fashioned puddings . . . for company in real old-fashioned style every day from 12 M. to 3 P.M." (Figure 2.13).[43] A moneymaking concession, the New England Kitchen was the brainchild of Miss Emma B. Southwick of Boston. Miss Southwick had visited the Vienna Exposition of 1873 and noticed there not only the various national houses set up on the grounds, fully furnished and tended by people in ethnic dress, but also restaurants selling ethnic foods, served, in appropriate settings, by waiters and waitresses in native outfits. In Philadelphia, she applied the notion to American history.

2.14
Revolutionary-era characters in costume at the Mississippi Valley Sanitary Fair, St. Louis, 1864

The Martha Washington Tea

Just as the final development of the period room appears to have had several points of origin, including the fireside of the Connecticut Cottage and the lifelike display of Washington's possessions at the 1876 fair, so the New England Kitchen had well-known American precedents in the Sanitary Fairs held in the cities of the North and West during the Civil War. Organized and directed mainly by women to raise money for care of the wounded, these fairs were decorous forms of entertainment that contrived to excite great interest without exposing true womanhood to the loss of gentility that theatrical endeavor might entail. At least six Sanitary Fairs—in Indianapolis, St. Louis, New York, Philadelphia, Brooklyn, and Poughkeepsie—took the form of "old tyme" kitchens of the colonial era (Figure 2.14).[44]

Typically, a kitchen exhibit invited two distinct kinds of activity, both of which could be conducted, if need be, with the same props and settings, although practicality favored separate groupings of artifacts. The first attraction of the Sanitary Kitchen was eating: "Yankee" food in Indianapolis, "Knickerbocker" fare in New York, "Pennsylvania"-Dutch dishes in Philadelphia. The joint Brooklyn and Long Island Fair that opened on Washington's Birthday in 1864 offered "repasts in the New England style." In a "Dutchess County Room One Hundred Years Ago," Poughkeepsie ladies in ancient petticoats guided guests through the split Dutch door toward "the huge fireplace with old Dutch tiles" and charged "fifty cents for a 'tea' in the rural style of a hundred years" past.[45] The second attraction of the Sanitary Kitchen was inspecting other people's family treasures or pointing with pardonable pride at one's own. In roomlike groupings next to or in the restaurant proper, displays of heirlooms stressed the antiquity of these United States and reasserted its stability in the face of the divisive conflict.

If George Washington finally became the Father of His Country during the years of the Civil War, a symbol of unity in a divided society, then his and his nation's familial home also became the "old tyme" colonial house, with a fireplace and a spinning wheel, lots of comforting things to eat and lots of old-fashioned things to admire. It is no accident that the abolitionist John Greenleaf Whittier turned in the immediate postwar years to poetic celebration of the snug ancestral home populated by the durable progeny of colonial sires. In *Snow Bound,* published in 1866, Whittier invokes the "old tyme" kitchens of the Sanitary Fairs as surely as he recreates the manses of his New England forefathers:

> Shut in from all the world without,
> We set the clean-winged hearth about,
> Content to let the north-wind roar
> In baffled rage at pane and door.[46]

The Sanitary Fair on New York's Union Square boasted of Peter Stuyvesant's mirror and antiquities from other prominent Knickerbocker families. The Poughkeepsie fair matched New York's, candlestick for silhouette, and also featured lady attendants who were "members of the oldest familes on the Hudson . . . in the costumes of their great-grandmothers . . . the genuine dresses[,] one spinning merrily on the great wool-wheel; another making thread with an ancient flax-wheel."[47] It was ladies of the first and oldest families, or those with social ambitions beyond their station, who ran the assorted kitchen exhibitions of the Civil War years in the name of expansive Christian charity. Indirectly, however, their efforts brought on the first constricting twinges of a new and increasingly self-conscious exclusivity, grounded in ancestry and a cult of "antiques" connoting hereditary superiority. But by the time of the Philadelphia Centennial and Miss Southwick's blatantly commercial New England Kitchen, the "collectors" whose zeal had provided artifacts for the Salem exhibition of local relics in 1876—people with or without distinguished ancestry, possessed of drive, pluck, and a little cash—had also helped to democratize the hunt for heirlooms.

In 1878 *Godey's Lady's Book* sniffed at antiquing, "the latest mania among fashionable people," because it seemed to boost a class of suspect individuals "desiring to lay claim to a respectable ancestry."[48] In 1876 almost anybody could aspire to finding a piece of "Mayflower furniture" in a hayloft, and anybody with the modest price of admission could live vicariously in the past, for an hour or so, amidst the relics displayed in the New England Log-House and Kitchen at the Philadelphia Centennial Exposition.

The log cabin, a farmhouse of "ancient aspect," contained two low, square rooms of "an exceedingly antiquated look" stuffed to the rafters with two kinds of curios: old-fashioned furniture and "Revolutionary relics" associated with particular well-known figures. Both species of Americana enthralled the paying guests:

The great open fireplace, which was adorned with appropriate paraphernalia, monopolized nearly all one side of the front room, while the narrow and low windows and doors shared with a few wrinkled pictures and relics the other wall. From the ceiling depended strings of dried apples and peppers, ears of corn and other emblems of the olden time. Here were shown General Stark's spurs, John Alden's desk, and the veritable cradle in which rocked Peregrine White, born in the "Mayflower," in 1620. . . . Here, too, was the silver pitcher used by Lafayette in Boston, Captain Nathan Barrett's sword worn at the Concord fight, Governor Endicott's folding chair, which was made for him in Dover more than two hundred years ago, . . . and a large number of other relics too numerous to mention. In the bed-room was an old-fashioned bed-stead, with a quilt of 200 years old, and a sheet belonging to a Lynn lady who received it from her great-grand-mother.[49]

Most of those who recorded in print their reactions to the Log-House displayed a remarkably elastic sense of history; the Revolutionary epoch stretched backward at will, for instance, to take in John Alden and Peregrine White and oozed forward again to accommodate a frontiersman's log cabin of nineteenth-century design.[50] If, as the more dedicated modernists in the journalistic ranks believed, the primary purpose of Emma Southwick's enterprise was to compare the amenities of American life in the present "with those of one hundred" or so years before, to the detriment of the past, then one old thing was just about as good as another.[51]

A typical tour guide, sublimely untroubled by a description that called the Log-House "an exact reproduction of the homes [of] the Minute Men of the Revolution" in one purple paragraph and conjured up visions of Pilgrim fathers nodding by its hearth in the next, thought that the Peregrine White cradle "remains a mute witness of the wonderful story of American progress with which all tongues are busy now. What a contrast between the scene when it held its little charge in the hamlet of Plymouth, amid the fierce storms that howled along the bleak and barren coast of New England, and the grand assemblage of the nations and wealth of the world in which it took its part!"[52]

Only William Dean Howells quibbled with the mode of construction—"it looks much like the log-cabins with which any dweller in the Middle West is familiar"—but he also suggested, turning a blind eye to Lafayette's pitcher, Barrett's sword, and the sheets belonging to the lady from Lynn, that the inside of the "Old Colony House of logs . . . aims at the accurate commemoration of Plymouth in its arrangement and furnishing":

There are many actual relics of the Pilgrim days, all of which the crowd examined with the keenest interest; there was among other things the writing-desk of John Alden, and at the corner of the deep and wide fire-place sat Priscilla spinning—or some young lady in a quaint, old-fashioned dress, who served the same purpose. I thought nothing could be better than this, till a lovely old Quakeress, who had stood by, peering critically at the work through her glasses, asked the fair spinster to let her take the wheel. . . . [The] good old dame bowed herself to the work, and the wheel went round with a soft triumphant burr. . . . That was altogether the prettiest thing I saw at the Centennial.[53]

Howells's not-so-oblique reference to Priscilla and the "Spinning-Wheel" segment of *The Courtship of Miles Standish* of 1858 is a reminder of Longfellow's role in stirring up nostalgia for things colonial and the influence of his word-pictures in arranging the fireside scene that aroused the "keenest interest" among the fairgoers of 1876.[54] Henry Wadsworth Longfellow had moved into the Vassall House in Cambridge in 1843 expressly because there "One whom memory oft recalls, / The Father of his Country, dwelt" during the winter of 1775–76.[55] An early if single-minded collector of antiques, the poet decorated the front hall of the Georgian mansion with a copy of the famous Houdon bust of Washington and an oil portrait finished off by Gilbert Stuart's daughter Jane. He filled his study—once the general's office—with Washington memorabilia of a more personal type, including a Chippendale chair once used by the Great Chief, and showed the room off to guests not as his workplace but as the birthplace of America.[56]

Longfellow's Priscilla, spinning at the ample hearth of a house built "solid, substantial, of timber rough-hewn from the firs of the forest," was an image of particular resonance for Howells, for his audience, for the ladies of the Sanitary Fairs, and for Miss Southwick, who installed the spinster in her New England Kitchen with a neat little wheel rumored to have been part of the cargo of the *Mayflower*. Such was the mystique of the spindle and the wheel that, in 1878, the modern women of Boston gathered in Old South Church for an "Aunt Tabitha Spinning Bee" to raise money for the preservation of the building.[57]

The spinning bee was a reasonable substitute for the "old tyme" kitchen because it embodied all the same overtones of feminine virtue while bearing even more pointed messages for contemporary females. Women writers on colonial culture—and the ranks of lady-historians swelled during the last quarter of the century—reminded their idle, pampered sisters that the colonial mothers once took a hand in the Revolution by forming societies called "Daughters of Liberty" whose principal activity was spinning, making homespun goods to take the place of British manufactures (Figure 2.15). In 1895 Anne Hollingsworth Wharton, author of *Colonial Days and Dames*, cited Longfellow's Plymouth heroine and then reminded her readers of the "pretty picture [that] has come down to us of the young girls sitting out upon Boston Common in the afternoon, with their spinning-wheels before them, industry being the fashion in Colonial days."[58]

"There was much public excitement over spinning," Alice Morse Earle declared in that same year. "Women, rich as well as poor, appeared in Boston Common with their wheels, thus making spinning a popular holiday recreation." But it was as a poignant reminder of honorable feminine industry and competence in bygone times that Morse cherished the juxtaposition of spinning wheel and hearth: "The associations of the kitchen fireside that linger in the hearts of those who are now old can find no counterpart in our domestic surroundings to-day. The welcome cheer of the open fire, which graced and beautified even the humblest rooms, is lost forever with the close gatherings of the family, the household occupations, the home-spun industries which formed and imprinted in the mind of every child the picture of home."[59]

2.15
The appeal of the spinster is illustrated by this photograph, staged in the east parlor of the historic Royall House in Massachusetts

In 1876 the brisk modernity of the Philadelphia Centennial was as alarming as it was enticing. In the new world of machines, in a culture that prized machine-made products, what would become of great-grandma's and grandma's mittens and the handcrafted things that mother used to make? What kind of urban home life could ever compensate for the loss of the old, self-sufficient country ways? What was the proper role of the spinster of yore in a changing pattern of economic and familial relations? Men, for the most part, doted on Priscilla spinning in her chimney corner; she was docile and unassuming in a way that Miss Southwick and the lady-managers of neo-colonial charity affairs were most emphatically not. Women like Candace Wheeler, who eschewed amateur handicrafting and went on to launch a legitimate professional career as a designer for Tiffany after inspecting the needlework displays at the Centennial, may have been just as nostalgic for a fictional past as Howells or Longfellow, but imagined it as a time when the Priscillas and Betsy Rosses did work that was respected and valued.[60]

The fundamental contradiction between seeing colonial history-in-the-round as a place of refuge from the present—a make-believe alternative to change—and viewing the past as a distant benchmark against which the giddy pace of progress could be measured was particularly apparent in the restaurant attached to the New England Log-House and Kitchen. Over the door hung a sign that read "Ye Olden Time" and a horseshoe to ward off witches. A Puritan Bible stood on the spindly old fireside table; a turkey turned slowly on the spit in the hearth; the porringers and caudle cups of yesteryear gleamed on the shelves. The charm of bygone days when ladies wore quaint gowns of linsey-woolsey was exclaimed over by almost every writer who ventured inside for a wholesome dinner of boiled meat, beans, and gingerbread. According to the press, the "New-England Ivy Cottage" was "always crowded with visitors eager to see the ancient costumes of the inmates," the young women who passed the coffee and explained the uses of the odd cooking utensils "whose very simplicity made them incomprehensible to the victim of modern improvements."[61]

Playing at rustic simplicity was healthful and beneficial for victims of strained modern nerves, too. Miss Southwick advertised her wares as the food "the old Puritans grew and waxed strong on."[62] "The erection of this temple to the viands of other days was a capital idea," effused a diner plagued by a sour stomach, "and a blessed one should it aid in the banishment of certain popular delicacies which afflict the digestive apparatus of to-day." The New England Kitchen was Longfellow, Whittier, and Lowell, all stirred and basted into one glorious, evocative feast for the palate and the spirit:

Crook-necks above the chimly hung,
    While in among 'em rusted
The old Queen's arm that Gran'ther Young
    Brought back from Concord busted.[63]

But the concession consisted of more than the log house with its cache of relics and the restaurant with its historical food and pretty colonial serving maids. Cheek by jowl with "the representation of a New England farmer's home 100 years ago" stood a modern kitchen, equipped with all the latest conveniences. Viewed in its totality, then, the display illustrated 1776 *and* 1876, set down side by side for purposes of instructive contrast and invidious comparison.[64] Everybody (except, that is, a few food faddists and dyspeptics) was expected to enjoy the colonial pageantry for its amusement value only; in the end, everybody was expected to prefer a bright and shiny today to a primitive yesterday. The so-called Modern New England Kitchen adjoining the farmhouse "contained all the improvements of the present age, and showed the progress of the century in this department of domestic industry," a technology especially fascinating to the men in the tourist throng, since cookery, like spinning, had been an exclusively female mystery.[65]

Power looms and patented cookers promised to change all that in ways the Philadelphia Exposition could hardly suggest, and other displays of the old technology also masked and moderated a pervasive anxiety about the ever-accelerating pace of change. A dominant attraction of the Agriculture Hall, for example, was the Old Windmill, erected by George V. Hecker & Co. of New York to promote the products of their Croton Flour Mills, including a new brand of self-rising flour (Figure 2.16). Crowds that ran into the thousands gathered around the mill at specified hours to gulp down the free cakes and biscuits baked on the spot from Croton flour. Apart from the treats, however, crowds gathered simply to watch the old blades go round, and to wonder.

2.16
The picturesque Old Mill, in the Agricultural Hall at the Philadelphia Centennial Exposition of 1876

It appeared extremely singular to the majority of visitors by contrast with the . . . machinery of the present day, and this novelty was greatly increased by the knowledge that, with all the mechanical devices of the last fifty years, thousands of mills, even ruder in their construction . . . than this, are seen in various parts of the United States . . . making noticeable dots in patches of beautiful scenery. When we see scattered throughout what should be prosperous localities such specimens of antiquity still in operation, it does not look as if the progress of civilization . . . has been quite as lively as is generally believed.[66]

Old mills were "specimens of antiquity" but they were also specimens of a wholly benign technology, reliable, familiar, and comfortable in a way that the awesome Corliss Engine that powered the exposition was not. Mills worked, but they never seemed to change. Mills were dots of happy human stewardship in lovely landscapes, picturesque, beautiful in their own right, infinitely paintable. As such, the old-fashioned windmills that made their appearance alongside an increasingly complex array of new machinery at all the great American fairs and expositions of the turn of the century—at Philadelphia, at Chicago in 1893, at St. Louis in 1904—helped to make modern apparatus less threatening by simple association: if the old technology had worked so well that the windmill had become a beloved landmark, then there was hope for its up-to-the minute counterparts. They, too, might leave the world of tomorrow substantially unaltered. The future might turn out to be pretty much like the blessed past.

Women rolled the biscuits at the Old Windmill. Women in Priscilla-the-Mayflower-of-Plymouth outfits spun the wool and sliced the brown-bread at the New England Kitchen, a product of female enterprise. Women invented the Sanitary Fairs with their old-time kitchens and relics disposed in roomlike settings. In the waning years of the nineteenth century, women were the primary custodians of the American heritage in its tangible manifestations, the keepers of the flame that burned upon the ancient hearth of the colonial past. And increasingly, as the centennial approached, the women of America had chosen to recreate colonial life in a unique, participatory ritual, a quasi-dramatic, quasi-social form of living for a few hours in a glamorized past called the Martha Washington tea.

In Philadelphia and elsewhere, women held formal teas in 1873 as an appropriate means of celebrating the hundredth anniversary of the Boston Tea Party.[67] Drawing inspiration from the success of these affairs, groups in Richmond and in Baltimore mounted Martha Washington tea parties in the spring of 1875 to raise an endowment for the repair and refurnishing of Mount Vernon in observance of the national centennial. The women of Ohio, meanwhile, garnered $2,000 from a "Washington Ball."[68] The lines of demarcation between the tea, the ball, and the pageant or playlet were not sharply drawn in the 1870s. Thus when the ladies of the New Haven Association, formed in 1875 to promote a wide range of feminine activity at the Philadelphia Fair, decided to present their own Martha Washington tea party in the Music Hall on the evenings of June 10 and 11, the correspondent for their journal, *The Spirit of Seventy-six,* found herself unable to characterize the proceedings succinctly.

Festivities in New Haven opened with a kind of tableau vivant as "the curtain rose upon a well filled gallery and floor. . . . After a few minutes, which were allowed the audience for observing the novel tableau, the queen of the evening, led by the gentleman who represented President Washington, advanced, and took her place upon the dais followed by the members of her suite."[69] The fancy dress that distinguished such affairs from an ordinary tea counted for a great deal in this rite, as did the real identity of the players and the provenance of their costumes. Most of the fifty-odd ladies and gentlemen taking part in the entertainment were assigned specific historical characters to impersonate. The more important the actor, the better the part.

George and Martha Washington were portrayed by Professor Norton (whose pleasantly "friendly spirit" had encouraged the ladies to undertake the project in the first place) and Mrs. Henry Trowbridge, doyenne of the New Haven social set. Mr. Alfred Bacon and his daughter got to represent Mr. and Mrs. Jeremiah Wadsworth largely because he promised to appear in "a suit descended from Col. Wadsworth, which was made in France, in 1784, to be worn [for] his presentation at the Court of Louis XVI, and was afterwards worn at the Court of George III." But ladies and gentlemen of lesser standing in the community were lost in the ranks of "other distinguished guests" despite their historic garments. As for the ostensible theme of the evening, the closest connection to the Washingtons was provided by the gowns of Miss Jocelyn and Miss Hayes (a.k.a. "Betty Washington" and "Mrs. General Hand"), which had once been "worn at the receptions of Mrs. President Washington."[70] Neither of these women received a featured role in the performance by virtue of the authenticity of her costume.

When Martha Washington mounted her dais, events moved toward their crescendo. Escorted to the platform one by one, the ladies of New Haven bowed before her, all the better to exhibit their finery:

Each made her obeisance with the formality of the ancient school. . . . The deep "curtseying" was occasionally and pleasantly varied by an amusing prim dip on the part of some ancient guest, very suggestive of the precise manners of the older regime. . . . [Then came] the dancing of the stately minuet, which occurred upon the conclusion of the presentation, and to which the showy and becoming costumes of the gentlemen added so much. . . .

Lastly, on the part of the entertainers, came the singing of the "Star Spangled Banner" by Mrs. George H. Blinn, whose magnificent voice . . . stirred the patriotism of all. Dancing to a moderate degree now commenced, and the numerous and becomingly attired flower-girls and waitresses began to flit among the crowd . . . proffering their tempting wares to eye and palate. Many from the galleries came down upon the floor to obtain a nearer view of the costumes, or to participate in the pleasures of the dance, and the evening ended in mutual satisfaction and congratulation.[71]

Those not fully absorbed by the spectacle were invited to slip down the block to "the new insurance company building," where they could inspect the Loan Exhibition of Relics opened in conjunction with the tea party. In among the family portraits of Connecticut worthies, the family silver, the ancestral swords and muskets brought home from the Revolution, the dresses too fragile for wear but showing "the luxurious tastes of our ancestors," and the huge display of chinaware, a few Indian artifacts were to be found, and a model of the original cotton gin. But otherwise the show was remarkable for its attempted fidelity to the Washington theme and to the loosely defined colonial era. George and Martha and their times were popular with the public, too: the combined receipts from the tea party and the loan exhibition totaled more than $4,000, of which $2,270.50 was pure profit.[72]

Throughout 1875 and 1876, Connecticut was ablaze with historical pageantry. The Women's Centennial Association of Hartford got up its own show in a local bank, a display combining Revolutionary artifacts, famous works of art, and amateur watercolors painted by local dabblers, both male and female. In aid of the Women's Building at the Philadelphia fair, the ladies of Greenwich had another Martha Washington tea, one without designated roles. Instead, the women (and a very few men) in attendance were distributed among thirteen tables representing the original colonies, decorated with the appropriate state emblems and dedicated to certain practical functions. Rhode Island's was the "ice cream table," for example; North and South Carolina dispensed the candy and the flowers. "The attendance was very large, everybody was inspired by the patriotic nature of the occasion, and ate, drank, and were merry over the achievements of their ancestors. Many of the costumes of the olden time were faithfully reproduced, causing much amusement. . . . The costumes were arranged with faithfulness to old times, and were very effective when contrasted with the modern costumes of the artists from New York, who represented the music of 1876."[73]

It was at Stamford, on the evening of April 28, 1876, that the Connecticut movement reached its glittering apogee with the "Lady Washington Reception" organized by the ladies in aid of the Women's Building at Philadelphia. The event was a pantomime, a ball, a gala dinner, and a traditional patriotic exercise combined in one stunning evening that began with a chorus of "The Star-Spangled Banner" floating over thirteen daintily appointed tables. Then, a curtain at one end of the new Town Hall rose to reveal "George Washington (Hon. M. F. Merritt) and Lady Washington (Mrs. W. C. Braclay)." Next, Colonel Humphreys (Mr. Alfred White) presented the make-believe personages from history "who were received with all the stately formality of our ancestors."

In all, some thirty famous pairs came forward to greet the Washingtons, including such intriguing duos as Madame Genet on the arm of Baron von Steuben, and Lafayette with Dolley Madison:

After presentation the couples retired to a group at the rear of the stage, a group noticeable for its elegant costumes, so different from the plainer apparel of to-day. Lady Washington's costume was a heavy gray silk; Mrs. John Adams . . . , who stood to her right, wore a silk of white and blue stripes, embroidered with bouquets in alternate white and red, and Mrs. Charles Burdett (Mrs. Morris), standing to her left, was attired in rich black velvet. . . .

A feature of rare attraction was the dancing by ten couples of the "Minuet de la Cour," a stately yet pleasing movement. After the supper had been served dances in the modern order continued until long after midnight, gracefully terminating one of the most delightful evenings of social life that Stamford had ever witnessed. Independent of the success in this way, the projectors of the enterprise had reason to congratulate themselves on a financial triumph, the treasurer being able to contribute several hundred dollars to the Centennial fund.[74]

The origin of the fancy Martha Washington "tea" or "reception" that figured so persistently in the far-flung preparations for the centennial is suggested in notices of an art exhibition held on Broadway in New York City in the fall of 1865. The painting on display was a large historical canvas by Daniel F. Huntington, president of the National Academy of Design. Entitled *The Republican Court in the Time of Washington, or Lady Washington's Reception Day,* the picture had occupied Huntington intermittently for four years (Figure 2.17). Now subscriptions were being taken for an engraving based on the scene, and the public exhibition was designed to stir up enthusiasm for that project.[75] According to the printed prospectus and a "key" to the characters supplied by the artist, his painting detailed not one single historical moment but the general tenor of all the Friday evening levees held from eight o'clock to ten or so by Martha Washington throughout her husband's presidency. Thus the painter was free to include a wide variety of famous people who might or might not ever have occupied the same reception room at the same time.

Reviewers thought that President Huntington had chosen this subject in a deliberate effort to pander to the snobbery of a class of well-

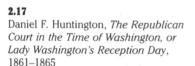

2.17
Daniel F. Huntington, *The Republican Court in the Time of Washington, or Lady Washington's Reception Day*, 1861–1865

connected "native Americans" from the cities, grown rich on wartime profits and tantalized by dreams that their children might one day be members of a new aristocratic caste of pomp and privilege. To such people, remarked the *New York Daily Tribune,* "the notion that once, 'in the good old days,' there *was* a Court, even though it was only a Republican one, gives a dreary sort of comfort":

If they cannot hope to see royalty . . . established in their days; . . . if the line of plebian Presidents is to stretch to the crack of doom, and murdered rail-splitters are to be forever succeeded by boorish tailors; at least they can turn their backs on these ignoble days and recall times when it was otherwise; times when . . . Presidents were dressed in black velvet suits, with swords and powdered-hair, and never smiled, nor made jokes, nor shook common people's hands; and when their wives received the cream of the cream of the land—standing queen-fashion on a dais, and looking with royal indifference on all the wealth, and intellect, and beauty that crowded their stately halls.[76]

The reporter's description of the sober-sided Washington, forbidding in his black velvet, came straight from the pages of Rufus Griswold's *The Republican Court; or, American Society in the Days of Washington,* a book published in 1854 and eventually reissued in 1868 on the wave of enthusiasm for aristocratic pageantry that swept the social enclaves of the North after Appomattox. Indeed, the theme of Huntington's opus also came directly from Griswold, along with his fixation on the social etiquette observed by colonial *grandes dames* paying their respects to Lady Martha and his minute attention to the details of their toilet.

Griswold thought nothing of interrupting an account of the ceremonies marking Washington's inauguration for an excursus on a particularly pretty gown of celestial blue seen in the crowd, a dress with a white satin petticoat and an Italian shawl-like affair at the neck. Although readers do not learn who wore this fabulous concoction, they do get a breathless, Frenchified report of the headdress that went with it, "a *pouf* of gauze, in the form of a globe, the *creneaux* or headpiece of which was composed of white satin, having a double wing, in large plaits, and trimmed with a wreath of artificial roses."[77]

Griswold's preoccupation with colonial haute couture was not unique. Mrs. Ellet's *Queens of American Society,* which reached its sixth edition in 1873, provided an exclusively social history of the Revolutionary and Federal periods: the American past, she argued by omission of all political and military events, was one long cotillion à la mode, one endless procession of elegant women in rich costumes of celestial blue. The "Republican Court," composed of the "principal ladies of New York" and raised to monarchial heights of refinement by Martha Washington, afforded, of course, "no places for the intrusion of the rabble . . . or for the mere coarse and boisterous partisan, the vulgar electioneerer, or the impudent place-hunter, with boots, frock-coat, or roundabouts, or with patched knees and holes at both elbows."[78]

Dress did make the man—and the woman by his side. "It is to meet a sentiment like this, and please such people," charged the *Daily Tribune*, "that 'The Republican Court' has been painted":

The treatment of the subject shows, plainly enough, that the sentiment is known to exist, and that the artist is of no higher mind than willingly to pander to it. To this end, women are made everywhere prominent, because their petticoats are picturesque and their costumes courtly; and in the grouping of the figures a wish to flatter the wealthy families of our own neighborhood is disagreeably evident. Their ancestors are put into the foremost places, and persons who were really of the greatest importance in the history of the country at the time, are shoved quite [out] of sight. . . . And what of the shining center of the picture itself? A bevy of ladies, whom Mr. Huntington has painted with whatever skill he is master of, and who present a sunny, cheerful enough appearance; but their names are not associated with any particular memories, that they should be made so conspicuous.[79]

Although Huntington's critic went on to lambaste him for botching the costumes—Miss Sophia Chew was wearing "entirely modern dress," and the female garments in general suffered from "tame monotony and want of richness," according to the savant from the *Tribune*—the paper was alone in finding the work deficient in that respect. On the contrary, the art critic Henry Tuckerman singled out the gowns for special praise, calling them "elegant, and as authentic as they are picturesque."[80] And it is clear that the popularity of the painting and the corresponding subscription print hinged on women's interest in two aspects of his opus: the dress and manners of their eighteenth-century ancestors, and a codified, Fifth Avenue social hierarchy legitimized by the precedent of Martha Washington perched on her elevated dais.[81]

Thus it came about, in February of 1875, that the fashionable ladies of St. John's Guild of New York, planning an event to support their charity work among the invalid poor, decided to hold a "Lady Washington's Reception-Day" at the Academy of Music and "to have the picture" by Huntington "represented by living characters," many of them direct descendants of the painted worthies. "The arrangement of the costumes and the stage," according to an announcement published a year in advance in *Harper's Weekly*, "will be under the general direction of MR. HUNTINGTON, by special request of the ladies interested."[82]

Meanwhile, sometime early in 1876, a second group of eighty-two New York ladies called upon Ward McAllister—lion of Delmonico's, social arbiter, founder of the Patriarch's Ball, and future codifier of the "Four Hundred"—with an urgent request. Would he kindly serve as manager of a ball they were "getting up at Chickering Hall, in aid of the 'Centennial Union,' to be called the 'Banner Ball'?" As McAllister tells the story in his reminiscences, *Society as I Have Found It*, he not only accepted their "flattering invitation to lead so fair a band of

2.18
C. S. Reinhart's drawing of the great Martha Washington reception staged at the Academy of Music, New York, 1876

patriots" but also hit upon the idea of dressing them up "in Colonial costumes, representing Lady Washington and the ladies of her Court."[83]

Whoever deserves the honor of having invented the classic Martha Washington society ball, with its arcane versions of historical evening dress and its intricate quadrilles, St. John's Guild and the Banner Ball committee both relied on Huntington's painting for pointers on costumes and for a proper aristocratic hauteur. McAllister, for instance, tells of one society matron asking a second, attired in a blaze of jewels and plumes, just what her various items of showy apparel were meant to signify. "What have I got on?" replied the bespangled belle. "Why, Madame, I had a grandmother!" "Had you, indeed!" huffed the questioner. "Then, if that was her garb, she must have been Pocahontas, or the Empress of Morocco!"[84] But such snobbery, according to McAllister, did nothing to detract from the high tone of the glittering evening, characterized by the gracious demeanor of a matriarch in "her great-grandmother's dress, pink and brown striped brocade, cut like Martha Washington's dress in the *Republican Court,* in which her great-grandmother figured. The wife of a prominent jurist, a remarkably handsome woman, with a grand presence and a noble carriage, representing Lady Washington, [she] wore, to all eyes, the most attractive costume there."[85]

At New York's Academy of Music, the "Martha Washington's Reception" as arranged by Mr. Huntington took place on George Washington's Birthday, 1876, with a corresponding emphasis on costumes that, judging from the woodcuts supplied in quantity to a curious readership by the illustrated papers, were no less capricious and 1876-ish than those seen in Chickering Hall (Figure 2.18).[86] And, as at the Banner Ball, "the wealth, beauty and fashion of New York were present in full strength and in all the glory of superb array." The program of events was more elaborate, however.

At ten o'clock in the evening, the curtains parted to reveal no less than forty-nine tea tables, emblematic of all the states and territories, with prominent costumed ladies ranged about them. Then, after the gasps of the audience and some patriotic airs by a choir, "twelve couples attired in the picturesque garb of a century ago made their appearance in the open space and proceeded in stately style to dance the minuet," and they led the company into an adjoining hall where hot tea was served "in white porcelain cups and saucers, [decorated] in green circlets, in perfect imitation of the service presented to General Washington by General Lafayette." The tea was for sale, and so were the souvenir cups and saucers.

At quarter to eleven, the last teacake having been dispensed with and the china tucked into pockets and handbags, the venue changed again. Governor Tilden headed a promenade of dignitaries back into the Academy for the ball proper, although the crush of more than eight thousand guests who crowded the boxes, vestibules, and corridors made dancing almost impossible and finally drowned out the music of Bernstein's Band.[87] But nobody really minded. With $15,000 raised in a single night and seemly deference paid to those who, by birthright or bank balance, claimed the honor of wearing the shorts of General Washington and the furbelows of his lady, the Martha Washington reception was a resounding success.

Order Versus Progress

Historical costume was a central feature of the centennial celebration. Washington's own clothes, tossed over a chair as if to suggest that he would return to camp and to his tea table in a moment, were the focal relics of the government's exhibit in Philadelphia. The guides and waitresses in the New England Kitchen wore the dresses of olden colonial times. The ladies and gentlemen who bowed and curtseyed their way through the gala charity affairs in New York and elsewhere that marked the hundredth birthday of the nation did so attired in the quaint kinds of garments once worn by the stately Father of His Country and the elegant Lady Washington.

The very coat and pants that once clothed the body of Washington established a special intimacy between the onlooker and the quasi-legendary hero; articles of common usage underscored the common humanity linking Washington with his modern-day countrymen. But wearing such apparel, or watching a contemporary do so, compressed the distance between 1776 and 1876 even more markedly. The local worthy who put on a powdered wig and items culled from the ancestral wardrobe to play George Washington for an evening *became* a human relic, an animate artifact, a living link with history and with the American heritage.

The passion for dressing up and the taste for heirlooms were promoted largely by women. Given that women were the titular custodians of nineteenth-century culture, their position of leadership in the colonial revival of 1876 is not surprising. What is nonetheless disconcerting is the pungent domestic flavor of centennial Washingtoniana: Washington's pants matrixed in a cozy camp-tent setting with the bed made and the table laid; his colonial epoch represented principally by a toasty hearth, a spinning wheel, and a pan of gingerbread; his social life recreated as a fancy-dress ball directed by Martha, with dainty souvenir cups and saucers for favors and an exquisite refinement of the rules of preferment.[88]

But excursions into the make-believe of historical kitsch were also gestures toward the special, material intimacy with the past that the centennial generation craved. It was expressed in other ways as well. Looking back on her own childhood, Mrs. Theodore Roosevelt, for instance, recalled that "Washington's portrait hung beside his wife's on our nursery wall. He was a beloved and familiar friend, and I was taught to throw kisses to 'George and Martha.'"[89] To the matron who, as a little girl, once blew bedtime kisses at the Athenaeum Portrait, a Martha Washington tea was no anomaly. It was part—an exciting and interesting part, to be sure, but just a part—of the normal order of things.

Orderliness provides another clue to what the neocolonialisms of 1876 were all about. Although stacked to the rafters with choice antiques and telling relics—and contemporary home interiors were decorated, by choice, according to the same aesthetic of profusion—the rooms created for the Sanitary Fairs, the exposition, and even the teas were models of orderly household arrangements. Every object had a firm rationale for being there, in its own place. The rich associations that adhered to the Peregrine White cradle or the suit Washington wore in Annapolis were ample reasons for their inclusion. So were the identities of the proud descendants (or possessors) who lent the artifacts. But so, finally, were the roles the tinned plate and the cup and saucer had to play in the plausible, everyday workings of the environments created, rooms in which George Washington might once have dined and Martha poured tea. Objects vivified the illusion of life, the sense that the Washingtons could go about their business in such places, much as the log cabin ladies of 1876 contrived to cook savory meals at well-equipped colonial hearths.

The housewife of 1876 might well have learned to prize modern technological advances when confronted with the cumbersome apparatus of the 1776 kitchen. Yet she also learned that tasks had changed by degree and not by kind, that the household of the past was not all that different from her own, that domesticity was a virtue inextricably tied up with the essence of the American past, and that the orderly home was the best refuge from the inherent disorder of rackety progress. Insofar as Martha Washington balls and tea parties carefully apportioned roles among the participants according to standards of birth and wealth and station, they also aimed at bringing an orderly hierarchy of relationships out of the social chaos spawned by progress—by urbanization, redistribution of wealth, and changing mores.

George and Martha stood for orderliness of all these sorts because they never changed as they blinked down from their frames upon the nursery wall. In books and paintings, as in modern-day recreations of them, Martha Washington forever stood on her dais in a gorgeous gown, acknowledging the homage of the fairest belles of the social elite, ignoring the common rabble. As for her husband, so "careful of little things," as fussy about his linen and knives and saltcellars as any centennial homemaker, George Washington—in his famous "shorts," of course—forever awaited the company at dinner of his progeny, the folks with their noses pressed to the other side of the glass, peering into that case in Philadelphia.

Colonial History Domesticated

3

The Restoration of Mount Vernon
1853–1890

3.1
A "Century Vase," exhibited at the 1876 Centennial Exposition by the Union Porcelain Works of Long Island and designed by Karl Mueller

Centennial Souvenirs for the Mantelpiece

In his mock oration for the Fourth of July, 1859, the humorist Artemus Ward spoke for those Union men who held up the august person of Washington as an object lesson in restraint, a rebuke to antebellum fractiousness and greed. "G. Washington," Ward insisted, "was abowt the best man this world ever sot eyes on. . . . He wasn't after the spiles. He was a human angil in a 3 kornerd hat and knee britches, and we shan't see his like right away."[1]

In 1876 Washington must have seemed to fairgoers even more like an alabaster "angil" or some other strange species of nonsectarian godling with a pigtail. His icons littered the grounds of the Philadelphia Exposition. His statue perched precariously atop the iron girders spanning the Main Building.[2] His features, modeled in sugar-candy, adorned a lavish confectionary grouping illustrating the signing of the Declaration of Independence; other events in the life of Washington were picked out in sweetmeats on the side of a pyramidal display assembled by a New York candy butcher.[3] And that was only the beginning.

Washington's bust adorned any number of special "Century Vases" proudly exhibited by firms both domestic and foreign (Figure 3.1). The centerpiece of the Gorham Manufacturing Company's booth was a solid silver vessel, over four feet high, at the center of which appeared in relief a fluttering angel bearing a silhouette of Washington. Commemorative urns of parian, porcelain, and earthenware came in sizes ranging from several inches high to the grotesque extreme of a twelve-foot pair contributed by the French. "The Stars and Stripes, the eagle; George Washington and the Goddess of Liberty," sighed a weary connoisseur of Centennial chinaware, "compose a quartet which, no matter how artistically they may be combined, pall at the present time

3.2
"Unpacking a Statue of Washington" at the Centennial

3.3
Guarnerio's *Apotheosis of Washington* in Memorial Hall

upon the general taste of the American public. . . . [Perhaps] Centennial fever will soon subside, and then it will be decided that in no more appropriate way than by these everlasting records [in ceramic] could the event be commemorated."[4]

Journalists touring the site to report on the bustle of last-minute preparations found pandemonium in Memorial Hall, where Italian workmen struggled to uncrate and reassemble a colossal half-length bust of Washington in white plaster, the work of one of their countrymen variously known to fairgoers as Pietro Guarneri or Prof. Guarnerio (Figure 3.2).[5] Executed especially for the exposition (in hopes of finding a rich American patron for a marble version), the sculpture was shown to advantage in an arch just inside the entrance to the south hall, where, alas, it was noticed chiefly for its size, an enormity that lent Washington's highly "particularized eyelashes" a strange aura of menace.[6]

Tourists who had suffered through the prayer offered during the opening ceremonies ("We thank Thee," droned Bishop Simpson, "for the fathers of our country, . . . for the immortal Washington," etc., etc.),[7] visited the Washington pantaloons, and inspected every one of the Washington vases were inclined to greet all this transatlantic enthusiasm for their hero with an air of stoic exhaustion: "Washington! . . . It is possible to have too much of a good thing, and judging from the every conceivable material in which the 'first in war, in peace, and first in the hearts of his countrymen' is represented to us, by foreign artists and artisans, one would fancy that we are a people who have never known the first president except by the page of history and the musty records of politics."[8]

Occasionally, however, as in the case of Guarnerio's *Apotheosis of Washington,* indifference turned to disbelief and scorn. In an attempt at poetic treatment, the sculptor had mounted Washington, Constitution in hand, on the back of an American eagle, which, large though it was, was not quite equal to the task of wafting its burden of parchment, powdered hair, and Pater Patriae to the stars (Figure 3.3). "A monstrosity!" cried sophisticates.[9] "The more ignorant surmised . . . that it must be 'Washington on a Lark!'"[10] William Dean Howells, cheered by the general unpopularity of this "Disgrace of the Art Hall," opined that aesthetic standards had apparently slipped a bit in Italy since Michelangelo's time: "The eagle [is] life-size and the Washington some six feet high from the middle up; having no occasion for legs in the attitude chosen, Washington thriftily dispenses with them. The poor man who made this thing is so besotted with it as to have placarded his other works, 'By the sculptor of the Washington.'"[11]

In fact, most of the samples of Italian statuary that turned up among the commercial displays in the Main Building and the artistic offerings in Memorial Hall (an annex was hastily constructed to hold them all) were hybrids, the combined work of art dealers—often Americans residing in Florence—and accomplished native stonecutters. Sculptors, in the conventional meaning of the term, had nothing to do with the humble craft of the imagemakers. And those prolific marblecutters and their cunning little statues, scaled for the mantelpiece or the parlor whatnot, were exempted from the disdain heaped upon the pretentious allegories of their betters by the fairgoing public (Figure 3.4).[12] John Sartain, the chief of the Centennial Bureau of Art, noted that the rooms in which this kind of mantelpiece statuary was displayed were the most crowded of the whole fair. As in one of the new department stores rather than a conventional art gallery, the aisles were always thronged with buyers. "The Italians . . . have struck out a new field in sculpture, and have succesfully treated in marble subjects heretofore confined to canvas—scenes from domestic life. Their execution is wonderful," Sartain insisted a little defensively, "and whatever the critics may say, the popular instinct recognizes and approves the truthfulness to nature manifested in these works."[13]

The works that won soft American hearts were sentimental statuettes executed with great technical panache. Cloth fell in lifelike folds. Locks of hair waved prettily, every strand delineated by the chisel.

3.4
Francis William Edmonds, *The Image-Peddlar* [sic], 1844. The kind of mass-produced patriotic statuary sold at the Centennial had been seen earlier in America; the difference was one of quantity and theme.

Baby flesh was as soft as butter: "Representing children at play, in grief, or in sorrow, or aping the vanities and faults of their elders . . . , these attracted considerable attention, and were by the mass of visitors, we think, preferred and better appreciated even than the generally solemn and mysterious productions of high art, which they had not the time to study or understand."[14] Preferred themes included a tiny girl who, in an excess of maternal devotion, attempts to nurse a baby bird at her own chubby bosom; a stubborn little boy in a nightshirt— all the better to show his dimpled knees—who refuses to say his bedtime prayers; and another little fellow, standing barefoot and abashed in his shimmy-shirt, who clutches a hatchet in one grubby fist. The latter came from Florence, from the workshop of Pietro Bazzanti and Sons, and depicted Washington and his hatchet, according to Parson Weems's beloved fable of the child-hero who couldn't tell a lie (Figure 3.5). Pasquale Romanelli of Florence had a baby Washington for sale, too, and both competitors recommended that the subject be paired with a *Franklin and His Whistle* available for on-the-spot purchase.[15]

The preference for the small and sugary in statuary, for the mischievous infant Washington over the ferocious general and the austere president, reinforces the notion that colonial history was a domesticated, even housewifely affair in 1876. The articles and images dominating the popular journals of the day only strengthen that impression. Washington and a complementary assortment of 1776 motifs were, quite naturally, seen everywhere. But the range of acceptable imagery was actually quite narrow and skewed in the direction of colonial sweetness and domesticity. Even Thomas Nast, in his famous cover cartoon for *Harper's Weekly*—an acid comment on the want of political honesty observable from the perspective of Washington's Birthday, 1876—chose Parson Weems's (and Pasquale Romanelli's) charming story of the dimpled child with the toy hatchet as his point of reference (Figure 3.6).

As the centennial year ran its course, the pages of *Harper's* were cluttered with glimpses of charming eighteenth-century interiors, backgrounds for scenes of dashing Continentals bound for the battlefield, embracing well-fed damsels whose correspondence to prevailing nineteenth-century canons of beauty was such that they might have posed for the illustrator on the afternoon of a Martha Washington tea (Figure 3.7). Fictional and factual selections alike were decorated with likenesses of Washingtonian gallants, in buff-and-blue uniforms with breeches, and ladies whose sumptuous gowns were arranged so that every possible detail of cut, trim, and fabric could be noted by the avid female reader awaiting an invitation to a Lady Washington ball.

Beginning in July of 1874, in anticipation of the anniversary year, *Harper's New Monthly Magazine* had run a series of illustrated pieces dealing with historical characters and sites. "One of the earliest," according to the historian Rodris Roth, "was Charles D. Deshler's, 'A Glimpse of Seventy-Six.' This article was a study of the social conditions of 'our ancestors of the Revolutionary period' in which the author 'crossed their thresholds and inspected the interiors of their households.' Using as source material the inventories of persons whose property was plundered or destroyed by the British, Deshler examined their parlors and kitchens, amusements, and privations."[16] Even travel writers for the monthly version of *Harper's* eschewed faraway places to concentrate on the ancient, colonial settlements along the eastern seaboard, just being rediscovered by urbanites seeking beauty spots for cheap, cool summer resorts.

In 1875 Charles Nordhoff compiled a list of amusing things to do in the unspoiled villages on Cape Cod, Nantucket, and Martha's Vineyard, recommending in particular the auctions that "have furnished recreation also to summer visitors, where they purchased curious old furniture, old china, old table gear; and I was even offered a magnificent brass warming-pan."[17] A long article on Lyme, Connecticut, published in the same magazine in 1876, was illustrated with pictures of furniture found in the manses along Lyme's tree-lined "Street," as if to suggest that the hamlet was a treasure-trove for seekers of antiquities.

One cut showed the writing desk Elder Brewster brought over on the *Mayflower* (his Mayflower tea set, it should be recalled, was on display in the Connecticut Cottage at the Centennial Exposition, and John Alden's Mayflower writing desk occupied a place of honor in the New England Kitchen there), "which is now in the possession of his

3.6
A Thomas Nast political cartoon reflecting on Washington's Birthday, 1876

3.7
Walter Saterlee, "Pro Patria—1776; Departure and Return"

3.8
Elder Brewster's writing desk, brought over on the *Mayflower*

granddaughter, Mrs. Daniel Chadwick, of Lyme" (Figure 3.8). Another showed the somewhat younger "Table of the Ex-Governors" that stood between the front windows in "the antique dwelling" of the Honorable Charles Johnson M'Curdy, LL.D., former justice of the Supreme Court and former lieutenant governor of Connecticut. That state had been served in the gubernatorial chair by no less than six M'Curdy forebears, whose table the present inhabitant of the old house regarded as a prize exhibit in his veritable "museum of souvenirs of preceding generations."[18]

Ancestry figured prominently throughout the descriptive tour of Lyme. Subtitled "A Chapter of American Genealogy," the *Harper's* article was a crazy-quilt mixture of gossipy tributes to the prominent descendants of good old families and their wonderful old furniture, anecdotes about romance in the olden times (illustrated with the requisite portrait of an embryonic Gibson Girl in a ruffled colonial frock), and local color of a dreamy, house-proud caste:

Turning north . . . you are confronted by a quaint homestead which seems to be taking life comfortably right in the middle of "The Street." . . . Its hall of entrance [is] of a pre-Revolutionary pattern, and its whole architecture one-sided; but it has an unmistakable air of gentility. If you enter, you are plunged headlong into an antiquarian mine; paneled walls, curious cornices, enormous fire-places, high mantles, and round tables all bring your forefathers and foremothers round you in their powdered wigs and high-heeled shoes. The chairs and pictures are many of them two hundred years old.[19]

The mania for Mayflower writing desks and for colonial bric-a-brac of all sorts, even that having the most tangential of associations with the vaunted Spirit of 1776, reached a crescendo in 1876. The antiques craze accordingly became the butt of much topical humor. The reigning centennial comic, for example, clearly expected his readers to get the joke when he tweaked that acquisitive frenzy in doggerel:

> In sixteen hundred twenty
> With good intentions plenty,
> From England came the Pilgrims, bringing heaps of things to wear,
> And such a lot of tables,
> Old clocks and chairs and cradles,
> That relics from the Mayflower are found most everywhere.[20]

Painting Daily Life in Colonial Times

Relics were found in lush profusion in the new crop of American history paintings that were among the popular favorites of the Centennial Exposition. George Boughton's *Pilgrims Going to Church,* also known as *The Pilgrims' Sunday Morning,* is a case in point (Figure 3.9).[21] The picture largely responsible for our persistent mental image of the New England Fathers, Boughton's canvas is suitably austere in

color and in the friezelike composition of gray-clad figures set off against the barren chill of the snow. As if in compensation for this miserly allotment of painterly charm, however, it is rich in local color, almost to the point of surfeit. The smallest detail of wimple, pleat, helmet, blunderbuss, and Bibleclasp is meticulously wrought. The sheen of polished leather, the itch of wool, the crisp snap of starchy linen, caress the senses.

Whatever one might deduce of the spiritual qualities of those worthies from examining Boughton's wintertime processional, the material substance of their lives seems ample, solid, even prodigal in its profusion. *Pilgrims to Church* suggests the relic room of a Sanitary Fair come suddenly to life; the lingering impression is that of most of New England's ancestral treasures assembled for some curious Pilgrim Ball.

The painting was frequently chosen as a guidebook plate and was the subject of extended commentary by Centennial art lovers:

The specimen of which we offer an engraving is taken . . . from the history of the Puritans [*sic*] in New England, which seems to have impressed Mr. Boughton as forcibly, considered as a repertory of art-effects, as it did Mr. Hawthorne the novelist. Our selection . . . represents a train of wayfarers passing with solemn caution through a snowy landscape, the men armed to the teeth, except the venerable pastor, whose defenses are the holy book he carries and the good angel who walks by his side in the person of a lovely daughter. . . . Each figure in the picture is seen against the snow—a sombre silhouette. Fathers, mothers, and innocent children proceed with serious, God-fearing expression through the desolate landscape. . . . It is strange and touching to watch these earnest men, in their peaked hats and leather jerkins, each with a Bible in his belt and a musket on his shoulder.[22]

3.10
Francis Davis Millet, *A Cozy Corner,* 1884

The writer speaks for the many delighted fairgoers who gave Boughton's painting a head start toward its eventual fame when he singles out for special notice the captivating details of costume, the pretty girl, the thrilling tinge of mock terror of the bedtime story variety, and the familial overtones of the scene—the very elements that made *Puritans Going to Church* the ideal subject for a framed sepia print to hang in the family parlor above a cache of Centennial souvenirs engraved with the bust of Washington, and adjacent to whatever ancestral relics the establishment could muster. Donald Mitchell, designer of the neocolonial Connecticut Cottage, spoke for countless others, too, when he admired "the modest piquancies" of Boughton's "well-authenticated pictures of the Puritan girls."[23]

Frank Millet of Boston, in his contribution to the Department of American Art at the fair, dispensed with the public portions of the historical record altogether and concentrated solely on the girls, their clothes, and their domestic paraphernalia (Figure 3.10). Although Millet's post-Centennial work consisted of genre paintings of the past—of young women actively impersonating his own ancestresses from the Plymouth Colony while wearing the costumes he collected, and posing among the specimens of Americana he purchased after his exposure to the antiques in evidence in Philadelphia—the lost *Lady in Costume of 1740* that hung in the exposition gallery made no such claim to be a magical glance backward in time. As the title specified, Millet's picture depicted the kind of 1876 make-believe practiced at Martha Washington teas: a lady of his acquaintance sat for Millet in his Tremont Street studio "in the dress worn by her great-great-grandmother . . . on the occasion of her wedding in 1740."[24]

Eventually, in aid of his historical reconstructions, Millet would pose the models in his own colonial kitchen, built into his house in East Bridgewater, Massachusetts; his popular Centennial painting was the first of many painstaking efforts to duplicate the daily life of the past, down to its most minute detail.[25] The exposition was both a rallying point for would-be revivalists like Millet and a source of inspiration for others, like the great Thomas Eakins of Philadelphia, to whom the colonial manner represented an important aspect of the contemporary experience.

Under the direct influence of the fair's organizers, Eakins, whose grimly contemporary *Gross Clinic* had been rejected by the Centennial jury, produced a series of watercolors in 1876 showing women in antique costume with spinning wheels and other props from a New England kitchen.[26] Although the American galleries contained their share of windy historical exercises in the grand manner—*Washington Welcoming the Provision Train, Washington as Ambassador to Fort Duquesne,* even Ritchie's steel engraving of *Lady Washington's Reception*—Enoch Wood Perry, Worthington Whittredge, Walter Saterlee

(the sometime illustrator of colonial themes for *Harper's*), Eastman Johnson, and E. Lamson Henry were merely the best known among the forty-odd native artists who elected to look instead at the spinning wheels, family houses, pretty girls, and wise old ladies of "one hundred years ago."[27]

In some respects, Henry is the most interesting of the lot. A conventional genre painter in the antebellum period, he served as a clerk in the Union army; on patrol in 1864 he first caught a glimpse of the old Westover mansion, colonial seat of the Byrds of Virginia (Figure 3.11). The sight of it, he later admitted, drove him "nearly crazy" with longing for that simpler age when planters offered bountiful hospitality to their neighbors and Washington danced at Williamsburg. Thereafter, the artist's standard presentation of Westover showed a colonial version of the heavenly Jerusalem rising, solid and serene, above the confusions of the Civil War.[28] In the same vein, Henry also combined contemporary and historical subject matter in his 1865 view of Boston's John Hancock House, the destruction of which, paradoxically, fanned the feeble flames of an active preservation movement. It is not entirely clear whether the artist sketched that old landmark just before it fell to the forces of progress in 1863, or worked from a photograph.

Using modern technology in the service of historical research, Henry had become an active photographer of colonial sites, and sometimes posed for the camera therein wearing colonial knee breeches. However old-fashioned in motif, therefore, his paintings of the haunts of the Founding Fathers are always resonant with a sad and thoroughly modern awareness that the merciless hand of time can be stayed only for a moment by the power of the artist's brush.

Time, in just that sense, was the theme of the picture that represented E. L. Henry at the Centennial Exposition. *The Old Clock on the Stairs,* based on Longfellow's 1845 poem of the same title, depicts the central hall of a Georgian house, aglow with the luster of old wood and the soft tones of old carpets (Figure 3.12). Through a low doorway under the staircase a distant room beckons the eye toward the fireplace, where a colonial grandmother slowly rocks—an early instance of the growing pictorial identification between women and the interiors they were expected to adorn in both the literal and the figurative senses. But the focal point of the painting is the grandfather clock in its case "of massive oak," looming over the landing at the turning of the stairs.

3.12
Edward Lamson Henry, *The Old Clock on the Stairs*, 1868

In Longfellow's poem, the clock serves as the repository for two distinct emotions: an almost sensual delight in aged things and a rueful awareness of loss, of a better world passing away with each tick, each sounding of the hour. The opening stanza is full of joy, adventure, and anticipation, as the poet walks down a quiet street somewhere in New England, finds the house, crosses the threshold, and finally sees the clock:

> Somewhat back from the village street
> Stands the old-fashioned country-seat.
> Across its antique portico
> Tall poplar-trees their shadows throw.
> And from its station in the hall
> An ancient timepiece says to all,—
>   "Forever—never!
>   Never—forever!"[29]

That verse is the rhymed equivalent of the *Harper's* writers' stroll down the tree-lined streets of Old Lyme, stalking antiques and a bond of blood between a gracious past and a problematic present. In Henry's painting, too, the viewer has just come through the door that opens off the street and the world of today. The clock and the founding mother by the fire are still a long way off; immediately at hand, however, is the old tilt-top table that gleams dully in the filtered sunlight spilling down the stairs—almost the same table old Judge M'Curdy cherished because his sainted grandsires and theirs once sat around it.

For Longfellow and for Henry the passage of the years enhances the loveliness of old things, like clocks and tables and aged ladies sitting by the chimneyside. They respect great age and honor the wisdom bred of long experience. Henry personifies wisdom in his grandmother with her mobcap and fichu. She stands for that whole generation of grandmothers in whose dresses Millet posed their pretty progeny. Maternal figures, they calm the unquiet spirit and nurture the careworn heart, much as their graceful houses brighten the jaded eye. But the painting, in its very airless stillness, also hints at the fragility of the moment. The clock will tick again, and the ancestral shades will vanish. When the light begins to fade, the old table will be just a piece of scarred and lifeless wood.

Toward the end of his poem, Longfellow gives vent to the hurt, the sense of betrayal by things that steals over the heart when neither antiquarian nor painter can stop the swift flight of the hours and the years:

> All are scattered now and fled,
> Some are married, some are dead;
> And when I ask, with throbs of pain,
> "Ah, when shall they all meet again?"

As in the days long since gone by,
The ancient timepiece makes reply,—
   "Forever—never!
   Never—forever!"[30]

Longfellow knew the seductive charm of antiquities at first hand because he lived in Washington's Cambridge headquarters, where Nathaniel Hawthorne had set the eighth chapter of his *Whole History of Grandfather's Chair* of 1841. If *The Scarlet Letter* and *The House of the Seven Gables* exude something of the eerie charm that infuses Boughton's Pilgrims, there is more than a touch of the story of Grandfather's antique chair in Henry's insistence on the soulfulness of tilt-top tables and pedimented clocks. The humble, inanimate object strikes Hawthorne the same way: it becomes a repository for the values of those who used it and a reminder of their virtues (Figure 3.13). So after the briefest of rhetorical pauses to wonder "if it might be irreverent to introduce the hallowed shade of Washington into a history where an ancient elbow-chair occupied the most prominent place," Grandfather resumes telling his grandchildren a Thanksgiving Eve's story of the progress of the nation to date. His narrative is couched in terms of the famous and no-so-famous Americans who once perched upon his own Washington relic:

3.13
Frank T. Merrill, "How to Capture the British Army," frontispiece to Hawthorne's *Grandfather's Chair*

"When General Washington first entered this mansion," said Grandfather, "he was ushered up the staircase and shown into a handsome apartment. He sat down in a large chair, which was the most conspicuous object in the room. The noble figure of Washington would have done honor to a throne. . . . Never before had the lion's head at the summit of the chair looked down upon such a face and form as Washington's."

"Why, Grandfather!" cried Clara, clasping her hands in amazement, "was it really so? Did George Washington sit in our great chair?"[31]

The children who listen to Grandfather's tales of George Washington and the heroic past are the America of the future and the subjects of Eastman Johnson's *Old Stage Coach* of 1871, a painting that received a prestigious Centennial award during its exhibition at the Philadelphia fair (Figure 3.14). Set in the golden sunshine of a long afternoon in the Catskills, the work depicts a group of children playing at make-believe around an abandoned stagecoach. The light, as well as the measured composition, suggest a kind of golden age of childhood and nostalgia for the joys of innocence, but the faded name along the roofline of the old coach—"Mayflower"—translates the artist's longing for his youth into the larger, national framework. The name harks back to Plymouth and the early settlers, and the coach itself belongs to that very preindustrial past with which the manufacturers assembled for the Centennial Exposition were at pains to juxtapose the splendors of a modern, technological present. Although Johnson evokes an idyllic

past, however, he also seems to foresee an idyllic American future when all the happy children—white and black alike—who work together to make the stagecoach in his picture "go," will have grown up at last.

America's Ruins

Eastman Johnson's mood of ebullient prophecy matched the optimism of the Centennial Exhibition. His use of the homey, undramatic theme of kids at play as a metaphor for great events allied Johnson with the wholesale domestication and feminization of historical imagery in the 1860s and 1870s, a trend he had helped to initiate in his own Mount Vernon paintings. In 1856 the artist's father had married a Mrs. Mary James, née Washington, one of the closest living relatives of the first president. Under the influence of that relationship and the beginnings of a drive to rescue the estate from "the squalor and general neglect everywhere apparent about the house and grounds" vividly described by the artist Thomas Rossiter in the columns of *The Crayon* in 1858, Johnson painted the tomb of Washington, moldering in picturesque decay, with lady-visitors sighing in the vicinity.[32]

That picture is known today only from written descriptions, and while the subject of a hero's tomb is a stock item in the vast store of nineteenth-century sentimentality, presentation of the grave in the form of a ruin, pleasurable to visit in its decay, taps another quite different convention of view painting. The treatment of the Washington vault as a ruin comparable to the mausoleums of the ancients gives the relatively short span of American history a sort of pseudo-antiquity, an intimation of duration and stable tradition at odds with the mercurial passions of those who would dissolve the Union in the heat of the moment.

While Rossiter produced metaphorical Mount Vernon scenes recreating the domestic life of Washington in order to emphasize the familial ties that bound the Union together—the pictures entitled *Washington Reading to His Family Under the Trees at Mount Vernon* and *Washington and Lafayette at Mount Vernon* were prepared from on-the-spot drawings well before the Civil War broke out—Johnson's works do not bring the hero back to life.[33] Indeed, the status of Washington as a remote and hallowed figure from long, long ago made the quarrels of Johnson's day, based on hot-tempered self-interest, seem all the more shameful. Great age contributes to the mood of meaningful, even enjoyable sadness that defines the nostalgia explicit in his views of ladies at the old tomb or a slave woman feeding her children around the gaping, ruinous hearth in the painting entitled *Washington's Kitchen at Mount Vernon.* Once upon a time, long ago, his imagery declares, there was a race of giants, big enough to need such hearths. Once there were Americans grand enough to fill the honored tombs of heroes.

Eastman Johnson added to the pathos of Mount Vernon by consigning the site to the keeping of women, children, and the humblest of domestics, but by introducing such figures to serve as the viewer's surrogate in the painting, he also gave the place a sweetness, a familiarity, and an approachable warmth missing from the stiff formality of Rossiter's *Visit of the Prince of Wales, President Buchanan and Dignitaries to the Tomb of Washington at Mount Vernon, October 1860* (Figure 3.15). Painted in 1861, as Huntington began his *Republican Court,* Rossiter's work described a real event. Throughout the 1850s, and despite the evident deterioration, Mount Vernon was a

3.15
Thomas P. Rossiter, *Visit of the Prince of Wales, President Buchanan and Dignitaries to the Tomb of Washington at Mount Vernon, October 1860*, 1861

place visitors to Washington, D.C., were taken to see. The house was off-limits but the grounds were not, and the tomb became a favorite stop on the tourist's itinerary. Twigs plucked from the willows in the vicinity were the customary souvenirs of such an outing. Prints showing the tomb circulated, as did puzzle pictures, issued by Currier and Ives as late as 1876, in which Washington's ghostly profile was formed by the outlines of the trees at the gravesite.[34]

People of all sorts traveled down the Potomac on their pious errand in the 1850s. But on October 5, 1860, the landing was thronged with guests who had sailed from the capital in the party of the president for an official state visit to the tomb. There were distinguished ladies in the company, wives of important men, hostesses of power and influence in their own right. They had all come to witness an important ritual. The guest of honor, the Prince of Wales, heir to the British crown and descendant of George III, concluded his tour of the United States by planting a symbolic tree in such a position as to cast a felicitous shade upon the final resting place of George Washington, the revolutionary who had driven the English from American soil. Albert Edward was the first distinguished visitor, although by no means the last, to be guided to Washington's grave with enormous fanfare. The fresh symbolic significance Mount Vernon acquired in the troubled political climate of years preceding the Civil War is demonstrated as much by that carefully staged bit of ceremonial tourism as it is by Rossiter's huge commemorative canvas.[35]

Symbolism did not stave off the Civil War. The next highly publicized visit to the tomb came in 1865, when the whole of Sherman's victorious army stopped there en route to a triumphal grand review in Washington. With the centennial year, however, the custom of foreign dignitaries planting memorial trees to shelter the remains of Washington was revived in earnest. And so, after helping Grant to start up the Corliss Engine in the tribute to technological power that opened the Philadelphia celebration of 1876, and after listening to Whittier's Centennial Hymn commend to the mercies of the Almighty a postwar nation where North and South met "united, free / And loyal to our land and Thee," Emperor Dom Pedro of Brazil went straight to the tomb at Mount Vernon and planted an elm in the name of his countrymen.[36]

As the centennial celebration neared, the primitive conditions at Mount Vernon were cause for worry among those who feared that the general dilapidation would give foreign guests a poor impression of an otherwise exemplary republic. There were Americans, a popular weekly editorialized, "to whom the memory of the men who established our independence is so precious that they would feel sincerely ashamed to have foreigners arrive and find that we honored the fathers so little as to leave their graves neglected and their monuments falling into ruins." Washington's estate was the worst of the lot:

3.16
Clark Mills's statue of Washington in 1860

Even Mount Vernon, the home and great monument of GEORGE WASHINGTON is tumbling to pieces, and its desolation and decay will offer a strange contrast to the fresh splendor of the Centennial buildings at Philadelphia. . . .

Extensive repairs are absolutely necessary. . . . The veneration for WASHINGTON in the hearts of the large mass of our foreign visitors, and the great curiosity in the minds of all of them, will undoubtedly make Mount Vernon a point of pilgrimage from Philadelphia. . . . Is there not enough self-respect to show [some reverence for Washington] by putting the country place which is his chief and most interesting monument in decent order? An opportunity will undoubtedly be given throughout the country to raise the necessary fund. Every body would be ready with his share if he could only fully conceive the amazement of strangers who would come to find us all agog about our divine WASHINGTON, and would then behold the unfinished chimney or shot-tower that is called his monument at the capital, and Mount Vernon, his homestead and his tomb, dilapidated and ruined.[37]

Anxiety over the reaction of visitors from abroad to shabby national monuments was a new, centennial concern, but sporadic bouts of guilt over a habitual indifference to the American past erupted whenever the unfinished Washington obelisk near the White House was mentioned. That stubby "chimney," fast assuming the status of a premature ruin, came into being as the result of a long, unseemly wrangle over the bones of poor Washington. In 1799 Congress had petitioned Martha Washington to inter her husband's remains in the capital city beneath a suitable sculptural tribute. She declined, as did Bushrod Washington, heir to the estate, when the idea cropped up again in 1816. In 1832 outraged senators and representatives from Virginia blocked a bill that would once more have called upon the Washington family to move the grave: Martha, it seems, was to have been left behind in the plot at Mount Vernon. But even when she was grudgingly included in the transfer, arrangements faltered on the terms of Washington's detailed instructions for his burial, which specified his desire to rest forever in Virginia soil within sight of his own house.[38]

Thwarted in its desire to create a national shrine around the tomb of the Father of His Country, Congress eventually opted for a piece of equestrian statuary by Clark Mills representing Washington, mounted on a terrified horse, rallying his panicky troops during the battle of Princeton (Figure 3.16). The cannonball that frightened the horse was included to show the general, in the teeth of mortal danger, "cool, calm, collected, and dignified, believing himself simply an instrument in the hands of Providence to work out the great problem of liberty, . . . firmly seated, like a god upon his throne."[39] Dedicated by President Buchanan on Washington's Birthday, 1860, when, according to the *New York Times,* "the clamors of sectional conflict and partisan animosity [were] at their height," the ceremony at the statue was only the first of several commemorations of Washington, father of North and South alike, that would eventually take the beleaguered chief executive to the tomb at Mount Vernon in the company of the Prince of Wales.[40]

On the day President Buchanan unveiled the equestrian tribute to Washington, the Episcopal divine who offered the invocation prayed that "this statue which the loving hearts and united hands of the whole nation now set up in honor of the faithfulness of our God and the loving Father of our Country may become a sacred shrine, before which the fierceness of sectional strife shall learn to chasten itself and where national unity and fraternity ever and anon, down to the latest posterity, shall renew their noblest inspiration and rekindle their intensest ardor." But the orator of the day, a Mr. Bocock of Virginia, before his mandatory plea for the cessation of "insurrectionary movements," gazed sadly southward down the Mall toward the tumbledown ruin that was meant to be the real Washington Monument and reflected on America's seeming inability to learn from history by paying fitting honor to her forefathers. "Yonder," Bocock observed, "in lonely isolation" and silent rebuke, stood the stunted marble shaft, "a structure whose incompleteness we regret."[41]

The audience had come for a spectacle, not a disquisition on forgetfulness. They tolerated the speeches. They cheered as a contingent of surviving officers and soldiers of the Revolution tottered by in their old uniforms. They looked interested as the visiting Masons from the lodge in Fredericksburg "in which Washington was initiated one hundred and six years ago" displayed the Bible used for that rite and tapped at the statue with the gavel Washington had used to lay the cornerstone of the Capitol. But they jeered when, despite the energetic tugging of the president and his military aide, "the statue's veil, instead of vanishing before the eloquence of Mr. Bocock like the mists of morning before the beams of the sun, [stuck] fast about its waist."[42]

In 1860 the Washington Monument seemed permanently stuck at 156 feet, or not quite a third of its projected height. Begun by a citizens' group formed in 1833, after plans for a mausoleum collapsed (and after it became clear that Congress, left to its own devices, would never get around to commemorating Washington), the structure had evolved in form slowly over the years from a temple complex with a tetrastyle portico and an empty, symbolic tomb into a single tall shaft of white marble. Contributions trickled in too slowly to sustain hopes for anything more elaborate. But in 1846, after a particularly disappointing solicitation, the Washington National Monument Society issued an urgent "Address to the American People" that hints at the persistent connection between the gravesite at Mount Vernon and the monument at Washington:

3.17
The unfinished monument, as it looked from 1859 to 1876

The pilgrim to Mount Vernon, the spot consecrated by Washington's hallowed remains, is often shocked when he looks upon the humble sepulcher which contains his dust, and laments that no monument has yet reared its lofty head to mark a nation's gratitude. [But the gravesite] can and does manifest the gratitude and veneration of the living for those who have passed away from the stage of life and left behind them the cherished memory of their virtues. The posthumous honors bestowed by a grateful nation on its distinguished citizens serve the further purpose of stimulating those who survive them to similar acts of greatness.[43]

With that salvo at complacency, the society printed up large copies of the Athenaeum Portrait for distribution to subscribers and set about laying the cornerstone. In 1848 Dolley Madison and Mrs. Alexander Hamilton turned out for the speeches, and Washington's famous gavel—it would be dusted off again in 1860—was wielded under a temporary arch, aflutter with cotton streamers and surmounted by the same live American eagle that welcomed Lafayette to Alexandria in 1824. From a podium located somewhere beneath bunting and bird, Robert Winthrop, speaker of the House, stressed the timeliness of the building program. "The Union, the Union in any event, was thus the sentiment of Washington," Winthrop thundered into a spanking breeze. "The Union, the Union in any event, let it be our sentiment this day! Let the column which we are about to construct be at once a pledge and an emblem of perpetual union!"[44]

For the next dozen years, almost nothing of note happened on the site (except the untimely demise of Zachary Taylor, who was felled by sunstroke while orating amid the foundation stones on a hot Fourth of July afternoon in 1850).[45] So when Mr. Bocock regretted the incompleteness of the Washington Monument in 1860 and when, in 1876, *Harper's Weekly* sniffed at "the unfinished chimney or shot-tower that is called his monument at the capital," both were expressing a marked turn in public opinion (Figure 3.17). Although people were not lined up to pledge their dollars to the cause, they were nonetheless offended by the dismal appearance of the excrescence on the Mall and receptive to the notion of direct government intervention. The impending national centennial helped to pressure Congress into belated if ineffectual action. But the society also began to link its fundraising drives to the Centennial Exposition, eventually garnering a substantial amount from collection boxes hung in the various state buildings after authorities denied permission for solicitation in the common areas of the fairgrounds.

There were those who thought the fuss unwarranted. In an editorial published in 1875, the *New York Tribune* deplored—on strictly aesthetic grounds—a recent Fourth of July appeal issued by the Monument Society:

Public judgment on that abortion has been made up. The country has failed in many ways to honor the memory of its first President, but the neglect to finish this Monument is not to be reckoned among them. A wretched design, a wretched location, and an insecure foundation match well with an empty treasury.

If the public will let the big furnace chimney on the Potomac Flats alone, and give its energies instead to cleaning out morally and physically the city likewise named after the Father of his Country, it will better honor his memory.[46]

Although several House members, taking their cue from the papers, proposed to blow the thing up and replace it with a nice Lombardic belltower, most were finally persuaded by a publicity campaign that sent the spellbinding Dr. Otis H. Tiffany on a national lecture tour to expatiate on the life and character of Washington. His lonely efforts were crowned by a gala benefit fete staged in June of 1876 in Washington's Willard Hall, a variant on the Martha Washington tea held under the auspices of ladies prominent in the social circles of the capital. On August 2, 1876, the funding bill breezed through Congress and was signed by President Grant. It directed that the monument be ready for final dedication in five years—or just in time for the centenary of the surrender of Lord Cornwallis to Washington at Yorktown, the closing act of the American Revolution.

The Historic House Movement

Predictably enough, the Washington Monument was not finished for the Yorktown centennial. All through 1876 and on into the middle of the next decade, it bulked there, ruinous and unsightly, reminding centennial patriots of the baleful condition of other American shrines, most notably Mount Vernon, for the preservation of which *Harper's Weekly* had suggested special donations in honor of the hundredth anniversary of American freedom.[47] Reports of the "sad state of decay" at Mount Vernon were indignantly squelched by "the highest authority" in a subsequent issue of *Harper's,* however. The denial was issued by a Mrs. Berghmans of Pennsylvania, regent of the Mount Vernon Ladies' Association of the Union.

Times *were* hard on the Potomac, according to Mrs. Berghmans. The enterprise was supported catch-as-catch-can by small profits from the sale of fruit and berries grown on the grounds, by a landing tax on passengers disembarking from the Washington steamer, by proceeds from the various Martha Washington balls and teas held by state chapters, and by contributions from members of the association. But the regent nonetheless took umbrage at "any implication . . . that the Association has not been diligent, or that it has suffered the estate to fall into decay through the carelessness of the officers." The tipsy colonnades, she noted, had been propped up. Several rooms had been repainted. The vice-regent for Wisconsin was restoring the lodges and gates at her own expense. The ladies of New York and Albany had resolved to repair the balustrade on the river front. And ladies representing the "old thirteen States," each state having been put in charge of a different bedchamber, were scouring their own bailiwicks in search of "appropriate old furniture" with which to furnish the almost empty house.[48]

Mrs. Berghmans did not comment on the Washington family vault, a plain red-brick affair flanked by the more showy obelisks of Bushrod Washington and his nephew, John.[49] The George Washington tomb at the head of the pathway running up from the boat landing still received its share of pilgrims, however. And those visitors, for the most part, were transfixed by the running monologue of the ancient William Burgess, a bricklayer who tended to the spot well into the 1880s, and told all comers that he had been the last living person to look upon the face of Washington during the transfer of the body from the old vault in 1831.[50] Given the slightest encouragement, the old man could expound upon the general's perfectly preserved features by the hour.

But the mood of the centennial year was neither elegiac nor funereal. Instead, interest in Mount Vernon and the bustle of activity afoot there in 1876 meshed neatly with the picture of the domestic Washington projected by the display of his "personal relics" at Philadelphia and reinforced by the conduct of a proper Martha Washington tea. Such George Washington humor as a respectful citizenry essayed in

3.18
Jasper Cropsey, *Washington's Headquarters on the Hudson*, 1850s

honor of the anniversary was also familiar in tone, like this popular specimen of bedroom farce entitled "Personal Characteristics of Gen. Washington":

> G. Washington did slumber
> In old houses without number;
> The list is said to be so long, that many have supposed
> That at night he changed his lodging,
> Into other houses dodging,
> Thus adding to the multitudes in which he had reposed.[51]

Despite—or perhaps because of—its comic intent, the ditty also shows that people were interested in the places Washington had visited and occupied during his lifetime, for the sake of personal associations still latent in the walls and furnishings. Tourists who had come to see the bits and pieces of Washingtoniana at the Centennial Exposition said that they had discovered a "past worthy of study."[52] But the mystique of spots where Washington had tarried predated the history lessons of the fair.

In 1850, when the little Hasbrouck House that had served as Washington's field headquarters in Newburgh was slated for demolition, Governor Hamilton Fish successfully petitioned the New York state legislature to buy it in the public interest (Figure 3.18). "It will be good for our citizens in these days when we hear the sound of disunion reiterated from every part of the country," Fish explained, "to chasten their minds by reviewing the history of our revolutionary struggle" as an antidote to bellicose and fratricidal thoughts.[53] The Stars and Stripes were raised by the village trustees over the Washington headquarters at Newburgh on the Fourth of July, 1850. With its flag and its cannon on the lawn, it became the first historic house museum in America.

Some of Washington's other wartime haunts were already revered as shrines. Although in private hands, the Vassall-Longfellow House in Cambridge, another temporary headquarters and the best-known house in New England, was also a midcentury shrine: the copy of the Houdon bust of Washington nestled in the turning of the staircase on a pedestal chosen to elevate the head to the precise height of the living general was almost as famous as the "Old Clock" on the landing above (Figure 3.19).[54] All up and down the East Coast stood houses with flags flying on the front lawn and similar stories to tell, saved from oblivion by what Charles Hosmer, Jr., historian of the preservation movement, calls "the golden aura" of Washington's touch:

With unerring instinct the Commander in Chief had selected for his headquarters the largest and finest buildings in every town he visited. As soon as Washington left such a house, no matter how short his stay, nothing was ever the same again. Frequently the structure became known simply as "Washing-

3.19
In Washington's former headquarters, the Vassall-Longfellow House in Cambridge, the bust of the general at the foot of the stairs rises to his exact height.

ton's Headquarters" (regardless of how many others may have been within twenty miles), and the owners often preserved the furniture and fittings that Washington had used.[55]

The residence of Henry A. Ford, in Morristown, New Jersey, was such a hallowed house, a graceful structure in its own right and a Washington command post for three long intervals during the Revolution. In the spring of 1873, following the death of its owner, local newspapers began to carry advertisements for a forthcoming auction of the property. The press confidently predicted a big turnout: "The Sacred Relic of Revolutionary Times should attract the attention of every lover of his country. The dwelling house, around which cluster the associations our memories delight to dwell upon, is 99 years old, and it is good for 99 years more. . . . The sacred associations of our Revolutionary days ought to secure a large and appreciative attendance."[56]

On the day of the sale, the crowd was huge and the bidding on contents—including a Masonic sash once worn by Washington—was spirited. When the time came for the house to go under the gavel, several gentlemen who had been competing for the prize joined forces to buy the Ford House along with all "the furniture of Washington's room, which had been carefully preserved since its occupancy by him."[57] Forming a hereditary Washington Association of New Jersey to serve as trustee for the site, these public-spirited citizens received a state charter and the pledge of annual help with operating expenses. Private donations of relics and cash were the mainstays of the new association, however, and a ladies' auxiliary served benefit teas in the colonial mode in the building.

On July 5, 1875, a rally in honor of the "Anniversary of American Independence" was held on the grounds to explain the mission of the group more fully. Former Governor Theodore F. Randolph, the new president of the Washington Association, addressed the holiday-makers at length on the value of historic places and artifacts:

The same oaken doors open to you as they did to Washington; the massive knocker his hand was wont to touch yet waits obedient to your wish. The floors he trod in anxious thought and with wearied brain, you may tread. The century has wrought no change in rafter or beam, or floor, or sheltering oak. Is there no significance in the remarkable preservation of this house?

This dwelling was for many months the home of Martha, the wife of George Washington. Within these rooms, with quiet dignity and grace, she received her husband's guests. Never idle, she set a constant example of thrift and industry. . . .

The curious old secretary he used, with its hidden drawers and quaint workmanship, stands here now as it did then. The mirrors used by General and Lady Washington you may see your faces reflected in. The old camp chest, heavy and solid, is yet good for a long campaign.[58]

By 1890, a year in which nine thousand visitors signed the guest-book, the association had restored the kitchen, putting a spinning wheel at the side of the gigantic hearth and an old grandfather clock in the corner, and hanging a long rifle over the mantel. It had bid successfully on the Washington table furniture sold in Philadelphia by the administrators for the estate of Mrs. Lorenzo Lewis, one of Washington's Custis connections. It had acquired, by gift of members, old china for the kitchen and autograph letters of Revolutionary days for the quaint old secretary. It had also come by the suit Washington wore to his first inauguration, "a unique marble bust of Washington, by Houdon," similar to the terra-cotta one at Mount Vernon, and a chair from the library there.[59]

The bust of Washington at the Longfellow House was positioned so as to suggest that the tall general was still patrolling the front hallway. The Washingtoniana in the Ford mansion consisted, for the most part, of mirrors and chairs and other functional objects that the museum-goer would use in precisely the same manner Washington had. In both cases the result was the same: an illusion of kinship between the 1770s and the 1870s, a heightened intimacy with the man, and a strong, lingering impression that his preoccupations—with his family and his daily routine—were those of less extraordinary figures, then and now.

So powerful was the connection between the hero and his physical surroundings, in fact, that during the centennial period the character of Washington was confidently deduced from the appearance of his home at Mount Vernon. A compilation of historical data produced for the fair under the title "Important Events of the Century" thus took the measure of the man from the spacious grandeur of his estate:

His inherited wealth was great, and the antiquity of his family gave him high rank. On his Potomac farms he had hundreds of slaves, and at his Mount Vernon home he was like the prince of a wide domain, free from dependence or restraint. He was fond of equipage and the appurtenances of high life. . . . This generous style of living, added perhaps to his native reserve, exposed him to the charge of aristocratic feeling. . . . His manner was formal and dignified.[60]

On the basis of such evidence the historian Michael Wallace and the architectural historian William Rhoads have both suggested that the American patriciate used the persona of Washington the eighteenth-century aristocrat as a counterbalance to the many forms of disorder rampant in the nineteenth century.[61] The gentleman-orators who unveiled the statues, dedicated the monuments, and opened the historic shrines prior to the Civil War, for instance, presented Washington as an unchangeable, inherently conservative force, a symbol and guardian of the Union. In the 1890s Washington and the ancestral style he represented would become symbols of an ancient and distinctively American heritage, antidotes to the poison of immigration. In 1875 the Washington Association of Morristown saw the very same Washington as a source of "grateful repose from life's turmoil," from the press of business, the racket of the factory, the crush and pace of urban living, and the forces of modernity in general, against which women, and a few enlightened men, stood charged with the defense of the frail structure of social solidarity.[62]

George Washington, his lady ever by his side, stood for order, for continuity, for things as they had been and always should be. Under the ministrations of the ladies, however, that courtly figure took on surprisingly egalitarian connotations. Washington was a principal actor in the balls and teas of centennial society; in his assigned role, he was the compleat aristocrat, at home in the genteel company of belles and matrons. As countless relic shows and teas and balls also suggested, the historical Washington had taken infinite pains with the splendid clothes he wore and the appointments of the drawing rooms he occupied, however temporarily. In that trait, he was not unlike the celebrants in Connecticut and Pennsylvania who dressed in ancestral finery for 1876 balls and fretted about the furnishings of his shrine at Morristown.

But it was over such little things that Washington and modern-day Americans of a less courtly sort were apt to meet on an equal footing. Dumb objects recognize no fine distinctions of social preferment, especially in a culture in which cash in hand can buy ancestral treasures. The same antique looking glass in Morristown that once reflected the face of Lady Washington could, a century later, mirror the features of a visiting washerwoman from the wrong side of Trenton. The armchair from Mount Vernon did not care if it held a mortal frame or the shimmering form of an "angil in a 3 kornerd hat." The historic houses of the heroic few cast a warming glow of secondhand nobility upon the touring many.

In 1874 Ann Pamela Cunningham, a frail spinster from South Carolina, bid a tearful farewell to the women of the Mount Vernon Ladies' Association, the organization she had founded in the course of her long and trying campaign to "save" Mount Vernon from the clutches of heartless speculators and businessmen determined to make it over into a fancy hotel. Resigning her regency in favor of Lily Berghmans—the same Mrs. Berghmans who bristled with righteous indignation at false reports that the place was "tumbling to pieces"—Miss Cunningham admonished her followers to guard the estate "religiously . . . from all change, whether by law or desecration." Mount Vernon should be kept exactly as Washington left it: "Ladies, the home of Washington is in your charge; see to it that you keep it the home of Washington! Let no irreverent hand change it; no vandal hands desecrate it with the fingers of 'progress'! Those who wish to go to the home in which he lived and died, wish to see in what he lived and died! Let one spot in this grand country of ours be saved from change! Upon you rests this duty."[63] Unlike the manufacturers and the prophets of progress who saw the Centennial Exposition as a last farewell to a primitive and unenviable past, she welcomed 1876 as an opportunity to expose the failings of a modern culture gone mad with the lust for profit: "When the Centennial comes, bringing with it thousands from the ends of the earth, to whom the Home of Washington will be the *place* of *places* in our country, let them see that, though we slay our forests, remove our dead, pull down our churches, remove from home to home, till the hearthstone seems to have no resting-place in America,—let them see that we do know how to care for the Home of our Hero! Farewell!"[64]

And with that final salvo at rapacious industry and migratory families, Miss Cunningham went back to the desolate ruins of her own ancestral home and died, leaving behind as her legacy the extraordinary shrine at Mount Vernon, the prototype for the historic house museum in America.

The story began romantically, even miraculously, just as rumors about the planned Mount Vernon Hotel were finding their way into the papers:

It was upon a clear moonlit night in 1853 that the mother of Miss Cunningham passed by Mount Vernon. The steamer's bell tolled out its requiem to the dead-hero, whose resting-place, even under the half-tones of the moonlight, revealed only neglect and desolation. Reflecting sadly . . . upon this melancholy scene as it faded in the distance, Mrs. Cunningham realized that unless some immediate effort were made for the preservation of this sacred spot utter ruin would result. . . . Suddenly, like the flash of the star which shot across the heavens, came the inspiration, "Let the women of America own and preserve Mount Vernon!"[65]

The idea was an audacious one for a woman of the 1850s whose name, decorum dictated, was not to be seen in the public prints except on the occasions of her birth, her marriage, and her demise. It must have seemed even more revolutionary to her invalid daughter, housebound and shy. Nonetheless, Ann Pamela Cunningham plucked up her courage and wrote an appeal to the "Women of America" (under the nom de plume of "The Southern Matron"); thanks to the new mass-circulation magazines, her call for contributions gradually reached a national audience. Originally, Cunningham admitted, "a Southern affair altogether," her movement aimed to raise $200,000; buy two hundred acres of the estate, including the tomb and the mansion, from the present owner; transfer the deed to the state of Virginia, so that it might be kept for a public resort; and put some ladies in charge of the operation "to adorn it if they could have the means."

Under the terms of her husband's will, after the death of Martha Washington the estate had passed to his nephew, Bushrod, a justice of the Supreme Court. Bushrod Washington left it to his nephew, John Augustine, who left it to his wife, Jane, who left it to her son, the second John A., the subject of the stealthy approach of the land speculators bearing a $300,000 offer for the property. While Virginia and the federal government both demurred at his asking price, the house and its surroundings crumbled away, little by little, under the onslaught of tourist feet.

Whether he liked it or not, Mr. Washington lived in a national shrine. Lafayette had called at the tomb during his triumphal tour of America in 1824 and found Mount Vernon much as he remembered it.[66] But when Benson Lossing passed through in the early 1850s, a mournful "silence pervaded the life-dwelling of Washington" and the historian pronounced himself "much disappointed in the appearance of the tomb, for it seems to me that in material and design it is quite too commonplace."[67]

Miss Cunningham's dream of restoring Mount Vernon to its former glory appealed to Mr. Washington, as did her pledge to meet his price. That price was high, however. Her appeal had raised some money, largely in the South, but when the Northern papers learned of the crusade and criticized its sectional exclusivity, financial necessity helped to create the inclusive structure of the Ladies' Association. Henceforth the officers of the organization would consist of a regent or head and a variable number of lady vice-regents, one from each state, to coordinate activities in their locales: "Washington belonged," wrote their leader, in a flurry of italics, "*not alone to the South!*" In 1855, under the leadership of the new Pennsylvania vice-regent, Philadelphia awoke to the cause. Clubs were formed. Collection boxes were installed in Independence Hall. The idea seemed to be working.

Then, suddenly, the "leading men" in the city withdrew their support "because it was a women's effort, and they disapproved of women mixing in public affairs."[68] But other men rallied gallantly to the support of Miss Cunningham and her intrepid sisters. Between 1856 and 1859 the popular lecturer Edward Everett, "Old Silver Tongue," delivered a two-hour disquisition on the character of Washington 129 times, before paying audiences assembled in lyceum halls from Massachusetts to Mississippi to Georgia, donating the proceeds—$69,294.54, or about a third of the purchase price—to the coffers of the Mount Vernon Ladies' Association.[69]

Everett seems to have regarded his performance as an act of devotion to the Union, although a few New York papers thought he volunteered in order to gratify his inflated sense of self-importance. Others justly held a low opinion of the speech, calling it insipid and repetitious, on the strength of such passages as this: "From beneath that humble roof went forth the intrepid and unselfish warrior—the magistrate who knew no glory but his country's good; to that he returned happiest when his work was done. . . . While it stands the latest generations of the grateful children of America will make this pilgrimage to it as to a shrine, and when it shall fall, if fall it must, the memory and name of Washington shall shed an eternal glory on the spot."[70]

Even Edward Everett's most rabid critics noticed "how the sea of plumes before us nodded—how the jewels flashed as snowy hands clapped—how brighter eyes gazed with admiration!"[71] The ladies went home, put their plumes and jewels away, and worked. All thirty state chapters worked together. They wrote letters. They harassed friends. They distributed color lithographs of the tomb and the big house, idealized and manicured as much by their own hopes as by an artist's fancy. On February 22, 1860, a little more than a year before the first shots were fired at Fort Sumter, John Washington moved out, leaving Mount Vernon the property of the association and its solemn responsibility.

The Meaning of Mount Vernon

Although the household gods of Mount Vernon failed to hold the Civil War at bay, the estate was treated as neutral territory by Union and Confederate troops, and the work of shoring up the walls went on. With the end of hostilities, the regent took up residence on the site and Benson Lossing returned to make notes for *The Home of Washington; or, Mount Vernon and Its Associations.* Published in 1870 and illustrated with the author's own pen drawings, the book was dedicated by the grateful author to Miss Cunningham and the ladies of the association, his "Patriotic Countrywomen, by whose efforts the home and tomb of Washington have been rescued from decay."[72] Lossing's volume did much to arouse a new kind of postwar interest in the site among those whose stake in Washington was less desperate than that of their prewar predecessors.

Edward Everett's set-piece, for instance, had quoted Jefferson telling George Washington that "North and South will hang together while they have you to hang to."[73] In 1859, the *Home Journal* had also tried to banish the clouds of disunity and war by a parallel logic. "The public *want,* at present," wrote the editors of behalf of their predominantly female readership, is "less to gaze upon the oft-repeated battle-fields and occasions of state and great event, than to have a nearer look at the *domestic daily life of the Great Chieftain.*"[74] Lossing had no such overarching spiritual reason to offer for why Americans should be interested in Washington's home. Instead, he assumed they would be (for more than four hundred pages) and concerned himself with a meticulous physical inventory of the few significant relics left inside and the many now dispersed among the various Lees, Custises, and Washingtons awaiting their return to Mount Vernon. Lossing also offered suggestions for future work.

The most immediate need, he thought—and Miss Cunningham agreed—was for an endowment fund at least equal in value to the purse raised to make the purchase. Much had been accomplished, but proceeds from the sale of souvenir canes, hatchets, and gavels made from "Mount Vernon Wood" collected in the hickory forest on the estate and from the sale of watch charms cut from the nuts of the "Lafayette Coffee-Bean Tree" went to a private concessionaire. The dribble of admission fees and returns from the sale of strawberries and garden plants were insufficient to the needs of the lady-preservationists:

The work of interior renovation has gone on slowly, until now, a greater portion of the wood-work has been painted, and the roof of the Mansion has been newly shingled. The whole building is now in a state of fair preservation. . . . Now, . . . from the Wharf to the Tomb and up to the Mansion, the visitor sees, at every step, evidences of poverty. The Tomb and its neighborhood have a most forbidding appearance; while the Mansion itself, bereft of nearly every thing mentioned in this work, is less attractive than it might be, if its surroundings could be beautified by Art and skilled Labor, and its rooms present an exhibition of objects of every kind, yet in existence, that were associated with Washington's life.[75]

When the new Regent wrote her tart rejoinder to *Harper's Weekly* in 1876, she described the status quo in much the same way: the fabric of the building had been saved from utter desolation, and the ladies were now seeking donations of antiques, mainly from within their own ranks, with the object of filling up the echoing chambers of "the home with appropriate old furniture."[76] The publicity given to the drive in *Godey's Lady's Book* and other sympathetic magazines helped. Lossing's woodcut of the "Room in Which Washington Died," prepared for his book in 1868 or 1869, shows an empty apartment, with four doors and a fireplace the only points of interest except for a tourist couple being lectured by a black guide (Figure 3.20).[77] Around 1855, while visiting Arlington House, Lossing had sketched the tall, mahogany four-poster that belonged in the room; in 1877 Washington's deathbed came back to Mount Vernon at last on an extended loan from General George Washington Custis Lee.[78] Nelly Custis's harpsichord soon followed.[79]

Piece by piece, bedstead by spinning wheel, the yawning spaces began to take on life and character. In 1889 a celebration of Washington's Birthday in the public schools of Kansas yielded $1,000 for building and equipping a replica of the servants' quarters, with its own bunks, hearths, and flax wheels. In 1892 the schoolchildren of St. Paul raised enough to restore the interior of the old spinning house

3.20
The room in which Washington died, as described by Benson Lossing in 1870

with equipment purchased from the Southern-born widow of one of the first serious collectors of Americana, a connoisseur who had decorated two parlors of his summer house in Massachusetts with "furniture from Mount Vernon, . . . bought . . . before the Mt. Vernon association purchased the real estate."[80] What the association could not wrest from the clutches of such collectors was replaced with a similar item or copied. The kitchen was finished in 1899 "in the Colonial manner" as the gift of Miss Amy Townsend, the vice-regent for New York. Harrison Howell Dodge, the new superintendent of the complex, recalled peering into innumerable old homesteads along the James River, looking for "heavy andirons, spits, tongs," and shovels to replicate.[81]

Mount Vernon slowly acquired a warmth and personality in keeping with the Centennial Exposition's version of the colonial home, a private, intimate place oriented to the fireplace and womanly economy, in which rooms invited such personalized titles as "Martha Washington's Spinning Room," "Martha Washington's Kitchen," and "George Washington's Bed Room." Although the gorgeous public rooms of the mansion would absorb more and more of the association's energy after 1886, the areas where life's little moments were passed maintained their hold upon the affections of lady-visitors like Ruth Lawrence, whose *Colonial Verses* of 1897 concern themselves wholly with Mount Vernon. There are poems about each of the state apartments, printed beneath photographs taken in such a way that even the spacious "Banquet Room" seems as cozy as the low-ceilinged spinning room. But the spinning room and the other nooks and crannies of Mount Vernon are the magical spots for the poet, where palpable memories gather in the half-light about the old, broad-breasted fireplace:

> Merry whirring of the wheel,
>   Loud the din!
> Twisting, turning speeds the reel
>   Maidens spin!
>
> Though the task their patience tax,
>   They are gay;
> Lightly drawing threads of flax
>   All the day.
>
> Half in shine and half in gloom,
>   Sit the throng;
> With the murmur of the loom
>   Comes a song.[82]

Some idea of what Mount Vernon was like in the years just after the war can be gleaned from Henry Adams's novel *Democracy*. By 1880, when Adams staged a key scene in his book there, Mount Vernon had become a popular and much-visited resort. One warm Saturday in

February, Adams's characters set out with a large crowd of fellow Washingtonians for a picnic on the grounds. They journey there aboard a Potomac steamer with "its small column of smoke as if it were a newly invented incense-burner approaching the temple of the national deity." And one by one, the merrymakers try to explain that "national deity" whose shrine is the goal of their pilgrimage.

The diplomat claims objectivity: Washington, in his detached opinion, is a synthetic icon—the bare-chested Jove of Horatio Greenough's Olympian statue with the frumpy face of Gilbert Stuart's Athenaeum Portrait. The Virginia girl speaks with the malicious authority of family tradition. Washington was, she chirps, "a raw-boned country farmer, very hard-featured, very awkward, very illiterate and very dull; very bad-tempered, very profane, and generally tipsy after dinner." The New England historian defines Washington as the embodiment of "Morality, Justice, Duty, Truth," all spoken in upper-case letters. The Western senator has learned a thing or two since the worshipful days of his boyhood with Parson Weems. Washington's skills at soldiering and politicking he now deems mediocre; the first president was, indeed, inferior to any one of a dozen public men of the present day. Such is American progress![83]

The diplomat, the saucy belle, and the historian stood for real enough attitudes abroad in the years between the two great Washington centennials of the waning nineteenth century—the 1876 Philadelphia fair and the gala celebration of the hundredth anniversary of the first inauguration, planned for New York City in 1889. Since the days of Noah Webster's first *New England Primer*, Washington had always been "great": by chanting "By Washington / Great deeds were done," several generations of youngsters had learned the letter *W*. But centennial fever brought amazing new facts about him to light. On March 30, 1877, the *New York Herald* printed the text of a supposed love-letter from Washington to Sally Cary Fairfax, his best friend's wife; sold at auction the next day, the manuscript promptly disappeared from view, although not from public memory.[84] Thereafter, abstract virtue and scurrilous folklore made up the recto and verso of the impenetrable icon now attached, on a regular basis, to the dollar bill.

The senator in Henry Adams's novel represented a real constituency of opinion about Washington, too, but it was a view that Adams, with his increasingly dyspeptic appraisal of progress, did not share. At the century's last massive commemorative fair, Chicago's Columbian Exposition of 1893, Adams encountered a force more sinister than the belching steamboat on the Potomac or the Corliss Engine from the 1876 extravaganza: he met the dynamo, the fearsome machine that symbolized for him the blind power of modern times and a mechanically induced rupture in the fabric of historical continuity. "Chicago asked in 1893 for the first time whether the American people knew where they were driving," he observed.[85] In a sense, the picnic at

Mount Vernon had posed the same question thirteen years earlier, and suggested an answer to it. The fervor with which Adams's senator boosted his political cronies—all intimates of the eminent Rutherford B. Hayes—at the expense of George Washington made the legislator appear shallow and foolish. Progress was the battlecry of the party hack, and Adams chose the setting for his exposure with exquisite irony. In the pages of *Democracy*, Mount Vernon was history's tacit reproach to progress and modernity.

However mean the design of the site, however meager its decor, most of the protagonists of *Democracy* preferred the bucolic Mount Vernon to the city and to the epoch they left behind them on the pier in Washington City. However regrettable the proportions of the tomb, it was "a simple misfortune which might befall any of us; we should not grieve over it too much. What would our feelings be if a Congressional committee reconstructed it of white marble with Gothic pepperpots, and gilded it inside on machine-moulded stucco!" As for the mansion:

Their eyes, weary of the harsh colors and forms of the city, took pleasure in the worn wainscots and the stained walls. Some of the rooms were still occupied; fires were burning in the wide fire-places. All were tolerably furnished, and there was no uncomfortable sense of repair or newness. . . .

"Is not the sense of rest here captivating?" [the girl said]. "Look at the quaint garden, and this ragged lawn, and the great river in front, and the superannuated fort beyond the river! Everything is peaceful, even down to the poor old General's little bed-room. One would like to lie down in it and sleep a century or two. And yet that dreadful Capitol and its office-seekers are only ten miles off."[86]

After 1874, Miss Cunningham's final exhortation to the Mount Vernon Ladies' Association on resistance to progress was read at every annual meeting. Every year the ladies heard her rail against the "vandal hands" that would seek to desecrate Mount Vernon "with the fingers of 'progress'!" Every year, they heard her plead that "one spot, in this grand country of ours, be saved from change."[87] The vandal fingers of time had been busy for nearly a century when the ladies' campaign began. Even the larger, public buildings of the eighteenth century had not been constructed to endure as historic monuments; with a few exceptions, the private houses of the Founding Fathers were not "built of the stuff which lasts through the ages."[88] Mount Vernon fell into grave disrepair shortly after the death of Martha Washington in 1802; the work of Cunningham's organization takes on heroic dimensions precisely because the membership began with nothing more than a heap of ruins.

The historian Daniel Boorstin has remarked that "the democratic past of a mobile people uses up, improves, and replaces its artifacts," a good definition of material progress in nineteenth-century America.[89] The Mount Vernon that Henry Adams saw in 1880, stained and worn though it was, was on its way to becoming a substitute artifact, a new and improved replacement for a used-up house. Miss Cunningham opposed progress and change in the name of Adams's picnickers. Pilgrims to Mount Vernon, she argued, "go to the home in which [Washington] lived and died . . . to see in what he lived and died." But increasingly, as the decades passed, they saw a scene like that presented in Daniel Huntington's *Republican Court,* a past reordered and rebuilt in the precise image of the contemporary imagination, the past as the present age wished to remember it. Preservation stood in rhetorical opposition to progress, yet Mount Vernon was a monument to change, a brand new birthplace of a dynamic culture—a culture that externalized its fears of social disorder and its exuberant material aspirations in the shrines and relics it elected to honor.

As the century drew toward its close, the mansion was packed with artifacts suggestive of wealth but also of how each incidental moment was passed from 1759 to 1799. Some were genuine bits of Washington property, bought or given to the association; some were replicas, like the kitchen utensils whose prototypes Colonel Dodge ran to ground; some were items thought to be "in period." Material stuff—the volumetric solidity of artifacts—filled up the emptiness of historical distance. The profusion of musical instruments, dental tools, firedogs, and decanters cast a spell over tourists like Owen Wister, Teddy Roosevelt's friend, who came away half convinced that Washington still prowled through the east parlor in his buckskin breeches, carrying his crabtree walking stick. The man who once slept here, and in an ever-growing number of other places, seemed not really to have gone to his final rest. "Everything, every subject, every corner and step seems to bring him close." Wister wrote. "It is an exquisite and friendly serenity which bathes the sense . . . , that seems to be charged all through with some meaning or message of beneficence and reassurance but nothing that could be put in words."[90]

Rustic serenity held out the promise of escape from urban life, a flight from modern times. But the sensuous appeal of Mount Vernon recognized and reinforced the modern acquisitive itch. It also lent fresh meaning to Regent Cunningham's analysis of the motives of tourists "who go to the home in which he lived and died [and] wish to see in what he lived and died." The plenitude and immediacy with which Mount Vernon described the "what" of Washington's home denied death by muffling the hero in the protective cotton-wool of domestic life by the fireside, a life relived at a hyperbolic pitch of ownership. A vigorous Washington thus lived on for his turn-of-the-nineteenth-century descendants in the cluttered Victorian interiors they themselves called home, alive and well and ready to attend his inaugural ball all over again, in the company of President Harrison and his wife, the charming Carolyn Scott Harrison, future founding president-general of the Daughters of the American Revolution.

Architecture, Ancestry, and High Society

4

The Uses of History
1876–1893

Living in the Past

In itself Mount Vernon was just the wooden house of a gentleman-farmer—the reverence of the lady-curators notwithstanding. It became a modest dwelling or a grand one according to the perspective and the income of each tourist. Only the knowledge that Washington lived there transformed the place into a shrine of national patriotism, but that made it no less important a symbol. As the annual report of the American Scenic and Historic Preservation Society once noted, "Men need these physical objects to stimulate their imagination and help them fix their thoughts on the ultimate ideas which they represent."[1]

If Mount Vernon was treasured because of its attachment to the mystique of Washington, it followed that the stylistic integrity of the building counted for less than its sheer survival. Accordingly, when the Philadelphia architect Samuel Sloan surveyed the ruins in 1856, he thought that the paramount object of the restorer should be to keep what remained safe from the further ravages of weather and tourism. After the war, in fact, Sloan proposed to take the house apart board by board, to number the pieces, and to reinstall the interior woodwork within an incorruptible new shell of brick with marble facings, a white roof of glazed tile, and a galvanized iron balustrade.[2]

Conversely, if Mount Vernon was prized only for its patriotic associations, then there was very little point to the growing concern of the Ladies' Association with historical accuracy. Any old furnishings of the eighteenth century had sufficed when the house stood empty and desolate. But as the rooms took on sparkle and color, the refurbished mansion came to demand Washington's own things, tracked down through painstaking detective work, wheedled out of distant relatives, and bought for high prices with slender resources. Indeed, across the whole spectrum of commemorative, celebratory, and preservationist activity, slapdash historicism gave way in the wake of the centennial to a more focused interest in the colonial past. Nor did the women who turned their attention to matters of provenance find such anti-quarianism arid or irrelevant. On the contrary, tracing out more precise genealogies for both persons and artifacts seems to have heightened a mounting enthusiasm for saving sites and collecting relics, especially those associated with George Washington.

A number of key buildings were renewed in the years just before and after the Centennial Exposition. Independence Hall, for example, was restored for the celebration under the tenets of that gospel of association whereby the legislators of New York State had believed that the pilgrim to Washington's headquarters at Newburgh would come away from the experience "a better man" with "a more devout mind." The prime mover behind the work at Independence Hall thought that "so long . . . as we can preserve the material objects . . . these great men saw, used, or even touched, the thrill of vitality may still be transmitted unbroken."[3] For similar reasons a committee of twenty Boston ladies, inspired by the memory of the great men who had passed through its portals and the great events it had witnessed, set out to "save" Old South Meeting House in 1876 by staging an "Aunt Tabitha Spinning Bee" as a fundraiser.[4]

In 1878, acknowledging the influence of Philadelphia and the Mount Vernon Ladies' Association, a group of Pennsylvania women tried to form a national society to buy the Washington headquarters building at Valley Forge in time for the upcoming centennial of the departure of the Continental Army from winter encampment. Like the Georgian houses with big American flags flying over the front door and signs proclaiming "Washington Slept Here" (there was a growing, and published, list of such houses), the Valley Forge site lacked the intensity of the associations concentrated in Washington's lifelong home. Nonetheless, the purchase was made. Speakers at the formal dedication even succeeded in making the military post sound like a kind of annex to Mount Vernon: "How precious are the old memories in our homes and households! . . . As with home, so with country. . . . Home and country! alike in the heart's best affections; present enjoyment and happy memory increase our devotion to both and intensify our patriotism. We are here to-day to illustrate history and perpetuate these memories. The ladies of this 'Association' by and through this organization, desire to accomplish this."[5]

The centennial spread the fever for collecting, too. If an afternoon's visit to Washington's headquarters could improve one's character, long-term exposure to colonial antiques could transform one's life. Or so the theory ran. Charles Eastlake and other arts-and-crafts proselytizers of the 1870s and 1880s argued that objects shaped the character of their users. Shoddy, machine-made goods of the type cranked out by the souvenirs-while-you-wait booths at the Centennial Exposition debased the wage-slaves who made them and the ignorant masses who bore them off to their dismal flats. The handmade spinning wheel or writing desk, on the other hand, insofar as it embodied the superior values of colonial craftsmanship and the enviable home life of its time, not only represented the spirit of the past but also transmitted that essence to its owner in some ineffable manner. In his influential *House Beautiful* of 1878, Clarence Cook discussed the incorporation of antiques into the modern home in just such terms: "There is . . . the pleasant knowledge that this furniture . . . was made for Americans, or bought by them; and there is a feeling that in going back to its use, in collecting it, and saving it from dishonor . . . we are bringing ourselves a little nearer in spirit to the old time."[6]

The rough democracy of the Centennial Exposition with its polyglot crowds of merrymakers turned the yearnings of the fastidious toward an American past in which a Virginia aristocracy and a "Republican Court" still flourished—and everybody else still knew their places. Mrs. Eliza Greatorix, who exhibited eighteen pen drawings of "Old New York" at the Philadelphia fair, had already used several of those works as illustrations to the second, 1875 volume of her *Old New York from the Battery to Bloomingdale.* In that text, Mrs. Greatorix did not hesitate to make a forceful connection between the old things she sought out, drew, and prized and the kind of life to which she aspired. In the colonial past, she wrote, thinking more of the elegant Chippendale of Mount Vernon than of the crude Pilgrim furnishings of the colonial kitchens, "social life was cultivated and enjoyed, and the distinctions of class were observed and acquiesced in . . . without any loss of self-respect or happiness to those who acknowledged the refined, the wealthy, and the intellectual superiority of others." In modern America, she continued, "many are questioning today whether, in exchanging this condition of society for a more levelling democracy, we have made any true progress in the higher life."[7]

Preservers and collectors of this stripe, Elizabeth Stillinger suggests in her fine history of American "antiquers," were often souls cast adrift without social or spiritual moorings in the get-rich-quick, cash culture of the centennial period:

Land had been the source of status and stability among the forebears of many in the new collecting generation; but with the Industrial Revolution and the urbanization of the East, those families had moved off the land and into the cities. The collectors had thus become interested in antiques partly as a replacement for the lost land—a symbol of their descent in old and respectable . . . American families. Because they could no longer define themselves in terms of farm ownership, they turned to a more abstract concept: the American past and the enterprise of [those] who had built and defended the nation.[8]

The antique hunters' interest in artifacts was not primarily aesthetic. Like the swelling fraternity of collectors of Washington portraits who wrangled among themselves over which was the truest likeness of the hero and counted one specimen better than another "if in contemplating it, we feel impressed with the nobility of his character, the dignity of his manhood, his truth and patriotism," they were seeking something that went beyond the distinctively American appearance of certain artifacts.[9] Indeed, the question arises: what's truly American anyway? Colonial materials were not universally regarded as American, for instance. Mariana Griswold Van Rensselaer, an influential critic of the 1880s, understood the reasoning of those who held that Americans should build modern copies of colonial structures simply because they were American. With the exception of the wigwam, however, Van Rensselaer was hard-pressed to find indigenous architectural forms in the colonies in the seventeenth and eighteenth centuries.[10]

It should come as no surprise, then, that those who seemed the most actively engaged in researching, promoting, and reviving the colonial manner of building were often indifferent to its innate artistic value. But what were they after? Thanks to Vincent Scully's study of the origins of the shingle style—one of the principal vehicles whereby the colonialisms of the centennial kitchens, in diluted and updated form, entered the mainstream of domestic architecture—the vacation trip taken by the youthful members of the architectural firm of McKim, Mead and White in the summer of 1877 has assumed the status of the quest for the neocolonial grail.[11] Dawdling along the East Coast in search of inspiration, the three partners made the sketches that laid the foundations for a full-fledged Colonial Revival in architecture, a movement showing few signs of exhaustion better than a century later. They even spent four days among the architectural fragments built into the fabric of Indian Hill, the estate outside Newburyport where old Mr. Poore still lived among the litter of authentic parlor sets he would not sell to the Mount Vernon Ladies' Association and the spinning equipment eventually installed there after his death. In his commentary on their progress along the coast, Scully suggests that the newfound colonial manner of McKim, Mead and White was an escapist reaction to the political corruption of the Grant administration and its successors. But it is also possible to argue that the motivations behind American revivalism in the 1870s and 1880s were far more diffuse in the social sense and far more narrow in their formal aspect.[12]

Whatever else McKim and company may have had in mind when they fled the city and its evil ways, they were also reacting against the medievalisms currently prevailing in their own profession, a taste that favored the irregular, the untidy, and the grotesquely picturesque. The regularity and restraint of the Georgian houses of New England represented, by contrast, a kind of classicism, a lost purity of shape, a hierarchical orderliness of form and design attached both to colonial models and to the Renaissance sources Beaux-Arts practitioners would soon adopt for important public complexes, like the palatial "White City" the partners built at the 1893 Columbian Exposition. The colonial style was interesting less for its own sake or for the sake of its wealth of associations than for its dissimilarity from current fashion.

The colonial and the classical—the former essentially domestic, personal, and small in scale and the latter public and official—both harked back to the honored past. But so did the popular Richardsonian Romanesque. Unlike the various medieval styles, however, the colonial and the classical answered the same instinctive need for order. McKim, Mead, White, their contemporaries, and their clients may have chosen visual order in direct response to the gaudy, messy spectacle of American politics, but if so, they were not alone. That need had also been articulated by ardent devotees of colonial Americana, like Mrs. Greatorix, who feared the cruder manifestations of the democracy of Grant and his successors.

Plans for the 1893 world's fair at Chicago were already afoot before the classicists fixed Imperial Roman as the official style for the pavilions of their "Dream City." The individual states, in fact, had been encouraged to choose "the Colonial" manner for their headquarters and were further instructed to consider housing themselves in reproductions of the historic buildings within their boundaries. Hence, while the important "palaces" of the exposition held in honor of Columbus resembled so many ancient baths interspersed with triumphal arches, the circle of smaller, cheaper, sometimes wooden structures erected by the states at the edge of Jackson Park summed up twenty years of experiments in housebuilding and historic preservation. The state pavilions exerted a powerful influence upon both movements for the twenty years to come.

The thirteen original colonies were especially eager to answer the call for colonial detail. The Connecticut and Delaware offerings were slightly enlarged versions of suburban homes with Georgian overtones outside and collections of period furniture (both real and reproduction) within; one guidebook justly described the former as "a type of the Connecticut residence."[13] Pennsylvania, by way of contrast, built an imposing edifice almost universally called "an 'exact' reproduction of Independence Hall in Philadelphia" to hold the Liberty Bell.[14] Exactitude seems to have described the builders' good intentions rather than the results, however, since the pavilion was semicircular at the base, topped off by a roof garden beneath a too-tall tower, and bristled with all manner of sculptural embellishment. Charles Follen McKim, with the disdain of a purist, called it "a sufficiently recognizable caricature of Independence Hall to make good Pennsylvanians blush."[15]

4.1
Peabody and Stearns, the Massachusetts building at the 1893 World's Columbian Exposition, Chicago; a copy of the John Hancock House on Beacon Hill in Boston, destroyed in 1863

4.2
Charles A. Gifford, the New Jersey building at the 1893 fair; a copy of Washington's Morristown headquarters

More successful as buildings and historic attractions were the pavilions of Massachusetts, New Jersey, and Virginia. For Massachusetts, the firm of Peabody and Stearns—Peabody had also made a colonial junket along the Atlantic coast in 1877—created a loose adaptation of the John Hancock mansion in Boston. Atop the flagstaff, it was said, "an aristocratic and golden cod-fish told which way the social wind blew in Boston" (Figure 4.1). The rooms inside "were filled with relics and autographs of great historic interest."[16] The nearby New Jersey building, "plain and unostentatious from the street," was also a free replica, this time "of Washington's headquarters at Morristown in the Revolutionary War," recently snatched from the jaws of desecration (Figure 4.2). On the exterior, the New Jersey pavilion was "a typical Colonial town house," hospitable and homelike, with broad, sheltering porches or verandahs where, Chicago's publicists imagined, Generals Greene, Lafayette, Steuben, Light-Horse Harry Lee, Mad Anthony Wayne, Putnam, Kosciusko, Benedict Arnold, and George Washington himself must have taken the evening air, in some vast, improbable council of war.[17]

That plain exterior hardly prepared the dazzled visitor for the interior appointments. Set off to one side were "a room . . . that was called Washington's bed-chamber and dining-room, and a wine buffet . . . set with fine cut glassware." The Washington quarters were relatively austere. But the rest of the house "startled the visitor . . . with the luxury and elegance of its furnishings, and the stateliness of its occupants. Colored servants to take the guest's card or lead him to the registry, silken ribbons across doorways and stair-cases, to remind him that he was not of the elect, pianos, chairs, tables and sideboards of rosewood, with carpets of deepest velvet . . . spoke of the wealth, pride and exclusive spirit of that little State."[18]

Virginia's offering was neither an adaptation "in the spirit" of the past nor a replicated shell with vintage High Victorian innards (Figure 4.3). It was, as advertised, "a fac-simile of Mt. Vernon, that historic structure so long occupied by George Washington," precise down to the very measurements of the rooms within and the dimensions of the dependencies without. Presided over by Mrs. Lucy Preston Beale, "Lady Assistant" of the Virginia Fair Board and a lady of impeccable Virginia lineage, a staff of "old Virginia negroes" served as guides to the exhibits.[19]

These attractions were a mixed lot. Although Mrs. Beale claimed that "nothing modern is seen in the building, except the people" and Virginians had made strenuous efforts to recreate both the death-chamber and Martha's little attic room overlooking her husband's tomb, few actual Washington relics were still available for loan. A family clock on the staircase; Mary Ball Washington's "time-stained chest of drawers"; Martha's tea caddy; George's table, his cup, saucer, sword, cane, his secretary, and a knife found in its drawer after his death: that was the lot. The curtained four-poster in the bedroom was a copy, as was the Nelly Custis harpsichord. Some rooms had to be closed up for want of displays. Yawning spaces were punctuated by Dolley Madison's piano, along with other miscellaneous articles—a remarkable "cloak made entirely from the feathers of the Virginia wild turkey, a bird now almost extinct in that State" among them—"which were collected from all over the State, [and] the heirlooms of old Virginia families."[20]

Although the American past was a dominant theme of the Philadelphia and Chicago fairs, the differences between the kinds and degrees of the colonialisms evident in each venue chart the rapid maturation of the historical imagination in less than two decades and the changing cultural uses of its contents. Washington is the great constant uniting the Philadelphia Centennial with the Columbian Exposition. In Chicago, the Spanish theme was roundly ignored by the same state exhibitors who went to great lengths to demonstrate some tangible connection with the first president. Massachusetts, with its Washington writing desk, is a case in point. By 1893 Washington had overshadowed the New England Fathers honored by the Mayflower relics and the Pilgrim foodstuffs prominent in Philadelphia. And his epoch—the more polished reaches of the eighteenth century—had displaced the cruder Puritan span in the affections of fairgoers who admired Virginia's facsimile of Mount Vernon and coveted the Georgian-style family houses sheltering the representatives of Connecticut and Delaware.

4.3
The Virginia building at the Columbian Exposition; a precise facsimile of Washington's home, Mount Vernon

The Changing Status of Women

Despite the objections of men who resented any public mention of their retiring wives and daughters, the colonial revival movement affected the status of women profoundly. Between the timid debut of female workers behind the scenes, colonial waitresses, and "old tyme" spinsters in 1876 and the emergence of highly visible Lady Managers of great neocolonial enterprises in Chicago in 1893, the politically disenfranchised women of America had contrived to waltz, all but unnoticed, onto the stage of public affairs, wearing their great-great-grandmothers' ballgowns and locks of George Washington's hair done up in brooches. The men were, at best, their escorts into the spotlight of history: the lady in the colonial pouf was sometimes, but not always, accompanied by a fidgety husband with powdered hair and satin knee pants.

The hereditary societies of patriots, male and female, founded in the 1880s and 1890s have for many years waged a battle of footnotes, unsupported recollections, and innuendo to establish the order of precedence among them. But the barrage of claims and counterclaims cannot obscure two facts. First, women were the instigators and the inventors of such organizations, even if they did not yet have the legalistic presence of mind to stake their claims with official-sounding charters. And second, their work with old houses and historic artifacts nurtured both the social rituals and the social aspirations manifest in the activities of organizations like the Sons and the Daughters of the American Revolution, the National Society of Colonial Dames, and the Mayflower Descendants. The exclusive Martha Washington tea of the centennial period, for example, became a regular DAR ceremony. The colonial tea was enacted with ancestral cups and saucers by members gowned in meticulously researched period costumes or in assorted articles of dress handed down in the family for several generations and thus, assuredly, "old."[21]

The same heady brew of fancy dress, antiquities, social standing, and family history also fortified the founders of the Association for the Preservation of Virginia Antiquities. The APVA began in 1888 as a Committee of Safety convened by a "little band" of well-connected Virginia ladies distressed by several recent developments on the pre-servation front.[22] Jamestown, sunk in a sleepy torpor since President Tyler had called there in 1857 to observe the 250th anniversary of the oldest settlement in America, "bade fair to ere long disappear forever under the encroaching waves of the James."[23] Worse yet, according to good intelligence, "unholy negotiations were being made to move the home of Mary, the mother of Washington, from its foundations, and to set it up in a distant part of the country for money-getting purposes."

Mary Ball Washington, about whom almost no solid fact was known, was on her way to becoming an object of intense veneration in the late nineteenth century. Scholars scrambled to identify some likeness of her. A Bible and a book of devotions said to be hers received much scrutiny.[24] The widow Custis gave the childless Father of His Country no offspring. Although Martha had been a mother before she married George, she made a poor maternal symbol when pitted against Mary, the mother of Washington, whose very name evoked memories of the biblical Madonna. On those grounds, and on the basis of legends of her piety and devotion to home and duty, Mary Washington was an ideal housewifely heroine; her virtues, unlike those of captains of industry or Revolutionary generals, had some bearing on the ideals against which true American womanhood was judged in the late nineteenth century. Furthermore, the rescue of her Fredericksburg house was the sort of thoroughly feminine occupation to which ex-emplary wives and mothers, stifled by the narrow compass of domestic affairs, might turn without reproach, thus evading the very strictures Mary Ball Washington's secular sainthood celebrated.

4.4
Miss May Handy as Queen Anne at the APVA ball, 1892

The "daughters of Williamsburg" who temporarily left the security of their own homes and hearths to meet together in that desolate old town in 1888 did not propose to sacrifice their domestic comforts entirely. Since "the pillared Capitol" and "lordly executive palace" were in ruins, they chose to hold council in "the dormer-windowed, colonial home of a Virginia woman" and from that cozy setting sallied forth to the executive mansion at Richmond. There the infant association proclaimed Mrs. Fitzhugh Lee, consort of the governor, its first president. An advisory board of powerful gentlemen was elected, a charter was incorporated in the names of fourteen persuasive ladies, "and the society entered immediately upon its gracious work."[25] And it takes nothing away from the solid accomplishments of the APVA to observe that in its first official history, published in 1894, tiny photographs of the drawing room of the Mary Ball Washington House, repaired and saved from a piecemeal trip to Chicago in packing crates, were overshadowed by pictures of Mrs. Lee, Mrs. John Bernard Lightfoot, and the other officers and former officers of the organization. Even more noticeable were glamorous, full-page portraits of the leading lights of the annual ball in all their finery, taken by "Foster of Richmond" (Figure 4.4).[26]

Although the patriotic societies taking shape at the same moment in time were not formed specifically to look after historic sites, their founders were also conscious of the niceties of social and economic stratification. Early accounts of the origin of the Sons of the American Revolution were not adorned with studio portraits of distinguished past members but did feature lists of illustrious recruits: in an 1899 compilation, William McKinley, Levi Morton, Chauncey Depew, Marcus Hanna, Henry Cabot Lodge, and Theodore Roosevelt were enumerated with pride. The official chroniclers of the all-male groups traced the impulse for the banding together of such prominent gentlemen on genealogical principle to "the renaissance of patriotism" that came to flower during the series of American centennials beginning at Lexington in April of 1875, when "under the potent influence of anniversary suggestion, people's thoughts were diverted from the rankling memories of the Civil War, then but ten years past, to the great events of a century before."[27]

Guided by that spirit of reconciliation, ten men calling themselves Sons of Revolutionary Squires met in a doctor's office on Kearney Street in San Francisco in 1875 and worked out the mechanics of a charter limiting membership "exclusively" to "*lineal* descendants from the heroes and statesmen of the American Revolution." Then, "dressed in the costume of the revolutionary period," they held a Fourth of July parade, ate dinner together, and hoisted a number of glasses in tribute to their own good breeding and patriotism.[28] The idea took hold rapidly in the East when a delegation from California attended the

Yorktown centennial celebration in 1881, inspiring New Yorkers of Revolutionary ancestry to claim a special role in upcoming ceremonies commemorating the anniversary of the evacuation of the city by the British in 1783.

By the spring of 1889, as New York City braced for another round of historic hoopla, this time to honor the inauguration of George Washington a century before, the competing groups—or most of them, at any rate—had coalesced into a single fraternity calling itself the Sons of the American Revolution. Their pact was solemnly ratified in the very room in Fraunces' Tavern where Washington had taken leave of his brother officers of the Continental Army, and the company settled down to the task of promoting patriotism by a round of jolly banquets with toasts and fine cigars and by the rescue, location, and marking of historic sites, a project appropriated directly from their wives as a kind of afterthought.

Despite an admittedly "rigid" set of standards for admission that refused membership, for instance, to those connected to the Revolutionary generation by simple collateral descent, the group claimed superiority to the ancient Society of the Cincinnati on the basis of greater openness. Formed in 1783, the Cincinnati enrolled only Washington's commissioned officers and later, following the strict rule of primogeniture, a choice selection of their offspring. By 1876, fewer than four hundred members remained and were objects of curiosity rather than influential voices in the affairs of the day. Their club, the Sons of the American Revolution charged, was "narrow and exclusive, and not in accord with the democratic spirit of the age."[29]

An organization that stood ready in theory to welcome men of any political persuasion, class, creed, or sympathy during the last war was also, in theory, entitled to crow about its egalitarian character; even if application forms demanded proof of direct, lineal descent from a patriot father, the accident of birth ultimately allotted memberships according to the democratic law of random selection. In practice, however, hereditary societies served to identify, exalt, and weld together a new class of old Americans. Old Americans were people whose family furniture had crossed the Atlantic beneath the decks of the *Mayflower*. They were people whose ancestry, possessions, and obsession with both set them firmly apart from brand-new Americans, the immigrants from Ireland and other dubious corners of Europe, fast overrunning the old Yankee and Quaker and Knickerbocker strongholds along the East Coast.

Even within the elect circle of old Americans, however, some sprigs on the ancestral tree were clearly superior to others. In 1890, although she was only a clerk in the Dead Letter Office of the postal service, Miss Eugenia Washington, a great-granddaughter of Samuel Washington, brother of George, was honored by being listed first on the roster of the newly constituted Daughters of the American Revolution, sister organization to the Sons. The Washington name covered a multitude of social sins. But Mary Lockwood, another of the founding mothers of the sorority, was allegedly passed over for high office because she ran a boarding house in downtown Washington and rented out rooms at $1.25 a night. And Mrs. Benjamin Harrison, the president's wife and the first present-general of the DAR, is said to have blackballed another founder from a position of leadership because she was only a clerk in the Pension Office.[30]

In 1876, a centennial story published by Henrietta M. Holdich in the *New York Observer* made no reference to the social standing of Hannah Thurston Arnett, colonial goodwife of New Jersey.[31] The story nonetheless seems to have been crucial to the founding of the DAR under Mrs. Harrison's benign and socially correct patronage (Figure 4.5). In effect, the saga created a new kind of active Revolutionary heroine for the American woman. Not simply another dutiful female like Betsy Ross, who plied her needle as usual but in the patriot cause, not simply another fecund female, like Mary, the mother of Washington, Hannah Arnett was seamstress, wife, mother, and much more.

When her husband and his friends considered accepting Lord Howe's offer of protection to those who would reaffirm their loyalty to Britain and swear not to take up arms against the mother country, she did something brave, unexpected, and entirely unbecoming to the stereotypical lady: Hannah meddled in the affairs of men for patriotic motives of her own. "If you take your protection you lose your wife, and I," she promised darkly through her tears, "—I lose my husband and my home."[32] At the time the tale appeared, it aroused strong feelings. Even though Henrietta Holdich was a great-granddaughter of Hannah Thurston Arnett, other great-granddaughters with loyalties to the Arnett side of the family sniffed at the story because it challenged the patriotism of the men in question. But for others, Hannah clearly served as a model of exemplary behavior, of a spunkiness and devotion to principle that ought never to have gone out of fashion.

In fact, the life of Hannah Arnett erupted into print again in 1890 in the pages of the *Washington Post* because Mary Lockwood—the boardinghouse keeper—was so incensed by the decision of the male descendants of Revolutionary yeomen and squires to ban women from their sanctioned bloodlines that she was driven to a public retort in the letters column. At a recent gathering of the local chapter of the Sons, Lockwood reported, sixty persons were in attendance, twenty of them women with precisely the credentials called for by such a group: their foremothers had been the wives and daughters of the Revolution. Yet they were treated as guests, observers whose ruffled feathers Senator Sherman, the presiding officer, did his best to smooth. Personally, the senator said, he approved of "any movement that would

4.5
Daniel Huntington, portrait of Mrs. Benjamin Harrison, the first president-general of the DAR. The painting was presented to the White House by the grateful members of that organization in 1894.

perpetuate the memory of the heroes of the Revolutionary War, and hailed with pleasure [an] organization composed of men and women of the descendants of Revolutionary sires. The women might not have done any of the fighting, but they took an equally important part in looking after the homes, that the men might absent themselves in their country's cause."

If so, retorted the furious Mrs. Lockwood, why was patriotism handed down exclusively from father to son?

If this is the case why do men and women band themselves together to commemorate a one-sided heroism? If these were true, patriotic women, why is not the patriotism of the country broad and just enough to take women in, too? It is a noble act for the descendants of the Revolutionary sires. But were there no mothers of the Revolution? Were these sires without dams? I trow not.

I have heard of a man who had a dam by a mill site, while he had "no mill by a dam site," but I have yet to hear of a man who had a Revolutionary sire without a dam by the home site. This is an opportune time to bring forward some of the women of "76" lest the sires become puffed up by vain glory. I will begin with a true story of the Revolution which can be backed up by scores more of equal patriotism.[33]

With that flash of risqué wit, Lockwood launched into the story of Hannah Arnett.

Lockwood's letter was the irritant around which her sisters came together to form their pearl of patriotism. A month after her statement appeared, the *Post* printed a report of a meeting of women calling themselves the Society of the Daughters of the American Revolution, who invited interested parties to write to Miss Eugenia Washington if they desired to "study the manner and measures of those days [and] to devise the best methods of perpetuating the memories of our ancestors and celebrating their achievements." *Any* woman could join, providing she could show lineal descent "from an ancestor who assisted in establishing American independence during the War of the Revolution, either as a military or naval officer, a soldier, or civilian."[34]

Civilians came in two genders, and the DAR flaunted its own. Almost immediately the ladies joined a new campaign to preserve the grave of Mary Washington from sale to a builder and to erect an obelisk above it, replacing an older marker "scarred by war" and hacked apart by a new breed of vandal relic-seekers.[35] Ancestral homes became another DAR specialty. By 1896 it was preserving a variety of Revolutionary sites, including the headquarters at Valley Forge—the Potts House—whose custodians had signed up as new members of the Daughters. By 1905 local chapters owned or maintained ten colonial house museums (many with very slight connections to military engagements), while the national office contributed cash and furnishings to restorations at the Paul Revere House, the Royall House, the Scotch-Boardman House, and other sites of antiquarian interest.[36]

The seal adopted by the group depicted a colonial dame and her spinning wheel ringed by the motto "Home and Country." The actual model was one of Thomas Jefferson's great-granddaughters, but the spiritual model was probably Hannah Arnett. In Mrs. Lockwood's account of her heroic deed, Hannah's husband tries to silence her by shouting, "My good little wife[,] you are making yourself ridiculous. Go to your spinning-wheel and leave us to settle affairs."[37] Affairs, as the ladies of America came to realize in the 1880s and 1890s, could often be handled quite nicely by the same hand that turned the spinning wheel or fluttered a pretty fan at a fancy ball.

Monuments and Patronage

Old buildings made new again in the late nineteenth century commemorated the deeds of America's ancestors. So did ornate sculptural markers, like the Yorktown Victory Monument dedicated during the centenary of the battle, in 1881.[38] Monument-building, an activity stimulated by the anniversaries of the centennial period, is a special form of retrospection: while the statue or the obelisk directs the attention of the viewer to events of the past, it is also an intrusive physical presence in the world of today. In content, but more particularly in style, that object must speak to the contemporary world in its own terms in order to fulfill its function.

Just as the colonial revival of the 1870s and the 1880s focused on home and hearth; just as preservationists found themselves drawn to the private haunts of the historic dead (including their dining rooms); just as the role of women shifted the prevailing view of the Revolutionary era from swords and battles toward spinning wheels and balls: so too did several important Washington monuments dedicated between the centennial year and the turn of the century reflect the unwarlike lives of their sponsors. By memorializing the statesman, the urbane gentleman, the first president, the Washington who was "First in Peace, First in the Hearts of His Countrymen," these monuments also commemorated modern-day lives absorbed in a prescribed round of social events and relationships, club meetings, fashion, the status conferred by lineage and a proper marriage, the rites of business and politics.[39]

Evacuation Day festivities in New York City in 1883, the centenary anniversary, were directed by the local Chamber of Commerce. The day was so named because it marked the retreat of the enemy from Manhattan during the Revolutionary War. After years of occupation by the British, the victorious George Washington had been formally received by the citizens of New York on November 25, 1783, at the site of Union Square in a ceremony marking the resumption of both peace and normal trade. It was altogether fitting, therefore, that the city's modern-day merchants and professional men should trace the origins

4.6

Evacuation Day, 1883; unveiling J. Q. A. Ward's statue of Washington in Wall Street

of their present prosperity to that symbolic event and should choose to commemorate it by suitable exercises centered on a twice-life-size bronze statue of Washington commissioned of John Quincy Adams Ward for the front steps of the Sub-Treasury in Wall Street (Figure 4.6).

In 1883 Wall Street was the throbbing heart of the financial district. In 1783, on the very spot where the marble pedestal for the statue was being built, stood old Federal Hall. And standing on the red sandstone flooring of the balcony—parts of the balustrade and the paving slabs were stored away somewhere in the bowels of Bellevue Hospital, old-timers thought—General Washington had become President Washington on April 30, 1789. By honoring Washington in his role as author of New York's future hegemony in trade, business, and finance and by anticipating the Inaugural Centennial that would add the luster of historic hegemony to the glitter of wealth and power, the Chamber of Commerce openly proclaimed the city's coming of age. In 1883 history would confirm the rectitude of modern business. The benign bronze gentleman in the suit of civilian clothes would henceforth stretch forth his right hand over Wall Street in a gesture of perpetual benediction.

At the eleventh hour, at least according to the *New York Times,* the wheels of commerce were turning almost too smoothly. The statue had arrived from the foundry in good order and awaited the great day beneath its shroud of canvas. Regiments from the old colonies, many of them now wearing parade dress based on the Continental uniform, had arrived in town and had received detailed instructions on where they were to form a line of march (Figure 4.7).[40] Little silk flags to wave during the festivities were at a premium. Official programs had been printed in the expectation that needy newsboys who sold them for a nickel along the various parade routes could keep a percentage of the profits. The reviewing stand in Union Square was done; tickets had been issued to select members of President Arthur's party. Meanwhile, for the various marine and street parades, entrepreneurs were selling private viewing stations on the roofs of office buildings, in store windows, and along the docks at prices ranging from $5 to $25. The German lager beer saloon-keeper now in possession of Washington's headquarters at Pearl and Broad Streets sat at Washington's old mahogany table in a corner of his dining room and hoped he could get a fire going in the old hearth in honor of the day: it would add a touch of authenticity to the setting and boost trade.

Private enterprise had also decorated the city, not always with unselfish patriotism guiding the aesthetic choices. A swank uptown haberdashery had installed a window display featuring "a bust of Washington, draped in the stars and stripes, . . . mounted on a pedestal beneath a gorgeous canopy and surrounded by tropical plants." But all such tributes were not executed in the same tasteful spirit of restrained civic-mindedness:

KNICKERBOCKERS.

In the Bowery . . . shopkeepers manifest a little patriotism, though here the advertising mania predominates. For instance, in connection with a huge portrait of Washington the wayfarer is informed that the Father of His Country never had an opportunity to purchase six linen shirts for $7, nor did his patriotic eyes ever behold such bargains in neckware as might be found inside the particular store displaying the picture. Second-hand shops have been ransacked for discolored busts of Franklin, Jefferson, and other statesmen. Noisy vendors are hawking libelous prints of Revolutionary heroes and battles. But they are dear at any price.[41]

Excesses among the merchants on the Bowery did little to reassure those well-placed observers who doubted New York's ability to provide a suitable climax to the string of observances that had begun in Philadelphia in September of 1874 with the centenary of the assembly of the Continental Congress. New York City was notorious for indifference toward its past, they said; that was the Dutch temperament of the place. But recent immigration was also a factor. "The mixed and cosmopolitan character of her subsequent population" boded ill for such events. "A large part of the crowd which will gaze upon the pageant of the celebration of Evacuation-day will wonder what Evacuation-day was," *Harper's Weekly* predicted, "and the electric national appeal of great national anniversaries, which brings homogeneous communities to their feet with pride and joy, will be wanting here."[42]

While the prognosticators envisioned failure, the Chamber of Commerce was facing immediate problems of finance and politics. Membership subscriptions to defray the mounting bills were slow in arriving. Two days before the main event, the Stock Exchange did come through with $1,000, boosting receipts in hand to $11,254, although Lord & Taylor in lieu of a check sent a note stating that the firm remained "opposed to" the celebration. The next day, society was heard from. From William K. Vanderbilt and William Astor came $250 apiece. Delmonico's and the Union League chipped in. Flushed with success, the Central Committee voted to furnish fourteen fifers and drummers to escort Washington's "chariot" (his coach), which was to be pulled by ten black horses supplied gratis by American Express.

Most of the businessmen fell into line just as the politicians were falling all over one another in their haste to break ranks. Roscoe Conkling, New York's political favorite, abruptly canceled plans to attend the banquet slated by the Chamber for the night of Evacuation Day to honor visiting state governors. Pleading a death in the family, pressing private business, a wedding, and even bodily distress caused by a recent roasting of the nether regions in the hot baths at Yellowstone, Conkling really begged off because he would "not cross his legs under the same table with Mr. Curtis," one of the guests of honor. General Grant, who was to have delivered a toast, also discovered a wedding that needed attending in Philadelphia at that very hour.[43] And the partisan subcommittee in charge of the unveiling of the statue huffily refused to postpone its appointed hour so that President Chester Arthur, whose itinerary placed him somewhere between a parade and a luncheon at the time, could attend.

On top of everything, it rained. It poured. It teemed. Organizers were glad that in an effort to unclog a crowded agenda one of the scheduled events had already taken place, under threatening but dry skies, several days before. A crowd of a thousand or so, pressed around the shrouded statue at the foot of Wall Street, had watched Royal Phelps, chairman of the unaccommodating subcommittee, remove a cap-piece from the pedestal and lower a time-capsule into the cavity beneath. The copper box, welded closed for posterity's sake, contained a list of the subscribers to the statue fund, copies of New York's daily papers, coins in current use, a special number of the souvenir program inscribed on parchment, and certain unspecified "records of the Chamber of Commerce." When the box was in place and the marble cemented over it, a chunk of the brownstone slab on which Washington stood when he took the oath of office was countersunk into the broad platform in front of the pedestal.

The sculptor sat off to one side supervising the whole operation and wondering if the storm would dampen his big moment.[44] On balance, reporters thought, it had not. Even the genteel *Harper's,* which had feared the worst from the polyglot crowds, came away moist but with a favorable impression of the day:

The chill November rain could not deprive the ceremonies of their greatest and best impressiveness—that which came from the evidence that the celebration was spontaneous and popular. Those who, with EMERSON, "have not the smallest interest in any holiday except as it celebrates real and not pretended joy," must have been cheered to see the universal glow of patriotism that many waters could not put out. . . . It was not the official but the unofficial celebration that was the most memorable, the tens of thousands standing their ground doggedly to see the great procession—of more than 20,000 men, it was reckoned—pass by, that they might not miss the memory of the centennial celebration soon to become legendary with the event it celebrates.[45]

In a separate article on the same theme, the magazine marveled at the good humor of the hundreds of thousands packed upon the sidewalks, pelted by the storm, and yet interested in what was happening and essentially orderly, an object lesson in "the effect of popular government in producing popular moderation and self-restraint." Swallowing its former thesis that immigrants would take no part in the commemoration, *Harper's* now prepared to account for the unaccountable enthusiasm of the Irish who figured mightily in the tally of spectators:

Of course the crowd, as must always be the case in New York, was a heterogeneous throng. It was composed of persons of many nationalities; for New York is the largest Irish city in the world, and almost the largest German city, and the numbers of natives of other lands are always large. The traditions of such a day are consequently unfamiliar to a great part of the spectators, to whom the pageant is pure spectacle, and who feel no thrill of patriotism in the associations of the hour. But, although this changes the nature of their pleasure, it does not destroy its zest, and they hear with the interest of novelty the story of the significance of the day. The Irish societies may be supposed to have had peculiar pleasure in recollecting that in some way the day commemorated British discomfiture. But the Irish societies may also wisely ponder the fact that, while British authority was happily expelled, the glorious British traditions of constitutional freedom remained, and are organized in new forms. It is the tradition of the English-speaking race that still dominates, as it has always controlled, our civilization.[46]

If Evacuation Day ceremonies stood for the rule of unaccented Anglo-Saxon law, so, in fact, did the statue of Washington in Wall Street. The dedication was the culminating event of the long day, and as the soggy canvas was stripped away, Roscoe Conkling's nemesis, the Honorable George William Curtis, told the assembly that the sculpture did not commemorate the advent of a conquerer but the inauguration of a president under the rule of law. It was not, said Curtis, as he gestured toward the bronze figure, the "sworded Commander-in-Chief of the Continental forces, but the first President of the United States with the fasces of magistracy, whom Mr. Ward's statue represents."[47]

More than anyone else in attendance that rainy afternoon in 1883, Ward had reason to appreciate the difference. On July 4, 1856, he had stood on a platform in Union Square beside then-Senator Fish and the Reverend George Bethune of Brooklyn, the principal speakers, looking down upon eight thousand spectators and three parading regiments of the National Guard, as dignitaries struggled with a tarpaulin that remained tangled around the fetlocks of an equestrian statue. The statue in Union Square was a Washington too, one also erected by public subscription to commemorate Evacuation Day at a time when some eyewitnesses—New Yorkers who had seen the hero enter the square at Fourth Avenue and Fourteenth Street in 1783—were still alive. High atop his granite pedestal, the general, with his hat tucked under his left arm and his right hand raised as if to restrain an army still clamoring for victory, rode forward to meet the new responsibilities of peace.[48]

John Quincy Adams Ward, who repeated that gesture in his own Evacuation Day statue some twenty-seven years later, had ample reason to recall the 1856 unveiling because his name—"J.Q.A. Ward, Ass't."—was carved on the base of the earlier sculpture alongside that of his teacher, Henry Kirke Brown, in honor of his tireless work at riveting the horse and rider together and chasing the surface during a strike by New York metalworkers (Figure 4.8). The ceremony was noteworthy on other grounds as well: Brown's was only the second American equestrian statue, and it had been paid for by ninety-seven individual and fourteen corporate donors recruited in an unprecedented campaign directed by James Lee, a commission merchant with offices on Wall Street. The corporate donors, whose contributions were often in kind, included builders, teamsters, a stoneware manufacturer, the carpenter who built the platform, the florist who supplied the turf to prettify the ceremony, and the sailmaker who made the "veil." Although some colleagues in the street rebuffed his plea for $400—"I will give nothing, sir," snorted one tightfisted patriot, "for Washington lives in my heart"—New York businessmen raised "a monument to him whom his countrymen," wrote Lee, "love to honor as the greatest man the world has ever known."[49] With their backing and with the help of Hamilton Fish, who lent the artist his own copy of the Houdon bust of Washington, Brown had begun his work on Washington's Birthday, 1853.

During the thirty years between the beginning of Brown's enterprise and the conclusion of Ward's, most of the major Washington monuments were equestrian statues. Boston unveiled Thomas Ball's horseman on the Common on July 3, 1869, after a decade-long delay caused by the War Between the States. The motive for showing the Virginian as he appeared on July 3, 1775, when he took command of his largely Yankee army beneath the Cambridge Elm, had been pacific and conciliatory: in 1859, the incident in Cambridge was read as a symbolic unification of North and South and the sculptor admitted to having been inspired by the Mount Vernon rescue drive. "Mr. Everett's efforts in behalf of Mount Vernon stimulated the veneration of the people for the name of Washington, and imparted, as it were, to the people a deeper reverence for the name than had manifested itself for many years," Ball recalled.[50]

Funds for the Boston Washington of 1869 were raised through public lectures. Robert Winthrop, who would later serve as the centenary orator at Yorktown, repeated a celebrated speech he had already delivered for the benefit of the YMCA in Baltimore, adding, here and there, references to a project for "placing Massachusetts by the side of Virginia in this precise mode of commemorating the Father of his Country." Rembrandt Peale, whose reputation hinged on his, his father's, and his family's numerous likenesses of the first president, repeated his famous disquisition on "the Portraits of Washington." Edward Everett spared the audience another warmed-over speech but donated a bound copy of the original manuscript of his Washington lecture, given frequently during the war in aid of the work of the Sanitary Commission. With his blessing, the "lady patronesses" of the statue fund had held a Statue Fair in 1859 that anticipated the creation of the Sanitary Fairs; as precedents for their forwardness, the women of the statue campaign felt compelled to cite their earlier efforts on behalf of the Bunker Hill Monument, the treasury of the Boston Provident Association, and the hospital for incurables.[51] In Washington's name some unaccustomed liberties were to be taken with impunity.

On Washington's Birthday in 1858, a day marked by rain, hailstones, and a furious snowstorm, Edward Everett attended the dedication of Thomas Crawford's equestrian Washington in Richmond, Virginia. The cornerstone, laid eight years earlier, contained a Bible, Webster's speller, an ear of corn, a piece of Washington's coffin, and a copy of the Farewell Address. The statue seems to have had an equally diffuse meaning. Commissioned at the end of the infamous dispute between Congress, Virginia, and the Washington family as to where the bones of the hero would finally rest, the Richmond monument was, according to Thomas Brumbaugh's reconstruction of its tangled history, a cenotaph, an empty tomb offering "at least a symbolic reassurance to 'the public' that Washington was buried in Virginia."[52]

Everett interpreted it in a different light. Between the unveiling and a bibulous ball that lasted until one in the morning, the old warhorse gave his standard Washington speech during a dinner at the American Hotel. Responding at considerable length to a toast, he searched the design of the statue for clues to its message. "That rigid arm," Everett ad-libbed, "shall point the unerring road to the welfare of the country more surely than any arm of living flesh; and a fiercer thunder than that of the elements shall clothe the neck of the monumental warhorse, and strike terror into the hearts of the enemies of the constitution and the union."[53] Even though some Virginians found his speech tedious—Everett also gave the patented lecture a second time, at a dollar a head, for the general public—courteous officials gave

4.8
"Spelter" statuette, ca. 1889, after Henry Kirke Brown's equestrian monument in Union Square

4.9
The *St. Nicholas* biography for children of 1886 featured Washington's camp chest and the cooking utensils shown in Philadelphia in 1876.

4.10
Washington's secretary, drawn for *St. Nicholas* by C. C. Cooper, Jr.

him Washington's cane in memory of his visit. But Southerners paid little heed to the warning supposedly conveyed by the position of Washington's hand. In 1862 Jefferson Davis delivered his inaugural address before the Washington statue in Richmond and put its likeness on the official seal of the Confederate States of America.

On his horse, Washington remained a martial figure, elevated and distant. When he stood on his own two feet, he became much like other men who tarried in the vicinity of Broad and Wall Streets. Those New Yorkers who looked searchingly at Ward's statue on the porch of the Sub-Treasury thought it a little large and glaring in tone, perhaps, although a growing familiarity and the effects of the weather would diminish its obtrusiveness in time. The face, a bit sour in expression if approached from the southwest, seemed unexceptionable from most other angles. Ward's customary facility with drapery had not deserted him either; the folds of the pants and waistcoat revealed enough anatomy to convince the passerby that Washington was no mere "stuffed suit of bronzed clothes, . . . a positive attainment in contemporary sculpture."[54]

But details like drapery and the bundle of fasces that helped to support the mass were most admirable in their subordination to the larger outlines. The severity and simplicity of the figure, standing large, serene, and free before the chaste façade of the Sub-Treasury, without tables, scrolls, horses, hats, or any of the usual impedimenta of nineteenth-century sculpture to compromise its grandeur, moved *Harper's* to impute a particular meaning to Ward's work with an aplomb that Edward Everett might have envied. "It is fortunate that Washington should have been commemorated by an effigy worthy of the duration that seems assured to this," the report stated. "It is especially fortunate that Wall Street should have a lasting reminder in a noble work of sculpture, as it had already in a noble work of architecture, that a man's life does not consist in the abundance of the things which he possesses."[55]

Governor Grover Cleveland, speaking at the banquet given by the Chamber of Commerce to conclude the festivities, also weighed nobility against materialism. Responding to an address in which Governor Butler had maligned "the merchants and professional men of the earlier day by saying they were not the men who carried on the Revolution," Cleveland suggested that the mercantile class of the ages past had sent men of the very best sort to represent the city's interests in the councils of state. In the performance of their political duties, Cleveland warned, "the citizens of New York should not fall behind the noble example of their forefathers" and then grumble because the Tammany Irish ran the show.[56] People of quality belonged in the political arena; worthy though their recent civic service in honor of Evacuation Day had been, the great decisions of the day were not

4.11

H. A. Ogden illustration of Washington rebuking Lee at Monmouth; the figure of the mounted Washington is based on Crawford's equestrian statue in Richmond.

made on the statuary subcommittee of the New York City Chamber of Commerce. The noble Washington, a man of every sterling quality, had come to Wall Street in 1789 to serve in government.[57]

The Best People Commemorate Washington

St. Nicholas, a magazine for children, serialized a long biography of George Washington in 1886. From January through October it ran, side by side with selections from *Little Lord Fauntleroy*, tips on the use of the fly-rod, and cunning pictures of baby bears. The illustrations chosen to remind boys and girls of the important episodes in the life of the hero constitute a compendium of Washington's best-known attributes and the most telling incidents in his career, as the period understood them.

The camp artifacts displayed at the Centennial Exposition were all there (Figure 4.9). So was the secretary where Washington's knife was found after his death (Figure 4.10). Larger plates betrayed an interest in balls and lavish costume; riders astride spirited horses, borrowed from Crawford and Brown (Figure 4.11); the Cambridge Elm; and the hardships of the winter at Valley Forge—Horace Scudder, the author of the series, gave a detailed account of Isaac Potts and the prayer in the snow.[58] The episodes from Washington's life singled out for pictorial treatment were chosen, it would appear, with the recent or upcoming centennials in mind: Cambridge, Yorktown, and the farewell at Fraunces' Tavern led to a final narrative plate introducing youngsters

4.12
Another of Ogden's splendid Washington illustrations, showing the first inaugural; the figure is based on the new J. Q. A. Ward statue of Washington.

to a Washington garbed just as Ward had left him on the porch of the Sub-Treasury, with his right hand outstretched in just the same manner, over a Bible on a velvet cushion. He was taking the oath of office on Wall Street in New York City (Figure 4.12). The date beneath the picture was April 30, 1789.[59]

The decision to celebrate that date as the culmination of the constitutional centennial came about through the efforts of J. E. Peyton, a transplanted Englishman from Haddonfield, New Jersey. In 1883 he induced the Tennessee legislature to pass a resolution calling upon Congress "to encourage an appropriate celebration of the inauguration of President Washington in New York in 1889." For the seventeen years previous, the tireless Peyton had roamed the land originating, proposing, and devising other centennials. He was rumored to have had a hand in events in Philadelphia and Yorktown, and in the Evacuation Day centenary of 1883. Whatever his earlier triumphs, however, the 1889 festivities in honor of the last of the great centenary years would represent the pinnacle of his career as a pageant-master.[60]

But even as Peyton argued his case in Tennessee, New Yorkers in 1883 were pondering the upcoming anniversary independently under the prodding of the orators speaking from beneath the sheltering hand of Washington on the steps of the Sub-Treasury. With George Lane, president of the Chamber of Commerce, in attendance, George William Curtis had stressed the theme of orderly, constitutional government and downplayed the usual military trappings of patriotic holidays:

The task upon which Washington entered here was infinitely greater than that which he undertook, when, fourteen years before, he drew his sword under the elm at Cambridge as commander-in-chief. . . . To lead a people in revolution wisely and successfully, without ambition and without a crime, demands, indeed, lofty genius and unbending virtue. But to build their state—amid the angry conflict of passion and prejudice and unreasonable apprehension, the incredulity of many, and the grave doubt of all, to organize for them and peacefully to inaugurate a complete and satisfactory government—is the greatest service that a man can render to mankind.[61]

Hence, practical steps were soon taken toward marking this wholly civilian occasion with suitable ceremony. In March of 1884, a formal meeting of the New York Historical Society resolved to do so largely on the basis of precedent. That organization, it seems, had orchestrated the Jubilee of the Constitution in 1839. The high point had been a two-hour speech by former President John Quincy Adams, who sat in Washington's own chair during exercises at the Middle Dutch Church on Cedar Street as the audience sang to the tune of the "Old Hundredth" an ode written for the occasion by William Cullen Bryant. A banquet at the City Hotel had followed the oratorical ordeal, and during the evening transparencies representing the first inauguration were unveiled at the back of the hall to loud applause.[62] In 1883 the presiding officer of the Historical Society recalled that evening while he conducted the meeting from the "Washington Chair" that stood on the platform at the front of the hall. A gift to the group in 1857, the ornate piece was made from the wood of the house prepared for the use of the first president on the corner of Cherry Street, in Franklin Square, and was decorated with a bust of Washington (Figure 4.13).[63]

But other, competing forces were also at work all over the city. The annual Washington's Birthday dinner of the New York Society of the Sons of the Revolution endorsed its own plan for an inaugural gala in 1885. In 1886 the Chamber of Commerce did likewise. In addition to sending copies of their minutes to state and local officials, the Chamber also petitioned Congress for a cash appropriation. Finally, Mr. Peyton himself entered the picture once more, calling a public meeting at the Fifth Avenue Hotel on November 10, 1887, for additional discussion. After a second such meeting—Daniel Huntington, the painter of *Lady Washington's Reception,* was a signatory to the call for a gathering of the civic-minded in 1887—all the interested parties were finally merged into one, great Committee of Citizens, two hundred strong, chaired first by Mayor Hewett and later by Hamilton Fish, former secretary of state. Included on its roster of luminaries were such distinguished New Yorkers as Richard Watson Gilder, William Waldorf Astor, William K. Vanderbilt, Stuyvesant Fish, and Ward McAllister, the social arbiter of the so-called Four Hundred, New York's social elite.[64]

Gilder promptly took himself off to Philadelphia under the auspices of a federal Constitutional Centennial Committee to trump up interest in the New York celebration and to recruit bands for the parade. In the meantime Ward McAllister lost no time in fixing the date for a ball, to be held at the Metropolitan Opera House exactly one year hence, on Monday, April 29, 1889. In his mind, at least, the civilian character of the event meant more than the participation of the Chamber of Commerce or the absence of military leadership. It meant that the best people—New York society as he had almost single-handedly defined it—would be the custodians of George Washington's public persona in 1889.

Choosing the date for the ball was of paramount importance, since the events of the whole Inaugural Centennial would revolve around it, just as the order of precedence in New York drawing rooms and banquet halls for years to come would hinge on the selection of the very best of the best ladies and gentlemen to open the ball by dancing the centennial quadrille in colonial costume. And despite some intimations on the part of those not likely to attend that McAllister's project was a strange way to begin the solemn celebration of the birth of a democratic nation, the agenda did appear to include something for everybody:

4.13
The Washington Chair at the New York Historical Society; gift of Mrs. Benjamin R. Winthrop, 1857

Such a celebration is in its nature a popular spectacle, and to be successful it must appeal to popular sympathy. Decorations and a procession are indispensable, and an oration and poem and dinner are made by custom essential parts of such an occasion. The provision for the arrival of the President in the city by the same route pursued by Washington gives opportunity for a striking aquatic spectacle, and a ball is one of the traditional forms of festal observance of Washington's birthday, and not inappropriately may be included in the scheme for the celebration.[65]

Eager to eclipse the ball "given to the Prince of Wales a quarter of a century ago far more grandly than that great assembly eclipsed all others that went before it," McAllister pressed forward with plans to swaddle the Opera House in "gaudy plush and shields and trophies, flags and bunting, the undertone being all garnet and cream-color," and to install Benjamin Harrison and his wife on a pair of thronelike seats "beneath a canopy of silks, satin, lace, velvet, and brass."[66] Cooler heads wrestled with the remaining slots in the three-day calendar of events: the exhibition of historical relics also slated for the Metropolitan Opera House; the progress of the president from Washington City, following the path taken by his predecessor en route to the first inauguration; the naval parade to accompany Harrison's water landing at the foot of Wall Street (Figure 4.14); a reception and luncheon for Harrison, hosted by the business community at the sumptuous Lawyers' Club in the Equitable Building; a public reception at City Hall; the ball; a symbolic reenactment by President Harrison of Washington's inaugural day, beginning with services at St. Paul's Church and climaxing with "literary exercises" planned for the porch of the Sub-Treasury; a parade of fifty thousand members of the several state militias; a banquet, which those excluded from dining could watch for a fee from boxes and galleries above; fireworks; and a concluding "pageant of peace," a civic and industrial parade said to be the largest ever mounted.

These diverse elements were held together by several common threads. One was a rigid adherence to the rules of etiquette. The preoccupation with the finer points of manners, precedence, table arrangements, orders of march, and rosters of dignitaries was not confined to the likes of Ward McAllister. An outbreak of punctiliousness infected the lawyers, the businessmen, the members of the official committees, the clergy, and the newspapers. It trickled down into the ranks of the ethnic societies whose participation had been carefully channeled into the parade tacked on to the ragtag end of things. It even affected the crowds who came to goggle at the whole wondrous carnival of class and patriotism. Whether that place was on the sidewalk or in the presidential box, in 1889 everyone jockeyed for a position precisely calibrated to his or her station in life.

4.14
De Thulstrup and Bodfish illustration showing President Harrison landing at the foot of Wall Street, April 29, 1889

Symptomatic of the obsession was an announcement from the White House, made several weeks before the Inaugural Centennial began, concerning the First Lady's researches into the matter of offering one's hand in greeting to those of lesser eminence. Mrs. Harrison had recently declined to shake hands with the three hundred guests at a Japanese reception and had persuaded her husband to do likewise on the basis of historical precedent. New York was therefore put on notice that because Washington didn't shake hands in 1789, Benjamin Harrison did not intend to do so in 1889:

It is announced that, in accordance with the practice at the reception of WASHINGTON in 1789, the President will not shake hands with the guests [at the Lawyers' Club reception], who will simply bow and pass on. The questions of etiquette in the approaching celebration have seemed largely to monopolize the attention of the managers, and the discussions have exploded in very severe remarks both in the Legislature and in public comment. But the tremendous controversy will not have been in vain if the centennial celebration shall lead to the abolition of the painful and cruel custom of Presidential hand-shaking at state receptions. The modern abuse—for it was not Washington's custom—is to be set aside at the Equitable under the plea of conformity to the "earliest and best precedent."[67]

The controversy in question had erupted across the headlines less than two weeks before Harrison was to be ferried ashore from a steam barge anchored in the East River by "the gallant old seadogs" of the Marine Society whose ancestors "rowed President Washington ashore a century ago" (Figure 4.15).[68] "Ward McAllister's Power Entirely

4.15
The official party being rowed ashore in the East River by the ex-shipmasters of the Marine Society of the Port of New York

Gone," crowed the *New York Times,* above an article that outlined the reasons for his "fall from high estate of practical boss of the ball to the nominal position of manager." The party line, emanating from Chairman Stuyvesant Fish and the remaining members of the Entertainment Committee, held McAllister insubordinate, high-handed, and secretive. Although he had gained some prominence as manager of the Patriarch's balls, said a hastily hired press agent for the other gentlemen involved, in this instance "McAllister went in regardless of the committee and sold boxes, issued invitations, and assumed general executive authority over the whole affair. He was called to account and ordered to make a report of all his doings. Such report as he did pretend to make was so garbled and indefinite that nothing could be made of it." Finally, McAllister added insult to injury by sending a prickly letter to the mayor asking for "a full definition of all the rights which I am to hold."[69]

Quite properly, that official shot the whole mess back to the committee, which met and reaffirmed its ultimate control over all balls, banquets, and similar functions. When asked by Mr. Fish if he intended to follow the instructions of his superiors in the future, Mr. McAllister uttered an emphatic "No," then muttered something inaudible and stalked off. When asked for his resignation, he denied Mr. Fish's right to request it. So, "to avoid a scandal," he was allowed to retain his title while his responsibilities were transferred to another.

Almost immediately his successor announced that flowers, decorations, and other sundries had been obtained at far lower prices than the careless McAllister had been able to negotiate. He also requested holders of ticket orders to present them promptly for redemption at the offices of the Madison Square Bank. The fracas, and the possibility of dramatic snubs all the way around, had put a real premium on tickets: as of April 10, with 5,022 already sold and 2,255 issued to invited guests, fewer than a thousand places remained at $10 a head.[70]

During the following week, Ward McAllister called in the *Times* to charge Fish and Elbridge Gerry, general superintendent of the Centennial, with animus and, oddly enough, with elitism. They were, he countered, "determined to run the ball and banquet for personal gratification rather than with an eye to making the affair a grand representative American celebration." Gerry, he added, was miffed because McAllister had denied him the place of honor between President Harrison and Vice President Morton at the banquet, assigning the chair to the mayor instead for, "as this celebration was given by the people, with the peoples' money, it was the people's right to have their representative in the position of honor, and . . . therefore Mayor Grant should be where Mr. Gerry wanted to be." As for Stuyvesant Fish:

The cause of his displeasure was even more ludicrous than that which raised the ire of Mr. Gerry. Mr. Fish insisted that, as Chairman of the Entertainment Committee, it was his privilege to dance opposite to President Harrison in the opening quadrille. Now, I consider Mr. Fish "a consummate ass," and told him that the position of honor he coveted should be filled by a man with some social distinction. Hence Mr. Fish has opposed me bitterly.[71]

When informed of McAllister's intemperate remarks, Fish responded in kind. The man was out of his depth as the czar of a hundred-thousand-dollar enterprise, involving eight thousand people! He was a lightweight, a butterfly, a fribble! And besides, "it is all nonsense to credit Mr. McAllister with the formation of the so-called 400. Mr. Charles Delmonico created the 400 when he built a ball room which would only accommodate that many persons!" Insulted beyond all telling, Ward McAllister finally tendered his resignation, pronouncing himself content with his accomplishments. He had secured the best Burgundy in New York for only $6 a bottle. He had contracted for Havana cigars "that cannot be beaten." The bill of fare was impeccably foreign and correct. The best boxes were safely in the hands of those "whom it was most desirable to have at the ball." Best of all, "Mayor Grant, as the representative of the people, will occupy the position of honor [and] the opening quadrille will be danced by the men and women who, after careful genealogical search, I believed should dance it." Box 12 was reserved for the McAllisters, but the deposed ruler of the ballroom did not plan to attend, pleading business out of town. Even "if he return[ed] to that city during the progress of the celebration," Ward McAllister vowed to boycott the Centennial Ball.[72]

The public relished the farce in its every sordid detail. An ostensible news report on the crush of visitors from "the country" upstate, come to witness the doings in the city, concocted rustic dialogue between a farmer and his wife, tramping along Broadway and Fifth Avenue in search of some remarkable sight to retail back home. "'John, I guess the 400 ain't out today,' sighed a stout matron as she toiled up the hill at Thirty-third-street, and her John coincided with her opinion."[73] *Life* ran a cartoon by Charles Dana Gibson showing McAllister, tricked out in a ballgown decorated with the heraldic shields of the nobility, leading the Four Hundred on leashes past the statue of Washington on Wall Street: the members of his flock are geese wearing crowns and medals (Figure 4.16).

The jesters at *Life* also claimed to have come into possession of a revised order of march for the parade. The president was at the head of the column, and toward the middle, high society appeared in the person of McAllister himself:

AN ELDERLY PERSON NAMED MCALLISTER
Arrayed in knee-breeches and on a platform wagon demonstrating to the assembled ruralists the proper way to dance the York.

THE FOUR HUNDRED
In closed carriages.
   . . . THE FOUR HUNDRED THOUSAND
Who knew the Four Hundred in the Codfish Days.
   THE PEDIGREES OF THE DANCERS,
Bound in Maroon Plush and carried on Golden Pillows.
   THE BOARD OF ALDERMEN,
Wearing Shamrocks and Shillelahs, and waving Green flags.
   A Portrait of George Washington.*

   *George Washington was the first President of the United States. He was not so great a man as Elliot F. Shepard, nor so exclusive as Ward McAllister, but was elected without catering to the Irish vote. By a peculiar coincidence, the procession will occur on the one hundredth anniversary of his inauguration. Out of deference to the State Legislature and the Board of Aldermen, it had been intended to hold it on St. Patrick's Day, but it was feared that the weather might prove inclement.[74]

The "tea-pot tempest" was a nine-day wonder. "Why did Fish call McAllister a caterer and a servant?" *Life* wondered. Because of jealousy, and pride of place? And "why was McAllister angered when Fish usurped his authority? Because McAllister desired to be, before the eyes of an admiring country and in the mind of another continent, supreme dictator of the celebration of an event, the significance of which has not once entered his thoughts."[75] Surely George Washington, the Constitution, and the inauguration of the American state were ill commemorated by haughty claims of rank and privilege and by the scramble for preferment at the Centennial Ball!

   Whatever doubts the celebrity-mad public may have harbored about the decorum of the Four Hundred's battle over the bones of colonial history were swept aside by the glamour of the event itself, "a brilliant social affair in point of numbers, the character of those who took part in it, and the decorations. It was graced by a larger number of distinguished men and fair women, and of representatives of families whose names are identified with the history of the country than has characterized any other similar event in the past" (Figure 4.17).[76] At eleven o'clock sharp, in a crush of spectators and potential dancers so dense that the temporary floor built out from the stage of the Opera House trembled with the weight, before fragrant cornucopias of roses and wildflowers ("indicative of prosperity"), the ladies Ward McAllister had selected on the basis of peerless ancestry and social standing worked their way to the center of the floor and, between walls formed by the backs of sturdy artillerymen holding the throng at bay, began the centennial quadrille. After all the fuss, the quadrille was disappointing, "a simple little contra dance," requiring only a bit of dignified shuffling on the part of the president, the vice president, the governor, and several of the spryer military officers.

But the costumes and the personages bedecked in them were engaging enough to merit whole, dense pages of breathless description in the major dailies. Mrs. William Astor wore a Worth creation, cut décolleté, and "the famous Astor diamonds, which commanded great attention because of their splendor," but she was the only member of the entourage to choose a gown that could not somehow be wrenched into verbal conformity with Washington's era. Mrs. Levi Morton, the

4.17
The Centennial Ball, as drawn by W. A. Rogers

vice president's wife, observed the eighteenth-century theme with a transatlantic twist: she danced in mauve faille decorated with Marie Antoinette bows and she carried a French fan.[77] Mrs. Edward Jones wore diamonds almost as impressive as Mrs. Astor's and ostrich feathers, lace, embroidery, and flowers, all attached by a miracle of dressmaking to a gown with a similar plunging neckline, described by its owner as a "colonial costume."

Women whose ancestry was more noteworthy than their wealth settled for less ostentation and more authenticity. Mrs. Robert Weir, wife of the famous artist and a great-granddaughter of Dolley Madison, turned out in a dress "copied after those of the colonial period" and "at the center of the bodice she wore a buckle containing the hair of Gen. Washington, whose great-grandniece" she also was. Miss Georgia Schuyler went her one better by appearing in a gown stitched from a length of heirloom brocade, more than a century old, taken from the wedding costume made for General Philip Schuyler's daughter in 1783. Her only ornaments were "a pearl locket, containing the hair of Gen. Washington, and a small diamond pin, in which was the hair of Alexander Hamilton, Miss Schuyler's great-grandfather."[78]

In the boxes nearest the stage, Worth creations and gowns "after the colonial period" were in vogue. In the farther reaches of the hall, however, fancy dress was more varied and the colonial period was pulled and stretched to cover a variety of centuries and continents. The English Empire style was much favored, as were the fashions of the courts of Louis XV and XVI and the Directoire. Diamonds were a universal mark of good taste and were all the more appreciated because they sparkled at a great distance. Under conditions of crowding that made dancing and virtually any movement more vigorous than a wave of the fan impossible, the social lions and lionesses were, therefore, confined to their boxes until released for a midnight collation in a jerry-rigged supper room planted in the middle of Thirty-ninth Street. In her costume "of white faille française" with a full train Mrs. Harrison led the way, no doubt grateful, in the heat generated by the closely packed bodies, for the ices of "ananas" and "framboises" that concluded the all-French menu.[79] Proud, touchy, hot, a bit thirsty from dainty servings of "jambons historiques," a bit bilious, perhaps, after the cold "pâté à la Washington": thus did America's reigning aristocracy of wealth and beauty welcome George Washington to New York City in 1889.

George Washington Humanized

5

The Inaugural Centennial of 1889

Artifacts and Masquerades

In the person of Benjamin Harrison, George Washington received a protracted welcome to New York in 1889. There was the ceremonial landing at the foot of Wall Street. There was the ball at which, for purposes of ready identification by the crush of spectators, the presidential party sat in a replica of the White House. And spectators, with or without tickets to the affair, were numerous.

Those who squeezed themselves into the hall found a "big grown-up fairy land . . . , peopled with substantial railway kings, princes of wealth, and men whose patents of nobility are known as bonds and other negotiable securities." Those left outside surged against the police lines only to be beaten back, "a vast open-mouthed and open-eyed wondering multitude" straining to see the famous Astor diamonds, to catch the melody of the infamous centennial quadrille as the music drifted from the open windows on a warm cloud of perfume, powder, and exotic posies.[1] Had the ballroom really been decorated with "a great display of such flowers as were cherished in our house gardens when Washington lived"? wondered readers of the morning papers.[2]

At first light that April morning the crowds had begun to collect along the railroad tracks in Trenton, New Jersey, to see a train provided at great expense by the Inaugural Centennial Transportation Committee. The parlor cars were said to be equipped with all "the comforts that attend life in a well-ordered rich man's house."[3] The papers ran descriptions of princely appointments including carved mantelpieces, weighty cornices and mirrors festooned with smilax and asparagus, a working "fireplace in the main saloon," electric lights, and rare glass and silver service in the dining car. But only "a few privileged persons were admitted behind the station gates and into the President's car," and from the outside the train was disappointingly ordinary.[4]

5.1
Silverware from the table of the
Honorable Elias Boudinot, used on the
occasion of Washington's progress
through New Jersey in 1789

Outside, along the tracks at Trenton, waited a troop of little boys in buff breeches and waistcoats. In Elizabeth the mob at the station included the history buffs who had researched every detail of Washington's luncheon there in 1789. For today's centenary repast, they had contrived to borrow from Miss Boudinot, a descendant of the general's host, Governor Elias Boudinot, the very chinaware and silver used during that earlier ceremonial feast (Figure 5.1).[5]

Since historical accuracy mandated a meal in New Jersey, Harrison left the train and breakfasted with Governor Green and the local elite in an old mansion made famous by the visits of Washington and Lafayette. Then he viewed a parade of some four thousand early-morning marchers. Civil War veterans, members of the state militia, Oddfellows, Hibernians, the Knights of St. John and Pythias, and the United Order of Mechanics marched shoulder to shoulder in a rare display of religious, ethnic, and ideological harmony, followed by "many farmers"—the descendants of the yeomen of '76—"attired as Revolutionary soldiers, as Indians, as boys going to mill, as old-time farmers, having dragged behind them several floats perpetuating the memory of the household and out-door scenes peculiar to the daily life of our patriot fathers."[6]

Nor were the patriot mothers forgotten: at least one float commemorated the art of spinning by hand beside the familial hearth.[7] But even before the last spinster had passed the reviewing stand, President Harrison was on the move again, headed for the harbor. As his carriage passed under a triumphal arch built after the model of one erected in the same place to honor the passage of George Washington, forty-nine little New Jersey girls representing the forty-two states and seven territories and dressed in colonial frocks showered fresh flowers down upon him.[8] Passing between "double rows of cheering, shouting citizens of New Jersey," he tipped his tall silk hat and marched on to the sea and to his rendezvous with New York society, both high and low.[9]

Despite its brevity, Benjamin Harrison's dash through New Jersey introduced a number of motifs that would figure in the round of ceremonies to come. The level of interest in Miss Boudinot's silver and the trappings of the presidential train was intense, for instance. What is more, that interest was neither heightened nor markedly diminished on the basis of the historical value of the table appointments and the monetary value of the private car. Thing-ness alone was ample reason for curiosity. Centenary artifacts—objects of all kinds and sorts, from the diamond necklaces and hothouse flowers seen at the Centennial Ball to the souvenir medals sold by street vendors at two dollars each in neat paper boxes of fake morocco leather lined in blue plush—were matters of the deepest concern and the subjects of exhaustive commentary, to which subtle nuances of worth were profoundly irrelevant (Figure 5.2).

In New Jersey and elsewhere, as a result, George Washington was appreciated mainly through the things associated with him: old silver, a fine old mansion, an arch of honor specially raised over Elizabeth Street, a splendid train, a glossy gentleman from the White House in a frock coat and a silk hat. In a world seemingly chock-full of one gorgeous, significant, or famous thing heaped upon another in undifferentiated profusion, it was not difficult for the Hibernian or the Oddfellow in the street to draw from his morning paper the inference that Washington, rich men, the days of the Founding Fathers, silver, jewels, important people, fancy trains, and President Harrison were all pretty much of a piece.

Of the whole range of emotions the printed word might have summoned up on such an occasion, published reports of Harrison's reenactment of the first inauguration unfailingly aroused the sense of touch, the impulse to hold and possess such objects of desire. The caress of silky gowns, the smell of rare blossoms, the taste of unimaginable delicacies, and the seductive glow of pearls against flushed bosoms slithered and wafted and oozed and spilled from the pages of the *New York Times,* the *Tribune, Harper's,* and the other official publications of the principal celebrants. The Inaugural Centennial imparted to history and to Washington a powerful sensuousness.

Washington's transformation from a remote, half-forgotten hero on a pedestal of moral rectitude to a kind of antique millionaire in the velvet and lace of fancy dress—the prototype for the distinguished dancers in the centennial quadrille—was helped along by President Harrison's willingness to participate in what amounted to a serial masquerade ball as he traveled up the Atlantic seaboard in pomp and luxury, following an itinerary worked out a century before. Although he would not repeat the oath of office on the site of Federal Hall while wearing Washington's short pants, Harrison would stand on the block of red stone embedded in the pedestal of Ward's statue where Washington had once stood. He would sit in George Washington's chair, use his writing table, and finger his Bible (Figure 5.3).

In playing at historical make-believe Harrison walked a fine line between respectful historicism and outright confusion of the past with the present. By bringing 1789 perilously close to 1889, those who participated in the Inaugural Centennial risked blurring real differences between colonial times and the late nineteenth century. If Washington was just another robber baron with a houseful of tasteful possessions and an aristocratic bearing, then Astor, Vanderbilt, Richard Gilder, Benjamin Harrison, and their contemporaries were his peers in every respect. But their faults and failings were his as well.

Once Washington stooped to the folly of Stuyvesant Fish and Ward McAllister, the storied past would cease to be a working model for the conduct of human affairs. The hero could no longer embody an

5.2
The centennial medal, designed by sculptor Augustus Saint-Gaudens

5.3
Washington's writing desk, used in Federal Hall in 1789 and retained in 1889 in the Governor's Room in City Hall, where Harrison greeted the people of New York

5.4
Spectators at the Inaugural Centennial of 1889

ideal for human conduct. Yet these strictures did nothing to lessen popular interest in history in McAllister's set. By enlisting in the cast of the great costume drama of 1889, the actors also betrayed a countervailing desire to evade the present, with its plethora of expensive trinkets, its rich social climbers of dubious breeding, its goggle-eyed mobs, and its marching Hibernians, in order to live according to the quaint and courtly customs of their forefathers. Viewed from the perspective of nostalgia, the historical Washington stood for the colonial aristocracy, the Republican Court. In contrast to the shapeless mobs of gawkers in the streets of New York in April of 1889, that Washingtonian social hierarchy was an order bred of fine distinctions between autonomous individuals of gentle birth. So, in his historical mode, Harrison did not shake hands with the riffraff because George Washington had declined to do so in 1789.

Fortunately, no ill-bred persons penetrated the chambers of the Lawyers' Club in the "eight-million-dollar granite" Equitable Life Assurance Society Building on Broadway to which Harrison, still playing the role of Washington, repaired his passage to Manhattan for an official reception in honor of the governors of the several states. He did not tarry among the estimated seventy thousand pent up behind barricades in the streets around the pier (Figure 5.4). He probably failed to notice little Bertie Webb, aged three, who slipped through the lines in a George Washington outfit and got as big a hand as the official Washington impersonator of the hour.

Before the president's carriage made its way up from the waterfront, another crowd had collected outside the Equitable Building. People of no distinction (including "not a few women") roamed through the lower floors: "The new-comers to the city could be picked out by the open-eyed wonder with which they gazed on the extensive corridors, the graceful pillars, the rapidly moving elevators and the glittering electric lights."[10] At twenty minutes to two, the police waded in to banish the interlopers to the pavement where troops kept sightseers on the curbs, church bells pealed, and three regimental bands played the "Old Hundredth," over and over again.

But when the president arrived to meet the governors, in official recognition of the second century of constitutional government, those officials were nowhere to be found. Although some news reports of the day's events mistakenly placed them on the scene, as the program dictated, they had never been invited to attend.[11] Instead, several thousand business and professional men filed by, representing pursuits that ranged from acting and insurance adjusting, to flour and metal wholesaling, to directing telegraph companies. Theodore Roosevelt was in the line along with the sugar magnate H. O. Havemeyer, several aged Cincinnati from Wall Street firms, descendants of French officers of the Revolution, drygoods merchants, furriers, and the officers of the General Society of Mechanics and Traders.

Held hostage by the monied interests, the president stood upon a little dais at the end of the room, like Lady Washington at her fabled reception in old Gotham, bowing to groups of two or three local luminaries as they were conducted into his presence. By accident or by design, the arrangement disguised the fact that Harrison was closer in stature to Martha than to George: "Following the custom in Washington's time, there was no handshaking. This not only facilitated the rapid passage of guests, but saved the President from much fatigue. . . . He bowed gracefully and a pleasant smile illuminated his face. . . . Though under average height, this was not noticed, because he was raised several inches above the floor of the room."[12]

A chosen group of sixty received the further honor of sharing a luncheon with the president in the private banquet room of the Café Savarin (Figure 5.5). Toasts were tendered to George Washington: "So beloved is he by all Americans that we call him 'Father'; so deified and sanctified in our hearts that but one other birthday is sacred to us!" A sumptuous French feast, the menu for which enjoyed wide circulation, was washed down with sherry, a nice Médoc, and imported champagne. A souvenir menu in a silver envelope was presented to the guest of honor. It contained the names of all the committeemen and a number of pictures. There was Washington being rowed ashore in 1789; St. Paul's Chapel, where he worshipped before the inauguration; old Federal Hall; Washington's residence at No. 3 Cherry Street; and, on the last page, beside the bill of fare, an engraving of the "splendid Equitable Building of to-day." The memento also included a list of members of the New York City Council a hundred years earlier, a roster that numbered "two Van Zandts and a Van Gelder among them, but . . . no Divvers, Flynns or Sheas."[13]

Guests received copies of the souvenir—minus the silver bindings— to help them remember a private function few photographers and illustrators recorded, although its every detail was spelled out in the papers. The table, for example, was reported to have been "the most magnificently appointed and decorated dining table ever seen in this country, if not in the world. Its ornamentation is said to have cost $4500." The centerpiece was a century plant hung with costly orchids and pink "electric jets" and surrounded by banks of fragrant roses nestled in beds of pink silk, all peppered with more tiny lights in pink globes. Massy silverware, "delicate shell-like crystal and artistic dishes" completed "a fairy scene" not too much out of the ordinary for the refined gentlemen who frequented such establishments as a matter of course. The Lawyers' Club, even when the president was not expected, was known for "quarters . . . more elegant and costly than those of any other club in the world."[14]

The George Washington of 1889, as far as the spectators with their noses pressed against the plate-glass windows of the Equitable Building were concerned, was muffled in a cocoon of pink silk. He was a

5.5
Banquet for President Harrison, April 29, 1889

rarefied being who fed on unpronounceable tidbits, subscribed to an unfathomable code of etiquette, and eschewed all but the costliest of table service, menus, and even envelopes. Nor was that impression altered by the press agentry laid on for Monday's Centennial Ball and Tuesday's Inauguration Centennial Banquet, both held within the exclusive precincts of the Metropolitan Opera. In addition to an assemblage of "more famous personages than were ever seen together in this country . . . the women [wearing] the most opulent, even gorgeous, attire," and a "display of diamonds . . . said to be the most magnificent ever seen," the ball was noteworthy for a certain gastronomical hyperbole in its provisions. The champagne bar was fully three hundred feet long, for example, and stocked with five thousand bottles of vintage wine of four brands. The supper centerpiece, once the property of Louis Philippe, was made of solid gold. The caterer's bill came to $55,000.

It is understandable, then, that the four thousand holders of tickets entitling them to watch the others dance and dine were often heard to gasp in wonderment. The five thousand paying observers at the banquet also held their collective breath as eight hundred men sat down to dinner at tables heaped with lilies, suspended, it seemed, on lakes of mirror glass. After dinner, from the tiers of "richly caparisoned balconies" above, "the flash of pink arms and the blaze of jewels were magnificent" as the ladies took their places for the speeches.[15] And, as if his recollections of his three glittering days in New York did not promise to gleam brightly enough, just before the parade on the following morning the mayor presented the president with a memorial scroll from the civic, industrial, and commercial bodies of the city, bound in a heavy silver cylinder designed by Tiffany (Figure 5.6).[16]

5.6
Tiffany silver case containing a souvenir scroll, presented to President Harrison at the beginning of the Civil and Industrial Parade, 1889

Jewels, lilies, silver: patriotism was a commodity of great price. Given the unflagging concern with costly products betraying the station and refinement of both givers and recipients, it is no wonder that copywriters for Pear's soap saw nothing amiss in an ad campaign geared to the festivities:

The centennial of Washington's Inauguration, which has been celebrated in such regal style . . . recalls another event for which all our loyal citizens should be thankful, viz.:—the invention of Pear's Soap. . . . For one hundred years Pear's Soap has led in the highest estimation in all parts of the civilized world . . . and [it] is now as much appreciated among connoisseurs in toilet necessities in the New World as it has been for a century in the Old.[17]

The Centennial Loan Exhibition

It was all too easy to confuse the Tiffany keepsakes the presidential train prepared to bear back to Washington City with the relics assembled in the Centennial Loan Exhibition on view in the assembly rooms of the Opera House. A novel feature of the show was a display of old gold and silver plate of the time of Washington put together by John Buck, an Englishman who once worked for the Gorham Company and was, in 1889, the volunteer curator of metalwork at the Metropolitan Museum.[18] By publishing a circular seeking contributions to this segment of the exhibition, Buck was able to mount an impressive presentation of silver that had come down in the great families of the East, each piece labeled as to maker, date, and place of origin.[19] As a result of the Centennial Loan Exhibition, silver (and other types of tableware) became the first "antiques" collected by substantial numbers of people.

Not all the novice collectors were wealthy, but they did share an interest in an American heritage the familial dimensions of which could be enhanced or even created by groupings of old porringers. Good families had fine old silver services rattling about their sideboards. Johnny-come-latelies did not. The earliest of the ancestral pieces located by Buck were accorded mainly curiosity value because of their age and family associations, and were credited with "little artistic merit." Silver from the time of Washington's inauguration, on the other hand, struck gallery-goers as delightfully and beautifully modern. "We may hear a great deal about the Spartan simplicity of those early times," wrote one reviewer after observing the profusion of florid plate surviving in the cases at the Metropolitan, "[but] all the tobacco that went to London from Virginia had not for return the absolute necessities of life."[20]

Unlike earlier gatherings of relics, the Loan Exhibition had aimed at a tight thematic focus from the outset. The objects displayed were to be related directly to Washington and to those involved in the first inauguration; the committee of selection promised "to exclude . . . such pictures or relics as properly belong to the Revolutionary period only, in order to avoid a repetition of certain features of the exhibitions held in connection with the Centennial Celebration at Philadelphia in 1876."[21] The result of these caveats was a picture gallery noteworthy for a systematic analysis of "the appearance of the first President at various periods of his life, and under the varying aspects in which the artists of his time viewed him" (Figure 5.7).[22]

Just as Buck's part of the show stimulated the collecting of silver, the portrait segment encouraged connoisseurs to look with favor upon the less familiar renderings of George Washington. The authority of the Gilbert Stuart image of an idealized Washington was challenged, in fact, by members of a generation of collectors schooled in photography and academic realism. The late nineteenth-century eye also relished variety and welcomed a shifting perspective on a hero much altered both by the vicissitudes of a long life and by the viewpoints of a host of observers. Collecting Washington portraits, an activity given a boost by Jane Stuart's 1876 and 1877 defenses of her father's accuracy of vision, was accelerated by the Loan Exhibition in New York.[23]

Paul Leicester Ford, an early collector of Washingtoniana (his father served on the Inaugural Centennial Art Committee), wrote biographical sketches for *Harper's* of all the members of the first Congress whose portraits were included in the Metropolitan Loan Exhibition. In the same journal, he also published a detailed account of the first inauguration, illustrated with pictures of Washington's coach and other

5.7
South Picture Gallery of the Loan Exhibition at the Metropolitan Opera House

relics.[24] Historical articles planted in magazines by members of the various Inaugural Centennial committees were invariably supplemented with illustrations of similar objects, which, in the context of the time, are best described not as relics but as antiques.

In *Century Magazine* Clarence Bowen, general editor of the volume recording the centennial activities, published an essay on the events of 1789 enlivened with loving renditions of the furniture in New York City Hall once used by George Washington.[25] That journal also supplied a bibliography of recent articles on Washington-related topics that readers might wish to consult in preparation for the upcoming celebration in Manhattan. The list included illustrated essays on "The Home and Haunts of Washington," "New York City Hall," "Mount Vernon as It Is," and "My Lord Fairfax of Virginia," and the issue closed with two contributions by Constance Cary Harrison accompanied by plates showing Martha Washington's silver tea set and George Washington's silver inkstand (Figure 5.8). The centennial history lesson thus became a compendium of up-to-the-minute decorating tips, and in the finicky draftsmanship of the period, the plainest vessel looked as ornate as the Tiffany case presented to President Harrison (Figure 5.9).

Constance Harrison's treatise was enhanced by a sketch of a fragment of the brocade worn by Mrs. James Beekman, a belle of the Republican Court, to a ball held in New York in April of 1789; the fabric, she took pains to note, was now in the possession of Miss Effie Beekman Borrowe.[26] In addition to the silver and the portraits, those who perused the cases at the Metropolitan Opera with care discerned an emphasis on the likes of the Mrs. James Beekmans of the colonial world. "One of the most pleasurable features of the gallery," remarked the scout for the *Tribune*, "was the large number of likenesses of bright and beautiful women who lent poetry and romance to the sternest realities of years of trial, . . . the belles of the Revolutionary epoch, women scarcely less distinguished than their fathers, brothers and husbands."[27] It was fitting, therefore, that distinguished ladies of the present day were among the chief lenders to the exhibition. A snuffbox with inlays of silver and pearl that Washington gave to his nephew was lent by Mrs. Roger Pryor; Baron Steuben's gold watch came from Mrs. Austin; Mrs. Pierrepont sent a gold ring concealing a lock of his own hair that Washington had presented to Mrs. James Madison; and Mrs. Lewis Washington was induced to part for a month with Mary Ball Washington's Bible, in which the birth of George had been recorded.[28]

Taken as a whole, the things that Mrs. Pryor, Mrs. Pierrepont, and their friends consigned to the Loan Exhibition presented a distinctive picture of Washington and his era (Figure 5.10). That picture was, if anything, even more domesticated than the image of Washington

5.8
George Washington's inkstand, included in the Loan Exhibition

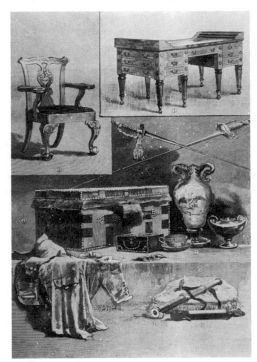

5.9
Washington relics in the Centennial Loan Exhibition, drawn by H. D. Nichols

awaiting his supper that was conjured up in Philadelphia in 1876 with many of the same artifacts: "In general, the collection of relics furnished a complete picture of colonial times, embracing as it did many specimens of the household furniture and implements, the dress and ornaments worn by men and women, . . . and something to represent nearly every phase in the life of the people."[29]

Washington memorabilia included the inauguration chair used in 1789 on the portico of Federal Hall, a china cup and saucer—lent by Mrs. Cleveland, wife of the former and future president—belonging to a service "much cherished by Martha Washington," a field glass used during the war lying upon a cushion worked by her hands, a piece of her ornamental netting, Valley Forge crockery of a certain "elegance," and a brown silk suit. "The stuff is excellent, looking in its tissue like a modern rep," a viewer reported. "Pater Patriae dressed well, and was particular as to material, fit, and cut of his clothes."

A cushion here and a desk there all added to a portrait of material abundance, fastidious good taste, and a certain artistocratic je-ne-sais-quoi associated as much with the persons who lent the relics as with the artifacts themselves. A few journalists feared that a materialistic age might confuse noble deeds with fine merchandise just because the latter had survived. But "in this hard matter-of-fact world, it is well that one should idealize something, be it the sword the hero has worn or the spurs he drove into his horse's flanks when he urged on his steed fighting for a just cause. . . . They are part and parcel of history."[30]

At least one admiring magazine, cognizant of the fact that the Loan Exhibition aimed to illuminate the inaugural period through these tokens of a time past, also realized that the kind of daily life suggested by the display of saucers and silk suits was beyond the reach of the majority. "Some day in the future," *Harper's* hoped, ". . . a loan collection may be made of the objects in use in ordinary life by the people of this country during the Colonial and Revolutionary periods."[31] But for the moment, George Washington was the antithesis of the ordinary American.

Preserving Colonial Values

Late in the afternoon of April 29, 1889, George Washington's double made his way from the posh upper reaches of the Equitable Building to the Governor's Room at City Hall, where ordinary Americans— schoolchildren, working men and their wives, ward heelers—had waited for hours to pay their respects. Along this stretch of Broadway, Tiffany keepsakes were not selling briskly. Although the venders would do most of their business the next day, here and there on the plaza in front of the steps onlookers brandished cheap souvenir hatchets, in bronze or silver finish, inscribed with the date of the first inauguration (Figure 5.11). A bust of Washington was inset in the blade but the likeness was almost redundant. In the folk wisdom, the hatchet meant Washington and the cherry tree fable that was taught, as a matter of course, in the grade school primer. The story of a very human little boy, full of mischief and prone to error, was valued for

5.11
Commemorative inaugural hatchet, silver finish

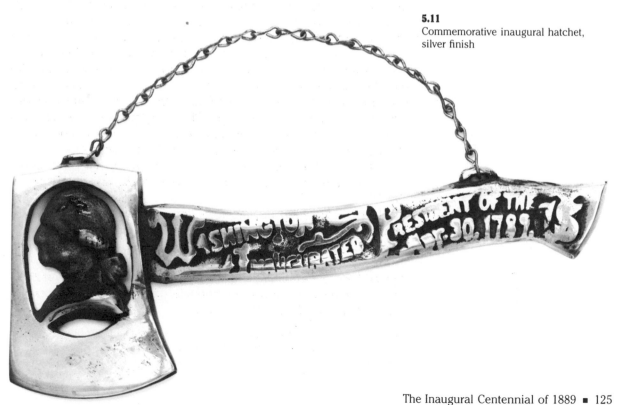

its moral. But the cherry tree fable owed at least some measure of its persistent appeal to the fact that the George Washington who committed mayhem with his little hatchet was not unlike the run of ordinary, everyday American children.

Little Dolly Keese, daughter of the janitor at City Hall, hauled the presidential banner to the top of the flagstaff when Harrison came into sight. As his carriage pulled to a stop, 180 schoolgirls from the public grammar schools, dressed in white in imitation of the maidens who had greeted General Washington in Trenton, strewed flowers in his path and formed a guard of honor, conducting him to the spot where Miss Annie Abrahams, class valedictorian at the Normal College, read an original address on the character of Washington. As if to demonstrate that the Lawyers' Club had no monopoly on worthy tokens of esteem, the girls then presented him with a copy of the speech written on parchment in an elegant script and "bound in soft Russian leather, lined inside with silk of a rich shade of purple."[32] Miss Martha Franklin, a pupil of the Colored School No. 80, wearing "her kinky hair [in a] Pompadour in front with a Psyche knot behind," expressed "the affluent spirit of the times . . . by sparkling diamonds in her ears"; she stood among the flower girls to typify "the advance in civilization since Washington was greeted here 100 years ago, when children of her race were condemned and foredoomed to slavery."[33]

The outdoor exercises concluded, the president disappeared into the building. Mounting a plush-covered platform in the Governor's Room, with Washington's own desk close at hand, Harrison leaned back against a brass railing and prepared to meet the public. When the doors were thrown open, the first man into the room leaped onto the dais and wrung his hand; several women in line just behind him did likewise before the guards intervened and put an end to such egalitarian liberties. For the remainder of the reception, functionaries posted by the entrance cried out, "The President is on the left; step lively," whenever a newcomer appeared, "and the procession moved along at almost a quickstep. Four hundred went by in five minutes, so that in the three-quarters of an hour the reception lasted, about thirty-five hundred citizens got a close view of Washington's successor."[34]

Skittering along so briskly, some among the multitudes who had waited in line all day missed the president altogether and bowed to the wrong dignitary. There was no time for an exchange of pleasantries with the elderly fellow who shuffled up to the podium and exclaimed, "I voted for your grandfather in 1840, and I voted for you."[35] And large numbers of restless, disgruntled hopefuls never got into the building in the short time allotted to the affair:

While the President was in the City Hall the crowd outside became so turbulent that it broke through the lines. The police rallied . . . and drove them back into place, but not until some very rough usage had been resorted to.

Clubs were uplifted and in several instances were brought down sharply on some of the more boisterous and disorderly members of the crowd. Later . . . the line was broken in several places, and the men, women, and children rushed wildly to the place where the school children had strewn flowers before the President, and there was the liveliest kind of scramble to pick up the leaves and twigs from the pavement.[36]

The vulgar mob was nowhere in evidence at St. Paul's Chapel early on the following day when Harrison took his seat in the pew occupied by George Washington on the morning of his inauguration (Figure 5.12). The Aisle Committee appointed for the reenactment had been charged with maintaining a goodly order and decorum. Otherwise, the positions were largely ceremonial ones, filled by Centennial organizers rather than men of the congregation, "to give prominence to the members of historical families" whose incomes and social position in 1889 did not guarantee their presence at ball, banquet, or private reception.[37] Such decayed gentlefolk were a major problem for the planners. Given the burgeoning interest in ancestry and societies of those who claimed superiority on account of it, living Van Cortlandts and Van Rensselaers and Livingstons needed acknowledgment. On the other hand, the future founder of the Daughters of the American Revolution, little Miss Washington from the Dead Letter Office—one admirer dubbed her the "unclaimed memory of departed glory"—was also a social liability who was fitted into the program in New York only with the utmost difficulty.[38] The chapel service was the ideal opportunity to honor the relatives of the mighty without beaming the spotlight of publicity upon their shabby gloves and ears bereft of diamonds.

Or so it must have seemed, before Bishop Potter climbed into the pulpit to flay "a generation which vaunts its descent from the founders of the Republic" for forgetting the "pre-eminent distinction" of their forebears—integrity, unselfish purpose, and devotion to the spirit of the Constitution. The bishop was an old hand at patriotic sermonizing; he had delivered the benediction during the Wall Street portion of the Evacuation Day rites of 1883. His bland appeals to the Almighty on that rainy day, however, gave little foretaste of the philippic he unleashed on the self-satisfied celebrants of 1889. Greed, corruption, and foreigners were assailed with equal vigor. "Poor in worldly possessions," Potter began, glaring down at the politicians fidgeting in their seats and amazing those who had visited the accumulated riches of the Centennial Loan Exhibition, the Founding Fathers could never have understood the spoils system. "The conception of the National Government as a huge machine, existing mainly for the purpose of rewarding partisan service—this was a conception so alien to the character and conduct of Washington and his associates that it seems grotesque even to speak of it."

5.12
The pew in St. Paul's Chapel that was occupied by Washington in 1789

But speak Bishop Potter did as he warmed to the task of admonishing his captive audience. Now it was the turn of "the plutocrats" to squirm about on the hard benches, for political corruption, he declared, went hand in hand with wealth:

Then ideas ruled the hour. To-day, there are indeed ideas that rule our hour, but they must be merchantable ideas. The growth of wealth, the prevalence of luxury, the massing of large material forces, which by their very existence are a standing menace to the freedom and integrity of the individual, the infinite swagger of our American speech and manners, mistaking bigness for greatness, and sadly confounding gain and godliness—all this is in contrast to the austere simplicity, the unpurchasable integrity of the first days and the first men of our Republic, which makes it impossible to reproduce to-day either the temper or the conduct of our fathers.[39]

Play-acting at life in the palmy days of Washington, he seemed to imply, was a futile pursuit because "to-day" was as vulgar as it was wanting in principle. Given the grand impersonation of which the service was a crucial element, that portion of Henry Potter's address was just controversial enough to set off a round of gratifying and wholly conventional lamentations on the conduct prevalent in the present day and its sad inferiority to the standards of a golden colonial age. But "let any man consider who were the actual political leaders of New York, and who are its actual leaders now," as the bishop's flock was quick to do, and it became apparent that the malefactors uppermost in his mind did not attend Episcopal services monitored by an Aisle Committee of sterling lineage.[40] No, according to the Reverend Mr. Potter, the real offenders had missed both the chapel ritual and the Loan Exhibition:

We may disinter the vanished draperies, we may revive the stately minuet, we may rehabilitate the old scenes, but the march of a century cannot be halted or reversed, and the enormous change in the situation can neither be disguised or ignored. Then we were, though not all of us sprung from one nationality, practically one people. Now, that steady deteriorating process . . . goes on, on every hand, apace. "The constant importation," wrote the author of "The Weal of Nations," "as now, in this country, of the lowest orders of people from abroad to dilute the quality of our natural manhood, is a sad and beggarly prostitution of the noblest gift ever conferred on a people. Who shall respect a people who do not respect their own blood? And how shall a National spirit, or any determinate and proportionate character, arise out of so many low-bred associations and coarse-grained temperaments, imported from every clime? It was, indeed, in keeping, that Pan, who was the son of everybody, was the ugliest of the gods."[41]

The "dense black human mass" that filled Broad Street in anticipation of the next stop on the historical itinerary was of a mixed and low-bred origin, for the most part. A babble of accents and languages could be heard above the squalls of babies and the shouts of barkers

5.13
"Seats 'ere now, gentlemen and ladies.
A few left."

renting lemon crates to perch on for a better view or selling seats in rickety stands thrown up along the route of the afternoon's parade (Figure 5.13). Although a million people stood about, jostled one another, and sweltered uncomfortably every time the sun peeped out to dry the bunting soaked in a week of steady rain, incidents were few and a cheerful holiday mood prevailed. "This city, always called so mercenary, so selfish, and so lacking in public spirit," adorned itself "in badges and medals struck for the occasion" and turned out in one, sprawling, good-humored, and curious lump of polyglot humanity to watch the climactic ceremony on the steps of the Sub-Treasury.[42]

Many wore little metal buttons bearing the inscription "Long Live the President," in commemoration of the words uttered by Chancellor Livingston after he administered the first oath of office. Washington's partisans had sewn them to their coats in 1789, but in 1889 people bought them as souvenirs of what promised to be an entertaining morning.[43] Already the temporary stage built out over Wall Street from the steps of the Sub-Treasury was filling up with personages worth a second look. Old Hannibal Hamlin, Lincoln's first vice-president, was recognized and cheered, as was Andrew Carnegie, the self-made millionaire. Which one was Chauncey Depew, the famous orator? Was Whittier, the aged Quaker poet, really going to read his ode? The ebony table, the plush cushion, the mahogany chair, and the big book that were being carried with reverent care to the front of the rostrum: what were they for? Who was the tall soldier standing at attention beside the statue of Washington? And didn't the statue look grand today, with a wreath of golden laurel leaves about its noble brow? (Figure 5.14).

The actual ceremony was brief: an invocation; the reading of Whittier's poem, a reaffirmation of national unity larded with references to the Civil War; Depew's thirty-two-minute oration on the lessons, chiefly economic, to be learned from Washington and the centenary of the Constitution; a few remarks from Mr. Harrison excusing his failure to address the same topic at length. The closing benediction was delivered by Archbishop Michael Augustine Corrigan, the Irish Catholic primate of New York, resplendent in his purple biretta and his great golden pectoral cross.[44] Those of his coreligionists slated to march in the parade the next morning then went home to get ready for the only active role in the proceedings reserved for the uncelebrated—for those whom Bishop Potter had lately dubbed "the lowest orders of people from abroad."

A "suggestive pageant," Mr. Depew had called it, "without which the commemoration would have been incomplete [because] it is to enterprise and industry, to peace and not to war, that the miracle of America today is due," the Civic and Industrial Parade had been organized by unions, working people, tradesmen, firemen, cops,

5.14
H. A. Ogden illustration, showing Harrison addressing the crowd at the Sub-Treasury

schoolboys, the Tammany Irish, Italian clubs, German marching and singing societies, and the representatives of lesser-known groups such as the Hebrew Orphans' Asylum Band.[45] As such, it was a chaotic affair, much different in character from the spit-and-polish military parade to which President Harrison repaired on April 30, immediately after Archbishop Corrigan's final "Amen."

The civilian order of march, with some notable exceptions, celebrated the present and looked forward to a prosperous future in which everybody could aspire to diamond earbobs and colonial ballgowns. The Military Parade looked backward. Many of the militia units that fell in behind the governors of their respective states wore Continental uniforms (Figure 5.15). Others were units remembered for distinction in the Civil War, the conflict with which Washington the unifier had come to have a connection so strong that more than twenty years after the end of hostilities, poet Whittier and the marshals of the eleven-mile, 52,000-man column were still invoking it as a matter of routine.

Looking back on the war as the Military Parade did was an exercise in nostalgia, too, for the generation of jowly, overstuffed gentlemen in Prince Albert coats who had fought at Gettysburg and marched through Georgia in the days of their beardless youth. Now grown to a man's estate, they took charge of the centenary. General William Tecumseh Sherman was cheered heartily by those gentlemen at the banquet, where he offered the toast to the army and the navy. They understood General Washington much as they understood Sherman, through their own wartime experiences and memories; they represented him to New York in several guises conditioned by that point of view. At the Lawyers' Club, for instance, Washington was urbane and aristocratic, like them. At the Loan Exhibition, he was tasteful, wealthy, well-connected, exclusive. At the Military Parade, he embodied power and order as the pseudo-Continentals marched smartly under triumphal arches adorned with his likeness, eighteen abreast, in time to the beat of "Yankee Doodle" with nary a hair out of place.[46]

Memory makes the past more orderly than the present can ever hope to be. Because history becomes predictable and rational in retrospect, nostalgia is an alternative to the uncertainties of daily living. Defensive nostalgia was an important factor in the creation of the hereditary societies that assumed final form in Fraunces' Tavern during the Inaugural Centennial of 1889; another was the fellow-feeling, a kind of exclusive camaraderie, also inherent in the military portion of the celebration. By going to war and by sharing family memories of an earlier one, Old Americans neatly differentiated themselves from immigrants beckoned westward by the new Bartholdi statue in the harbor, immigrants who had arrived on these shores too late to grasp the import of the Military Parade.

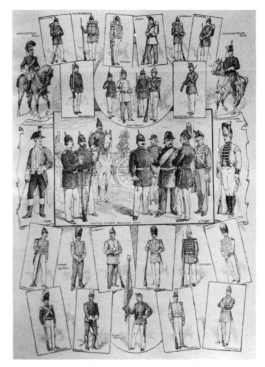

5.15
Uniforms of the Military Parade, April 30, 1889

The Washington whose statue beckoned the marching units onward with his sword from high atop the arch at Fifth Avenue and Twenty-third Street was an object lesson to the wealthy, the powerful, and the well-connected. He was the finest product of a colonial nobility brought to dazzling perfection in New York in 1789, with the first inauguration and with the subsequent creation of the Republican Court. He was also a defiant symbol of their hegemony over the million or so oddly assorted commoners who milled about in a holiday mood, applauded the bands that played the loudest, and awaited the start of the largest and gaudiest of all the Centennial events set for nine o'clock on the morning of May 1.

The Parade as Popular History

5.16
"A Thompson Street display": Washington tributes from ordinary people

Predictably enough, the Civil, Industrial, and Commercial Parade straggled off about an hour late, in some disarray. Daniel Butterfield, ex-general and director of the order of procession, arrived on the scene at dawn to find over a hundred thousand potential marchers waiting to form up. Dashing from the piano-makers to the New York Turn-Bezirk, from the Ancient Order of the Hibernians to the Garibaldi Guards, he discovered every unit swollen with supplementary members, all eager to take part. It was only by a heroic feat of persuasion that he managed to reduce the total force "to 75,000 souls" before the unwieldy column headed out by fits and starts, in no discernible order, with many of the heavy floats stranded in peculiar surroundings.

The main body of the Italian division, for example, lost its place in line by dallying in a side street and trotted down the street at a run in a futile effort to catch up with a horse-drawn float called "Columbus Discovering America," for which it was to have served as an escort. When the Italians were nowhere to be found, the *Nina,* the *Pinta,* and the *Santa Maria* set sail down Fifth Avenue accompanied by a stray band that played "Away in Dixie Land" over and over again.[47]

"It was the people's day," chortled the *New York Tribune,* anticipating a wealth of human-interest stories. "They who had enjoyed the spectacles of the naval parade and the marching troops on the previous days . . . were themselves to make up the spectacle that was to be the great feature of the last day of the celebration." The parade celebrated the outcome of the great events of 1789 and the establishment of constitutional government: flourishing industry, prosperity, and, under the influence of the latter, an influx of new Americans of foreign birth, in whose quarters "decorations, modest though they were," fluttered as bravely as they did on Wall Street (Figure 5.16). Wall Street with all its bright adornments "brings no better testimony to the affection of American citizens for the institutions of free republican government," the *Tribune* continued, "than the portraits and flags and cheap festoons which were to be found by the thousands in the streets where the toiling mases live who came to this country as to a haven of rest from political serfdom and social oppression."[48]

Judging by the startled reactions of the fourth estate, before the parade wound its erratic course through the city the swarms of naturalized Americans who competed for places in George Washington's parade had been invisible, except as a vague, generic menace or a specific political faction to be deplored. Their sheer numbers were amazing and perhaps more than a little alarming:

Few parades . . . have seen so large a body of foreign-born citizens in the ranks. Probably half of those who marched yesterday were born on foreign soil. . . . Yet on this distinctively American holiday, representatives of all races and nationalities, Germans, French, Italians, Austrians, Scotchmen, Irishmen, Poles and Scandinavians, joined in, many of them at a considerable expense, to hold up the reputation of civic against military patriotism. No feature of the procession was more striking than the share the so-called foreign element had in it, and no assistance from foreign-born New-York in a similar way has, perhaps, been so extensive, so timely, and so grateful.[49]

At times their behavior gave cause for worry, too. Although their right to a place in the unit dedicated to the industrial progress of New York over the past century was open to dispute, the cheeky Irish-American braves of Chief Tammany turned out nonetheless, in the tall silk hats of the swells, marching behind their own Johnny Cochrane. When they passed the president and the reviewing stand, the toppers stayed glued to their heads until indignant voices of protest coaxed some few to salute halfheartedly. But for the most part, and despite mix-ups that assigned troops of Teutonic warriors in fur leggings to walk beside floats picturing "Old Virginia" or "Mount Vernon," the parade lurched forward without untoward incident in three loose and by no means mutually exclusive thematic divisions.

The first division consisted of New Americans, represented by ethnic societies, their bands, and a series of floats interpreting American history as successive waves of immigration. Groups of various national and religious backgrounds followed wagons on which were mounted tableaux—complete with scenery, props, and elaborate costuming—showing events having a special bearing on their own tenure in the United States. A Catholic organization, for instance, commissioned a float titled "Maryland," reminding onlookers of the role played by colonial worthies of their own faith in early American history.

The Germans, who were particularly adept at float-building, enumerated their contributions to American culture with parade wagons illustrating Wagnerian opera, fairy tales, and even Santa Claus. They also sponsored a number of historical floats that directly addressed the topic of naturalization. These rolling history books included "Immigration One Hundred Years Ago" (a little Dutch sailing ship), "Pioneer Farmers" (migrating west in a prairie schooner), "The Quakers" (persecuted in the Old World and preparing to flee to America), "A Revolutionary Council" (attended by Von Steuben, De Kalb, Herkimer, and Muhlenberg), "Lincoln" (a bust of the martyred hero, surrounded by the flags of German regiments of the Civil War), and "Immigrants of the Present Time" (an ocean steamer and a customs agent on a wharf).

The second division was made up of tradesmen and workers, some of whom, like the Rhine-wine makers with their mounted arbors and cellars, and the brewers flanking the chariot of King Gambrinus, were also affiliated with ethnic societies. The most ingenious of the industrial floats tried to situate the history of the trade in question within the broader sweep of American history: "[Float] No. 53 was the 'Art

5.17

In the front, the floats of the ship-joiners; behind them, the floats of the Operative Plasterers' Society, manufacturing busts of George Washington

Two tableaux rolling by: Washington's farewell to his officers at Fraunces' Tavern in 1783 and the balcony of Federal Hall in 1889

of Cooking,' showing the culinary advance in America since its discovery. In the front part of the wagon was a group of Indians gathered about an old kettle, while the rest of the wagon was taken up with a modern kitchen, with all its improvements and appliances. The contrast was striking."[50] Some were simply eye-catching, like the pork-packers' float with its four big nickel-plated statues of the American hog glinting fatly in the sunshine as a company of butchers in knee breeches fingered plump sausages. Others were technological wonders: thirty manufacturers pooled their resources and demonstrated, aboard several contiguous floats, how a piano was made. Workmen on the wagons of the Plasterers' Society, each in his white coveralls and cap, made small plaster busts of Lincoln and Washington as the parade clomped along, and tossed them to the bystanders; when they reached the reviewing stand, "a halt was made, and a plaster cast of the President was struck off" (Figure 5.17).[51] Samples of their wares were passed to Mr. Harrison, who bowed and departed for the train station long before the people's parade was properly begun.

The third and final division—nothing, of course, appeared on Fifth Avenue in precisely the scheduled order—included a medley of floats depicting the life of Washington and the history of New York, with particular emphasis on points in time at which those two stories overlapped. Henry Hudson was shown coming ashore near a clump

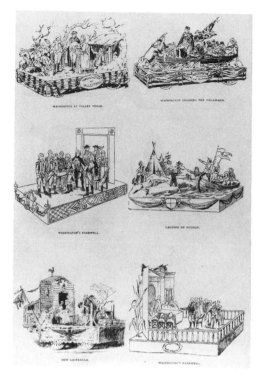

5.19
Historical floats in the Civil Parade,
May 1, 1889

of tepees on the banks of the river that bears his name. New Amsterdam in the early days was represented by a prisoner in stocks, a log cabin, and a woman sitting in the doorway spinning. The imagery was simple, direct, conventional. Like illustrations in stories for children, the iconography of parade floats is a good gauge of what scenes were part of the historical consciousness of the day—of what scenes the greater number of the million New Yorkers cheering on the sidewalks could reasonably be expected to recognize, even though many of them were not Americans of the old stock.

And so the historical floats lumbered by. A copy of the balcony of Federal Hall with Washington taking the oath essentially recreated the recreation Benjamin Harrison had just completed. A depiction of Washington's farewell to his officers at Fraunces' Tavern reminded spectators of another local landmark in which meetings of patriotic societies were taking place in honor of the centennial and to which sightseers had been directed since the Evacuation Day centenary of 1883 (Figure 5.18). The float entitled "Washington Crossing the Delaware" was a tribute to the fame of Emanuel Leutze's picture of the same name, well known to immigrants from the artist's native Germany, where the painting had been created as a rallying symbol for the 1848 revolution.[52] Last came the float featuring Washington, dressed in the famous buff-and-blue uniform exhibited in Philadelphia, resigning his commission at Annapolis. It honored the renunciation of despotic power that both defined American democracy and separated Washington from Napoleon, Bismarck, and the other European supermen of the eighteenth and nineteenth centuries who were his nearest rivals in fame.

The wigwams, the spinning wheel, the log cabin, the landmarks at which New York's several recent anniversaries had been observed, and historical episodes familiar to the foreign-born were not surprising ingredients for a popular celebration held in 1889. More interesting were the four remaining Washington floats, which, despite their wide range of subject matter, contrived to present a courtly, domestic Washington, a creature of lace and gold braid with an eye for colonial ladies. In the ranks of the elite, where Washington was commemorated by fancy-dress balls and ancestral silverware, that sort of Father of His Country was the order of the day, but his presence on parade floats built by and displayed to a mass audience shows just how commonplace the figure of Washington as gentleman of wealth and refinement had become (Figures 5.19, 5.20).

The "Washington at Valley Forge" float, for instance, consisted of ragged Continentals lying about in the snow and being inspected—not prayed over—by the standing general, decked out in his full dress uniform with cape and hat; Martha, richly gowned, was on his arm. A kind of American *caritas* image, with George and Martha Washington

5.20
Float depicting Washington's inauguration, passing Union Square

cast as the parents of the suffering troops, the arrangement nonetheless set Washington apart from the soldiers in bearing, dress, and his strong identification with the gentler, distaff virtues. The sumptuous Washington Coach, used in New York during his presidency, also became a parade float, containing wax figures of George and Martha gliding along in semiregal state with footmen, outriders, and two hundred marching Continentals in their retinue. A replica of the stately Mount Vernon rolled past too, followed by a scale model of a mansion on Washington Heights that once served as his New York headquarters. The trees and the shrubbery on the float were relics in their own right, "taken from the neighborhood of the house."[53]

These houses on wheels underscored the importance of the movement to preserve historic homesteads and the significance attached to understanding the hero through the trappings of his daily life. That the character and standing of the man could be read from the façade of his house was axiomatic both to builders of stately chateaux for fin de siècle millionaires and to those who peeped through their iron fences with awe and envy and deciphered the message inscribed in the ornate pilasters. Authors who wrote about George Washington in the late 1880s and the 1890s subscribed to the theory with a vengeance. Mount Vernon was scrutinized down to the last silver candlestand for clues to the personality of its occupant and loving rebuilder.[54]

Because they were taken for signs of worth in the modern world, certain objects of virtu, like old silver, and certain qualities, like ample size and formality, were apt to interest people rummaging through the colonial past for proof that the human Washington was somebody who might have carried off the 1889 version of his inauguration with at least as much aplomb as his successor brought to the task.

From Mount Vernon, the search for talking sites widened to include the myriad Revolutionary headquarters, the abodes of his relatives and childhood friends, the many houses in which he once passed a night on sundry tours of the colonies. The New York house with the fringe of live bushes carried aboard the float in the inaugural parade was among several associated with his comings and goings through the city. The Washington imagery deployed on New York's parade floats appeared there because it was already familiar to the man and woman in the street. In 1889 the floats depicted a man of a recognizable type: successful, rich, refined, swaddled in beautiful and costly possessions. What they could not show, however, were the deepest emotions of the private self—what set the man apart from others of his type and class in the privacy of his stately home.

Yet increasingly, the nature of that inner life came to be of interest to Americans typed and stereotyped by the strictures of mass culture. One historic home in New York, for instance, a house not so very different from the buildings simulated on the floats, had witnessed the pangs of the great, unrequited love of Washington's young life, and a second—that Tory lady's mansion—had become, by a cruel trick of fate, General Washington's headquarters on Harlem Heights, high above the city and the British lines. In the centennial era, the house stood for the private person who repaired there after the toil of public life. And the feelings displayed behind closed doors of such Georgian mansions were almost as appealing to Washington's latter-day countrymen as the houses themselves or their treasure troves of family silver.

Washington's Centennial Romance

The lady-householder of Harlem Heights was Mary Philipse, a wealthy heiress from the Hudson Valley; her family was so prominent in the history of the region, in fact, that in 1868 the town of Yonkers bought Philipse Manor with its quaint Dutch door and painted ceilings. In 1872 it became City Hall, and a decade later, during celebrations of the city's bicentennial, visitors clamored to see two rooms redolent with the fragrance of romance. In the first, located in the southwest corner, Washington once passed the night as a houseguest. In the other, adjacent to it, Mary Philipse had married a Royalist, a one-time friend and comrade of her former suitor, George Washington. The army of that disappointed swain would in 1776 drive Mary and her husband from their home overlooking New York.[55]

The star-crossed story of George Washington and his Tory sweetheart began twenty years earlier, when the young Virginia colonel met "Polly" Philipse in New York City on his way back home from Boston, where he had been transacting military business. Washington spent his twenty-fourth birthday in the city as the guest of Colonel Beverly Robinson, Mary's brother-in-law; he also spent one pound four shillings treating the ladies of the house to a "microcosm" (a pantomime) in a wasted effort to impress the young mistress of Philipse Manor.

The trip and Washington's dalliance in New York were known to early nineteenth-century historians, although details varied greatly from account to account. Washington Irving, one of the last survivors of the crowd that witnessed the inauguration at Federal Hall, took a special interest in a story that linked George Washington to a famous colonial belle, daughter of one of the great families of old New York. In the 1850s he concluded that the soldier had left the lists of love too soon in order to answer the call of duty, surrendering the field to his successful rival, Colonel Morris; the subsequent wooing of Martha, he thought, was conducted all the more briskly for that sobering experience.[56] In 1862 Evert Duyckinck accepted the story Irving published as "historical fact," largely because Washington was known to have been "by no means insensible to female charms" and "had also a prudent regard for fortune." And, although it was difficult for writers of the period to find a fault—even a lack of charm—in the hero's makeup, or to admit that he had failed at anything, "the story is sometimes added," Duyckinck allowed, "that he sought her hand and was rejected, but this [Irving] discredits as impossible."[57] Benson Lossing included Mary's portrait in his biography of Washington and in 1870 added that the young officer would have married the girl with the "bright eyes, blooming cheeks, and winning ways . . . but his natural diffidence kept the momentous question unspoken in his heart, and his fellow aide-de-camp in Braddock's family, Roger Morris, bore off the prize."[58]

Before the Civil War, Bishop Meade reported hearing stories—all untrue, of course—that Washington used intemperate language with a panache befitting a hero: he "swore like an angel," according to the gossips. The bishop condemned such prattle and fulminated against those who would bring Washington down to the "common level by representing him as passionately fond not merely of the chase and much addicted to it, but also of the dance, the ballroom, . . . the theatre," and the ladies.[59] Yet chivalry and civility, foxhunting, squiring lovely ladies to balls, and even a bit of genteel profanity were part and parcel of the dreamy picture of life among the Virginia aristocracy painted in strokes of vibrant nostalgia in the 1870s and 1880s when the "colonial court" of an antebellum yesterday became a staple of popular history.

Mrs. Ellet's widely read treatise, *The Queens of American Society,* which had gone through six large editions by 1873, describes Martha Washington traveling with postilions in white-and-scarlet liveries "in something like feudal state," through a cultural landscape of privilege and almost unimaginable sumptuousness:

In the second or third generation, a class of "first families" was built up [in Virginia], and the best education was limited to them; for there were no schools for the masses. There existed, therefore, a broad line of distinction between the wealthy proprietors and the common people. The planters had their tenants and slaves, and lived luxuriously. . . .They were "horse-racing, cock-fighting Virginia squires." Visiting was done in ponderous emblazoned coaches. The hospitable board was loaded with terrapins, shad, salmon, wild geese, pigeons, plover, canvas-back ducks, venison, and every variety of bread, with "that delicious hotch-potch," gumbo, and other country dainties. The . . . lappets of sleeves were turned up to carve, and guests were pressed to demolish the various meats and wash them down with cider, ale, brandy, and Bordeaux wine.[60]

In Mrs. Ellet's breathless prose, George Washington the ardent suitor, Washington the husband, Washington the general and the president, always bows courteously as the music begins; he moves through an endless succession of intricate figures, always in the company of "the most beautiful woman" of the hour. With the war raging about him, he dances at a camp entertainment, partner to "a circle of brilliants" that includes Martha, Mrs. Knox, and Mrs. Greene. He opens a grand ball in the Annapolis State House in 1783 with Mrs. James Macubbin, the reigning belle of Maryland, on his arm. At a ball in the Assembly Rooms on Broadway just above Wall Street, held to mark the inauguration—and here Mrs. Ellet relies on the testimony of no less an authority than Thomas Jefferson—Washington danced "two cotillions and a minuet" with beautiful women carrying fans hand-painted in France in cunning designs incorporating his own portrait.[61]

Female writers invariably took an interest in George Washington's relations with the fair sex. But although it was women who described the first inaugural ball and its decor for readers preparing to celebrate the centennial of 1889, men also were intrigued by his social life.[62] A note submitted by a gentleman to the *Magazine of American History* in September of 1888, hard on the heels of a searching inquiry into whether Washington ate "green peas with a knife," cited a little-known letter by General Greene describing a three-hour "frisk" in his quarters. "The record of the Father of our Country for patriotism, piety, and fishing, has passed into history, but if the [letter] correctly describes his endurance, in dancing he takes the cake," the contributor declared.[63] Mention of the Greene letter, written from New Jersey in the spring of 1779, prompted a second amateur historian to supply details of Washington's "pretty little frisk." The house in which the marathon took place, he wrote, still stood on the banks of the Raritan. Mrs. Greene, Washington's dancing partner, "was then about twenty-five years of age, [and] is said to have been singularly lovely in character."[64]

The documentation for Washington's ability to dance the night away was no more solid or extensive than new evidence for his dalliance with Mary Philipse that also came to light in 1889, at the height of New York's bout of centennial fever. A playful letter to Washington from Joseph Chew speaking of the assault on that lady's affection in terms of a military campaign was the basis for most of the stories. But as an indignant respondent to an article on the Philipse family noted, there was also a persistent body of legend including "the baseless tradition of Washington's having been refused by Mary Philipse"; the faithful subscriber hoped, with the help of his fellow readers, to assign blame for the dissemination of that rumor.[65]

In February of 1890, his query was answered. Attributing the Philipse stories to General George T. Morris on hearsay alone, William Pelletreau cited an 1848 report in a New Jersey newspaper to the effect that Mary had already given her heart to Morris when George Washington came to Yonkers a-courting, a neat and romantic explanation for a situation from which Washington might otherwise have emerged a failure: Mary was promised to another, nobly honored her commitment, and thus regretfully surrendered the future hero to Martha and to history.

Not content with leaving matters there, General Morris (or was it Mr. Pelletreau?) also had her form a warm friendship with the unfortunate Major André and come to Washington's tent in disguise to plead for his life, only to find "too late that the face and voice that once charmed him [had] lost all power to influence the acts of one who only lived for his country. Such is the substance of the romance that has been copied time and again till at last it has been received as truth by the popular mind."[66] The appetite for Washington trivia was, to all appearances, insatiable.

Shortly after the turn of the century, the editor of the posthumous revision of the Schroeder-Lossing *Life and Times of Washington* rightly traced an unwholesome strain in historiography back to the anniversaries lately observed in Philadelphia and New York:

Several recent works have aimed, more or less openly, to apply a method of detraction to the character of Washington, and to reduce his greatness to the common level, upon the theory that we gain a man while we lose a hero. The utterances brought out by the Centennial celebrations which culminated in that of 1889 at New York were almost universally at the level of exceedingly deficient knowledge and profoundly unfortunate misapprehension, even on the part of men of highly representative position and character. An edition of the writings of Washington under the editorship of Mr. W. C. Ford, begun in 1888, was executed on lines deliberately and avowedly intended to bring Washington down from his high historic pedestal; and in sequel Mr. Ford's brother undertook a popular volume, designed to reduce Washington from the heroic, almost godlike level, to that of a common historic character.[67]

It was Worthington Chauncey Ford, for instance, whose edition of Washington's letters gave wide circulation and respectability to an ambiguous missive Washington sent to Mrs. George William Fairfax in September of 1758, not long after his passage at arms with Mary Philipse. In that letter, declaring himself "a votary of love," the young Washington confirmed his engagement to Mrs. Custis but, in the eyes of many startled readers from that day to this, hinted at an unquenchable passion for Mrs. Fairfax herself.[68] W. C. Ford also sorted out the cryptic allusions, buried in Washington's letters, to his other heart-throbs. Ford's final roster of sweethearts included a mysterious "Lowland Beauty"; a certain Miss Betsy who refused his hand; Sally Fairfax, whose intriguing correspondence with her neighbor from Mount Vernon first came to light in 1877 in the pages of the New York *Herald* (only to be auctioned off and so to disappear again the next day); and Martha Custis, the plump widow who brought to him in marriage her not inconsiderable fortune.

In 1897 Paul Leicester Ford, brother of W. C., reviewed each of these affairs of the heart in *The True George Washington*, a book devoted to such human aspects of Washington's story as his "physique," his "social life," "tastes and amusements," and "relations with the fair sex," to cite the topics of several key chapters. The lady-loves discussed by the younger Ford were, to the woman, far more interesting than his wife. Indeed, a contemporary witness described Martha as a dismal creature "not possessing much sense"; in the words of others more favorably disposed to her, she was "petite, over-fond, hot-tempered, obstinate, and a poor speller."[69]

But the Fords' claims to originality in the field of Washington romance were shaky. An unsigned article on "Washington as Lover and Poet" printed alongside news coverage of the Inaugural Centennial in *Harper's* made reference to the fact that "the most mysterious" of the Sally Fairfax letters would shortly appear in the second volume of W. C. Ford's *Writings of Washington*.[70] *Somebody* knew about the Fairfax correspondence, and *Harper's*, in the meantime, was prepared to supply the lowdown on all known objects of Washington's boundless affections. On the identity of the "lowland beauty" the adolescent Washington had praised in a note to a friend, there was much speculation: Bishop Meade thought she was Mary Cary, Sally's sister, who married Edward Ambler; Lossing said she was Mary Bland; others were partisans for Lucy Grimes, mother of Light-Horse Harry Lee and grandmother of Robert E. Lee; for a Miss Eilbeck, the Charles City beauty who married George Mason; for Anne Daniel, one of his Stafford cousins; and for Sally Cary Fairfax herself. But the evidence favored Miss Betsy Fauntleroy, to whom the schoolboy lost his heart at the tender age of sixteen. Denied her hand, George Washington sought military glory instead. When the conquering hero of the western territories returned to Williamsburg, Betsy, now a married lady, fainted dead away at the window as the triumphal procession passed by and her George saluted with a wave of the sword—or so it was said.[71]

Sally, "a famous beauty," was merely a sympathetic older friend to the youthful bachelor-hero. She was a confidante, a mender of shabby clothes who sewed on loose buttons. Fine clothes were always important to the Virginia aristocrat. Although "the romantic days may have been over for them both" when George met Martha, she must have "satisfied Washington's fondness for beautiful raiment if she wore her splendid brocades, fans, old lace, and ornaments found packed away in the garret at Arlington." As for his lifelong attention to prettier women, his contemporaries gave him the benefit of the doubt; such admiration, idolaters said, was "a proof of his Homage to the worthy part of the Sex, and highly respectful to his wife." And as for Mary Philipse, the New York charmer resuscitated for the 1889 centennial, the nation could only be grateful for her strongmindedness and Washington's awkward courtship: "Long after she had become Mrs. Roger Morris, a little niece said, 'Mr. Washington wouldn't be a rebel if he'd married aunty.' Perhpas, indeed, we have to thank this Tory dame for not smiling on the young Colonel's suit."[72]

For good or ill, during the 1890s Washington the lover, the dancer, and the courtly aristocrat displaced the rather abstract figure who once stood for national unity, moral rectitude, self-denial, and stoic devotion to duty. It is true that even before the Philadelphia Centennial, Benson Lossing had named the objects of Washington's schoolboy crushes and cited letters indicating his passion for apparel made of "the best superfine blue Cotton Velvet" London had to offer. He also documented Washington's fondness for the minuet and made mention of the Fredericksburg celebration of the defeat of Cornwallis, said by some stiff-necked hagiographers to be the last ball at which the future first president danced.[73] But these were passing references in a book on Mount Vernon and its romantic associations.

After 1889, even sober political and military biographies of Washington—and a great number of them were issued with clamorous fanfare between Harrison's departure from the reviewing stand and the turn of the new century—labored under an obligation to include analysis of the hero's innermost feelings about issues far removed from the battlefield and the halls of power. Woodrow Wilson's biography, serialized in *Harper's New Monthly Magazine* in 1896 after an elaborate ad campaign, ran under the title "In Washington's Day" and introduced a princely sort of Southern colonel in the March issue. "Passionate and full of warm blood," he careened from the perils of the forced march to the romantic dangers of the drawing room, perfectly dressed for all occasions "in proper uniform of buff and blue, a white and scarlet cloak upon his shoulders, the sword at his side knotted with red and gold, his horse's fittings engraved with the Washington arms." So attired, he set out for the Wilsonian version of his fateful rendezvous with Mary Philipse in 1756 (Figure 5.21):

With him rode two aides in their uniforms, and two servants in their white and scarlet livery. Curious folk who looked upon the celebrated young officer upon the road saw . . . a Virginian gentleman, a handsome man, and an admirable horseman,—a very gallant figure, no one could deny. Everywhere . . . he showed himself the earnest, high-strung, achieving youth he was. In New York he fell into a new ambush, from which he did not come off without a wound. His friend Beverly Robinson must needs have Miss Mary Philipse at his house there, a beauty and an heiress, and Washington came away from her with a sharp rigor at his heart. But he could not leave that desolate frontier at home unprotected to stay for a siege upon a lady's heart; he had recovered from such wounds before, had before left pleasure for duty.[74]

Vaporous passages like that one—the historian Garry Wills is being kind when he labels the book "silly"—alternate with lengthy descriptions of the barbaric splendor in which the Virginia squirarchy dwelt.[75] The text was also larded with illustrations, some drawings and engravings, some paintings, some photographs, showing Washington's own luxurious silver and dishes, the recently manicured historic homes in which he and his friends once gathered for business or balls, and the women in his life, from the blue-eyed enchantress of Philipse Manor to Nelly Custis, his pretty ward and the delight of his final years.

Thanks to a full-page plate by Howard Pyle, the Fredericksburg ball mentioned in passing by Lossing is elevated in the Wilson biography to the status of a major incident in a Washington iconography increasingly devoted to three principal features of that illustration (Figure 5.22). The first consists of silks, satins, fans, and vast rooms, richly appointed. The second is Washington's personal and emotional life, represented by his aged mother, leaning on his arm. The third is his social life, a formal, elegant affair of minuets, lived among "the elite of the Virginia" and the colonial aristocracy.[76]

The 1889 campaign to reconstruct the tomb of Mary Ball Washington at Fredericksburg and the mounting interest in this obscure figure signaled by the appearance of Marion Harland's brief biography in 1892 are also symptomatic of a new trend in Washington scholarship grounded in the popular forms of centenary history.[77] Washington historians were aware that they were breaking with the traditions of their discipline by prizing intimate detail above conventional analysis.

5.21
Washington wooing Mary Philipse, an illustration for Woodrow Wilson's biography

At the end of the 1880s, in his eight-volume *History of the People of the United States*, John Bach McMaster had been the first to assert that although "the outlines of his biography are known to every schoolboy in the land, . . . his true biography is yet to be prepared. General Washington is known to us, and President Washington. But George Washington"—the *true* George Washington—"is an unknown man."[78] When that figure emerged at last, McMaster argued, "we shall read less of the cherry tree and more of the man. We shall behold the great commander. . . . But we shall also hear his oaths" and, presumably, read a great deal about those "pretty little frisks" of his.[79]

Woodrow Wilson's ill-advised excursions into deep romantic goo have something to do with McMaster's challenge. So does Henry Cabot Lodge's two-volume *George Washington* of 1891, which opens with a promise to find the "true" man. In this instance, the true Washington turns out to be an uneasy mixture of the perfectly ordinary with the surpassingly heroic.[80] Like his future political nemesis, Woodrow Wilson, Lodge sought out this strange, bifurcated Washington in the parlor of Mary, rich and beautiful descendant of the patroons Frederick and Adolphus Philipse, Dutch colonial magnates of a hundred years past:

5.22
Howard Pyle illustration for the same text, showing Washington escorting his mother into the ballroom in Fredericksburg

How much this little interlude, pushed into a corner as it has been by the dignity of history, how much it tells of the real man! How the statuesque myth and the priggish myth and the dull and solemn myth melt away before it! Wise and strong, a bearer of heavy responsibility beyond his years, daring in fight and sober in judgment, we have here the other and the more human side of Washington. One loves to picture that gallant, generous, youthful figure, brilliant in color and manly in form, riding gayly on from one little colonial town to another, feasting, dancing, courting, and making merry. For him the myrtle and ivy were intertwined with the laurel, and fame was sweetened by youth. He was righteously ready to draw from life all the good things which fate and fortune, then smiling upon him, could offer, and he took his pleasure frankly, with an honest heart.[81]

Lodge's reviewers treated his book as an answer to McMaster, whose call for attention to issues heretofore excluded from the canon had not met with universal approval. Leonard Irving, writing in the *Magazine of American History*, thought very highly of the Lodge biography, for example, but wondered at the author's frank admiration for his predecessor and the quest after the "true" George Washington that Professor McMaster had launched with assorted "sneers," innuendoes, and disingenuous half-facts. Irving was particularly troubled by McMaster's desire to rehabilitate a Washington who swore—although profanity is always abhorrent, Washington's rare oaths "seem to us simply evidences of [his] vigorous . . . manhood," Irving opined—as if to imply that oaths were habitual to him, and a secret vice practiced exclusively by the Father of His Country. "He hints and insinuates at possibilities of ugly discovery," wrote the critic, whereas "there are moments in such a life as his when the volcanoes of human nature must find an eruption in some such way."[82]

Word of Washington's explosion of wrath at Monmouth and his curses over St. Clair's defeat had already appeared in print. Lodge highlighted the incidents not to hint at some dark streak of baseness concealed beneath Washington's excellences as general and president but rather to prove that the hero was tenderhearted about his troops and anxious for their safety: "What could be more intensely human that this? What a warm heart is here, and what a lightning glimpse of a passionate nature bursting through silence into burning speech!"[83]

Historians such as Paul Leicester Ford and the many authors of popular books on colonial times who were quick to follow in the footsteps of Lodge and McMaster did not turn up much new data either. The Sally Fairfax letters were the singular "find" of the nineteenth century. But they combed what stories and snippets of hearsay lay buried in the existing literature for clues to the contents of Washington's heroic heart. Determined to capture the true Washington in all his human glory, they walked a fine line between scandalmongering and canonization, between spice and marmoreal dullness.

"One of Washington's Sweethearts," a note on Mary Philipse that appeared in a respectable historical journal in 1893, rehashed Washington Irving at great length before retailing one nugget of hearsay about her character, not his: "Besides her wealth and beauty she was credited with possessing a strong mind and imperious will; so much so that it was freely hinted at that time that if Washington had married her he would never have been the leader of the patriots."[84] In the same decade Moncure Conway, a descendant of one of the much-wooed Cary sisters, tried without much success to spread the rumor that "Martha Washington was always rather cool to this beautiful Mrs. George William Fairfax of Belvoir," but he had no moral to draw from that arguable observation.[85] General Bradley Johnson, on the other hand, used in his *General Washington* of 1897 the by-now-familiar list of girlfriends—the Misses Bland, Grimes, Cary, and Fauntleroy, Mary Philipse, and "the hundred other girls from Boston to Annapolis with whom the young Virginia colonel flirted and made love"—to prove that Washington was "a man all over, a man with strong appetites, . . . positive, belligerent, and aggressive" in the manner of the planter-aristocrat. He was the toast of the Tidewater; "what wonder, then, that he fell in love with every pretty girl and told her so."[86]

From the point of view of the women who came to dominate the production of this kind of humanized, romanticized history in the 1890s, Washington's interest in the ladies was no more than they deserved, and certainly no sign of moral weakness. A particularly zealous member of a women's club, who delivered a paper proving from Washington's own letters that "the hero of the hatchet story was not unlike the generality of sons" in his shameful neglect of his aged mother, received attention in the daily press because of the oddity of her conclusions. More common was the tortured logic of the woman who thought that "Washington had much of old-fashioned gallantry in his treatment" of damsels young and old, and that even the disturbing tenor of the infamous letter to Sally Fairfax on the occasion of his engagement to another (a missive "supposed to indicate that he was really in love with the wife of his friend") expressed "only the customary gallantry of an old-fashioned Virginia gentleman toward ladies."[87]

Not every authoress was as sweetly trusting, but Alice Morse Earle, in her *Colonial Dames and Good Wives* of 1895, and Anne Hollingsworth Wharton, in her *Colonial Days and Dames* of the same year, both doted on the semilegendary accounts of his flirtations with Lucy and Betsy and Mary Philipse, the future Tory, even though Earle was quick to note the rapid transferral of Washington's warm regard from the haughty Mary to "the inevitable widow," the agreeable Martha, "with a fortune of fifteen thousand pounds sterling."[88] Because "such associations bring the old life before us with a sudden crowding upon the canvas of historic scenes and figures," Wharton openly preferred legends like the stories the Mount Vernon blacks told about the "magic rose" in the garden, a courting charm that marked the spot where Lawrence Lewis proposed to Nelly Custis.

She also recognized the mystery and the evanescence of human emotion. Well versed in the more than five decades of speculation as to why George Washington did not wed Mary Philipse—was it she who rejected the Father of His Country? Who but an incipient Tory could do such a thing?—Wharton delicately conjoined the end of the flirtation with Washington's later seizure of her house on Harlem Heights, and left the rest to the imaginations of her proper lady-readers. "There being no positive data on the subject" of who ditched whom, she wrote, "and the spirit of a love-affair being about as difficult to transmit from one generation to another as the tone of a voice or the glance of an eye, we feel free to put upon the affair the construction that detracts least from the dignity of the American hero."[89]

A thinly disguised version of the Philipse-Washington romance became a play in 1901. *Washington and the Lady* by Mrs. Edmund Nash Morgan implicated "Marion Morris" in Benedict Arnold's treachery and gives her a climactic scene in which she dashes a cup of poison from her former suitor's hand; the general permits her to escape to England on the warrant of a pledge of loyalty made twenty-odd years ago and sealed with a faded rose he has carried in his pocket ever since.[90] But equally sentimental glosses on the brief meeting at Beverly Robinson's New York house also cropped up in popular and semischolarly

5.23
Mary Philipse's home on Harlem
Heights: the Morris-Jumel mansion, once
used as Washington's headquarters

books with some pretense to credibility. Thomas Glenn's social history
of colonial mansions, a combination of architectural criticism, genealogy, and quibbles with the conclusions of Conway and P. L. Ford,
is a case in point. Although it is possible to question the sagacity of
one who decides, for no better reason than to keep the breath of
scandal from the hero, that the Sally Fairfax letters must have been
written to her unmarried sister, Mary, Glenn did know the difference
between fact and fancy. He had also made a conscientious survey of
the oldest accounts of Washington's wooing in New York. Thus he
questioned the tradition that Washington "was refused point-blank by
the haughty heiress, who was then thirty years of age and getting
rather passée," because the story had been passed down through Tory
sources (Figure 5.23).

That did not deter Glenn, however, from stringing together a compendium of other suspect yarns about the abortive romance, each one
given a touch of plausibility gleaned from another page in Washington's biography. His whirlwind courtship of the widow Custis in a
single night, his youthful shyness, the terrible temper he revealed in
the heat of battle, and his lifelong interest in his property were all
applied to an amorphous idyll of courtly love, a saga to which the
reader was invited to supply the ending of his or her choice:

One version of his historic love-affair tells how they sat together in conversation until daybreak, and, as the gray light of morning crept in, mocking the
flickering light of the candles burning low in their sockets, Washington at last
found courage to propose, only to be refused. The story continues that the
handsome young Virginia colonel grew ashy pale—and rushed out of the

house, upsetting one of the slaves who was getting breakfast. Another account tells us that Washington, always on the lookout in his younger days for a rich wife, paid considerable attention to Mary Philipse, but never summoned up courage to propose—a fact that was always extremely regretted by the heiress of Frederick Philipse.[91]

And some stories, although "manifestly untrue," were just "too picturesque to omit." Glenn therefore leaves Mrs. Mary Philipse Morris, "heavily cloaked and masked," stealing into the American camp with her brother-in-law in secret to try to save Major André from the gallows. "George," she murmurs huskily, much to the chagrin of the steely commander in chief. "He called loudly for an officer of the guard. 'Show these persons through the lines!' [Washington] exclaimed, and left the room abruptly in disgust."[92]

As the new century dawned, some wondered if the purveying of historical fluff had not gone too far and if, in the process of gaining a man, the nation had not lost a hero. Edward Towne typifies the dilemma of those who had followed the lead of McMaster and the Fords, dug up the dirt on the "true" George Washington, and found themselves with a fox-hunting, hand-kissing, powdered Virginia dancing-master on their hands, a pleasant enough chap but one whose expertise at the minuet and whose keen interest in ladies' gowns hardly qualified him for the pedestal on which national heroes customarily resided.

In 1889 Towne had been the correspondent who provided *Harper's* with the scoop on "Washington as Lover and Poet." In 1903, as he finished revising and editing the old-fashioned, worshipful Schroeder-Lossing biography of Washington for a twentieth-century audience, Towne had come to wonder what he and his kind had wrought with their searches for portraits of the elusive Mary Bland, their collections of Mary Philipse lore, and their heated debates over the identity of the "lowland beauty."

In his amendments to the older text, Towne had gone farther than his revisionist predecessors toward recognizing that the Sally Fairfax correspondence indicated something more than chummy camaraderie—"There is no evidence that to either the whole experience was more than a transaction of silence or of dumb distant signals, with no effect upon the actual life of either"—but in the end he abjured such trivia. His book did not aim to reduce George Washington to the status of a business and social leader of good family, escorting a lovely woman draped in ancestral diamonds and lace to the Centennial Ball at the Metropolitan Opera House. Nor did it aim to convince America that a Washington who loved and lost and loved again, on Harlem Heights and elsewhere, was worthy of emulation on that account; that a hundred-year-old encounter between girlish coquetry and Southern gallantry deserved one more gooey article or play or sermon on the splendid human qualities of the first president. Instead, his work "aimed to strengthen the proof that the worship almost by the fathers of Washington was but simple justice, and that lapse of time but casts new lights on the colossal and splendid figure which Washington must ever be in the history truly told."[93] But for many Americans the play-acting, the pageantry, and the parades, the relics and the romance, were infinitely more appealing in their own right than any hero. Although the quest for the true George Washington had created the colonial revival, Washington himself would rapidly become extraneous to the historical thinking manifest in turn-of-the-century parlors adorned in the new colonial mode.

The Colonial Revival

6

Heroic Imagery for the American Home
1893–1924

The World's Columbian Exposition of 1893

American cities other than New York also observed April 30, 1889, as a patriotic holiday—the birthday of constitutional government—with or without large doses of Washingtoniana. "Here in Chicago," a correspondent to a New York magazine remarked sanctimoniously, "the observances of the day were marked by a fervor and an enthusiasm which borrowed nothing of vinous or alcoholic inspiration."[1] But the fireworks did fizzle out there in the West, a disaster more readily excused by drunkenness than by incompetent sobriety: despite a homegrown reproduction of the inaugural chapel service in St. James's Church, remembering George Washington in a place so far removed from the familiar haunts of the Founding Fathers was no easy matter. Indeed, the after-dinner speaker at Chicago's civic banquet felt constrained to remind his auditors that it was "in every sense appropriate to connect the name of Washington with the Constitution" and the government of law being honored in the observances of 1889.[2]

Nonetheless Chicago nosed out New York in the competition for the distinction of hosting the World's Columbian Exposition.[3] And the fair that opened on the shores of Lake Michigan on May 1, 1893, reflected the importance of Washington as a cultural symbol whose potency was not confined to a specific state or region. Christopher Columbus was the eminence grise of Chicago. The gala ostensibly commemorated his discovery of America in 1492, but except for a seventy-one-foot duplicate of the *Santa Maria* anchored in the lake and copy of the "weather-beaten old" Convent of La Rabida housing such relics of the explorer as survived through four hundred years, the theme was mainly American colonial in the eighteenth-century sense, and the hero of choice was still George Washington.[4]

As Susan Prendergast Schoelwer has recently shown, "Every major eastern state, in addition to others, such as Louisiana, displayed George Washington relics and, whenever possible, a reproduction of some room in which he had slept within the state boundaries."[5] New England, the South, and the Midatlantic states all erected structures in more or less Georgian styles, popular in his era. New Jersey replicated Washington's headquarters at Morristown, complete with his bedchamber on the second floor. Virginia reproduced Mount Vernon and the room in which he died.[6] But bits and pieces of colonializing ornament also turned up on the buildings calling attention to the beauties of such uncolonial locales as Utah, the Indian Territories, the Dakotas, and Wisconsin. Even though they could not boast of Washington's fish knife, his pewter plates, and a pass signed by his hand (these items had been lent by proud New Yorkers to the big thirteen-colony heritage display held in the Government Building) or the authentic mementos of "home life of the past" in Washington's day featured in the "relic room" of New York's otherwise neo-Imperial palazzo, the plains and prairies had become fervently neocolonial.[7]

Unlike the Philadelphia fair, Chicago's attracted an audience drawn from the western side of the Appalachians. Of the twenty million who trooped through the various state buildings en route to the larger-than-life copy of the Liberty Bell made from such historic scraps of salvage as surviving fragments of Jefferson's kettle and Washington's surveying chain, few had ever seen a real colonial building. Of the twenty million who gawked at commercial displays dignified by reproductions of colonial furnishings, most were not familiar with the kinds of old houses and public buildings that defined the landscape of the urban and suburban East. Descendants of long-ago migrants from the Atlantic coast might treasure pieces of ancestral china brought west in a covered wagon—Alice Morse Earle's *China Collecting in America* of 1892 had recently set those who lacked properly equipped forebears hunting for the blue-and-white dishes of other people's great-grandparents anyway—but few had ever seen the profusion of fireplaces, spinning wheels, Brewster chairs, sideboards, and other relics distributed among twenty-two separate buildings that reflected the colonial ethos in some way.[8]

Inside these ill-assorted mansions, manors, farmhouses, cottages, cabins, stately homes, and adobe missions in the Colonial Revival manner lurked several thousand such artifacts, looking strange but powerfully attractive.[9] Revived after its success in Philadelphia, for example, the "Old Tyme" New England Log Cabin restaurant of Mrs. Brinton (née Southwick), serving pork and beans to the whir of a flax wheel by the crackling hearth, was brand-new here in the hinterlands.[10]

That so many diverse agencies and institutions built along Lake Michigan in the colonial manner was a tribute of sorts to the fashionability of colonialism. Out of the shattering disunity of the Civil War and the cultural diversity fostered by immigration on a large scale, a national style nonetheless emerged in 1893. And it is fitting that such a mode should have taken hold first in Chicago. On a patriotic holiday Wall Street's Bishop Potter had cited Washington's alleged bias against foreigners and their evil entanglements and pointed to the "steady deterioration" evident in New York life because of the importation of "the lowest orders of people from abroad." Chicago, by contrast, had aimed its observance of the same Inaugural Centennial specifically at foreign-born communities.

In fact, the celebration had become a means of attempting to educate newcomers into American citizenship though foreign-language addresses on the virtues of George Washington.[11] At the Chicago fair, the parochial colonialism of the Eastern centenaries lost its English and New England biases and acquired Spanish, French, and heavily regional overtones: if the Old Tyme Kitchen and a copy of the much-lamented John Hancock House were colonial, why then so were Mount Vernon, a Creole mansion with a gallery, and an adobe hacienda. So was a modest wooden house of painted clapboards with gables and broad porches built by West Virginia to represent a typical residence in that state and said to be "in the Colonial Style."[12] For if the colonial style was a truly national vocabulary, as indigenous to West Virginia, Arkansas, and California as it was to Massachusetts and Pennsylvania; if the colonial style gave visible testimony to the American heritage of places far from Jamestown and Plymouth Rock, then it was also well suited to the adornment of the modern American home because pilasters, hearths, and Palladian windows were fiercely up-to-date.

Like all the great fairs of the last century, Chicago's Columbian Exposition had less to do with historical retrospection than with machinery, technology, trade, and the latest commercial products. Juxtaposed with unfamiliar goods and apparatus and amazing devices for accomplishing the work of twenty men with the flick of a finger, buildings "in the Colonial Style" looked every bit as strange, new, and amazing to most fairgoers. By association and by ideology, nostalgia—a backward glance at the early days—became part of the great American push forward: an edenic past bolstered the drive toward a utopian future.

Imre Kiralfy's "grand historical spectacle," *America,* was playing at the Auditorium Building in downtown Chicago during the run of the fair. Kiralfy hope to lure fairgoers away from the Ferris wheel and from the eighteenth-century parlor the Essex Museum had set up in the Massachusetts building, in order to demonstrate in dramatic form just how the colonial past pointed toward a future of mechanical marvels like the great revolving wheel. *America* was not exactly a play; many of the principal characters were silent throughout, leaving the progress of the plot to choruses sung by groups of Spanish maidens or dissident Pilgrims cavorting about a Maypole. Although allegorical figures of "Progress" and "Perseverance" did utter lines from time to time, for the most part the "spectacle" was grand opera without arias, a pageant held indoors with music, dance, and breathtaking sets.

Kiralfy's contribution to the genre consisted of twenty-one lush scenes, divided into two acts tracing "Progress, Civilization, Liberty of Mind and Action, and Arts and Sciences of America" from the meeting of Columbus and Isabella to the opening of the Chicago fair.[13] In common with the fair, then, *America* celebrated progress. In fact, "Progress" was personified as the spirit who greeted the victors at Yorktown; banished the religious and ethnic bigotry brought to America by settlers from the Old World; assembled dancing reapers, incandescent lights, sewing machines, typewriters, lightning rods, steamboats, and cotton gins for a "Ballet of American Inventions" in the "Palace of Progress," his "Magnificent Modern and Somewhat Fantastic Home"; and helped to marshal the cast for a finale in which all the nations of the world gathered at the feet of Columbia in Chicago in tribute to American genius (Figure 6.1).[14]

In its clear articulation of the importance of immigration and modernism, and the relationship of both to the sweep of American history, Kiralfy's production differed markedly from the popular entertainments associated with earlier commemorative festivals. Only the cover of the program retained the character of those earlier celebrations. Although Washington was by no means the central character in the script, his face, surrounded by rondels bearing the names of the thirteen colonies and plaques enumerating his military victories, appeared there—the consummate emblem of *America* (Figure 6.2).

6.1
"Columbia's Triumph," the finale of Imre Kiralfy's 1893 "spectacle," *America*

But inside, Washington figured only in two brief scenes, little tableaux vivants in which the curtain opens, the hero is revealed in a characteristic pose for a moment of oohs and ahs, and the lights go out again. In the Yorktown scene he sits on his horse surrounded by his generals, all posed after Trumbull's famous painting of the ritual of surrender. The stage directions for Act I, Scene VI, do not specify exactly what the hero is to do. Presumably, he just stands there in the boat, bravely facing the future, as Leutze had once depicted him:

American side of the river on the memorable night of December 25, 1776.
The patriot troops are conveyed across the river, and amid the packed ice, and in the bitter cold, the future Father of his Country,
THE IMMORTAL WASHINGTON, CROSSES THE DELAWARE.[15]

But these set-pieces from well-known cultural icons were obligatory tributes to a vision of history dominated by heroes and their decisive acts. Although there was no abrupt diminution in the number of reverent biographies of Washington published annually after 1893, the times that shaped the figure and were influenced in turn by him came to be almost as engaging as the hero himself. This shift from idolatry to a more diffuse sort of interest in the texture of the past can be detected in the program for *America,* with its traditional George Washington cover and a novel text that pays as much or more attention to Miles Standish, Priscilla, Paul Revere, and the anonymous farmer-patriots of Lexington.

The change was not, however, a uniform one affecting all heroes and epochs simultaneously. Washington's was a special case. For one thing, he had been drawn and described and talked half to death in the past decade. For another, habitual reverence for the persona of Washington had already led by degrees to an interest in his relics, his physical surroundings, his friends and associates, and his milieu in general. The growing appeal of the colonial setting—American to the core, comforting to those caught up in the swift current of change, homey and old-fashioned yet oddly progressive—promised to eclipse his popularity. In the hands of Bishop Potter and a legion of other Washington experts, his deeds, if malleable to the touch of an orator with a cause in mind, still proved resistant to outright fabrication: his stolid features were difficult to recast for every occasion.

But as vague a thing as a stretch of time, especially when the era in question was the notoriously elastic colonial epoch, could signify almost anything to a commentator with imagination and a pressing need to find particular messages in history. In truth, then, the colonial style no longer required the stately figure of Washington as its principal ornament. And in Chicago, far to the west of the fabled Delaware River, George Washington was fast becoming another cunning prop in a colonial parlor, a picture hung over the mantle of the house everyone suddenly wanted to live in. The picture was more interesting,

6.2
The cover of the program for Kiralfy's
America

6.3
The "Colonial" Arkansas building at the 1904 Louisiana Purchase Exposition in St. Louis

perhaps, than the reeded molding around the fireplace, but it was also somewhat less attractive to the eye of the decorator than the blue-and-white plates and the quaint furniture ranged about it. The stories—the lovely, romantic stories—that such things could tell, if only they could speak!

The Louisiana Purchase Exposition of 1904

George Washington was hardly to be seen in St. Louis when the Louisiana Purchase Exposition opened there in 1904, in tribute to the farsighted bargain Jefferson had struck with France just over a century before. President Theodore Roosevelt, the adopted Westerner who spoke at the dedicatory ceremony, compared this centenary with the Washington anniversary celebrated earlier in his native New York: "We have met here today to commemorate the hundredth anniversary of the event which more than any other, after the foundation of the Government . . . determined the character of our national life—determined that we should be a great expanding nation instead of a relatively small and stationary one."[16] Roosevelt's words captured the expansive spirit of the occasion, too. The St. Louis fair, even more than the expositions at Philadelphia and Chicago, was a grab bag of modern inventiveness, boosterism, and booming optimism, a vast entertainment to which a dollop of history lent some semblance of high-minded dignity.

Monticello, the home of Thomas Jefferson, ostensible patron saint of the fair, was faithfully copied in the Virginia pavilion, where state chapters of the Daughters of the American Revolution and the Colonial Dames of America joined forces to serve gallons of "Old Richmond Punch" to homesick natives. Because he was also known as the father of the University of Virginia, his gravestone had been borrowed for exhibition in the Education Building.[17] But like Washington, Jefferson himself was by no means easy to find in Forest Park, where he shared the honor of being cast in a colossal plaster effigy with Louis IX, de Soto, Joliet, Daniel Boone, Pierre Laclede, Lewis and Clark, Robert Livingston, and Napoleon.[18]

Colonialisms, on the other hand, all but obscured the wedding-cake classicism of the chief exposition buildings. One of the main thoroughfares was Colonial Avenue, which began at Commonwealth, ran gently downhill from the Plateau of States, and lost itself in the wooded Trail. The Arkansas building, located at the Commonwealth intersection, was an ample Georgian residence with balustrades atop a hipped roof, pediments and Corinthian columns on three sides, and fanlights and Palladian windows everywhere. Painted white, the mansion was said to be of a "quaint" style "popular in . . . little interior towns" of Arkansas, and therefore "strongly suggestive of the State's typical architecture" (Figure 6.3).[19]

New Hampshire put up a plain, boxy house with a high-pitched roof, massive central chimney stack, and "old-fashioned windows with small panes of glass." It was, the sign over the front door announced, the "Birthplace of Daniel Webster" in facsimile. A second sign, lettered in old-fashioned style, protruded from the corner of the structure and announced the presence within of "ANTIQUES." In fact, the interior rooms were full of "quaint New England furniture. There are mahogany tables and old fashioned sideboards and straight backed chairs of one hundred years ago."[20]

More than any other type of display, architecture and its associated artifacts carried the forward-looking message of the fair. Because domestic architecture was an element in everybody's visual culture, everybody could be relied upon to recognize the change between houses of 1803 (when the Louisiana Purchase was made) and those of 1904, and to note the remarkable progress achieved in the interval, even when a straightforward comparison was complicated by the newly minted splendor of structures like the Arkansas building, designed after much older prototypes. Size was one important way of telling the old from the new: dwellings of the early nineteenth century copied for the fair were very small by modern standards. And the more primitive the house, the more likely it was to be venerable.

6.4
The Old Virginia Homestead, a money-making concession that did not fare too well in St. Louis

The Old Virginia Homestead, a profit-making concession not far from California's Spanish colonial copy of the Jesuit mission of La Rabida, emphasized the hardships of the past by showing the drawbacks of housing and housework in "colonial" 1803, the year in which a windowless log cabin with a wooden chimney, its walls chinked with clay, had been built on the farm of Patrick Henry. The Homestead Corporation brought that cabin to St. Louis complete with the horseshoe over the front door and a split-bottomed chair at the doorstep holding a 101-year-old great-grandmother, "knitting after the fashion of one hundred years ago" (Figure 6.4). The gloomy interior contained relics: "a flint-lock gun over two hundred years old which was owned by Governor Berkely and a chair brought over in the Mayflower." In a shed next door other grannies in ancient dress demonstrated carding, spinning, and weaving "all by hand . . . for the amusement and for impressions instructive as well, of the younger generation."

In contrast to the Abraham Lincoln Cabin (its front door was flanked by a pair of spinning wheels), which made $2,099.14 on receipts of over $6,000, the Old Virginia Homestead did poorly, with a profit of $1,600.[21] Although the West's own colonial period of pioneering fared best in paying displays, the biggest crowds along Colonial Avenue and environs came to see state and territorial headquarter-houses in the new, neocolonial style. These differed somewhat from the usual replicas of historic sites used to represent the states. True, Louisiana recreated the old Cabildo, where the purchase treaty was signed.

6.5
The Rhode Island pavilion at the Louisiana Purchase Exposition, with its unusual colonial gables

Virginia had its Monticello. Vermont had the Old Constitution House from Windsor "of Puritan plainness . . . in strong contrast with the nearby palatial mansions of other States." Tennessee had Andrew Jackson's Hermitage, and New Jersey camped out once again in its traditional copy of the Ford mansion, with relics and the Washington bedroom upstairs. "To those whose interest in things colonial is keen," one guidebook stated, "the Old Ford Tavern is a Mecca" because of its collection of antique furniture and cut glass "of colonial pattern."[22]

But the buildings that attracted the most attention were free variations on the colonial manner—bigger than the originals, more ornate, and far more individualized. The custodians of the Rhode Island Colonial Mansion, for instance, took pride in explaining that they had combined the curious circular gables of the historic Smith House, said to be "the only examples" of that peculiar form "now to be seen in New England," with the piazza of the old Carrington House in Providence to create a traffic-stopping hybrid (Figure 6.5). By painting the outside walls to look like masonry laid up in multicolored courses, the architects also emphasized the distinction of this house from all the gray and ivory and white state pavilions, colonial or not, painted in conformity with the prevailing beaux-arts color scheme.

One woman, upon entering the Rhode Island building, purportedly exclaimed, "Why, this is the stairway in my grandfather's old home!"[23] Details like that stairway, details suddenly considered to be "antiques" detachable from the fabric of the building, could be reassembled to make what would nowadays be called Colonial Revival houses, old in their every part but oh-so-smart and modern as sprawling wholes. Massachusetts dispensed hospitality from such a big, comfortable white house. The façade reproduced features of the Old State House in Boston, but the long porches at the sides came from the Longfellow House in Cambridge. And on the second and third floors, the ornate Georgian scheme gave way to the rude vigor of Puritan furniture in dark woods and simple forms.

Strolling past a specimen of the third generation of the Charter Oak planted on the front lawn, "the wandering Nutmeg" abroad in St. Louis entered the Connecticut building through an Ionic doorway from the old Slater residence at Norwich, recently demolished. The door adorned a façade reminiscent of the historic Sigourney mansion at Hartford. Taken as a whole, said the publicists, the house was "typical of the ancestral homes of Connecticut gentlemen."[24]

In reality, each state building that was not an outright copy of some stately home resembled *somebody's* home, and they all fairly dripped with ancestral charm. The Michigan building, grouped with the Cabildo and the octagonal wooden wigwam of the state of Washington, looked vaguely colonial in that company. The squat Corinthian col-

6.6
In the heart of the Plateau of States at the St. Louis World's Fair, 1904; the scene could be a residential neighborhood anywhere

6.6
In the heart of the Plateau of States at the St. Louis World's Fair, 1904; the scene could be a residential neighborhood anywhere

umns and the heavy colonnade might just as readily have earned it the "classical" sobriquet, however, had it not been for the low lines and verandahs of domestic usage. "Of Colonial style of architecture, the building," the commissioners noted, "was planned for the comfort of those who make use of it": it was just too homey and cozy to be anything *but* colonial![25] Hemmed in on all sides by swan's-neck pediments, freshly painted clapboards, and green shutters, the tourist walking down tree-shaded Colonial Avenue was also walking back in time into an age of ample hospitality signaled by the welcoming reach of porches and the tall, broad doorways that beckoned the passerby to enter (Figure 6.6).

There were Georgian public buildings in America; the Massachusetts pavilion copied features of one of the more prominent of them. But the style had been essentially a domestic manner, enlarged, when necessary, to answer civic needs. Public buildings built in the colonial or neocolonial modes also retained the scale and the arrangement of rooms peculiar to homes. Hence, visiting the Arkansas or the Michigan pavilion was more like paying an afternoon call on the well-to-do lady down the block than it was like transacting business in the average state capitol or city hall with its lofty chambers, its gilded decor, and its grand, echoing corridors. She might have been a long way from her own tidy house on a Colonial Avenue just off Commonwealth somewhere in Minnesota or Kansas or even, perhaps, Rhode Island, but the turn-of-the-century fairgoer was never far from a reasonable substitute: the colonial era whence the nation came was also the place it collectively called home.

6.7
A patriotic ad for Liebig's Extract of Beef

Souvenir Spoons and House Museums

About the time the St. Louis fair ended, so did a craze for souvenir spoons that had begun fifteen years before.[26] In the advertising pages tucked away in the back of family magazines—alongside offerings of watches and building plans, next to illustrated testimonials for a patented extract of beef hailed as an example of scientific achievement comparable, in its own realm, to Washington's passage of the Delaware (Figure 6.7)—stay-at-homes were urged to buy spoons in tea, orange, or coffee sizes (with or without golden bowls) commemorating the silver triennial conclave of the Knights Templar in Denver, Colorado.

It was also possible for those unable to attend the Chicago and St. Louis fairs to obtain spoons adorned with the official symbols thereof.[27] Established firms made such spoons (Figure 6.8). The respected Gorham Company of Providence, maker of almost a thousand different keepsakes of this kind, is credited with starting the boom when it introduced a line of Salem witch spoons in 1890: her broom

6.8
Souvenir spoons: 1893 Chicago fair (by Standard), 1904 St. Louis fair (by Connecticut Silver), and Mount Vernon (by Rogers)

formed the handle, a cat grasped the bowl, and the crone on the finial was about to soar past a Halloween moon.[28]

In later years, items like witch spoons would look tawdry and hopelessly romantic even to such entrepreneurs as Wallace Nutting, whose line of products eventually included almost anything that could be described as colonial. Nutting peddled flatware, reproduction furniture, wrought iron, and even hand-tinted photographs of his family and friends dressed up in costume, playing at being squires and dames sitting by the hearthsides of the several historic house museums he owned and operated in New England. But in his popular picture books, Nutting still deplored Salem's concessions to the tourist trade. Caroline Emmerton's private management of the House of the Seven Gables was praised for attention to "the romantic and literary tourist," even though that had meant turning the place into a high-class boarding house with antiques for sale in the parlor and hot lunches served in the Pyncheon garden, where Hawthorne's Phoebe once read to Clifford.[29] The updated Witch House, however, was too much for even the most profit-conscious merchant to swallow. Nutting pronounced it utterly "disfigured by the wart of a modern shop added to its front," in which witch paraphernalia could be had for a modest price.[30]

Wallace Nutting issued his judgment in the 1920s; by that time, a few quaint tearooms capitalizing on witch lore, a few shops that stocked souvenirs, a few antique stores, and a fine museum had grown into a tourist trap draped in orange and black. Every corner, it seemed, bristled with stocks in which daytrippers might have their pictures taken, brandishing their witch spoons. Yet despite such touristic excesses, the popularity of the spoon as a souvenir and collector's item merits serious attention.

There is nothing inherent in the shape of the spoon that would seem to warrant its selection as a good keepsake. With determination, a designer could reinvent the spoon to accommodate the attributes of a witch, Columbus and the Chicago fair, or views of St. Louis, but the results were aesthetically and functionally uneven. Unlike the paperweights, belt buckles, and other objets d'art retailed by the souvenir trade before 1890, however, the spoon nicely suited the character of the emerging colonial revival. As a piece of household apparatus, it reflected the domestic side of the colonial style, embodied in kitchens, hearths, and the overblown family houses erected at the major expositions of the period.

And thanks to years of relic displays, magazine illustrations, and the inventory of historic American metalwork attempted in the Metropolitan Opera Inaugural Centennial show of 1889, silver already carried with it connotations of educated taste and gentility. The serious collector of old silver was, more likely than not, a gentleman or lady affiliated, if only by the act of acquisition, with old families and thus with the old American virtues of the days of the Founding Fathers. The collector of souvenir teaspoons, by aping the preferences of an elite in a lower price range, contrived to bask in the rays of glory that shone from the polished surfaces of American silverware.

Small, lightweight, and unbreakable, spoons were also eminently portable. They could be mailed to customers unwilling or unable to come to Forest Park in person. But they could also be tucked away in the reticule of the avid tourist. The fact that major national celebrations were held far from the Atlantic seaboard in 1893 and 1904 indicates that travel presented no real obstacle to attendance. Americans were willing to go great distances to see something of interest to them and existing means of transportation—the railroad, mainly—got them there.

In 1895, as one historian of the historic house museum has noted, there were four automobiles in the United States; by 1910, half a million such vehicles tootled down the backroads. "The same years that saw this miracle saw also . . . the rise of historic houses, from about 20 open in 1895 to nearly a hundred in 1910."[31] The originals after which the houses occupied by the states at world's fairs were modeled, such museums were generally colonial and often contained a savory mixture of relics of former inhabitants, original furniture, and curiosities deposited by interested neighbors. Joining the other Washington shrines in the region—his headquarters at Valley Forge, at Newburgh, and at Morristown—the Wallace House, his command post in Somerville, New Jersey, opened to the public in 1897. In 1904 Whittier's home in Amesbury, Massachusetts, became a museum. Among the more famous American homesteads, the Memorial Association acquired the Betsy Ross House in Philadelphia in 1898, although the title would not be secure and the restoration would not be complete for several years to come, and in 1910 the House of the Seven Gables in Salem became a guesthouse *cum* museum.[32] Most historic houses were promptly pictured in the bowls of souvenir spoons.

A house might be "colonial" without being museum material, of course. What made the difference were historic associations, the more romantic the better. In 1889, when Lucia Ames Mead, a writer specializing in such subjects, read that the Old Wayside Inn in Sudbury, Massachusetts, was on the block, she submitted an article to *New England Magazine* suggesting that local government acquire the property and use it as a memorial. In honor of the town's sesquicentennial, she observed, Milford, Connecticut, had recently done just that with an old stone bridge. Citing as proof of the practical benefits of refurbishing ancient landmarks the much-visited museum of colonial Americana recently established in an abandoned structure on the grounds of the Deerfield Academy, Mrs. Mead thought that "the restoration of the Wayside Inn as an old colonial tavern" would be an especially rewarding venture because of the universal popularity of Henry Wadsworth Longfellow.

According to her research, the poet had driven out from Cambridge to Sudbury one Sunday afternoon in the fall of 1862 in the company of his publisher and, on the basis of his inspection of the "tumble-down" Red Horse Inn, kept by the Howe family for 175 years, wrote his *Tales of a Wayside Inn*.[33] "The Landlord's Tale," the first of the versified stories recounted therein, was the Revolutionary legend that began with the injunction "Listen, my children, and you shall hear / Of the midnight ride of Paul Revere," and was, after Julia Ward Howe's "Battle Hymn of the Republic" and Emerson's "Concord Hymn," the best-known patriotic rhyme of the nineteenth century.[34]

Thanks to Mead's efforts, the property passed first to a Salem collector, Edward Lemon. He filled it with period furniture and, for a fee, entertained there an odd mix of artists, Universalist ministers, bicyclists, and sleighing parties from Boston. In 1923 the automaker Henry Ford bought the Wayside Inn from Lemon's widow, after his agents established the bona fides of the place. "Longfellow slept here at least one night—undoubtedly more," they reported, "on the authority of his daughter Alice who slept in the smaller room adjoining his, as related by her to Mrs. Lemon."[35]

Using Wallace Nutting as an intermediary, Ford acquired enough old furniture of his own to turn it into a museum-hotel-restaurant, in the dry taproom of which he invited wayfaring members of the clergy to dine free of charge (Figure 6.9). The real purpose of his tourist attraction on the highway to Boston, he said, was to give "foreigners who come to us . . . a way of finding out what is the real spirit of this country."[36] As if to show that he meant what he said, Ford opened the Wayside Inn Boys School on the property in 1928 and in its eighteenth-century quarters taught young hyphenated-Americans English and a trade. The virtues of the Founding Fathers they were expected to absorb by sheer propinquity with antiquities during hearty colonial meals and Thursday-night frolics in the inn.

Patriotic societies also believed in the efficacy of exposing all comers, but immigrants in particular, to the spirit of Americanism stored up in the pores of old wood. The Daughters of the American Revolution brought busloads of Italian youngsters to the Wayside Inn on a regular basis as part of an ongoing program of "Americanization" that appeared on the agenda of the Colonial Dames as well.[37] Both societies ran, contributed to the support of, or donated furnishings for historic home museums. In the case of the Paul Revere House in Boston's North End, for example, DAR members joined the Memorial Association formed to work toward its restoration and the local chap-

6.9
The taproom and bar of the Wayside Inn in 1898

ter supplied many of the interior appointments. The lovely Royall House in Medford, Massachusetts, was sold by Miss Kathleen Geer, a member of the Sarah Bradlee Fulton chapter, to a similar association formed in 1908 largely through the efforts of her DAR sisters. When the Scotch-Boardman House in Saugus was purchased by the Society for the Preservation of New England Antiquities, the Daughters' Faneuil Hall Chapter contributed to the purse.[38] Not to be outdone by the ladies, the Sons of the Revolution made rescue of New York's Fraunces' Tavern from the hands of cynical profit-mongers their project for 1907.[39]

The Good Dames of the Colonial Revival

Colonial Days in Old New York was dedicated "to the Society of the Colonial Dames of the State of New York . . . by a loyal and loving member," Alice Morse Earle.[40] Like her other popular books of the 1890s, this one dealt with the terms whereby American life had been lived at the level of the individual household. What kind of clothes did the wives of plump Dutch burghers wear? What were the social customs of those times? Could a profusion of objects sharpen the picture of the past in the mind's eye of the reader, if he or she came to understand the uses of the domestic clutter collected in historic houses, the function of mysterious objects ranging from a candle snuffer to a door hinged in the middle?

These were the questions Earle addressed time and again in a series of volumes absorbed with the private world of the home, the women and children who gathered about its hearth, the industries they practiced, the implements they used, and the social practices observed there. She wrote whole books on old china, dress, colonial children, famous colonial ladies (including Washington's romantic attachments), and the customs and fashions of old New England.[41] And in 1898 she published the first edition of her influential *Home Life in Colonial Days*. Grounded in the kinds of objects displayed in the recreated environments of the new museums, Earle's treatise on seventeenth- and eighteenth-century American households exerted an enormous influence on what the American home of the next several decades would look like.

In her preface Earle thanked Deerfield Memorial Hall, the Bostonian Society, the American Antiquarian Society, and many state historical societies and associations for their assistance, but for "the artistic and photographic reproduction of many of these objects" she also thanked the technicians who had helped her capture historic relics and interiors in groupings suggestive of their actual use.[42] The subtitle of the volume stressed the pictures, described as "photographs, gathered by the author, of real things, works and happenings of olden times." True to that billing, flax- and wool-spinning, silk-braiding, operating the

6.10
"Making Thanksgiving Pies," a typical
arranged "colonial" photograph
published by Alice Morse Earle

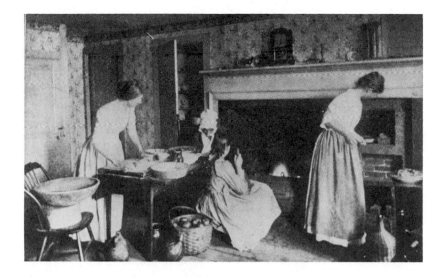

garter loom, candle-dipping, and even the making of Thanksgiving pies in the brick oven let into the side of the hearth were illustrated by photographs of women in colonial garb perched on Windsor chairs and posed against backgrounds of old beams, highboys, and grandfather clocks, where they worked away, oblivious to the camera (Figure 6.10).[43]

The effect of the pictures was somewhat strange: how, one wondered, had the camera operator managed to take that apparatus back in time, to catch America's great-great-grandmothers in the bloom of their once-upon-a-time youth? Earle's plates were as enticing as they were peculiar, however, for the illustrations also gave a clear sense of how colonial bits and pieces from the antique shop could be placed to advantage in room settings, and how milady might look presiding over the historic treasures in her own living room.

The ideology of Alice Morse Earle's domesticity is almost as odd as the imagery in which it is couched. Although she clearly enjoyed a flourishing career and, on the basis of imaginative research into colonial ads for women teachers, hardware dealers, reporters and the like, emphatically disputed the almost universal belief "that the 'business woman' is wholly a product of the nineteenth century," her eye-catching illustrations depicted women as homebound creatures. The characters in Whittier's "Snow-bound," a poem she admired and quoted, were released from the fireside by spring, or a thaw, whereas the women in Earle's plates are perpetual shut-ins, enchanted by the homey contentment of colonial rooms.[44]

There they work daintily, at pretty piecrust tables, at pretty tasks rendered artistic and antiquarian by the passage of time. They are hobbyists, lady-amateurs, women of leisure, and their world is entirely a feminine one; into its murky kitchens no colonial worthy in short pants is invited to stray. Indeed, the feminized colonial home built in words and pictures by Alice Morse Earle might almost serve as a metaphor for the genre of literature of which she was the reigning queen at the turn of the century, when historic house books—compendia of the lore and legend associated with relic-filled sites—were written almost exclusively by women for other women.

From the beginning, Alice Earle had her competitors, women like Anne Hollingsworth Wharton who could also serve up a heady mixture of nostrums on the racial purity of old New Englanders and the love life of George Washington, spiced with charming drawings of the mantelpiece of the Robinson House in Newport.[45] Marion Harland (her given name was Mary Virginia Terhune) and Mary Harrod Northend were the best of the lot. Harland began her career dispensing advice to women. *Common Sense in the Household: A Manual of Practical Housewifery* of 1877 was followed by *Eve's Daughters; or, Common Sense for Maid, Wife, and Mother* of 1882. At the turn of the century, however, she merged her expertise in the mores governing the lives of modern women in the home with the rising national interest in the colonial period. The result was a series of articles in *Harper's Weekly* and *Cosmopolitan,* shortly gathered into a series of illustrated books each of which passed into several editions.

Some Colonial Homesteads and Their Stories of 1897 and its sequel, *More Colonial Homesteads and Their Stories* of 1899, consisted of generous helpings of sentimental storytelling interspersed with photographs of the restored interiors of historic homes on the tourist circuit. Her explanation for the migration of aristocrats to the New World typifies the Harland approach: "Some one of the many delvers in the strata of colonial history may beguile the tedium of statistical labours by computing what proportion of well-born pioneers were driven across the sea by unfortunate love-affairs. The result would show that a Cupid-in-tears, or a spray of Love-lies-bleeding, might be incorporated with the arms of several of our proudest commonwealths."[46] Choice tales, such as Washington's supposed passion for Mary Cary and his courtship of Mary Philipse—"rebel and Republican 'though he was, Washington was a patrician at heart!"—were, of course, reviewed at length. "The stories that make romantic the Colonial Homesteads described [here]," Harland wrote, "were collected during visits paid by myself to these historical shrines."[47] Architecture, then, became a link between the past and the domestic interiors of the present day that were, her readers clearly hoped, still redolent with the borrowed romance of yesteryear; in the room in which Miss Philipse was married, for instance, the author paused to examine a ceiling "elaborately decorated in the much-esteemed 'putty-work' of those times, which is also a popular fad of ours."[48]

Mary Northend was a native of Salem, a descendant of Governor Dummer of colonial days, and blood kin of the Longfellows and the Lowells. She was also one of that breed known in the nineteenth century as "decayed gentlewomen." An invalid for most of her girlhood, "she had reached a mature age, when," according to Northend's biographer, "after various efforts toward self-support" she finally entered "the literary field" around 1903. Her first subjects were the sights to be seen in Salem; she supplemented her prose with snapshots taken with her own Kodak. By the time *Massachusetts Magazine* ran an interview with Miss Northend in 1915, she was a minor celebrity.

A constant contributor to the *Ladies' Home Journal, Outlook,* and *Century*—in 1914 alone, she claimed to have sold 150 articles—she employed a stenographer, several file clerks, and a full-time photographer, and already had two books to her credit. At the urging of her publishers, Northend had written the first of them, *Colonial Homes and Their Furnishings* of 1912, "in seven weeks time, an act made possible only by the existence of the most wonderful collection of negatives in the country, bearing upon colonial and historic homes, which now numbers nearly sixty thousand" (Figure 6.11).[49]

Begun with shots made in Salem by the author herself, this collection was enlarged on summer expeditions into other parts of New England, trips on which Northend was accompanied by a salaried camera operator. She owed her success, she said, to the collectors who welcomed her into their houses, especially "the citizens of my

6.11
A Mary Northend view of an inviting dining room doorway with George and Martha portraits, a plate rail bearing antique china, and, over Washington's left shoulder, a Wallace Nutting "colonial" photograph of a similar interior

home town, Salem. Had they not thrown open their homes for my inspection and reproduction, I would have been nothing." Her admirers thought that the debt was a mutual one: "Modest and grateful as the little lady is, had not her own perseverance and hope won for her sufficient evidences of success-attaining ability, Salem pride would not have allowed mediocre efforts to have given publicity to its firesides; but now the owners of those beautiful Salem mansions are as proud of the fame and authority of their author as they are of her subject matter."[50]

In the very years in which Mary Northend was embarking upon her career as a neocolonialist, Salem was awakening to its own status as a center for antiquarians, collectors, and dreamers in search of picturesque scenes from the long-ago. The witch spoons are one significant measure of Salem's pivotal role in the colonial revival. The other is the suite of period rooms—a kitchen ca. 1750, a parlor and a bedroom ca. 1800—installed by George Francis Dow on the second floor of Salem's Essex Institute in 1907.[51] Although Melinda Young Frye has recently disputed the primacy of the colonial suite at the Essex Institute, citing as precedents the "primitive Bedchamber" recreated in 1880 at Deerfield and a colonial kitchen installed in a private home in Lyme, Connecticut, in 1906, the picture of Early American life presented by Dow did shape Mary Northend's vision of the past.[52]

Three-sided affairs with a fourth wall of glass, the period rooms in Salem were not duplicates of particular old chambers but reproductions, instead, of the typicality of colonial parlors, bedrooms, and kitchens. Whereas it was difficult (as the ladies of Mount Vernon knew) to track down all the objects that once embellished a given historic site, it was relatively simple to assemble a variety of artifacts loosely related by function and by a period that might take in the several generations resident under one roof. Besides, environments recreated with archaeological precision leaned toward a certain sparseness and formality of appearance, often evident in today's public, largely ceremonial chambers of state. In Dow's hands the period room became a cluttered and homey place, looking for all the world as if the colonial goodwife whose gloves lay forgotten on a settle might rush back to retrieve them at any second. The transient effects, the litter, and the true-to-life mismatch of artifacts that avoided the impression of sterile grandeur made the rooms look more like the home of a Salem resident of 1907—an avid collector, Miss Northend lived in the "quaint old side street of Lynde in Salem . . . surrounded by her inherited and accumulated treasures"—than like a typical museum display.[53]

The interiors shown in Mary Northend's photographs resemble the period rooms at the Essex Institute in that lived-in quality. And taking them to achieve that effect was no easy matter. She often spent "from an hour to an hour and a half in one room, arranging small and insignificant details, to make a complete whole."[54] The results were worth the trouble. In her first book, the picture of the "colonial fireplace" in Gove House (on Lynde Street, Salem) with a portrait of Washington decorating the chimneypiece shows the beginnings of a personal collection of Washingtoniana and the legs of comfy chairs that carry the imagination out of the black-and-white photograph, into the hospitable room and the home that shelters it. The Sheraton chair of ca. 1795 that she calls a "Martha Washington" sits for its portrait wearing a frowzy cretonne slipcover. The eighteenth-century four-poster in Middleton House shares the room with a spinning wheel placed at the foot of the bed for effect and with pictures draped in palm fronds, another affectation of the late nineteenth-century decorator.[55]

6.12
Mary Northend photograph of a "colonial fireplace" in the Dorothy Quincy House, Quincy, Massachusetts

Unlike the photographs staged by Alice Morse Earle, pictures that set up a confusion between past and present by putting costumed ladies in old-fashioned settings, the Northend shots are unapologetically of the moment. They are pictures of modern homes in which heirlooms and old woodwork are shown up to advantage, and they are full of visual tips for antiquers wondering what on earth to do with a recently acquired spinning wheel (Figure 6.12).

Northend's forte as a writer was her ability to explain the "indescribable charm" the colonial setting held for the collectors then scouring New England for *Mayflower* relics. Such treasure-hunters, she correctly surmised, would be her readers:

The wonderfully good collections of antiques for which Salem is noted was of great interest to me, being owned by personal friends who kindly consented to allow me for the first time to go through their homes and pick out the cream of their inheritance. If the readers are half as interested in these objects as I have become,—growing enthusiastic in the work through the valuable pieces found,—they will enjoy the pictures of colonial furnishings, many of which cannot be duplicated in any other collection of antiques. Family bits, wonderful old Lowestoft, and other treasures are included, all brought over in the holds of cumbersome ships, at the time when the commerce of Salem was at high tide.[56]

Among the private dwellings photographed for her second book, *Historic Houses of New England,* Northend also inserted shots of museum rooms in such shrines as the Longfellow House and the House of the Seven Gables. But even these views are domesticated for the camera. A droopy fern obscures the lines of a rare console in the parlor of the House of the Seven Gables, and a vase of flowers on a linen cloth adorns the dining room table: these are touches suggestive of life and habitation, if only by Miss Emmerton's paying guests.[57] Minimizing the differences between the house museum and the private home, Northend arrived at her rationale for studying historical remains in the first place: "Houses such as these possess the greatest charm—

ancestral homes that have descended from generation to generation in the same family since their founding. . . . Through pictured homes like these one is given a deeper interest in the early life of our country and realizes more than ever before what the colonial period stood for in home building."[58]

In the 1920s Mary Northend actually wrote a practical manual on the art of home decoration (dedicated to her friend Bruce Barton, the man who thought that Christ and the modern-day business executive were a lot alike.) By then, "the Colonial house," she noted, had "come into its own" again. That style was "wrapped inseparably with the history of our country," and because it was democratic, it was suitable for "either mansion or cottage." Her advice in the matter of coloni-alizing the American home leaned heavily on her own experience with creating, or finding, particularly "artistic groupings" in the eclectic New England interiors of the past twenty years that were furnished with new things and old ones from "great grandmother's hoard."[59] It also drew on the strengths of her archive of negatives. Thus colonial doorways, overrepresented in the collection because of connotations of invitation and mystery—"Is it not symbolic of the most dramatic scenes in life? The coming of the bride, the christening party, the bitter end of a quarrel, the return of the prodigal"—merited a chapter of their own, as did fireplaces, which "arouse . . . tender visions of homely joys and pleasant commonplaces elevated to a romantic plane and endowed with witching charm by the ruddy aura of lambent flames."[60]

The pictures of colonial portals inspired her *Historic Doorways of Old Salem* of 1926, her last major work, and the hearth became the centerpiece of *We Visit Old Inns* of 1925, a book recounting stories told around the fire at the Wayside Inn.[61] Lacking the sense of novelty and discovery that her first attempts at integrating colonial culture with modern living conveyed, these late works preached colonialism to the converted, to persons who had already decorated their fire-places with portraits of Washington or old samplers mourning his demise. "In addition to the fun of hunting out these different antiques," Northend remarked with a bogus air of surprise after mentioning the Paul Revere lanterns on display in the Wayside Inn, "we learned to our amazement the story of furniture, glass and china, many pieces of which are still found not only in colonial homes but those of modern-day architecture. It is the grouping of these old historic pieces with present-day designs that give[s] to our houses a most distinctive charm."[62]

Nor was that elusive quality called "charm" confined to the firesides and the hospitable entryways of spanking new neocolonial houses on the Atlantic seaboard:

6.13
A Mary Northend photograph, taken in the gardens of the Ward House in Salem, showing the colonial guides

On the western coast, particularly in and about Los Angeles, there are whole districts of the most adorable Colonial cottages. For the most part, these are small, having but one story, with exteriors of white clapboards or creamy white stucco, with green blinds. Oftentimes, the door, with its divided sidelights and fan-shaped transom has before it a raised red brick terrace large enough to accommodate chairs and the entrance is ornamented with an arched trellis of white over which the crimson rambler or creamy pink rose is trained.

To drive down an avenue between rows of feathery pepper trees and tropical palms, lined with homes of this type leads one to realize that at last Americans have come to differentiate between what is really good and what is bad in architecture.[63]

Wallace Nutting's Snapshots of History

Under titles such as "The Coming Out of Rosa" and "Nantucket Gossip," Wallace Nutting was offering hand-colored photographs of colonial doorways wreathed in rosebuds for sale from his restored farmhouse in Southbury, Connecticut, as early as 1910 or 1911, when his list already ran to some two hundred subjects.[64] Apart from the faint blush of color, the main difference between Nutting's doorways and Northend's was that Nutting's pictures included women in period dress miming conversation or colonial comings and goings.[65]

Alice Earle had demonstrated the use of colonial apparatus through photographs of costumed models who wove or spun. George Francis Dow dressed resident manager Sarah Symonds and her assistants in period costume to guide visitors through the newly restored Ward House in Salem in 1912.[66] And Mary Northend staged a number of photographs showing "Puritan girls" at their leisure in the gardens of the Ward House and youngsters in satins and periwigs at holiday costume parties elsewhere doing the minuet or pretending to spin (Figure 6.13).[67] All these pictures were rather self-conscious affairs, however: hairpieces were askew, dresses drooped, flivvers were parked at the curb just off-camera, and the enjoyment of the scenes hinged on the pleasurable realization that it was all a game, being played by real, live people.

The "Wallace Nutting Pictures," colored by the so-called Nutting Girls, signed by the master, and shipped to art-goods stores by the thousand from his workshops in Southbury, Saugus, and Framingham, were far more solemn in effect and intent. Meant to be used as works of art on the walls of middle-class Colonial Revival homes, Nutting's products were of two principal types. First, there were the landscape pictures, always taken with a view toward the sentiment conveyed by places long under the gentle dominion of the farmer: old stone walls crumble away, avenues of ancient oaks flank a narrow road, apple trees nod under the burden of their blossoms. It was during his years as a minister, in 1897, that Wallace Nutting began to photograph such outdoor scenes, as a hobby. In 1904, in early middle age, he retired from the pulpit to a Connecticut farmhouse to make a living from his pastime.[68] In his first catalogue of offerings, issued in 1912, he particularly commended for a bridal offering a rural scene called "Honeymoon Drive": dappled with sunshine, a peaceful road overarched by a bower of apple blossoms meanders into the distance beside a stone wall. As John Freeman, a specialist in the decorative arts, observes, "One of the most popular wedding gifts of the first third of our century was a Wallace Nutting print."[69] In 1933 Nutting himself estimated that his works were hanging in ten million American homes.[70]

The second type of Nutting print was the period interior. These he called his "personals" or his "colonials," and he began to take them in 1904, almost by accident. When rain forced him indoors one day, Mrs. Nutting suggested that he stage a scene around a few antiques. He was so pleased with his success in recreating early American life that he began to collect furniture and restore historic houses to serve as backgrounds for such pictures. By the time World War I broke out, he owned a chain of five house museums in New England, open to the public at twenty-five cents a head.

Fully one-third of the inventory listed in his first catalogue consisted of pictures of women in long dresses and bonnets trading news, reading, or standing under a trellis in a framing doorway. Some stood outdoors, with their historic houses in the background. Most kept to kitchens and parlors clogged with colonial bric-a-brac (Figure 6.14). Available in sizes to suit any spare wall space, the smallest ones (5″ × 7″) cost $1.25 and the biggest (20″ × 40″) were $20.00, mounts included, but the proportions of the prints were very often long and narrow, to reinforce the sense of womblike enclosure and protection in the snug, low-ceilinged rooms depicted. He urged his agents to stock them in quantity. "The average dealer will wish about one-third

6.14
A typical Wallace Nutting "colonial"

6.15
A pseudo-Nutting pin tray, a salesman's sample for Fred Thompson, proprietor of "Pictures—Oddities," of Portland, Maine

of his order in 'Colonial' pictures," Nutting advised. "To give the finest variety, some of these should be interiors. . . . The balance should be strong in apple blossoms (for weddings)."

Speaking in the third person, as was his wont, he also supplied a rationale for the "personals":

These figure subjects were conceived by Mr. Nutting for the sake of preserving the historical charm of the life of our fathers. Thus we present some two-hundred old-fashioned or "colonial" themes, showing old-fashioned girls and grandsires at the center of our ancestral life, that is the hearth, and at the hospitable and beautiful front doors, and on the winding stairs and old settles of our ancestors. Some imitations of this work are now being brought forward[;] in some cases posing and titles have been copied as nearly as the law will allow.[71]

The popularity of his scenes is, in fact, best demonstrated by the large number of copies, adaptations, and outright forgeries still in circulation today (Figure 6.15).[72] The skullduggery inspired by the "colonials" is not without a certain ironic charm, however, since Nutting frequently touted his own, authentic products on the basis of their innate "honesty." Honesty was one of the tenets of the arts-and-crafts ideology to which he and any number of other defenders of the unpremeditated directness, simplicity, and purported ethical upright-ness of colonial artifacts subscribed. According to this gospel, much in vogue among American designers and social workers in the last quarter of the nineteenth century, factory-made gimcracks were inferior to hand-wrought products bearing the mark of the maker's hand. In practice, however, a colonial chair cranked out by a furniture factory in Grand Rapids, since it looked a great deal more "honest" than one made by the same machines in the manner of Louis XIV, was a more acceptable addition to a moral household.

Although he would in time change his mind, when Nutting issued his first catalogue of reproduction furniture in 1922 he rejected imported mahogany and cabriole legs on the basis of overrefinement and championed the oak furniture of the "pilgrim century" for its native crudity: the traditional Puritan ethic and the national identity (both endangered propositions in the eyes of conservatives) were to be protected and revived by equipping the American home with moral oaken tables and the proper pictures. Thus Wallace Nutting was careful to inform his retail outlets that his photographs in the colonial style "produce scenes that are historically correct and have charm which no meretricious background can give. . . . He never uses models for posing, but always persons who still live in the midst of the dignified and beautiful surroundings of our fathers."[73]

Nutting was altogether too clever a salesman to offend potential customers by bursting into tirades in the midst of the placid generalities that made up the texts of the illustrated gift books through which a market for his pictures was created. But from time to time he would break off a tribute to old roads "eloquent with the echoes of ancient marches to liberty and light and power" to fulminate against the awfulness of contemporary life. In *Massachusetts Beautiful,* the travel volume containing some of his most famous nature studies—these include a view of Whittier's home adrift in a field of grass, the "great Wayside Oak" outside the inn in Sudbury, and his own shop in Framingham seen through a screen of trees and titled "Massachusetts, There She Stands!"—modern cities, skyscrapers, immigrants, Boston Irish politicians, and roadside advertising signs are all vigorously deplored:

New York is frankly constructed of pyramids of masonry and the writer is so averse to such Babel structures that the work of an etcher like [Joseph] Pennell cannot lure him to believe in their beauty. . . . Within Boston very little remains of the earliest days. The Paul Revere House has been rescued but such was its condition and such is its setting that it loses much of the nameless charm afforded by mellowed age and freedom from encroaching modern edifices.[74]

On the other hand, he has nothing but praise for old fireplaces and doorways, the private, interior iconography he shares with others of his tribe similarly devoted to the regeneration of American virtue through the restoration of the American home. Beneath all the mystic claptrap and sonorous phrases, Nutting sees the very primitivism of the hearth as a defiant symbol of order in the face of change—the order of the generations, uniting old-stock Americans with their Pilgrim roots; the orderly relations of family member to family member, and family to the outside world; the architectural order that makes the arch above the fireplace the foundation for the rooms above; the order of simple chairs and tables grouped around the fire for warmth and hospitality:

Our word "hearth" goes back to the roots of our language. . . . Its play of colors and fantastic shapes, its spit-fire and its glowing embers are invitations to dream. Back of this, of course, lies the completest chain of heredity known to human beings. The oldest of all sentiments has grown at the hearth into human consciousness. Warmth and protection, a sense of home, the memories of every progression of age in a single human life and in all life are gathered into the . . . web of unconscious memory. From the hearth came the savory dish after a day of fierce battling with wild beasts and wilder elements. The earliest waking of knowledge and dawning affection were born at the hearth side. The boy there learned the lore of his tribe. There the family councils were held. In their old age our fathers sat huddled in the chimney corner, fondling their grandchildren upon their knees.

The hearth was the focus of the house. In its modern significance there is a fine flavor. It was the fountain, the center, the core of life. It was the glowing source whence emanated all humane civilizing currents, and there at last our fathers were gathered to their fathers.[75]

Even though his pictures of grizzled "fathers" and "grandsires" huddled by the fire are by no means as numerous as his references to these worthies would imply, one of the best-loved Nutting "colonials," taken in 1917, showed a pretty miss of Revolutionary times, "a young lady who perhaps would not like her name mentioned." She was seated on a high-backed settle near the hearth in the company of one of the photographer's aged relatives, a skinny old gentleman with a little tuft of beard. A pair of crude turned chairs with rush seats, a wrought-iron candlestand, two braided rugs (Mrs. Nutting took charge of that department of the family business), and a Tudor court-cupboard complete the ensemble. Taken in the hall chamber of his restored Iron Works House in Saugus, the photograph served to illustrate "Pine Settle, Carver Chairs, Roasting Jack, [and] Candle Box" in the second edition of Nutting's famous *Furniture of the Pilgrim Century* of 1924, the perennial bible of decorators and antiquers. But the print was also available in a hand-tinted version under the title "Knitting for Uncle Sam," a reference to the women all over America who, thanks to the Red Cross, were busy "knitting socks for soldiers" in the Great War.[76] No embryonic flapper ever knit a sock in Wallace Nutting's version of the American home. No jaded career girl dared to swig a cocktail on the premises. If the nation took his pictorial advice, the doughboy would come marching home to find family and loved ones waiting at the door or gathered about the quiet hearth, just as they

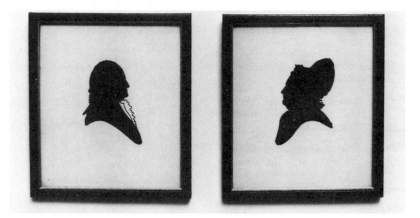

were in his mind's eye: gentle, warm, happy, eternally serene. Nothing ever changed in Nuttingland, except, perhaps, the master's prices.

At the peak of his influence, in the decade just after the war, Wallace Nutting Inc. could supply every want of the home-loving revivalist: copies of old furniture, in oak, maple, or even mahogany; colonialized versions of modern pieces, such as telephone stands, swivel chairs, file cabinets; rugs; framed "personals" to complement mixed roomfuls of family treasures, brand-new colonial heirlooms, and other samples of Nutting's wares; paired silhouettes of colonial couples; notepaper; foot-scrapers, door-knockers, and fireplace tools (Figure 6.16). As the acknowledged leader of the movement's folksier side, he warned weekend antique-hunters against fakes in the pages of the *Saturday Evening Post* and pestered Henry Ford with gratuitous advice about the restoration of the Wayside Inn.

That was at the beginning of the colonial mania that swept the country in the 1920s. But as a genuine expert and a collector of some discrimination, he also sold his own accumulation of seventeenth-century furniture to no less discriminating a buyer than J. P. Morgan (who gave it to the Wadsworth Atheneum). And just as the tide of mass enthusiasm for things colonial finally began to ebb, Nutting produced the elegant armchairs ordered by John D. Rockefeller, Jr., for the Council Chamber of the recreated capitol at Williamsburg in 1933.[77]

Brand-New Colonial Relics

Nutting was by no means the first to manufacture copies of colonial furniture priced for the average pocketbook. Some firms, makers of specialty items for the most part, never abandoned old, traditional designs that began to look like neocolonial ones as the revival picked up steam. With no fanfare at all, for instance, the Wakefield Rattan Company of Boston was selling cradles for babies in the 1890s that resembled the Peregrine White relic widely exhibited at turn-of-the-century expositions: the type had survived from the days of the Pilgrims in a conservative craft milieu.[78]

Among firms prepared to produce completely new designs in order to capitalize on the renewed interest in the seventeenth and eighteenth centuries, those that made small items of occasional furniture were able to introduce new styles more quickly and with less risk of ruin should the taste for the colonial prove short-lived. Leo Austrian & Company of Chicago, a factory specializing in hat racks and music cabinets, unveiled around 1905 a hall stand of quartered oak loosely based on the shape of a ladder-back chair. Even though that old-fashioned touch was almost lost in a welter of turnings and scrollwork with less precise connections to the past, the $20 piece would in its day have been taken for colonial.[79]

The Piedmont Red-Cedar Chest Company of Statesville, North Carolina, did not leave the character of its products in any doubt, however. Introduced by a glowing testimonial from J. D. Rockefeller, "the multimillionaire, President of Standard Oil," its 1910 catalogue was full of aromatic storage chests for woolens distinguished the one from the other mainly by size, number of drawers or compartments, and the use or omission of decorative metal banding and studs. But the various models have wonderful, colonial names and chatty captions describing their colonial credentials. The Patrick Henry Old-Fashioned model is "a pure Colonial chest, representing strength and stability, and built to last for many generations. It's the kind your great grandmother knew all about." Benjamin Franklin, Miles Standish, James Monroe, John Alden, Martha Washington, Nelly Custis, Alexander Hamilton, Virginia Dare, Priscilla, Captain Kidd, John Hancock, Thomas Jefferson, Lafayette, Roger Williams, Ethan Allen, Dolley (*always* spelled "Dolly" in the 1920s and 1930s) Madison, Paul Revere, Longfellow, Nathaniel Hawthorne, John Adams, Betsy Ross, the *Mayflower,* and Janice Meredith, colonial heroine of Paul Leicester Ford's 1899 novel of the same name, all lent their monikers to tall chests and short ones, some Sheraton in feeling, others more hazy in pedigree, each exemplifying "the honest craftsmanship of furniture of the Colonial period," every one a piece worthy of being "handed down as an heirloom to future generations."

The pièce de résistance was the George Washington Highboy (Figure 6.17). It cost $116.75 if adorned with copper strips and slightly less plain. But when the pair of short drawers at the top was omitted and wooden pulls substituted for brass or cut-glass ones, the George Washington became the Alexander Hamilton Old-Fashioned Colonial

Highboy, for a mere $82.25: "The design of this [George Washington] Highboy is noteworthy, being constructed along the clean, plain, straight lines that made the furniture of that master craftsman, Sheraton, so famous and popular. It is colonial in effect, and embodies the plainness of design, sturdiness and honest craftsmanship that made furniture of the Colonial period so beautiful and everlasting."[80]

A Cedar Chest Pays for Itself in What it Actually Saves

No. 135. GEORGE WASHINGTON HIGHBOY

This Highboy is made throughout of Solid Southern Red Cedar. No other wood is used in its construction but Red Cedar,—even the drawer bottoms, sides and backs are of Red Cedar. Finished in either natural or mahogany, hand-rubbed and polished. The mahogany shade is medium dark, and given a soft, piano polish finish, and will tone with any shade of mahogany furniture. Our natural finish is much the same shade as Tuna mahogany and has a soft, rich, piano polish finish. The design of this Highboy is noteworthy, being constructed along the clean, plain, straight lines that made the furniture of that master craftsman, Sheraton, so famous and popular. It

is Colonial in effect, and embodies the plainness of design, sturdiness and honest craftsmanship that made furniture of the Colonial period so beautiful and everlasting. This Highboy has six capacious drawers, graduating in size, the smallest being at the top. The two short drawers at top will be found convenient for storing many small, necessary articles, and the simplicity of design is a relief from over ornamentation, which is now so common. No. 135 is heavily bound with wide bands of dull finish copper, and studded with old-fashioned copper rivets, while No. 136 is perfectly plain and without copper trimmings. It is one of the finest pieces of cedar furniture ever designed, and material, construction and finish are the very best. It's built to last not for a few years, but for generations, and to be handed down as an heirloom. Moth, mice, dust and damp-proof. In the construction of this Highboy we

have made a regular frame from 2-inch stock, and run a panel in the frame between each drawer. This panel forms an absolutely dust-proof partition, and means that the drawers are entirely separated from each other by this dust-proof panel partition. It forms the most rigid and strongest possible frame. Fitted with brass casters and sanitary legs, brass sockets on end of leg, Roman gold finish. Each drawer has a strong cylinder lock, and the cedar or cut-glass knobs add a pleasing touch to the decoration. Inside dimensions of top drawers are: Width, 20¼ in.; depth, 20 in.; height, 6 in. Inside dimensions of next two drawers are: Width, 43 in.; depth, 20 in.; height, 7 in. Inside dimensions of two lower drawers are: Width, 43 in.; depth, 20 in.; height, 8 in. Outside dimensions, Nos. 135-136: Height, 56 in.; width, 50 in.; depth, 24 in. **$116.75**

No. 136. GEORGE WASHINGTON HIGHBOY

The height includes casters, and measurement is from floor to top of Highboy.

The large drawers are deep enough to accommodate a lady's hat without crushing plumes or trimming.

Either No. 135 or No. 136 Highboy can be furnished dull instead of with polished finish when desired. Customer has option of mahogany or natural finish. For No. 135 we recommend natural finish, as it harmonizes perfectly with the copper bands. We recommend dark mahogany finish for No. 136. The grain of cedar closely resembles mahogany.

The description of No. 135 also applies to No. 136. No. 136 is exactly the same Highboy as No. 135, only it is without copper trimmings, and has old-fashioned cut-glass knobs — or can furnish with solid cast brass knobs, if preferred. These cut-glass knobs give it a unique appearance, and make it distinctly Colonial.

6.17
Pages from a furniture trade catalogue of 1910, describing several models of a George Washington Highboy

It exemplified, said the copywriters at Piedmont, a brand-new trend in American taste: "Furniture with straight lines, sturdy and substantial, without unnecessary ornamentation, is being appreciated by the American people more and more."[81]

By 1915, when a Chicago business issued a catalogue called *Things Colonial, Being a Few Illustrations of the Reproductions Made and Sold by W. K. Cowan & Co.*, the colonial style had ceased to be a novelty. The text describing the features of the moderately priced line boasted of Cowan's ability "to undertake the complete furnishing of a house in the Colonial style" and invited further inquiries "on this subject" from interested parties. Although the company specialty was said to be the adjustment of "the Colonial style to articles of furniture not in use in Colonial times, . . . adaptations in consonance with the period while suited to modern surroundings and modern needs," the only indisputably colonial example among the assorted Greek Revival and eclectic specimens reproduced was a slavish $150 copy of the much-illustrated writing desk used by George Washington in New York in 1789 and preserved in the City Hall there. "The 'Father of his Country,'" read the squib below, "has certainly given us the ideal library table. Fourteen commodious drawers, a spacious top and the shelves at the ends leave little to be desired."[82]

The young Franklin Delano Roosevelt, in his capacity as assistant secretary of the navy, was entrusted with the task of refitting the U.S.S. *George Washington* to carry Woodrow Wilson to the peace conference at Versailles in December of 1918. Taking his cue from the name of the ship, he decided that the décor should be colonial and personally scoured the New York department stores for suitable accessories. His idea was not as peculiar as it might appear. Several of the World War I troop ships refitted as passenger liners after the armistice were given colonial staterooms and public facilities to "express throughout, Democracy, as against Imperialism." Because the style was both inexpensive and emblematic in "its simple character . . . [of] American development," ships like the S.S. *Hawkeye State* put to sea with colonial tearooms and paneled men's bars featuring "motifs used in the architecture which recall Washington's house at Mount Vernon—the mantel and the window treatment."[83]

In 1918 the big New York stores were also heavily involved with the colonial revival. Wallace Nutting's collection of Windsor chairs and most of the eighteenth-century mahogany pieces displayed in his now-defunct house museums were sold off by John Wanamaker's when the Society for the Preservation of New England Antiquities failed to meet the asking price, and other leading stores had their own heavily promoted colonial nooks and ells, full of reproductions.[84] In one such cozy recess, Roosevelt bought a copy of the desk that stood in George Washington's study at Mount Vernon and dispatched it to the ship for the president's use.

6.18
Olin Dows's rendition of Franklin D. Roosevelt sitting at his George Washington desk in the office wing of the Roosevelt Library, Hyde Park, New York.

6.19
A Martha Washington Sewing Cabinet offered for sale in the 1923 Sears, Roebuck catalogue

Some time later, after the defeat of Wilson's Fourteen Points, when the U.S.S. *Washington* was decommissioned and its fittings sold at auction at the Navy Yard, Secretary Roosevelt notified the president of the sale, but receiving no reply, attended and bought the desk for his own. He installed it in his study at Hyde Park, where it may have helped to inspire his wife's interest in making similar pieces (Figure 6.18). At any rate, in the 1920s Eleanor Roosevelt also sold her Val-Kill colonial furniture through the same New York City department stores in which her husband had once shopped for pieces sufficiently American in appearance to grace the cabin of the president of the United States.[85]

Franklin Roosevelt's preference for colonial desks was slightly ahead of its time. In 1916 Peck & Hills of New York supplied Louis XIV, Louis XV, and Louis XVI—along with Adam, Queen Anne, William and Mary, and Charles II—furniture to those wishing to stay well within the accepted bounds of good taste. "Historic designs are those that have stood the test of time," the firm allowed, and "a knowledge of Period Styles in Furniture is essential to those who would correctly and properly furnish a home." Native designs, not always in favor, were currently correct: "In addition to the styles mentioned above, we now have the Colonial, the Arts and Crafts, and the Mission, which originated in the Spanish Missions of California. These styles are purely America."[86]

Despite all the fuss about adding some down-home touches to the canon of approved foreign modes, the Peck & Hills catalogue contained few actual examples of American styles, and most of those were designs not for impressive suites of parlor furniture but for little sewing cabinets, the lightweight, portable stands used at a chair-arm to hold needles and thread for darning. The cheapest, called the Betsy Ross Cabinet, was a plain, hexagonal drum with a single drawer elevated on stocky rails. The fanciest—the Virginia Lee—featured many tiny drawers supported by an elaborately turned frame.

The Martha Washington Sewing Cabinet, a tambour model perched on spindly legs, occupied the intermediate price range and, unlike the others, was not inconsistent in shape and spirit with historic pieces actually associated with that lady.[87] In 1923 the Sears Roebuck catalogue offered a slightly larger, slightly less elegant Martha Washington Sewing Cabinet, an imitation of the Peck & Hills design, to a far-flung mail order clientele at a cut-rate price. In birch mahogany finish, the high-style piece sold for $19. The knockoff was only $15.85 in mahogany and a dime more in a walnut finish (Figure 6.19).[88]

And so it went. Pieces enjoying a great modern vogue, such as the chaise longue, were often the first to be colonialized. The Danersk line, manufactured by a consortium of Scottish cabinetmakers and Austrian benchmen working in the Carolina mountains, featured whole roomfuls of "quaint painted furniture of the Colonial days that brought charm into the New England home," including such a daybed, available in the older "Venetian" as well as the newer colonial version.[89] By the middle to late 1920s, however, the sorts of reminiscent pieces once described as "Early New England" had been superseded by a vast range of items adhering faithfully to distinguished prototypes. The Virginia Craftsmen Inc. boasted of "the exclusive privilege of reproducing the historic antiques of Thomas Jefferson's famous home—Monticello" when those exemplars continued to be useful in the contemporary home or office. And when, as in the case of heavy executive furniture and typing stands, designers "conceded that there were no desks of this type in Colonial times," they undertook to supply them only after remarks calculated to expose such hybrids for the solecisms they were.

But frazzled businessmen, or a harried housewife demanding a colonial cabinet for her Edison phonograph (Figure 6.20), might be forgiven their naiveté given the popularity, the appeal, the snob value, and the almost contagious restfulness of the colonial style:

Authentic, Hand-made Reproductions of the furniture known to us as "Antique" have a definite place in the decorative scheme of the modern home. In producing the charming pieces illustrated in this catalogue our craftsmen have followed the same ideals that motivated the Colonial craftsmen. They have striven for beauty, for character, for utility. They have re-created for you the atmosphere of stately yesterdays. Most of us in this modern age willingly confess our fondness and admiration for the quiet, restful charm which seems a part of every Colonial interior. Few there are who are able, by virtue of inherited antiques, to produce, in their own environments, this same beauty. But now, with reproductions that are minutely faithful to originals long admired, every house will find it possible to echo a true Early American atmosphere—inexpensively. [And] it is interesting that today, in the accelerations of a machine age, there are men who are willing to devote their skill and their sympathy to the creation of hand-made furniture.[90]

6.20
Period cabinets for the Edison phonograph were fashionable in the 1920s.

Little by little, however, the associational value of a specific artifact used by Washington or owned by Jefferson was displaced by the authority of style itself, subdivided into aesthetic categories and attributed to certain celebrated craftsmen by connoisseurs and by a new breed of curators more concerned with the lines of a cabinet than with its role in the life of a famous American. With choice pieces copied from important orginals, the Century Furniture Company of Grand Rapids catered openly to the needs of those whose ancestors had neglected to leave them roomfuls of colonial booty: a Windsor chair after a "rare example . . . from the collection of Ex-Congressman Hayes, of Lexington, Massachusetts," and a wing chair of similarly "rare design" taken from an original "in Kittery, Maine," were included in the 1927 collection, but they were overshadowed by several costly and impressive articles commended for derivation from signed works by Duncan Phyfe and William Savery in the collection of the new American Wing of the Metropolitan Museum.[91]

Building Modern Colonial Houses

Architectural design of the period follows the same pattern, although the early revival of colonial elements by the builders of exposition pavilions dating back to 1876 meant that architects were somewhat in advance of furnituremakers in codifying the style.[92] A so-called colonial bungalow built in 1908 in Corsicana, Texas, with a Mission interior, was constructed again in Englewood, New Jersey, with "a strictly simple Colonial interior, . . . all the trim . . . white, with mahogany doors, old-style Colonial mantlepieces with open brick fireplaces, oak floors in the main rooms and a generally complete eighteenth century aspect." A bizarre merger of the Greek temple and the Asiatic house form, this bungalow was colonial mainly in its militant homeyness, the fanlight in the pediment over the front door, and the architect's unswerving belief that he had produced an example of the "style which we moderns call 'Colonial' simply because our 'first settlers' were so fond of building in it."[93] But the plans for complete colonial houses, cottages, and bungalows published by M. L. Keith several years later already showed the gambrel roofs, diamond-pane casement windows, turned balusters, and regular room arrangements that, while oddly combined in some examples, would constitute the vocabulary of Suburban Subdivision Colonial from 1912 until Levittown and beyond.[94]

Manuals for those about to build new houses—*Inexpensive Homes of Individuality* of 1912 was one such architectural guide—recognized a defined "Colonial Revival" style as one of the options facing the potential owner. Although its Georgian manifestations were deemed "out of place on wild cliffs," there were few other locations for which the ancestral style, so closely associated with the social and the aesthetic character of the American home, was judged wanting.[95] A 1913 text, *Colonial Architecture for Those About to Build,* stressed the need for householders to select the proper subspecies of the colonial manner in order to express their own ideals: the symmetry of a Georgian manse, for instance, would bespeak a sedate temperament and clarity of vision, whereas the Gothic irregularities of the Puritan cottage "abounding in nooks" hinted at a more romantic, mysterious bent of mind.

The same rules of expressiveness that governed the use of colonialisms on the part of the businessman at his leisure were extended to cover his office, the public facilities he frequented, and even his place of worship. "Individuals and corporations, who contemplate building and are sensible of the merits of the Colonial style, are presented in this volume with the best examples of that style from a locality that possesses, of domestic, religious and governmental architecture, examples inferior to none," the authors declared, as they prepared to analyze historic shrines of the Midatlantic states in search of design features useful to the contemporary builder.[96]

Joseph Everett Chandler's *Colonial House* of 1916 used old buildings as models too, but as cautionary examples of what to avoid: "There is at the present time a fortunately widespread and increasingly intelligent interest in the so-called Colonial Style, and particularly in its application to home-building. This book has therefore been compiled in the hope that it may be of use to those who admire the old examples and who wish to avoid in their possible building operations, certain short-comings recognizable in much of the supposedly in-the-old-vein modern work."[97] The omission of closets and modern conveniences in the name of historical accuracy was the sort of foolishness that Chandler, himself a builder of colonial houses, found distasteful. He also railed against the inept architect who, having botched such a commission badly, calls the results "Georgian" instead: "Better than Colonial, . . . more virile and compelling!"

The day was over when it sufficed for Washington to have slept in a bed, looked in a mirror, or dined in a house to lend it distinction forever, Chandler declared. Since 1876, "the variousness of the 'colonial'" had indeed been rediscovered with some exactitude, and good architects, like good museum curators, were expected to differentiate among periods, geographic areas, and known builders when matching a house to the personality of the client. And not every client was a candidate for a historic house:

The Colonial type of house is not for every one. For this much thanks! The houses of our forefathers bespoke a fearless honesty characteristic of themselves,—a lack of pretense and sham, but with a diffident expression of a love for the beautiful which, if somewhat severe and subdued, was their rightful heritage, and made their homes express the limitations forced on them by the country of their adoption. It would, however, be well to-day if the rank and file of our nation could return in marked degree toward this simplicity and again have a life approximating the sane life of our Colonial forebears.[98]

Chandler understood old buildings in the technical as well as the spiritual sense. Much praised for painstaking restorations at the Old State House in Boston and elsewhere, he exemplified a new, scientific attitude toward the artifactual remains of the past that stood in obvious contrast to the hearts-and-flowers approach of Marion Harland. Whereas the latter was apt to describe a doorway by an anecdote— preferably one featuring George Washington and a well-born lady— without any reference to its mode of construction, Chandler's followers were just as likely to treat Mount Vernon as the exception to the rule that true colonial houses seldom employed the two-story column so common in the Greek Revival period.[99]

Harold Eberlein's 1915 *Architecture of Colonial America,* a work clearly written under the new dispensation, used Mary Northend's romantic photographs of cozy hearths to prove that "architecture is crystallized history" of an epoch of hardship and unremitting toil, the rigors of which were amply demonstrated by the cumbersome technology of baking bread in a colonial oven. He came away from his confrontation with the New England kitchen "with a keener veneration . . . [for] the men and women of by-gone years," but he still persisted in looking for functional explanations for details others misused and romanticized. The decorative cuts on shutters currently nailed up beside the windows of modern homes once admitted air and light when they were folded across the openings; far from indicating some star-crossed affair, the stars, hearts, half-moons, and pots of flowers cut into the shutters told Eberlein a tale of how to cool a hot room gracefully in a properly built neocolonial home.[100]

By the time Joseph Jackson came to write his *American Colonial Architecture: Its Origin and Development* in 1924, however, his subject was no longer the preserve of fablists or builders of suburban villas. "In the majority of books dealing with so-called Colonial architecture," Jackson observed with some heat, "more attention [was] paid to the genealogy of the families occupying the houses regarded as historic, than to the history of the building of these houses."[101] He did not propose to do likewise.

He had harsh words for the relic hunters who literally pulled the ancient Barker House in Pembroke, Massachusetts, to pieces in their eagerness to own a real antique. He had no tips to offer those wishing to dwell in copies of the Fairbanks House, calling it "not convenient, comfortable, nor artistic." To the sober architectural historian, the most that could be said of his colonial subject was that it was "a native style, just as individual to this country as is the 'skyscraper.'"[102] And that was the only, tenuous link between Washington's day and the frenetic modernism of the 1920s.

Washingtoniana

7

Biography, Pageantry, and Good Taste
1896–1924

The Colonial Revival Comes of Age

The drive to understand colonial culture in a more precise way spilled over into many corners of American life during the first two decades of the twentieth century. Legend had once made old buildings interesting. Now sheer age, the state of preservation, and particularly "good" details of finish became reason enough for a new breed of connoisseur to look with favor on a house that could boast of no visitations whatsoever from George Washington. As architects and their clients made finer and finer distinctions between the Connecticut and the Massachusetts saltbox, the High Chippendale Georgian and the Mercantile Palladian, or the work of a Bullfinch and that of a McIntire, the amorphous colonial style once characterized by fireplaces, spinning wheels, and yearnings after a wholesomely simple yet elegant past fell out of favor.

Although slapdash colonial—a green shutter here, a white clapboard there—could still be found in builder's subdivisions in the less pricy recesses of suburbia, the trend ran to more "correct" colonialisms. For the living room of an honest-to-gosh, Philadelphia-circa-1773 interior, for instance, furniture identified with the colonial era by a general knobbiness and the manufacturer's decision to name a fumed oak sofa after Martha Washington would no longer do. New settings called for brand-new old furniture, line-by-line reproductions of authentic artifacts given an added cachet by their inclusion in the collections of prestigious museums.

Nor were collectors of antiques quite so apt to be dazzled by the merest hint that a mediocre snuffbox once belonged to a shirttail relative of the Washington family, that an otherwise undistinguished bed was once slept in by the peripatetic general. The lines of the headboard suddenly counted for more than the bloodlines of its former users. In that sense, the sea changes in Wallace Nutting's taste chart the maturation of the colonial revival movement as a whole. At the turn of the century, Nutting was an enthusiast for crude Pilgrim furniture of oak because it bespoke the hardy self-reliance of those days, and so he despised the effete wares of the eighteenth century. Just twenty years later, he could argue the evolution of the cabriole leg with the best of them and had reversed himself completely on the subject of the decadence of mahogany. By 1924, when the American Wing at the Metropolitan Museum threw open to the public a pair of doors borrowed from the façade of the old Assay Office on Wall Street, the delicacy and refinement of an American Adam mantelpiece attracted as much admiration as the cavernous brick fireplace in the keeping room of the Parson Capen House.[1] Polish and sleek sophistication had become chic.

While it was still of considerable importance to the Metropolitan and its potential visitors to note that George Washington had once danced with Ben Franklin's daughter in one of the period rooms recreated there, and had in 1798 attended a ball in honor of his birthday in another, respect for the Father of His Country did not lessen the zeal of the curators for an accurate replication of those tasteful environments.[2] And written studies of Washington exhibited the same penchant for accuracy at the expense of the usual deferential mythology. If no man can be a hero to his valet, still less could Washington be an idol to a scrupulous biographer: as more and more of the minute details of his life came to light, the hero came to seem more and more like the sort of ordinary fellow who might fuss over the appointments of a new tract house in the Mount Vernon manner.

Paul Leicester Ford's biography, which was published in 1896 and widely read and cited for the next thirty years, set the standard for an apolitical, nonmilitary approach to its subject; *The True George Washington* stressed the unbuttoned patriot at home and at his leisure. The book explored Washington's personality and quirks of character, not all of them admirable or conventionally pleasing. To the dismay of the many who followed the revived cult of Mariolatry, it was Ford who first suggested that the closeness between Washington and his mother had been much exaggerated. Her son's active neglect of Mary Ball Washington was richly justified, too, for the old lady was, Ford quipped, "illiterate and untidy, and moreover, if tradition is to be believed, smoked a pipe."[3]

From Ford came the first commonsensical—albeit erroneous—explanation for the puffy-faced Washington of the Athenaeum Portrait: Gilbert Stuart, he reported, had filled out the president's toothless gums with wads of cotton.[4] From Ford came the first open discussion of the Sally Fairfax affair. In the end and with some reluctance, it seems, the author came down on the side of propriety in the matter of Washington's relations with Mrs. Fairfax but not before airing the supposed dalliance in a manner ill calculated to put the rumors to rest for good:

It has been asserted that Washington loved the wife of his friend George William Fairfax, but the evidence has not been produced. On the contrary, though the two corresponded, it was in a purely platonic fashion, very different from the strain of love. . . . Thus the claim seems due, like many another of Washington's mythical love-affairs, rather to the desire of descendants to link their family "to a star" than to more substantial basis.[5]

By introducing old Tory libels about the mistress General Washington was supposed to have stashed in a New Jersey boarding house (to which he repaired under the cover of darkness in heavy disguise) and "pretty little Kate, the Washer-woman's daughter," allegedly procured on his chieftain's behalf by a brother officer, Ford effectively reopened "the question of whether Washington was a faithful husband." That issue might better have been "left to the facts already given were it not," said Ford, "that stories of his immorality are bandied about in clubs, a well-known clergyman has vouched for their truth, and a U.S. senator has given further currency to them by claiming special knowledge on the subject."[6]

Evidence supporting the back-room stories was finding its way into print in the 1920s. An edition of Washington's own diaries, issued under the auspices of the august Mount Vernon Ladies' Association in 1925, made it clear that contrary to the fervent assertions of Bishop Meade, Washington had been fond of plays, the hunt, and dancing the night away with handsome women. Books like the 1925 *Love Stories of Famous Virginians,* written by the national historian of the Colonial Dames, took up the cause of Sally Fairfax with a vengeance: "I consider his early romances but zephyrs to this one crimson whirlwind passion of his life," gushed Mrs. Sally Robins.[7] Meanwhile, in the same year, J. P. Morgan let it be known that he had bought up a number of autograph Washington letters of a "smutty" nature in order to suppress them forever. "Could we afford to pay the price and destroy our investment? We could and did," said the millionaire's private librarian, who had probably burned some of the many forgeries in circulation in a period that craved sensational keepsakes a more innocent age would have recognized for fakes.[8]

When George Washington was stricken with the foibles of mortal men, he also adopted their petty snobberies. Thus it took Henry Van Dyke the whole of a slender volume published in 1906 to prove the "Americanism" of Washington, against the contentions of Anglophiles who used foxhunts and love letters quoting Addison's *Cato* to prove that the first president was "a very decent English country gentleman" laboring under the misfortune of having been born in Virginia.[9] In the course of his literary shadowboxing with such unnamed slanderers, it became clear that Van Dyke had written his book to ward off recent attacks on Washington from two directions. One camp was disputing Washington's greatness because, unlike Lincoln, he had died a rich man and money, among some segments of the great unwashed, was un-American. "I am sick of the shallow judgment that ranks the worth of a man by his poverty or by his wealth at death," Van Dyke fumed. "Many a selfish speculator dies poor. Many an unselfish patriot dies prosperous."[10]

But the notion that the Englishness of life among the colonial upper crust, of which Washington was a member, disqualified him from Americanism had already been debated for several years by people who had no objection to acquired wealth. Washington's Birthday of 1890, for instance, had elicited a disquisition on the theme from Henry Cabot Lodge, whom *Life* added to a growing list of notables—Matthew Arnold and James Russell Lowell had already addressed the subject— convinced of Washington's temperamental kinship with members of the British peerage. That the editors found the brouhaha over Washington's native credentials a good target for humor confirms its currency:

What is really in question is at what time tail feathers worn in the hair ceased to be an essential qualification of the true American and what distinguishing characteristics took their place. Whenever doctors can agree whether there was such a thing as a Caucasian American in the latter half of the eighteenth century, and what were his dimensions and symptoms, it will be a simple matter to measure our father, George, by their standard and see if he fits.[11]

When invited to speak before the national convention of the American Institute of Architects in 1907, Henry Cabot Lodge—historian, senator, well-known Anglophile—had further allowed as how colonial architecture derived its principal elements from English sources but had managed to transform them in a vague, unspecified way into something distinctive and American. "Old Colonial forms" were "so agreeable," Lodge thought, because instead of imitating imported ideas slavishly, the colonists "tried to apply forms which had been tested elsewhere in a way to make them represent the New World."[12] Thus the lifestyle of the colonial aristocracy was, if English in its taste for the finer things, still American somehow in the manner of displaying them.

A part of the broader argument over whether there was such a thing as a national culture, the dispute about Washington's American bona fides also reopened a question tacitly broached during the festivities of 1889: what was the man in the street to think of a hero whose manners and possessions were so patently unlike his own? Of a hero honored by diamonds and champagne at a Centennial Ball the average American could only glimpse from the curb when the door to the special supper room swung open for a moment? Did wealth and all that it implied disqualify Washington from greatness in an America of vast economic inequities?

Van Dyke, for one, thought the issue serious enough to merit a book-length rebuttal and a stinging indictment of a Darwinian social order which, unlike that of Washington's day, worshipped wealth and ignored true character, "an age of greedy privilege and sullen poverty, of blatant luxury and curious envy, of rising palaces and vanishing homes, of stupid frivolity and idiotic publicomania, in which four hundred gilded fribbles give monkey-dinners and Louis XV revels, while four million ungilded gossips gape at them and read about them in the newspapers."[13]

Owen Wister's *Seven Ages of Washington,* a book begun in 1907 as the annual Washington's Birthday address at the University of Pennsylvania and published later in that year, was, like Ford's and Van Dyke's efforts, more involved with the man than with the commander or the president. Commander and president rated a chapter apiece while the remaining "ages" were assigned to Washington's boyhood, his young manhood, "The Married Man," and his posthumous immortality.[14] The man Wister was interested in was plainly not the frozen idol grown "rigid with congealed virtue," the prig who cut down the cherry tree, or the paragon of virtue whose letters Jared Sparks once pruned of human signs of impatience and bad temper as diligently as Morgan would later search them for hints of sexual indiscretion. Instead, Wister was concerned with a person not very different from his own readers, a man who could laugh or boil with anger, a practical individual with a strong "business bent . . . [in] the line of bonds and receipts" and little use for literature, a nitpicking householder from whose Mount Vernon journals "you would scarce guess that the public life engaged a moment of his thought or that he had ever seen a day's fighting."[15]

Visiting Mount Vernon in the course of his research, Wister came away half-convinced that Washington still prowled through the east parlor in his buckskin breeches, carrying his favorite crabtree walking stick. "Everything, every subject, every corner and step seems to bring him close," Wister confessed. "It is an exquisite and friendly serenity which bathes the sense . . . , that seems to be charged all through with some meaning or message of beneficence and reassurance but nothing that could be put into words."[16] When all the evidence was weighed without prejudice, Wister's George Washington of Mount Vernon was no plaster saint but a figure not unlike the brisk, present-day man of affairs pacing the floor of his office, a pungent individual, neither perfect nor deeply flawed.

Washington's religious attitudes were a case in point. Although those demanding a saint assembled proof of his devoutness and those desiring a rogue seized upon evidence of his atheism, Wister preferred to face the facts as they were. To admit that "he gave up taking Communion in middle life; he attended church regularly as President, and not at all so when living at Mount Vernon; [and] in dying, he said nothing about religion," was merely to allow that Washington steered a middle course through the shoals of conventional piety, as any sensible person might.[17] Americans perplexed by the casual religiosity of Washington and the Founding Fathers had only to translate a document like the Declaration of Independence into the language of 1907:

Let us suppose that some leader of our own times were to write: "Three dangers today threaten the United States, any one of which could be fatal: unscrupulous Capital, destroying man's liberty to compete; unscrupulous Labor, destroying man's liberty to work; and undesirable Immigration, in which four years of naturalization are not going to counteract four hundred years of heredity. Unless people check all of these, American liberty will become extinct."[18]

Wister's text enlarged upon two aspects of the Washington story: the factual circumstances of his private life and the direct applicability of his precepts to the modern age. Both would shortly become the themes of major contributions to the swelling corpus of Washingtoniana. Washington's faith, his love life, and his domestic arrangements all received book-length treatment. *Sally Cary: A Long Hidden Romance of Washington's Life* (1916), *Mount Vernon: Washington's Home and the Nation's Shrine* (1916), *George Washington the Christian* (1919), *George Washington as a Housekeeper* (1924), *George Washington: Country Gentleman* (1925), and *The Family Life of George Washington* (1926) answered an insatiable demand for popular works describing his everyday life and his innermost thoughts and feelings with a realism hitherto wanting in both the old, worshipful biographies and in the newer, romantic fluff heaped liberally upon descriptions of historic sites visited by the hero.[19]

Merchandise and the Movies

So delineated, George Washington seemed to be the archetype of the anonymous modern man of the 1920s whose public existence was formulaic, circumscribed, and inauthentic but whose private life, as if in compensation for the strictures imposed by the corporate world, was rich in philosophical speculation and powerful emotion, family activity, and ardent pruning of the vine and the olive. George F. Babbitt, titular hero of Sinclair Lewis's 1922 novel, was just such a person, engaged in a furtive affair that enlivened an otherwise conventional round of backslapping conformity, and obsessed with his sleeping porch, his nickel-plated bathroom fixtures, his new car. "The Babbitt whose god was Modern Appliances," if he had read anything other than magazines and the works of "T. Cholmondeley Frink, the poet and advertising-agent," might have found the current crop of studies of George Washington among his imported firedogs and wine coolers both instructive and heartening.[20]

Babbitt was also a red-white-and-blue patriot. A member of the Good Citizen's League, he was suspicious of foreigners, strikers, and radicals of all stripes. And bigotry, too, was the leitmotif of much Washington literature of the period. In the 1890s, the ancient custom of marking February 22 with oratory on "The Character of Washington" had been revived by Senator Lodge and President McKinley.[21] Following their example, former Senator Albert Beveridge, Republican of Indiana, used the occasion of a 1921 Washington's Birthday gala held by the Sons of the Revolution in New York to enlist Washington in a renewed struggle against "the insidious wiles" of foreign radicals in the cities.[22] His formal address at Carnegie Hall, his off-the-cuff remarks at the Plaza Hotel banquet concluding the ceremonies, and a poem by Thomas Bailey Aldrich amplifying his message were printed together in booklet form. Ten thousand copies were distributed to members of patriotic organizations including the Colonial Dames, the DAR, the Society of Colonial Wars, the Daughters of the Cincinnati, and the Military Order of Foreign Wars.

The principal address began with a tirade against postwar alliances with European nations and a call for a return to the "prophetic chart of national conduct" recommended in Washington's "immortal Farewell Address." At the very summit of his long career, when Washington stood "alone and unapproachable like a snow-clad peak rising above its fellows in the clear air of morning," bellowed the senator as he pointed manfully at the gilded ceiling, the first president had foreseen the danger of future foreign entanglements.[23] Beveridge wanted the nation to regain the insular, all-American purity of George Washington and his era: "At no time have the well-being and security of the United States more thoroughly required that every citizen of the Republic shall be American, wholly American, and nothing but American—exclusively American in body, mind and soul, heart so overflowing with patriotic devotion that it can hold no other love."[24]

The enemy, "a motley throng" of immigrants, had already stolen through the "unguarded gates" described in Aldrich's graphically jingoistic poem:

> Featureless figures of the Hoang-Ho,
> Malayan, Scythian, Teuton, Kelt and Slav,
> Flying the old world's poverty and scorn;
> These bringing with them unknown gods and rites—
> Those, tiger passions, here to stretch their claws.
> In street and alley what strange tongues are loud
> Accents of menace alien to our air,
> Voices that once the Tower of Babel knew![25]

Thus it was that George Washington, patron saint of flag-waving, one-hundred-percent Americanism and household god of a cozy American fireside decorated with talismanic objects in the Mount Vernon mode, led his progeny into the easy-credit, go-go 1920s and the great "antiques craze" generally said to have been touched off by the creation of the new American Wing at the Metropolitan. The art historian Russell Lynes, one of the first to analyze the reasons for that fresh burst of general enthusiasm for cobbler's benches and Nutting silhouettes of spinsters at their wheels, argues that a generation earlier "the past was a convenient point from which to measure progress, but progress was more important than nostalgia."[26] In the 1920s, however, the dubious benefits of progress had manifested themselves in unlivable urban centers filled with the restless, alien workers Senator Beveridge feared. The green fringes of the city alone seemed immune to the blight of factories, to the march of angry strikers, to disruption and constant change.

There the neocolonial house with its appliances and nickel-plated bathroom fixtures, and its reproduction relics, presented a symbolic alternative to progress: the benefits of modern times could be enjoyed in a seemingly changeless setting, virtuously antimodernist in its unelectrified candlesticks and wood-burning hearth. Throughout its history revivalism had always been a response to an irritant of the time. But in its 1920s phase, the colonial revival moved out of the narrow confines of the society ball and the once-in-the-lifetime commemorative event to encompass the smallest everyday detail of American life. The neocolonial home became a psychic safety valve: beyond the fanlight and the paneled front door, American progress might do its worst. Within the sacred precincts of the pseudo-ancestral abode in suburbia, the rewards of progress were burnished to the glowing, silvery luster of a Revere bowl—a new species of *genuine* reproduction, just like the valuable and tasteful original in the museum.

If artifacts provide a reasonable index to attitudes, then it is clear that minority reservations about progress—the conservatism prevailing among the socialites who were the first prominent collectors of their ancestors' booty—had come to be shared by the majority in the early 1920s, even before Mrs. Russell Sage and her well-connected peers gave their treasures to the American Wing at the Metropolitan Museum. Sears, Roebuck sold walnut sewing cabinets named after Martha Washington. Mass-circulation magazines of the day retailed a variety of colonial thingamabobs that, while they were not the line-by-line reproductions of authenticated originals preferred in middle-class suburbs, approximated the flavor of the real thing well enough to satisfy customers earnestly invited to return the products for a full refund, no questions asked, if they failed to delight. These pseudo-antiques were cheap; they were, ironically enough, mass-produced by the same industrial system the colonial revival questioned; and they were marketed among present-minded, up-to-the-minute movie star fans, drawn mainly from the polyglot working-class walkups of the cities.

A display ad in a 1923 issue of *Movie Weekly* is typical (Figure 7.1). The Hartman Furniture & Carpet Company of Chicago offered a "110-Piece Martha Washington Blue and Gold Decorated Dinner Set" for the bargain price of $32.85. The charge included personalization: every last saucer and sauceboat would be stamped with two "pure gold" initials of the buyer's choice "in Old English design with gold wreaths." Interested parties were invited to send "$1.00 now" and the balance in easy monthly payments. The first fifty thousand readers to mail the coupon back were entitled to a free gift: six dainty doilies, a table runner, and a partial service of silver-plated knives and forks in the complementary "fleur-de-lis pattern."[27]

The illustration of the "beautiful Colonial shape" of the dishes—the cream jug and sugar bowl *do* look vaguely like pewter tankards—and the text of the fine print beneath reflect an eclecticism accommodating enough to include a touch of the Old English and a soupçon of the Old French. The dishes were not designed to fool the likes of Mrs. Russell Sage, of course. But the "Colonial" shape was indeed more Federal in character than not and patently unlike the design of competing "modern" china services. For those lacking colonial ancestors and the wherewithal to buy up real ancestral relics, Hartman's dinner service had the added advantage of the initials that designated each monogrammed plate as an instant family heirloom.

The family name of Washington was not unfamiliar to the movie-goers being wooed by Hartman & Co., either. One of the principal means by which consumers learned to spot and to covet a "beautiful Colonial shape" named in honor of Lady Washington was the motion picture. Historical movies traded on the popularity of novels set in the colonial period, and both reflected the current state of Washington hagiography. Books like Paul Leicester Ford's *Janice Meredith,* Silas Weir Mitchell's 1908 *Red City: A Novel of the Second Administration of President Washington,* and Thackeray's *The Virginians,* reissued with great fanfare in 1923, helped readers to see silver knives and the golden wreaths on china plates glistening in the candlelight of the mind's eye.[28] They also created a market for the spate of Washington films that appeared just as the talkies prepared to revolutionize the industry. In general, although brash Hollywood moguls preferred to leave George Washington clothed in some few shreds of old-fashioned decorum, they were not insensible to the contemporary interest in the love affairs of movie stars and presidents and the lust for vicarious adventure that Lindbergh would soon tap. So adventures and amours were found for George Washington.

Winners of the Wilderness, a 1927 MGM melodrama centered on Braddock's defeat, starred Edward Hearn as the dashing young colonial volunteer who emerges from the debacle at the head of the

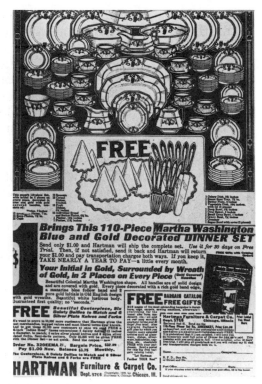

7.1
Movie-magazine ad for a mail-order "Martha Washington Dinner Set"

Virginia militia, ready to command the Revolutionary armies in days to come. That was the blood-and-thunder side of the cinematic Washington. In D. W. Griffith's *America* and in *Janice Meredith,* Washington was the presiding cupid of hearts-and-flowers romance. Both movies—and earlier, stage versions of Ford's 1899 bestseller—managed to shift canards about Washington's flings with Tory ladies and the perpetual lovesickness of his adolescence from the general to his junior officers.[29] Thus, after lump-in-the-throat but incidental recreations of Paul Revere's ride and the crossing of the Delaware, *Janice Meredith* concludes with an avuncular Joseph Kilgour, as Washington, beaming down upon a reunion of star-crossed patriot sweethearts at a Mount Vernon awash in antiques.[30]

But another crop of movies starred a fiercely updated Washington, a Sunday-school hero caught up in the moral ambiguities of modern life in city and suburb. Warner Brothers' *George Washington, Jr.* opened in time for the Washington's Birthday holiday in 1924. Based on a hit George M. Cohan play of 1906—he introduced "You're a Grand Old Flag" in the first act (Figure 7.2)—the film was a patriotic farce set in a variety of high-class drawing rooms, some of them neocolonial in decor. A bogus European count steals a vital treaty from a senator. To the rescue comes the senator's jazz-baby son, "George Washington, Jr." With the help of Ham, the Negro butler, Junior gets at the truth, recovers the document, saves the republic from shifty foreigners, and, in the end, permits himself one large white lie when he gives his father credit for the coup. That lie—the lie the truthful little George Washington of cherry tree fame could not tell— saves the senator's career.

On the opposite end of the social spectrum, *George Washington Cohen* pits George Jessel against overweening ambition. An immigrant tailor's son from the East Side, G. W. Cohen is determined to climb the ladder of success. He finds a bulging wallet in the gutter and, recalling his American namesake's penchant for honesty, returns the money to its owner, a Wall Street broker. Virtue is rewarded; George Washington Cohen becomes the speculator's right-hand man. His employer is rich but shifty, and the climactic courtroom scene finds the modern hero torn between telling the truth about the boss's wife, thus serving the ends of Wall Street and earning another cash reward, or telling a lie to ensure the happiness of a child. George Washington Cohen tells the lie and goes to jail.[31]

It is not surprising that these movies of the 1920s were based on popular stage productions of 1906 and 1915. The sense of an unbroken cultural continuum running from the turn of the century through the glory days of the great bull market is reinforced by other Washington ads, keepsakes, and celebrations, all of which show that colonial personages were major icons of popular culture throughout the

7.2
Sheet-music cover for a George M. Cohan song from the 1906 play *George Washington, Jr.*

roughly twenty years in question. They were almost as familiar to the public at large as trademarks or the media celebrities of the day. And like a Hollywood lover or an ethnic comic on Broadway, whose personality was larger than the part he played, colonial characters represented certain clusters of easily grasped ideas to the readers of newspapers and magazines. The Martha Washington dishes of 1923, for instance, presuppose a ready identification of that name with a desirable product for the well-appointed home. And the connection between the Washingtons and domestic ease was already a given in 1909 when newspapers across the Midwest, including the *Dodgeville* (Wisconsin) *Chronicle,* carried an advertisement for "Martha Washington Comfort Shoes," a brand of house slippers with elastic gussets guaranteed to "fit like a glove and feel as easy as a stocking" (Figure 7.3).

"If you will send us the name of a dealer who *does not* handle Martha Washington Comfort Shoes," the F. Mayer Boot & Shoe Company promised those who read the fine print beneath the smiling likeness of the first First Lady, "we will send you free, postpaid, a beautiful picture of Martha Washington, size 15×20."[32] As for George, the Modern Woodmen of America, a secret beneficiary society of white Midwestern males of sound health, exemplary habits, and good moral character, sent delegates home from a 1901 conclave in St. Paul, Minnesota, with gilded matchholders for the kitchen wall in the shape of hatchets to remind each member of his obligation to be truthful and honest in the discharge of his "duties as a man and patriot." The blade of the hatchet bore a profile of Washington wreathed in symbolic cherries (Figure 7.4).[33]

7.3
Newspaper ad for "Martha Washington Comfort Shoes"

7.4
Souvenir matchholder distributed by the Modern Woodmen of America, 1901

Signs and Symbols of Colonial Days

By the first decade of the century, George Washington, Martha, and a select number of their colonial compatriots had become stereotypes, emblematic figures equipped with certain stock physical attributes, like knee breeches and frizzy hair, recognizable whether the image appeared on official currency, on the stage, or in the advertising columns of a small-town weekly. They were associated with certain familiar concepts, such as domestic comfort and unswerving honesty, that clung tenaciously to the colonial eminence in question whether he or she trod the boards of Broadway disguised as a poor Jewish boy on the make or purveyed carpet slippers in a murky reproduction. The process of identifying and exploiting such valid cultural stereotypes was the basis of the advertising and entertainment industries. These trades came into their own in the twenty-odd years that also witnessed the climax of the colonial revival, and their techniques, in a very real sense, came from the theatrical branch of revivalism, the American pageant movement. Pageantry helped to create the repertory of colonial symbols exploited by the mass media in the 1920s.

Although important earlier and later examples can be cited, the heyday of pageantry lasted from 1905 through the mid-1920s. Trudy Baltz and other recent historians of that organized community ritual have stressed the painterly and dramaturgical aspects of these spectacles, which were generally (but not always) held outdoors in broad daylight with huge casts of volunteers and without much in the way of props, lines, and scenery.[34] Those circumstances bred particular kinds of images. Because the dramatis personae of the pageant had to be identified, without benefit of explanatory speeches, by audiences drawn from the community as a whole, and because the man in the street often had to do so from a considerable distance with the sun in his eyes, the characters in such performances tended to be people or types already familiar to everybody. Short pants and a white X on the chest made a Continental soldier, for instance. A white wig, the same pants, and a cape, perhaps, for foul-weather scenes—and voilà! George Washington.

Given the difficulty of wordless plot development, it was also crucial for the various principals to carry their own meanings with them to a pageant. Hence the use of the allegorical ladies in cheesecloth bearing wheat sheaves or railroad cars who conveyed the ineffable spirit of agriculture, transportation, and the like in murals, civic sculpture, and community festivals in the city park. Hence, too, the use of Washington and his retinue, to whom adhered a whole cluster of other hard-to-define imponderables such as the dignity and serenity of the American home, and a natural, democratic variant on aristocratic grace.

By the time the movement came to be codified by such promoters as Ralph Davol and Esther Willard Bates, who published handbooks of pageantry in 1914 and 1912 respectively; by the time an American Pageant Association, with its own journal, had been founded, in 1913; by the time popular magazines—*American Homes and Gardens,* for example—had taken up the cause, between 1909 and 1914, pageants had evolved into mute plays. "Masques" (the quainter and more elegant term was adopted by Percy MacKaye, Thomas Wood Stevens, and others of the new fraternity of pageant-writers) were plotted by the historical events they commemorated.[35] Sometimes, as in the case of the Jamestown, New York, centennial pageant of 1927, which opened with Indians filing through the woods and settlers arriving and ended with scenes of the present day, pageantry stressed the contrast between the good old days and modern times to the disadvantage of the latter.[36] More often, however, pageant-masters left the present out, effectively dissociating the glory days when Washington came to town from the mercurial, rackety world outside the town park. The performance became an antimodern gesture comparable to that made by the householder who chose to retreat into the candlelit recesses of his or her neocolonial abode.

Despite brief turns by World War I doughboys, Virginia Tanner's *Pageant of the State of Maine,* presented in Bath in 1928 by the combined citizenry of four nearby towns, her 1923 *Pageant of Portsmouth,* which enlisted nine New Hampshire communities in the production, and her Albany tercentenary pageant of 1924 all reached their dramatic finales in eras removed from Tanner's own by a century or more.[37] Stevens's *Pageant of Newark,* mounted in 1916, starred Washington and Lafayette, jumped forward for a glimpse of Lincoln, and

7.5
Frontispiece to Ralph Davol's book, showing American pageantry's standard version of the Pilgrim father

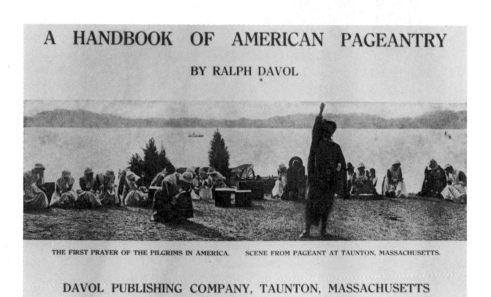

A HANDBOOK OF AMERICAN PAGEANTRY

BY RALPH DAVOL

THE FIRST PRAYER OF THE PILGRIMS IN AMERICA.   SCENE FROM PAGEANT AT TAUNTON, MASSACHUSETTS.

DAVOL PUBLISHING COMPANY, TAUNTON, MASSACHUSETTS

7.6
A scene from a pageant by Emily A. Strong, staged in Oxford, Massachusetts, showing the funeral honors for George Washington

7.7
"No pageant is complete without a charming colonial wedding."

then stopped dead; in the scene that followed, timeless allegories of Commerce, Civic Beauty, Ignorance, and Invention were shepherded about by a "Puritan Spirit" dressed like one of Boughton's churchgoing Pilgrims or the twelve-foot bronze *Puritan* designed by Augustus Saint-Gaudens for the park in Springfield, Massachusetts, in 1887.[38] Simplifying them to a new imagistic clarity, pageantry translated the colonial conventions of art and historical literature into the domain of mass culture (Figure 7.5).

Production photographs of the major pageants emphasize the generous size of the greenswards where Washington's funeral, the signing of the Declaration of Independence, the surrender of Burgoyne, the welcoming of Lafayette, and the battle of Lexington were recreated (Figure 7.6). Too far from the action to be visible in most of the photos, the spectators could have spotted marks of identity only if they were writ very large indeed. Close-up shots of Washington's crossing of the Delaware as interpreted by children in a New Jersey playground, Paul Revere's ride reenacted in Arlington, Massachusetts, and an unidentified colonial wedding—Davol says that "no pageant is complete without a charming colonial wedding"—confirm the fact that pageant costumes were larger than life, conceived in terms of strong color contrasts, and bold in cut (Figures 7.7, 7.8).

The faces of Revere and the farmer-soldiers of 1775 are all but invisible. The overscaled hats, the long pigtails, the big, baggy knee breeches and the muskets—enlarged versions of the chief attributes of *The Minute Man,* Daniel Chester French's statue which had stood at the bridge in Concord since 1875—make sense of the scene.[39] The children pretending to cross the Delaware in a cardboard boat draped in the American flag assume poses loosely based on Leutze's famous painting and are muffled to the eyebrows in dark drapery highlighted by enormous white wigs: those popular trademarks of the waterborne

7.9
Newark, New Jersey, boys recreating Washington's heroic crossing of the Delaware

patriot were the means by which the pantomime could be connected with a specific historical event (Figure 7.9).

The design of pageants indicates that shorthand symbols for colonial life were just about universally appreciable. Or so believed those who earned their bread by coaxing hundreds of busy women to stitch breeches and fluff wigs and hundreds of reluctant husbands and children to wear them.[40] Pageantry shows that the colonial revival produced popular heroes and heroines as well as a stock of tasteful merchandise. And the attenuated plots of the pageants disclose further affinities between the antimodern ideology of these playlets and the tenor of the colonial revival in architecture, decor, and popular historiography. For example, the intense localism of many productions, drawn from incidents forgotten in general histories of colonial times, meant that pageants dwelt on trivia, on out-of-the-way facts of the kind being turned up by contemporary seekers after the "true" George Washington. The participatory nature of the pageant form meant that regardless of story lines tacitly critical of the present, those who impersonated minutemen and colonial goodwives gave witness by the very act of make-believe to the affinity between the past and the present. When he hinted at real similarities between Washington and the American businessman, husband, and owner of Martha Washington dinnerware, ca. 1907, Owen Wister was making the same connection.

Nor were the theorists of American pageantry insensible to linkages between on-stage roles and real life, although Ralph Davol, for one, denied that contemporary feminism and the colonial heroines redis-covered by the revival movement had anything to do with each other even as he proved the opposite point in his horrified disquisition on such females:

Dramatis personae to-day are mostly feminine. Pageantry in America is dom-inated by a handful of men and several hundred women. It is a demonstration of the fermenting feminist movement. Is there any form of patriotic expression higher than the service of motherhood? . . . Those inspiring, well-rounded heroines whom the pageant revives—Priscilla Mullins, Betsy Ross, Martha Washington, Dolly Madison—inevitably raise the question: Should the pag-eant, as an expression of community ideals, exalt the denatured feminist who sniffs at responsibilities of home as a light and airy fiction, or should the pageant throw the weight of its influence to uphold the sweetness, charm, and sanctity of the home, on which America was founded and has been preserved! Pageantry is not intended as a satire upon modern High Life.[41]

Davol invokes the home, one of the oldest and the most potent symbols standing for colonial America. And the home, or a simplified version of the colonial building at any rate, was also the emblem that gave rise to the key feature of American pageantry—the float.

During the teens and twenties, pageantry had evolved in the direc-tion of the stage drama, particularly the musical revue and the movie epic, with their casts of thousands; the narrative had gradually sub-sumed the emblematic features of the genre. But in 1908, when the form had not yet jelled, wide variations were still possible. That summer, on the Plains of Abraham, Frank Lascelles directed some-thing called "a pageant . . . after the English plan" in honor of the tercentenary of Quebec. An English pageant consisted of "historical scenes enacted within a limited area to which admission was re-stricted by ticket." It was fine for small towns and stratified societies but inappropriate for big American cities, where planners were man-dated to admit all comers and spaces large enough to hold a sizable hunk of the populace were at a premium.[42] What would come to be called the "American plan" pageant was invented to cope with the demands of live mass entertainment. The American pageant was a parade with symbolic floats, distinguished from the format of the civic parade at the Inaugural Centennial of 1889 mainly by nomenclature and by arrangement of the mobile tableaux in a strict chronological order that gave the procession a rudimentary story line.

Springfield, Massachusetts, put on an especially memorable Fourth of July pageant-parade in 1908, with floats made by the grammar schools and marchers representing thirteen different nationalities. In February 1909, the Central High School in Springfield gave a colonial pageant in its assembly hall that was a kind of cross between an indoor parade and a play tracing "the progress of the country through episodes of colonial times to national independence"; in August, the nearby town of Hadley observed its 250th anniversary with bands, marching militiamen, a mile-long column of pioneer settlers, colonial worthies, and other characters from the American past welded into a coherent account of local history by a succession of floats representing "Ye Old Time Kitchen" and "Ye Log Schoolhouse."[43] Houses, cabins, kitchens, and other slices of colonial architecture remained central to the American pageant and thus contributed, not so very indirectly, to the design of the American Wing at the Metropolitan, the model of colonial good taste for the 1920s.

The best of these hybrid events was the Philadelphia Historical Pageant of 1908, a parade "which proceeded along the city's leading highway for a distance of four miles." According to one curbside admirer, "it was viewed by a multitude of people—as many as could find space to see from the starting to the dismissing point. Vast labor and a vast sum of money were expended to secure artistic excellence and historical truth in representation."[44] That observer, Ellis Oberholtzer, was so impressed by the lovely costumes and the aura of bygone times evoked by the architectural set-pieces that he spent two summers in England studying historical pageantry at its source. He would return to mount a great British-style pageant-play in Philadelphia in 1912, in honor of the 125th anniversary of the adoption of the Constitution, backed by a committee that included such ardent revivalists as the colonial historian John Bach McMaster and the neocolonial architect Wilson Eyre.

The Hudson-Fulton Pageant of 1909

The more immediate impact of the first Philadelphia Historical Pageant was felt in neighboring New York. New York City had been designated by the state legislature as host to twin observances of the discovery of the Hudson River by the explorer whose name it bears and the first trial of the steamboat *Clermont* in the same waters. The combined Hudson-Fulton Celebration would last from 1907, the centennial of Robert Fulton's invention, through 1909, the tercentenary of the *Half Moon*'s voyage northward from Manhattan. It would affect communities from the Battery to Albany. The culmination of the festivities would be a week-long series of exhibits, performances, and land and water parades in the city, from which point a great historical parade—a "pageant-parade" of fifty-four massive floats—would proceed up the river by barge, calling at Yonkers and Brooklyn, Richmond Hill, Hastings, Dobbs Ferry, Irvington, Tarrytown, Nyack, Ossining, Peekskill, Poughkeepsie, and other communities en route (sometimes the flotilla put in at five or six stops in a single day), until it reached the capital at Albany.[45]

In New York City proper, festivities opened with a kind of water pageant, a naval parade featuring replicas of the *Half Moon* and the

Clermont that set sail at dawn on Saturday, September 25. The state commission in charge of the various events, like other such bodies before and since, was wary of the big city but determined to bring "visual instruction" in its history and development "to the great population of New York's foreign-born population. It is a question," confessed the official chronicler of the Hudson-Fulton ceremonies, "if such instruction is not needed quite as much by the native population of a city which, more than any other probably, is concerned with the present rather than with the past."[46]

The natives were interested. On the morning in question, a million spectators gathered for instruction or entertainment in the streets facing the river, from 72nd to 130th. At 10:40, after interminable delays, the *Clermont* limped into view, broke down, and stopped dead in the water to make repairs. The *Half Moon*, meanwhile, was becalmed downriver, her crew, despite their ancient costumes, unfamiliar with the workings of canvas and rope (Figure 7.10). Refusing a tow, the angry captain finally got under way, dropped his great sails into position, and slapped her full into the wind: "Whether it was that the Half Moon caught the spirit of unrest that pervaded the city or decided to become a warship on her own account, she suddenly was seized with a fit of cantankerousness on the very morning that opened the celebration, and came very near to spoiling it by her extraordinary exploits."[47]

As the crowd roared with horrified laughter, the *Half Moon* bore down on the *Clermont*'s port quarter, rammed her abaft the boiler, shattered twenty feet of rail, and staved in a section of the hull. Her own figurehead and some of her stays were also lost in the collision. A tug rushed to the rescue but accidentally rammed the *Half Moon*, bringing down the main boom. Although the meeting of the two vessels "caused more amusement than damage, suggesting the idea that the spirit of the old Half Moon rather resented the new-fangled idea represented by the Clermont," it was an omen of things to come.[48]

The Hudson-Fulton Celebration in New York City opened with the naval parade. It closed, on the following Saturday, with a so-called "carnival pageant," a parade designed to celebrate the cultural aspects of life neglected in other facets of the observance and to recognize, in a context quite distinct from the pageant of American history, the ethnic diversity of the urban melting pot. In fact, however, the Germans—12,500 marchers strong, blessed with a "heritage of pageantry"—dominated the day. Thus the fifty floats of the carnival pageant (said by publicists of native birth to "illuminate that great body of Old World folklore . . . and Old World Culture" appropriated by Americans too busy with the "material facts of . . . our progressive civilization" to develop one of their own) were almost exclusively Nordic in character. As it was defined by the floats, American high culture consisted

7.10
A floating replica of the *Half Moon* built for the water parade at the Hudson-Fulton Celebration of 1909

of Wagnerian opera, gnomes, elves, Alpine Gods, and the fairy tales of the Brothers Grimm. The rest of the world had to settle for a rolling tribute to "Egyptian Art" in the forty-first position, escorted by students of the liberal arts from Columbia University; a float adorned with "symbols of good luck among the peoples of both hemispheres"; and, bringing up the rear, "Uncle Sam Welcoming the Nations."[49]

In between the lopsided tribute to Teutonic culture and the naval calamity came a spell of foul weather and the main event, the historical parade through the streets of Manhattan scheduled for September 28. Preparation of the "historical scenes upon moveable 'floats' in a procession moving through six miles of the principal thoroughfares of the city" took a full year. During the previous September, A. H. Stoddard of New Orleans, long-time master of the Mardi Gras parades—he termed *them* "pageants"—was imported to explain his methods. In November he was hired away with the title of "Captain of Pageantry," set up a New Orleans–style "den" or workshop, and signed on 160 papier-mâché workers, carpenters, costumers, modelers, and watchmen, many of them recruited in Louisiana.

B. A. Wickstrom, a Swedish artist who had made his living for many years by designing Mardi Gras floats, came north with Stoddard and drew the first rough "plates" submitted to a citizens' committee of prominent New York State residents that included the historical painter Frank Millet; they were supposed to check for accuracy in pictorial details. By the time Wickstrom died in New York in April of 1909, the sketches had been corrected and in the casting studio every conceivable object "from imitation flames and cabbages to heroic figures of men and women, a life-sized cow and horse, or an eagle that stood 18 feet high and measured 15 feet from [wing]tip to [wing]tip" was being stockpiled against the final assembly of the floats. These mule-drawn floats or "cars" were unusually large and substantial. Their sturdiness was a plus, since they were to be manhandled on and off barges and hauled over back roads in their eventual progress up the river. Their great scale—at fourteen feet across, thirty-two feet long, and from twenty to forty feet high, they were the largest of their kind ever built—was the designer's concession to the scale of New York's rising skyscrapers, with which, he calculated, his rolling history lessons would have to compete for attention (Figure 7.11).[50]

In retrospect, the decision seemed ill-advised. In the canyonlike streets, hemmed in by tall buildings and two and a half million jostling celebrants, the effect was claustrophobic. Because of their perilous height, the floats pitched and swayed as they lurched down the pavement, causing George Washington, Martha, the usual spinsters, and a witch on her dunking stool to clutch at the colonial scenery, lest they be toppled from their lofty perches into the thoroughfare. And the floats were slow and hard to maneuver. Because of threatening

7.11

The "Manor Hall" float coming through the temporary arch on Getty Square, Yonkers, during the traveling version of the Hudson-Fulton pageant

weather, the decision to start the pageant had been delayed until ten o'clock on the fateful Tuesday morning; in the rush to get going at last, the lumbering floats had got out of line. Once in motion, they proved almost impossible to rearrange within the confines of New York streets, and some drivers panicked:

In her hurry, the "Half Moon," true to the ill luck of her floating prototype on Saturday, promptly collided with a lamp post, and proceeded on her course minus part of her canvas sea; and the Statue of Liberty ceased to enlighten the world since, through a similar casualty she lost her torch. . . . [The] "Erie Canal" and "Fulton Ferry" were in line with "The Destruction of the Statue of George III" and "The Capture of Stony Point," while Washington took the oath of office as first President of the United States seven blocks ahead of Henry Hudson discovering the Hudson River.[51]

Had it been carried out as planned, the rolling pageant would have illustrated the history of New York—a selective and partial narrative, to be sure—through four successive divisions: "the Indian, with ten floats; the Dutch, with twelve; the English and Colonial with eighteen; and the United States, with thirteen[,] each division preceded by a title car and one grand title car preceding the whole."[52] But the schedule of events published by the *New York Times* a week before suggested certain conceptual difficulties in melding the goals of historical accuracy and communal inclusivity. Even at that date, for example, the Friendly Sons of St. Patrick, the Hibernians, and smaller, ragtag troops of Italians, Bohemians, Poles, and Hungarians were slated to march with the "Indian" division; other Irish and Huguenot societies were, just as inexplicably, instructed to march with the Knickerbocker floats of the second division. And so it went.[53]

When, however, on the morning in question, Syrians in red fezes turned up toward the end of the Dutch floats and "the escort of the old Dutchmen playing the first game of bowls on Bowling Green was a French society enthusiastically shouting 'The Marseilles,'" even officials who should have known better assumed that the marching units had become as snarled as the floats they were supposed to accompany. When the car honoring the delivery of water to New York from the Croton Reservoir, a refugee from the fourth division, strayed into colonial times "just ahead of the float on which Nathan Hale was being brought before a British General, who, seated in front of his tent, was having a nice bottle of wine, . . . the crowd enjoyed the mistake. It cheered the girls on the Croton float, and commented facetiously on the suggestion of 'wine and water mixed.'" But when the Hibernians of Kings, Queens, and Richmond counties swung by in their duly appointed places, wits on the reviewing stand were heard to laugh, and to remark that "more Irishmen have discovered America than Dutchmen."[54]

Filing its fourth and final report in Albany in 1910, the Hudson-Fulton Commission stated that the historical pageant had aimed at two goals:

One was to illustrate by moving tableaux memorable scenes in the history of the City and State for public education and entertainment. The second object was to unite in the procession the representatives of as many as possible of the nationalities comprising the cosmopolitan population of the State, so as to make them feel that the heritage of the State's history belonged to them as well as to those more distinctively American.[55]

Although organizers found it hard to integrate real-life marchers with the unfolding story of faraway times in old New York—the Tammany Society, in their top hats and tails, marched among the Indians because of their totemic connections to wigwams and sachems—the patriotic and ethnic units were better received than the floats, the wild disorder of which, in both sequence and construction, branded the pageant a failure in the eyes of officialdom.

A souvenir booklet hawked in the streets for fifty cents a copy and the free programs printed in the papers had foretold marvels of beauty and inventiveness, unfolding the epic of America in terms that can only be called cinematic. Brief takes, describing "A Dutch Doorway," "A Colonial Home," "Old Manor Hall in Yonkers," or "Washington's Coach," would pass before the spectator's eyes, each one a cliché, a soundless drama for which the script was clearly understood, each one an episode in a grand, cumulative saga of popular history. On Christmas Day of 1908, the New York police had swooped down upon the 550 nickelodeons and movie houses in the city, establishments that catered largely to ethnic Americans, and closed them for violations of blue laws.[56] But the aesthetic of the silent screen had already filtered into the streets and parks, and specifically into the set-pieces of American pageantry, with their overstated costumes and props, their stereotyped themes, and their rudimentary narratives, the latter often little more than the eternal story supplied by the passage of time.

The conventions of pageantry would, in turn, reinfect the cinema (see, for instance, the massing and movement of crowds in D. W. Griffith's *Birth of a Nation* and the prayer-in-the-snow tableau in *America*), a medium scorned and feared by the same native-born, establishment Americans who complained bitterly about the fiasco of the floats at the Hudson-Fulton historical pageant. The crowd, by and large, watched the "successful parts" of the parade—the individual floats, the bands that introduced them—carefully and even solemnly. As the float with the colonial balcony showing Washington taking the oath of office at Federal Hall creaked past, "both foreign and American spectators," many of them familiar with the subject from its previous reenactments, "rais[ed] their hats respectfully" (Figure 7.12).[57] As for the ludicrous juxtapositions, the lost units, and the breakdown of the chronology calculated to instruct, the spectators on the sidewalks recognized the humor of the situation and treated it "as comedy" or farce, in good-natured contrast to the sour reactions of those occupying the places of honor alongside Julia Ward Howe on the reviewing stand.[58]

"Childish" and "undignified" were the words disappointed critics of the pageant most frequently applied to the colonial scenes on floats when they wrote their memoirs in later years. The New York *Evening Post,* the day afterward, was almost as harsh:

7.12
"Washington Taking the Oath of Office," with a famous football hero of the day aboard the float

The floats yesterday were fearfully unreal. A glaringly twentieth-century Peter Stuyvesant on a precarious balcony, a benevolent gentleman in spectacles storming Stony Point, are obviously not conducive to the development of the historical imagination. As against the bulky and incongruous float, we cast our vote for costume in parade and pageantry. Yesterday, the mummers in colonial costume pleased whenever they could be disassociated from the "scenery." The Knickerbocker group in front of Washington's balcony was charming; so was Martha Washington in her coach. Clothes, after all, appeal to a very fundamental passion in us, and when you put pretty clothes on animated beings, and place the wearers in a living posture, you have as elemental and sure an appeal as a brass band. . . . That is pageantry; but for the several dozen ambulatory specimens of Coney Island sculpture we have, with a few exceptions, little to say.[59]

Yet the fellows in glasses who stormed forts and swore oaths in colonial costume were important to the participatory dynamic of the pageant. The spectators' surrogates in the action, they wore their uniforms on behalf of onlookers who fully expected to recognize the six-foot-four-and-a-half-inch-tall Richard Sheldon, former Yale tackle, decked out in Washington's brown suit and standing, with one hand raised and the other clamped to the swaying papier-mâché balcony, on the float entitled "Washington Taking the Oath of Office."[60]

The Colonial Home on Wheels

Part of the meaning of the pageant surely inhered in the fact that the companies of uniformed colonials leading "Washington's Coach" and the Fraunces' Tavern scene of "Washington's Farewell" were chapters of the Sons of the Revolution, men of the present whose attitudes toward the American past were almost as plain to those who cheered them as the significance of the events chosen for depiction on the fifty-odd floats. The present struck its own peculiar bargain with the past in the pageant. The crudity and simplicity of the float-mounted tableaux were, if not wholly deliberate, then fortuitous. Had the actors played their parts better, their identity as representatives from the world of 1909 would have been compromised; the sense that this was *our* self-created past—the past that a collective "we" concocted of and for "ourselves" in 1909—would have been lost. The pageant-goer understood the pertinence of the past because its houses, its props, and its principals had all been plucked from the modern present.

Yet as evidenced in the floats, the historical perspective of the period was skewed toward the good old days. Gustav Kobbé, whose account of the Hudson-Fulton gala was commissioned by New York's Society of Iconophiles, made a decent effort to show that the entire program recapitulated the progressive premise of the 1876 exposition. The pageant, that is, hinged on a manifest contrast between primitive

7.13
Artist's rendering of Float Number 20, "Dutch Doorway"

yesterdays and a glorious today. He pointed out that in the naval parade, the ill-fated *Half Moon* replica led a flotilla of spanking new warships; that its dim lanterns were eclipsed by the million-candle-power battery of searchlights mounted above the Hudson and by the new electric billboards in the streets; that its slow and erratic voyage was mocked by Wilbur Wright's soaring flights around the Statue of Liberty and Grant's Tomb; that the *Half Moon* float, despite its ungainly bulk, was dwarfed by a modern urban marvel, the skyscraper.[61]

Although onlookers were free to shuffle the disparate elements of the week-long spectacle into that configuration, the pageant-parade itself, taken as coherent whole (however incoherently executed), avoided the modern epoch almost totally. In its nearest approach to contemporaneity, the pageant hardly crept past the age of Jackson. After the "Erie Canal" scene in the final division came the reservoir float and two others with undatable, once-upon-a-time motifs that evoked the sorts of memories an oldster might tell his grandson when a fire alarm rang or the snowbanks mounted. "An Old Time Broadway Sleigh" and "The Old Volunteer Fire Department" suggested the nineteenth century in terms as vague and shadowy as those by which the era of the Indians in the first division had been conjured up with a few rocks and feathers.

Indians, fire wagons, sleighs: these were aspects of a murky once-upon-a-time distinguished by that very lack of precision from the colonial days, the real focus of the pageant. Colonial floats outnumbered all the rest. The motifs themselves possessed a clarity and precision evolved during a thirty-year process of winnowing that broad field of history down to precious kernels of imagistic truth. Dominated by George Washington and by symbols of home, the floats represented the distilled essence of the colonial America perceptible to and cherished by a modern America in 1909.

A high percentage of the floats depicted colonial houses or genre scenes only tangentially related to the stirring events of the conventional histories. For every "Bronck's Treaty with the Indians" in the second division, there was a "Bowling on Bowling Green," a "Reception to Stuyvesant," a "Dutch Doorway" (Figure 7.13). Sketches for the "Dutch Doorway" showed a steep, tile-roofed cottage with bottle-glass window panes and the date—1679—inscribed on one wall. A papier-mâché cow and some chickens occupied the front yard; the garden bloomed with papier-mâché cabbages. A stout burgher stood in his half-door, smoking a clay pipe and contemplating the peaceful scenes around his home: his wife milking, a daughter feeding the poultry, two rosy children at work nearby.[62] A "typical" Dutch family riding the float became its own historical prototype, its own justification for purveying a particular hierarchical and housebound ideal of the nuclear family.

The situation was much the same in the third section of the parade, the English and colonial division, in which even the story of the capture and execution of Nathan Hale was presented as a sort of eighteenth-century cocktail party. The "Old Manor Hall in Yonkers," a reminder of Washington's dalliance with Mary Philipse, and "Fraunces' Tavern," the scene of his farewell (the building had just been restored and reopened in 1907 by the New York Society of the Sons of the Revolution), were two of the more prominent floats to flaunt the architectural symbols of the ongoing colonial revival.[63] Number 27, "The Colonial Home" (Figure 7.14), had nothing but such domestic symbolism—a heady mixture of Puritan hearthside severity and aristocratic Virginia charm—to justify its inclusion in the pageant: "This was designed to give an idea of domestic life in New York City during the English period near the time of the Revolution. It represented both the exterior and interior of a house of the period. Indoors a woman sat spinning. On the porch, beside the mistress of the house, stood the master, just returned from the hunt, while before him in the foreground stood a colored servant, holding the hounds."[64]

The Patriotic Order of the Sons of America provided the spinsters, servants, lords, and ladies who teetered on the float. The citizens who stood below the rickety balcony on which Washington took his oath were members of the Washington Continental Guard, and they were cheered on by the music of the Sons of the American Revolution

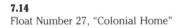

7.14
Float Number 27, "Colonial Home"

7.15
"Washington's Coach" in Yonkers

Band, fifty members strong. The last-named group supplied the pretty Martha who peeped from the recesses of "Washington's Coach" (Figure 7.15), while the Sons of the Revolution, on the basis of their stewardship of the site, claimed the honor of staffing "Fraunces' Tavern."[65]

These essentially conservative societies were not breaking new ground in the image of history endorsed by the floats they chose to sponsor. On the contrary, the tried-and-true iconography of many of the Washington scenes had been used for parade floats in 1889 and therefore had the peculiar virtue of the cliché. The sight of the tall gent swearing an oath on the balcony was enjoyable both as a reminder of Yale's gridiron heroics (and the heroism of modern life) and as a sign that the very stones of modern-day New York—the paving blocks of Wall Street—were part of a historical continuum linking a home-loving, patriotic, industrious, yet elegant past with the age of electric lights, Wilbur Wright, Wallace Nutting chairs, college football, patriotic societies on the march, and apple-cheeked families aspiring to neocolonial homes. That was the birthright of the marchers of the Washington Continental Guards and the ladies they cajoled into riding their floats.

Although these societies and the designers of the floats they rode did not explore new reaches of colonial history, they did give the period fresh nuances, most particularly in the prop-laden tableaux representing daily life in the days of George and Martha Washington. It was no longer sufficient to display a few Washington relics on the balcony of the Sub-Treasury and tell people about them in newspaper stories. Visible, tangible detail counted. Papier-mâché cabbages, spinning wheels, and tankards gave the arid reaches of history the rich texture of the real-life present.

The Past as the Present in Costume

Pageantry and patriotic ritual as a whole moved in the same direction in the epoch of the Hudson-Fulton Celebration. Most of the state pavilions at the Jamestown Tercentennial Celebration held at Hampton Roads, near Norfolk, Virginia, in 1907, for example, were careful recreations of the haunts of the Founding Fathers. Eschewing the usual evocative oddities "in the manner of" an unspecified segment of the colonial period and the replicas of designated historical landmarks, architects for Maryland, Georgia, and Ohio copied stately homes distinguished mainly for their beauty.[66] It was easy to imagine someone really living in a house like "Homewood" or "Adena," and easy, too, to find decorating hints for somewhat smaller, newer premises.

Similarly, photographs of pageant costumes included in the official

Charles H. Stephens, watercolor study
for Episode VI, Scene 2, of the Philadelphia Pageant of 1912: "Washington at
Gray's Gardens"

program for the Philadelphia Historical Pageant of 1912 were indistin-
guishable in manner of presentation from ads for contemporary
gowns. Moreover, the dresses for each episode were carefully differentiated according to criteria also used by the editors of modern-day
society and the women's pages: rank, class, and the slightest shift in
the tides of fashion. The past was as real as the present and it was
responsive to the same conventions, prejudices, and enthusiasms.

After due consideration on the part of the organizers, Philadelphia's
pageant commemorating the 125th anniversary of the ratification of
the Constitution adopted the dramatic format rather than the processional one especially to achieve a more convincing rendition of the
flavor of colonial times in Pennsylvania. As the lush watercolor studies
for the key episodes in the story show, the desired sense of the
concrete and tangible favored the recreation of incidents about which
local historians could provide the most minute of records. Not surprisingly, the grandest of these featured Washington and his lady in a
suburban genre scene calculated not only to deploy all the hackneyed
Washington iconography of the past thirty years—the Martha Washington tea, the coach, the Federal aristocracy, and so forth—but also
to comment on the act of mounting a pageant (Figure 7.16).

The subject was a parade of sorts, complete with a historical float,
held in Gray's Gardens by the banks of the Schuylkill early in George
Washington's first administration:

Tea tables are set upon the green. . . . The federal ship "Union" which was
used in the Federal Procession in 1788 and for several years afterward was a
popular attraction at Gray's Gardens [is pulled in by a team of horses]. The
ladies and gentlemen representing the best Colonial society at the "Republican

Court" enter and await the arrival of Washington. He comes on a white charger. Mrs. Washington rides in the famous family coach. . . . As he dismounts "God Save Great Washington" set to the tune of "God Save the King" is sung. . . . Children wave a welcome from the ship "Union" which is entwined with French and American flags.[67]

Other equally lush scenes showed Washington coming to Philadelphia in November 1790 to take up residence; Washington leaving town; and Washington returning. His every move, it seemed, had been accompanied by a colonial-style parade made for the pageant-master's script. "The President," noted that document, "was everywhere acclaimed as 'the hero of the Western world,' and was the mark for many popular demonstrations. His arrival and his departure for his 'seat' in Virginia, his birthday, the Fourth of July and other occasions received ceremonious observance."[68]

Just as much of the Philadelphia Historical Pageant of 1912 self-consciously replicated the pageantry of the past and thus asserted a commonality of interest with colonial times, the pageant program conflated the colonial past with the neocolonial present in its hefty advertising section. At two dollars per volume, J. B. Lippincott Company of Philadelphia offered the bound script for sale in a new "true" history series that included the latest edition of Paul Leicester Ford's *The True George Washington,* Sidney George Fisher's *True History of the American Revolution,* and George Morgan's *The True Patrick Henry.* The back of the book was full of neocolonial advertisements for Philadelphia businesses. Under a drawing of a figure that closely resembled Washington holding a bayonet in one hand and a vault key in the other, the Colonial Trust Company stressed the security of savings accounts to provide for one's old age. The registered trademark of Quaker Maid Stockings ("for those who *will* have the best") was a photograph à la Nutting of a young woman wearing a colonial costume identical to the pageant outfits illustrated earlier in the text. Seated in a meeting house, she peeped at an offstage beau from beneath the brim of her bonnet with the brazen calculation of an incipient flapper.[69]

The accelerating tendency of the pageant to garb the present in the dresses and uniforms of colonial times meant that World War I spawned a fresh outburst of Washingtoniana focused on that conflict. Dixon Wecter has described a quasi-religious, quasi-patriotic service called "The Worship of the Flag" prescribed by the Episcopalian Diocese of New York during the war and the Red Scare that followed. In this rite, the seven red stripes of Old Glory were personified by communicants dressed as Washington, Jefferson, and other great American leaders down to Woodrow Wilson, and the congregation recited a responsorial psalm as each of them appeared.[70]

Percy MacKaye, folklorist and soon to be luminary of the movement, wrote *Washington: The Man Who Made Us*, a pageant or "ballad-play" for civic performance by a hundred volunteers, after hearing the real Woodrow Wilson address representatives of thirty-three nations gathered at Washington's tomb on July 4, 1918, for another colorful service. With the war raging in Europe, Wilson characterized the Revolution Washington had led not as a revolt but as "a step in the liberation of [America's] own people," and concluded with the "confident hope . . . of the spread of this revolt, this liberation of the great stage of the world itself."[71] In the finale of his third act, MacKaye reenacted that modern-day pageant of nations in order to demonstrate the meaning of Washington for the war-torn world of 1919:

Today, Washington—dead—is for most people a figure remote, statuesque, dignified, cold, almost mythical; one to be revered, but not warmly loved. But in his own day—alive—he was a magnetic human being, passionate, patient, resourceful—a rugged personality, lovable and greatly beloved.[72]

It has been, then, my aim so to portray him in his strong prime, with truth to reality, that we of today (and especially our young men of America, fighting today for what he fought for) may be led to feel a more intimate affection for "the man who made us," and for the still contemporary cause which he espoused for mankind.[73]

Roused to a positive fury of activity by the impending war, the patriotic societies undertook projects designed to turn every motor trip and stroll into a historical pageant. The Congress of the National Society of Sons of the American Revolution, meeting in Chicago in May 1913, voted to mark the route taken by George Washington from Philadelphia to Cambridge to take command of the American forces. Local chapters hunted down each of his landing spots and places of entertainment and bedecked the sides of the highways with historical markers, whitewashed rocks, arrows, and flags designating a special processional way leading backward in time as well as northward along a 1913 route map.[74]

Roadside markers designating otherwise invisible points along the colonial itinerary came to occupy more and more of the attention of such groups as the miles of paved highway multiplied and the configuration of ancient urban areas changed to accommodate traffic. A subcommittee of the prestigious Committee of One Hundred chartered by Mayor Gaynor to observe the tercentenary of "duly chartered commerce in New York City" in 1914—Cornelius Vanderbilt was president and the Morgan firm acted as the official treasurer—took notice of the general disrepair of such plaques and tablets within the city limits. Particularly shocking was the news that "the tablet at No. 255 West Street . . . marking the landing place of George Washington in 1775" had been carried off by vandals some ten years earlier without arousing any public outcry.[75]

The Commercial Tercentenary was marked by a general refurbishing of historical markers as well as by more ephemeral forms of civic ceremonial. Highly placed members of the Merchants' and Manufacturers' Exchange donned feathers, swords, wigs, and leather pants and, clutching the legendary strings of beads once exchanged for Manhattan, put on a pageant of trade with the Indians on a windswept Staten Island beach. As a prelude to that dumbshow, they arranged "safe and sane" Fourth of July festivities at City Hall in 1913 that included a pageant-parade of marching units garbed as New Yorkers of '76 and before.[76] But in comparison to the Hudson-Fulton Celebration the hoopla of 1913 and 1914 was only a distant echo, drowned out by debates over pacifism, preparedness, and possible war.

Back in 1909 the American Scenic and Historic Preservation Society had erected tablets in several locations, including one at the site of Fort Tryon where the Daughters of the American Revolution held rites to honor Margaret Corbin of Pennsylvania, said to have "fought for her husband in that engagement." Her name, at the behest of the DAR, figured prominently in the text inscribed thereon.[77] Honoring the only female soldier in Washington's forces, a woman who was hardly a model of stay-at-home domesticity, hints at some shift in the definition of femininity deemed acceptable by the membership. Indeed, in contrast to previous practice, officers of the organization delivered public speeches before mixed crowds of men and women at both Fort Tryon and Stony Point.

And contemporary feminism was justified by historical example. Helen Varick Boswell, principal orator at the laying of the Corbin plaque, dwelt upon "the illustrious deed which has inscribed the name of Margaret Corbin not only upon this bronze memorial behind me, but upon the yet more enduring tablet of the hearts of the American people":

I thought of the many thousands of women who are today standing side by side [with men] in the industrial world as truly heroines as she who long ago shared in the gallant defense of this historic ground. ... It is indeed the "women's invasion" in time of peace, but she fills her role with credit to her own energy, her own ability, and with honor to the country whose flag and the deathless principles it stands for has [sic] made her emancipation a reality.[78]

But for the most part women played more conventional roles in the pageantry surrounding the Hudson-Fulton Celebration. As indulgent teachers and settlement workers, for instance, they marshaled three hundred thousand schoolchildren for pageants in the city parks. On Washington Heights, little boys dressed as Redcoats and Continentals contended for "a stone house of the Revolutionary Period." In Battery Park, the "Little Mothers' Aid Association, whose officers had drilled the children," presented a parade of "little ones" attired as colonial dames, Dutch settlers, Indians, and the like; they also performed synchronized marches and reenacted a series of historical scenes: at the conclusion of the program "on the greensward, George and Martha Washington served tea." In Brooklyn, a ten-year-old Cornwallis capitulated to an eight-year-old Washington: "With the surrender of his sword . . . , a band hidden somewhere in the crowd struck up 'America' and all removed their hats and joined in the song." In DeWitt Clinton Park, Mrs. Russell Sage, known for her philanthropic nature and an inheritance of $70 million from her late speculator-husband, was the guest of honor at the moppets' dramatized history lesson.[79]

The Hudson-Fulton Celebration Exhibition

Along with the members of the Colonial Dames of New York and the venerable Mount Vernon Ladies' Association, Mrs. Sage would help to make the Hudson-Fulton Celebration a watershed in the history of American taste, for it was a special exhibition of the decorative arts at the Metropolitan Museum, held in concert with the speeches, parades, and pageants, that, according to its curator, Henry Watson Kent, created "a veritable renaissance of the so-called Colonial style."[80] The exhibition would show the originals on which those papier-mâché icons borne through the streets of Manhattan had been based. "This was the first time American 'antiques' were ever shown in New York," Kent later recalled in a pardonable overstatement, "and they made a great hit with the public and dealer alike. The Hudson-Fulton effort resulted eventually in the American Wing."[81]

The evolution of this seminal exhibition—attracting almost three hundred thousand visitors, it was also one of the more popular events held in conjunction with the festivities—is chronicled in the pages of the museum's monthly *Bulletin*. At first it seemed as if the staff was planning another relic show, since the museum was pleased to note the temporary loan of the sword Washington wore at Annapolis in 1783 from the ladies of Mount Vernon, who had only recently acquired it as a gift from J. Pierpont Morgan of New York, one of the members of the New York State Hudson-Fulton Celebration Commission charged with the supervision of "arts and historical exhibitions."[82] But it soon became clear that something more ambitious was in the offing.

As it was described by Robert deForest, chairman of the official exhibition committee, Mrs. Sage's lawyer, and secretary of the Met, the Hudson-Fulton Celebration Exhibition was a two-part affair in keeping with the bifurcated nature of the anniversary itself. In addition to a display of Dutch paintings of the period of Henry Hudson, "examples of the American industrial arts dating from about 1625 to 1825, with paintings by American artists of Fulton's time," were also to be shown.[83] The Colonial Dames were responsible for turning up paintings by American artists of the eighteenth century that might set off roomlike displays of pewter, glass, pottery, and most especially silver, grouped with furniture of the appropriate date.

The silver show, which included pieces by Paul Revere, was itself an event in the annals of American collecting. A major exhibition of American pieces at the Museum of Fine Arts in Boston in 1906 had set a new standard for the appreciation of silver not simply as an ancestral relic or a nostalgic token of vanished wealth and luxury, but as a source of fine proportions and pleasing lines, an object lesson in superior taste for designers and consumers. With a catalogue by R. T. Haines Halsey, who lent much of the silver shown in New York in 1909 and who would eventually install the American Wing at the Met, the Boston show brought into prominence a new breed of collector, distinguished by a fine eye rather than great wealth or superior breeding.

In her recent study of American "antiquers," Elizabeth Stillinger contends that as antiques became works of art instead of armorial symbols of good lineage, aesthetic appreciation for a silver vessel could be shared by immigrant and by native-stock American alike. That shift was fostered by the ideology of the genteel tradition in force in the American museum. The custodians of culture thought that seeing objects of excellence would elevate the taste of the working classes and, in time, stamp out the market for the shoddy, mass-produced goods factory hands were forced to make and consume. It is ironic, therefore, that material for the joint exhibition of American ecclesiastical silver held by the Metropolitan and the Museum of Fine Arts in 1911 would be assembled by the Colonial Dames just as the old associational and familial reasons for cherishing silver were being challenged by a new philosophy of collecting.[84] But in 1909, despite the participation of hereditary societies, the Metropolitan stoutly disavowed such connotations of class or birth as might continue to

7.17
Installation of the American section of the Hudson-Fulton Celebration Exhibition at the Metropolitan Museum of Art, New York, 1909

adhere to American-made silver. "The arrangement" of this segment of the show, Mr. deForest insisted, "will bring out the story of the development of the industrial arts in this country before 1815."[85]

The real attraction of the exhibition in the public estimate and "the most important group shown" from the point of view of the museum's board was the furniture owned by Eugene H. Bolles of Boston, who lent "examples of oak chests, chests of drawers, 'turned chairs,' 'wainscot chairs,' etc., from his remarkable collection."[86] His seventeenth-century pieces, acquired by Mrs. Sage in September of 1909 for $125,000 on the advice of her attorney and promptly presented to the museum, would become the nucleus of the American Wing.[87]

Whether the workmen who shuffled past Mrs. Sage's wainscot chairs went away determined to make no more shoddy cigars or unaesthetic shirtwaists thereafter is a matter of conjecture. Indeed, there is no reason at all to believe that the crowd abounded in such persons, despite the lack of an admission fee. But what was most appealing to most of the visitors, whoever they were, can be deduced from the fond recollections of the Hudson-Fulton show dusted off by commentators when the new wing finally opened in 1924, and from the features of the new facility derived from that earlier exhibition.

Installation photographs show that the objects on exhibit in 1909 were grouped in float fashion, on a shallow platform running along the gallery walls (Figure 7.17). Copleys, Smiberts, and other period paintings, as well as mirrors and clocks, were hung from the walls in the conventional manner. But the furniture, wherever practicable, was presented in organic groupings. Chairs were canted at an angle to tables, as though the occupants had just stood up. Large vessels and Bible boxes were displayed on surfaces where they might once have stood, and in natural positions. Only smaller pieces of silver were sealed in glass cases, and the cases were for the most part unobtrusively positioned within the ensembles.

At several points in this pageantlike procession of interior fragments, however, the cadence was broken by what seemed to be real, though narrow, rooms (Figure 7.18). The similarity between these abbreviated symbols for the colonial house and the architecture of parade floats like the "Dutch Doorway" is obvious. Set against the wall of one gallery was the woodwork of an early eighteenth-century room with a fireplace and cupboards forming a context for a spatter of chairs, candlesticks, and mugs the *New York Times* later identified with "the homes of our ancestors" and mistakenly called "Dutch."[88] The so-called Dutch chamber, actually the Newington Room from Connecticut, detached and rebuilt specially for the Hudson-Fulton show, later became a permanent feature of the American Wing (Figure 7.19). Reporters touring the galleries in 1924 remembered that "pine room which was first shown in the Hudson-Fulton Exhibition, . . .

7.18
An American interior reconstructed for the Hudson-Fulton Exhibition

used to represent the housing of the descendants of those who hewed their way through the forests from the vicinity of Boston to the shores of the Connecticut River. It contains," the *Times* noted, "a beautiful fireplace, which has been reproduced many times in the making of present-day rooms for those to whom the charm of this particular type of early eighteenth century architecture has appealed."[89]

In all, fifteen such rooms made up the bulk of the permanent display that opened at the Metropolitan Museum in the autumn of 1924, in a three-story addition at the north end of the Morgan Wing. Although the period room was not a new feature of exhibition design, the predominance of that method of display in the American Wing suggests that Americans now preferred to envision relics as components in a total domestic environment appreciated less for its novelty and its evocation of great historical events than for its resemblance to the contemporary home. Familiarity and comfort were the watchwords of neocolonialism in the 1920s. Press releases about the American Wing stressed inclusion of "the handiwork of the old American craftsmen who made the furniture and built the comfortable and artistic houses of early days. The new wing of the Metropolitan Museum . . . will be devoted to the art of the American home and here will be assembled the intimate things of generations that have passed—a remarkable collection that is certain to be one of the greatest attractions of the metropolis, for love of old furniture and art objects seems universal."[90]

By showing such rooms, the Metropolitan was throwing its prestige behind a radical assertion: raw, crude America indeed possessed an indigenous art of quality, associated with types of objects accessible to anyone. The American Wing, therefore, added fuel to fires blazing in neocolonial hearths across the land, where householders at their leisure perused the pages of *The True George Washington,* sewed colonial pageant costumes, or merely dozed in a Windsor rocker made by Wallace Nutting.

Previewing the opening and the response of critics to the whole enterprise, the *Times* harked back to the old notion that the annals of American history offered models for virtuous living:

It is, of course, excellent that we should praise famous men and our fathers that were before us, and the best way to praise them is to preserve and display their creditable works. But we can do more for them than this—we can emulate them. We can furnish our houses, or those slices of houses that we get in apartment houses, with objects that are sound in craftsmanship. . . . And we can learn to do this by studying the collections in the new wing of the Metropolitan Museum.[91]

Although the Metropolitan showed real rooms, R. T. Halsey's tastefully austere arrangements of furniture and silver still emphasized the preciousness of each piece and its formal properties, much as showing a perfect rose alone in a vase or hanging paintings in a balanced pattern against a neutral ground will direct attention toward uniqueness and quality. Despite inclusion of a homey context, the Halsey approach did not, apparently, create a demand for modern-style goods fabricated in accordance with sound American principles of the past. But American antiques like those displayed in the Metropolitan were assuredly "American" all the same, insofar as they betrayed "one of the qualities for which Washington himself has been both praised and blamed, a close exacting attention to excellence in small matters."[92]

Above all else, period rooms confirmed the desirability of *new* houses, apartments, business offices, and steamship cabins in the colonial style. They both stimulated the market for period reproductions and sent collectors into paroxysms of dissatisfaction with their own authentic finds. "The several thousands of us who have picked up antiques, who have congratulated ourselves on our 'collector's luck,' who have gazed lovingly upon the piecrust edge of our tiptable and the sheaf of wheat rather crudely cut on our Hepplewhite backs," said a confessed addict, "should approach the exhibition in dead earnest, not for a smattering of styles, but to let sink into the soul that indescribable difference between the first and second best which sets them worlds apart."[93]

Elihu Root, who spoke at the official housewarming ceremony for the American Wing, toured rooms plucked from Washington's old Philadelphia headquarters and from the tavern a scant eight miles beyond the gates of Mount Vernon, and saw "the ghosts of early Americans" all around him, sitting, chatting, reading their books, and nodding by the fire: the settings contradicted the old, history-book images of unyielding rectitude, of dry, cold lives. "No one can go through the new wing," Root said, "without learning that there was warmth in their lives, that their interests centered about the hearth-stone, and that there were qualities in their character that made for love of beauty."[94]

Their bric-a-brac told the story, and its price was on the rise, according to Robert deForest, a prime mover in the campaign to build the American Wing, who rose to comment on the unforeseen consequences of the long-ago Hudson-Fulton Celebration: "Since our plans were first made American art, American domestic art, has come into its own. Perhaps it has a little more than come into its own. Perhaps, at the moment, it has more acclaim than future generations would think it ought to have had. It has filled the antiquity shops, it has crowded the auction rooms, it is a vogue. And the price which it has gradually come to realize . . . has been somewhat paralyzing."[95] Antiques were the last word, a fad of the kind with which America's acquisitive forefathers were familiar. Seeking the lessons of the American Wing, social critics hit repeatedly on that same theme:

[The period rooms] tell us how interested the men of the eighteenth century were in the beauty of their homes, what close attention they paid to the detail of making them beautiful. Few of them equaled Washington in such ways, but it was a prevailing trait. . . . Our ancestors were [not much] different from ourselves in their liking for novelty, in their acceptance of ultra-modern design in order to be in the van of fashion, in their innocent desire to surpass each his neighbor in the decoration of houses.[96]

By 1924, when the Metropolitan Museum suddenly recognized that the decoration of the contemporary American home demanded the discernment and high seriousness of a Washington (and the bankroll of a Mrs. Russell Sage), the colonial craze had already reached its dizzy height. Madison Avenue auction rooms were crowded with rich swells, but those of lesser means, doing their "antiqueering" at country auctions, could learn the techniques of effective bidding from the weekly section of the *Saturday Evening Post* devoted to the newest national mania.[97] Alongside ads commending phonographs and steam radiators on the basis of their tenuous connections with the colonial era (Figure 7.20), the *Post* showed the middle-class reader in step-by-step detail how to build or buy a heritage house in the Early American mode, "a home of peace and beauty"; how to be a keen "junk snupper" on a par with Mrs. Sage, Mrs. Theodore Roosevelt, and the ladies of the DAR, whose expensive escapades on the collecting front were cited in order to hint that sheer dedication could still turn up treasures on the cheap; how to tell Sheraton from Chippendale from "Magoofus"; how to avoid decorator's clichés in arranging antiques about the electrified hearth; and how to spot collectible items whose prices had not yet risen, things like windowshades with paintings of Washington crossing the Delaware on them or "browny" printed handkerchief-pictures of Washington and Lafayette.[98]

The historical novelist Kenneth Roberts, who had collaborated with Booth Tarkington and Hugh Kahler on a pseudonymous book-length parody of the craze—*The Curator's Whatnot: A Compendium, Manual, and Syllabus of Information on All Subjects Appertaining to the Collection of Antiques, Both Ancient and Not So Ancient* appeared in 1923—was a frequent contributor to those pages, too,[99] The ins and outs of the quest for "Chippendale coat hangers, Adam andirons, Nebuchadnezzar whatnots, rare old New England carriage seats decorated with original tobacco juice, . . . graceful old Haig & Haig bottles, and . . . the old Coolidge sap bucket" from the incumbent president's ancestral homestead in Vermont were just familiar enough to the contemporary reader to be very funny.[100]

And while the Colonial Dames might devote themselves to the dogged pursuit of costly mourning samplers made by proper young women in 1799 to mark the passing of Washington, there were objects of lesser status to be collected and displayed in a half-mocking, half-serious vein—things such as "a pint flask of deep blue, with Wash-

7.21
A George Washington Cut Plug Tobacco can; except for the dome on the lid (ca. 1935), the design of this package varied little after the turn of the century.

ington's head like a smooth, masterly cameo."[101] A find of that order, bubbled a student of "Glass Mania" in the columns of the *Saturday Evening Post,* could make "anyone, collector or no, appreciative."[102] With the Volstead Act in effect and prohibition a topic of conversation almost as commonplace as colonial antiques, collectors discovered that George Washington had topped all other favorites in the designs for nineteenth-century whiskey bottles and that the "first great temperance crusade in America, started in 1840 by six liquor addicts of Baltimore . . . called itself 'The Washington Society.'"[103]

Ancient Washington flasks were still thick on the ground in 1924, and Washington was still being enlisted by canny entrepreneurs to hook Americans on nasty habits. Every corner drugstore had its red-white-and-blue cans of George Washington Cut Plug Tobacco for smoking or chewing (Figure 7.21). The slogan on the back of the can read "Greatest American." Whether the phrase better described the George Washington of the portrait thereon or the weed therein was left to the taste of the discerning customer, puffing thoughtfully on a pipe before a neocolonial hearth.

Neocolonial Politics

8 / / / / / / / / / / / / / / / /

The Presidency of Warren Harding
1921–1923

8.1
The Warren G. Harding House in Marion, Ohio, built ca. 1890. The "colonial" porch was added later.

A Front Porch in the Colonial Revival Style

Warren G. Harding came to the White House from a big green-and-white house on Mount Vernon Avenue in Marion, Ohio. Designed around 1890 in a vaguely Queen Anne style by the president-to-be and his intended bride in anticipation of their marriage, it was finished a few years later with the addition of a fashionable Colonial Revival porch, a huge excrescence with stubby white columns and a semi-circular bulge just to the right of the front door (Figure 8.1).[1] The door of the Harding home at 380 Mount Vernon Avenue opened directly upon a capacious front hall, and there hung an elaborate glass globe, a wedding present to Warren and his Florence: when the light went on, the little colonial boy in the painted tableau on the lampshade bowed toward his little colonial miss and wooed her eternally with a nosegay. The house was just quaint and colonial enough to be very, very modern.

In Harding's cluttered study, an alcove off the parlor, a battered copy of a 1902 bestseller by Gertrude Atherton, *The Conquerer: A Dramatized Biography of Alexander Hamilton,* shared a shelf with Jared Sparks's venerable *Life of Washington.*[2] Washington biographies were standard features of the turn-of-the-century home library. In the austere farmhouse in Vermont where Harding's vice president and successor, Calvin Coolidge, was reared, J. T. Headley's hoary *Washington and His Generals* was deemed suitable fare for bookish boys, and by the time the lad went off to Amherst to study history, he had also "learned to cherish the works of the great prophet of the gods of prosperity, Alexander Hamilton."[3]

Warren Harding's murky syntax would betray his more rudimentary education, but he could digest lighter fare, especially dime novels, and he devoured the Atherton book, which, he said, reawakened an

8.2
A Washington's Birthday cartoon from
Life, February 1902, in which the hero
tells a "fish story" instead of his
customary whopper

"early passion" for Hamilton. "It riveted me," Harding confessed.[4] For years thereafter he toured the summer lyceum circuit, at $100 a week, "bloviating" (as he put it) in vague, romantic terms about George Washington's secretary of the Treasury. In a florid set speech entitled "Prophet of American Destiny," Harding's Hamilton bcame the spiritual founding father of the GOP, herald of "the gospel of American optimism," and a paragon of honesty, the virtue that, according to the future twenty-ninth president of the United States, was "the greatest essential" of American progress. But as President Harding would later tell the annual convention of the Chambers of Commerce of the United States with an ingratiating frankness, he himself often tempered his platform opinions on Hamilton, truthtelling, and other such weighty matters to the beliefs of the more "commercially-minded" in his audience: today, sound businessmen surely understood that good public relations sometimes demanded an honesty of a different order.[5]

Truthtelling was the traditional attribute of George Washington in the McGuffey Readers and in the popular imagination although, in the interests of one of those higher truths, Sparks's 1839 biography had deftly excised both the cherry tree lies of Parson Weems and such mild crudities of prose expression as Washington had in actuality permitted himself.[6] There were facts that defied the editor's pencil, however, and Sparks betrayed some anxiety over the undeniable childlessness of the Father of His Country.[7] Like Warren G. Harding of Mount Vernon Avenue, the George Washington of Mount Vernon was nobody's real papa—merely stepfather to the issue of his wife's previous marriage. Or so it seemed, in both cases.

Since Revolutionary days, the "left-handed side of folklore" had given the honest Washington an assortment of shady assignations with octoroon and Tory mistresses and numerous illegitimate offspring, including Alexander Hamilton, the "Prophet of American Destiny."[8] The illustrated papers still honored Washington's Birthday every February with reminders of the boy who could not tell a lie, but increasingly the prodigy with the little hatchet who appeared in the seasonal cartoons seemed to resort to the truth only in the absence of other options (Figure 8.2). Washington's Birthday greeting cards popular at the turn of the century also grew more and more flip. A humorous postcard copyrighted in 1905 used the cherries and hatchets that served as the decorative emblems of Washington (Figure 8.3) to suggest that the infant "George almost ruined this country" with his axe by wiping out the trees that supplied the fruit garnish for cocktails (Figure 8.4). "Nancy A." of Springfield, Illinois, who mailed that card to her friend Betsy Peel in 1906, added this irreverent toast as a postscript: "Here's to the memory of George Washington, the childless father of eighty millions."

The historical climate was one of affectionate familiarity: the popular view of the past was colored by a knowing skepticism about the ways of heroes. In such an atmosphere, it is small wonder that *The True George Washington,* Ford's sober biography, first published in 1896 and reissued at regular intervals up through the 1920s, had candidly recited the stories of his deceitfulness, his immorality, and his bastards "being bandied about in clubs," including the Senate of the United States.[9] Thanks to nearly half a century of revivalism, George Washington had become something less than a hero, and something more like Senator Warren G. Harding of Marion, Ohio, a bluff and ebullient hail-fellow-well-met, a tippler of fruited cocktails.

By the time the 1924 edition of *The True George Washington* appeared in Marion, Ohio, Warren Harding had already been buried there. Despite the peroration of his standard campaign speech in which he had asserted that "Washington, Lincoln and Roosevelt are the three greatest men in American history," Harding seems to have known very little about the first of those heroes.[10] There is no evidence that he read anything on Washington beyond what appeared in the magazines, for instance. And in all likelihood Harding never opened his own edition of the Sparks *Life of Washington,* a book that, like John Marshall's leaden, multivolume work of the same name, was to be found in the parlors of a thousand Mount Vernon Avenues, moldering in unopened righteousness.

But the George Washington scandals whispered about the enclaves of the American male were almost certainly a different matter, for Warren Harding dearly loved a club, any club: the Moose, the Sons

8.3
A Washington's Birthday postcard, mailed 1908

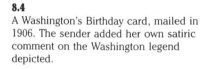

8.4
A Washington's Birthday card, mailed in 1906. The sender added her own satiric comment on the Washington legend depicted.

of Union Veterans, the Concatenated Order of Hoo-Hoos, the U.S. Senate. Senator Harding, it was said, belonged in a fez—or a toga: "He was superbly handsome; his face and carriage had a Washingtonian nobility and dignity."[11] As the amiable Senator Harding once confessed to his fellow members of that most august of gentlemen's clubs, "I like the fraternity of this body. I like to know that when the waters are muddy, I will be considered. I like to participate in the 'Booster' proposition."[12]

In 1910, at the climax of his unsuccessful gubernatorial campaign, a parade of hometown admirers wound down Mount Vernon Avenue, chanting "Boost a Booster . . . Vote for Harding . . . a Marion County Booster." Pine though he might for their fellowship, however, the archbooster and clubman was blackballed by the local Masons until the sedentary "front porch" campaign of 1920 made Marion the focus of national attention (at which time the neighbors built a neocolonialish colonnade along Mount Vernon Avenue leading to his residence). Only then was Harding inducted, with curious haste. And only after his inauguration did he gratefully accept membership in the Rotary, the Kiwanis, and the Marion Eagles with "no niggling afterthought about why he had not been asked sooner."[13]

The Left-Handed Side of Colonial History

Racial and sexual rumors—some of them, as time would show, fact rather than malicious gossip—had barred Warren Harding from the choosier clubs in Marion, Ohio. Although evil reports about public figures were nothing new in the American political arena, the Harding stories mirrored the Washington slanders current in the 1920s to an uncanny degree. It was as if the George Washington tales preserved in the subterranean lore of the lodgehalls Harding frequented had oozed out of the historical past and attached themselves with modern tenacity to his own imposing person.

Like Warren Harding's forebears, for instance, Washington was supposed to have consorted with Negro women. According to the historian Francis Russell, the charge that the Harding family was descended from fugitive slaves and mulattos predated Warren's birth and accounted for his exclusion from the choosier clubs in Marion. At the Republican convention of 1920 crude fliers circulated bringing the supposed facts of his blackness to wider attention. Most newspapers ignored the issue. When the *New York Times* ran a veiled account of the accusations, the GOP commissioned on behalf of the nominee an elaborate family tree adorned with blue-eyed pioneers, and mailed out pallid, full-page portraits of his father and mother.

Since few Americans apart from Marion natives and Chicago delegates had heard the gossip in the first place, sudden publication of this lily-white genealogy might have been a calculated risk had such tables not become a routine feature of the formidable "cult of ancestors."[14] So, for every voter who wondered why the folksy candidate on the neocolonial front porch in rural Ohio "should be going ancestral," for every party functionary who wondered whether Harding was running for election to the presidency or the Sons of the Revolution, there were others to whom it mattered greatly that the Republican standard-bearer was a direct descendant of the Anglo-Saxon Stephen Harding of Massachusetts Bay.[15]

The hereditary societies placed a premium on blood descent from the colonial fathers even when racial purity was not at issue and they constituted a powerful political lobby, well worth cultivating by senators with higher aspirations. One sure sign of Harding's rise toward the status required of a Republican hopeful had been his invitation to deliver a Washington's Birthday address before a joint meeting of the Sons and Daughters of the American Revolution assembled in the capital in 1918. But among the great and famous orations on the virtues of Washington, Harding's is unique for an almost total absence of facts, myths, half-truths, or outright lies about the Father of His Country.

After the vaguest of references to Washington's Farewell Address and its warnings against factionalism, the speaker instead began to sputter darkly about God, progress, anarchy in revolutionary Russia, and wartime interests—"commercial, industrial, agricultural and professional"—whose ambitions ought to be curbed, or perhaps promoted. The text invited either reading and closed with the enigmatic observation that "no people shod in $18 shoes is equipped for the conquering march of civilization."[16] The Sons and Daughters, by all reports, went away reassured that the philosophic pillars of the republic still stood.

Their preoccupation with bloodlines flowing back to the Founding Fathers was symptomatic of the filiopietism that also affected political parties, lyceums, and less savory organizations in the years around World War I. During Harding's presidency, the Ku Klux Klan was naming its local "dens" in honor of Revolutionary patriots and William Allen White was shortly to accuse the DAR of turning red-white-and-blue ancestry into a weapon against "colored people, Jews and Catholics, enemies of the KKK."[17] But distinguished ancestry was also the traditional weapon against any charges of impiety leveled against heroes.

During the first spate of Washington revelations elicited by the various Philadelphia and New York centennials at the turn of the century, for example, pious genealogists had responded with weighty tomes on the *fathers* of the Patriot Father, tracing his forebears back to the entourage of William the Conquerer and, in one memorable instance, to Odin, the mythological Scandinavian god.[18] The longer the lines of descent, the more respectable the progeny. And as factual data shaded by degrees into the quasi-divinity of Anglo-Saxon hero legend, ancestor-hunters sought to preserve both Washington and the "Washingtonian" Warren Gamaliel Harding from the frailties of mortal American men.

Warren Harding's brand-new, colonialized family tree, omitting as it did several recent shoots, still afforded little refuge from spicy stories that were demonstrably true. On the eve of his nomination, the Republicans sent an emissary to call upon their future standard-bearer. "Before acting finally," the visitor declared, "we think you should tell us, on your conscience and before God, whether there is anything that might be brought against you that would embarrass the party, any impediment that might disqualify you or make you inexpedient, either as candidate or as President."[19] The inquiry was unprecedented but thoroughly expedient. Since 1905 Warren Harding had been embroiled in an affair with the elegant wife of one of his closest friends, a Marion merchant.

Distant supporters who wrote indignantly to Marion during the long summer on the front porch reported whispering campaigns about Harding's "nigger" blood and told of hearing stories that "you are chasing around with another woman."[20] The scenario hinted at in George Washington's notorious letters to Sally Fairfax, *his* best friend's wife, seemed to be providing the script for a furtive modern-day romance in the Midwest. William Allen White and Mark Sullivan, covering the doings in Marion for their respective papers, caught the odd whiff of gossip seeping from the fastness of Marion's fraternal enclaves, too. Chasing after married women was bad enough, but in 1910 or thereabouts, according to local word of mouth, Harding had also begun to cast frisky glances at a neighborhood teenager who longed to be a film star. In 1919, in the heat of the primaries, the would-be movie queen had given birth to Harding's natural daughter amid threats of exposure from the discarded mistress cooling her heels back in Ohio.

Harding had gamely tried to stave off disaster with five-pound boxes of Martha Washington chocolates; these he routinely dispatched to all the women he might have wronged. Colonial chocolates notwithstanding, however, the Republican convention was still alive with rumors about the first of his liaisons and written "testimony" about the baby. Sizzling letters penned to a third lady would soon appear for sale in New York at an extortionary price met, in due course, by party leaders. Nevertheless, the GOP hierarchy swallowed Harding's sincere assurance that his conscience was clear. It was their candidate, after all—the clubman's clubman—who spoke so often and so eloquently on honesty, the "great essential" of American progress.

When the candidate, dogged by the nation's press corps, settled in on Mount Vernon Avenue, the situation worsened. William Allen White noticed one lone store in Marion innocent of the boosters' bunting draped everywhere in honor of the hero's return. White asked the owner to explain his lonely boycott and heard the sordid story of Harding's most durable affair from the mouth of the aggrieved husband.[21] The fellow's errant wife, in the meantime, was being chased off the famous Harding front porch by Florence in a hail of piano stools and feather dusters. At this dangerous juncture, the Republican National Committee sent a public relations expert to Ohio. Albert Lasker, the advertising genius responsible for Palmolive's "schoolgirl complexion," the "film" that Pepsodent banished, and the flapper's sudden craving for Lucky Strikes, paid off knowing locals, planted fresh genealogies in press packets, and set about restoring Marion to that blessed condition the candidate called "normalcy."

Harding had coined the word during a primary speech in Boston. "America's present need," he pontificated, "is not heroics but healing; not nostrums but normalcy; not revolution but restoration; . . . not surgery but serenity."[22] Faintly heard beneath the alliterative tinkle was an ancient siren song, wafting out of the good old days, that vague, eternal American dreamtime before things always went awry, when life was simple and truth was truth, when the skies above the big front porch were unclouded and bright. "Normalcy" summoned up a roseate vision of all the good years, back there before the Great War, a domain of memory untouched by the spiritual rigors of war and the intellectual challenges of a society transformed in its aftermath. No heroics, no revolution. Poised between nostalgia and uncertainty, Harding proposed a stately retreat into the serenity of tradition. The man from Mount Vernon Avenue proposed to become America's first neocolonial president.

Looking back at "normalcy" from the perspective of the 1930s, the novelist John Dos Passos would fix this decisive point of choice as the moment when the American Dream went sour. In his *1919,* prewar reform yielded to postwar anarchy because the world of normalcy had no room for authentic, demanding heroes. One of Dos Passos's extraneous, martyred heroes was Wesley Everest, a doughboy who "came home from overseas and got his discharge from the army, [and] went back to his old job of logging" in the state of Washington. Castrated, hanged, and finally shot to death on Armistice Day by a businessmen's club and its mercenary army of "hundred per cent" veterans, this IWW organizer was an old-style hero as Dos Passos described him. He was a man of action, a doer, heedless of the status quo. Everest "was a logger like Paul Bunyan. . . . When Paul Bunyan came back from making Europe safe for the democracy of the Big Four, he joined the lumberjacks' local to help make the Pacific slope safe for the workingstiffs. The wobblies were reds. Not a thing in this world Paul Bunyan's ascared of."[23]

In that subtle shift from simile to metaphor, Dos Passos linked his Wobbly protagonist to the tradition of mighty men of legend, whose deeds reverberate through history to inspire modern heroism. The American tradition, he argued, was a call to change, to perpetual struggle and revolution. This invocation of heroic mythology made the finale of the novel, with its pair of juxtaposed burials, catastrophically bleak. "Nobody knows where they buried the body of Wesley Everest," wrote Dos Passos; Paul Bunyan, and the very possibility of change revivified by the American heroic tradition, vanish without a trace. And meanwhile, at Arlington Cemetery, the Unknown Soldier is laid to rest as "Mr. Harding prayed to God and the diplomats and the generals and the admirals and the brasshats and the politicians and the handsomely dressed ladies out of the *Washington Post* stood up solemnly and thought how beautiful sad Old Glory God's Country it was to have the bugler play taps."[24]

The bugler's dirge honored a dead hero. For the writer, the notes also signaled the death of heroism, or rather its safe interment in the realm of "Old Glory" sentimentality, where the old heroes stood frozen on their pedestals, debarred from meddling in the real-life business of "normalcy" and casting a feeble glow of righteousness upon their progeny. Normalcy drew a meticulous distinction between the active heroics of a modern-day Paul Bunyan, the "heroics" Warren Harding rejected, and the moribund heroes, the household gods of Mount Vernon Avenue at whose altar he paid symbolic homage with his talismanic *Life of Washington*, his colonial chandelier, his Colonial Revival porch, his lectures on the honesty and prophetic vision of Hamilton, and, of course, his palliative shipments of Martha Washington chocolates to irate sweethearts.

As he fulminated against disruptive heroics, the candidate may have overlooked the obvious parallels between his own adventures to date and the odder recent twists in the legend of the heroic Washington. Yet Warren Harding lived a life haunted at every juncture by heroes, heroines, and their historic relics. The walls of his sanctum at the *Marion Daily Star* bore lithographic likenesses of Lincoln and General Grant. Opposite his desk hung a carbon print of Napoleon at the tomb of Frederick the Great. In the office down the hall, his father proudly displayed a Lincoln print and another of Betsy Ross inventing Old Glory for General Washington.

In the parlor on Mount Vernon Avenue stood *Priscilla the Puritan Girl,* a marble sculpture carved in Pisa, Italy, and purchased by Florence Harding in retaliation for Warren's excessive interest in a genuine work of art, a statue of a stark naked dancing girl. The alcove off the parlor harbored (beneath a portrait of Hamilton and alongside the

Hamilton and Washington volumes) a well-thumbed copy of *Imperial Purple,* a potboiler on the career of Julius Caesar. Of the three great builders of the three greatest republics in all of history—Caesar, Napoleon, and Alexander Hamilton—Harding still thought the last was best.

But in the smoke-filled back rooms of the Chicago convention, hard questions were being asked about the earthy realities of Warren Harding's private life. On the public floor of the convention, stump orators all but ignored the present to meander instead through the annals of a glorious, hero-ridden past. Tradition formed a seemly backdrop for the nominee, casting the kindly, amber haze of heroism over his mundane virtues, lending them a proper weight and magnitude. "After reading these nominating speeches," the *Boston Transcript* chuckled, "Washington, Lincoln, Grant, Roosevelt, Julius Caesar and Napoleon feel like pretty small potatoes this morning."[25]

The technique was no novelty. William Allen White remembered that his first job with the *Kansas City Star* in the 1890s called for liberal doses of incense to be wafted over political figures beloved of the editor. White and his friends made a game of escalating their heroic allusions, a reductio ad absurdum in which Grover Cleveland became first the new Washington, next a second Lincoln, and finally Christ returned to earth.[26] But the 1920s would find nothing absurd about such similes; they were among the usual props in the public relations man's bag of tricks. Bruce Barton's runaway bestseller, *The Man Nobody Knew,* even described Christ as a successful and inspirational business executive who used clever ads to get his message across. In readers' eyes the comparison flattered both God and the contemporary Rotarian.[27]

Harding himself was another rallying symbol for modern go-getters. Twenty-five hundred traveling salesmen once paraded through Marion behind six brass bands, confident that Harding was their hero. Unlike Cox, his Democratic opponent, Harding had never called America's peripatetic drummers "parasites and public menaces"; in fact, the affability and glibness of the drummer were qualities he had cultivated during his years as a Marion clubman. Hard on the heels of the salesmen came a high-stepping column of stars. During the front porch campaign Al Jolson, Texas Guinan, and forty other celebrities of the hour held a parade in Marion, too, marching under the banner of the newly constituted Harding and Coolidge Theatrical League.[28] Their up-to-the-minute "jazz campaign" on behalf of the Republican candidate served as a kind of counterbalance to the stodgy image created for Harding by Lasker and the public relations experts.

The word "jazz" connoted snap decisions and the harried tempo of postwar America, or just those signs of modernity the front porch strategy was designed to conceal. The house on Mount Vernon Avenue was as much a part of the Harding image as his Washingtonian self, and big houses with green lawns and Colonial Revival porches meant something quite specific to those who followed the stately progress of the campaign in the pictures carried by their hometown newspapers. "In these days of jazz bands, bungalows, chewing gum and other nervous disorders," wrote a practicing architect in 1917, "it is a relief to discover evidence of a return to the simpler ways of the forefathers of our country. There is no more refreshing indication of this than . . . the renewed interest in Colonial architecture."[29]

So, from the portico of an old-fashioned house in a nice little town, Florence Harding gave interviews punctuated with asides about her statue of Priscilla, recipes for waffles, and tidbits about her "nice little cretone curtains," and fended off amorous threats to the stability of her home. The candidate's aged father was photographed having breakfast there, looking every inch the Wallace Nutting grandsire by the hearth, in order to portray "the ancestral home atmosphere."[30] If not exactly a log cabin, the house on Mount Vernon Avenue and all the appurtenances thereof suggested the rise of a boy-hero out of a history book, the apotheosis of the American Dream, "the reestablishment of the old order of elevation from rural obscurity," the Country Boy who had scrambled up from obscurity toward the highest office in the land trailing clouds of homebound, hearthside virtue in his wake.[31]

The same fraternity of marketing geniuses who were working so diligently to touch up the neocolonial portrait of Warren Gamaliel Harding being etched into the public consciousness would also, in the 1920s, sell quaint colonial houses on the basis of their association with the blameless joys of close-knit family living. Thus the ad copy for a typical Dutch Colonial model—it was called "The Washington"—produced by the Standard Homes Company appealed to the consumer's higher instincts and to nostalgia for an imagined prewar past: "When one looks . . . at the Colonial style . . . as shown in The Washington, his thoughts go back to the days when love of home and family were the most sacred emotions in the hearts of men. There are yet many with a steadfastness of purpose who inwardly long for the colonial days, and to such The Washington will be an inspiration."[32]

In the changing world of big business, big labor, and big cities, the Harding persona being assembled on Mount Vernon Avenue in Marion, Ohio, stood for once-upon-a-time. The small-town candidate, Mark Sullivan observed, "loved an orderly world, a neat world, a world of carefully gravelled paths and nicely clipped hedges—above all, a world that stays the same from day to day."[33] According to *Literary Digest*, Harding's campaign staff took pride in the fact that, despite their prompt attention to a multitude of daily problems, "there [was] no jazz" in their management of his publicity: "The tranquillity of the

Harding offices is taken by some to indicate the sort of an administration the Ohioan would give the country if elected. 'He'll take the jazz out of life and bring us back to sane living once more,' one man is quoted as saying."[34] Jazz was the last word in modernity, but the official Republican fight song, composed by Al Jolson for jazz performance, demanded "another Lincoln, to do the country's thinkin'." That hero for modern times was "Mis-ter Hard-ing," whose election landed his jazz-age presidency squarely in the midst of an endless costume pageant of American history.[35]

The Plymouth Landing Tercentenary

The rapidly closing distance between the jazz era and the make-believe past, a gulf "normalcy" promised to bridge, found expression in the Plymouth Landing Tercentenary ceremonies. Festivities began in December of 1920, just after the national election (Figure 8.5). Senator Henry Cabot Lodge, archfoe of Wilsonian internationalism, student of the Farewell Address, and a popular historian with texts on Hamilton and Washington already to his credit, made a speech about the Pilgrim fathers. Among New Englanders like Lodge, Washington and the patriots were Johnny-come-lately freedom fighters responsible, at best, for a kind of "second founding" that fulfilled the prophetic act of 1620 when the fathers of Massachusetts had claimed Plymouth Rock. But the Plymouth Colony Pilgrims, in mystical anticipation of Washington's warnings against foreign entanglements, also assured the senator "from their own experience that the economic and political system recently raised up in Russia by the Bolshevik Revolution was fated to fail and that capitalism and the right to personal property were the only true economic expressions of the will of God."[36] The gray-clad Pilgrims of 1620 had something germane to tell the fearsome Reds of 1920. What was more, Lodge's rhetoric made it sound as if those Pilgrims were still hovering around their rock, fretting over twentieth-century radicalism and coaching the senior senator from Massachusetts in ways to combat it.

Governor Calvin Coolidge of Massachusetts, Harding's running mate and vice president–elect, took the podium next to boast, in the face of clear genealogical evidence from Marion to the contrary, that it was no real distinction to have come over on the *Mayflower*—or to own furniture that looked as though it might have made the trip—because, although, "men trace to them their lineage as to a royal house," the Pilgrims were actually "oblivious to rank."[37] Coolidge, of course, could afford to be oblivious to the benefits of a New England heritage: he was a dyed-in-the-wool Puritan throwback from the picturesque reaches of rural Vermont. But Warren Harding, with his mythical Massachusetts forebears and his storebought colonial bric-a-brac,

8.5
Bronze medal, cast in honor of the Plymouth tercentenary by the Boston Numismatic Society in 1920; Harding received a copy of the medal in gold on August 1, 1921, during his visit to the Pilgrim pageant.

could not ignore the manifest advantages of ancient bloodlines. Within days after the circulation of his new family history, he had joined the Sons of the American Revolution, and his advancement through the degrees of Freemasonry was accelerated to win him the endorsement of the Sons and Daughters of Washington and membership in the Alexandria, Virginia, lodge to which George Washington had once belonged.[38]

Voters fearful of immigrant conspiracies, labor unrest, and bolshevism could find stability in the image of Plymouth Rock, still resting on its beach along the Atlantic, and in the comforting words of Lodge and Coolidge, twin pillars of austere Yankeedom. At the conclusion of his remarks, however, Calvin Coolidge departed from tradition by placing a newfangled long-distance telephone call to Governor Stephens of California. The call was by way of fulfilling Daniel Webster's prophecy, delivered on the same spot during the 1820 bicentennial. Webster had predicted that a hundred years hence "the voice of acclamation and gratitude, commencing on the Rock of Plymouth, shall be transmitted through millions of the sons of the Pilgrims, till it lose itself in the murmurs of the Pacific Seas."[39] Calvin Coolidge meant to prove him right with the help of twentieth-century electronics.

Albert Lasker and his team of ad men back in Marion could have found much to envy in the razzle-dazzle rhetoric of the Plymouth Tercentenary whereby the rightness of Manifest Destiny was confirmed by the modern technology of 1920. But the geneaological conceit hinged on aligning type with antitype—Plymouth Rock in 1620, Coolidge-as-Webster standing for 1820, and California in 1920—in an electrified chain that, alas, was subject to the vagaries of contemporary politics. And so the prophetic voice of the ages was, if not lost in the Pacific, then somewhat misdirected: the governor of California went hunting that day, and unbeknownst to the solemn throng assembled at Plymouth Rock, a lowly secretary answered the call of the centuries!

That was the least of Plymouth's problems. The most mortifying involved technical difficulties in moving the sacred rock back to a spot near the water where a Pilgrim father could, at some point in history, have stepped on it. Hence the celebration dragged on into 1921 and resumed with the arrival of Warren Harding, who sailed up to the relocated rock in the Presidential yacht *Mayflower*, bloviated before an audience of one hundred thousand, reviewed a parade of colonial worthies, and settled down as dusk fell to watch *The Pilgrim Spirit*, a pageant with a cast of thirteen hundred.[40] The principal events of August 1, the day of the Harding visit, were formalized components in a rite of patriotic ceremonial and pageantry Americans now thought essential to moments of deepest historical retrospection.

The president and his party arrived even as members of the local arrangements committee and the town fathers squabbled amongst themselves for the honor of greeting him first. There was a historical parade up from the harbor, with floats depicting "dramatic episodes relating to the history of the pilgrims in Massachusetts." The famous landing was restaged before a large pasteboard rock; the first house built by the Pilgrims on Leyden Street was honored by a lifelike replica on wheels; passing units from the lodges, patriotic orders, and fraternal organizations of Plymouth elicited much enthusiasm from the president, who was an active or aspiring member of most of them; and the women who marched with their men to the loudest cheers of all "wore the costumes of the Pilgrim women—simple gray gowns, white sleeves, collars and cap."[41] The floats in the industrial division, the largest in the parade, traced the histories of such firms as the Standish Worsted Company and Puritan Mills. The town of Rockland, represented by a twenty-foot car showing the manufacture and sale of shoes from the days of the Plymouth Colony to the present, included so many figures ("all . . . descendants of colonial ancestors") that rehearsals were required.[42]

Corn of the golden bantam variety, picked on Adams Street in Quincy, "The City of Presidents," was served at a luncheon for the guests of honor in a hotel dining room decorated with colonial flags assembled by a historian hired to do just that. But the meal was particularly noteworthy for the exclusion of almost everyone customarily honored in the pantheon of Plymouth society. According to the *Boston Globe*, "the other guests of the town," who were legion, "went to Ye Pilgrim Tavern." In fact, Senator Lodge was almost arrested as an intruder when he tried to join the president's party at the landing site.[43]

Before the day was out, Henry Cabot Lodge might have wished that he had stayed at home. His own biography was a late addition to the fabric of Washington hagiography woven by grateful New England poets and historians to honor the leader who drove the enemy from their farms and towns and pursued the Revolutionary War at points far removed from Plymouth. As chief orator of the Plymouth Landing Tercentenary of the previous December, he had enlarged on those beliefs and stressed the spiritual linkage between the Pilgrim fathers and Washington's generation of Founding Fathers. As chairman of the Senate Committee on Foreign Relations, Lodge also advanced a vision of foreign policy consistent with his understanding of Washington's Farewell Address in his opposition to the League of Nations.[44]

His position on the relevance of Washington to contemporary America was the GOP position about colonial history, and was stoutly maintained at a time when political parties were fully expected to articulate such attitudes toward the heroes and the issues of the past. The dire warnings about radical agitators, immigrants who maintained their ties with the "old country," and schoolbooks infected with foreign propaganda delivered by Republican spokesman Albert Beveridge to the assembled Sons of the Revolution on Washington's Birthday of the year in which Harding spoke at Plymouth Rock sprang from the same historical sensibility. "Every word of the Farewell Address might have been written in 1921, so peculiarly applicable is that great state paper to condition that afflict the American people today," Beveridge had insisted.[45]

For all the evidence of due caution in the matter of alien entanglements finally offered by his public statements in Plymouth, Warren Harding might never have heard of Senators Beveridge and Lodge, the ideology of his own party, or his own previous speeches on the greatness of Washington when he announced plans for a speech on an international theme, calling for a new "World Brotherhood." After dispensing good citizenship medals to "children of humble foreign birth" from New Bedford (thus setting them on the path to one-hundred-percent Americanism), President Harding launched that day into a prepared text that promised to offer an extremely un-Republican interpretation of the colonial past by which nativism and isolationism in their most virulent forms were so often justified. But as he stood there, looking his most Washingtonian, silhouetted against a replica of the old wooden *Mayflower* afloat in the harbor, it soon became apparent that Harding's fuzzy rhetoric was, after all, calibrated to please the throng with a litany of all the old bromides and benevolent sentiments. He opposed any "superstate," he announced with a flourish (as though expecting that his opposition would come as a revelation to his auditors); the crowd applauded politely. His evocation of New England, the birthplace of religious freedom, elicited cheers. So did his insistence that the American Revolution was a New England affair from the first and his appeals to a "community of free people of our race" founded at Jamestown and Plymouth.

Colonial history did have a lesson to teach, the president sensed dimly—a moral of high-mindedness and tolerance which his tenuous grasp on just what had transpired at Plymouth Rock and his inability to translate such intimations into prose left stranded on shoals of verbiage far less secure than the rock:

The perspectives of history are not safely to be judged save from the loftiest peaks of human experience. It is the dearly bought privilege of our generation to stand on one of these heights of the long ages, to look back over the pathways by which we have come thus far, to see clearly what have been the main traveled roads and what the by-paths.

We cannot lift the veil to the future, but we can analyze what had gone before. It is good to keep our feet firmly on the earth, though we gaze in high hope for human brotherhood and high attainments. Just as the Pilgrims had a practical mind for material things amid the effective pursuit of their higher ideals, so must we with our inheritance.[46]

H. L. Mencken called such stemwinding "Gamaliese." "It reminds me of a string of wet sponges," he quipped. "It is so bad that a certain grandeur creeps into it."[47] But the crowd in Plymouth hooted with pleasure throughout the oratorical ordeal. Although the theme of world brotherhood had gotten lost in heavy grammatical seas, it was pleasant to think that the Puritanism Harding routinely confused with the Pilgrim fathers somehow justified not a new round of postwar asceticism but the material preoccupations of a nation that wore Miles Standish worsteds, ate neocolonial Jell-O (Figure 8.6), and aspired to cottages reminiscent of the Pilgrim houses hauled along Water Street in the tercentenary parade. For his part, the president was gratified by his warm reception. He waved, beamed, put his glossy top hat back on, collected his wife, and left for dinner at the Hotel Pilgrim.

Dinner was brief. At dusk, the dignitaries were hauled back to the waterfront for "the most gorgeously impressive spectacle ever offered the people of America"—*The Pilgrim Spirit*. Slated for just twelve performances because of the logistical problems involved in bringing together the huge volunteer cast, the seventy-piece symphony band, and the three-hundred-member chorus, a Sunday daylight run-through scheduled for the benefit of the motion-picture cameras had been rained out by a bad thunderstorm.[48] But Monday night was lovely, and as the sun set, the first scene of the pageant opened with music, electric campfires glowing in the gathering darkness, and ten frightened Indians spying a Norse vessel just off Plymouth Rock.[49]

Despite the movie crews in attendance, the special trains and boats from major cities for advance ticket-holders, and the aura of big-time show biz that clung to the production, the pageant was no jazz-baby revue cooked up by ad men. Written by a Harvard drama professor, it had a reverential tone, and its principal character was the backward-rolling panorama of American history, personified by a sonorous "Voice from the Rock."

A sequence of tableaux came to a crescendo in Episode IV, Scene III: while the band struggled through MacDowell's "1620" and the chorus delivered itself of Hermann Hagedorn's "Hymn of Praise," Priscilla ("the Puritan girl"), John Alden, and Miles Standish landed on the rock and fell to their knees in prayer, illuminated by the searchlights of World War I battleships anchored in the harbor.[50] In the grand finale, the Pilgrim fathers emerged from the night of history and beheld, in a blinding flash of electric light, the figure of George Washington.

"The basis of our political system is the right of the people to make and to alter their constitution of government," Washington told them. The lights went out again. A hush fell. "Suddenly from far out on the Mayflower [replica] a bugle calls in the darkness," and something "begins to glow on the vessel, but very faintly." The pageant ended

8.6
Norman Price's 1921 illustration for a neocolonial ad for Jell-O® Gelatin Dessert

with colored light everywhere and the whole cast singing Robert Frost's "The Return of the Pilgrims."[51] Wires, bulbs, and hidden amplifiers had brought the Pilgrims back to Plymouth in the company of George Washington. The technology somehow suited the whole tercentenary enterprise. Searchlights saved Pilgrims, Puritans, and Continental general alike from the darkness of time. Thanks to their earnest descendants in the electrified age of normalcy, the founders of America were as factual and palpable and alive as Warren G. Harding.

Building a Presidential Birthplace

The whole of President Harding's public life was lived in the reflected light of that recreated history.[52] During the ancestral phases of the 1920 campaign, public relations experts planted a story in the *Boston Evening Transcript* with the intriguing title "Harding as Washington's Double." The headline captioned two pictures: one was the famous Athenaeum Portrait of George Washington, and the other was a retouched version of it with Harding's florid features beaming out from beneath the frizzy wig of the Father of His Country.[53] If the result was ludicrous or merely puzzling, nobody said so then or later when the dignity of the presidency elicited only slightly less fulsome comparisons between Harding and the heroes of American history from his hyperbolic countrymen. The citation accompanying his honorary doctorate from Princeton, for instance, equated the Bible with the U.S. Constitution—both were Harding's infallible guides—and then pressed on to liken the incumbent to a global Lincoln, "a man of the people, leading the people, heeding the will of the people and the need of the world."

Folksy fence-mending among the people brought Harding back to Marion in the second year of his term for the local centennial gala. The parade there began with a prairie schooner and some semblance of historical accuracy: covered wagons *had* once pushed through Ohio. But another float, to which an anonymous wit had attached the legend "No Flapper Rocked This," carried a colonial mother tending her baby's cradle by the hearth.[54] History manufactured as a rebuttal to contemporary mores and a buttress against change was as fluid and chaotic as the jazz-age culture that demanded it. Having moved once, nothing prevented the Rock of Plymouth and its sundry colonial attendants from migrating once more into the history of an Ohio town founded in 1822. History was not rocklike fact. History was a kind of modern decorating style that could be applied to a speech, a float, or a house as the mood of the embellisher dictated. Differences between colonial Mount Vernon and Mount Vernon Avenue were, at bottom, trivial.

Harding's last editorial, written for the *Marion Daily Star* during that centennial week in 1922, took pains to demonstrate that the myth of the heroic yet perfectly regulated past justified confidence in a future made in the precise image of the good old days before the flapper kicked up her heels and threw off her bonnet and shawl:

Sturdy men pioneered the way to early settlement and sturdy women too. . . . Resolute and able men made secure the social order here. . . . Let Marion preserve every good lesson of the yesterday and resolve to go on, adding to the stride of industry and commerce, and determination that every enlargement in material growth shall reflect larger progress in the finer attainments which make a community worthwhile. The fit counterpart to the city of material success is the city of happy homes.[55]

The past was a slightly less prosperous version of 1922, and the ancient homestead on the float in the historical parade, be it a log cabin in Ohio or a Pilgrim cottage on Leyden Street, served as a metaphor for rootedness and for the traditional family values Warren Harding of Mount Vernon Avenue honored more in the breach than in the observance.

And so it was that Warren G. Harding, whose colonial front porch helped to send him to the White House, became the first American president to build his own birthplace. When the opportunity arose—his Carnegie Hall appearance of 1919 is one excellent example—Harding was fond of delivering homely rags-to-riches parables about poor lads from Marion who went on to win glory as bankers and the like by dint of pluck and hard work. Despite the Lincoln correlations routinely made by his fans, however, Harding's was not the classic log cabin story; in unguarded moments he even admitted as much. "The log cabin stuff makes good copy," the former editor told favored members of the press corps camped in his Marion backyard, "but unfortunately it is not true."[56]

Samuel Hopkins Adams, author of the 1926 novel that began the posthumous demolition of the Harding myth, said, "He came up the easy way. To draw a copy-book moral from his career, one must reverse the formula."[57] Besides, the restrained graciousness of the eighteenth century squared more readily with those facts about Harding known to the public at large in the early 1920s than acts of Lincolnian rail-splitting. Thus the president hired a Columbus architect to gussy up the surviving fragments of his great-grandfather's "little old house" and provided himself with a suitably presidential birthplace, in the prevailing Mount Vernon style.

Harding was not the progenitor of the fanciful neocolonialisms that flourished during his administration. His "birthplace," his house, his rhetoric, his library, and the events in which he appeared as a casual actor all show that the stage was set long before he made his genial entrance into this cultural drama. Nor was Warren Harding responsible for a pseudo-aristocracy of *Mayflower* descendants, popular interest with the private lives of the Founding Fathers, cults of historical fetishism and hero-worship, or mass play-acting in the precincts of a crazy-quilt heroic past. "The apotheosis of the average American," Harding succeeded by following a script his fellow Americans already knew well. As an aspiring public figure, he played a familiar and reassuring part, one polished by public relations experts and applauded by celebrities and boosters. Indeed, Harding seemed to have been born to fill the social role which, above all others, demanded that the modern star, like the little colonial boy on his chandelier, bow knowingly toward the costumed heroes in the wings of history. If he did not *really* look a great deal like George Washington, Warren Harding did, according to his chief political backers, "look . . . like a President" in the grand old manner.[58]

When Warren and Florence Harding hung their colonial chandelier in the front hall on Mount Vernon Avenue in 1891, the underpinnings of that grand historical manner were already in place. The Civil War had confirmed American nationhood and reconfirmed the importance of its architects. Lincoln emerged as the premier national hero of the postwar years. In his roles as martyr, healer, common man, and exemplar of the Horatio Alger success formula, Abraham Lincoln continued to be honored—he figured in Harding's own collection of icons—and he continued to be invoked, never more earnestly than at the moment of Harding's sudden death in 1923. The Lincoln Memorial, supported on thirty-six columns symbolizing the restored union of the states, was completed in 1922, during Harding's term.[59]

Analysts of the American temperament, pondering Warren Harding's victory at the polls, also brought Lincoln, the rustic rail-splitter, into their discussions of how old-stock, middle-class Americans—most of them born in small towns, if they no longer lived in them—had seen the Ohio editor as a replica of themselves, their inherited, rural values, and their sense of community and identity.[60] But the Washington of the hatchet and the cherry tree came from the country too, and unlike the crusading Lincoln, George Washington was an altogether less demanding hero for a generation sick of war, duty, and an intrusive wartime government. Washington had grown pliant in the several generations since his rumpled trousers went on display in Philadelphia; the butt of postcard humor, he and his stern visage had acquired the beginnings of an accommodating grin.

When a wisecracker in Marion asked the candidate, "Do you know the difference between you and George Washington? George Washington couldn't tell a lie and you can't tell a liar!" people just laughed.[61] And even the most stalwart members of the GOP, the party of Lincoln, were forced to notice that Honest Abe's rawboned person did not project a sense of the easy amplitude, the well-fed, comfy, upholstered well-being, that the times demanded. Even before World War I, a Washington biographer exercised by persistent Lincoln-worship based on the humble origins Honest Abe shared with most Americans took pains to demonstrate one significant but frequently overlooked point of similarity between the eighteenth century and the present: the log cabin myth notwithstanding, it was possible in colonial times for an "unselfish patriot" to have lived and died prosperous.[62] Placid prosperity was the chief desideratum of the voters "Washington's Double" wooed from his Colonial Revival porch in 1920.

Modern Progress and the Colonial Revival

Washington's latest successor in office had discovered one fine morning "that he and his chauffeur belonged to the same lodge, regarding this purely fortuitous fact as a symbol of the healing power of the Fathers and of American Democracy."[63] By the time of Warren Harding's ascent to Washingtonian grace, the otherwise troublesome aristocratic connotations of the Virginian's life and legend had undergone a curious process of democratization. Every facet of that life was an open book, for one thing, as accessible to the casual magazine reader as to those whose stock of Washington lore had been handed down from generation to blue-blooded generation. George Washington had become a sort of common man writ large, an ordinary Joe with a flair for dress-up and ritual that would do a Shriner proud. Rituals associated with Washington, once reserved for the ballrooms of the upper crust, were now being carried out in ordinary public meeting rooms by persons whose only claim to social distinction rested, in many cases, on events several centuries distant when their great-grandsires debouched from the *Mayflower.*

Sinclair Lewis, the greatest satirist of the day, had a sensitive ear for the cadences of American speech: the sloganeering, boosting, and bloviating of the recent campaign informed the passages of bravura dialogue that made his *Babbitt* of 1922 seem uncannily true to life.[64] Lewis's eye was every bit as sharp as his ear. What it observed in a Midwestern town a lot like Marion, among plump, middle-class professional men much like Warren Harding in their zest for lodges, creature comforts, frisky women, and progress, in the "autumn [when] a Mr. W. G. Harding, of Marion, Ohio, was appointed President," was a culture in frantic pursuit of the last word in modern colonialisms.[65] Lewis's George Babbitt—a realtor and a Republican—lived in a five-year-old Dutch Colonial house, painted green and white, in a tract known as Floral Heights. There were two other such wooden boxes in the same block of Chatham Road, and all of them were equipped with "the latest conveniences. Throughout, electricity took the place of candles and slatternly hearth-fires," although electric tapers and logs maintained the illusion of a picturesque yesteryear. Nor were Wallace Nutting's wares in short supply in the living rooms of Zenith:

Among the pictures . . . were a red and black imitation English hunting-print, an anemic imitation boudoir-print with a French caption of whose morality Babbitt had always been rather suspicious, and a hand-colored photograph of a Colonial room—rag rug, maiden spinning, cat demure before a white fireplace. (Nineteen out of every twenty houses in Floral Heights had either a hunting-print, a *Madame Fait la Toilette* print, a colored photograph of a New England house, a photograph of a Rocky Mountain, or all four.)[66]

When Babbitt dines out in the Art Room of the Zenith Inn, he finds "waitresses being artistic in Dutch caps" copied straight from Washington Irving. When he visits the Athletic Club, with its Gothic lobby, Roman Imperial washroom, and Spanish Mission lounge, he is vaguely pleased by the cozy Chippendale reading room, although busy businessmen like himself get most of their printed culture from thumbing through the picture magazines. And when Babbitt acquires a mistress, at least part of her appeal rests on her taste in home decor. "It was luxurious," Babbitt thought, "to loll in a deep green rep chair, his legs thrust out before him, to glance at . . . the colored photograph of Mount Vernon he had always liked so much."[67]

But he is rarely absent from Chatham Road for long: the Dutch Colonial house with its prescribed Nutting print is too important an emblem of its owner's identity to be abandoned. The house bespeaks Babbitt's standing in the community, his success in business, his conformity with prevailing tastes, his kinship with his peers, his aspiration for the latest in modern conveniences and comforts (albeit styled to disguise their contemporary origins), and his status as a respectable, God-fearing, home-loving family man. The big Dutch Colonial on Chatham Road, like the big Queen Anne with the bulbous "colonial" porch on Mount Vernon Avenue, was an exercise in public relations. Alas, Lewis remarks, "there was but one thing wrong with the Babbitt house: It was not a home."[68]

In *Main Street,* too, Sinclair Lewis makes physical surroundings comment on his characters, their place in the social scheme of things, and their personalities. Carol Kennicott, his city-bred heroine, comes to the Midwestern town of Gopher Prairie from a collegiate atmosphere the gentility of which is suggested by "the portraits of Whittier and Martha Washington" on the walls of the library. Although the principal intersection of Gopher Prairie is the corner of Main Street and Washington Avenue, the name of that colonial hero was clearly bestowed in tribute around the time of the Philadelphia Centennial, for the first wave of the fashionable colonial revival, ca. 1913, is nowhere in evidence. Instead Carol and her husband settle down in a house adorned with Victorian jigsaw ornament on the outside and the plush and horsehair of a generation past on the inside.

But Lewis establishes his protagonist's modernity—her rebellion against the mid-Victorian mores of the village—by having Carol launch a scheme to beautify Gopher Prairie after rifling through the new magazines at the public library. Her vision of a modern town is, paradoxically, a make-believe colonial New England hamlet translated to the wheat fields of the Midwest:

> She found pictures of New England streets, the dignity of Falmouth, the charm of Concord, Stockbridge and Farmington. . . . Assured that she was not quite mad in her belief that a small American town might be lovely, as well as useful in buying wheat and selling plows, she sat brooding. . . . She saw in Gopher Prairie a Georgian city hall: warm brick walls with white shutters, a fanlight, a wide hall and curving stair. She saw it the common home and inspiration not only of the town but of the country about it. . . . Forming about it and influenced by it . . . she saw a new Georgian town as graceful and beloved as Annapolis or that bowery Alexandria to which Washington rode.[69]

After inspecting the parlors of her neighbors (here, a "steel engraving of Grant at Appomattox, . . . a basket of stereoscopic views"; there, a Yard-of-Roses and a bank made in the form of a Swiss chalet), she tries to inveigle her husband into trendsetting alterations of the dowdy family manse. "She babbled of a low stone house with lattice windows and tulip-beds, of colonial brick, of a white frame cottage with green shutters and dormer windows," but all in vain. Her failure to make Gopher Prairie over in conformity with the pictures in the magazines stands for her more significant failure to adapt to the social strictures of small-town life, and eventually, using war work in Washington as her excuse, Carol flees.[70]

Her ultimate reconciliation with her husband, presaging her return to Main Street, is signaled by their visit to Mount Vernon. Dr. Kennicott comes to Washington to woo her back:

> "You'd like to motor down to Mount Vernon this afternoon, wouldn't you?" she said.
> It was the only thing he had planned. He was delighted that it seemed to be a perfectly well bred and Washingtonian thing to do. . . . At Mount Vernon he admired the paneled library and Washington's dental tools.[71]

Mount Vernon remained the source for Mount Vernon Avenues everywhere. On a scale of artifactual involvement with the colonial past that runs from a handful of 1876 Centennial Exposition mementos, through cast-iron souvenir hatchets and satin ballgowns, to a bumper crop of antiques and make-believe antiques, like the Martha Washington sewing cabinet of 1923 and Babbitt's Wallace Nutting print, the colonial chandelier in Warren Harding's Mount Vernon Avenue house illuminates the far end of that spectrum while his birthplace project occupies the nearer, more crowded margin. By the time of Harding's death in 1923, the colonial revival had passed beyond the stages of souvenir kitsch and high-society exclusivity. It was the province of Main Street now. The middle-class suburb was on the drawing boards—if not already fully occupied—and the appurtenances of neocolonial life had already flooded the marketplace on easy credit terms. And Mount Vernon, "Washington's Home and the Nation's Shrine," was the permanent and readily accessible mecca for a cult of family living in the colonial manner.[72]

As Sinclair Lewis and Doc Kennicott both realized, excursions down the Potomac were Washingtonian signs of a taste and an aura of breeding to which all could readily aspire. In the early 1920s, some four hundred thousand tourists visited Mount Vernon every year. According to sightseeing experts in the capital, they were "brought by the desire to see the home, rather than the grave of the first President. It was Washington's mansion, not his tomb, that was the shrine," now that the war and Woodrow Wilson's martial exercises at the Washington vault were over.[73] That expert opinion was confirmed by a substantial volume that appeared in 1924 under the title *George Washington as a Housekeeper with Glimpses of His Domestic Arrangements, Dining, Company, Etc.*[74]

In the teens and twenties, the swelling crowds of tourists who boosted Georgian civic improvements, coveted Martha Washington sewing tables, and followed the latest twists of the colonial craze in the pages of the *Saturday Evening Post* continued to love the mansion for its exhaustive display of colonial drygoods. Scholar and tourist alike were most awed, however, by the spit-and-polish perfection of Mount Vernon. The grounds were a case in point. A visitor of 1916 poked into the corners of the same gardens Owen Wister had earlier explored and was surprised, at first, to find them so clean. "There is perhaps," he mused, "a trimness to the walks and a smartness to the cropped lawns and an absence of littered corners which even the old General could not have wrung from his shiftless slave labor."[75]

The comment reveals a growing awareness of history as a deliberate construct. Grounds sanitized and manicured to the gloss of a Hollywood movie set were not, perhaps, quite authentic. Yet, if "George Washington never saw such perfect gardens in all his life," surviving drawings showed that they were the kinds of flower beds he wished for. Naturally, the plantings of the 1920s were better than his "because gardeners have learned better methods."[76]

The benefits accruing to Mount Vernon as a result of modern-day know-how were discussed at length in several popular histories of the Ladies' Association. Much was made of the fact that in 1924 Henry Ford had presented the association with a firetruck and the latest motor-driven equipment to go with it.[77] But machinery aside, the formal order imposed upon an infinity of firedogs and blades of grass by the present custodians of Mount Vernon was an object lesson in its own right and a source of pride. Chaotic energies had been governed here by a modern generation of business and boosterism. Material abundance was held in check by a restraint possessed of its own beauty. To Mount Vernon's visitors in the 1920s, history was perfectible, and change, initiated by business and industry, moved the wheels of historical progress toward perfection. "American business is not a monster," President Harding once remarked, "but an expression of [a] God-given impulse to create, and the savior of our happiness."[78] Mount Vernon therefore condoned the rackety progress of the 1920s by investing the machine-made profusion of mail-order Martha Washington dinner sets with the luster of a grave, formal dignity. The ads were the heralds of progress, and business the handmaid of history. In 1923, Emile Coué urged the gospel of modern perfectibility upon his American disciples: "Every day, in every respect, I am getting better and better."[79] George Washington's faultless but ever-improving mansion proved the boosters right. As Warren Harding planned a new Mount Vernon of his own, the shades of the nation's shrine blessed his dreams.

Celebrating Washington's Birthday in the Suburban Home

To the regret of the management, the genial Harding was the first president in a generation who did not manage to work a visit to the real Mount Vernon into his schedule, although "he had been a frequent visitor as a Senator."[80] With cameras clicking and reporters scribbling, such executive excursions contributed more than their share to the prevailing sentiment that Mount Vernon was not simply the nation's shrine but its home as well. The sense of close kinship with the first president fostered by the ability of the tourist—or the vicarious tourist, shopping for Washingtoniana in the local Bon Ton—to rummage, as it were, through his personal effects was also enhanced by an easygoing attitude toward traditional celebrations of Washington's Birthday. Until the end of the nineteenth century, observances of the day had been public or quasi-public in nature: speeches, dinners, balls, and rallies of patriotic societies were in order, and cards decorated with cherry boughs were often exchanged. But the holiday lacked a cohesive program of celebration as late as 1893, when Mrs. Burton Kingsland, writing in the *Ladies' Home Journal,* bewailed the fact that American businessmen did not know what to do with a day off.

She proposed, by way of a novel and more unbuttoned approach to the remembrance of Washington on February 22, a luncheon (a rare chance for busy fathers and husbands to spend time with their wives in the familial informality of life before the dinner hour) with special foods, decorations, and games. It had not yet been decided that cherry pie was the correct fare on Washington's Birthday. Mrs. Kingsland, at any rate, decreed whortleberry and pumpkin tarts for dessert and "only such dishes as are notably American" for the preceding courses. Hence the menu ran to blue-point oysters, canvasback ducks, and celery salad served on a dainty table embellished with place cards bearing the Washington coat of arms in watercolor and a "Cherry Tree and Hatchet" centerpiece. The latter was to be concocted from a miniature potted palm with a toy hatchet affixed to its base. To the pointed leaves of the plant, Mrs. Kingsland's readers were instructed to tie caramel-candy cherries—cherries "like those of the tree so famous in the history of the Father of his Country."

After lunch, games were urged upon the celebrants. A conventional question-and-answer quiz with historical topics was recommended, as was a new diversion from Paris involving secret, written answers to suggestive questions such as "What is the most absorbing love affair?" An appropriate prize, Mrs. Kingsland suggested, "might be a copy of Irving's 'Life of Washington,' and after such an entertainment the friends would, I think, take leave of each other with mutual congratulations that they were Americans."[81]

Although the theme-party craze had reached its climax in the 1920s, the 1932 bicentennial of Washington's birth called for rekindled celebratory fervor. And so the weary editors of those departments of women's magazines devoted to clever ideas for parties resumed the task of dreaming up something new for the February issue. *Good Housekeeping* trotted out red-white-and-blue crepe paper, blue-and-white china, baked beans, gingerbread (the most popular ready-to-use mix claimed to be made from Washington's mother's private recipe), and the ubiquitous celery salad. The meal was inexpensive, in recognition of hard times and the Depression, and those who wished to press the point could even ask guests to wear old clothes— *not* their great-grandmothers' ballgowns!—and form "a bread line" to get their colonial-style beans.[82] The *Woman's Home Companion* adapted Martha Washington's recipes to modern measurements and ingredients.[83] Believing that "every American woman . . . will want to plan at least one patriotic party in her own home" during the bicentennial, *McCall's* (for ten cents) would forward a leaflet—*In Honor of George Washington*—containing "suggestions for patriotic decorations, menus, games, etc., which may be adapted to an evening party for a mixed group or a Colonial Tea for the women's club."[84].

The science of giving a Washington's Birthday party is yet another demonstration of the ongoing domestication of Washington. And since by 1932 any women's club was presumed conversant with and thus entitled to mount the "colonial tea"—the old Martha Washington tea— the history of such unofficial forms of celebration also illustrates a shift in the composition of groups of celebrants. Mrs. Russell Sage, benefactor of the American Wing at the Metropolitan, founder of the

Society of Mayflower Descendants, and a member of the Colonial Dames, represents the old-American and high-society strains of fili-opietism. Separately and acting in concert, these aristocracies of wealth and birth first brought George Washington into the ballroom and the clubhouse, where, in time, he joined the company of lady-editors and became a colonial homebody, like George Babbitt. In the 1920s, Mrs. Sage and her sisters were still very much on the scene, but so was Mrs. Kennicott, with her drives to Mount Vernon and her party plans cribbed from the *Ladies' Home Journal*, and so was a relentless band of schoolteachers, armed with manuals of organized juvenile fun for February 22.

During World War I, Rose O'Neill's famous Kewpies, who appeared monthly in *Good Housekeeping*, began celebrating Washington's Birthday with the younger set. The February "Kewps" thought that children, shown committing acts of mayhem with a hatchet, "had not quite grasped the idea" of that story.[85] If so, it was certainly not the fault of the public schools. Specialized books of "recitations, plays, dialogues, drills, tableaux, pantomimes, quotations, tributes, stories, and facts" for Washington's Birthday, the main patriotic holiday on the academic calendar, had been available for classroom use since 1910, and skits were carefully and democratically framed to include every available child.[86] Small boys with powder in their hair swung cardboard hatchets. So, infrequently, did small girls, attributing little George's attack on the tree to a preference for fresh cherry over dried-apple pies, with the wisdom of seasoned housewives. The pieces in the manuals often originated with the women's magazines and their traditional February features. "Truthful George," for instance, began as a poem in the *Woman's Home Companion*. In the hands of a determined and sentimental teacher, the verse was easily adapted into the kind of tableau vivant calculated to break a mother's heart:

> The old-time garden path they paced
>   In days of long ago,
> His arm encircled Martha's waist,
>   Their steps were staid and slow.
> Said she, "Pray tell me, I implore—
>   George Washington, confess—
> Have e'er you kissed a girl before?"
>   Quoth truthful George, "Oh, yes!"[87]

By 1920, the neocolonial frame of reference in which grown-ups and presidents operated was known to the most backward six-year-old. On the adult level, the equivalent to the hatchet drill was the 1921 Plymouth tercentenary and *The Pilgrim Spirit*, with its cast of thirteen hundred costumed extras and its audience of one hundred thousand; the Marion centennial parade, with its colonial mother at a papier-mâché fireside; the Fredericksburg sesquicentennial parade of 1921, with floats showing "George Washington and his Cherry Tree" or "Washington Dancing at the Peace Ball" mounted on the beds of Ford's motorized trucks.[88] In Warren Harding's administration, the colonial fathers and mothers lived again—along with their colonial kids. Anybody with an inclination to do so could become an American aristocrat, his or her own ancestor. In fact, the scheduled high point of the Marion centennial was a dress-up pageant, with parts for a thousand local somebodies. In addition to the usual troop of colonials and pioneers, the finale was to have introduced Warren G. Harding, playing his modern, presidential self in the latest chapter of Marion's foreordained historical progress to greatness. There was some disappointment when the hero declined to display his Washingtonian features to pageant-goers as a living symbol of progress.

Presidential Venality and Debunkery

Warren Gamaliel Harding died on August 2, 1923, his colonial birthplace still unbuilt. He had been making a goodwill tour through the West, in flight from imminent revelations of graft and official misconduct on the part of friends he put in high places. His secretary of commerce, Herbert Hoover, was aboard the presidential train. Hoover counseled honesty, "the great essential" of Hamilton and of the copybook George Washington of the little hatchet and the kiss in the garden. "Open it up completely and without delay," he urged.[89] Instead, the president fretted and temporized his way through Alaska and the state of Washington.

He died suddenly in San Francisco. The cause of his death was a mystery. Conflicting reports cited tainted crabmeat, pneumonia, a heart condition; Florence refused permission for an autopsy. She rode the funeral cortege back to the White House and began a systematic destruction of Warren's papers. Newsboys all across the nation were collecting pennies to be melted down into a statue of "Laddie Boy," the presidential pooch; Florence gave Warren's dog away and decamped for Marion to resume the task of burning his letters as the Teapot Dome scandals began to unravel across the headlines.

In life, the man who "looked like a president" was an American hero in the epic mold, a genial Founding Father reincarnated with a box of Martha Washington chocolates tucked jauntily under his arm. In death, Warren Harding seemed fated to play the leading role in a new Washingtoniad of disillusionment. As the venality of his Kitchen Cabinet associates came to light, the quirkier aspects of Harding's life and death were pounced upon with glee by a vengeful public. Their hero was a humbug: what had been taken for perfection was sham; apparent honesty had masked a tissue of lies. Harding's posthumous and sensationalized fall from grace was understandable. More difficult to explain is the fact that each seamy revelation and every sordid innuendo corresponded to a story about George Washington put into circulation at the same moment.

From the beginning, the manner of Harding's passing invited speculation. In 1926 Samuel Hopkins Adams's *Revelry* proposed a solution to the apparent mystery; Harding, thinly disguised as the fictional President Willis Markham, had done away with himself to avoid exposure. The novel sold one hundred thousand copies. Sales were stimulated by bans imposed by the District of Columbia and several state legislatures.[90] The book became a hit play and a movie, and the story of the bibulous Willis Markham passed quickly into the realm of folklore. People who had not read *Revelry* heard about it and passed the word that Harding had been murdered. Murder or suicide, the conclusion was the same: Harding richly merited his end.

So had the George Washington of 1926. Throughout the nineteenth century, Washington's manner of dying was variously cited as a model of patient stoicism, Christian resignation, or virtuous confidence in celestial reward. Felled by a chill, the old general suffered the primitive ministrations of Dr. Craik and "breathed his last without a groan."[91] According to the memorial eulogy preached by Timothy Dwight of Yale, Washington had even closed his own eyelids as he died, in a masterly display of the orderliness which marked his character.[92]

Dwight got that story from the same wellspring of idolatrous tradition Parson Weems later tapped, but Weems dared to follow the deathbed scene with a heavenly apotheosis. "Swift on angels' wings the brightening Soul ascended," he rhapsodized, "while voices more than human were warbling through the happy region and hymning the great procession toward the gates of heaven," where Washington was embraced by his old patriot comrades.[93] But the gates of heaven seemed to have clanged firmly shut in 1926 with an article in *Scribner's Magazine* suggesting that Washington's fatal chill "was the result of an assignation with an overseer's wife" in the Mount Vernon gardens on a cold afternoon.[94] Like Willis Markham (or Warren Harding), George Washington, it appeared, had got his just deserts.

The author of the *Scribner's* piece cited that scurrilous tidbit in order to prove it untrue, but similar anecdotes found their way into print in the mid 1920s with growing frequency and increasingly savage intent. Florence Harding's swift and peculiar actions in regard to her husband's papers made a neat reprise, for example, to a newly painted picture of Martha Washington, closeted in the death chamber, silently feeding her letters from George into the fire. What, the 1920s asked, did Martha have to hide?

Ernest Prussing published a study of Washington's finances in *Scribner's* in 1921 and subsequently examined the "Sally Fairfax letters." In 1925, on the basis of his research, Prussing delicately hinted that the letters Martha burned disclosed a chill formality in what had been a marriage of fiscal convenience. If George Washington had married for money, and if he was hopelessly in love with someone else, then Martha had disposed of the telltale letters to spare her husband's reputation.[95] In 1924 J. P. Morgan had performed a similar patriotic service for Washington by buying up and then destroying a group of his "smutty" letters.[96] Prussing also adopted a defensive posture toward Washington. Having made his deductions, he turned his store of poke-and-wink evidence into a soapy melodrama of Washington's unrequited love for Mrs. Fairfax, a passion vanquished by the hero's stoic fidelity to the marriage vow.

In *George Washington in Love,* Prussing nowhere introduced the contemporary analogue, although Mrs. Harding's incinerations were a matter of public comment and it was generally known that Florence was the Harding with the money. But in 1925 love letters had not yet become a key feature of the Harding scandals. Harding's love life and his "smutty" correspondence burst upon the scene only in June of 1927, with the publication of *The President's Daughter.* Timed to take advantage of the latest round of Teapot Dome indictments, the book was a disingenuous confession by Nan Britton, mother of little Elizabeth Ann Harding. If Nan could not become a movie star, she could and did become a celebrity by claiming that she told all for the benefit of wayward mothers and unacknowledged babies everywhere: the profits from the book were earmarked, she said, for a charitable trust to be known as the Elizabeth Ann Guild.

At first, booksellers "kept it under the counter as if it were a collection of French postcards"; only the iconoclastic H. L. Mencken ventured a review.[97] But by September *The President's Daughter* led the bestseller lists. The *New York World* would call it "a highly romantic and thrilling story of a love affair with . . . the ring of truth in it."[98] The truth, according to Nan Britton, included passionate assignations on the floor of the Senate cloakroom closet (upon a bed of rubbers) and Keystone Kop chases through the White House with Florence Harding in hot pursuit.

Nan's brand of truth worked a delicious revenge on her late lover, the fraudulent apostle of honesty. While the wanton "ring of truth" stimulated sales, however, the product was a familiar one. Popular history in the 1920s also marshaled intimate facts of precisely this order as a corrective to the odious lies of mythology. Lacking factual support, history was, as Henry Ford had succinctly put it in 1919, "more or less the bunk."[99] A hard-headed commitment to the "facts," however unsavory or inconvenient, was the hallmark of the modern mind. Habitual readers of bestsellers, therefore, must have experienced a giddy sensation of déjà vu as they reviewed the spicy, modern facts disclosed in *The President's Daughter.* The same chips of truth had fallen where they might in 1926 in two bestselling biographies of George Washington.

Between them, W. E. Woodward's *George Washington: The Image and the Man* and Rupert Hughes's *George Washington: The Human Being and the Hero* credited to their subject nearly every failing with which Warren Harding would be charged. As their titles suggest, the authors set out to demolish the frozen "image" and the copybook "hero" with factual ammunition. The "human being" thus disclosed was a man who died from a dalliance with his overseer's wife and drove Martha to burn his letters.[100] He carried on with married ladies under their husbands' noses; the husbands were, of course, his friends. He wrote letters of such gross indiscretion as to merit page upon page of direct quotation. He resorted to the truth only when circumstances removed the alternative: "His honesty was combined with shrewdness; and that is the kind of honesty admired by the average American."[101] The average American, if his taste for facts had not been satiated by Washington's latest biographers, could find equally sensational nuggets in the reviews of the two volumes and in competing exposés commissioned by a whole range of highbrow and popular periodicals.

However repelled by the antics of Woodward and Hughes, the critics nevertheless contrived to highlight and supplement the facts already in evidence. "Pretty little Kate, the Washerwoman's daughter," Mary Gibbons waiting for her general-lover in a New Jersey boarding house, and scores of "lowland beauties" from the South were exhumed from the files, along with Alexander (a.k.a. Washington) Hamilton and other fleshly tokens of stolen love. The Sally Fairfax letters were dissected once more. Much was made of a secret code of dots and hash marks in the margin of his diary: had Washington kept score of his conquests? The distinction of being the Father of His Country, quipped one authority, "might take on a new meaning."[102]

Profligacy did take on fresh dimensions as the catalogue of Washington's sins mounted: immoderation in drink and in card playing, betting on horses, and cursing were among the least of his failings, and new sources of "tradition" hinting at vices as yet unplumbed were alluded to knowingly. *The Nation* summed up the sorry state of Washington hagiography in 1926 by quoting an after-dinner speech by Rupert Hughes, delivered before an apoplectic chapter of the Sons of the American Revolution. Washington was, said Hughes, "a great card player, a distiller of whiskey, and a champion curser . . . and he [often] danced for three hours without stopping, . . . never prayed and persistently avoided any participation in communion."[103]

The brash tone of Hughes's remarks (oddly ill suited to a patriotic rally) left the impression that this hard-drinking, foul-mouthed Washington might have been very much at home at a different kind of male gathering—at an all-night poker session of Harding and his Kitchen Cabinet, or the annual convention of the Concatenated Order of Hoo-Hoos, for instance. Indeed, several commentators on modern specimens of Washington biography detected a certain contemporary flavor in both the literary style and factual preoccupations of the authors.

The historian Allan Nevins, making a retrospective survey of the genre for a Washington's Birthday issue of the *Saturday Review,* cited "a constant mixture of trivial everyday facts (the heat, the roads, the color of a waistcoat) with momentous historical facts in order to give the latter a new luster of reality."[104] That reality was up-to-the-minute, Nan Britton reality, as *Catholic World* noted with pious revulsion in a 1927 analysis of Woodward and Hughes. The reviewer, Charles Phillips, was disgusted with both books because of an all-inclusive "pruriency," comparable in effect to Horatio Greenough's nineteenth-century statue of the "naked Washington" once seated outside the east entrance to the national Capitol. That neoclassical statue had at least left Washington covered in a scrap of Roman scarf which had been snatched away, as it were, by modern biography in a "phallic caper" that confused overstuffed fame with headline notoriety. A laudable attempt to humanize the "canting prude" of legend had gone awry when Washington was stripped of his mythic garments and equipped with all the more loathsome traits of the contemporary smart set.

Phillips based his contention on a choice of language geared to "the 'perhaps' of back-stairs insinuation"—the argot of the flapper, the pulps, and *The President's Daughter:* "They are writing for a public so unconventional that it demands from its servitors the utmost in suggestiveness and blasé innuendo." Peekaboo in details of a private nature was bad enough, but Phillips reserved his choicest invectives for the treatment of the "momentous" and heretofore unquestioned historical facts discussed by Allan Nevins: "I get the impression that what Woodward wants as a revolutionary army is a mob like Budienny's Bolshevik cavalry." According to *Catholic World,* modern realism was a mess of modern "spiciness" larded over with a modern coat of "radical-red" gravy.[105]

Phillips had a point of sorts. In 1925 *Literary Digest* ran an article about the apparent crusade to remake the prunes-and-prisms Washington into a modern "man's man." Entitled "Washington Dismounted from His High Horse," the piece consisted of extended quotations from a review of George Washington's diaries, preserved by the Mount Vernon Ladies' Association and just released in a four-volume set edited by John C. Fitzpatrick of the Library of Congress. The reviewer was Claude Bowers, whose own recent bestseller, *Jefferson and Hamilton: The Struggle for Democracy in America,* had elicited a glowing review from Franklin Delano Roosevelt and was said to be "as readable as a good novel." Bowers's book received an especially warm welcome in Democratic Party circles "as an antidote to the one-sided productions of Hamiltonian hero-worshippers," chief among whom had been the late President Harding.[106]

Because Bowers was a moderate member of the biographical camp of the "moderns" and believed that history always had a contemporary resonance, his analysis of the Washington diaries is instructive. He passed lightly over the women, the rum punches, and the dancing, all of which would captivate Woodward and Hughes. Such details were important, but only in the context of sketching a holistic portrait of a naggingly familiar character who thought two and only two aspects of his daily life worthy of recording. One was amusement. The other was business. The primary evidence, Bowers argued, revealed "a rather hard business man, a forerunner of the modern captain of industry."[107] And when the veneer of slick sensationalism was peeled away, that "modern captain of industry" emerged as the antihero of W. E. Woodward's "radical-red" 1926 biography. *George Washington: The Image and the Man* was, in fact, a scathing critique of the contemporary businessman, dressed for the occasion in a George Washington pageant costume borrowed from the late President Harding.

Woodward's Washington, for example, was badly educated as a child and made little effort to improve himself in later life: "How familiar this seems to any one who knows modern 'captains of industry.' Economy of effort is a basic trait of their character, as it was of Washington's. The typical financial magnate never goes to the trouble of learning a foreign language, no matter how much business he does with people who speak it. He does not learn it because it is not necessary and he is devoid of intellectual curiosity."[108] Woodward's biography captured more than its share of attention because of the snappy tone of the prose and the explicit parallels with stock figures of twentieth-century life, but his basic argument—that George Washington was a fiscal conservative with strong business interests— had already made the first president a symbol of the triumphant Republicanism of McKinley, Taft, and their successors. Although he did not intend to assign high praise by so doing, Charles Beard's controversial *Economic Interpretation of the Constitution of the United States* of 1913 had also stressed Washington's personal stake, as a successful businessman, in the establishment of a strong, stable government.[109] And William Roscoe Thayer's 1922 *George Washington,* even though it was enlivened with pictures of the hero riding to the hounds, courting Mary Philipse, and agonizing over his velvets and laces, was, at bottom, a life-sketch of a reactionary gentleman of affairs, a courtly specimen of the business breed.[110]

But Thayer and the Republicans admired the tycoons whom their Washington resembled. Woodward did not. In his emerging portrait, George Washington closely resembled the auto-crazed George Babbitt, Sinclair Lewis's businessman hero of 1922. Both fellows were chronic joiners with a weakness for "ne-oo" household gear, smutty stories, and a well-turned ankle, and possessing a level of intellectual sophistication calibrated to the minimal demands of chitchat at a boosters' luncheon: "If [Washington] lived in this present age his library would probably contain many books on money and investment, besides, of course, such sterling works as *The Gasoline Engine in Sickness and Health.*"[111]

An apostate businessman himself, Woodward knew whereof he spoke. The former banking executive and advertising man turned to fiction writing in 1922 and fled to Europe to nurse his muse in isolation from the business-driven culture he despised. The hypocrisy of advertising, he thought, had poisoned American life: "Illusion, that's it. It's a big thing in life. Millions of people make their living with no other asset." The projected novel involved the exposure of a thoroughly vile character (a financial magnate, of course) by an expert, a newfangled and as yet nonexistent professional in the art of truthtelling. When he sailed for New York, Woodward was still casting about for a word to describe such a paid specialist in the business of honesty—the ad man's opposite.

The answer came to him from the editorial page of the London *Times.* A reference to delousing trench soldiers in World War I triggered a chain of associations: "If you could delouse a man, you could also debunk him." The 1923 novel acquired the pithy title *Bunk,* and the expert was christened a debunker. In Henry Ford's business lingo, bunk meant bunkum, pretense and trickery. "Debunking," Woodward wrote, "means simply taking the bunk out of things, . . . an intellectual deflation. It is the science of reality."[112]

Woodward's coinage was quickly applied to himself, Rupert Hughes, and the other popular historians bent on tossing patriots off their pedestals. The term first entered the common parlance, in fact, as a synonym for slanders committed against George Washington.[113] Questioned about the debunking mania of the day, Calvin Coolidge quickly glanced out the window of the Oval Office toward the Mall and the glistening shaft of the Washington obelisk and chirped, "Well, I see the Monument is still there."[114] Yet the growing celebrity status of the hero who once seemed to be as spotless and immovable as that monument of stone was changing Americans' attitudes toward the "great white ghost" whose commemorative column brooded over the capital city.[115] And if the cold perfection of that symbol of Washington's rectitude seemed to shimmer and quaver in the sunlight nowadays, Calvin Coolidge was partly to blame.

The Washington Bicentennial Bill of 1924

In December of 1924, serving out the final year of his predecessor's unexpired term, Coolidge had signed a measure of which Harding would surely have approved, for it promised nothing less than a full decade of the neocolonial pageantry he once loved, stage-managed by the federal government. That joint resolution of Congress created the United States Commission for the Celebration of the Two Hundredth Anniversary of the Birth of George Washington. The legislation authorized $10,000 in seed money. It identified a group of nineteen commissioners which included the president, a clutch of key senators and representatives, and eight illustrious citizens of Coolidge's choosing, to be drawn from all sections of the country. And it directed the new commission to meet immediately.

February 22, 1932, was the official bicentennial birthday. But the grand scale of the planned celebration mandated seven years of preliminary festivities and allowed the commission, providing that its energies and the nation's enthusiasm had not flagged in the meantime, to continue the gala through December of 1934.[116] Foreign nations were to be asked to participate; state, civic, and territorial subcommittees were to be established; the citizenry at large was to be polled for suggestions; historical data "about Washington and his times" were to be collected and disseminated.[117] In short, the Washington bicentennial was to be the most glorious and all-encompassing hero-tribute in American history. It was also to lend the force of national policy to the popular colonial revival.

Calvin Coolidge signed the bicentennial bill in 1924, when a hero was still a hero and patriots (both ancient and modern) still occupied their pedestals with reasonable aplomb. By 1925, when Coolidge was asked to deliver the annual Fourth of July address in Cambridge, Massachusetts, those pedestals were beginning to tremble in the winds of a jittery suspicion that the old verities were mere bunk. A miasma of mystery and intrigue was creeping over the noble profile of Warren Harding. Popular magazines were exploring strange interludes in the life of the noble George Washington. And certain keen-eyed observers of the American panorama thought that those developments might not be unrelated.

Lowell Schmaltz, hero of Sinclair Lewis's 1928 novella, *The Man Who Knew Coolidge,* came to that conclusion even as his putative acquaintance prepared to depart for Massachusetts. Although Schmaltz reveled in the "New Era" of "Henry Ford, . . . Andrew Mellon, and other such rulers of modern industry and commerce," he still appreciated American history, especially when he saw it in the guise of "a dandy up-to-date hot-dog stand—some like log-cabins and some like . . . Indian wigwams or little small imitations of Mount Vernon about ten feet high."[118] And so he was properly shocked by the things being said about departed American heroes, both colonial and almost up-to-date:

I am reliably informed—though certainly I have not sullied my self-respect by reading any of them, but I have been informed of their contents by criticisms given in various sermons—I am informed that during the last year or so there have been published two books purporting to show that George Washington was not the great hero we all know him to be but a man that smoked, drank, used bad language, and flirted. . . . And no less than three disgraceful books, two of them novels and one a screed by a woman claiming to have known him too intimately, have dared to hint that our Martyr President, Harding himself, was a dumb-bell surrounded by crooks.

Well, I've got the answer for all these authorial gentlemen! And my answer is that it is not worth the while of a serious and busy man of affairs to pay the slightest attention to notoriety-hunting hacks, who creep out of their fetid holes to bay the moon, who seek by filthy and lying accusations to keep a foothold in the public eye.[119]

Historian-moralists seemed to be rushing Washington to the bar of modern judgment even as the government officially took note of the fact that he had been born almost two hundred years before. He was fast becoming a schizophrenic modern man, part pleasure-seeker, part hard businessman. Like Henry Ford or Warren Harding, George Washington was a 1920s celebrity, subject to conflicting appraisals of contemporary mores in the public sector. The speech Calvin Coolidge made in Cambridge in 1925—the first speech of the George Washington bicentennial period—only reinforced the mounting confusion between the past and the present. The stainless Father of His Country, the American immortal, was a kind of marmoreal manager in Coolidge's script, a benevolent magnate in a three-cornered hat. In Washington, the orator of the day concluded, "we see . . . the qualities of a great man of business which he brings to serve the vast task of organizing and equipping his armies."[120]

When heroes become mere businessmen, history no longer protects them from the scorn heaped upon erring members of their tribe. By 1926, when Coolidge glanced out his window for the benefit of the assembled press corps, the storm of debunkery had broken over the Washington Monument and howled with unabated fury about the vast cylindrical tomb in Marion, Ohio, that was to have been a grateful nation's monument to Warren G. Harding.[121] Designs showed a tholos ringed by a colonnade; the forty-eight pillars represented the homage of the sorrowing states. With each startling revelation about the late hero's pleasures—the women, the graft, the poker sessions, the flagrant violations of the Volstead Act—contributions to the memorial fund dwindled. By 1927 what tribute monies remained flowed, instead, into the coffers of the Elizabeth Ann Guild, and construction of the Harding mausoleum was halted with forty-six columns in place.

By 1927 Calvin Coolidge had had ample time for meditation on the vicissitudes of the American hero and the fate of his predecessor, once the quintessential modern hero, the man's man, the hail-fellow-well-met. The Washington Monument still stood, but Coolidge testily declined to dedicate the funerary monument to Warren G. Harding. Harding's marble monument remained, like his "birthplace," unfinished and unhallowed. Twin symbols of a bright beginning and an inglorious end, these structures offered mute testimony to a past and a present now conjoined in a paroxysm of doubt that allowed neither to stand complete and whole.

Heroes, History, and Modern Celebrities

9

"Puritanism de Luxe"
1923–1929

Modernizing Old Heroes and Antiquing New Ones

The George Washington of the 1920s was a peculiar mixture of solid, Republican business acumen and petty Rotarian vice. The former made him great; the latter made him accessible to modern fans on a common ground. The hero gave way to the celebrity who was applauded for some special skill that was exercised in the glare of the spotlight on behalf of all, but was cherished because, apart from that single, magical quality, he was just like everybody else. With a little luck, with one spark of talent above the run of the ordinary, anybody could be that star.

As William Woodward put it, George Washington was "the American common denominator, the average man deified and raised to the nth power."[1] With that phrase, Woodward could just as easily have been describing George Herman Ruth, the Sultan of Swat, the spindly-legged, dough-faced star who set the celebrity pattern for the decade. In Yankee Stadium the Babe was the home-run king, a figure of preternatural powers. Off the field he was disappointingly mundane— a prodigious eater and guzzler of illicit needle-beer, "a large man in a camel's hair coat and camel's hair cap, standing in front of a hotel, his broad nostrils sniffing at the promise of the night."[2]

In May 1927 a new star appeared in the American firmament. Charles Lindbergh, the Lone Eagle, made a solo airplane flight from New York to Paris in pursuit of the Orteig Prize. Lindbergh was the most famous American of the decade, *Time*'s first "Man of the Year," and a hero with no perceptible flaws, unless his disdain for the rites of celebrity could be counted against him by a culture that wanted headline insights into the personalities of its idols. In June, Calvin Coolidge welcomed "Lucky Lindy" home at the base of the Washington Monument, which editorialists labored to adorn with the American-bred virtues of the young aviator.

The *Washington Post* compared Lindy's spirit to that of the Pilgrims and George Washington. Unlike Babbitts abroad, crowed the *St. Louis Star,* the modest lad from the Midwest was neither a windy booster nor a money-mad grabber: "The last man of his type that Europe knows anything about was George Washington."[3] Lindbergh's picture, wrote a startled European pilgrim to America, "stares at you from over the reception desks of Midwestern hotels. It is hung at the entrance to railway stations, draped in flags. It smiles at you from inside taxicabs, it is stuck to the walls of elevators, it brightens the desks of countless stenographers. It is placed in schoolrooms, side by side with Lincoln and Washington."[4]

The 1920s adored celebrities. That fact, John Lardner posits, "meant that people were not disposed to look at themselves, and their lives in general, and therefore ran gaping and thirsty to look at anything . . . that was special, and apart from the life they knew."[5] Queen Marie of Rumania, who was fulsomely welcomed to New York in 1926 by Grover Whalen (Whalen was a full-time professional greeter retained by the mayor to cope with the celebrity problem), was one such "special" personage.[6] Marie was royalty, the one distinction even Babbitts could not claim for their republic, thanks to George Washington and the Constitution. "Howdy, Queen!" was Coolidge's reported salute to her at a White House banquet.[7] The president, of course, had said no such thing. His apocryphal gaucherie was much applauded, however, and public delight in the story suggests that "special," backhanded appeal of the monarchy to a democratic society. Less exclusive was the pile of debts the queen was trying to pay off on the hustings of media stardom.

What set Lindbergh apart from competing celebrities feted by Grover Whalen and Calvin Coolidge was not so much a "special" distinction from the common life of his adorers as his infinitely heightened ordinariness, a quality appreciated by the reporters and foreign observers who instinctively juxtaposed Lindbergh with Washington, "the average man . . . raised to the nth power." Jimmy Walker and Rudolph Valentino; Queen Marie of Rumania; Marion Taley, the homegrown opera star from Kansas City; Gene Tunney and Jack Dempsey, whose first matchup in Philadelphia's Sesqui-Centennial Stadium all but overshadowed the historical observances of 1926: each reigning celebrity of the 1920s had a singular source of charisma—a devastating left, a crown, a way with the ladies. That mark of distinction was always counterbalanced, however, by a set of ordinary defects called "personality"—scampishness, penury, effeminacy.

The hero with the devastating left or perfect pitch was hard to imitate, despite the foibles that encouraged a relationship between star and fan premised on the shared trivia of personality. But identification with the celebrity was the real key to the popularity of boxer and singer alike. By seeing him- or herself in the idol's shoes, the fan shared in feelings of uplift and triumph that in turn promoted a sense of personal security and well-being.[8] And so, in a roundabout way, Lardner's hypothesis is a useful one. If Americans of the 1920s found it painful to "look at themselves and their lives in general," identification with celebrities soothed the modern insecurities that had created such celebrities in the first place. Charles Lindbergh was the most soothing of them all because the special talent that brought him into the limelight was nothing really special: "The biggest news about Lindbergh was that he was such big news."[9]

Lindbergh's fame rested on a marvelous stunt, a feat completed forever at Le Bourget field before anyone knew much about it. The performance was over when Coolidge met the hero at the Washington Monument and, when analyzed in retrospect, the spectacular deed seemed to have required no particular, noteworthy gift on Lindbergh's part. Rushed into print in 1927, his memoir, called *We,* was a laconic recitation of facts about fuel capacity, tachometers, and navigational aids.[10] That title referred to the pilot and the equipment; the book left the distinct impression that anyone who followed the instructions on the operator's manual and minded his p's and q's could also have leapfrogged the Atlantic.

Unlike the superb eye-hand coordination of Babe Ruth or the brilliantined sizzle of Valentino, the skills that propelled Lindbergh to the top were accessible to the ordinary conscientious pilot of the last of Henry Ford's old Model T's, which rolled off the assembly line in May of 1927, ten days after the Lone Eagle landed in France.[11] For the budding celebrity to match the colossal impact of his act therefore required a flight into the cloudy realm of qualities of character that led Lindbergh and *only* Lindbergh to fly the ocean alone.

What invisible trait of mind or soul made Lindbergh great? Nobody seemed able to give the public a simple, direct answer to that important question. And so the *Washington Post* waxed lyrical over Lindy's "spirit," a gaseous ineffable also accruing to George Washington, the Puritans, and other notable Americans. The *St. Louis Star* resorted to a negative definition that stressed the lad's refreshing lack of the boorishness sometimes noted in Midwesterners abroad. And sensing that their crack analysts had collectively overlooked some crucial component in the rotogravure formula for heroes, the press in general hounded Lindbergh to distraction trying to find out wherein this elusive greatness lay.

Lacking signs of positive genius or special gifts, negative definitions—what Lindbergh was, or seemed to be, unlike—prevailed. *Unlike* run-of-the-mill joiners, ballplayers on teams, prizefighters with opponents, and movie stars with supporting casts and platoons of supernumeraries, Lindy went alone. Despite his own deference to his airplane as the better half of "we," his individualism became Lindbergh's special mark of grace, a symbolic virtue confirmed every time he evaded a reporter or his adoring public and one that, in a stunning paradox, undercut but somehow beatified the collective, corporate system that had manufactured his airplane.[12]

The spare grace of the Lone Eagle—the American individualist writ large—was, no doubt, a welcome antidote to the rococo transgressions committed en masse by Warren Harding and his Kitchen Cabinet. Lindbergh was young, photogenic, and modest (or shy); with the late, venal president he shared only good looks. But the personality created for Lindbergh by a subtractive process was faultless by default, stainless by omission, and curiously blank.

His nullity invited the public to attach his name to almost any passing fad. The dancing fools of the Nightclub Era named the Lindbergh Hop in his honor, for instance, while humble taxpayers suggested that his portrait be put beside Washington's on the three-cent stamp, and corporate heads scrambled for the honor of advertising their soap, their ink, and their airplanes as Lindy's favorites. Overnight, Trans-World Airlines had become "TWA, the Lindbergh Line" and the list of potential endorsements excluded few products of American enterprise. The celebrity personality of Charles A. Lindbergh, it seemed, accommodated the whole mad gamut of hearts' desires with an obliging and featureless plasticity. Modesty, individualism, and sporadic irritability were, at best, unobtrusive ripples on a flat surface of deified ordinariness: in 1927 Lindbergh was a hero waiting to be made in the image his worshippers wanted or needed to project upon the empty screen of his personality.

The Washington of whom Lindbergh was the streamlined model was himself being girded in a modern, chromium-plated business suit in 1927 to withstand the onslaughts of the debunkers. President Coolidge launched the counterattack on impiety from Capitol Hill. Addressing a joint session of Congress on Washington's Birthday, 1927, in his capacity as titular head of the Bicentennial Commission, Calvin Coolidge began by paying a sour compliment to the researches of Woodward and Hughes. "No great mystery surrounds" George Washington, he maintained, Nor should prurient allusions to mysterious love letters and the like be allowed to obscure hard facts about the hero's life and character.

"He was a man endowed with what has been called uncommon common sense," Coolidge declared. "His estate was managed in a thoroughly businesslike fashion. He kept a very careful set of account books for it, as he did for his other enterprises, . . . constantly on the outlook for sound investments and for ways to increase his capital." George Washington was, in sum, "the first commercial American."[13]

This was an expansive tribute indeed from the president known as Silent Cal, and one in keeping with the widely quoted aphorism with which he began his own four-year term in the office once held by Washington: "The business of America," Coolidge told a group of bemused editors in 1925, "is business." That was his article of faith and each pithy new White House motto further adorned the litany of commerce. "Brains are wealth and wealth is the chief end of man!" he quipped. "The man who builds a factory builds a temple; the man who works there worships there!"[14]

So later in the same speech, when Coolidge found it "doubtful if anyone outside the great religious teachers ever so thoroughly impressed himself on the heart of humanity as has George Washington," he was actually preaching a modern gospel of business service to which recent disclosures about Washington's aversion to prayer were irrelevant. The past was being rewritten to conform with the ideals and interests of the present. In any event, Congress had itself debunked charges of Washington's irreligiousness in 1927 by authorizing a new two-cent stamp that pictured not Lindbergh and Washington conjoined (as a vocal segment of the public had urged) but rather Calvin Coolidge's businessman-general praying alone in the snows of Valley Forge.[15]

When the president sounded the drumroll of Manifest Destiny in his Washington's Birthday speech to Congress, the clamor of the cash register almost drowned out the patriotic airs customary at such solemn gatherings. George Washington was great, said Coolidge, because he brought free enterprise and profitmaking endeavor to his nation: "That [Washington] should have been responsible in large measure for the opening of the West and for calling attention to the commercial advantages the country might derive therefrom is by no means the least of his benefactions to the nation. He demonstrated that those who develop our resources, whether along agricultural, commercial [or] industrial lines . . . are entitled to the approval, rather than the censure, of their countrymen."[16] The American heritage was a simple matter of dollars and cents.

Another oft-quoted Coolidge aphorism held that "no people can look forward who do not look backward."[17] His own interest in history and historical sites and his knowledge of the edifying facets of the character of Washington were, in contrast to Harding's fuzzy references to the greats of the colonial past, both genuine and deep. And if Amherst's former medalist in history sometimes invoked a conservative, Republican version of Washington that went back to Henry Cabot Lodge's biography, he did so with full knowledge of other competing points of view. In his Cambridge address of 1925 commemorating the 150th anniversary of Washington's assumption of command, for example, Calvin Coolidge acknowledged the existence of the sugar-coated myths about Washington currently nettling the debunkers and even sympathized with the difficulty of creating "a satisfying picture of him" at a remove of almost two centuries. But despite a promise to avoid "the vain speculation of what [Washington] might do if he were living today," Coolidge did not hesitate to redraw the hero along thoroughly contemporary lines, as an enterprising engineer and "a great man of business" whom sound businessmen of the day could readily claim for one of their own.[18]

The Cambridge speech called for words of presidential wisdom specifically *about* George Washington, and Coolidge obliged with an impressive display of historical acumen. In addition to questionable claims for Washington's having been the chief corporate executive of colonial America, he also examined the Trenton and Yorktown campaigns in detail and demonstrated an awareness of volumes lately written "on Washington as a pioneer of modern scientific agriculture." But on other occasions, when he was under no compulsion to rehearse the biography of the first president at all, Calvin Coolidge betrayed a canny appreciation of the historical sensibilities of his countrymen. He knew that people admired celebrities vastly. He also knew that George Washington qualified as a genuine celebrity—the Babe Ruth, the Charles Lindbergh, the Calvin Coolidge of the American past. His invocations of that famous name were, accordingly, both fervent and frequent.

In a radio address to the nation from the White House on the subject of "the duties of citizenship," for instance, he cited Washington's praise for the revolutionary zeal of the fair sex as his authority for urging women to exercise their hard-won franchise. "Without doubt," Coolidge concluded, "the intuition of the women of his day was quick to reveal what a high promise the patriotic efforts of Washington and his associates held out for the homes and for the children of our new and unfolding republic." Speaking before the New York Chamber of Commerce on the "service" rendered by business to the community, he dragged in Washington to justify a special relationship between government and the capitalist pursuits that were, Coolidge cried with rare passion, among "the greatest contributing forces to the moral and spiritual advancement of the race."

Greeting delegates to the American Farm Bureau Federation convention in Chicago, he reminded them that "it was the loyalty and perseverance bred of the home life of the American farmer that supported Washington through seven years of conflict and provided the necessary self-restraint to translate his victory into the abiding institutions of peace." Before the thirty-fifth Continental Congress of the Daughters of the American Revolution, he summoned up the names of heroines who "helped the sorely tried army of George Washington." He called the members "sentries" guarding the memory of Washington and "the sacred heritage bequeathed to us in the Declaration of Independence and the Federal Constitution" against the assaults of aliens, urged them to vote, and praised their work in preserving historical sites and rearing monuments.[19]

That was the public Coolidge. In such private moments as became part of "the great Calvin Coolidge myth" of the taciturn Yankee, he was also wont to make pithy statements about the first president. When Bruce Barton came to visit him in his retirement, Coolidge cited two letters by Washington dictating domestic arrangements to make a point about his own habit of working out the smallest detail in advance. "Coolidge was silent a moment" after that, Barton recollected, "and then said deliberately, 'He was the only man in American public life who never made a mistake.'"[20]

The Coolidge autobiography ends abruptly with his startling decision to give up the office—"I do not choose to run"—just as Washington had done: "Although I did not know it at the time, nine months later I found out that Washington said practically the same thing. Certainly he said no more in his Farewell Address, where he announced that 'choice and prudence' invited him to retire."[21]

For her part, Grace Coolidge "often said she meant to have a dress like the one Martha Washington wears in the portrait hanging in the White House—with a quilted satin petticoat, an overdress with panniers and elbow sleeves, lace ruffles, and a lace fichu." In later years Mrs. Coolidge was heard to regret that she had never got around to having such a grand garment made.[22]

Building a Birthplace for Washington

During their tenure in the White House and the vice presidential interlude preceding it, the Coolidges spent a substantial portion of their public lives honoring Geroge, Martha, and the colonial fathers and mothers in various ways. They visited both the 1920 and 1921 versions of the Plymouth tercentenary. In 1922 they appeared in Fredericksburg, Virginia, to launch a national drive to save and refurbish Kenmore, the home of Washington's sister Betty—the sister who, when muffled in George's big military cloak, was said to have looked just like him, and whose son married Martha's granddaughter, Nelly Custis.

Betty Washington herself had married Fielding Lewis, the hero of Vice President Coolidge's speech that day. "Colonel Lewis," he said, "was a patriot who sacrificed a fortune in supplying the Revolutionary forces with arms and ammunition": "The mansion not only has these associations, but it is a good example of Colonial architecture, well fitted to rank with the home of Jefferson, of Mason, of Lee, and Mount Vernon itself. It ought to be preserved for its own sake. It must be preserved for the sake of patriotic America."[23]

Although his qualitative reference to colonial architecture was an acknowledgment of the new, aesthetic criteria now being applied to sites previously valued only for a contagious atmosphere of patriotism, Coolidge had no intention of giving up that time-honored justification for a restoration project endorsed by the powerful board of directors of the DAR and supervised by a committee that included the journalist and popular historian Mark Sullivan.[24] Atmosphere and relics were still needed, he claimed: "A people who worship at the shrine of true greatness will themselves be truly great men." And about Kenmore's silent chambers, Coolidge thought, "the incomparable patriotism of George Washington" still hung like the old blue cloak Betty used to like to wear.[25]

In the fall of 1923, shortly after the rustic swearing-in ceremony hastily conducted in his father's Vermont farmhouse, President and Mrs. Coolidge brought friends who were staying with them at the White House down to Mount Vernon for a typical tourist's afternoon of "inspecting the Mansion, gardens and relics."[26] On another Sunday afternoon during the following summer, they sailed down the Potomac on the presidential yacht *Mayflower* and landed on a sandy beach near a ruined wharf at the mouth of Bridge's Creek. From there they "motored for a mile or more along an unimproved road reminiscent of Colonial days" through herds of curious cows, grazing in the lane. The car rounded a little graveyard in the middle of a turnip field and came upon a listing obelisk erected in 1896 to mark the site of Wakefield, the birthplace of George Washington.[27]

The story of the visit made the papers because as Coolidge, his wife, his aged father, and the Coolidges' son John prepared to make the return trip, they discovered that the outgoing tide had stranded their landing craft on the beach. So the party drove on to Colonial Beach, a nearby resort where the *Mayflower* could anchor close to shore, and stirred up much excitement among bathers suddenly confronted, in the midst of their weekend ablutions, by a celebrity of the first order.[28]

That impromptu visit drew attention to Wakefield and to the recently constituted Wakefield Memorial Association, founded to buy the thousand-acre tract surrounding the Washington family graveyard and the obelisk from the Latane brothers, the self-styled "collateral descendants of the father of his country" who raised sheep, pigs, and poultry on Wakefield Farm. Periodically, the Latanes threatened to sell the property to a crass developer with plans for neocolonial subdivisions or a honky-tonk resort like Colonial Beach.[29] The house in which Washington was born no longer stood. Even enterprising Virginians, the kind who in 1923 made a good living by directing gullible tourists to a gnarled tree beside the Rappahannock which they swore was the very "descendant of the cherry tree described by Parson Weems," could not find one brick standing upon another at the point where the State Department had claimed to have traced out the foundations in the 1880s.[30]

Several sketches purporting to show the original farmhouse were in circulation, including one that hung in the Mount Vernon collection, but since these various likenesses corresponded only in their mutual conformity to ideas of "quaintness" current at the moments when they were drawn from the imagination, a proper recreation of Wakefield was generally counted among the most worthwhile projects the newly appointed United States George Washington Bicentennial Commission could undertake.[31] The late President Harding's analogous building scheme was not discussed at plenary meetings of the commission held in the Crystal Room of the White House. During the administration of his successor, however, constructing a suitable birthplace for George Washington rapidly became an item of the highest national priority.[32] Staffers scrambled to assemble the requisite facts on farmhouse architecture in Virginia in the early eighteenth century.

Coolidge, Washington, and Old-Fashioned Virtue

The commercial Washington of Calvin Coolidge was based on facts, too—facts that stood in sober contrast to the gaudy innuendo of the debunkers. Indicative of a steady competence on Washington's part rather than any epic romance, the facts about the first president were as modestly modern as Lindbergh's explanation of his carburetor. And they were almost as dull. H. L. Mencken, sharing some censorious "selected prejudices" with the "booboisie" in 1927, acknowledged that new dispensation for up-to-date heroes:

Only an overwhelming natural impulse . . . can urge on America into the writing of fugues or epics. The pull is toward the investment securities business. . . . The successful businessman among us . . . enjoys the respect and adulation that elsewhere bathe only bishops and generals of artillery. He is treated with dignity in the newspapers, even when he appears in combat with his wife's lover. His opinion is sought upon all public questions, including the aesthetic. In the stews and wineshops he receives the attention that, in old Vienna, used to be given to Beethoven. He enjoys an aristocratic immunity to most forms of judicial process. He wears the *legion d'honneur,* is an LL.D. of Yale, and is cordially received at the White House.[33]

Mencken preferred the epic mold for heroes, of course, and was particularly intrigued by a hot-blooded, pugnacious Washington who regularly appeared in the pages of his *Smart Set,* doing battle against "the Money Power and the Interests." Mencken's George Washington was nothing like Coolidge's prim accountant *cum* gentleman-farmer. Despite a documented "still at Mount Vernon," neither was he the latter-day robber baron of the debunkers, although he was "the Rockefeller of his time, the richest man in the United States, [and] a promoter of stock companies." According to legends that reached Baltimore, Washington "was not pious, . . . drank red liquor, . . . and knew more profanity than Scripture." But these pungent facts merely went to show that, in this modern age of business plutocracy, he would be a pariah, a scandal to the "uplift magazines," and "ineligible for any public office of honor or profit."[34] If Washington were alive today, "where would he go on idle nights?" Mencken acidly inquired. "To a patriotic meeting of the American Legion?"[35]

The warring factions within the Washington-as-businessman camp agreed on one thing: if their hero were to be reborn in the 1920s, he would head straight for a Rotary luncheon—either to join in the merriment or to chastise the members. *Smart Set* thought Washington an unmodern and therefore praiseworthy foe of corporate lunchtime twaddle about "service" and the like. "Nothing could have been further from the intent of Washington . . . than that the official doctrine of the nation . . . should be identical with the nonsense heard in the Chautauqua, from the evangelical pulpit and on the stump," Mencken sneered.[36] Yet *Collier's Weekly* and the leading newspaper of Muncie, Indiana, both envisioned the reborn idol as a mainstay of the local business establishment (despite his quirky penchant for colonial dress). Their Washington "would undoubtedly have been a realtor. Because that is precisely the kind of man he was. . . . He joined everything there was to join. If there had been a Rotary (or Kiwanis or Lions or Civitas) or a real estate board or a chamber of commerce, George Washington, the 'regular fellow' would surely have been a member."[37]

The "regular fellow" was an ordinary fellow, a slightly more gregarious Lindbergh. A regular, ordinary, businesslike demeanor was the chief attraction of Calvin Coolidge, too. Walter Lippmann realized that the president's personality fascinated the public, and a year before Coolidge met Lindbergh beneath the Washington Monument, the journalist found himself struggling to explain this unlikely hero. The difficulty of doing so is reflected in Lippmann's use of the kind of imprecise symbolic language reporters assigned to penetrate the soul of the Lone Eagle would shortly replicate in sheer despair. The simplicity of Coolidge, Lippmann argued, and the bland assurance of his belief in business as the steady heartbeat of American history, had clothed the man in an aura of old-fashioned serenity otherwise associated only with the canonized figures of American myth, like Washington.

In actuality, of course, "Washington . . . was a rebel against constituted authority," something that Coolidge most emphatically was not. But like a quaint and curious picture in an old history book, Coolidge soothed the voters. Frenetic buyers of Martha Washington china, behind on their installment payments, "are delighted with the oil lamps in the farmhouse at Plymouth, and with fine, old Colonel Coolidge and his chores and his antique grandeur. . . . They are delighted that the President comes of such stock, and they even feel, I think, that they are stern, ascetic and devoted to plain living because they vote for a man who is. . . . Thus we have attained a Puritanism de luxe in which it is possible to praise the classic virtues, while continuing to enjoy all the modern conveniences."[38]

Apart from his laconic refusal to run for a second term of his own and his wry dismissal of debunkery, the best-known thing Calvin Coolidge ever did was to have himself sworn into office at 2:47 in the early morning of August 3, 1923, just after word of Harding's death reached remote Plymouth, Vermont. His aged father, Colonel John Coolidge, the local notary, administered the oath by the light of a kerosene lamp. The colonel and his neighbors, it seems, hadn't much use for electricity, phones, and other modern fripperies, and so, among the little clot of witnesses assembled in the sitting room to make it all official, stood the delivery man who had been compelled to drive over from the next town bearing the news of the president's sudden passing (Figure 9.1).

An artist named Keller also made tracks for Plymouth to record the scene for posterity and found himself on the ground floor of a whole cottage industry in prints and doctored photographs of the impromptu inauguration. These reproductions fed an apparently insatiable public appetite for every quaint detail of the predawn swearing-in.[39] And whether or not they appreciated the symbolism of the Coolidge oil lamps, virtually every commentator on the succession from that day to this has attributed the remarkable popularity of the silent Yankee from Plymouth to a certain seventeenth- or eighteenth-century patina of rustic dignity that clung to his person thereafter.

Coolidge became an "authentic hero" to his age, writes one student of the period, because of "a strange nostalgia for old-fashioned and virtuous ideals." He was a "real, live Puritan"; he fulfilled a longing "for a past that never was, for a world that would stand still" forever. He was, in the words of William Allen White's famous title, "a Puritan in Babylon."[40] "Just as public heroes endowed with the old virtues of strength, courage, and probity once acted as surrogates in penitential rites," reasoned another seeker after the source of Americans' fervent admiration for this chilly character, "the prim and parsimonious Coolidge in the White House sat silently doing nothing as the nation indulged itself in an orgy of wealth-making and wealth-spending."[41] Gamaliel Bradford, writing in 1930, highlighted the "contrast between the mad, hurrying, chattering, extravagant, self-indulgent harlotry of twentieth-century America and the grave, silent, stern, narrow, uncomprehending New England Puritanism of Calvin Coolidge."[42]

9.1
The Coolidge Homestead Room, where he took his oath of office by the light of an "antique" oil lamp

9.2
Calvin Coolidge in his antique work smock: "Puritanism de luxe"

Coolidge was not averse to polishing his image as a living symbol of ancient days and virtues. For all his ascetic reserve, he was also fond of dressing up in the paraphernalia of various communities and orders: aboard the *Mayflower,* for instance, he wore a yachting cap, and in the summer of 1927, when he announced his decision to retire, he appeared before the newsreel cameras in the Black Hills wearing a full Hollywood-style cowboy suit, with "CAL" emblazoned on the chaps. Candidates for office often indulged in such antics for the benefit of the press. Hoping to garner popular support against revelations to come, Warren Harding stopped in Hutchinson, Kansas, on his last trip west and after making a long speech on a day of killing heat, shed his city duds, strode into a wheatfield, and drove a binder to remind folks of his honest, rural roots.[43]

Coolidge went him one better by donning historical dress when the reporters came calling. During his years as governor of Massachusetts, it was his habit to go up to Vermont at the turning of the seasons to help with the chores. Mrs. Coolidge later insisted that he was mortified to be discovered there, one day in 1919, togged out in a quaint homespun garment woven by his grandmother:

The news photographers came to Plymouth to take some pictures of him performing the various farm duties to which he had been accustomed in his youth. He wore the frock and the high leather boots which he was also in the habit of wearing. When the pictures were published, criticism developed, and his friends protested that the world at large thought it was all for effect. After that he hung the coat away in the back chamber closet and set the boots on the floor beneath it. He could never be prevailed upon to get them out again.[44]

But the photographic record shows that he willingly resurrected the woolen smock—the sort of outfit worn in the fields of Vermont a century and a half earlier—in the summer of 1923, too. So adorned in the luster of age and custom, he posed for reporters and casual tourists alike, pantomiming the steps in the process of cutting hay (Figure 9.2).[45] Like his father's oil lamps, pictures of the president acting out a sort of colonial pageant all his own in the back forty suggested that thrift, hard work, self-denial, and the other components of the old Puritan ethic were viable still in a world of easy credit, loose morals, and abundant leisure.

Even as his tractors and automobiles were changing the mores of the countryside, Henry Ford turned up in the newspapers doing precisely the same thing—"working" by hand in an imagined past, with traditional agricultural tools.[46] One of the most highly publicized "events" of the Coolidge presidency was the ceremonial visit to Plymouth by Ford, Harvey Firestone, and Thomas Edison. The three industrialists were treated to a trip to the little cheese factory behind the farmhouse and ate curds with spoons whittled from shingles. And as a climax to this orgy of rusticity, "Mr. Coolidge," Ford said, "spoke about an old sap bucket which his [great-great-] grandfather had used, and offered it to me for our collection at Dearborn" (Figure 9.3). Delighted to add that prime specimen of "Puritanism de luxe" to the hoard of Americana shortly to become the museums of Greenfield Village and the Edison Institute, Ford suggested that the party commemorate the afternoon by signing the bucket while the cameras rolled.[47]

In 1927 the magazine of the Daughters of the American Revolution observed that "patriotic Americans who treasure the memory of our forefathers can do no better today than to reproduce in their homes the furniture and decorations" of those historic times.[48] Henry Ford eventually built a whole Coolidge Collection around his bucket in the name of that brand of patriotism. "We have his cradle," Ford noted with pride in 1935, "the first baby carriage in which he rode, the 'settle' from the old Coolidge kitchen, and various household objects connected with his boyhood. He was one of the most American men I have ever known."[49]

Much to their surprise, Grace and Calvin Coolidge found the autographed bucket "swinging from an iron arm attached to a side wall in the barroom" of the Wayside Inn in Sudbury, Massachusetts, where the couple spent their twenty-fifth wedding anniversary in 1930, en route to an American Legion convention in Boston. The Coolidges

9.3
Autographing the old Coolidge sap bucket for Henry Ford's collection of historic relics

were the honored guests of the inn's proud new proprietor, Henry Ford. Purchased in 1923, the historic tavern where Longfellow set his *Tales of a Wayside Inn* ("Built in the old Colonial day, / When men lived in a grander way, / With ampler hospitality") became, in Ford's hands, a kind of living museum. Although he brought in job-lots of antiques after consultation with such experts as Israel Sack and Wallace Nutting and amassed an amazing collection of treasures there— among them was a relic from George Washington's fateful cherry tree, displayed with an affidavit declaring that the heart-shaped "piece of cherry wood came from a stump which, according to tradition, was left from the original cherry tree chopped down by our first president as a boy"—the Wayside Inn was a working hostelry that accepted overnight guests (Figure 9.4).[50]

But the inn did not cater to the average, casual tourist (Figure 9.5). Staying there, as Mrs. Coolidge's account of her weekend suggests, was very much like becoming a figure in a Wallace Nutting hearthside photograph, acting in a pageant, or playing at haymaking with Calvin in a Vermont meadow:

Dinner [was] being prepared for us in the old kitchen of the inn. A beef roast was turning on the spit in front of the huge fireplace; vegetables in iron pots hanging from the crane were steaming off delicious odors; there were mince, apple, and pumpkin pies in the brick oven, and hoe cake in the ashes. Presently we were sitting down in front of the fire at a tavern table set with old pewter, steel knives, and three-tined forks. In the center was a wooden bowl filled with rosy-red apples polished to a gleaming brilliancy. A kitchen maid in a print dress of the period carved the roast on a wooden block.

. . . It was not difficult to turn back the pages of the years and fancy that we were living in a bygone day when the Wayside Inn was new and its rooms were peopled with others who, like ourselves, were celebrating an occasion which was a landmark in their lives.[51]

9.5
The parlor of the Wayside Inn, ca. 1926

The celebrities of the 1920s and the early 1930s—and ex-President Coolidge was such a figure—went from ritual to historical ritual, often in one another's company. Ford went camping with Harvey Firestone and Thomas Alva Edison, for example, in an effort to recreate the simplicity of American life in the preindustrial era. Noting that important "men of business," like Firestone, Ford, A. P. Giannini, Owen D. Young, J. P. Morgan, and Lewis Pierson of the Chamber of Commerce, made the White House guest list resemble a "chart of interlocking directorates of high finance" when Queen Marie or Lindbergh was in town, a cub reporter once asked the president on a slow news day why he didn't have artists and poets around the place, too.[52]

According to one version of the story, when the names of Frost and E. A. Robinson were mentioned Coolidge professed never to have heard of them. In another retelling, he did bring to mind the name of the class poet at Amherst: "Haven't heard of him since, either!"[53] De luxe Puritanism was for the famous or for those who aspired to be. When Coolidge did at last invite an artist to stay at the White House, it was Howard Chandler Christy, a well-paid magazine illustrator who had also designed the famous "Uncle Sam Wants You" poster and the official Harding-Coolidge campaign banners. And according to published reports, the high point of the visit was not her husband's artwork but Mrs. Nancy Christy's homemade old-fashioned apple pies.[54]

Walter Lippmann's analysis of the Coolidge brand of old-fashioned, historical charm—his Puritanism de luxe—was meant to flatter neither the poker-faced Republican president nor the nervous voter who made his living in the securities business. But Lippmann's knowing commentary on a captivating new celebrity personality sprung like a neocolonial genie from an antique oil lamp does help to explain the *Washington Post*'s reaction to the sight of Coolidge greeting Lindbergh at the Washington Monument. In that context and company, Lindbergh did seem to evoke the "spirit" of the Pilgrims and George Washington—the simple, time-honored values embodied by his host, Calvin Coolidge, antitype and heir apparent of George Washington, the modernized colonial tycoon. And like Coolidge himself, Lindy proved that "the good old days" were not really gone beyond all recovery and that, despite appearances to the contrary, the nation was still "morally sound and sweet and good . . . at the core."[55]

Along with George Washington, Lindbergh and Coolidge were separate manifestations of a common personality, an American type. The personality craze of the 1920s centered on such celebrities, their stunts, and the public events at which they could be observed. According to Emily Post, however, "personality" also meant expression "of . . . *your* old-fashioned conventions, . . . your emancipated modernism—whichever characteristics are typically yours," through the appointments of the private home.[56] In practical terms, the interior decorator took "personality" as a license to order Early American furniture and accessories; all across the land, electrified models of old Colonel Coolidge's ancestral oil lamps lit up spanking new pseudo-farmhouses. And the juxtaposition between "modern conveniences" and antiquity in discussions of Coolidge's charm, Lindbergh's flair, and the taste of the average suburbanite measures the degree to which those were synonymous and mutually dependent propositions in the period.

The president in the modern celluloid collar who flatly asserted that "the business of America is business"; the dashing young aviator who proved the worth of the most advanced species of modern technology: no two "personalities" seem more remote from the Mount Vernon plantation in the national salad days of the eighteenth century. Yet in the tense, idiosyncratic merger between utopian futurism and nostalgic historicism that characterized the decade, Calvin Coolidge and Charles Lindbergh *were* George Washington, reincarnate in multiple versions. And George Washington, for his part, was a madcap modern in knee breeches.

The year 1927, for example, found George Washington setting the beat for the Lindbergh Hop in a popular jazz lyric that paired the American Revolution with hot new trends on Tin Pan Alley:

> Washington at Valley Forge
> Freezing cold, but up spoke George
> He said: "Vo-do-de-o, vo-do-de-o-do."
>
> Crazy words, crazy tune
> All that George would croon and spoon
> Was: "Vo-do-de-o, vo-do-de-o-do."
>
> On his ukulele, daily
> He would strum:
> "Deedle-dum-dum."
> Dancing, prancing
> Then he'd holler:
> "Red hot mamma!"[57]

If Washington was a kind of colonial flapper, he was also associated with ultramodernity of an altogether more respectable sort. In Minneapolis in 1927 the first steel went up on the skeleton of a structure billed as the apogee of modern commercial architecture. A thirty-four-story Art Deco office building equipped with every corporate amenity and loudly said to be the tallest skyscraper between Chicago and the Pacific, the Foshay Tower was also a grossly inflated copy of the

9.6

Cover of the issue of the *Foshay Spot Light* commemorating the dedication of a new Minneapolis office building designed after the Washington Monument. Modern technology and know-how improved on the model.

Washington Monument. The design for its sloping walls and pointed top—crowned with electric searchlights—was pending at the patent office, since the developers confidently expected duplicate obelisks to be built far and wide (Figure 9.6).

According to the public relations firm charged with explaining the anomalous structure to the public at large, the concept of a memorial office building sprang from the imagination of Wilbur Foshay, its builder and financial backer. At the age of fifteen, Foshay, then a would-be architect, had found himself at "the structure that is the Mecca of all who journey to the nation's capitol city. A visit to the Washington Monument." The seed was planted:

At last, the inspiration to build a commercial building as a memorial to George Washington. . . . America, pioneer in so many things, also was to be the pioneer in an architectural project never even remotely approached in daring simplicity. Putting it in terms of equal simplicity, it meant that young Foshay was thinking ahead of the then existing architectural ideas by a matter of two or three decades; because it was not until comparatively recently that the adoption of plain, geometric surfaces was undertaken whole-heartedly by modern architects and builders.[58]

At least insofar as its commemorative aspects were concerned, Foshay's weird design never did catch on. More useful and up-to-date versions of the Washington Monument housing public utilities firms, investment companies, choice shops with streamlined façades, and the like did not sprout up across the land. And shortly after the 447-foot Foshay Tower was dedicated before twenty thousand spectators (including the Minneapolis regent of the DAR) with a special Foshay March performed by John Philip Sousa's band, Foshay went bankrupt from the expense of it all. In the end, he went to Leavenworth for fraud, a strange fate for one whose devotion to the memory of Washington and to a Washingtonian honesty in business practices were made quasi-legendary by his busy publicists.[59]

The Philadelphia Sesqui-Centennial of 1926

The same uneasy juxtaposition between historical retrospection and modern technology dominated the pages of the Philadelphia newspapers in 1926 when the Sesqui-Centennial International Exposition was being planned, vigorously promoted, and opened at last to disappointing receipts during the rainiest summer in memory.[60] The anniversary year began with several "lovely descendants" of the signers of the Declaration of Independence—all members of the city's madcap "younger set"—reenacting the signing in a New Year's pageant held in Independence Hall. Organized by the Colonial Dames, the ceremony spotlighted fourteen young ladies of high social standing in the community. With their fashionable freshly plucked eyebrows and lac-

9.7
Frances Bayard, Alice Carter, and Elise du Pont, wearing 1926 makeup and colonial dresses

quered cupid's-bow lips, they acted as witnesses to the signing, "garbed in the costumes of their illustrious ancestors, in some cases genuine silks and satins of the period." Their masquerade neatly fused the modern world with Philadelphia's ancestral past.

The newspapers noticed that these were modern young women accustomed to lipstick and marcel waves, and reported the story largely in terms of their reactions to wearing clothing that, in the postwar period of shortened skirts and skimpy lingerie, had become far more exotic than it had seemed to the young du Ponts, Carrolls, and Chews who had attended colonial balls a generation before (Figure 9.7). "I don't think the old-fashioned garb was uncomfortable by any means," stated Alice Carter, a descendant of Benjamin Rush, who wore the costume of her great-great-great-grandmother. Mary Spencer of Haverford, a descendant of Charles Carroll, wore the gown Harriet Chew once donned for "Washington's ball." "This costume is very well preserved," she said. "We consider it one of the family's most priceless possessions." But even when pressed, none of the debs could tell just how old their heirlooms were or when the Revolution happened, for that matter, although they were sure that their pretty dresses had been "handed down from Revolutionary times."[61]

Philadelphia's January headlines also featured the annual mummers' parade, in which bands wearing capes emblazoned with the Liberty Bell marched along with units of "Charlestown Babies" imitating the latest dance craze (a news report from New York that morning printed alongside the list of local parade themes had a twenty-four-year-old mother of three swearing off the Charleston after breaking her leg doing the intricate steps at a New Year's Eve party!). Other mummers' routines poked fun at football hero "Red" Grange and the current crop of unsuccessful swimmers of the English Channel.[62] On a stage "set in Early American furniture over which shone lights denoting the dates 1776–1926," the Hibernians performed their own signing-of-the-Declaration pageant during an intermission at the annual ball; an added scene, showing the delivery of the document to the English king, was wildly cheered by the Irish-Americans.[63] In the Philadelphia commemoration of 1776, celebrities past and present mingled at will under the electric lights.

If the lightbulbs, the lipstick, and the Charleston all reminded celebrants that this was 1926, the content of the news stories with which accounts of such pageantry shared the headlines suggested that the past was at least as important to the average Philadelphian as the cautionary tale of the dancing mother from Manhattan. Among those stories was a report of the arrival in the city of a Dr. Penniman. Author of several books on George Washington—some of them had been published by the Mount Vernon Ladies' Association—Penniman held a press conference to clarify certain murky points in the biography of the first president. Washington was, Penniman attested, "probably the richest American of his day," but his riches were honorably acquired. "I do not know of one unethical act ever done by George Washington," said the good doctor, whose purpose, it developed, was to portray the hero of the Delaware as a kind of premature foe of bathtub gin.

"George Washington served wine to his guests" as the customs of the day dictated, Penniman disclosed, "and drank wine himself. But he was most abstemious."[64] In much the same vein Mrs. Charles L. Purnell, formidable president of the Philadelphia Federation of Women's Clubs, made a splash at an otherwise unremarkable ladies' luncheon by linking Washington to the berouged flappers and their sheiks, when she told social critics and debunkers alike to "stop vilifying the Father of Our Country, and let us cease our attacks on the younger generation. If it continues we shall have to page Diogenes to find an honest man."[65]

Penniman and Mrs. Purnell were both reacting to Rupert Hughes's debunkery, word of which first reached the *Philadelphia Public Ledger* several weeks after the mummers' parade in reports of the writer's controversial speech before the Sons of the Revolution and President Coolidge's highly quotable dismissal thereof. "I am asked to comment on George Washington," Coolidge had remarked in reply to a written question submitted by a reporter, and turning toward the south window of his office, the president had looked out at Wilbur Foshay's guiding inspiration and noted that the monument was still standing, despite charges that Washington swore, smoked, drank, danced, and placed bets. Hughes, Philadelphians learned, believed "it would be much better to teach children what Washington really was like than to teach the ridiculous story of the cherry tree."[66]

But judging by the tenor of Mrs. Purnell's remarks, the younger set was already well acquainted with drink and other personal vices, and according to several Washington descendants run to ground by the Associated Press, their ancestor had been laudably modern in that respect, too. The aged John Washington, a peppery retired editor and the great-great-grandson of George Washington's eldest brother, seemed amazed anyone would think that Washington favored Prohibition before its time. "Why, certainly George Washington drank," he snorted. "Why try to place a halo around him? He was a man, a soldier and a capitalist. He typified the true Southern gentleman." The other Washington relative interviewed about the matter was even more blunt: "George Washington was 'well up' on the follies of his time, and although it is questionable whether he ever indulged in many of them, he 'cussed' and drank like a gentleman and 'made some of the best whiskey in Virginia,' John Thornton Washington, great-great-grandnephew of the general, said . . . in indorsing Rupert Hughes' address to the Sons of the Revolution in Washington."[67]

Remarks like these, of course, only elicited stronger retorts from Dr. Penniman. For the benefit of the Philadelphia papers, he drew up a list of texts from Washington's own hand warning against the evils of the rum trade and forbidding gambling in the army. "Much of the recent discussion of Washington's standards of personal conduct" had not been based, he claimed, "on bed-rock stuff. . . . No one seems to have tried . . . to look up the original sources" that proved Washington superior in every respect to the rackety moderns who claimed he caroused like a bewigged jazz-baby.[68]

Whether the "drys" wished to recognize the fact or not, drinking establishments were a part of the colonial heritage, although a tavern could, in the hands of someone like Henry Ford, exude an aura of wholesomeness at variance with the depraved atmosphere of the average speakeasy. In the midst of the Rupert Hughes flap, the *Public Ledger* also ran stories about Ford and his flivver being snowed in at the Wayside Inn, en route to the automobile show in New York. As oxen were pressed into service to plow the highway outside, Ford perched on a high-backed chair near the fireplace and "told reporters he thought his business deals, manipulations of the market, and the amassing of fortunes by individuals were good for the country": "He was interrupted by a cook entering the room with a huge pan of Indian pudding, and Mr. Ford jumped to his feet to open the door of an oven at the side of the fireplace. 'You should have seen the pies that came out of that oven this morning,' he said."[69]

The inn did not cater to dancers of the Charleston, gyrating to a chorus of "vo-do-de-o-does." "Reporters were admitted to the ballroom on the second floor of the Inn to be regaled with an old-time concert performed by eight New England fiddlers," including "John Wilder, of Plymouth, Vt., uncle by marriage of President Coolidge." They received Ford's official denial of rumors that he intended to "reconstruct an old New England village around the inn where 300 persons would live." And they heard his plan to move the section of the old Boston Post Road immediately in front of the Wayside Inn some five hundred feet back, at enormous expense to himself, "because the vibration of traffic is injuring the venerable inn." In one of the many striking paradoxes of the day, Ford's own principal occupations—preserving the past and, through his automobiles, reshaping the future—had come into sharp conflict.

The irony of the situation was largely lost on Henry Ford's contemporaries, however. At week's end, the rotogravure section of the *Ledger* was full of pictures intended to be amusing because the Flivver King, who was shown putting on his ice skates during the interlude in Sudbury, had adopted for the moment a gasless form of locomotion, or because the man whose career stood for modern industry, restless movement, and a radical transformation of American life chose to pose motionless in a Carver chair before the fireplace at the Wayside Inn with a copy of Longfellow's poems in his lap (Figure 9.8).[70] The Philadelphia fair, opened in the spring of 1926 and officially rededicated by President Coolidge on a steamy Fourth of July, was a similar welter of the opposites the papers had already taught Philadelphians to regard as inherent in the natural order of things.

The two greatest attractions of the "Sesqui" illustrate that forcible blending of old and new. One of them was "the tremendous illuminated Liberty Bell, suspended over the plaza on South Broad Street, north of the main entrance to the grounds." A $100,000 replica of the old bell suspended from a framework duplicating the original support at Independence Hall, it was eighty feet tall and made of steel studded with sockets for 26,000 fifteen-watt bulbs. When the juice was turned on, it lit up the length of Broad Street; the amber glow could be seen "from every vantage point in Philadelphia" and from parts of New Jersey. Electricity—a lavish expenditure of candlepower putting the glitzy new "White Ways" of a thousand commercial strips to shame— was one of the chief selling points of a fair that declared itself open by broadcasting the numbers 1-9-2-6 by radio throughout the nation as they were tapped out in code on the rim of the old bell.[71]

The second big draw was High Street ("the Street" for short), a slightly underscaled ensemble of twenty houses, a marketplace, and a town hall laid out to suggest the appearance of Market Street, the first thoroughfare in the country to have been paved and lighted by fixed street lamps.[72] Since none of the originals survived, Sarah Lowrie and the Women's Committee responsible for "the Street" could rebuild vanished landmarks pretty much as they fancied and invent others to take advantage of the Washington craze in progress in 1926. So there was a "Washington House," fashioned after his Philadelphia residence and scene of the president's formal levees, "undoubtedly the most visited of any house on the Street, [which] embodied most perfectly the spirit of Colonial architecture." It was placed in the charge of the DAR, and regents from each of the thirteen original states acted as resident hostesses for two-week periods during the run of the fair.

Next door, the Washington stables housed the Little Theatre—"appropriately enough, for Washington himself was a great patron of plays." And further down the block, past the log cabin and a dame school where the Teachers' Association gave out copies of the old New England primer, stood other buildings made legendary by the presence of Washington:

[Here] the visitor actually found himself in early Philadelphia with a vivid visualization of the United States Capital when George Washington was President; a masterpiece of art, architecture and patriotism over which, because of its transitory character, one might reasonably weep. It was an inspiration lovingly executed; had the public realized its message beforehand, its great

9.8
Henry Ford, seated at the fireplace of the Wayside Inn during a press conference

educational importance as a picture of public and private life in the infancy
of our country, it would surely have been built of permanent material, a lasting
memorial of Old Philadelphia.[73]

Near "the Street" but not part of it there were, on adjoining lots, a
reproduction of Sulgrave Manor, the ancestral home of the British
Washingtons, contributed by the Colonial Dames, and a replica of
Mount Vernon fitted out as a cafeteria by the YWCA (Figure 9.9).
Indeed, the presence of Washington—and Calvin Coolidge, his real-
life celebrity counterpart—was felt throughout the fairgrounds. The
presidential motorcade that rushed through the exposition on July 5
under threat of severe storms passed the intersection marked by
Sulgrave Manor. It zipped past New York's replica of Federal Hall with
its inaugural balcony (a not-so-subtle reminder that New York had
preceded Philadelphia as the nation's capital). It skirted the Coolidge
inaugural farmhouse sent by the state of Vermont. The entourage
finally stopped at Washington House to receive keepsakes from the
Women's Committee.[74]

On the same day, Benedict Arnold's "patrician" mansion in Fairmount Park was opened for public inspection by a coalition of female
members of patriotic organizations who dressed as ladies of Washington's day and posed for photographers. Miss Bernice McIlhenny,
however, exercised her rights as a New Woman of the 1920s by
strolling about the gardens in knee breeches, silk hose, and a gentleman's wig, with Miss Mary Sailor, in a dress of Revolutionary vintage,
on her arm (Figure 9.10).[75]

Miss McIlhenny and her social-register friends were well-known
local figures. But the throngs that turned out to mob the Coolidge car
as it inched down High Street toward Washington House were out for
bigger celebrity game. The directors of the Philadelphia "Sesqui"
obliged. Gertrude Ederle, fresh from her conquest of the Channel,
posed in a rolling chair with a brace of famous aviators; film star
Gloria Swanson fired off a Revolutionary field piece to open the
National Air Races above the grounds. The rodeo stopped at the

exposition, with a $50,000 purse. The world's heavyweight title passed from Jack Dempsey to Gene Tunney on September 22 in "the fight of the century," held outdoors in the rain under the fair's dazzling electric lights, before 122,000 fans: the $1,700,000 gate broke all records. As if sports heroes and celebrated Hollywood idols were not enough, Queen Marie and the beautiful Princess Ileana received full honors too, in a hastily constructed "royal box" erected in their honor.[76]

The prettiest, the strongest, the bravest, the richest, the most titled: they all passed through Philadelphia in 1926—and through a sesquicentennial setting geared to honoring the celebrities of American history. On the most banal level, there was the Newsboys' Harding Memorial, a statue of the late president's famous Airedale, Laddie Boy, cast from 19,314 pennies donated by the nation's paperboys. The pooch's renown rested on a sentimentality relentlessly exploited by the press, and something of that same gush and goo spilled over the old Betsy Ross House, designated one of the "Seven Wonders" of historic Philadelphia and the site for the adulation of visiting female celebrities, be they down-at-the-heels monarchs or visiting movie queens.[77]

In the ragtag band of dogs, seamstresses, and electrified kites that defined the parameters of sesquicentennial history, however, George Washington was the supreme hero, as he had been in Philadelphia in 1876. Recreated bits of his physical environment were among the major architectural attractions of the fair. The Patent Office exhibited documents bearing his signature. On his birthday—his 194th, to be exact—the Women's Sesqui-Centennial Committee entertained club-women and officers of patriotic groups representing the thirteen colonies and reenacted the meeting of the Second Continental Congress. The official exposition pageant called *Freedom* (more often canceled than performed during that summer of downpours) devoted fully half of the historical scenes to Washington taking command of his troops, watching Mistress Ross cut her stars, praying in the snow, leaving Mount Vernon, and taking his oath of office.

Although President Coolidge was slated to watch the spectacle during his visit to the exposition, he and sixty thousand other disappointed visitors were driven indoors by bad weather and missed the dramatic compression of all of the early American past into the easy-to-follow life of one figure, George Washington: a star, a personality, a historical celebrity of the first magnitude. But Calvin Coolidge, whose Plymouth farmhouse was considered every bit as worthy of replication as Mount Vernon, was a celebrity of sufficient stature to ease the disappointment. In honor of the Philadelphia Sesqui-Centennial of 1926, a likeness of Coolidge appeared on the obverse of special commemorative half dollars, the first time a living president had ever been seen on the legal coinage of the United States.[78] But he was not

9.10
Miss Bernice McIlhenny and Miss Mary Sailor costumed for the opening of the Benedict Arnold Mansion, 1926

alone. The profile of George Washington was superimposed on that of his Yankee successor, a second Washington, a peerless American personality, a celebrity who provided living proof that the sterling business leader and the heroic political leader were still attainable American ideals.

Public Opinion Polls

W. E. Woodward had once claimed that debunking heroes was "the science of reality." The ad men and pollsters who struggled to gauge public opinion in the 1920s, the better to take advantage of crazes and shifts in taste, could have claimed the same honor for their new science. Popularity polls were an invention of the 1920s and an index to those celebrity personalities eliciting the most intense public interest. While anybody was fair game for the pollster, surveys taken among the young of the nation were analyzed with special care. The flaming youth of the American campus were vanguard moderns, liberated from the inhibitions of their elders. As such, college students were apt to be advanced and prescient in their views on almost any subject, including the most common areas of inquiry: sex, cars, and heroes. Grade-school tykes, on the other hand, parroted opinions so widely held that they had even percolated down to the level of the nursery.

It was news, therefore, when a 1928 poll taken among New Jersey schoolboys and closely scrutinized by the *New York Times* disclosed that the great majority of kids wanted to grow up to be just like Lindbergh. Next on the list of contemporary exemplars came President Coolidge and Henry Ford. "My Dad" ranked last, along with Benito Mussolini. A much larger grammar-school sample was taken in a 1929 poll conducted in Alabama. Invited to select the greatest idol of American youth from amongst all the heroes, living or dead, boys picked George Washington and Charles Lindbergh overwhelmingly, although an impressive number of diehards held out for Henry Ford and Babe Ruth. Girls selected George Washington, Clara Bow, and Lindbergh, with Betsy Ross trailing the pack.[79] Asked to identify the three greatest figures of all time, collegiate opinion-makers of the late 1920s settled on Christ and Napoleon Bonaparte, closely followed by Henry Ford, the Good Businessman who had achieved astounding material success without sacrificing the old-fashioned, commonsensical grit required to tell their sniggering, debunking profs that "history is more or less the bunk."[80]

Henry Ford loomed large in all the polls. While their votes went to Coolidge, Lindbergh, and George Washington, mere children paid Ford the homage due Babe Ruth, and peppy collegians made him their number-one living hero. For his part, however, Henry Ford held a mechanical hero in almost sacrilegious awe: "Machinery," he solemnly intoned, "is the new Messiah." And, had the pollsters' questions been phrased differently, perhaps Ford's own auto would have topped the list instead of Washington and Lucky Lindy.

But in human terms, Ford stood for his popular machines and for the assembly lines that made them. "Dazzled by the prosperity of the time and by the endless stream of new gadgets," says the historian William Leuchtenberg, "the American people raised business in the 1920s into a national religion and paid respectful homage to the businessman as the prophet of heaven on earth. As government looked only to the single interest of business, so society gave to the businessman social preeminence. . . . To call a scientist or a preacher or a professor . . . a good businessman was to pay him the most fulsome of compliments, for the chief index of a man's worth was his income."[81]

And if Henry Ford was the premier business celebrity of the 1920s, then all the greatest popular heroes of the hour basked in the reflected light of his highly individual achievement as the technological benefactor of the emergent modern age. Magnates and machines were the twin lodestars of modern America. Idolizing businessmen like Ford, Calvin Coolidge, for instance, regarded his and the country's business as business; Fordian equations between factories and temples of worship rolled smoothly from his tongue. Hence the George Washington conjured up by Coolidge and the debunkers alike was a businessman, a joiner of service clubs. Charles Lindbergh, the poet of the carburetor and the consummate lone individual, flew one of American industry's "new gadgets" to celebrity. Coolidge, Washington, and Lindbergh, in fact, each magnified an aspect of Ford's personality.

In 1922 a Ford-for-president boom started, only to "be skillfully pricked behind the scenes by another crackerbarrel philosopher, Calvin Coolidge."[82] In 1923, according to the papers, a "Ford craze" broke out: millions of admiring fans followed his every move in wire-service pictures.[83] When he bought the Wayside Inn and the old Botsford Tavern on the road to Detroit with an eye to restoring them to their original glories, public announcement of the purchases helped to start the "antiques craze" in earnest.[84]

What brands Ford the authentic hero of the Coolidge years, however, is not his ubiquity, his ranking in the polls, or his affinity with other contemporary celebrities. Rather, it is his Janus-faced approach to time. The Father of the Flivver was a natural hero to present-minded young people in Model T's. But a youth cult embodied in Lindbergh, the athletic star, and the matinee idol spread beyond the province of an underage public. A pervasive social factor, it attempted nothing less than the obliteration of history. Those supporters and detractors of corporate capitalism who made Washington an up-to-date businessman were youth cultists, for example, insofar as they denied the process of national maturation over time as consciously as Mary Pickford staved off the physical signs of grown-up womanhood. Living in and for the budding now, and its ever-new gadgets, the present-minded substituted the primal innocence of youth for mature awareness of the problematic aspects of their own new chromium-plated culture.

Despite easy credit terms, there were monstrous inequities of wealth in the America of the 1920s. Despite gleeful mobility, the auto was changing family structures and courtship patterns in disturbing ways. Attempts to legislate morality—Prohibition, for instance—were a bad joke. But the childlike innocent was absolved from making hard judgments about the grimy innards concealed beneath the auto's shiny hood. Youthfulness became a moral position, or rather a posture geared to the avoidance of moral choices. A wide-eyed "gee whiz" was its response to the declaration that "the business of America is business." The successful businessman was the Good Businessman, a Santa Claus to all good American children. And his gadgets were their lollipops and the sugarplum fairies. Or, as Henry Ford put it, "Machinery is the new Messiah."

Ford's statement exuded the breathless naiveté of innocence. So did his appearance in a Mount Clemens, Michigan, courtroom in 1919. The *Chicago Tribune* had been irked and finally alarmed by the dramatic gestures through which Ford expressed his pungent individuality—his high wage scales, his short work days, his low prices, and his Peace Ship. The paper called him an anarchist and Ford filed a libel suit. Thanks to a battery of lawyers assembled in his twenty-five-room suite at the Colonial Hotel, Ford won a six-cent judgment against the *Tribune,* in pursuit of which he spent eight days on the witness stand testifying on any theme that promised to elucidate his philosophy.[85]

Because he was a celebrity, Ford's every word was reported by the *Tribune*'s rivals. During his long moment in the spotlight of publicity, Ford failed to distinguish Arnold Bennett from Benedict Arnold. He confused the Revolutionary War with the War of 1812. His statements "proved what ought to have been obvious—that he was an imaginative mechanic with an eighth-grade education."[86] Beyond simple ignorance, however, Ford's fund of colorful misinformation about the past, upon which he drew with some relish, was symptomatic of a schoolboy's contemptuous pride in ignorance, a present-mindedness that thumbed its nose at fixed, unchangeable historical facts. At this libel trial, goaded by defense attorneys intent on proving that even the richest man in the world could not alter history, an exasperated Henry Ford reiterated his famous anathema: "History is more or less the bunk."

Henry Ford's Greenfield Village

For all his bluster, Henry Ford would not leave American history alone. What he called "bunk" became his obsession in 1919, when he began to collect Early Americana on a modest scale, a whale-oil lamp here, a spice mill there (Figure 9.11).[87] By the time Lindbergh came home from Paris, Ford was the proprietor of the Wayside Inn, which he promptly equipped with electric lights, indoor plumbing, central heating—those hearths were largely symbolic—and spacious closets.[88] And there he amassed a staggering number of curios plucked with eclectic abandon from the seventeenth, eighteenth, and nineteenth centuries on the warrant that they were old-timey and American.

The Wayside Inn showcased the settles and the highboys of Mrs. Post and the domestic "personality" cult; it was an object lesson for decorators everywhere. And that was just the beginning. Ford took an interest in Mount Vernon and donated state-of-the-art firefighting equipment to the Ladies' Association in 1924. But the ladies were firmly in charge in Virginia and the mansion had already reached its definitive state of embalmed perfection. Mount Vernon did not welcome the attentions of a present-minded billionaire who was not quite convinced that history was a matter of settled facts, resistant to modern improvements.

9.11
Henry Ford gazing into the hearth at the Botsford Tavern near Detroit. This was the second of his restored "colonial" inns.

Rebuffed in his efforts to improve upon perfection, Ford turned his attention to neglected monuments. He restored the humble farmhouse in which he was reared so that the place would look just as it had in 1876, when he was thirteen years old and "the saner and sweeter idea of life that prevailed in prewar days" was still lived in rural America: assembly workers were plucked from the line to dig for fragments of his mother's china and the rusty old skates he wore as a boy.[89] When everything had been found, he located a distant relative who looked like his mother, dressed her in the garments of 1876, had her spin by the fire, and made a film of it all.[90] Thanks to modern technology, it really was possible to turn back the hands of time.

In the barn, he invited his friends to dance the reel, the quadrille, and the gavotte wearing the costumes of the centennial era; the old rounds and squares were wholesome, folksy antidotes to the Charleston, he suggested in a 1926 manual entitled *Good Morning: After a Lapse of 25 Years, Old-Fashioned Dancing Is Being Revived by Mr. and Mrs. Henry Ford.*[91] In a spanking new birthplace not unlike the one Warren Harding had pined to build for himself, the cough and chug of the auto were drowned out by the kind of sweet music Cal Coolidge's uncle used to play for old-time kitchen dances in Plymouth, Vermont.

Ford bought the so-called Noah Webster Cottage and Patrick Henry's house, dismantled them, and shipped them off to an empty factory shed at the Ford plant in Dearborn. He bought the little red schoolhouse where he had learned his curious historical malapropisms (along with the bowdlerized version of Parson Weems's fable of "George and the Hatchet" prominent in the third volume of *McGuffey's Eclectic Reader*) and sent it to Dearborn, too. He made an offer for Independence Hall, and when brusquely told that it was not for sale at any price, he thumped the table in frustration and ordered construction of a brand-new Independence Hall in Dearborn, bigger and much better than the one in Philadelphia.[92]

Michigan's electrified, modernized Independence Hall and the 125-acre tract surrounding it came to prefigure the famous warehouse scene from *Citizen Kane* as Citizen Ford's Americana purchases moved into the wholesale category. There were hundreds of old guns, fifty spinning wheels, a score of music boxes; there were heaps of army boots, a fleet of Conestoga wagons, daguerreotype machines, hoop skirts, and wheat flails in serried ranks; and there were more and more crated-up buildings, with barrels of antique equipment to go with them—a general store, a courthouse, a post office, a firehouse, a tavern, a depot. When the novelist Hamlin Garland visited the old tractor plant that housed most of the collections in 1925, he saw "only an immense warehouse of discarded furniture, . . . the storehouse of the outworn." But when he looked more closely, Garland found himself strangely moved by "the homely character of the objects": "Here was the long-legged stove under which, as a boy of five, I had laid to learn my letters. . . . I took into my hand the tin lantern which I had so often held while my father milked the cows. [Here were] all the time-worn, work-worn humble tools and furnishing of the average American home."[93]

By the time Ford was canonized by college students as the third-greatest figure of all time, the grand design for the historical flotsam and jetsam strewn about Dearborn was beginning to take shape, in fact. He first outlined his plan to his secretary, Ernest Liebold, as the pair motored home from the infamous libel trial:

We're going to start something. I'm going to start up a museum and give people a true picture of the development of the country. That's the only history worth observing, that you can preserve in itself. We're going to build a museum that's going to show industrial history, and it won't be bunk. We'll show the people what actually existed in years gone by and we'll show the actual development of American industry from the early days, from the earliest days that we can recollect up to the present day.[94]

In June of 1929, Ford bought Thomas Edison's Menlo Park laboratory from General Electric, privy and all, along with several tons of red New Jersey dirt dug up from under the old floorboards. The purchase was no simple financial transaction; it amounted to a vast corporate scavenger hunt. Parts of the abandoned building had been reused in local houses and businesses. Every rafter, door, and brick was hunted down by Ford agents. What could not be found was replicated precisely using the latest techniques. A case in point was the only surviving shutter. It was minced up so that an authentic fragment could be incorporated into each one of the duplicate shutters needed to fill out the set.

Ford excavated the Menlo Park dump and came up with 125 boxfuls of broken glass bulbs and crockery, all preserved and catalogued by his minions. He located Edison's old supplier and reordered every chemical the Wizard of Menlo Park had ever stocked. The first light-bulb factory, more recently the home of squatters and chickens, had already been salvaged by General Electric and reassembled at its corporate park in Mazdabrook. Ford took the building, lock, stock, and barrel, and shipped it west.

As newsreel cameras recorded the acquisition, Ford unveiled his master plan with the help of Edward L. Bernays, a public relations consultant retained by GE to restrain the Flivver King from any faux pas damaging to its corporate image. Bernays and Ford announced a gala celebration of the Golden Jubilee of Light to be held in Detroit on October 21, 1929: on that occasion Edison would reenact his epochal invention in the very building where electric light came into being in 1879; and that building, its privy, and its coating of New Jersey dirt would occupy a small corner of Ford's new Greenfield Village, slated to open to the public on the day of the jubilee.

Ostensibly, the village and its depositories of accumulated loot were simply adjuncts to a $5 million Edison Institute; like the Wayside Inn project, Greenfield Village was an element in Ford's crusade to Americanize immigrants and uplift promising young mechanics housed amidst his collections. But the educational aspects of the institute paled in comparison to the popular entertainment provided by the historical hodgepodge of Greenfield Village Square, where the worlds of Edison, Noah Webster, Patrick Henry, little Henry Ford, and the Founding Fathers of Philadelphia mingled in an antic recreation of the entire American past.[95]

Accuracy in detail was important to Ford: he held the last Menlo Park shutter as dear as a sliver of the True Cross. Scrupulosity in small things was also the watchword of Ford's friend and fellow billionaire John D. Rockefeller, who had lately succumbed to historical fanaticism under the prodding of a clergyman from Williamsburg, Virginia. The pastor dreamed of restoring his tumbledown parish to its glory days in the 1700s. "I am convinced that from a historical point of view this is the greatest teaching opportunity which exists in America," he told potential backers.[96]

In 1928 a staff of experts suddenly appeared in Williamsburg and land was purchased by shadowy middlemen. Newspapers speculated on the identity of the silent benefactor. Was it Henry Ford or George Eastman of Kodak Camera?[97] As preparation of the site began in 1929 with the laying of concealed power lines and the construction of a modern water and sewage system, Henry Ford came calling, in search of tips for Greenfield Village. Rockefeller stressed the need to get the facts straight.

At Williamsburg, Ford found reinforcement for his own interest in accuracy of detail. From Mount Vernon he had already learned the lesson of profusion and had taken it rather too much to heart: if one spinning wheel was a good thing, why, fifty must be that much better! What made Greenfield Village unique, then, was not the plethora of authentic artifacts or the care with which missing elements were replicated. Each discrete fact was impeccably right. But the ensemble as a whole was wildly and gloriously wrong, a potpourri of gripping moments and patently quaint sights wrenched from any page of history ripe for the pillaging, without much regard for temporal distinctions between colonial times and the life and times of Henry Ford.

A watch supposedly carried by George Washington on his nocturnal excursion across the Delaware interested Ford when its owner offered to part with the relic for a mere $1,000, but he was just as pleased to accept a not-so-old, broken-down threshing machine tendered as a gift by an admirer and operated by Ford when he, like Harding and Coolidge before him, played at "working" in the fields adjacent to the village.[98] It was, all of it, "Early American," "old-fashioned," "colonial": Greenfield Village, in other words, was colonial by virtue of *not* being modern and up-to-date.

Exactly what Henry Ford was up to in Greenfield Village is not easy to ascertain, despite Bernays's fusillade of press releases. The artifacts of his school days and of Edison's early years suggest that Ford was making his boyhood memories concrete and paying compensatory tribute to a world his automobile and Edison's lightbulb had helped to vanquish. The fanciful juxtapositions of centuries and once-distant sites summoned up a child's-eye view of a hundred separate half-remembered history lessons. Greenfield was steeped in sentimentality and awash in the nostalgia of a rich old man's recollections of his robust youth. The greedy acquisitiveness of a monied culture also figured in the aesthetic of Ford's tourist attraction. Although Ford by no means initiated the rush to buy back items homemakers had been tossing away ever since a modern consumer culture began the long march out of the handicraft era, those roomfuls of Terry clocks and china hens for storing eggs helped spread the antiques craze to a much larger audience. On one level, Greenfield was simply the biggest antique shop in a nation bursting with Martha Washington china.

It was a new kind of museum, too, a far cry from the marble halls and naked Grecian gods of curators who regarded high culture as a purgative for the unwashed. Greenfield Village was a homespun, down-to-earth collection of objects that came, for the most part, from the everyday lives of people, with a perceptible emphasis on the simple and ingenious technology of the past. Finally, Greenfield was, as Edison is said to have remarked upon visiting his old lab—he would also light an illuminated, electrified copy of the Liberty Bell later in the day—much too clean.[99] In that respect it resembled the typical half-timbered colonial in the suburbs or the family car parked in the drive, fenders always polished to a mirror shine.

Yet for all his purchases and researches, the man who planned and paid for Greenfield Village seemed to hold the past in utter contempt. History was bunk to him. "We want to live in the present," he insisted, "and the only history that is worth a tinker's dam is the history we make today."[100] Thus Greenfield Village was history remade by today for today—for the present-minded 1920s. Like Williamsburg, it was improved with every subterranean convenience; unlike Rockefeller, however, Henry Ford was too much the creative industrialist to be stifled by adherence to the facts of what had happened at one place in a given stretch of time. He tinkered with the facts by rearranging them here and there; he improved them. The avaricious eclecticism of Greenfield was as modern as its plumbing.

Because of its determined modernism, Henry Ford remained true to his announced principles: Greenfield Village was not an exercise in pious bunk. It was instead a kind of *anti*history in three dimensions, a bricks-and-mortar proof that the present was superior to a past which could be subordinated, tamed, reshuffled, and cleaned up at will. And history could be taught to tell modern stories. Mount Vernon convinced tourists that the eighteenth century was an endless tea party for the gentry, a ritual of Byzantine complexity involving whole pantries of odd silver implements. Greenfield Village proclaimed that America's present-day love affair with clever gadgets, ever-faster modes of transportation, and even larger heaps of stuff to buy was the real legacy of American history. Ever since colonial times, Ford's artifacts seemed to say, America had been pretty much as it was in 1929. Spice mills, locomotives, and antique skirt-hoops from Appalachia told the story with an adamantine force the printed words in textbooks could never hope to match.

The "Usable Past"

When Van Wyck Brooks called for the creation of a "usable past" in 1918, he did not envision Henry Ford as the answer to his prayers. Brooks and his cadre of young intellectuals despised the "commercial mind" they attributed to the movers and shakers of the late nineteenth century. They were equally disenchanted with modern America. "The present is a void," Brooks wrote, "and the American writer floats in that void because the past that survives in the common mind of the present is a past without living value." His point was that a native literary tradition was unlikely to flourish in the shallow soil of American culture unless artists discovered an alternative to technology and utilitarianism. As it was, Americans coped with the "Puritan" taboo on instinctual pleasure by channeling all their orgiastic, creative drives into the pursuit of material things. By leapfrogging over the moralistic Victorian past that "our professors offer us," Brooks hoped to discover fresh sources of community in a new past, a past "of our own."[101]

Although Van Wyck Brooks and Henry Ford made strange bedfellows, Greenfield Village did answer that call for a usable past. Appealing to the "common mind" of the 1920s through projecting modern preoccupations back upon the past, Ford manipulated artifactual history to bring a homogeneous blend of "Puritan" and Victorian settings into alignment with the values of the present-minded. He used history to prove that all was well in the world of "modern conveniences." The past was just like the present: clean, prosperous, busy, mobile, and stocked with every imaginable consumer durable.

The usable past resembled a new suburban subdivision outside Kansas City or Minneapolis, each home and shop decked out in a distinctive, old-fashioned slipcover and appointed with the tasteful marks of "personality."[102] In a sense, then, Greenfield Village was a personality in its own right, an inanimate celebrity. Celebrities soothed their fans. Greenfield Village soothed the tourist, who had no reason to doubt the righteousness of modern ways when technology and consumerism were shown to be the precepts of the Founding Fathers, a legacy endorsed by every generation since.

The Fords and the Edisons were links in a great chain of historical progress that stretched from the colonial cottage to the Model A. If people felt ascetic and virtuous when they voted for Calvin Coolidge with one eye on his father's oil lamps and the other on their own modern conveniences, Greenfield Village made them feel just as good, and for the same reasons. If the masses worshipped themselves—the ordinary American writ large—when they anointed celebrities like Lucky Lindy, Greenfield Village, too, emphasized the normal, workaday texture of history, only occasionally enlivened by strokes of luck and pluck. Henry Ford came from the ordinary little red schoolhouse that every American lad once endured, and the rubbish from the Menlo Park dump showed just how many ordinary, uneventful days preceded October 21, 1879.

9.12
Advertisement for Monarch Foods; note the juxtaposition of Lucky Lindy, Honest Abe, and George Washington, idols of modern youth.

Finally, Greenfield Village shared with the human celebrity a certain plasticity of character, a passivity that allowed for modeling and shaping to suit the needs of the idolater. When Henry Ford moved buildings willy-nilly to Michigan, he effectively wiped away the context and meaning once determined by their sites and associations, and rendered them featureless. He was free, therefore, to arrange the building blocks of Greenfield just as he wished, endowing a colonial house or a nineteenth-century factory with a fresh meaning arising from whatever physical juxtapositions he fancied. Van Wyck Brooks proposed to tailor a "usable past" that could serve as an alternative to modern ballyhoo, but Henry Ford beat him to the punch.

The author of *The Wine of the Puritans* probably knew the old adage that says the devil can quote Scripture to further his wicked ends. By the same token, Henry Ford could make a "colonial" monument the birthplace of crass American boosterism. Descended from the skies and scrutinized in isolation from his flight, in the airless arena of celebrity, Lindbergh became as nondescript as one of Ford's historical relics. A blank slate—an American for all occasions—Lindbergh could stand for Ford's individualism, or present-minded, gilded youth, or the taciturn charm of Coolidge, or the promise of modern technology and business. He could even stand for the colonial spirit of the Puritans and George Washington (Figure 9.12).

Washington, for his part, could play the same roles to perfection in jazz songs, in speeches praising his business sense, and in the "usable," antihistorical history manufactured with present-minded fervor by debunkers and boosters alike. In the 1920s, American history *was* bunk. But the usable past was a vital component of up-to-date Americanism in the prosperous days of the Coolidge regime. Like George Washington, the polls never told a lie. Every celebrity was really a new Washington, and the first president was also the first American individualist, the first service-minded, commercial American. As such, he was worthy to stand with Calvin Coolidge, Charles Lindbergh, and Henry Ford in the pantheon of American heroes for the ages.

Herbert Hoover and the Cherry Tree

10 ′ ′ ′ ′ ′ ′ ′ ′ ′ ′ ′ ′ ′ ′ ′ ′ ′

Modern Mythmaking
1928–1932

Culture, History, and the Victorian Hero

Early in his career Will Rogers discovered that his newspaper columns were much funnier when cast in the form of friendly letters to reigning celebrities. Thus Rogers told the folks back home about his 1927 tour of Europe in a series of weekly articles entitled "Letters from a Self-Appointed Ambassador to His President," whom he addressed as just plain "Calvin."[1] The merchandising strategy was not unique. Ice cream manufacturers also boosted sales by pointing out that George Washington invented their product and Calvin Coolidge loved it; in 1926 the dairy industry even marketed the treat briefly under the name "President's Pudding."[2] Calvin Coolidge sold chocolate, vanilla, strawberry, and newspapers, too, and so, with studied irony, Will Rogers directed his voluble correspondence to Silent Cal in order to cash in on the popularity of that crackerbarrel hero.

Rogers reached Europe shortly before Lindbergh did and surveyed the scene through the eyes of an American innocent from Oklahoma. The Old World, or so he had been told, was awash in culture, a commodity often said to be in short supply on his side of the Atlantic. Rome, he confided to his erstwhile pen pal, the president, did have a little "more culture than Minneapolis or Long Beach, California":

They live there in Rome amongst what used to be called culture, but that don't mean a thing. Men in Washington you know yourself, Calvin, live where Washington and Jefferson and Hamilton lived, but as far as the good it does them, they might just as well have the Capitol down at Claremore, Oklahoma—and, by the way, I doubt if Claremore would take it; there is a town that has never had a setback. So, you see, Association has nothing to do with culture.[3]

Rogers poked some fun at the notion that America's political elite had gained much in the way of culture from residence in the august haunts of the Founding Fathers. But his willingness to broach the subject of culture at all indicates that Van Wyck Brooks's highly literate despair at the low estate of American art had filtered down into the bastions of chipper Philistinism and newspaper chatter. Brooks's work (unread, to be sure, by the largest segment of Will Rogers's audience) intimated that if America was to acquire a culture consisting of more than new cars and ice cream ad campaigns, a "usable past"—a source of inspiration in the void of what passed for contemporary culture— would have to be assembled from a very few bright interludes in American history.

The era honored by the Plymouth tercentenary was first among the *un*usable patches of the past. In his *Wine of the Puritans* of 1908, Brooks had introduced the theme of cultural repression and traced it back to the New England pioneers of his title: the sanctimonious, industrious Puritan of official American mythology was pictured as the forefather of modern capitalism. And so the Puritan, in turn, became the real villain of *The Ordeal of Mark Twain,* Brooks's 1920 indictment of the Gilded Age, a period he called the final "twilight of the human spirit" in America.[4] Puritanism and the capitalism that followed from its tenets had stifled the artist and stunted the flowering of American culture.

Yet the Puritans and American history clearly mattered deeply to Brooks; in his view, history was a dismal record of missed opportunities but it was not bunk. Had Van Wyck Brooks not believed that history was an active, "usable" force, capable of generating change for the good and solving the social and cultural problems of the day, his attack upon the slumbering dead would have been pointless. But stylish debunkery was not Brooks's game. And much of his vehemence might have been misdirected in the end, since the real quarrel was not with the Puritans of old New England but with the high-Victorian captains of industry whose pet professors had expounded prudery, commerce, hero-worship, and laissez faire in the name of the same kind of mythical Puritanism that pictured those worthies as stern Pilgrim fathers tramping through the snow toward church, dressed in somber garments and wielding large Bibles like weapons against the ungodly. In the popular imagination and in the history paintings popular at the turn of the century, such was the canonical portrait of the Puritan. By the 1920s, the historian Charles Beard observed, "Puritanism" had come to signify almost "anything that interfere[d] with the new freedom, free verse, psychoanalysis, or even double entendre."[5]

The despairing intellectual of the 1920s (Sinclair Lewis's Carol Kennicott was a small-town parody on the type) thought both freedom and free verse impossible in the land of the Puritan, although just who might be responsible for continuing the tradition of censorship and prudery was often unclear until Thomas Beers's *Mauve Decade* appeared in 1926. In his viciously unflattering portrait of the entrepreneurial 1890s, Beers squarely hit the target Brooks had missed. And, like many writers and critics in the brave new world of the 1920s, Beers articulated a postwar reaction against the turn-of-the-century idealism that sent Americans to the trenches and the profiteering industrialists who kept them there. Unlike the more conventional, goldfish-swallowing youth cultists of the day, then, Beers and the Young Intellectuals "spat squarely in the eyes of the older generation . . . who had started the war. The values they had been brought up to accept with blind faith, if indeed they had ever existed, had been blasted forever by the war. The ultimate damning epithet was 'Victorian.'"[6]

Biological fathers and proto-Founding Fathers—the Victorians and the Puritans—thus shared the blame for the malaise that hung over Greenwich Village during the 1920s as Lindbergh fiddled with his tachometer, Coolidge glanced knowingly at the Washington Monument, and Henry Ford bought spinning wheels in job-lots, built Greenfield Village, and crept steadily up in the popularity polls. A cash-mad society transfixed by the antics of such celebrities had little use for the serious artists of New York's bohemian quarter, of course. And American artists knew it. The painter Charles Demuth used an acerbic version of the European cubist style to comment on the foibles of American fame in his "poster-portraits" of the late 1920s. *I Saw the Figure 5 in Gold* of 1928, for example, showed the marquee lights of a glitzy movie première; a shiny red firetruck beneath it symbolized the mechanical cacophony of the excited city. But Demuth's pseudo-billboard honored the poet William Carlos Williams, whose difficult verse (and complex treatment of George Washington) aroused no hubbub at all outside his tiny circle of admiring friends. Above the wasteland of American culture, Demuth's galaxy of neglected "stars" of painting and belles-lettres would never twinkle in the firmament of popular adulation.[7] Art and what passed for culture in the mass media were conjoined only in the painter's ironic vision.

As long as the millions ran gaping and thirsty after gadgets and heroes, ersatz antiques, and make-believe history, the "cold lethal simplicities of American business culture" would prevail, wrote the critic Waldo Frank.[8] But suppose Americans were to discover their *real* history? According to Van Wyck Brooks, the artist's best hope for creating a genuine, unified culture lay in the truths of American history: a communal wellspring of reassurance and inspiration, the "usable past" could unite artists and the people in a cultural renaissance grounded in memories and in a mythology both groups shared.

In his day, however, history was still firmly in the hands of "Victorians." Even the celebrity craze of the 1920s was a hangover from Beers's Mauve Decade, when an elite impersonated Washington and his circle for the edification of immigrants who flattened their noses in wonderment against the windows of society ballrooms. Victorian youth had been expected to have heroes to admire and emulate. Movies like *George Washington Cohen* acknowledged the practice by poking fun at it, and live tycoons of the 1920s were fond of citing heroes whose examples had guided their own steps to wealth and fame. Samuel Insull, the self-made former officeboy who became the "Electric Utilities Czar" and head of GE, had worshipped Edison from boyhood and succeeded royally.[9] According to the polls, contemporary children took Insull's example to heart. Coolidge, Lindbergh, and Ford placed high on their hero lists; Van Wyck Brooks, Waldo Frank, and William Carlos Williams did not.

Artists were competing none too successfully with commercialized popular culture—with lavishly colored magazines, bestsellers sold by master advertisers, the movies, the radio, and Tin Pan Alley. The media used history cannily, appealing always to the historical imagery freshest in the "common mind." Hollywood took on the Puritans in 1926, for instance, in *The Scarlet Letter*. What Brooks had taken for repression of the spirit, director Victor Seastrom turned into a racy exposé of adultery in olden times, with Lillian Gish lending modern, celebrity overtones to the role of Hester Prynne.[10] Henry Ford, whose historical benefactions to the nation were slickly packaged by public relations experts, used the movie-set razzle-dazzle of the Wayside Inn to illustrate the "Victorian" precepts of industrious consumerism and limitless material progress, with up-and-coming young mechanics on the premises to drive the history lesson home. Media history was steeped in the Victorian attitudes that had blighted American culture.

So was the realm of popular art. Young Norman Rockwell rocketed to the top of his profession designing ads for *Collier's, Liberty,* the *Saturday Evening Post,* and *Good Housekeeping* that showed white-haired old ladies with spinning wheels recalling their first order from Montgomery Ward back in '72. Rockwell also drew old codgers who resembled Henry Ford sitting by the hearth instructing apple-cheeked Boy Scouts in the wisdom of using Colgate Ribbon Dental Cream and adhering to other wholesome American traditions. One of his most successful promotional formats, adopted during the 1920s and used regularly until after World War II, pictured a modern boy dreaming of an inspirational American hero—Daniel Boone, Ethan Allen, George Washington. As the lad dreamt, his hero rose genie-like over a nice new Underwood typewriter or a yellow Ticonderoga pencil. Alternatively, the same little fellow made off with the Del Monte Royal Anne cherries intended for the pie and told his mother, "I cannot tell a lie— I did cut it with my little can opener."[11]

The Rockwell formula (Figure 10.1) shows how easily the McCann-Erickson ad agency and other venders of popular imagery were able to preempt the historical themes that, according to Brooks's doctrine

10.1
This 1932 calendar illustration for the Boy Scouts of America typifies Norman Rockwell's inspirational formula. It was published by Brown and Bigelow of St. Paul, Minnesota.

of the "usable past," would someday allow the painter, the sculptor, and the poet to reenter the mainstream of American culture. The "usable past," was out there, all right, vibrant and verdant in the common mind, but vast tracts of that historical terrain had already been taken and occupied by an army of salesmen, copywriters, and illustrators.

Furthermore, the real artists—the painters and the poets, that is—had left themselves very little room for maneuvering in the Elysian Fields of American history. The taboo on Puritanism eliminated colonial New England from their consideration, for example, and "Victorianism" tainted the industrial Northeast for the better part of the nineteenth century. The South remained, however. And although D. W. Griffith had introduced controversial aspects of the theme to moviegoers in 1915 with *The Birth of a Nation,* the writers known as the Vanderbilt agrarians reclaimed the cavalier tradition for high culture in the early 1920s.[12] Almost by default, the Revolutionary South in particular and the period of the Revolutionary War in general became attractive to exponents of the "new freedom, free verse . . . or even double entendre," despite their disillusionment with World War I.

But the Philistines got there first. Every new poll showed that George Washington of Virginia, the patriot father of America, the leader of the Revolution, rivaled Henry Ford in popularity and mass appeal. Modern celebrities were doomed to rapid eclipse unless they partook of his spirit and character. Movies, ditties, advertising slogans, and magazine features proved Washington's preeminence in the common mind. Raging battles over his sex life and his sobriety kept him in the news, alongside Prohibition and the Snyder-Gray sex murder of 1927. Mild-mannered realtors were pleased to elect him to their ranks, in absentia. George Washington was, in short, chief among the celebrities of commercial America, the star of a popular, usable past. It is a measure of the importance of George Washington to the ethos of the 1920s that the avant-garde, with full knowledge of Washington's status as a "great man of business," nonetheless set out to woo away him from the embrace of Calvin Coolidge and the lethal grasp of business culture.

William Carlos Williams on the Colonial Hero

William Carlos Williams led the mission to rehabilitate "The Pap of Our Country." *In the American Grain,* a collection of essays with a brilliant central chapter on George Washington, was published in 1925 and sank like a stone into the morass of popular indifference. Undaunted, Williams pressed on with a libretto for an opera called *The First President* (it was never produced) and a tart essay incorporating his earlier Washington research that did attract some attention in the 1930s as an antidote to the saccharine flavor of the George Washington bicentennial festivities.[13] But Williams's work on Washington was important not because it wowed the masses, changed their minds, or ushered in the cultural renaissance; the author's virtual obsession with his personal hero accomplished no such feats. Instead, *In the American Grain* marks a significant juncture in the evolution of a unified culture because Williams expressed the thinking of an articulate and critical minority as ferociously enchanted with Washington as were the present-minded capitalists they excoriated. On the centrality of that one personality to American culture, Philistine and artist cheerfully agreed in the later 1920s.

As it turned out, Williams was even more present-minded than Calvin Coolidge or Henry Ford and a great deal more eloquent about it than either of those purveyors of up-to-date history. Official history that "portrays us in generic patterns, like effigies or the carving on sarcophagi, which say nothing save, of such and such a man, that he is dead" was a lie, the poet argued. And a dead past is a dangerous past since, if a culture buries its history, it also forgets that "what we are has its origins in what *the nation* in the past has been." That ignorance, Williams concluded, deprived the present decade of "our greatest well of inspiration, our greatest hope of freedom (since the future is totally blank, if not black)."[14]

Like Van Wyck Brooks, then, Williams needed a usable past. And he was no more sanguine than Brooks about the usability of Puritanism, at least insofar as the New England heritage was understood at that time by Hollywood and Greenwich Village. Williams's Puritans are his villains. *In the American Grain* posits two distinct strains in colonial history, the English and the French. The English or Puritan strain retained its European identity and eschewed contact with the essentials of the New World. That is, the Puritans shunned the Indians, branding them a satanic remnant of the lost tribes of Israel (infidels who, not incidentally, held the land the newcomers wanted). The French, on the other hand, mingled with the natives and married them. Their joie de vivre pointed up the joyless fervor of the moralistic and capitalistic English; the Puritan saga was a story of the repression and extermination of the Indian (with biblical license) for the sake of ownership. In his Manichaean version of the history of colonization, Williams sided passionately with the vanquished—the Indians and the French—because he recognized the deformities wrought by Puritanism in himself and his fellow Americans.

Williams felt that his own late-Victorian youth had been misshapen by spiritual and emotional repressions akin to the horrors visited upon the Indians by the Puritans; in both cases a rigid order had been imposed on natural impulses in the name of a spurious conception of virtue. The dead hand of the past, as Brooks maintained, *had* left its deforming mark on the America character. But, said Williams, off in a recess of history, shunted aside for generations by the professors and the popularizers, there still lay untouched "our last great hope of freedom" from the tyranny of capitalist values. That forgotten historical element was America—its essence, its spirit. The Puritans, he maintained, were *not* Americans at all! Nor were they any kin to the American Founding Fathers. By the simple expedient of reading the Puritans out of the record, Williams finally bypassed the thicket of recrimination in which his peers had been stuck for a decade and blazed a fresh trail to George Washington, his first real American.

Not long before, Calvin Coolidge had described George Washington as a frontiersman in order to praise his business acumen. But the pioneers, in Williams's opinion, were not accountants in buckskin; rather, they were the poets, the first to apprehend the real essence of the New World. In search of that essence, Daniel Boone and Davy Crockett turned their backs on the repressions of the East and headed West, toward a raw, untamed something that was America. The Puritans never touched the secret soul of the continent; they killed off the natives, scoured the land clean, and subdivided the plots like so many colonial realtors with an eye on the balance sheet. The Puritans, in sum, remained Europeans although their transplanted culture was what the masses later mistook for the genuine article. The Puritan strain in American thought was imported and false. The *real* America—indigenous, aboriginal, true—still remained out there somewhere, where the frontiersmen once went in search of it.

As Williams described him, George Washington was the father of frontiersmen, the living father of a still-unrealized America, an America still struggling to be born. A tragic hero, Washington mediated between the intrinsic vigor of the New World—his own emotional authenticity was profoundly American, hot temper and all—and the English strain of manners and airs that cosseted him and finally offered him up, "the typical sacrifice to the mob":

Here was a man of tremendous vitality buried in a massive frame and under a rather stolid and untractable exterior which the ladies somewhat feared, I fancy. He must have looked well to them, from a distance, or say on horseback—but later it proved a little too powerful for comfort. And he wanted them too; violently. One can imagine him curiously alive to the need of dainty waistcoats, lace and kid gloves, in which to cover that dangerous rudeness which he must have felt about himself. His interest in dress at a certain period of his career is notorious.[15]

William Carlos Williams was doing research on Washington's waistcoats, kid gloves, and colonial sweethearts at the New York Public Library in 1924, while Woodward and Hughes were working on their books. The kinds of facts all three writers culled from the record were remarkably similar and militantly untraditional. William Woodward had marshaled new evidence to show that Washington was a captain of industry whose interests and traits of character were those of the average American of the 1920s. By stripping away the coating of moralistic myth that had made Washington into a Victorian priss, a Protestant saint of the nineteenth century, Rupert Hughes had hoped to reveal a plausible, even lovable human being, of interest to the modern man in the street. Humanizing, for critical or laudatory ends, entailed discovery and presentation of facts that described Washington's private habits, things he said and did in unguarded moments, the details of the common life he and all men must lead.

At the Centennial Exposition of 1876, Washington's breeches were historical relics even though their manner of display hints at an emerging inclination to regard them as a hero's pants. Woodward, Hughes, and Williams all took pants and other items of apparel seriously; like the decorative signs of "personality" Mrs. Post was finding in the neocolonial home in the suburbs, intimate detail diagnosed the inner, human personality of Washington for would-be historians of the 1920s. To Woodward, attire connoted avarice; to Hughes, a warming touch of self-conscious vanity; to Williams, a figleaf, a straitjacket of phony culture barely containing the rude vitality of the American Adam.

But the facts signified all the same, no matter what construction the investigator put on them, and so Williams concentrated on turning up the more obscure fables of history: Washington's "club life in Alexandria, as a Mason," his temper tantrum at Monmouth, "the obscene anecdote he told that night in the boat crossing the Delaware." And there were always the ladies: "Some girl at Princeton, was it? And some joke about a slipper at a dance. He was full of it."[16]

Williams was a poet. He argued his case by allusion and juxtaposition rather than logic and chronology. The meaning of George Washington's passions and pleasures is clarified for the reader of *In the American Grain* primarily by the organizational framework of the biographical chapter. The disquisition on waistcoats, for instance, is followed by a passage on Washington the young surveyor bound for Fort Duquesne. "The wilderness," says Williams, "was . . . the other side of the question." The frontier was the place where "he must have breathed a more serious air which cannot but have penetrated to the deepest parts of his nature." Although Washington went back to "his 'vine and fig tree,'" to "a sloping lawn with a river at the bottom," and to his widow-wife, "there must have been within him a great country whose wide paths he alone knew and explored in secret and at his leisure."[17]

Washington the frontiersman touched the wild heart of America the Puritans never knew and heard it beating in his own bursts of wanting, rage, and lust. The frontier lay deep within, along the secret pathways of the self, where only the poet dared pursue him. Washington the internal frontiersman was, in fact, a poet who, like Williams, was driven back upon himself by the niceties of an alien and repressive culture:

America has a special destiny for such men, I suppose, great wench lovers— there is the letter from Jefferson attesting it in the case of Washington, if that were needed—terrible leaders they might make if one could release them. It seems a loss not compensated for by the tawdry stuff bred after them—in place of a splendor, too rare. They are a kind of American swan song, each one. The whole crawling mass gnaws on them—hates them. He was hated, don't imagine he was not. The minute he had secured their dung heap for them—he had to take their dirt in the face.[18]

W. E. Woodward gave the popular culture of the 1920s George Washington the typical American businessman. Rupert Hughes added George Washington the regular fellow, who put on his breeches one leg at a time. William Carlos Williams had the audacity to unveil George Washington the embattled modern poet, the alienated truth-seeker, despised by the hypocritical, Puritanical herd because he dared give free rein to the appetites and instincts of the true America. The whiskey and the wenches unearthed by the debunkers were impertinent insults to the pieties of the older generation. In that sense, Woodward and Hughes were bright young moderns and Brooksian anti-Victorians like Williams. But their biographies ultimately consigned Washington to mass culture on its own terms.

What was perceived as cultural and historical criticism in the Hughes and Woodward biographies was largely a matter of style: their veneer of knowing sophistication made the past a familiar, if quainter, version of 1926 or 1927, and Washington a quirky celebrity, as enjoyable as Silent Cal, the mercurial Henry Ford, or any one of the ill-assorted gaggle of modern newsmakers. Williams, however, used the same shocking details to emphasize sexual and emotional freedom and a singular individuality at odds with the socially approved individualism of a tycoon or an aviator. The heroic tragedy of freedom denied made Washington larger than and different from the crowd: he was "in a great many ways thoroughly disappointing," Williams concluded, because he felt compelled to don his stylish waistcoat.[19]

So William Carlos Williams claimed Washington for a modern, anti-Victorian minority of intellectuals who stood apart from mass culture, by choice—and sometimes by the choice of a hostile public—in order to pursue the secret pathways within. The freedom they cherished was not the freedom to consume in a free-market economy but an intimate mental and behavioral liberty. A real American culture, as distinct from the prevailing mass culture, would embrace those liberties in the name of George Washington, if Williams were to be believed. It would neither condemn them nor sweep them under the latest thing in neocolonial carpets.[20] There were no carpet wholesalers, no businessmen, in the usable past created by William Carlos Williams. In his utopian vision of an American culture for the 1920s, everybody was a poet and George Washington was the inspirational father of American free verse.

The "Great Engineer," a Hero for Modern Times

It is unlikely that Calvin Coolidge read *In the American Grain*. It is even more improbable that when he peered through his window at the Washington Monument in 1926, the president saw in his mind's eye a nation of lusty, bohemian poets scribbling away beneath the obelisk. After the Crash of '29 and the long business depression of the 1930s, however, many wondered just what Coolidge *had* glimpsed beyond his window. "The Washington monument pierces five hundred and fifty-five feet into the sky to symbolize the greatness of George Washington's contribution to his country," Irving Stone acidly recounted. "Calvin Coolidge's monument could be a hole dug straight down into the ground to commemorate all the things he failed to do for his country; a railing should be built around this monument to protect the beholder from vertigo."[21]

In 1926, of course, Coolidge had no reason to see himself as a vacuous negation of George Washington: the business of America was business, by presidential decree, and George Washington was the greatest exemplar of the president's own business principles. The year ahead promised to be the best of all possible times. The nation was blessed with the great Coolidge prosperity, the movies would talk, Lindy would fly to Paris, and Babe Ruth would hit sixty homers. If Mr. Coolidge sensed any portent of disaster, it was not a tremor on Wall Street but a crack in a levee that foretold political doom. In April of 1927, the Great Mississippi Flood devastated seven states, killed five hundred people, and ruined 162,017 homes.[22]

To the rescue rushed Herbert Hoover, the perennial secretary of commerce, the Reliever, now the Great Engineer, a new national hero. Thereafter Hoover's name rose inexorably in the polls. Calvin Coolidge went to the Black Hills to face that unpleasant truth squarely; a second Washington, after all, could do no less. His idol, as even so unconventional a biographer as William Carlos Williams had conceded, "was too strong to evade anything. That's his reputation for truthtelling."[23] And so, on August 2, 1927, Calvin Coolidge laid down his fishing rod and told the reporters, "I do not choose to run."[24] The Washington Monument still stood firm, but with a change in national leadership, George Washington the businessman and sometime poet was about to become George Washington the benevolent engineer.

Coolidge had no monopoly on Washingtonian virtue. Evoking the spirit of a George Washington who could not tell a lie, Herbert Hoover had advised Warren Harding to tell the truth in 1923. "Keeping Your Word" was the subject of the commencement speech the earnest young Hoover delivered to his fellow graduates of an Iowa high school in 1887.[25] Adherence to those copybook maxims had carried him no farther than the Commerce Department, however, until the Great Mississippi Flood of 1927 made him a national hero. "At last," wrote Will Irwin, his official campaign biographer, "his own country turned to Hoover the Reliever" and wonder-worker:

Hoover touched flood-relief with his magic hand. Ahead of the flood moved Hoover's forces in perfect coordination. . . . I, who have followed Hoover on his great European jobs, would like to leave him as I saw him one May morning in 1927—standing on the tottering Melville levee, his aeroplanes scouting overhead, his mosquito-fleet scurrying below, a group of prominent citizens about him listening to the wise, quick, terse directions which were bringing order out of chaos. It symbolizes the man, that scene—"The one tranquil among the raging floods," the transmuter of altruistic emotion into benevolent action.[26]

Newsreels showed the Great Engineer atop the levee, with a clipboard full of facts and figures, synchronizing the movements of Red Cross volunteers and military experts. Orchestrated by his staff, the image of Herbert Hoover reconstructing the social and natural order with a wave of the hand impressed itself deeply on the national imagination. The author of a popular children's book, *Heroes of Today,* rushed a revised edition to press in 1928 to append a new chapter on Herbert Hoover. In her foreword to the young reader, Mary Parkman recalled telling "stories of the heroes of old" to some little friends. One boy bewailed the dearth of "*real*" heroes" in modern times. "Great men who do important things" were legion, the lad complained, but they failed to equal "the daring deeds of the knights and vikings, or of the American pioneers."

The author agreed that "our complex modern life with its many duties, its new conscience, [and] its new feeling of individual responsibility for the welfare of all" was different from the glorious days of yore. Nevertheless, the career of Herbert Hoover proved to Parkman that old-fashioned heroism was not dead. Nor was his heroic and beneficent mastery of the Mississippi flood an isolated act. Just as Will Irwin's panegyric had none too subtly brought up Hoover's "great European jobs" of the past, so Parkman introduced the younger set to his service as head of the American Commission for Relief in Belgium during World War I.

Feeding the children of war-torn Belgium was a modern problem, and Hoover's self-appointed mission testified to the "new feeling of individual responsibility for the welfare of all." Responsibility and service, Parkman maintained, were the legacy of Hoover's career as a "really successful man of business."[27] The Good Businessman idolized in the 1920s was a wartime invention. Dollar-a-year executives went to Washington, kept goods moving to the Western front, or organized relief efforts at home, demonstrating what the Rotarians and the ad men had been saying all along: namely, that business was itself a form of public service and that right-thinking tycoons were those best equipped to grapple with the complexities of doing good in a complex world.

Herbert Hoover had been a conventional business success; when the war broke out, conservative estimates put his earnings from mining enterprises at $4 million. He was also a Good Businessman. In Parkman's telling, he renounced the profit motive without hesitation: "I have all the money I need, I want to do some real work; it's only doing things that counts."[28]

Unselfish volunteerism was one component of this "Hero of to-day." The other was engineering genius, the noblest expression of the machine age. When Hoover entered Stanford to study engineering in 1891, the profession was new and glamorous. Engineering, and mining engineering in particular, promised an adventurous life in wild corners of the world. Richard Hannay, the hero of John Buchan's 1915 mystery thriller, *The Thirty-nine Steps,* was a mining engineer.[29] Zane Grey projected the modern construction engineer back into the 1870s and made him the dynamic hero of *The U.P. Trail* of 1918: engineering, along with pluck and grit, had won the West, according to Grey. Copywriters of the 1920s used the same cliché to sell rugged trousers for engineers (and sedentary he-men reading the magazines in their own living rooms).[30] *Pioneers All! Achievements in Adventure,* an inspirational giftbook for boys published in 1929, ranked the heroic engineer and the aviator up there with the explorer, the cowboy, and the trapper of American legend.[31]

To schoolboys and their parents alike, a "master of vast engineering projects, . . . a man used to handling great enterprises—a captain of industry and a master of men" was ideally equipped to contend with crisis or with the day-to-day operations of the presidency. Belgian relief had succeeded, Parkman concluded, because the service instincts of the Good Businessman were tempered in Hoover's personality by the rationality of the Great Engineer, in command of all the salient facts: "He can grasp the most complex problems, wheels within wheels, and get all the cogs running in perfect harmony."[32]

Although boilerplate American heroes had not hitherto been equipped with engineering credentials, voluntary service and a head for sound business practices were among the characteristics attached to George Washington under Republican auspices during the 1920s.

His was also a success story that, if not precisely a scramble from rags to riches, still justified confidence in Fords, Edisons, and Hoovers, modern-day men of affairs who had made money, reputations, or both. As Alan Holder has pointed out, however, William Carlos Williams's treatment of historical heroes in *In the American Grain* was a critique of such conventional measures of success. Williams selected for attention figures more likely to tell an "American failure story," and when confronted with Washington, whose attainments were impossible to minimize, suggested that "success came at too high a cost" since it was purchased at the expense of suppressing the anarchic passions within the man.[33] But while unknown poets in garrets could afford to snigger at wealth and celebrity and gauge success by subtle measurements of the soul, the public preferred hoopla and hyperbole.

In addition to engineering, Herbert Hoover was also master of a second modern science—that of public relations. The Hoover Publicity League, organized to stampede the 1920 Republican convention, was a case in point. Hoover succumbed to Harding in 1920 and retired to the Commerce Department as the leading Good Businessman of the land—until the Mississippi Flood, that is. But the image of "the Chief" created for the 1920 campaign, and scrupulously maintained in the interim, provided the story line for the newsreel footage of 1927 and wrote script for the efficient and magnanimous leader who would win the presidency in 1928. That Herbert Hoover was a patented reincarnation of George Washington. The George Washington of the Hoover drive toward the White House was a new creation, however, concocted for the occasion from one part "Washington, Captain of Industry" and one part "Washington the Engineer."

The principal architect of the new Hoover personality was Eugene Prussing. Prussing was not a GOP stalwart; instead, he seems to have been a sincere progressive who admired the mild progressivism of the presidential hopeful: his humane sympathies, his horror of radicalism, and his skeptical approach to coercive social panaceas. At any rate, Prussing dedicated his George Washington biography of 1925 to Woodrow Wilson, the Democrat—"your friend and mine"—and leaned heavily on Wilson's 1896 study of Washington (reissued in 1924) for his own assessment of the hero's character. Wilson's Washington had been a progressive leader, "the Happy Warrior" who lived to serve, and so was Prussing's.

In addition to the service philosophy Hoover shared with that version of George Washington, Prussing also admired another of Hoover's progressive traits—the belief that collection and publication of verified facts was the best modern corrective to social ills. According to progressive thought, those who knew the facts could act upon them, calmly and rationally. Believing biography to be a model for action,

Prussing aimed to reconstruct the true George Washington solely on the basis of "the facts as written by Washington himself."[34]

Eugene Prussing undertook his studies for Hoover's benefit, however, and so began with research on Washington's sporadic work as a surveyor and a kind of engineer on the Potomac Canal:

"The Engineer" [chapter] was first sketched to aid Herbert C. Hoover's campaign for the Presidency in 1920, he being contemptuously referred to at that time as a "mere engineer." Later he urged me to complete it in the public interest, as he phrased it, and . . . Dr. Frank W. Gunsaulus, when he heard of it, practically compelled me to "come down to the Armour Institute of Technology on Washington's birthday and give that message to my six or seven hundred young would-be engineers," which I did on February 21, 1921, and repeated the experiment at the California Institute of Technology later.[35]

The engineering "sketch" was, in fact, based on scanty and unfamiliar material, and candor compelled the author to acknowledge that when 115 million Americans laid their work aside once a year to honor Washington on his birthday, few thought they were expressing gratitude "for the fact that George Washington was an engineer." But the facts disclosed to Prussing a young surveyor with an "engineering mind," absorbed in practical questions of "what would work." Whether paying off the national debt, laying out the capital city, or ordering the first departments of government, he was an engineer-president, using the habitual skills of that nascent profession: "Washington began, developed and ended his life, not as a soldier or a statesman, but as an engineer."[36]

Parson Weems Creates a Hero

At Hoover's request, Prussing reworked a second campaign piece, too. "The Captain of Industry" had appeared in *Scribner's Magazine* in 1921.[37] It covered the same ground as the profile of the engineer-president—that is, the nature of Washington's hitherto unknown activities in private life and their impact upon his presidency. But this time Prussing portrayed a Washington wrapped up in business—or, better, agribusiness—for the fifteen years preceding the Revolution. His father, Augustine Washington, from whom the future president had inherited Cherry Tree Farm on the Rappahannock and the skills to manage the property, was presented as America's first Good Businessman.

In bringing new data about the business activities of the family to light, Prussing was generally scornful of legend because it obscured fact. On the subject of fact, he followed McMaster's famous call for historical realism and cited with approval the older scholar's contention that when the facts about the unknown Washington were brought to light, "we shall hear less of the cherry tree and more of the man."[38] But Prussing was not prepared to jettison that most familiar of all Washington myths when the parable of the hero's boyhood could be used to advantage. The rustic cherry tree legend, along with the apple orchard and cabbage seed fables amassed by Mason Locke Weems, were introduced into a purportedly factual biography expressly to show that business was an exemplary and ethical pursuit.

"Parson Weems' legends," Prussing insisted in full knowledge of their unreliability, "indicate that [Augustine Washington] took a keen interest in the moral training of his son and was one of the chief factors in his mental and moral development. No doubt his mental characteristics descended to and were developed in the boy." Thus, he concluded, by training and genetic inheritance George Washington became a businessman-president of dauntless rectitude, a president "who determined the fate of the nation by deciding on business principle the question of narrow or broad construction of the Constitution." It was the timely application of business principles by Washington back in the eighteenth century, Prussing contended, that had made "this country today one of the best governed, happiest and richest in the world."[39]

Prussing's historical researches for Hoover were atypical of Washington biography in the 1920s in several important respects. His interest in the boyhood of Washington as a formative period was consuming, for instance: in all of Prussing's essays, Washington zips from young manhood, passed as a master builder, adventurer, and sagacious marketer of farm produce, to the presidency, with hardly a moment to spare for the Revolutionary War. Hoover's official George Washington, then, is clearly not a revolutionary in any sense of the word, nor is he a supporter of war. So described in the absence of discussions of generalship, this Washington was responsive to the sharp reaction against World War I that may have been a factor in making Hoover, the savior of Belgium, less appealing to the GOP in 1920 than the stay-at-home Senator Harding.

The campaign-literature Washington was also young—Lindberghian, in that respect—and the values he acquired in his youth were said to have remained the lodestar of his presidency. For political purposes, a peppier Washington than the elderly man on the stamps was clearly usable in promoting Herbert Hoover. At forty-six, Hoover was a very young candidate in 1920; Harding looked more like an average president because he was a mature, silver-haired fifty-five.

In stressing and attributing positive qualities to the boyhood of George Washington, Prussing moved his hero into closer alignment with the youthful aspirations of the day—with physical culturists, admirers of Lindy, the nicer kind of jazz-babies, energetic movie idols, and bright young things of all stripes: if Washington no longer stood for insurrection, he did hint at change of the mild, organic, unrevolutionary sort that comes about when the older generation lets its juniors take a hand in things. But in dwelling on Washington's almost undocumented youth, Prussing walked and sometimes crossed the fine line between the myths he rejected and the facts he espoused in the name of modern realism.

Parson Weems was the dubious authority for most of the stories about Washington's youth. And in the years between the centennial and World War I, McMaster's low regard for Weemsian mythmaking was widely shared by Washington biographers. In 1889, for example, Henry Cabot Lodge had called Weems's parables "turgid, overloaded and at times silly."[40] In 1907 Owen Wister had poured contempt upon "the priggish, sickening cherry-tree invention."[41]

Printed in 1800, Mason Locke Weems's original pamphlet on George Washington opened with the French and Indian War and was a swashbuckling, blood-and-thunder military yarn, hallowed by divine interventions and biblical-style concordances. Seventeen separate bullets missed their mark when George Washington did battle with the Indians, for example; when he slipped from a raft into the raging torrent, he was rescued miraculously, to cross the Delaware in good order later in the story. Despite such flourishes, however, early editions of Weems's *Life* always claimed that the incidents presented were factual, and based on "authentic documents."

Scenes from Washington's childhood and a clutch of parables about little Georgie the truthful boy appeared for the first time in the fifth edition of 1806, and mention of "authentic documents" duly vanished from the title. Thereafter, the author called the book *The Life of George Washington, with Curious Anecdotes Laudable to Himself and Exemplary to His Young Countrymen.*[42] Weems's didactic purpose was explicitly revealed in the new title. And throughout the rest of the twenty-odd editions issued during the parson's lifetime, the cherry tree Washington was an *exemplum virtutis,* a pasteboard hero who always told the truth (even when that entailed tattling on his little schoolmates), who routinely performed rustic feats of strength (the boy Washington tossed stones—sometimes dollars—across the mighty rivers and rode unruly horses to death), and who obeyed his sainted mother in all things.

The much-maligned Weems had a good deal in common with Prussing and the realists who would struggle to flesh out a believable and interesting figure a century later. For he told (and in some cases invented) his boyhood-of-the-hero tales in order to humanize Washington, the cold and colorless statesman of John Marshall's imposing biography, a book that the good parson, an itinerant book peddler, had found impossible to sell. The fame of General Washington and President Washington, said Weems, were well known: "True, he has been seen in *greatness*: but it is only the greatness of public character, which is no evidence of *true greatness.*" In the case of lesser men, it was often dangerous to look beyond the "authentic documents" in the public record, for let the average hero "be thrust back into the shades of private life; and you shall see how soon, like a forced plant robbed of its hot-bed, he will drop his false foliage and fruit, and stand forth confessed in native stinkweed sterility and worthlessness." The test of greatness, Weems decided, lay elsewhere: "It is not, then, in the glare of *public,* but in the shade of *private life,* that we are to look for the man. Private life is always *real life.*"[43]

With that caveat, couched in the language of the farm, Weems launched directly into his stories of cabbages, apples, and cherry trees and three new chapters on the rural boyhood of Washington. The heavy-handed moralism that offended Wister and Lodge did not deter Weems's customers, but the key to the remarkable and persistent popularity of the book in a rural, nineteenth-century America was his vivid portrayal of an idyllic country childhood. The most enduring of the Lincoln legends pictured Honest Abe, the country boy from New Salem, reading a copy of Weems by firelight. Even the critical Owen Wister felt the charm of Weems's extended passages about life at Cherry Tree Farm. While rejecting "the untrue and fablish story of the hatchet and cherry tree," Wister quoted the other tales of Washington's schooldays and adventures on the plantation with open approval. "The value of the legends is not their individual authenticity," he allowed, "but their united testimony" to a quality of experience that shaped a demigod.[44]

Debunking the Cherry Tree

As described in Weems's florid prose, Washington's rural experience was the American equivalent of life in the Garden of Eden. The farm was a "wide wilderness of fruit" where "trees were bending under the weight of apples, which hung in clusters like grapes." The house was ringed with "a gooseberry walk . . . well hung with ripe fruit." Ever-warm breezes spread the sweet music of nature—"the busy humming [of] bees, . . . the gay notes of birds."[45] This paradise of lush innocence was made by God for little six-year-old George, or so said Augustine Washington in the overblown speech Weems wrote for him: ". . . and up in the *trees* there are apples, and peaches, and *thousands* of sweet fruits for him! and *all, all around* him, wherever my dear boy looks, he sees every thing he wants and wishes;—the bubbling springs with cool sweet water for him to drink! and the wood to make him sparkling fires when he is cold!"[46]

In this peaceable kingdom of God-given abundance, where humanized apples "hide their blushing cheeks behind green leaves," it is scarcely possible to disbelieve in little George, blushing "with the inexpressible charm of all-conquering truth," as he tells his pa the facts about the cherry tree. The crime was an offense against the bounty of nature, a plenitude rendered all but palpable by Weems's overripe language. And while Augustine Washington's retort to the confession of the little criminal disavowed all interest in fruit trees, the moral precept he intended to draw from the incident was over-shadowed by an image of botanical marvels that, in retrospect, seem no more implausible additions to Weems's *hortus conclusus* than the sacred cherry tree itself: "Such an act of heroism in my son," his proud father avers, "is worth more than a thousand trees, though blossomed with silver, and their fruits of purest gold."[47]

The debunkers of the 1920s had no use for Mason Weems (Figure 10.2). Indeed, as exponents of fact and "the science of reality," they

10.2
Albert Levering drew this 1904 cartoon for *Harper's Weekly*: "George Washington Had He Only Waited for the Help of Modern Inventions."

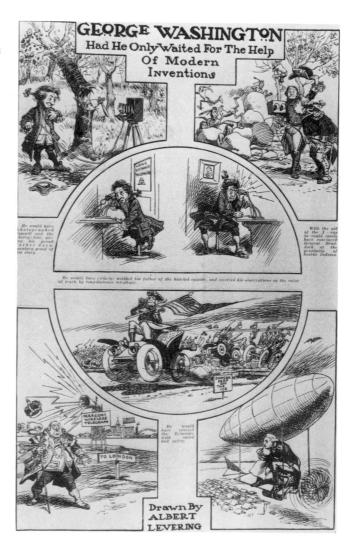

took special pleasure in debunking a notorious fantast in the spirit of the cynical school-boy poet created by the old *Life* magazine for the Washington's Birthday issue of 1904:

My pa ain't like Washington's pa.
When I cut down our cherry tree,
And said I did, pa walloped me.
And I went up to bed and cried
And golly, how I wish I'd lied![48]

Before Hughes and Woodward arrived on the scene, opinion on the veracity of the story was divided, but its merit was more often than not acknowledged. In the 1890s, for instance, proponents of the new realism perpetually demanded by biographers of Washington believed that "the mythical hatchet story" arose from the more credible narrative of the headstrong teenager killing his widowed mother's fiery colt in the process of taming it, confessing his misdeed, and thereby turning parental anger to moral approval.[49] "The point" of the horse parable, surmised one writer who had already noted Weems's propensity for deviating from the truth when a good story was in the offing, "resembles that of the hackneyed little hatchet tale, and perhaps they both grew out of one incident."[50]

By and large, the writers of the 1920s were of two minds about the parson's pleasant fiction, too. As one of them put it, "We do not know whether to 'uproot the tree or bury the hatchet.'"[51] William Roscoe Thayer, a member of the faction in favor of plucking the cherry tree from the record, was sure that the accumulation of such fictional incidents was what had made poor Washington unpalatable to clear-eyed moderns:

Owing to the pernicious drivel of the Reverend Weems no other great man in history has had to live down such a mass of absurdities and deliberate false inventions. At last after a century and a quarter the rubbish had been mostly cleared away, and only those who wilfully prefer to deceive themselves need waste time over an imaginary Father of His Country amusing himself with a fictitious cherry-tree and hatchet.[52]

Yet others took the story as a welcome glimpse into a period in Washington's life about which military and political records were silent. Fact or fiction, the story pictured close and loving familial ties that warmed the marmoreal image of the hero on a pedestal. "He cut down the cherry-tree," said an author who patently disbelieved in the fable, "and was on such friendly terms with his father that he confessed the crime."[53] Washington's father would certainly have set out cherry trees upon moving to a new farm, a thirsty Weems apologist of the Prohibition era theorized, because "every Virginian of those days grew cherries and operated a liquor still for the purposes of his household,—cherry brandy being favored for a medicine as well as a beverage."[54]

But whether the cherry tree story was true or not, a third analyst submitted, it should be cherished for its inspirational value and for its familiarity to several generations of American children who had learned the rudiments of public speaking by declaiming an endless jingle entitled "Georgie's Hatchet." Those verses followed the little miscreant as he fondled his new "red hatchet with handle, smooth, and round, and white." They looked in upon him as he "chopped about on board and stick, and tried it once upon a brick" before spotting the ill-fated tree. They registered proper anxiety as George watched "his pa and dear ma" coming upon their seedling "all wilted down and sad to see, the tender bark all newly chopped," and as he cried out, "I chopped it Father, It was I. I cannot, cannot tell a lie." Then, in the dramatic finale, Augustine Washington smiled:

> And kissed and kissed his darling child
> While tears of joy like rain he shed;
> And thus to little Georgie said,
> "My precious child, my noble boy,
> Now ten times told my pride and joy!"
>
> . . . This little boy grew up to be
> The greenest branch on freedom's tree,
> His country's battles fought and won,
> His name it was George Washington.

"If the tale isn't true," insisted a lady who remembered every verse from her days at school, "it should be. It is too pretty to be classified with the myths."[55]

The debunkers took Weems's fictions personally, however. Rupert Hughes devoted a whole appendix in his first volume (and a twenty-eight-page chapter in his third) to demolishing the Potts myth, a relatively late embellishment worked into Weems's ninth edition. The prayer-in-the-snow story was nettlesome to realists of the day for two reasons: first, because the eyewitness form in which Weems couched the tale made a mockery of historical fact, and second, because the story was the only "evidence" of Washington's orthodox religiosity and was, accordingly, cherished under the same dispensation that allowed the Betsy Ross legend to flourish because it provided an active role for women in the cycle of Washington mythology.

Prints showing the general on his knees reached a new peak of popularity during and after World War I (they would be reissued during World War II) and, given the pacifistic character of the unseen observer, proved resistant to postwar reaction. But to Woodward, "the idea of this two-fisted man going about bellowing in the woods" was "grotesque."[56] And Hughes's even greater hostility to the episode only served to make the picture into an emblem of God-fearing anti-debunkery; hence, in 1927, the Weemsian Washington, "with a countenance of angel serenity," prayed fervently in the snow on the two-cent stamp as much to confound his irreverent biographers as to move the nation's mail.[57]

For the most part, the debunkers left the boyhood of Washington alone except to snipe at the most unlikely hero-tales of Weems and George Washington Parke Custis, or to introduce portents of a certain sleazy normalcy in his mature business dealings and sexual pursuits. W. E. Woodward placed a low value on the boy's Washington heredity: the family "must be called undistinguished, unless a persistent mediocrity, enduring many generations, is in itself a distinction." Washington's ramshackle birthplace, he sneered, was "not an impressive structure."

In his description of Augustine's plantations, Woodward methodically defaced Weems's word-portrait of rich pastures and wind-rippled fields. The paternal lands were "primitive clearings, pockmarked with holes and spotted with stumps" and punctuated at intervals by "crazy structures of undressed boards." Nowhere in evidence was the stately Weemsian homestead, rimmed by a gooseberry walk. As for Weems himself, Woodward skewered him on a single pointed phrase. "The Cannot-Tell-a-Lie incident of the cherry tree and the hatchet," he chortled, "is a brazen piece of fiction."[58]

Rupert Hughes opened his biography with two salutary facts that cast serious doubt on Weems's credibility. The first concerned the character of "Mary, the Mother of Washington," an American Blessed Virgin, to whose honor Presidents Jackson and Cleveland had solemnly dedicated successive miniature obelisks near Fredericksburg. Mary Ball Washington could not spell and liked to dance, Hughes claimed to have discovered; although these tendencies were neither reprehensible nor shocking, they were suggestive, somehow, since her youngest child had inherited both. Legend had made her some kind of paragon (a good speller, no doubt; a woman indifferent to low amusements such as dancing), but according to Hughes, "it is a cruel truth that she was chiefly remarkable as a very human, cantankerous old lady." She also smoked a pipe. The second significant fact concerned Washington's birthplace at Wakefield. The miniature obelisk erected to mark that sacred spot, said Hughes, had been set by mistake "over what was probably an outhouse."

Having laid his scientific groundwork of unimpeachable data, Hughes turned to the fables and devoted several pages as well as a long footnote to the cherry tree myth on the warrant that the familiarity of the legend necessitated factual clarification. On balance, although he dubbed Weems's book a "slush of plagiarism and piety," Hughes rather enjoyed the old rascal's "hilarious style" and was almost alone among his contemporaries in crediting the parson with a purposeful literary technique. Hughes noticed that Weems had used natural imagery in his early chapters to good effect and acknowledged the pungent memorability of "the parental voice sounding like Jehovah's over Eden, after the apple incident," with little George improving upon Adam's performance.[59]

On balance, however, the debunkers seem to have regarded the Weemsian boyhood of Washington as a case study in willful ignorance, of interest chiefly as an easy target for their fusillade of facts. Humanizing the hero, à la Professor McMaster, meant reducing Mary Ball and Augustine Washington to human dimensions at the earliest possible opportunity. By contrast, although Prussing was equally concerned with facts, he was also convinced that the human George Washington disclosed by patient inquiry would be a worthwhile human being. While he was preparing his Washington profiles for the Hoover forces in 1920, Prussing was also finishing an essay called "George Washington in Love," a detailed but high-minded treatment of the Sally Fairfax letters collated in 1916 by an "unidentified friend."[60] By providing them with facts amenable to more than one interpretation, Prussing thus became an unwitting source for the debunkers' unflagging interest in Washington's sex life.[61]

Woodward wisecracked about the Sally Fairfax affair; it confirmed his cynical view of the habits of captains of industry. Hughes meant to be more objective but piled up details and present-minded speculation about their meaning with the smarmy glee of a tabloid gossip columnist. The end result was hardly romantic. But the same facts painted a different picture for Prussing and one altogether consistent with his factual presentations of "The Engineer" and the "The Captain of Industry." Washington's youthful admiration for a kind and cultivated older lady and his lifelong devotion to the memory of their friendship constituted, he insisted, "the finest love story in the world." Loving from afar with boyish ardor taught a grown-up Washington how to love his family and his country. A romantic story and traits of character well established in the historical record provided mutual corroboration. In the boyhood of the lovesick Washington, fact and myth coincided.

The Ideal Rural Boyhood of the American Hero

Prussing accepted the cherry tree myth and with it Weems's controlling megamyth of an edenic boyhood. Whatever Washington achieved in later life as the patriot-lover of his country, the engineer-president, or the Good Businessman, Prussing intimated, was traceable to his formative years in a particular moral and physical environment not dissimilar to that limned by the good parson. The cherry tree fable stood for the pastoral setting of colonial Virginia, and Augustine's teachings about seedlings and saplings typified the simple, innocent life of the countryside, when the country was innocent and very young. In factual terms, Augustine functioned as the human father of an apple-cheeked country boy who made mistakes. But in a legend tempered by the facts of knowing retrospection, Augustine also functioned as God did in the Book of Genesis: he was the Father of the Father of the race.

And so Augustine further served to beatify the sequence of moral inheritance that ran from himself to his son to the modern-day American; the Good Businessman became the holy grandsire of a nation. The Good Businessman and the Great Engineer thus sprang from the virgin soil of Cherry Tree Farm as surely as Henry Ford had arisen, full blown, from the little red schoolhouse in Dearborn. Written to further the political interests of Herbert C. Hoover, the collected essays that made up Prussing's *George Washington in Love and Otherwise* tracked the highest virtues of an urban, commercial, and industrial nation straight back to the farmlands of rural America.

Prussing's book was published on Washington's Birthday in 1925. In 1928, after the platform adopted at the party convention reaffirmed "the American Constitutional Doctrine as announced by George Washington in his Farewell Address," Hoover accepted the Republicans' presidential nomination by letter.[62] Letters made good press releases. He was, Hoover wrote with a newfound humility, just "a boy from a country village, without inheritance or influential friends."[63] Attentive readers of Ernest Prussing could have grasped the underlying meaning of that statement and the urgency with which the nominee strove to impress it upon the public consciousness. Mention of the "boy from a country village" signaled a new direction in the thrust of the Hoover campaign based on a new and different Washington analogue.

Despite extensive publicity and wide dissemination of facts supporting his kinship with George Washington, the engineer-president, the Great Engineer was not a very popular personality in 1928. In the spring *Time* had dubbed him the "beaver-man":

Material well-being, comfort, order, efficiency in government and economy—these he stands for, but they are conditions, not ends. A technologist, he does not discuss ultimate purposes. In a society of temperate, industrious, unspeculative beavers, such a beaver-man would make an ideal King-beaver. But humans are different. People want Herbert Hoover to tell them where, with his extraordinary abilities, he would lead them. He needs, it would seem, to undergo a spiritual crisis before he will satisfy as a popular leader.[64]

The crisis came in the early summer of 1928. The Mississippi flood episode was proving more of a liability than an asset. Planted newspaper and magazine articles on Hoover the Reliever elicited yawns. Will Irwin's special campaign movie, *The Master of Emergencies,* and some ten miles of additional footage going back to 1914 and the Belgian war relief effort were having no effect upon the electorate.[65]

"All his advertising has made him appeal to the American imagination," wrote the inveterate campaign-watchers at *Time,* "but not to the American heart."[66] If Washington the engineer was dull beyond all telling, his alter ego, Hoover the engineer, was too efficient to be human.

Thus it came to pass that tiny West Branch, Iowa—and moviegoers everywhere—witnessed a peculiar ritual on a summer afternoon in 1928. A "serious, square-set man in a double-breasted suit, a rich and famous man who had come home for a day" was awkwardly poking about the banks of the Wapsinonoc Creek, shadowed by a squadron of reporters and upwards of fifteen thousand curiosity-seekers.[67] Herbert Hoover had returned to his country birthplace for a carefully orchestrated assault on the heartstrings of his countrymen. The cameras caught him in the act of looking for the old swimming hole under the willows down by the railroad trestle, but he was in fact looking for a shady spot beneath Parson Weems's old cherry tree, a magical myth to clothe the "beaver-man" in the roseate glow of humanity. A down-home George Washington from Iowa—Prussing's country innocent—was about to enter the political arena.

Hoover's birthplace was a snug white cottage on the creek: columbine, phlox, and Sweet William grew all around; rows of portulaca flanked the walk; and the front lawn was dappled with fruit trees, the most prominent in memory a red Siberian crabapple.[68] Tiny, humble, yet perfection itself in the descriptions of the publicists, the house became as symbolic in its way as the Coolidge farmstead or the log cabins of Old Hickory, Tippecanoe, and Abe Lincoln. Whereas Hoover's engineering background suggested the triumph of newfangled things—dams, levees, new chrome bathrooms, scientific nutrition—it also bespoke a tradition of American empiricism and a concern for material well-being going back to Washington himself. Hoover's white frame birthplace in verdant Iowa took the edge off his modernity and humanized him. After his campaign stop at the old place in West Branch, as the *Los Angeles Times* was quick to grasp, Hoover became, however briefly, an "engineer with a heart."[69]

As part of a campaign the *Saturday Evening Post* called "humanizing the Commerce Department," Secretary Hoover had become leader of a national Better Homes movement that, in 1925 alone, proselytized an estimated three million people on zoning laws, construction methods, and home purchase with a movie *(Home Sweet Home),* lectures, ads in the papers, and a popular pamphlet called *Own Your Own Home.*[70] For the American family such a home was, and still remains, a powerful assertion of its own stability, prosperity, and rooted values. Furthermore, as the frenetic 1920s drew to their close, the old-fashioned house redolent with associations had become an accepted totem of those personalities who professed to carry with them into the modern world the spiritual baggage of the Founding Fathers.

Thus began the mushroom growth of the period subdivision and a half-serious drive to establish new Salems or Fredericksburgs or Plymouths here and there, where modern life would become sweeter and slower. One Manhattan romantic proposed a wholesale retreat to an enclave of phony central-chimney New England farmhouses to be built in wildest New Jersey:

Our village will be called the Plymouth Colony of New Jersey. It will have a big village green in the centre with a community church at one end (a replica of that one in Concord would be a peach). And the post office and the garage will be in keeping, and maybe a copy of the Wayside Inn at Sudbury will serve for our hotel. For our little houses where the chaps live who catch the 5:15 . . . we would have little gardens and lawns and picket fences so that if you wanted to grow hollyhocks, and I wanted to grow Plymouth Rock chickens, we would have mutual protection. We wouldn't have many laws. . . . We would try to contrive some place where there would be an old swimmin' hole.

If this early American Village could have some local industry like a furniture factory, for example, dedicated to making authentic reproductions of some of the treasures of the past, it would not need to be near a metropolis. The colony would be self-supporting. The world would make a beaten path to its door. The Plymouth Colony! That's not such a bad idea after all. It may happen. Who knows?[71]

Little by little such make-believe communities, with their connotations of self-reliance and neighborly nurture, were indeed rising from Massachusetts and Virginia to Michigan as challenges to the corporate impersonality of the twentieth century. The Wayside Inn, already in operation, was the hub of a growing village of mills, schoolhouses, and other historic buildings grouped on the site. Colonial Williamsburd and Greenfield Village were nearing completion. In 1930 the Massachusetts Bay Colony Tercentenary was introduced by Samuel Eliot Morison's encomium to the influence of the Puritans on modern business practice but was tangibly commemorated for the ages by replicas of the wigwams and cottages of early colonial Salem arranged along streets and greens.[72]

But the thirst that drove Americans to construct such elaborate monuments to their past was not wholly slaked by visiting a Salem village. Curators soon learned what home builders already knew: that the tourist peering around a reconstructed colonial house was, in imagination, gauging his chances of moving in—or rather, of moving out of a time rife with challenges to those beliefs and institutions that the house seemed to stand for. The Wayside Inn catered to the Coolidges and the exclusive few who could afford to dine on roast beef before an open fire. But by the late 1930s, Williamsburg had recognized a widespread desire to migrate backward in time by building "a new air-conditioned hotel of 'early Republic' architectural design" on the outskirts of town.[73]

At the same time, on the road to Greenfield Village, Charles H. Hart designed for the lot behind the Dearborn Inn ("Colonial Inn and Motor House") a village of seven miniaturized and electrified replicas of famous American homes, furnished with period reproductions. For a fee, the motorist could check into the Barbara Fritchie House, Walt Whitman's birthplace, Patrick Henry's home in Red Hill, Virginia, or the Litchfield, Connecticut, residence of Governor Oliver Wolcott, where George Washington once slept.[74] The village fantasy was complete when the average American could spend the night in George Washington's bed, dreaming of the saner, simpler days of yore.

Will Irwin made the most of Hoover's Iowa birthplace fantasy in his campaign biography: the swimming hole under the willows, "sliding down Cook's Hill in snow-time, ranging the spring fields in vain pursuit of baby rabbits, gathering wild strawberries in summer, the sonorous roll of the English Bible at family prayers."[75] The barefoot boy from the country was steeped in the traditions of rural America; like Weems's boy Washington, who scratched the soft ground beneath an apple tree with his "little naked toes" while his pa taught him to be generous and kind, Hoover too absorbed the Bible in the perfume of the springtime blossoms.

It was a simple, even humble boyhood that, like Washington's, harked back to the days when America was very young. There were pigeons to shoot with a bow and arrow borrowed from a real little red Indian boy; there were long, hot afternoons along the Wapsinonoc and fat angleworms dangling from bits of butcher's string on homemade willow poles. And every lovely vignette was true. The facts set down in Irwin's campaign biography were all repeated verbatim by Hoover in August of 1928 as he addressed his former neighbors in West Branch, and again in 1931 as he paved the way for a second political contest with publication of his own reminiscences, *A Boyhood in Iowa.*[76]

The Birthplace of Herbert Hoover

In 1922 Hoover had written a book called *American Individualism.* In that text, the West Branch he remembered from the first eleven years of his life was a place where people grew the food they ate, "made their own clothes, . . . boiled their own soft-soap, tried out their own lard."[77] People were self-reliant; they were, he said, American individualists, throwbacks to the age of legend and myth. The tightly scripted pageant prepared by his political functionaries for the homecoming of the native son in 1928 took pains to dwell on especially photogenic evidence of old-time values. After the search for the swimming hole came Hoover's speech in the big Chautauqua tent pitched on the grass and a reunion with Mrs. Molly Brown Curran, his first teacher at the prim country schoolhouse. The press was given ample opportunity to badger Mrs. Curran for picturesque incidents in the youth of the only local prodigy West Branch had ever produced. Meanwhile, the candidate and his retinue sped away, bearing on film an image of a country cottage in a bower of leafy trees, a precious piece of the period's "usable past."

"West Branch made a good symbolic beginning for Herbert Hoover," the historian David Burner remarks.[78] The ingenious little boy who fashioned rabbit traps out of cracker boxes translated readily into the Great Engineer. The self-reliance and sturdy morality of pioneer Iowa gave rise to the Good Businessman, the doer and the charitable humanitarian. West Branch was a symbol of simplicity, like Colonel Coolidge's oil lamp, a myth of the rural heritage in which success was tempered by un-Darwinian goodness, and nature itself—the steady rhythm of the seasons and the tidy beauty of floral walks—bespoke prosperity and social order. The story of West Branch was the George Washington myth as Prussing had rewritten it.

The cottage in West Branch went with Herbert Hoover the way a hatchet went with George Washington. The story of his legendary Iowa boyhood among the posies and the bunnies was parroted, for instance, by William J. Marsh, Jr., aged eleven, putative author of *Our President Herbert Hoover,* a slender biography that appeared in 1930. Master Marsh's pamphlet was larded with innocent tributes to boys who came up the hard way—"Do you know it seems as if all our famous men are self-made!"—and to the kind of God-fearing Iowa mother who "don't [*sic*] spend all her time at dances," but "teach[es] her boys to be good."[79] By 1931, the structure of the myth of country boyhood had become firm enough for Iowa's own Grant Wood, having been asked by a group of local businessmen to paint the birthplace of Herbert Hoover, to set about demolishing it with the wit of a painterly debunker (Figure 10.3).

In the 1920s Wood's literary counterparts had already extended their rude remarks about the character of George Washington to cover Wakefield, his long-vanished birthplace on Pope's Creek in Virginia. More recently, however, Wakefield had become the focus of respectful federal interest. The official literature issued by the celebratory body established by Coolidge and nurtured by President Hoover was filled with fanciful illustrations of Wakefield, showing a kind of Early American fairy-tale cottage. As if to demonstrate the symbolic importance invested in the American home, an official United States George Washington Bicentennial Commission pageant entitled *Wakefield: A Folk Masque of America* would star a symbolic genius loci. And with the assistance of technicians from Colonial Williamsburg and a $50,000 appropriation from Congress, a red-brick Wakefield was built de novo in 1931 at a discreet distance from a commemorative obelisk that was

erected over what might have been the plantation privy.[80] Grant Wood's *Birthplace of Herbert Hoover* was painted against that tapestry of revivalism and reverence.

Some commentators feel that Wood's picture mocks the log cabin legend and the obligatory humble origins of political figures. There is some support for this view in the preliminary cartoon; at the lower left, Wood had originally inserted a vignette showing the tiny Hoover cabin, an unprepossessing shack foiled off against the ample dwelling that had swallowed it whole. But the finished painting has another point to make. A gesticulating tour guide—the prototype for the neo-colonial Parson Weems in Wood's 1939 version of the cherry tree legend—directs attention to a preternaturally tidy and prosperous complex of buildings set in a verdant garden. The scene is, of course, a kind of Iowan Williamsburg, the bicentennial Wakefield translated to the prairies—a manufactured, fully modernized birthplace mythos. The synthetic history cranked out by campaign flacks and government commissions, a history laundered and cosmetized for popular consumption, is Wood's real target, even as the title of the painting evokes longing for the rude legends displaced by the exigencies of politics. Wood's smiling lawns are sinister, somehow, because they too orderly to be true—too perfect to tolerate the intrusion of barefoot boys with rabbit traps or little axes.[81]

For his part, Grant Wood of Iowa never warmed to the candidate from West Branch and went on to become a fervent New Dealer. And Herbert Hoover proved skittish when confronted with visual evidence that his boyhood was a self-generated myth: although the business community had hoped to present it to him during a mandatory campaign swing through West Branch in 1932, he rejected Wood's picture because the lowly cabin of the Great Engineer—obligatory, of course, in an election year—was obscured from public view by an ordinary modern house facing the street.[82] When fact and myth came into conflict, the candidate found it prudent to choose the latter.[83]

If Hoover would leave Iowa in 1932 without a picture by Grant Wood, he had left West Branch four years before in possession of a new, rural image and a historical pedigree of devastating power in the impending struggle against Al Smith, his Democratic rival from the sidewalks of New York's immigrant East Side. Urban Republicans sometimes mocked the historical trappings in which the Old Guard were wont to swaddle party heroes. In 1922 Fiorello La Guardia, Republican of New York, told a reporter, "I stand for the Republicanism of Abraham Lincoln; and let me tell you that the average Republican leader east of the Mississippi doesn't know anything more about Abraham Lincoln than Henry Ford knows about the Talmud."[84] La Guardia overstated his case. Senator Beveridge's 1921 Washington's Birthday tirade against "the insidious wiles" of foreign radicals in the cities had shown that the GOP could use historical heroes to good effect in the ongoing struggle to maintain the status quo.[85] In 1928, when the alien accents of New York and the rites of popery were assailed by the rustic nativism of West Branch and "the sonorous roll of the English Bible," the cherry tree myth lent tacit support to a countryside traumatized by the candidacy of a "wet" Catholic Irishman from Manhattan, with a cigar and a derby.

The new Hoover appealed to the bruised fundamentalism of Dayton, Tennessee; to the xenophobia and the anti-Catholicism of the Midwestern Klan; to the punitive, small-town hysteria of the Anti-Saloon League. Traditional farm values were passing away in the late 1920s; even Hoover admitted that folks back home no longer rendered their lard and boiled their soap. A cash income, a radio, and a Model A were modern rural desiderata. The farm had always prided itself on antimaterialism and charged the city with amoral money-grubbing, however, and so the longing for consumer durables posed something of a philosophical dilemma for Smith's city-hating opponents. But the character of Herbert Hoover that was fashioned out of components of the George Washington personality accessible to the period reinforced traditional values while licensing change in the name of time-honored virtues. Rural America was the birthplace of the Great Engineer *and* the Good Businessman. The most advanced technological and commercial realities of modern America were sanctioned by the earliest and simplest of her myths.

Hoover at Valley Forge

On March 4, 1929, Herbert Clark Hoover became the president of the United States, thirty-first in the line of succession that stretched back to George Washington. On Wall Street the "inaugural market" surged; the new order of limitless prosperity and gadgetry was firmly supported by the old order of West Branch and the cherry tree.[86] On Monday, October 21, that alliance of history and modernity was celebrated in Detroit at Henry Ford's great Edison Jubilee. President Hoover was the guest of honor. Bernays, the public relations genius, escorted him to Greenfield Village aboard an antique train; guides dressed in nineteenth-century costumes drove him about the hodgepodge of colonial and pioneer settings in a horse-drawn carriage; he lunched in a reconstructed tavern of the stagecoach era, a Midwestern Wayside Inn.

In the evening Thomas Edison reenacted the invention of electric light for five hundred guests who arrived in Michigan from the pinnacle of American success. Herbert Hoover and Henry Ford were joined by Will Rogers, Samuel Insull, and Walter Chrysler; by Charles Schwab of Bethlehem Steel, Owen Young of GE, and Otto Kahn of the investment house of Kuhn and Loeb. The program for the dinner, prepared by Bernays, defined the significance of the occasion for any dignitary who might have missed the point: "Never before perhaps has a group met under similar circumstances, to give homage to a simple citizen whose right to homage is based on inventive skill and mechanical ingenuity. Here at last is a democracy that rates greatness of achievement principally in terms of social service."[87]

From recent personal experience, Hoover had ample reason to agree. As the nostalgic strains of "Oh, Susannah" faded, NBC and CBS broadcast the toasts of the Great Engineer and of all the good captains of industry and finance forgathered in a new and better version of Independence Hall. A splendid time was had by all. And three days later, on Black Thursday—October 24, 1929—the market crashed and the Great Depression began.

Candidate Hoover once envisioned a "New Era" in which the good businessmen, industrialists, and financiers who joined him at Ford's banquet would assume voluntary responsibility for keeping the economic ship of state afloat. Yet barely eight months after the New Era dawned, the country's self-regulated prosperity had foundered, abruptly and mysteriously. Nor did the wise captains of industry seem to have any grasp on the causes of the problem or its possible solution.[88] In November 1929 Henry Ford tried to incant the nation's troubles away. "Things are better today than they were yesterday," he swore in the face of ample evidence to the contrary. A week later Charles Schwab told the press that "never before has American business been as firmly entrenched for prosperity as it is today."[89]

Shortly after the election, *Time* had characterized Hoover as "a trained engineer about to sink a new shaft in quest of buried facts."[90] But a year later the facts merely baffled the engineer-president. "*All* evidences indicate that the worst effects of the crash upon unemployment will have been passed during the next sixty days," Hoover promised, and fudged the April unemployment statistics to support what amounted to a desperate dream of prosperity. Hoover, it seems, had begun to believe the myths he helped to create.

Will Rogers cast a jaundiced eye upon the headline pronouncements of his former dinner companions. "There has been more 'optimism' talked and less practiced than at any time during our history," he complained.[91] On February 22, 1931, Rogers's gall spilled over into his column as he cited grim facts the White House denied. "Here is what George Washington missed by not living to his 199th birthday," he wrote. "He would have seen our great political system of 'equal rights to all and privileges to none' working so smoothly that seven million are without a chance to earn their living. He would see 'em handing out rations in peace time, that would have reminded him of Valley Forge. . . . I bet after seeing us, he would sue us for calling him 'Father.'"[92]

Speaking of George Washington at Valley Forge on Memorial Day of that same grim year, President Hoover begged to differ:

On the eve of the celebration of the two hundredth anniversary of the birth of George Washington . . . it is . . . appropriate that our observance . . . be at this place, so intimately associated with the moral grandeur of the Father of Our Country. Here Washington and his little band of hungry and almost naked patriots kept alive the spark of liberty in the lowest hours of the Revolution. They met the crisis with steadfast fortitude; they conserved their strength; they husbanded their resources; they seized the opportunity . . . which led on to victory. It was a triumph of character and idealism and high intelligence over the counsels of despair, of prudence and material comfort. . . . Without such victories the life of man would descend to a sheer materialism. . . . God grant that we may prove worthy of George Washington and his men at Valley Forge.[93]

The Washington bicentennial year was indeed at hand. In spite of—or perhaps because of—the continuing depression, the celebration would be grandiose in scale. And if the somber president had his way, it would be profoundly serious, for as he anticipated the start of the festivities in his Memorial Day address, Hoover was clearly speaking not of Washington's dilemma and the "hungry" patriots of Valley Forge but of his own and his country's current crisis.

Rogers's acidic levity and the lavish materialism of Ford's Jubilee gala were inappropriate to the tone of the moral renewal Hoover had in mind. Official bicentennial history and pageantry, insofar as the celebration was meant to contend with a social and economic calamity of unprecedented magnitude (and one that often raised the unwelcome specter of a second revolution), were solemn responsibilities. If the president's historical vision proved truly "usable," then Washington would inspire another victory in 1932 in the hearts of his demoralized descendants. Fortitude, self reliance, the husbanding of scarce resources, and turns of luck were what America needed once again. Character, idealism, and intelligence, the Washingtonian attributes of the current occupant of the White House, would, when fully appreciated, rally the nation.

Up to that point, however, Hoover's leadership had been strangely ineffectual. Like the exhortations from Wall Street's fallen Lords of Creation, the measured, intelligent reports from the presidential chairman of the board had failed to inspire. Because the significance of his facts and ideals was not generally understood, Hoover blamed inaccurate reporting. "Losing faith with the Press," said *Time,* "he has come to think of himself as a martyr in a hairshirt, misunderstood and misinterpreted by the People."[94]

"Valley Forge," the president declared in the address delivered on that sobering site, "is our American synonym for the trial of the human character through privation and suffering, and it is the symbol of triumph of the American soul."[95] As his remark demonstrates, Hoover understood symbols and how to manipulate them. And so, on the eve of the most thoroughgoing observance of Washington's Birthday ever mounted by his grateful countrymen, Hoover proposed to retire the Washington of 1928, that sweet "St. George . . . moving through an orchard of ever-blooming cherry trees," in favor of the stern general at prayer in the snow.[96]

Who Was the Real George Washington?

History shows that the symbol of Washington at prayer did not keep the incumbent in office in 1932, nor did the exchange of one Washington image for another do much to defeat whatever mysterious forces were responsible for the Depression, although Franklin Roosevelt would use another cast of historical figures—Lincoln, Jackson, and Jefferson, most notably—to advantage in conveying to the electorate a sense of the populism, the compassion, and the ebullient style of his New Deal.[97] Historical symbols, those wishful pictures of the past shaped in the image of what the present and the future ought to look like, had not grown suddenly ineffectual in 1932. But the particular symbolic value of George Washington had, it seems, suffered a marked decrease.

Since the days of Benjamin Harrison, George Washington had stood for the presidency and growing presidential power, for Old Americans and the speedy "melting" of immigrants, for "home" and the varying list of traditional values attached to the domestic realm. Since Harding's term at least, he had also stood for conservative Republican leadership; indeed, the listless GOP convention that nominated Hoover for a second term would do so in the bicentennial year beneath a canopy of shield-shaped portraits of the Father of His Country, each one draped in swags of bunting.[98] But at the same time Washington conveyed a whole panoply of other ideas, ideological positions, and vague feelings. He legitimated modern business practices, boosterism, service clubs, and the rising new profession called engineering. Any number of social novelties, from the romance of the engineer to modern poetry, from sexual freedom to jazz to the Broadway musical and the movies, sought respectability (and heightened shock value) by incorporating his good gray self into their agendas.

As a standard-bearer for the new, Washington was the prototype for Lindbergh; he was the inspiration, in 1926, for Henry Woodhouse's giddy scheme to combine on a mile-square section of the Washington "ancestral homelands near Alexandria, Virginia" a shrine containing his personal collection of Washingtoniana with the George Washington Air Junction, an airport, a flying school for kids, and an "artists' airpark" where painters would gain inspiration from the intoxicating mixture of history and futuristic technology.[99] When not otherwise engaged in aerial promotions, Washington sold ice cream, canned vegetables, and steam radiators in the magazines. He promoted with equal aplomb the colonial asceticism of old Colonel Coolidge's oil lamps and the material profusion of Greenfield Village, wherein were gathered, alongside the Coolidge sap bucket and Lindy's motorcycle, samples of Washington's china, the chair he sat in in Cambridge, his mother's highboy, a spare camp bed, his bookplate, and an 1848 patent press bearing his picture.[100]

In an analysis of the 1928 election published shortly thereafter in the *New York Times Magazine,* Anne O'Hare McCormick complained that a "lack of precision and color made Hoover's campaign 'blend' perfectly with the furnishings of any comfortable and refined American living room."[101] Those furnishings, of course, were neocolonial, and in his eagerness to stand for all the best things the times had to offer, Hoover managed to equip the conceptual keeping-room his agents were constructing in the American imagination with Washingtoniana of every possible description.

He greeted the voter in the guise of Washington the businessman, Washington the engineer, the farm boy *cum* country squire, the success story, the gifted administrator, the harbinger of the new, the defender of the old. By putting on almost all the available faces of

Washington, Hoover raised the maintenance of the status quo to new heights of imagistic intensity; like the biographers of the 1920s, however, he also helped to reduce the potency of any one of those George Washington masks. The surveyor, the lover, the stoic, and the tycoon ran together into a puddle of colorless imprecision reflected in the Hoover campaign.

Who was George Washington, after all? The more eagerly he was invoked, copied, exposed, and exploited, the less clear the features of the puffy-faced old fellow sitting by the fireside became. The hero was in grave danger of vanishing into the mists of his own complicated mythology. Or had another fate overtaken poor Washington? Had real, live people—Harding, Ford, Coolidge, Lindbergh, and Herbert Hoover, most recently—tried so valiantly to fill his niche and succeeded so well that their failures had become Washington's? that when they stumbled, when the system faltered, Washington was discredited along with his legion of impersonators?

Whatever the reasons for his abrupt reversal of fortunes, they had reached a low ebb in 1931 when President Hoover put Washington back on his knees in the snows of Valley Forge. With the official United States George Washington Bicentennial celebration at hand, the culminating event in a half century of heretofore unflagging interest in the Father of His Country, that cold and lonely prayer assumed overtones of baffled despair.

Popular History

11 *✻ ✻ ✻ ✻ ✻ ✻ ✻ ✻ ✻ ✻ ✻ ✻ ✻ ✻ ✻ ✻*

The George Washington Bicentennial of 1932

Congressman Sol Bloom, Bicentennial Pageant-Master

What Herber Hoover and the United States George Washington Bicentennial Commission needed in those dark Depression days was a good public relations man, another Bernays or a Will Irwin skilled in scientific techniques for educating and wooing the bewildered public. Late in 1930 the commission was nearly as dispirited as the populace at large, and with the anniversary only two years away, inertia threatened to blight the observance.

A membership roster top-heavy with figureheads was no help, either. The Congressional delegation included Senators Fess of Ohio, Glass of West Virginia, and Tydings of Maryland, but they were busy men absorbed in the same national crisis that plagued Hoover. Commissioners chosen by the president included Bernard Baruch, George Eastman, and Henry Ford, busy magnates whose celebrity status and fitness for leadership had been compromised by the Crash. And day-to-day management of the commission's operations was further crippled by divided responsibility vested in two coequal associate directors. One was Colonel Ulysses S. Grant III of the U.S. Army, an engineer and a dependable bureaucrat. The other was a rambunctious Congressman from New York, a Tammany Democrat named Sol Bloom.[1]

Previously in charge of the commission's tiny Publicity Department, the colorful New Yorker was an unlikely instrument of the drab president's will, but early in 1931 Colonel Grant was suddenly ordered away to perform other "official duties" and Representative Bloom became the czar of the official United States George Washington Bicentennial celebration. He would prove more than equal to the urgency of the challenge, since, whatever other roles he might have played in a colorful career till then, Bloom was a public relations genius.[2] That flair for promotion let his backers overlook certain indiscretions which, in a man of lesser talent, would have merited the scorn of the righteous.

The press always called Sol Bloom "flamboyant" or worse, while acknowledging his "genius of publicity."[3] The son of Jewish immigrants from Poland, Bloom had been born in Pekin, Illinois, in 1871, and like George Washington Cohen of the movies, had set out to climb the ladder of success as quickly as possible. He manufactured brushes, managed a theater in San Francisco, and claimed to have built the Midway Plaisance at the Chicago World's Fair of 1893 single-handedly. He almost certainly did help to erect the first Ferris wheel there, introduced the "Hootchy-Kootchy" to salivating fairgoers, and, notwithstanding later protests of complete innocence, sponsored the gyrations of the notorious "Little Egypt."[4] When the Spanish-American War erupted in 1898, Bloom turned his attention to pop music: on the day news of the disaster broke, he completed and published a song called "The Heroes Who Sank with the *Maine*" and secured his fortune. In 1903, after dabbling for a time on the seamier fringes of show business, he moved to New York City to become a movie millionaire "widely known in amusement circles as a builder of theatres."[5]

In 1920 Bloom retired from business (like Hoover before him), eager to bestow his varied talents upon public service. First, he joined the Mayor's Committee to Welcome Distinguished Guests, a flying squad of professional greeters who whipped up organized enthusiasm for visiting celebrities. But entranced by the obvious glamour of politics, he ran for the Congressional seat in Manhattan's Nineteenth District—the so-called silk-stocking district—with Tammany backing in 1923. It was a special election and the results were disputed by a partisan House committee. At stake was the outcome of the presidential election of 1924, or so fearful Republicans thought when they backed the incumbent, Walter Chandler: if the contest between Coolidge and Al Smith were to be thrown into the House for a final decision, an extra Democrat would tip the New York vote to Smith. In the ensuing squabble, Bloom became an overnight sensation, a minor celebrity in his own right.

When he cheerfully accepted the directorship of the Bicentennial Commission from President Hoover, Sol Bloom probably recalled that he had won his fight to stay in Congress in the first place only by virtue of support from a few fair-minded Republicans. Thereafter, in any event, his political career continued to make headlines because of Bloom's ongoing battles with political adversaries. The Sixty-ninth Congress became known as "the fighting Sixty-ninth" thanks to the antics of Senator Carter Glass, "lightweight, of West Virginia," and Representative Sol Bloom, "light-heavyweight, of New York." In 1927 the *Marion* (Ohio) *Star,* the paper once owned by the late Warren

Harding, nominated Gene Tunney for public office, reasoning that the sorry pugilistic shows on Capitol Hill could be improved by a bit of professionalism. "If the halls of Congress are to be the scene of almost daily fistic encounters," the paper quipped, "the ideal candidate for a place in Congress is the world-champion heavyweight."

Carter Glass, it developed, had attacked Burton Wheeler of Montana at the door of the Senate cloakroom after a debate on the banking bill, and a proposed blue law for the District of Columbia resulted in an exchange of punches between Bloom and Representative Blanton of Texas, in which, according to Washington gossips, "the chief sufferers . . . were the bystanders." After that bout, an envious Congressman told the *Literary Digest* that "if Rep. Bloom had gotten in one good punch in his set-to with Blanton, he could have been elected Mayor of New York!" "What's a sock on the jaw," asked another, "if you can get on the front page of the country's newspapers?"[6]

Getting on the front page was what Sol Bloom did best, and it was his unerring instinct for attracting attention, along with the boundless energy he brought to the task of making George Washington "live again and become a vital force in the minds and hearts of the American people," that made him the perfect choice for the job of chief historical ringmaster of the Hoover administration.[7] An editorial cartoon put Bloom in a Valley Forge uniform above the caption "First in War, First in Peace, First in Bicentennial publicity." When the festivities were finally over, Will Rogers was the first to recognize a hard job well done. "You are the only guy who ever made a party run nine months," read Rogers's congratulatory wire, "and you did it in dry times, too. Sol [,] you made the whole country Washington conscious. . . . We had just pictured him as a man standing up in a boat when he ought to be sitting down."[8] A Democratic party official teased a Republican colleague by asking, "Can't you do something about Sol Bloom's starting to look so much like George Washington?" (Shot back the object of the taunt, a Congresswoman from California, "I wouldn't worry about that. I don't think any of us will have real cause for alarm unless George Washington starts to look like Sol Bloom!")[9]

Those jibes were affectionate tributes to the success of his crusade on behalf of Washington. But more recently, scholars looking back on the bicentennial with the wisdom of hindsight have tended to treat Bloom as an impresario run amuck, a ridiculous figure whose presence in the Hoover camp in the bleak days of 1932 was an anomaly. Marshall Fishwick, a historian of popular culture, describes the commission's appropriation of "Mother's Day, Memorial Day, Independence Day, and Goethe's Birthday" for the Washington effort as though a practice common enough among advertisers of drygoods and canned cherries had been the distasteful invention of Sol Bloom and inappropriate for the selling of dry-as-dust bicentennial history. Bloom even had the affrontery, Fishwick notes, to "set up his own radio station, with an antenna on top of the Washington Monument. Never, but never, has one man said so much about Washington to so many. . . . By the time Bloom left Congress, Washington was almost better known than Mary Pickford."[10]

The historian Dixon Wecter cites other Bloom-instigated gimmicks with bemused condescension, among them George M. Cohan's official bicentennial song (Figure 11.1), Phyllis-Marie Arthur's official bicentennial ditty, and Edwin Markham's official bicentennial poem.[11] "Father of the Land We Love" by Cohan was a jazz march with a snappy chorus:

> Whenever drums begin to roll
> Within the nation's heart and soul
> A patriotic something seems to say:—
>   First in War, First in Peace,
>   First in the Hearts of His Countrymen.[12]

Miss Arthur's "What He Means to Me" had a slower, homey tempo:

> Oft as I work to fill the cookie-jar,
> I see his noble face there on the wall,
> Smiling upon the laundry calendar:
> Saying, it seems to me, "I've suffered all."

And Edwin Markham, always cited in commission press releases as the "author of 'The Man with the Hoe,'" contributed a turgid poem called "Washington the Nation-Builder." He was a "silent man" said Markham, who reinforced his contention by comparing George Washington to a number of cold, inanimate objects, including Mount Washington, the tallest peak in the Presidential Range, and a celestial body:

> He did the day's work that was given him;
> He toiled for men until he flamed with God.
> Now in his greatness, ever superbly lone,
> He moves in his serene eternity,
>   Like far Polaris wheeling on the North.[13]

But the intrinsic aesthetic merits of these products—or the lack thereof—should not obscure the motives that governed their dissemination by Sol Bloom and his Bicentennial Commission. The director was, after all, a one-time songwriter and author of "The Heroes Who sank with the *Maine*"! At the risk of offending future highbrow historians (and devotees of William Carlos Williams, whose few readers were already well acquainted with the "Pap" of his country), Bloom had calibrated lyrical tributes to Washington to the tastes and preferences of a mass audience: a little women's-magazine doggerel, something snappy for the younger folks, and a bit of serious poetry. Other sanctioned activities also aimed at grabbing public attention through

11.1
James Montgomery Flagg, sheet-music cover for George M. Cohan's "Father of the Land We Love" (1931), one of several "official" George Washington bicentennial songs

staging the kinds of tried-and-true stunts the newspapers loved to cover because they involved famous people doing odd things or ordinary folks doing the same peculiar things en masse.

The historian Marcus Cunliffe pokes fun at Bloom's official bicentennial flight, an inspired piece of period showmanship of just this sort. On July 25, 1932, Jimmy Doolittle loaded into his mail plane Miss Anne Madison Washington, "a middle-aged great-great-great grandniece of the General," and flew 2,600 miles between dawn and dusk, following the exact route of Washington's known travels within the continental United States. Those trips had been mapped out in detail in the official *George Washington Atlas* published by Sol Bloom.[14] The nation guffawed, gasped, and noticed the name of Washington—almost everywhere. For the better part of 1932, for example, the name of Washington was synonymous with holes that appeared mysteriously in parks, picnic grounds, and sometimes in the front yards of the unwary. The Boy Scouts were the culprits. They were to be found underfoot from coast to coast, planting black walnuts gathered from the trees at Mount Vernon in honor of the first president, whose shadowy likeness guided the actions of the fresh-faced calendar boy Norman Rockwell designed for the 1932 edition of the official Scout calendar (see Figure 10.1).[15]

Foreign nations did not escape the media barrage. In Paris, Bloom persuaded Sacha Guitry and Yvonne Printemps, stars of the Comédie Française, to play a Gallic George and Martha in a Mount Vernon pageant. In Saigon, children attired as "Marianne" (the symbol of revolutionary France) and George Washington consecrated a bronze bust of the Father of Liberty donated for the purpose by Sol Bloom (Figure 11.2). All told, eighty-one countries were cajoled into mounting exercises in honor of Washington. As a result, the fourth and final volume of the commission's exhaustive records is peppered with strange photographs: Winston Churchill looking bilious at a George Washington colonial banquet given by the Pilgrims of Great Britain; a grim byway in Hamburg about to be christened "Washingtonstrasse" by order of Hitler's Reichstag (Figure 11.3); a desolate concrete overpass in Turin bearing a "Via Washington" by order of Benito Mussolini, whom Bloom admired inordinately.[16]

Elsewhere, Americans abroad were expected to inspire the natives. Sheepish embassy staffers therefore posed for government cameras in homemade variants on colonial costume, whipped up from sewing patterns supplied by Bloom. For a bicentennial party in Foochow, China, Vice Consul and Mrs. Gordon L. Burke impersonated Washington and Columbia, respectively. In Chihuahua, Mexico, one William Pole was Washington while a Mrs. J. W. Goodard did the honors as his Martha. In Tokyo, Japan, so many expatriates turned out for the festivities that the ambassador-director ran out of meaty roles. Several

11.2
The dedication of a 1932 George Washington monument—one of Sol Bloom's "official" busts—in Saigon, French Indochina, by children representing Washington and "Marianne"

11.3
The new "Washingtonstrasse" in Hamburg, Germany, renamed as a result of the Bicentennial Commission's foreign observances

young military attachés were forced to play the Mount Vernon house slaves in blackface, and spare debutantes milled about as Sally Fairfaxes, Mary Philipses, and a bevy of anonymous beauties of the Potomac (Figure 11.4).[17]

A special edition of the *Bulletin of the Pan-American Union* was issued, containing the remarks of twenty Latin American heads of state conveyed to Mount Vernon on Pan-American Day, 1932, to eulogize the hero. Venezuela noted that she had already done her part in 1883, during the Bolívar centenary, by dedicating the first monument to Washington ever erected in Spanish America; a floral tribute had recently been added. Brazil and Bolivia seemed unsure of what was expected of them in the way of Washingtoniana, and rationed out a single sentence apiece expressing "to the American government . . . the sincere admiration and the friendship" of their respective regimes.

Rafael Trujillo was fervent and personal. "I have the honor, as a faithful interpreter of my Government and my people," he declared, "to associate the name of the Dominican Republic with this tribute." Haiti paid its pointed tribute to the living rather than the ineffectual dead, hoping that President Hoover as "heir to the great tradition of George Washington . . . will take up his responsibilities and confront the obscure forces which desire to prevent his Government from permitting the idea of sovereignty to prevail over private or individual interests or over 'benefits to foreign countries.'"[18]

Americans read about foreign tributes to their first president in the newspapers. Thanks to the hyperactive Publicity Service of the Bicentennial Commission, they also saw innumerable photographs of

11.4
Tokyo observances of the Washington anniversary of 1932

Chinese, Poles, and Germans spiritually united with Americans in a kind of global Mount Vernon pageant. Suddenly, in fact, the fearsome and "featureless" ethnics of Thomas Bailey Aldrich's poem and Senator Beveridge's perfervid oratory had become friendly folks in powdered colonial wigs, in which guise they closely resembled red-blooded Americans. Through its overseas programs the commission embraced a tentative and largely ceremonial internationalism.

More important, however, the pictures of Italian and Chinese George Washingtons were the means by which the bicentennial enterprise reached out to those foreign-accented urbanites abandoned to the mercies of the Democrats in 1928. Bicentennial history was for all the people, regardless of national origin or taste in commemorative poetry. It is hard to believe that between February 22 and November 24, 1932—the official celebration began on Washington's Birthday, of course, and ended with a Thanksgiving Day dedicated to national gratitude for his life and benefactions—any American citizen, native- or foreign-born, in city or countryside, failed to be touched by some aspect of Bloom's promotional extravaganza.

His mistakes, as it turned out, were by-products of too fervent a devotion to his cause. Staffers learned not to remind their boss of misbegotten plans for a George Washington Letter-Writing Contest for Illiterates (Bloom was astonished to learn that they couldn't read and write), his reckless offer to supply a relief map of Washington's military operations to every schoolchild in the land (the maps would have cost more than the $328,000 grudgingly allocated by Congress to cover the entire operation), or his plan to affix George Washington's picture permanently to every tire-cover sold in the United States (motorists protested loudly).[19] If his zeal cloyed at times, Bloom's skill and patriotic piety were obvious. Furthermore, the Democratic Congressman with the show-business background was ideologically predisposed to represent Hoover's views on the significance of Washington and to implement them within the framework provided by the president's Memorial Day address at Valley Forge.

Austere Hoopla

"The Heroes Who Sank with the *Maine*" gave an early sign of Bloom's appreciation of hero-worship: he understood the necessity for heroes, their inspirational uses, and their popular appeal. Indeed, he considered himself something of a self-made hero, in the Hoover mold—an American success story who came up the hard way and a Good Businessman who devoted himself to public service once his bankroll had been made. In the 1920s, the advertising man had often seemed to represent the service ideal of American business best: the folk art of promotion, so its apologists maintained, provided free and useful information to the consumer and was, therefore, a "vital cog in the great prosperity machine."[20] In his new role in the chastened 1930s, Sol Bloom simply had a different concept to push. He was advertising heroism and historical facts—and the product came free of charge.

The early press releases through which Bloom introduced himself and the George Washington Bicentennial Commission to the public accepted the challenge of making "this great man live again and become a vital force in the minds and hearts of the American people." Bicentennial history would be usable, useful, present-minded, and shaped by the business ideals that packaged it for mass consumption. Bloom also acknowledged that the campaign would be "a project of magnitude" and some difficulty.[21] Speaking of himself in the third person, the then-associate director set it as his goal in 1930 "to make this celebration nation-wide and all-American."[22]

The difficulty, in 1932, arose from doing so within the framework of the disdain for "sheer materialism" expressed in President's Hoover's recent Valley Forge speech on Washington. The political wisdom of Hoover and the Republicans in Congress cautioned them against any appearance of government extravagance during a period of economic depression.[23] The fact that it was an election year also dictated a bicentennial that would not place financial demands on the average taxpayer.

The licensing of quasi-official souvenir items was approached with caution.[24] Events requiring admission tickets or travel to distant sites were disallowed with a great show of indignation. By renouncing costly ceremony, the George Washington Bicentennial Commission called attention to the fiscal prudence of the administration. The commission also became a model of the thrift and restraint now expected of business, showing the private sector how to make promotional virtue of penurious necessity. Finally, by avoiding the occasion of the new sin of materialism, the commisssion converted poverty into an object lesson in consumer stoicism, a sign that Americans had brought the Depression upon themselves with their reckless, easy-credit ways but now, inspired by the example of George Washington, were prepared to come to their senses and repent.

For these reasons, Bloom harped on the fact that there would be no central festival site in 1932, "no world's fair, no concentration of material evidence of the Nation's growth."[25] American fairs had always celebrated material progress as lustily as possible, whatever the historical excuse tendered for having fun and showing off the latest thing in carpet looms, gear shafts, and neocolonial durable goods. In the iconography of fairs and expositions, the picturesque crudities of the past provided firsthand assurance that progress had indeed occurred, since advancement meant the proliferation of the newfangled stuff of which the nation's forefathers had been deprived, judging by the contents of their frequently recreated houses.

But in the sober context of 1932, materialism no longer signified progress. Instead, it meant silly gadgets or light-minded whims, whereas the Washington bicentennial was a serious affair despite such occasional miscues as the pictorial tire-covers. "Instead of inviting the people to a physical memorial—a transitory gesture of homage—this celebration," Director Bloom insisted, "will be in the minds and hearts of the American people, in their own homes, churches, schools, fraternities, clubs. . . . It will not be in the form of an exposition [of] what Americans can do now, but what our fathers did to make possible the United States of the twentieth century. Its purposes are entirely patriotic and will be in keeping with the event it signalizes."[26]

The vehemence with which Sol Bloom rejected a "world's fair" that was never seriously considered by the Bicentennial Commission in the first place is interesting in light of the several ambitious expositions on the drawing boards in the early 1930s. In 1931 the Chicago business community was planning a Century of Progress Exposition for the summer of 1933. Chicago's fair would be awash in "materialism" and would use history chiefly as an illustration of the quaint backwardness of yesteryear. The Century of Progress aimed to stimulate retail sales and the construction industry; backers made no bones about their intentions. Although gate receipts fell below expectations and the fair was held over for another year to recoup losses, it did save some Loop hotels and department stores from bankruptcy. Because of glowing financial projections, the activities in Chicago drew the attention of Grover Whalen and the New York merchants and bankers who were beginning to consider a comparable fair—The World of Tomorrow—to revitalize New York City business in 1939, the sesquicentennial of Washington's inauguration there.[27] It was possible, they thought, to honor Washington, celebrate American history, and make money, all at the same time.

As the chosen theme showed, Chicago was interested in the past only insofar as a crude reconstruction of Fort Dearborn, when juxtaposed with the futuristic pylons of the General Motors pavilion and the "rocket cars" that zoomed above the grounds on suspended cables, could help to illustrate the material progress of the city over a hundred years (Figure 11.5).[28] In keeping with the commercial drives of the fair, souvenir items abounded. Each one expressed the dreams of the planners in graphic terms.

Inexpensive trinkets ranging from pasteboard coasters and trivets to tiny boxed sets of photographic views, money clips, hankies, compacts, and playing cards were all decorated with the official Century of Progress trademark: a whirling planet Earth trailing a dynamic, triple stream of cosmic energy (Figure 11.6). Other mementos—machine-woven tapestries and doilies, for instance—subordinated old Fort Dearborn to a sci-fi array of planes, rocketships, pylons, dirigibles,

11.5
A souvenir plaque showing the "Sky Ride" at Chicago's Century of Progress during its second season (1934)

11.6
A Century of Progress souvenir compact, with the official futuristic logo

FORT DEARBORN·A CENTURY OF PROGRESS·CHICAGO 1933

and spinning globes (Figure 11.7). Tomorrow was right around the corner, said the comet-strewn shot glasses and the postcards: this was the Century of Progress.

Special exhibits and daily shows conveyed the same message. A popular attraction of the 1933 season was a pageant called *Wings of a Century: The Romance of Transportation,* written by Edward Hungerford. For ten cents the fairgoer could watch 102 actors, 17 locomotive engineers, and 28 horsemen and drovers working their way out of the slough of history toward interstellar prosperity. After a prologue illustrating the "Indian Retreat," scenes and interludes whisked by during which canalboats, the Iron Horse, the Pony Express, and finally the automobile ("Interlude IV, the Horseless Carriage, 1905–1925") were each rendered obsolete by the romance of technological progress. A crude biplane appeared in the penultimate episode; in the grand finale, glimpses of a world of the future—a world just around the corner—made the audience gasp in anticipation: "And so the motor car. And so, these great and birdlike creatures overhead. All move at [man's] command—upon his pleasure. Together, they are the lifeblood of the nation. . . . Transport is more than the right hand of the land. It is its very heart and soul. Wings of a Century! It is no idle phrase."[29]

The Baltimore & Ohio exhibit for the 1934 season was a shade less dramatic but equally determined to show that the Depression was only a momentary hitch in the forward sweep of material progress—that the immediate future still held marvels in store. The B&O display included a few old railway cars refurbished for the railroad's hundredth birthday in the happier year of 1927. Offered for sale were sets of centenary china, just like the dinner service "used in [the] beautiful Colonial Dining Cars" on the line. But the real focus was on progress and the key evidence thereof: five new, experimental freight cars made of Cor-Ten steel.[30]

Not all the fun on the fairgrounds came from buying compacts adorned with Buck Rogers–style emblems of a happier tomorrow or imagining cities of the future abuzz with rocket cars. Thanks to a Bicentennial Commission that purported to abhor the materialism of fairs, the colonial past also became a source of general hilarity in Chicago. In the art exhibition—such places, even at fairs, had always tended to be a little stuffy—tourists giggled and gawked and bought up picture-postcards of one of the paintings on exhibit in such quantities that the supply never quite kept up with the demand.[31] The picture was called *Daughters of Revolution*.

Grant Wood's *Daughters of Revolution*

A recent work by Grant Wood, *Daughters of Revolution* showed three Iowa matrons celebrating their annual Martha Washington tea in front of a steel engraving after Emanuel Leutze's famous *Washington Crossing the Delaware*; the engraving, not unlike the ladies themselves, was "mottled grey with age" (Figure 11.8). The 1932 work is generally held to commemorate the artist's personal squabble with the Cedar Rapids, Iowa, chapter of the DAR, which had objected to his plan to have his memorial window honoring the dead of World War I fabricated in Germany, homeland of the enemy.[32] But the instant popularity of the picture and the laughs it elicited from fairgoers who had never

11.8
Grant Wood, *Daughters of Revolution*, 1932

11.9
A purple Washington Crossing the Delaware plate, one of a set of twelve issued in honor of the bicentennial

heard of Grant Wood's troubles back home suggest that what was funny was really George Washington, teetering manfully in his boat at dead center.

Because of the general's prominent position in the middle of the painting, it is tempting to believe that artist Wood had heard a story or two about Washington's smutty remarks on the Delaware. Isolating the standing hero from the rest of the composition, for instance, meant zeroing in on Washington's heroically splayed legs. He is not, therefore, the foggy old gentleman of the canonical Stuart portrait of whom Gertrude Stein could remark with some justice in 1931, "She is very sleepy, George Washington."[33] Instead, the Washington enshrined by Wood at the center of the painting is a vigorous, virile man, a plausible Father of His Country, rendered all the more masculine by the polite tea party he is forced to attend.

Given the painter's emphasis on the lavender-and-old-lace domesticity of the "Daughters," with their tatted collars, fussy print frocks, and blue-willow china, George Washington becomes a macho bull in a thoroughly feminine china shop by contrast alone. As the men's club legends of Washington's "obscene anecdote" on the Delaware filter through the dainty, ladies-only atmosphere of genteel rectitude, one laugh—an earthy guffaw—is on those prim and proper ladies. But the bigger laugh is on Sol Bloom and his minions.

In order to make Washington appreciable to twentieth-century realists and to those who, having seen the economic worst, had given up on fairy tales, bicentennial workers were inclined to be pedantic about historical facts. Not only did commission functionaries prize scraps of information for their authenticity but they actively despised legends for sugar-coating the harsh realities of life. And excepting perhaps the cherry tree fable, no legend was more thoroughly trounced in 1932 than Leutze's rendition of Christmas night, 1776 (Figure 11.9).

That painter's depiction of Washington's dramatic passage of the Delaware led the list of damnable errors dismissed in a corrective catechism of "Questions and Answers Pertaining to the Life and Times of George Washington" issued free of charge by Director Bloom to any individual, club, church group, or organization expressing a glimmer of interest in the theme:

Q. Is the Leutze picture of George Washington Crossing the Delaware in the Metropolitan Museum of Art in New York, authentic?
A. This picture is not authentic because it shows the American flag which was not adopted until the following year. Also, it shows Washington standing in the boat. While there is no evidence available to prove that Washington did not stand in the boat, it is much more likely that he was seated.[34]

Even if the Leutze scene had not automatically raised the specter of William Carlos Williams and "the obscene anecdote [Washington] told that night in the boat," the tableau would have failed to meet modern standards of authenticity. Captains of industry did not stand up in rowboats; nor did smart Kiwanians, and Bloom—himself a Shriner, Elk, Moose, Red Man, and thirty-second-degree Mason—had just assured a conclave of them that Washington was "our kind of man. If George Washington were alive today . . . he would be a proud member of such a splendid group."[35]

Sol Bloom's attack on the authenticity of a cherished American icon in the name of reverent honesty provided as fertile a field for satire as any off-color George Washington story. Grant Wood painted *Daughters of Revolution* in parody of that combative spirit of truthtelling, although his immediate target was the established institutions that guarded America's symbolic past. And it is crucial to remember that Wood selected this particular icon—a much-beloved image of the hero, under heavy fire in 1932 from George Washington's bureaucratic custodians—in preference to a wide range of other pictorial symbols that could have served him well had his goal been a straightforward contrast between the glorious heritage of the nation and Iowa's perverters of that "democratic birthright."[36]

As Wood organized his painting, much of the Leutze composition is hidden from view. The top of Leutze's scene is radically cropped. The flanks are covered by the heads of two of the women. Thus Washington's reckless marine posturing is spotlighted with some care; the error Bloom abhorred is exalted. And by bringing his head to the very top of the canvas, Wood makes the hero and his reowned-in-history pose the axis about which the picture revolves, both spatially and spiritually. In effect, Wood makes popular legend dominate reality, neatly reversing the drive of the bicentennial crusade. Authentic facts—the carefully delineated, full-color figures in the foreground of the picture—are tested against enduring myth and found wanting in 1932, in the midst of a much-publicized debate over the issue of fact versus legend.

Choosing an "Authentic" Likeness of Washington

The first pictorial skirmish in the battle of the facts opened with a mandate from Congress authorizing the Bicentennial Commission to select from among "the many more or less authenticated portraits of George Washington . . . painted by contemporary artists . . . the one portrait which will have official sanction and be issued in hundreds and thousands of copies as part of the observance of 1932."[37] The chosen likeness would appear on stamps, a bicentennial medal, and commemorative quarters "with a profile relief on one side." Even more important, it would serve as the official logo for the United States

George Washington Bicentennial Commission, be printed on its letterhead, and be the symbol by which the diverse features of the celebration would be identified and remembered (Figure 11.10).

Whatever the image finally picked, it would be reproduced on an unprecedented scale: in addition to its use in ads, promotions, and merchandising schemes, the ebullient Bloom had also pledged to distribute "1,000,000 pictures of Washington to the country's schools" as soon as the definitive portrait was found by a committee of seven expert "critics," including several delegates from the stodgy Commission of Fine Arts, two historians from the Bicentennial Commission staff, the chief of the Fine Arts Division of the Library of Congress, an academic painter from Virginia, and Harrison Howell Dodge, the resident superintendent of Mount Vernon.[38]

Given the composition of the group, quarrels among the jurors were almost inevitable, as the fine arts contingent discoursed knowingly about color and style while the historians, mistrusting the wayward vagaries of taste, preferred to debate the factual accuracy of the pictorial evidence offered for their consideration. Had the artist really met Washington? they wanted to know. Did the picture under examination agree at key points with other works also executed from life?

11.10
The letterhead of the Bicentennial Commission

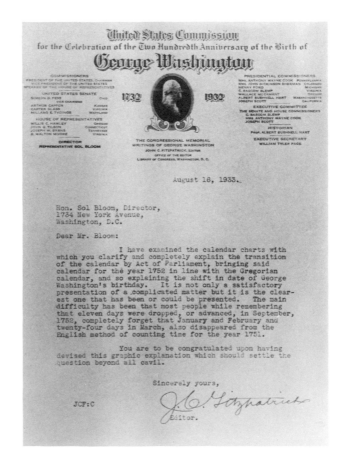

To facilitate such comparisons, the committee had begun its work by making a thorough examination of every available likeness of Washington taken during his lifetime. They looked at oil paintings, sketches in pen and ink, pastels, profiles in cut paper, watercolors, prints, miniatures on whalebone, and bits of needlepoint. But as the weeks and the meetings dragged on, they failed time and time again to reach a unanimous verdict.

In every Peale or Trumbull or Gilbert Stuart portrait, Washington looked different somehow. Subtle variations created by an assortment of media, techniques, and styles did not trouble the real art "critics" overmuch but seem to have distressed the historians deeply. The makers of these portraits had actually sat in the presence of the living Washington; Albert Bushnell Hart, John Fitzpatrick, and the other commission researchers had the hard historical evidence to prove it. Yet their pictures did not agree. By want of skill or honesty, they had apparently failed to record the absolute truth, since no two images matched exactly. As documentary fact, the painter's art was defective, untrustworthy, and probably unworthy to serve as the official symbol of the bicentennial.

Hopelessly divided in their choice of a factually dependable picture of Washington among the two-dimensional remains of an era without cameras, the committee perked up suddenly at the prospect of simulating a photograph of the hero. According to Superintendent Dodge, whose memoirs contain the fullest account of what happened behind the closed doors of the jury, he had thought all along "that the Houdon bust at Mount Vernon was the only really satisfactory likeness of General Washington" but kept his tongue lest he be accused of special pleading for his own collection. Besides, it was clear that for reasons of practicality alone "the committee was certainly not in favor of a sculptured head," a million copies of which would have bankrupted the commission many times over.[39] But when "Mr. Kent, the head of the Metropolitan Museum," told the group in passing of an "Austrian named Jaffé who, in his opinion, was the world's most skillful photographer of sculpture," Dodge made his case for the Houdon. Without further hesitation, his weary colleagues commissioned Jaffé to go to Mount Vernon immediately to take pictures of the bust.

From a factual point of view, the statue Jaffé photographed under bright spotlights (while he himself lay on the floor at the foot of the pedestal) could satisfy the pickiest historian. Its pedigree was immaculate: Jean-Antoine Houdon made the bust during a two-week visit to Mount Vernon in 1785, in preparation for modeling a full-length bronze commissioned by the state of Virginia. Even allowing for the artistic license to which image-makers of the period seemed addicted, the commission's jurors were struck by the similarity between the life-size bust in the Mount Vernon collection and a life mask of George Washington, also taken by Houdon. The mask preserved the very imprint of the subject's flesh—the dimensions, the wrinkles, and even the smallpox scars of Washington's face—with an infallible precision surpassing in detail even the mechanical silhouettes made with a machine called a "physiognotrace."

The jury had studied Washington masks and facial molds before, of course. It had also examined Houdon's Richmond bronze as a kind of standard against which the accuracy of other likenesses could be judged. Whatever its documentary merits, the Richmond statue was also an extremely popular image of Washington from which the Gorham Company, of Providence, Rhode Island, by act of the Virginia legislature, had been authorized to make bronze copies for various units of government, educational institutions, "any patriotic society, or for presentation to any duly organized board, commission or society having in charge the care and preservation on any historic spot closely related to the history and achievements of George Washington" upon application to the governor and payment of a fee.[40] Although their deliberations sometimes suggested indifference to questions of popular appeal, the experts did sense that a factually correct Washington who did not look anything like the George Washington in the nation's collective memory would be of questionable value to the anniversary program for 1932.

In 1932, truncated busts made from the uppermost sections of the Gorham mold sold for $450 and turned up in such far-flung spots as Indochina; thanks to novelty manufacturers, dismayed by the commission's failure to designate an official Washington likeness in time for their workshops to churn out souvenirs, pirated versions of the bust also filled dime-store cases in the United States (Figure 11.11). Gorham's own full-length reproductions, at $4,500 apiece, had already found their way into the Washington Memorial Chapel at Valley Forge and the DAR collection in San Francisco, and were about to be seen in Lima, Montevideo, Versailles, and Trafalgar Square.[41]

Because that Washington—the Richmond type, with his sword discarded and his plow at the ready—was so famous, Bloom later had it incorporated into one of the two official bicentennial posters. Drawn by the cartoonist Albert T. Reid, a GOP stalwart famous for his likenesses of "Uncle Sam," it was circulated through Boy and Girl Scout units, "given wide general distribution," and even supplied to youth-oriented organizations preserved under glass, in an impressive oak frame (Figure 11.12).[42] The poster depicted Reid's genial Uncle Sam, resplendent in his flag-striped trousers, introducing a modern American boy to the bronze Houdon Washington, elevated on a plinth above the old man and his awestruck young companion.[43]

11.11
A Richmond-style bust after Houdon, a miniature keepsake version of the Gorham type, ca. 1932

The poster illustrates clearly enough that the bronze Houdon was an entity set apart from daily life by its uniform brown color, its pedestal, and even its elegant pose, an ungainly one by later norms of pleasing male posture.[44] But photographs of the pale Mount Vernon terra cotta (which had been painted white to resemble marble or patriot skin) had no such off-putting defects, even though Jaffé had taken the best shots of the lot—a profile and a three-quarters view, both showing the right side of the face—from below, to emphasize the visionary quality Houdon sought to impart to the great Washington. Indeed, except for the absence of a stiff Hoover collar and tie at the naked throat, the man in the pictures presented to the committee could have been any vigorous, middle-aged executive staring fearlessly into the corporate future (Figure 11.13).

If the conventions of 1930s portrait photography—the averted gaze, the absence of color, the stylishly vaporish quality of the upper torso—looked slightly incongruous in the old-fashioned Georgian egg-and-dart frame with which the image was most often surrounded, those same tricks also made an eighteenth-century statue look like a "fact," a publicity portrait of a contemporary American, somebody real and consequential in the bicentennial year of 1932. When the weary experts gathered to inspect the photographs, it took them only minutes to designate "the Houdon bust of George Washington at Mount Vernon . . . as the subject for the official portrait which [the Bicentennial Commission] will distribute over the country." The reasons were obvious:

Selection of this [statue] was . . . determined by the fact that, as modeled from the living figure of Washington, it has every guarantee of absolute accuracy in presenting Washington at the prime of his life and because the bust is beyond question a great artistic masterpiece in every respect. Finally the bust was chosen because, by being photographed from several angles, it provides a variety of portraits, all artistic and all authentic.[45]

Souvenirs of the Washington Bicentennial

Secretary of the Treasury Mellon lost no time in making one of the commission's "authentic" photographs of George Washington the model for artists competing for the design of the bicentennial quarter, the numismatic plum of the decade.[46] But private enterprise also pounced on the designated Washington portrait. Despite the Depression, there was still a market for inexpensive Washingtoniana, and its manufacturers had followed the search for an official likeness impatiently. The Almar Metal Arts Company of Point Merion, Pennsylvania, is a case in point. Although the firm lacked the kind of sanction Gorham had from the state of Virginia, Almar began to produce four-inch cast-iron miniatures of the Mount Vernon bust anyway; the legend

11.12
"Uncle Sam" poster for the Bicentennial Commission, drawn by Albert T. Reid and painted by Henry Hintermeister

11.13
The official George Washington portrait of the United States George Washington Bicentennial Commission

on the base—"George Washington, 1732–1932"—made the bicentennial connection clear, and the price was modest (Figure 11.14). With every purchase of a pint of vinegar during the year of celebration, H. J. Heinz gave the customer a decorative glass dispenser absolutely free. On the back a cherry tree surmounted a scroll bearing the significant dates, and on the front was the official profile view of the official Houdon bust (Figure 11.15). Before the year was out, the bare-chested Washington in profile was also available on liquor bottles, funeral-parlor paper fans, hatchet-shaped ice cream molds, plaques, and posters of every description (Figures 11.16, 11.17).

11.14
Bust after the official Mount Vernon likeness, by Almar Metal Arts, 1932

11.15
A Heinz Washington bicentennial commemorative vinegar cruet

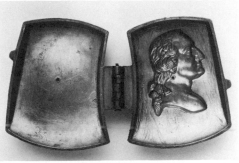

11.16
A bicentennial ice cream mold

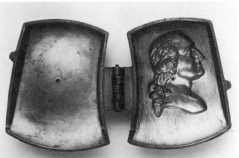

11.17
Manufactured by Brown and Bigelow in 1932, this Washington fan was given away by the Economy Furniture Upholstery Company of Austin, Texas.

A second Bicentennial Commission poster, this one by Norman Rockwell, showed the typical besweatered all-American youth of the day doing his history homework at a student desk littered with books, an inkwell, an apple, a discarded football, and a plaster copy of the Mount Vernon bust (Figure 11.18). The bust serves as "the guiding inspiration"—the title Sol Bloom gave the poster—for the lad's essay. To drive the point home, the dome of the Capitol and George Washington in the military uniform he wore at Annapolis appear magically in the ether above the little statue. Since it was the commission's policy to make pictorial materials available to all comers, a version of the Rockwell poster once handed out free by the government to interested parties eventually made its way in the world of commerce as a framed lithograph, suitable for the decoration of a boy's room and advertised in the "art goods" pages of mail-order fliers. But if the commission supplied the marketplace with profitable commemorative products, that body was also willing to accept such materials as donations from the private sector. In fact, *The Guiding Inspiration* (subtitled *At Work on His Washington Essay*) began life as the cover of the famous Sears Roebuck catalogue for 1932. In its first appearance, the picture was overprinted with directions to "See Page 87" for a nice selection of bicentennial mementos and a list of planned events.[47] Bloom borrowed the design from Sears because the conceit perfectly reflected his views of the efficacy of the official bicentennial likeness.

Because he believed that the sight of George Washington could shape a child for a lifetime, Bloom had rashly promised a million free Washingtons to the nation's schools in honor of the anniversary. In the *Handbook of the George Washington Appreciation Course* provided to educators, a staged photograph closely resembling the Rockwell poster pictures a little boy standing eye-to-eye with a copy of the Mount Vernon bust ensconced on the corner of a schoolroom desk (Figure 11.19).[48] The other children are gathered about as their teacher points to Washington; on the blackboard behind them, another little fellow has painfully scrawled an inscription in white chalk: "George Washington, Born February 22, 1732." "A Good Example," reads the caption, is "the Best Instruction."[49]

Posed and heavily retouched though it is, the photo is a disarming commentary on Sol Bloom's personal crusade to bring the *exemplum virtutis* into the classroom in human form. Not to be outdone by the vinegar or mail-order industries in facilitating that decisive confrontation between the American child and the official effigy of an avuncular first president, he ordered copies of the designated Washington by the gross, in a variety of media. The *New Yorker* found his penchant for the bust amusing: "He early fell under the sway of the Houdon bust, and plaster-of-Paris reproductions are to be found in every

11.18
Norman Rockwell, *The Guiding Inspiration,* 1932; this version of the motif that also served as a government poster and a Sears catalogue cover was sold framed and ready for hanging in a boy's room.

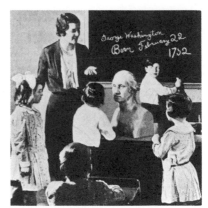

11.19
"A Good Example Is the Best Instruction": the photograph reflects Bloom's belief in the efficacy of images.

11.20
Calendar-thermometer-mirror giveaway plaques like this one came in blue or yellow; the firm's message was imprinted in the blank at the lower center.

schoolhouse, public office, and library in the land. The government pays for both, besides shipping. This idealized sculpture of Washington has come in for considerable criticism from many authorities."[50]

By the time the period of celebration began in earnest, however, Bloom had actually been forced to become a great deal more catholic in his taste in Washingtons. For one thing, busts were too expensive to be distributed on a grand scale. For another, "official" photographs of the statue were by no means popular, perhaps because of their lack of color and somewhat daunting nobility of gaze. Finally, as the director wistfully remarked when he opened a commission-sponsored exhibition of George Washington paintings at the Corcoran Gallery, the Athenaeum Portrait by Gilbert Stuart—the one on the two-cent stamp—was still the "most famous and perhaps the most familiar of all the Washington likenesses."[51]

His best efforts to replace the frowsy Gilbert Stuart with a *real* Washington had failed utterly. And since, despite the fiasco with the relief maps and the plaster busts, he still hoped that "in 1932 there will not be a school room or school building in the United States without its picture of George Washington," Bloom bowed to popular

11.21
A 1932 blue Washington at Valley Forge plate by Crown Ducal features a sumptuous Della Robbia border that contradicts the iconography of the image.

preference and printed up 750,000 Stuarts for a start.[52] By November 24, 1932, a big, full-color reproduction of the Athenaeum Portrait, duly framed in fumed oak, blinked down on every schoolchild in the continental United States and its territories and possessions. Adults got another look at the elderly Washington every time they licked a stamp, and the unlikely pinup boy with the "letter-box mouth" also graced any number of cardboard trivets, fans, and promotional calendars with inset thermometers doled out by public-spirited merchants (Figure 11.20).[53] The nation had chosen its own official bicentennial George.

Although his unsmiling "photograph" appeared as the frontispiece to many weighty and serious tomes published during the bicentennial year, the grim-looking George Washington also had a lighter, more relaxed side to his 1932 personality.[54] Thanks to the tireless Congressman Bloom, Washington's likeness adorned not only quarters, stamps, calendars, thermometers, and vinegar bottles but china plates, carnival prizes, and premiums for enterprising newsboys (Figures 11.21, 11.22, 11.23).[55] A short story in *Good Housekeeping* even dealt with a copy of the Stuart "Portrait of Washington" given to a pair of newlyweds who would have preferred a "Yard o' Pansies" print:

11.22
Bicentennial chalk figures of Washington were popular carnival prizes for years after the anniversary year; this example is inscribed on the base with its date of acquisition—August 22, 1935.

"How did the girls happen to send this one?" he asked.

"Oh," Essie's mouth trembled childishly, "I suppose it's my fault. They asked me what I wanted for a wedding present, and I said a picture. . . . And they asked what our furniture was like, and I said," a shade of pride here, "that it was kind of Colonial."

"And so," Bill grinned, "they sent you a picture of George Washington—as large as life, and twice as ugly!"[56]

The role of the omniscient portrait in keeping the jobless Bill from turning to a life of crime might have stretched the implications of Rockwell's *Guiding Inspiration* to the breaking point, but the notion of Washington's overseeing the daily doings of Americans everywhere was not inherently far-fetched. Bloom's Bicentennial Commission had, in the end, contrived to insinuate a big, color reproduction of the Athenaeum Portrait into more than a million schoolrooms, lodge halls, and bureaucratic enclaves. In 1939 Grant Wood chose *that* face for the smug little brat with the hatchet in his *Parson Weems's Fable* because a misuse of the canonical effigy was acutely funny at the end of a decade of Stuart lookalikes (Figure 11.24).[57]

For the same reason, Stuart's puffy and powdered image dominates *Daughters of Revolution,* painted at the height of bicentennial hysteria. Modern eyes can readily enough discern the irony in a situation that pits the hero, standing up in his boat in an act of Revolutionary bravado, against a trio of timid old dears who, despite their devotion to the legacy of history, would faint dead away at the mere mention

11.23
The Day's Beginning, after a painting by Ferris, was thought sufficiently edifying to serve as a prize card for good school performance or devotion to one's paper route; it was also used on calendars.

of a revolution. But it takes an eye inured to the pictorial ministrations of Sol Bloom to recognize that the dottiest of Wood's "Daughters"— the frizzy-haired fright with the letter-box mouth at the left edge of the picture—is none other than Gilbert Stuart's George Washington in drag (see Figure 11.8).

Tricked out in a flowered dress and planted smugly before his truer, mythical self, this Washington was a deliberate affront to the supposedly authentic bicentennial hero of 1932. And judging by their enthusiasm for the painting, Chicago's fairgoers of 1933 were better equipped than today's critics to appreciate a picture that offered political and social satire on current events along with a truly hilarious sight gag.[58]

A Bicentennial for the Foreign-Born

Possible correlations between the George Washington celebration and the upcoming Chicago fair were of particular interest to the poet Vachel Lindsay, a Midwesterner. Lindsay, who had published *The Litany of Washington Street* in 1929 to explain the incidence of such street names in the West—"a Gilbert Stuart kind of book," he called it in the opening paragraph—believed, like William Carlos Williams, that Washington contained within himself two warring cultures, the English and the American. But unlike his Eastern counterpart, Lindsay thought that the Founding Fathers had somehow cast off their "Anglo-Saxon" heritage on the frontier before they ever launched the Revolution:

This soil had given [the American] its special vitamins, the blood of its wild animals; he was acquiring a tomahawk skull and cheekbones, a face that distinguished him forever from the Englishman, and a tomahawk way of thinking that distinguished him forever from Europe and made him no longer a Colonist.

Of all this, George Washington was the great chief, disguised at Mount Vernon in silk stockings and velvet breeches, in carefully powdered hair and a three-cornered hat, in Virginia greatcoat, and Virginia high boots, but not a colonist, rather a native in his own right.[59]

On those grounds (and after years on the lecture circuit delivering a prepared talk about Gilbert Stuart's portrait), Lindsay dismissed "the efforts of the new Washington scholarship . . . to destroy the meaning of the Gilbert Stuart portrait" by reducing its mysterious subject to the level of common humanity. "Gilbert Stuart," he concluded enigmatically, "is the only human being who ever painted a portrait of a red Indian chief. All other attempts are art calendars and railroad advertisements."[60]

Eagerly anticipating a different kind of fair, Lindsay died shortly before the Century of Progess opened. But in a proposal published in the *Christian Century* in July of 1931, Lindsay argued that Chicago's vague observance of American progress should be conflated with "the two centuries of progress celebration" of 1932, the Washington bicentennial. Such a spillover would probably happen anyway in the normal course of things, he thought. Since the bicentennial was scheduled to conclude on Thanksgiving Day of 1932 with a national inquiry into "why we are thankful for George," and since advance publicity for the fair would move into high gear at the same time, "the Chicago group will be obliged to take over George Washington, bag and baggage," Lindsay predicted:

We may expect the Century of Progress men to accept the situation gracefully, and whether the present committees so design it or not, the George Washington celebration will probably continue on, with increased momentum, with Chicago as its center, through 1933. Having learned again the trick of colonial pageantry . . . we will not at once abandon the habit. . . . Virginia and the tidewater families will move into Fort Dearborn at the mouth of the Chicago River and again we will behold the winning of the West.[61]

Vachel Lindsay's deduction proved very wrong, of course. In conception, the exposition on Lake Michigan resembled Greenfield Village, stripped down and streamlined for ideological efficiency. The Century of Progress used just enough history to conjure up prospects for more and better material prosperity to come, and no more. Except for his cameo appearance in Grant Wood's painting, George Washington was not a potent presence on the fairgrounds.

The commercial interests in Chicago rejected Washington. And Sol Bloom had forsworn world's fairs because of their materialism. But the Bicentennial Commission was not averse to taking other tokens of material progress under its official wing when they were free, or cheap. Thus the great span between Fort Lee, New Jersey, and Fort Washington, New York, begun in May of 1927, was called the George Washington Bridge at the suggestion of the DAR, with the assent of Sol Bloom.[62] A boulevard under construction between the District of Columbia and Mount Vernon was named the George Washington Memorial Parkway, after patriotic societies agreed to supply all the necessary signs and plantings.[63]

The commission lent its moral support to the Wakefield National Memorial Association, a nonprofit group engaged in recreating the birthplace of Washington from a small pile of rubble. With the exception of a modest appropriation from Congress—Bloom discussed it infrequently and apologetically—"every dollar" spent on Wakefield was raised by public subscription. The site had been purchased on behalf of the association by John D. Rockefeller, Jr., "at a cost of $115,000" of his own money, and the bricks were being manufactured gratis at Williamsburg by Rockefeller employees.[64]

The Washington currency and the coins routinely produced by the government anyway were also acceptable to the Bicentennial Commission: materialistic though they were, Bloom couldn't really quarrel with a traditional usage of the man whose features already graced the dollar bill. The bicentennial quarter was designed and minted along with a special 1932 issue of Washington portrait postage, which included a green one-cent Houdon and a brown one-and-a-half-cent Peale in addition to the customary two-cent Stuart.[65]

But the products of the private sector were accorded more gingerly treatment. Bicentennial Commissioner George Eastman volunteered the services of Eastman Kodak Teaching Films for the production of an official talking picture on the life and times of George Washington, for example. Bloom agreed to coproduce the movie but only on condition that no costs accrue to the commission, that the film be provided free of charge to schools and colleges, and that stills become part of the commission's massive pictorial archive, available without royalty payment to any publisher in need of instructional illustrations.[66]

The commission, Bloom stated in the press release announcing the joint venture with Kodak, "is a government agency which consistently refuses to be connected with any commercial or profit-making projects. . . . The United States George Washington Bicentennial Commission emphasizes the fact that it has at no time, nor will it become in the future, affiliated with any commercial project." Bloom and his staff stood "ready to cooperate with business firms, but at no time will they compromise the Commission with an official approval of, or responsibility for, any money-making enterprise."[67] Accurate information was the only commodity in which the commission wished to trade overtly.

Vachel Lindsay's anticipated alliance between Sol Bloom and the profit-mongers of the Century of Progress did not come to pass, but the poet's 1931 essay did hit upon two points that figured prominently in Bloom's plans. One was ethnic participation. The other was the eradication of myth so that the true facts about George Washington might finally emerge.

The prospect of George Washington being honored and reinvestigated in Chicago intrigued Lindsay because he thought that local immigrants and the descendants of immigrants would probably greet the old-style, mythical Washington with a healthy skepticism. Calling Parson Weems "the first and most outrageous liar about George Washington, possibly the greatest liar the world has ever known, certainly the most unkillable liar the world has ever known, except the father of lies," he chortled to think what would happen when the Italian, Scandinavian, Irish, Jewish, and German communities of Chicago heard "all the rotting pieties, all the sniffy priggishness, all the waxworks perfection . . . all the emasculation, stupidity [and] cheap hypocrisy" of popular legend.

What, for example, would a Norwegian-American with salt water in his veins think of a man who purportedly stood up in an open boat and quoted the Bible to the sailors wisely sitting at their oars as a gale raged over the Delaware River? Could they accept the river depicted in Leutze's famous painting, a gentle stream choked with cakes of ice that resembled bars of "Ivory-Soap-it-Floats"? Accustomed to the hot-blooded gods of the ancients, what would Italian-Americans make of a sugar-candy hero? Could a rabbi or an Irish Catholic stomach the "vile Protestant" pieties of "the heretic Parson Weems"? On balance, Lindsay thought not:

If we can only summon the courage to rally all those races who have come to the United States since the Parson was consigned to the uttermost depths of hell, races untainted by his smirking lies, we may, at the end of the Century of Progress exposition at Chicago in 1933, have a George Washington who is a real hero, who will make all the Pilgrim fathers groan in their graves and the F.F.V.'s die of shame. It is a consummation devoutly to be wished.[68]

Bloom set great store by foreign tributes to Washington and saw to it that news items about the commission's overseas activities were planted in the media. The foreign program reflected his eagerness to make the bicentennial meaningful to hyphenated Americans like himself, who had been regarded as dangerous aliens or candidates for melting-pot acculturation in earlier patriotic observances. But Bloom did not adopt Vachel Lindsay's approach to the very real problem of America's newcomers. Although he would prove just as committed as the poet to purging myth from the historical record, the publicity Sol Bloom directed specifically at ethnic communities was notable for avoiding all but the most casual references to Washington, the native-born American.

Instead, in the interests of including all "the people" in the bicentennial, Bloom beamed the spotlight on Washington's gallant allies from across the Atlantic:

Not only do we want to impress upon the nation its debt to George Washington, but also our debt to other heroes associated with him. We want to remember those splendid men and women, many of them of foreign birth, who offered up their lives upon the altar of American independence. We want to remember Von Steuben, De Kalb, and the Muhlenbergs, . . . Carroll, Barry, Knox and the host of Irish patriots, . . . Kosciuszko, Pulaski, [and] Benjamin Nones, who has been called "the Jewish Lafayette."[69]

True to his word, the commission's publicity machine churned out fact sheets about Madame Lafayette's gift of money to the new nation; about French, Polish, German, Swedish, Irish, and Jewish "Colonial Patriots"; about Von Steuben; and about Rochambeau's amazement at the patriotism of foreign volunteers.[70] Even in his retirement at Mount Vernon, readers of the morning papers learned, George Washington still relied on the assistance of foreign powers: thanks to gifts from abroad, he planted Siberian and South African strains of wheat, for example, and bred Spanish jackasses. And he had first been called the Father of His Country—"Der Landes Vater"—in a Pennsylvania Dutch almanac printed in Lancaster in 1779.[71] In all these stories Washington played a highly specific role:

George Washington was the magnet who drew all those brave men to him. George Washington was a man above all others who inspired confidence and devotion among those ragged, hungry, and suffering troops who struggled . . . forward under his leadership. We Americans today still have our differences in origin and in character. We still struggle for various ideals and principles, but we can all rally today under the leadership of George Washington, as did those splendid Americans 150 years ago. In honoring the memory of George Washington there can be no division and no dispute.[72]

By drawing a parallel between the Revolutionary epoch and his own time, Bloom simply assimilated those fractious minorities who differed from DAR members in their origins and were widely supposed to differ from Old Americans in character and political beliefs as well. According to the George Washington Bicentennial Commission, *all* Americans made up that "we" born in a crisis of hardship and hunger that, in the telling at least, seemed a lot like the Great Depression—

a derevolutionized Revolution. Whereas Washington's methods of resolving that historical crisis were not specified, both national unity and ultimate triumph were attributed to his symbolic presence. Without much subtlety, then, Bloom was suggesting that Washington provided the ideal of leadership demanded by the present circumstances. His analysis of Washingtonian leadership in fact mirrored President Hoover's thinking on the nature and value of historical heroes.

The Lessons of 1932

Herbert Hoover's views on the qualities essential to the Washington persona around which the nation might rally once again were spelled out for the Bicentennial Commission in two documents quoted, paraphrased, and praised repeatedly by Sol Bloom. The first of these, dated November 19, 1930, was the president's foreword to a special bicentennial edition (in twenty-five volumes) of the writings of Washington compiled by John Fitzpatrick, late of the Library of Congress, a commission historian and a contributor to Bloom's popularized series of "Honor to George Washington" pamphlets. Hoover's reading of the diaries and letters was matter-of-fact but highly self-referential:

The materials on his activity as a man of affairs, which are brought into relief, bring home to the reader the picture of Washington as a landowner, land developer, and land cultivator. A much neglected side of his character is Washington as an engineer. His countrymen have not realized how modern he was in his engineering operations—as a reclaimer of the Dismal Swamp; as advisor and engineer of the Potomac and James River Canal; as the first advocate of a combined highway and waterway from the Atlantic Coast to the Ohio River; as a bank director; as an inventor; as one of the earliest Americans to recognize the possibilities of power transportation by water; and the first to suggest that air navigation might be very useful to the people of the United States.[73]

In this stage in the maturation of his thinking about Washington, Hoover was still Ernest Prussing's apprentice, singling out engineering and business data pertinent to his own career and to an understanding of modern life justified by the interests of the first Good Businessman. Representative Bertrand H. Snell, standing beneath a huge George Washington banner at the 1932 Republican convention, would say pretty much the same thing about the incumbent, "the engineer President of the United States [who] is solving, and will solve, stupendous and vexatious problems, as did out first engineer President, for the benefit of our mankind."[74] In his agrarian references Hoover also recalled the rural Washington of his 1928 campaign.[75] If anything set Herbert Hoover apart from his more lyrical publicists, it was the dryness and businesslike tone of his report.

On February 22, 1932, something much more dramatic was called for. From the outset, the Bicentennial Commission had planned to kick off its allotted nine months of intense tribute with a presidential address to a joint session of Congress. The Washington's Birthday message was to be broadcast nationally; after the speech, as the Marine Band played "America," a mass singing of the anthem in front of every radio set in the land was urged upon auditors.[76] Hoover's speech for that important day borrowed whatever eloquence it achieved from a long, prefatory quotation from Daniel Webster's famous centenary oration of 1832. Since the "masters of art and poetry" had eulogized Washington for a hundred years, "to what they have said I attempt to make no addition," Hoover announced. Besides, the bicentennial could succeed without art or artifice; what the occasion did demand, he said, was "time . . . to recall for our own guidance" the practical lessons of Washington's life and the unique strengths of the republic he founded.[77]

11.25
A Washington party favor, copyrighted in 1926 by the Beistle Company, reflects the home- and school-oriented pageantry of the observances.

In 1932, just what those lessons were depended on the age, temperament, and media-resistance of the pupil. The children of the bicentennial year learned that cherry tarts were eaten on Washington's Birthday and that appropriate decorations featured hatchets and tricolored bunting (Figure 11.25). More knowing kids—or their elders, who wrote school exercises to teach the young about heroes—were amused by the debunkers and the fanatical Washington worshippers alike. A considerable body of bicentennial literature prepared for youngsters thus endorses the traditional iconography the bureaucrats condemned while maintaining a healthy skepticism about the blandishments of revisionists:

> Let others echo Rupert Hughes
>   And mix up motes and beams—
> The anecdotes that I peruse
>   Were told by Parson Weems.
> Above iconoclastic views
>   That little hatchet gleams!
> "I cannot tell a lie," I choose
>   The Washington of Weems.[78]

Readers of the humor page in the *Saturday Evening Post,* meanwhile, were learning a new version of the old story:

A frock-coated secretary touched young Washington on the arm.
"The tree is ready, Master George."
The boy yawned. "Are the cameramen here?"
"Seven of them from the leading newsreel companies, Sir, and there are also nine press photographers."
"And the microphone for the sound films? . . . All right, I'll go on out. Tell dad to be ready for his cue. . . . I cannot tell a lie, father," he enunciated. "I

did it with a Model A-12 superforged, American-manufactured CHOPZ KWIK hatchet—The Hatchet That is Making History."[79]

Little girls whose mothers took the *Woman's Home Companion* learned how to embroider hankies with a bunch of red cherries in the outline stitch.[80] In the same magazine, if they were avid readers of fine print, their mommies could learn something of "Our Heritage from Washington" from James Truslow Adams, who quoted President Hoover on his nobility of character but stated as unremarkable fact that "his heart had long been hopelessly pledged to the beautiful Sally Fairfax whom he first met as the wife of one of his best friends."[81] Women who preferred cuisine to fine character could learn just how Martha Washington made "Sally Lunn" for George's breakfast. And women who preferred looking at pictures could learn from a photographic spread in the same issue that Washington had slept in a variety of remarkably scenic spots.[82]

On balance, the history lessons imparted by that segment of the publishing industry catering to women concerned one of two issues: better household management or management of affairs of the heart. *Good Housekeeping* observed the Washington bicentennial with a feature on certain inexpensive but "charming" colonial homes that gave the impression of spaciousness in rooms of Lilliputian dimensions. The "Forgotten Facts About Washington" disclosed by the *Ladies' Home Journal* in honor of the patriotic anniversary were mainly amorous. "That his proposal of marriage was refused by several women has been established," wrote the female author of the article with a hint of pride in the power of her colonial sisters. "Mary Philipse, belle of New York, was one of these—although the debunkers are now trying to destroy this legend" (Figure 11.26).[83]

For those determined to learn even on that subject, steamy historical novels were also available. There was Bernie Babcock's *Heart of George Washington: A Simple Story of Great Love,* a torrid retelling of the Sally Fairfax story dedicated to the "thirty-first president of the United States" on the warrant that Hoover, like Washington, was an engineer, and that "each man, in his own way, had to learn that in affairs of love and labor, Human Nature must give way to Destiny" (Figure 11.27).[84] And there was Ralph Bradford's *White Way,* set on Christmas Eve, 1783, when Washington returns home after the war still sick with love for the absent Sally, and sadly remembers her every smile and word.[85]

In order to engage Americans in the celebration at a basic emotional level, the Bicentennial Commission had taken over Mother's Day, "with all its tender significance to each individual," for consideration of a little boy named George who once loved his mother.[86] For that reason, the mothers and children of 1932 stood to learn a great deal more

11.26
Norman Rockwell, *When Washington Failed,* a 1932 rendition of the Philipse courtship for the *Ladies' Home Journal*; this page was clipped, colored, and framed by a reader.

11.27
A bicentennial novel, with the official profile on the cover

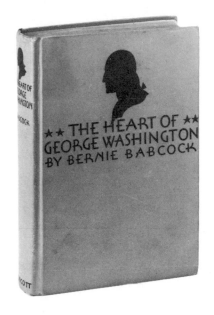

11.28
George Washington memorial knife,
1932: "Always Obey Your Superiors"

than was strictly provable about Mary Ball Washington. A "pageant-play" for youngsters called *The Redbud Tree,* published under the auspices of the commission and recommended for the holiday, recounted one of the several legends woven about Washington's various partings from his mother. At fourteen, according to the script, George determined to seek his fortune as a midshipman in the British navy: "George Washington wanted to go to sea. But his mother, Mary Ball Washington, didn't want him to go. . . . Why, if she had allowed him to go to sea he would never have become the great man we know of today."[87]

He minded his weeping mother, of course, and as a reward she gave him a little knife bearing on the blade the inscription "Always Obey Your Superiors." To the son of a saintly mother, God—and not the Continental Congress—was the ultimate superior, and in 1932 such quasi-religious, quasi-patriotic relics played a prominent role in the souvenir market. Inspired by the commission's pamphlet on Washington's "Fraternal Life," with its special section on Freemasonry, the George Washington National Masonic Association issued replicas of Mary's gift for distribution to members of their order.[88]

A wide-awake firm in St. Paul copyrighted the design for an otherwise ordinary penknife (Figure 11.28), its celluloid handle embossed with the message: "1732–1932 / A knife like this George Washington received from his mother on the pledge to 'Always Obey Your Superiors.' / That pledge and a knife saved the nation at Valley Forge," when Washington fingered the memento in his darkest hour, obeyed his charge from heaven, and attacked (or so ran another legend revived in 1932 over the protests of Washington's official keepers). On the opposite side of the handle, a space was reserved for a suitable corporate message. In 1932 the Brainerd Foundry Company of Brainerd, Minnesota, was among the many firms sending season's greetings to their customers with this timely and sentimental token of esteem.

The nation's dads, leafing through their fat Sunday papers, were liable to notice pictures of the sculptor Gutzon Borglum dangling from the face of Mount Rushmore out in South Dakota, a mountain that had lately begun to resemble the face of George Washington. Calvin Coolidge had blessed the enterprise in 1927, when the artist still had hopes of finishing the first of the four massive heads by 1930.[89] The Crash slowed things down, however, and for his bicentennial Washington was still not quite done. There was probably a lesson about hubris and human folly in the story of the unfinished Washington bust on Mount Rushmore; those were subjects churchgoers learned all about in a special George Washington sermon preached by Father Fulton J. Sheen to the Catholics of Washington, D.C. Calling the Revolution "America's Calvary" and likening George Washington to the suffering Jesus—among the churchly, the prayer in the snow inevitably called to mind Christ's prayer in the garden of Gethsemane—the spellbinding young priest taught his flock that by virtue of the purifying sacrifices of the Depression, the nation was ready to become "not only the economic, but the moral leader of the world."[90]

President Hoover drew quite a different moral from his Washington's Birthday homily. The nation was durable and progressive: "What other great, purely human institution, devised in the era of the stagecoach and the candle, has so marvelously grown and survived into the epoch of the steam engine, the airplane, the incandescent lamp, the wireless telephone, and the battleship?" he asked with a reminiscent nod to the Edison Jubilee and the technological optimism of 1929.

As for the qualities in Washington that made the nation great, "they were not spectacular" ones. The hero's greatest assets were "the strategy of attrition, the patient endurance of adversity, steadfast purpose unbent by defeat. The American shrine most associated with Washington," Hoover concluded, "is Valley Forge, and Valley Forge was not a place of victory—except the victory of Washington's fortitude triumphant above the weakness and discouragement of lesser men. Washington had courage without excitement, determination without passion."[91]

Tentatively introduced in Hoover's Memorial Day speech of the previous year, the beleaguered Washington of Valley Forge—as distinct from the enterprising young farmer or the courtly gentleman of Mount Vernon—was a hero, a hero for a crisis. Washington's life, or so the president asserted, taught that bad times demanded passionless and stoical forbearance; leadership under such conditions was a matter of enduring the barks of critics and the trials of adversity. The bicentennial Washington was, therefore, a reflection of Hoover's own subdued style of presidential leadership in a worsening depression. The address constantly refers to a Washington beset by catastrophe and by the numerous "early crises of the Republic." But throughout the text, the chosen examples of Washington's supreme accomplishment in the face of difficulty have a contemporary resonance.

Hoover's Washington, for instance, "established the nonexistent credit of an insolvent infant nation." He kept order and so built a nation that was "not a momentary flash of impulse in a people rebellious . . . destined to fade into a dictatorship, and the chaos so often born of revolutions." Washington was, in short, no rebel, no radical, no innovator. He was a successful business leader of magnetic, self-abnegating calm. His legacy was a stable "economic system based upon the largest degree of freedom and stimulation to initiative and enterprise which can be permitted and still maintain the ideal of equality of opportunity among men."[92]

To instill that economic and political vision in the "minds and hearts of the people," the media engineers of the bicentennial celebration needed only a supply of simple, straightforward facts. "We need," said Hoover, "no attempt at a canonization of George Washington." The worshipful myths of Parson Weems detracted from knowing him as a real man (like the sitting president, perhaps) who "never lost faith in our people." And although he despised the nineteenth-century myth-makers, Hoover did not think highly of the factual research of the twentieth-century debunkers. Modern historians had defiled the old, mythical image but substituted instead a highly colored portrait of a mendacious businessman—and a rake. Neither picture squared with Hoover's understanding of the inspirational Good Businessman, past and present. In the sharpest passage of his speech, Hoover declared himself out of "patience with those who undertake the irrational humanizing of Washington. . . . He had, indeed [,] the fine qualities of friendliness, of sociableness, of humanness, of simple hospitality; but we have no need to lower our vision from the unique qualities of greatness, or to seek to depreciate the unparalleled accomplishments of the man who dominated and gave birth to the being of a great nation."[93]

Hoover's Washington's Birthday address of 1932 offered a precise blueprint for the construction of a resolute leader whose stoicism would inspire a business culture to endure its latest crisis. History guaranteed the eventual triumph of the enterprise: Washington's success proved that a second Washington who matched his every virtue would also prevail in his name.

As the Marine Band prepared to strike up the chorus of "America," it was fitting that the Great Engineer concluded his speech with a tribute to a feat of engineering and sound construction. Herbert Hoover described the view from his window, the same prospect Calvin Coolidge once invoked to quash the debunkers and the humanizers:

From the room where I conduct my high office I hourly see the monument which Washington's proud and grateful countrymen have raised to his memory. It stand foursquare to the world, its base rooted steadfast in the solid substance of American soil. Its peak rises toward the heavens with matchless serenity and calm. . . . Beyond any other monument built by the hand of man out of clay and stone, this shaft is a thing of the spirit. . . . It is a pledge in the sight of all mankind, given by Washington's countrymen, to carry forward the continuing fulfillment of his vision of America.[94]

The metaphor described the dematerialized but stable edifice of salient fact that Sol Bloom, the public relations engineer, had been engaged to build to exact and demanding specifications.

The Bicentennial's Official Historians

Since the Bicentennial Commission had no rooted monument to solidify the celebration, and since its mission was to bring the still-living inspiration of Washington into the people's own environment, fact was Bloom's principal instrument of persuasion. His was to be a paper monument, an edifice of words and images fashioned out of radio shows beamed from atop the Washington Monument, the Eastman Kodak film, the fiction in the magazines, the photographs of costume parties in Tokyo, and press releases on topics ranging from Count Pulaski to a history of active American corporations founded during Washington's lifetime.[95] A coherent structure of fact held these varied endeavors together. And the sanctioned facts were all set forth in fifteen booklets published and distributed by bicentennial headquarters; these tracts made up the "Honor to George Washington" series.

The pamphlets were edited by Albert Bushnell Hart, professor emeritus of Harvard College and official historian of the commission from 1926 onward. Hart was a conservative scholar; debunking reportedly enraged him and he regarded Charles Beard's *Economic Interpretation of the Constitution* as little short of indecent.[96] Nor did he have much use for stories of "the boy who chopped down the cherry tree."[97] Hart had no objection to historical hucksterism, however. His nephew, Laurance C. Hart, made his living as a George Washington impersonator.[98]

In 1930 the professor (who sometimes dressed up in a Continental uniform himself) had served as the adviser to the Newburyport, Massachusetts, Tercentenary Committee, then under investigation by Lloyd Warner and the pioneer sociologists of the "Yankee City" project. According to Warner, Professor Hart persuaded the leaders of Yankee City to use their festival as a means of "establishing understanding among . . . citizens of diverse racial origins and points of view and demonstrat[ing] their relationships and importance to community progress."[99] This notion is nowhere in evidence in Hoover's state papers, but the idea is repeated constantly in similar language in Bicentennial Commission press releases. It is reasonable to conclude, then, that Albert Hart, Sol Bloom's private tutor in Washington history, was the moving force behind Bloom's considerable effort to ensure ethnic participation in the Washington observances.

He may also have had something to do with Bloom's fixation on facts. In his advisory capacity with the Newburyport committee, Hart Massachusetts had made sure that George Washington figured prominently in the ceremonies. But he was not willing to tolerate cherry trees and storm-tossed boats. Instead, Hart ascertained that exacting standards of factual accuracy were applied to the main event, a Washington parade said to be a precise recreation of the famous presidential tour through New England, with authentic costumes for as the actors and genuine period settings aboard the floats. In Hart's role as bicentennial historian, too, his watchword was fact.

Of the fifteen historical brochures issued under his direction, three were written by Professor Hart himself; Fitzpatrick, Bloom, and the recently deposed Colonel Grant also contributed texts.[100] Sol Bloom covered "Washington the Business Man." Grant dealt with "Washington as Engineer and City Builder." Hart wrote on "Washington as President," compiled a group of "Tributes to Washington" from the famous orators and writers of the past, and reserved for himself one of the three major topics of the series—"Washington the Man of Mind."

Concerned with the subject of education, this pamphlet was a crucial entry because the "Honor to Washington" project was the backbone of the commission's informational mission and of its myriad curricula for grade schools, academies, colleges, clubs, lodges (Professor Hart belonged to almost as many of those as Sol Bloom did), and independent-study courses. The *Handbook of the George Washington Appreciation Course for Teachers and Students* was keyed to the pamphlets and to a parallel sequence of a dozen "George Washington Programs" that translated the texts into exercises, such as map-reading, art appreciation, and keeping a running count of places where Washington might actually have slept.[101]

The quality of Washington's own education and the proper educational role of heroes in the training of young Americans had both been keenly debated for several years. The *Handbook* suggested that even when reference books were in short supply, instructors and pupils would find Washington an ideal theme for classroom discussion because, "as Calvin Coolidge says, 'the subject of Washington never seems to be exhausted.'"[102] Speaking on behalf of the bicentennial planners, William John Cooper, the U.S. commissioner of education, labeled the study of Washington imperative for modern youngsters because "this country is passing through a serious crisis. . . . If our country is to survive this economic and social storm, we must have some careful thinking and patriotic activity." Hence teachers of Washington courses had an important role to play if the nation was "to discover the kind of leadership which successful administration of our democracy demands."

But there were dangers in the ample stock of misinformation that made classroom discussion deceptively easy, said Cooper. To instill proper appreciation of the true lesson of leadership, "Washington and his generals must be stripped of all the myth and legend which have been accumulated for nearly two centuries and their sterling human qualities allowed to appear." Otherwise, the commissioner warned, the bicentennial Washington might turn out to be the "'Great Father' of a race of dependents" and "a generation of weaklings."[103]

Misinformation about Washington's own education was rife and was regarded as especially pernicious to modern schoolchildren in search of heroes because the old stories and the new exposés both presented Washington as an indifferent student. Parson Weems delighted in recounting George's brush with learning Latin under the tutelage of a semiliterate master. The humanizers cited as a "human quality" of Washington his chronic inability to spell. Albert Bushnell Hart's pamphlet set out to reveal the errors of Weems and "this so-called modern school of Washington biography" and to correct mistakes by drawing a fine distinction between a practical and an academic education.

Washington was the product of a practical self-education. And autodidacticism, according to Hart's fuzzy reasoning on the subject, had somehow made him more cheerful and better-looking than the run-of-the-mill scholar: "Some modern so-called biographers attempt to make out that Washington was a slow young man, rather hardheaded, but gloomy, disappointed, discouraged, and unhappy because he was not getting on well [in school]. On the contrary, he was the liveliest, handsomest, most successful young man in Virginia."[104]

Hart opposed the humanizers but urged his readers to reject the mythical Washington also: once upon a time, people had mistaken Weems's "artificial figure" for the genuine article, but "nowadays," or so imagined the Harvard historian who didn't read the *Saturday Evening Post* and *Good Housekeeping,* "people pay [it] little regard." The choice between virtue established by lies and heroism compromised by illusory facts was not an easy one to make. In the tussle between myth and fact characteristic of bicentennial history, Professor Hart found himself caught in the middle without a great deal to say and without much fresh evidence to bolster any argument. Indeed, his two principal acknowledged sources were Coolidge's Washington Birthday addresses of 1926 and 1927, the former to Congress and the latter to the National Education Association. In order to create a Washington almost as perfect as the parson's, yet one acceptable to clear-eyed students of the modern day, Hart was forced to resort to windy assertions having little bearing on George Washington's education, practical or otherwise.

According to Hart's undocumented flight of fancy, Washington somehow taught himself something that fitted him for the two significant roles he played in history. Projected back upon the eighteenth century, the careers of modern American celebrities of industry and public affairs demonstrated, rhetorically at least, that Washington was a professional engineer and a good organizer—that he was a businessman capable of directing vast enterprises:

He was the first professional engineer . . . and added the suggestion, revived by President Hoover, that there should be a system of canals connecting the

Great Lakes with the Ohio River. . . . Washington was a founder, an organizer. He could have set up a university, or a social science association or an engineer's club or a Rockefeller foundation. He had within himself that incomprehensible power which enabled him to run anything from a flour mill to the United States of America. . . . If George Washington were alive today, he would be the president of a locomotive works, or a railroad, or steel works. . . . The educated man is the man who knows how to do things that have never been done before. . . . Henry Ford, once a laborer, developed into what a wit calls an "automobillionaire," [and] is an educated man.[105]

In this curious inversion of historical reasoning, Professor Hart seemed to be urging students to lay aside their Washington appreciation courses and head instead for the idle factories in hopes of becoming new Henry Fords, or so many George Washingtons in modern attire. It amounted to much the same thing!

It was Albert Bushnell Hart's kind of present-minded perspective that Grant Wood parodied in his several historical canvases of the 1930s. *Parson Weems's Fable* (Figure 11.24) and *The Midnight Ride of Paul Revere* (Figure 11.29) both tell stories out of the American past. But the viewer is constantly being reminded that these tired old yarns are being respun in modern, not historical, times. In Wood's version of Longfellow's ditty of Lexington and Concord, for example, the houses of colonial New England are lit up by glaring electric bulbs and linked by a smooth concrete highway, vintage 1931. According to Grant Wood, Parson Weems is a colonial showman, a clerical Sol

11.29
Grant Wood, *The Midnight Ride of Paul Revere,* 1931

Bloom who pulls aside a velvet stage curtain to reveal his patently bogus historical pageant of the dreadful little Georgie with the sixty-four-year-old, picture-in-a-million-classrooms face. The parson's glance at the viewer shows that he knows that we know the hoary old tale for what it is: a pious fiction for small fry, a national fairy tale, akin to Longfellow's harmless ditty about the exploits of Paul Revere.

Viewer and painter and painted protagonists: in a Wood picture, all share a mild joke especially contrived for grown-ups done with schoolrooms and poetry about the bravery and honesty of America's forebears. But the grown-ups of the period were also being reeducated by Professor Hart and Congressman Bloom. The barrage of radio addresses and planted news stories and the torrents of free pamphlets that emerged from the headquarters of the United States George Washington Bicentennial Commission all aimed to show that the "real" Washington was a far more useful exemplar to a stricken nation than the insufferable boy prig of the tales. So Grant Wood's Parson Weems emerged from Bloom's question-and-answer guidebook to Washington hagiography as a well-meaning and vaguely amusing fraud:

Q. Who originated the Washington cherry tree story?

A. It was originated by the Reverend Mason Locke Weems, in his *Life of Washington*. It is interesting to note that this yarn did not appear in the first few editions, but was added in a later edition. . . . No evidence to prove this story has been found. In writing this work, Weems gave full play to his imagination, without very much regard for historical facts, even acknowledging that he did this for moral purposes.[106]

In the last analysis, then, *Parson Weems's Fable* lampooned hypocrites and official historical hypocrisy, Weems and Bloom, and generations of classroom drills in civil morality. It even mocked Iowa and Iowa's own Grant Wood, insofar as the idyllic manse before which the epic-making revelation is made—"Pa, you know I can't tell a lie. I did cut it with my little hatchet!"—is, with a nod to the Wakefield reconstruction and *The Birthplace of Herbert Hoover*, the artist's own newly purchased and fashionably old-fashioned house in Iowa City. By incorporating his own neocolonial house into the picture, the painter inserts himself into a witty meditation on truthtelling wherein the artist paints a liar introducing the viewer to a concocted scene that has been further falsified by the combined artistic contrivance of Father Time, Grant Wood, and Gilbert Stuart. Art is the lie that reveals the truth about history and about those who would reject sweet and "historic bits of American folklore" in favor of the collected platitudes of Calvin Coolidge.[107]

Albert Bushnell Hart had quoted Coolidge as a reputable authority on Washington. In "Washington the Business Man," Sol Bloom cited the presiding authorities of New Era history, Ernest Prussing and

Halsted L. Ritter. Ritter's *Washington as a Business Man,* with a windy introduction by Professor Hart, appeared in 1931; it was the business community's rejoinder to Woodward. But unlike the pamphlet by Hart, this book was amply researched and documented with quotes from Woodrow Wilson, Stuart Chase, *Middletown,* and obscure studies of Washington's management of his farms, as well as obligatory references to the collected speeches of Calvin Coolidge. Even Charles Beard was used to advantage. And although Ritter's sunny assumptions about the way America worked, was working, and would work might have had a hollow ring in 1931, he asserted them boldly enough.

"Business," Ritter declared, "is the obsession of the North American": the businessman had ousted the priest and the scholar from the position of setting contemporary "standards of ethics and behavior." In "this age of big business in which men are constantly judged by their power to carry on large enterprises . . . and to create immense plants employing large numbers of men," Ritter proposed to evaluate Washington according to such business standards in order to ascertain if the Father of His Country really was, as Woodward had argued, a grasping buffoon.[108]

Modern biographers had been too preoccupied with colorful incidents, love stories, and other appealing moments to risk such a "practical, unromantic" reckoning, he reasoned, but Ritter dared to be deadly dull. So he took up Washington's ledgers, his performance as president-administrator, and his agricultural balance sheets with meticulous deliberation—and arrived at a foreordained conclusion: "George Washington was in reality a great businessman. He is the prototype of the modern man of business." The facts proved the case. Washington's records revealed a self-made man of affairs. The history of his plantation showed that "he lifted farming into agriculture, and agriculture into an industry." Furthermore, his state papers disclosed that George Washington efficiently managed a government that was and "is, in fact, a great business enterprise."[109]

Colonial business was not entirely without romance, either—the romance of heroic virtue. Ritter believed that somewhat colorless traits of personality such as Washington's habitual efficiency and acumen were best dramatized not by a recitation of colorful parables and fables about the hero, but rather by sober consideration of "the ideals of American business, and the successful use of fortitude, intelligence, patience, and will power in their realization." Will power, for example, enabled Washington to "establish good rules, and a regular system . . . , the life and soul of any kind of business." All the dusty facts and figures pointed toward a fresh appreciaiton of the human dimensions of the Good Businessman. Washington "exemplified the patriotism and human service of wealth—demonstrated the worth of business ideals. The making of money did not smother his soul. Ambition was held in leash. . . . His true biography must portray the union of a social conscience with a successful business career. His type is still the standard in the United States of America."[110]

Sol Bloom had little to add to Ritter's encomium to business except the useful notation that, since "the modern era of commerce and manufacturing was beginning" during the lifetime of Washington, it was entirely fair to appraise him in modern terms. With his customary energy, Bloom marshaled a battery of facts his predecessors had missed: Washington's stock portfolio, his theories of sound currency, his relations with "the canny merchant classes of New England," and his predictions about the commercial potential of Detroit.[111] But with his sensitive nose for public relations, Bloom also sniffed out a troublesome fact Ritter and Hart had somehow overlooked: George Washington the businessman was rapidly becoming a daunting figure, elevated on a modern pedestal as lofty as his former podium of Weemsian priggishness.

The Twilight of the Heroic Tycoon

Incessant comparisons to the likes of Ford and Rockefeller placed Washington in a class remote from ordinary experience. It was all well and good to ballyhoo the self-made man when a schoolboy could readily find a job working in a Ford plant or guiding tourists through the Wayside Inn. In 1932, however, such advice seemed calculated to repel wise youngsters and enrage their elders. As a business celebrity, Washington also labored under the disadvantage of the once-omniscient contemporary tycoon whose nostrums had been blasted by the Depression. Business celebrities were in short supply. Because popular idols magnified the aspirations of their devotees and illustrated ways in which anybody could participate in the dream of endless prosperity, when the dream became a nagging nightmare, the business hero ceased to be a soothing ideal. He seemed instead inhuman, bloodless, remote, and indifferent to the painful realities of daily life.

For all their disclaimers, Hart and Ritter had been humanizers: they wanted to replace the flawed humanity of Woodward's Captain of Industry with the sterling humanity of the Good Businessman. In more favorable economic circumstances, they might even have succeeded. In 1932, the "Honor" series took up the cause of a human, even lovable, Washington in business. Therein, Washington's humanity was established by his small and average virtues; he was honest and thrifty, and he acted prudently after all the facts were in. He troubled himself with humble details of seed corn and fish nets. His social conscience was manifest in his dealings with his neighbors. In Bloom's booklet, at any rate, these were not the attributes of a Henry Ford but the unheralded merits of the average small businessman of Main Street,

11.30
Early planners envisioned Washington as the chief symbol of the 1939 World's Fair; this commemorative plate stresses the sesquicentennial of his inauguration in a way that the fair did not.

USA, the mainstay of the local Rotary: "One of the evidences of modern business organization is the growth of service clubs and other associations of business men for mutual acquaintance and the furthering of common ends. Despite the massiveness of his character, Washington was a natural 'joiner.'"[112] Washington's humanity was such that it sanctified even the traveling salesman of doubtful reputation:

If Washington possessed no sample case, he went through all the manoeuvers of the proficient traveling man of nowadays. He made journeys to meetings of the boards of which he was a member. . . . He also had the official traveling man's intimate knowledge of the roads, the inns, the hospitable houses, and the food and drink of his country.[113]

In the interest of humanizing, Bloom was further prepared to permit Washington—that colonial Duncan Hines—an occasional tipple in a hotel bar. And it was this swell guy with the invisible sample case that Bloom was determined to propel into the hearts of lodge brothers, clubmen, and conventioneers. The Kiwanis basked in his assurance that "if George Washingtopn were alive today . . . he would be proud to be a member of such a splendid group as is assembled here."[114] Addressing the country at large on the Fourth of July over an NBC hookup, Bloom gave his hero yet another meeting to attend: Washington, of rural Virginia, if he were to return to earth today, would undoubtedly join the ranks of the American Farm Bureau Federation.[115]

As Sol Bloom took to the rubber-chicken circuit with his amiable hero, a group of worried businessmen, gathered for luncheon in New York City, fretted about their dismal profit-and-loss figures for the past three years. Herbert Hoover's chances of reelection looked dismal, too, and what the ouster of the party of business would mean for Wall Street, the city's hotels, the department stores, and the building trades could only be imagined with horror.

Out west, Chicago had taken matters in hand: the Century of Progress would open soon and tourism was expected to revitalize the Loop. Could an exposition lift New York out of the economic doldrums? And the occasion? Well, 1939 was going to be some sort of historic year. It marked the 150th anniversary of Washington's inauguration, and George Washington was still big box office. Picture it! A sixty-five-foot statue of George Washington, gleaming white in the sun, welcoming huge crowds to—how about a world's fair in honor of George, out at the old city dump on Flushing Meadow? (Figure 11.30).

A George Washington
for All Occasions

12 ✸ ✸ ✸ ✸ ✸ ✸ ✸ ✸ ✸ ✸ ✸ ✸ ✸ ✸ ✸ ✸

From the 1939 World's Fair
to Superbowl XIX

History and the Common Man

The 1930s were an epoch of history: after a decade of Babbittry, boom, and business punctuated by the sullen yowls of the Young Intellectuals who bemoaned a national lack of tradition—the rootless shallows of the native "commercial mind"—America found her heritage again.[1] Buffeted by the cyclone of Depression, "driven . . . by a pressing need to find answers to the riddles of today," America salvaged and clung to the "usable past." "We need to know," wrote the novelist John Dos Passos, "what kind of firm ground other men, belonging to generations before us, have found to stand on."[2]

Debunking national heroes went out of vogue. Wisecracking cynicism about Puritans and presidents no longer seemed so smart. As the literary historian and critic Alfred Kazin put it in 1939, "Where the generation of the twenties wanted to revenge themselves on their fathers, the generation of the thirties needed the comfort of their grandfathers."[3] The American past offered a firm footing in the midst of social and economic chaos. History tendered comfort and solace, and it provided a model for building a utopian future.[4]

And so the marble columns of the National Archives rose on Federal Triangle near the White House. The new building was a monument to the documents that certified America's heritage. In the public lobby on the main floor, a pair of lackluster murals by Barry Faulkner reminded aspiring historians of the importance of the Declaration of Independence and the Constitution. In the clot of lookalike colonials of solemn demeanor assembled by the artist to signify the contributions of the Founding Fathers, a Stuartian George Washington was the only figure who could be recognized with ease.[5]

Over the course of the next decade, the Roosevelt administration would send other mural painters into hundreds of post offices, into thousands of high schools and libraries from Maine to California, to

12.1
Victor Arnautoff, detail of fresco in the George Washington High School, San Francisco, painted in 1935 under the auspices of the WPA's Federal Art Project

picture for local residents their own unique chapters in America's "usable past" (Figure 12.1). Usually that hometown chronicle did not involve scenes from the life and times of George Washington or other famous Americans. Instead, the pictures showed the historic moment when a given town was planted and its future secured by energetic, capable pioneers, made in the image and likeness of their modern-day descendants. People like these, or so the iconography of New Deal murals implied, were not liable to succumb to a depression.[6]

All Depression history had a populist bent. Because Andrew Jackson had championed the interests of ordinary people, Franklin D. Roosevelt reviewed his second inaugural parade from a scale replica of the Hermitage perched on the White House lawn.[7] For similar reasons, raw-boned Abe Lincoln loved and lost Ann Rutledge on Broadway and on the silver screens of Main Streets everywhere.[8] Jackson and Lincoln were common men writ larger than life in the heyday of the common man; they reminded America that greatness often comes in plain wrappers and prevails against great odds.

Franklin Roosevelt also made it a point to appear at Mount Rushmore for the unveiling of Thomas Jefferson's head.[9] The New Deal put Monticello on the nickel and built the Jefferson Memorial temple on the Tidal Basin to honor that champion of the American yeoman-farmer. The Sage of Monticello, to be sure, bore more than a passing resemblance to the Squire of Hyde Park. Clever men who, in the words of Stephen Vincent Benét's sprightly verse, could turn "From buying empires / To planting 'taters, / From Declarations / To Trick dumb-waiters" were the national stock in trade.[10]

But the decade did not belong exclusively to the clever, the compassionate, and the companionably common. Colonial wigs and courtliness were also in evidence. In addition to his *Young Mr. Lincoln* of 1939, for example, director John Ford released *Drums Along the Mohawk*, a Revolutionary costume saga based on the Walter Edmonds bestseller; trading in his stovepipe hat and side-whiskers for a pair of knee breeches, the durable Henry Fonda starred once again.[11] Fonda's colonial hero remained Lincolnesque, however—a lowly but quick-witted farmer not unlike the lovesick young Lincoln of the Federal Theatre Project's hit play, *Prologue to Glory.* In the summer of 1939 *Prologue to Glory* moved from Broadway to the fairgrounds at Flushing Meadow on the outskirts of New York City for the season. There, the populist hero of the Great Depression could be measured against the massive dignity of the mature George Washington whose 1789 inauguration in New York the 1939 World's Fair ostensibly commemorated.

Most students of the New York World's Fair of 1939 have disputed the sincerity of the organizers' dedication to the memory of the first president. The broad thoroughfare of Constitution Mall at the heart of the Theme Center was indeed dominated by James Earle Fraser's sixty-five-foot plaster effigy of Washington in his campaign cloak, "said to be the largest portrait statue of modern times." George Washington's name and face appeared elsewhere about the grounds, too. But the World's Fair historian Stanley Appelbaum correctly notes that "the only real George Washington memorabilia were relegated to a modest and remote pavilion in the Amusement Area, the Sons of the American Revolution Building."[12]

Those visual disparities reflect a real enough indecision among the visionaries charged with building a World of Tomorrow on a garbage dump in Queens. Records of preliminary meetings show that the planners of the fair were of two minds about Washington from the beginning. Among the artistic consultants to the Board of Design, for instance, the landscape architect Gilmore Clarke—he would later work on Constitution Mall—observed vehement opposition to "the representation of George Washington alone because . . . this important plaza could not be made sufficiently significant if it contained the figure of but one man."[13] Yet it was unthinkable that Washington should *not* be prominently represented in any public commemoration of 1789: in 1937 Congress had funded a full-blown United States Constitution Sesquicentennial Commission under the direction of the unsinkable Mr. Bloom, who had seized the opportunity to dispose of his remaining store of George Washington anecdotes and pictures in a fresh outpouring of publicity and patriotic pamphlets.

Bloom even published an atlas tracing the precise route of Washington's inaugural journey from Mount Vernon to Wall Street. Local pride was thereby hitched to a proper memorial of Washington's advent in New York. Since the year 1939 would both inaugurate the projected New York World's Fair and mark the birth of the new national government under law in New York City, Arthur Sulzberger of the *New York Times* agitated for incorporating Washington into a sculptural group representing the Constitutional freedoms of press, speech, religion, and assembly.[14]

But when the debates were over, Fraser's gigantic Washington stood alone, foiled off against the futuristic Trylon and Perisphere "on the principal axis of the Mall, . . . the most important and dominating figure in the composition" (Figure 12.2). At night, red, white, and blue lights played over his ashen corpulence, and fairgoers bound for the Billy Rose Aquacade, the General Motors Futurama, or Ford Motor's Road of Tomorrow were invited to pause and glance up at a sound-and-light show called "The Spirit of George Washington" projected on the side of the Perisphere.[15] According to the master plan of the Fair Corporation, the big white Washington who stood there stolidly amidst the multicolored lights and the portents of the future was playing an important dual role in the iconographic program of the Mall. He was "First President of the United States," of course, but he was also "first

12.2
James Earle Fraser's huge Washington statue, silhouetted against the Trylon and the Perisphere at the 1939 New York World's Fair

champion of the provisions set forth in the Constitution."[16] He was the first principle and the moving principle, iconic essence and symbolic force. Perhaps *that* explained why he had to be so large!

Big did not necessarily mean interesting, however. With his grim slit of a mouth by Gilbert Stuart and his body by Houdon out of J. Q. A. Ward, George Washington never ceased to strike the advisory panel as a dull subject. As William Delano told the sculptor Lee Lawrie when their attempt to ban the overscaled Father of His Country from the grounds came to grief, "Washington is Washington and there is very little that can be done to conventionalize him further."[17]

A Private Symbol in a Public Crisis

Delano's estimate was shared by many artists in the aftermath of the exhausting Washington bicentennial of 1932. Grant Wood, whose *Parson Weems's Fable* was directly inspired by plans for the colossus on Constitution Mall, had to resort to pictorial shock tactics in order to detach Washington from the plaster cloak of dullness in which he had been swaddled by James Earle Fraser. Florine Stettheimer, the eccentric New York painter who kept a bust of George Washington in a niche in her bedroom as a votive image of a nice, sexless male (and painted persons she especially liked wearing his lace stock), was also moved by the fair to reconsider the meaning of her hero.

Instead of Grant Wood's malevolent child with a wizened head, Stettheimer's Washington became a great, glowing face turning its unsettling glance upon a shrunken Manhattan. In its private significance, Florine Stettheimer's visionary image shared some common ground with the treatment of Washington by Frank Weston Moran, a Vermont hermit and untrained sculptor, whose bicentennial statue of 1932 with its swollen head and shriveled limbs is said to have borne an eerie resemblance to its maker (Figure 12.3).[18]

That same overheated atmosphere of personal emotion surrounds Alfred Maurer's *George Washington* of 1932 (Figure 12.4). The last major work completed before the artist hung himself in the doorway of his bedroom, the portrait was a protest of sorts against the George Washington bicentennial: abstractionist though he was—and derided for it by the ignorant—Maurer seemed determined to do better for old George than had the commission with its portfolios of anecdotal prints.[19]

The souvenirs and the bicentennial hucksterism offended him, too. "George Washington, symbol of our country's beginnings," Maurer fumed, "a commodity sold over the counter, like a pound of sausage!":

I will paint the true George Washington. I will paint him free from tainting and corrupting entanglements. I will paint him as big as the years from Valley Forge to now. I will paint him as the unvanquished. He knew the tears of

12.3
George Washington by folk artist Frank Moran, 1932

12.4
Alfred Maurer, *George Washington,* 1932

things. He suffered the bleeding feet of untrained warriors, the lack of guns and powder, treachery behind the lines, traitors at home, faint-hearted lieutenants. All that he overcame.

Not the wars of the soul hidden from all others. Not the wounds which are invisible. Not the conflict lost in silence. Not inner and private battles. Not these will I paint. I will paint man's hope, in the wars and victories of life.[20]

Yet there was also something inward and autobiographical about Maurer's identification with Washington. In a statement published in the picture pages of the *New York Post* during the worst year of the Depression, Maurer stressed the hero's conquest of adversity and then offered to trade the painting for $500 worth of clothes or a supply of canned goods. Maurer vowed not to paint Washington's "private battles" but depicted him nonetheless in the form of a psychological jigsaw puzzle, pieced together out of several portrait heads.

In a series of agonized works marking the much-reported one hundredth birthday of the elder Maurer, the artist had depicted himself and his far more famous father, Louis Maurer, "America's oldest living artist" and "last of the painters of the famous Currier and Ives lithographs," using the peculiar technique of the Washington picture. In honor of Louis Maurer's birthday, the Old Print Shop had exhibited sixty-seven prints by Currier and Ives tracing the progress of George Washington from cradle to grave. Human-interest reporters delighted in linking the Louis Maurer centenary to the Washington bicentenary: the anniversaries fell only a day apart and the old artist like the old pictures in the exhibition best. "He doesn't think much of modern art," the father was said to have remarked of his son's career, while posing beside his own portrait of Buffalo Bill.[21]

The Statue on Constitution Mall

Alfred Maurer's unhappy death over art and George Washington almost certainly went unnoticed by impresario Grover Whalen and the circle of New York merchants and financiers who, at the beginning of 1934, had already been meeting weekly for several months to "work out some form of promotion to attract new business and bring visitors to New York."[22] Nor were they much interested in George Washington. Instead, their eyes were fixed on the books of the Chicago businesses that claimed to have been saved from ruin by the Century of Progress Exposition, despite its own financial failure. Only in 1936, when Whalen required an act of Congress to deal with potential foreign exhibitors, did someone think to ask what the fair was to stand for. Only then was Washington pushed forward as a historical figurehead fronting a blatantly commercial venture:

The New York World's Fair will appropriately celebrate the one hundred and fiftieth anniversary of the launching of the Government of the United States under the Federal Constitution and the inauguration of George Washington as President in New York City, the first capital of the New Nation, on April 30, 1789. The New York World's Fair will be a fair for "everyone"—today, tomorrow and a century hence. It will present a clear, unified and comprehensive picture of the epochal achievements of a century and a half of modern civilization in the fields of art and literature, of science and industry, of government and the social services. The past will be depicted to give an understanding of the richer and more complicated present, with all its seriousness and gaiety, its varied colors,—rhythms and movements. By showing how the present has evolved out of the past—by giving a clear and orderly interpretation of our own age, the Fair will project the average man into the World of Tomorrow. . . . It will give a compelling impetus to that to which President Washington exhorted his inaugural audience: "The discernment and pursuit of the public good."[23]

In this preview of future world's fair press-agentry, the name of Washington serves to bracket a statement about modern accomplishments, tomorrow, and the average—the forgotten?—man. If the content of Whalen's statement is taken seriously, it also suggests that unlike the personalized Washingtons of Wood, Stettheimer, Moran, and Alfred Maurer, the monumental George Washington on Constitution Mall would serve as a highly depersonalized symbol for history and the passage of time. In contrast to the Washington of the several previous decades, the figure discussed in Whalen's prospectus was neither average nor particularly human; if he was "usable," it was in the same way that a tree or a rock is useful to the traveler on unfamiliar terrain. Washington was a usable landmark on the horizon of time, a distant spot in the American heritage from which progress could be measured by gazing backward.[24]

Presumably, it was only against a meager colonial past—against the nullity of an old-fashioned marbleized hero in lace cuffs and a tricorn hat—that the "richer and more complicated" present of 1939 could be endorsed and celebrated. The fair's planners therefore agreed with their Board of Design. Washington *was* Washington, but against all odds Grover Whalen had managed "to conventionalize him further," into statuesque inertia, even before James Earle Fraser set to work on his plaster president.

The World's Fair opened on April 30, 1939, with a speech by President Roosevelt. His address of greeting was a valiant effort to breathe life into the George Washington so recently petrified upon his pedestal. Washington was more than a patriotic pretext, more than a mute historical marker on the highway of time, Franklin Roosevelt insisted. The George Washington of 1939 was a symbol of "the destiny of the nation."[25]

Perhaps this latest Washington came from the pages of the *Official Guidebook* of the fair. In it, seeking to provide some explanation for

Fraser's neocolonial giant standing almost alone in the futurism of its setting, Grover Whalen strained to remake Washington into the father of the official fair slogan, "Building the World of Tomorrow":

The founders of the Fair were early persuaded that this anniversary was more than an opportunity to build a great exposition with a purely commemorative theme. To them the future, pregnant with high destiny, seemed even more meaningful than the past with all its fateful achievements. Washington and his colleagues had with courageous vision, charted a course out of dangerous seas; they planned better than even the most optimistic dared hope. Those who formulated the theme determined that emulation was the highest tribute—that the Fair should attempt to accomplish in our day what Washington and his contemporaries did in theirs. . . . The eyes of the Fair are on the future.[26]

The historian James Truslow Adams, reviewing "that fateful" inauguration day of 1789 "which the New York World's Fair will celebrate," put the case more succinctly in the *New York Times*: "After a century and a half of achievement we need not believe in the prophets of doom."[27] George Washington's heroic yesterdays guaranteed that the nation's glorious tomorrows were imminent.

Perhaps the leap of faith required to envision the wooden-faced Washington in his funny clothes as a symbol of the technological miracles of the future was just too great for most people to make. For all of Roosevelt's ceremonial attention to Lincoln and Jefferson, perhaps the New Deal was simply too dynamic, too concerned with leapfrogging out of the Depression into a prosperous tomorrow, to encourage genuine retrospection. Whatever the cause, the Constitution Sesquicentennial Commission, bent on disposing of its remaining stock of Washingtoniana, did no better at resuscitating fading interest in the first president than the fair did. Bloom's agency went out of business the day the fair opened, leaving it to the ceremonies inaugurating the World of Tomorrow to pay proper homage to the past.

Governor Lehman unveiled Fraser's George Washington on Constitution Mall, the first inauguration was reenacted at the foot of the statue, and the Chamber of Commerce and local patriotic societies sponsored concurrent exercises in New York City at the foot of the old Ward statue on Wall Street.[28] Out in Flushing, thanks to the excitement of opening day and a spirited performance in the role of Washington by cartoonist Denys Wortman, things went reasonably well. But in Manhattan, nobody turned out for the ceremony; the Sunday morning lethargy of the financial district went almost undisturbed. Despite a fresh batch of question-and-answer pamphlets, the planting of "Constitution trees," George Washington radio addresses rewritten from a fresh point of view, and a vigorous push to distribute replicas of the case or "Shrine of the Constitution" almost as widely as Stuart Washingtons, the sesquicentennial was something of a bust.

12.5
We the People, the official Constitution
Sesquicentennial poster designed by
Howard Chandler Christy, 1937

Admittedly, the Constitution was harder to publicize in everyday language and anecdotal imagery than Washington had been, but the document was only part of the problem. Howard Chandler Christy's *We the People,* the official sesquicentennial poster, pictured a gauze-draped female allegory wafting toward heaven on an eagle with Old Glory streaming out behind her (Figure 12.5). Down below sat a crowd of anonymous colonial signatories of whom George Washington alone could be identified with certainty, thanks to his official 1932 profile. Despite wide distribution, the poster was not a popular success; nor was Christy's Boy Scout picture (based on Rockwell's earlier bicentennial poster), which showed a Scout seeing a vision of George Washington and the other framers while he dreamed over a copy of the Constitution. Christy's 1939 mural for the east stairway of the House wing of the Capitol was his Congressional reward for serving as the sesquicentennial painter. Called *Scene at the Signing of the Constitution,* the mural contained few memorable passages except for the familiar figure of the presiding Washington, in a position not unlike that of a crooner at an invisible microphone (Figure 12.6). That likeness was as poorly received as the huge canvas itself.[29]

A popular illustrator, Christy did not fail because of a sudden fit of ineptness. His failure was, rather, symptomatic of the failure of all enterprises premised on Washingtoniana in the later 1930s. Before the magnitude of public lack of interest became apparent, the souvenir industry had already geared up for commemorations of the Declaration and the Constitution in Philadelphia. That city had seemed determined at first to rival New York's coming fair (the Mayor testily refused to

12.6
Howard Chandler Christy, *Scene at the Signing of the Constitution* for the U.S. Capitol, 1939

lend Whalen the Liberty Bell, even though Pennsylvania did, in the end, build a replica of Independence Hall at Flushing Meadow in 1939) but produced instead a water carnival and a number of localized events, spoiled, it was said, by too much rain or excessive heat. In any case, the latest crop of George Washington paperweights went begging (Figure 12.7).

In vain did Sol Bloom broadcast a tribute to the drafters of the Constitution from Washington's tomb at Mount Vernon and another from the shoulder of the George Washington Parkway, where trees from the thirteen original states were being planted. In vain did Washington Hall at the New York fair try to tempt visitors bedazzled by visions of a Buck Rogers World of Tomorrow to savor a close inspection of George Washington's razor, his surveying gear, and the silver buckles from his shoes (Figure 12.8). In 1939 Washington had finally become a bore, fancy buckles and all.

With his big shoe dangling over the edge of his pedestal and his sword swept back at his side, Washington graced the cover of the special World's Fair issue of the *New York Times* in which James Truslow Adams described him as a kind of guarantor of happy days to come (Figure 12.2). In the picture, in a deliberate inversion of local geography, Washington was set off against a background of the Trylon and the Perisphere, themselves hovering magically above the storybook clouds and fantastic turrets of a World of Tomorrow. His eyes, like those of the compliant fairgoer, were fixed "on the future"; his gaze, therefore, conjured up a vision of the nation's destiny. Like the little boys in the posters by Norman Rockwell and Howard Chandler Christy—the ones whose patriotic thoughts coaxed George Washington back to life—Washington's glance created an American future. Before the tangibility and the enchantment of his prophetic dream, the "prophets of doom" seemed feeble prognosticators indeed.

In reality, of course, the great statue on Constitution Mall directly faced the Trylon and the Perisphere, the fair's "moderne"-style symbols of an aspiring and pregnant tomorrow. And the finished statue was not without its own kinetic qualities of pose and attitude. With his shoe poised on the edge of his pedestal, Washington seemed to have just yanked off his hat, all the better to climb off his perch and go thundering down the Mall, straight into the future toward which he stared so fixidly. The inherent dynamism of this Washington was fully appreciated only by the souvenir industry. Alongside the ever-popular Trylon and Perisphere salt and pepper shakers, venders offered a white china George Washington toby jug with a streamlined profile that lent the Father of His Country the rakish air of a neocolonial hood ornament (Figure 12.9).[30]

The worst was yet to come, however. Even when they were streamlined and futurized, historical souvenirs still went begging (Figure

12.7
George Washington paperweight by Brown and Bigelow; on the reverse, the dates 1776–1936 and the Liberty Bell

12.8
A nineteenth-century English-made razor with Washington on the blade; replicas were sold in the twentieth century.

12.10). Admissions to the fair were so sluggish the first summer that a Jubilee campaign was organized to sell six hundred thousand tickets in two weeks:

Three hundred Fair employees—police, cashiers, guides, Haskell Indians, information clerks, and actors and actresses from Fair attractions—proceeded from the Fairgrounds in a vast motorcade to Wall Street and the very spot at which Washington's inaugural ceremony had been held. There songs and stunts were performed at the base of the Washington statue; the music of the Trytons, the Fair band, and the Dagenham Pipers (from the entertainment "Merrie England") helped to delight the crowd of over 10,000.[31]

New York had seen nothing like it since World War I, when Douglas Fairbanks and Charlie Chaplin had cavorted on the steps of the Sub-Treasury to sell liberty bonds. As banker George McAneny reminded onlookers from a roost just below the silver shoe buckle of J. Q. A. Ward's big Washington, buying a ticket to the '39 fair was tantamount to a patriotic duty, too.[32]

But as for Washington himself, his modernistic manifestation at the fairgrounds out in Queens failed to convince. The recent efforts of Sol Bloom—to whom George Washington was truly a man for all seasons, occasions, good causes, and uplifting sentiments—were only the latest in a long series of improvements to Washington's estimable person. After many decades of purposeful tinkering with the life and character of the Father of His Country, whatever meaning his trusty old self conveyed to most Americans in the late 1930s was shaded, unclear, problematic. Perhaps that sleek, white Washington on Constitution Mall was, as Grant Wood strongly intimated in his *Parson Weems's Fable* of 1939, a bit of an embarrassment, a national joke.

12.9
George Washington toby jug, produced by American Potters in 1940; the trademark is superimposed upon a likeness of the Trylon and the Perisphere. This was a souvenir of the 1939 fair's second summer.

12.10
Keepsake from the 1939 fair—a token with the 1789 inauguration on the obverse

Communist, Fascist, or Capitalist?

To Groucho Marx, playing Rufus T. Firefly, king of Freedonia, in the 1933 comedy *Duck Soup,* Washington was the funny fellow in the uniform with the smooth line of jazz patter who dispatched Harpo on his own "midnight ride."[33] To Arthur Rothstein, photographing the human toll of the Depression for the Farm Security Administration in 1937, Washington was a grim reminder that suffering was as much a part of the American heritage as Grover Whalen's optimism: in Rothstein's powerful picture of old John Dudeck, out of work in Dalton, New York, the Stuart Washington hanging over his head looked enough like him to be his father, or his brother from the breadline (Figure 12.11).[34] To Laurance Hart, whose fading career of Washington mimicry "in a white wig, three-cornered hat, velvet coat and knee breeches, lace collar and cuffs, silver buckles, and a sword" revived with the 1939 fair, the first president meant debunking the Parson Weems

cherry tree story before several thousand fourth- and fifth-graders in twenty-two states, at twenty-five dollars a crack.[35]

To a top official of the Popular Front, attempting to prove that communism was really "Twentieth Century Americanism" in the days before the signing of the Nazi-Soviet pact, Washington was a home-grown radical, commander in chief of a workers' Continental army in which young "Littleberry Browder . . . [of] Dinwiddie County, Virginia," forefather of Comrade Earl Browder, had served with distinction.[36] To the anti-Semites of the German-American Bund, gathered for a Washington's Birthday observance in New Jersey in 1938, he was "the first Fascist."[37] To those who attended the Bund rally in Madison Square Garden in 1939, the thirty-foot image of George Washington surrounded by swastikas hanging from the wall behind the podium gave proof of their earnest patriotism (Figure 12.12).[38]

Washington's frozen countenance endorsed a broad range of products, events, and political positions in the 1930s, although, toward the end of the decade, colonialisms came to signify not conservatism exactly, nor the authority of tradition, but the musty lure of the status quo back in the fat and distant 1920s, before the Crash of '29. It is perhaps indicative of the appeal of nostalgic stuffiness in some circles that in the 1937 (and last) edition of his famous furniture catalogue, Wallace Nutting tried to sell neocolonial tables and chairs by invoking the names of the deposed greats of Wall Street. Nutting boasted of the past patronage of J. P. Morgan, for instance, and called his pieces "investments that count." "A broker whose office was furnished by us," Nutting reported, "said he believed the prestige derived from the equipment . . . would pay for it in three months. Anyhow, he died rich."[39]

In Maxwell Anderson's *Valley Forge*, a three-act play written in 1934, the Continental Congress wages war for "profits, not freedom." If Anderson's tatterdemalion troops resemble FDR's "forgotten men"—working stiffs debating politics in their drafty cabins with the passion of union organizers—Washington, who is distracted by the entrance of an older and wiser Mary Philipse, is governed by an old-fashioned code of gentlemanly honor that makes for an unexciting evening on Broadway. Only as the curtain falls does this bland managerial presence catch fire from the defiance of his men, just in time to refuse Lord Howe's offer of a surrender.[40]

As John Ford told it later, he and Frank Capra bought the rights to Anderson's play, probably in 1937, with the intention of codirecting a movie version. But backers flatly refused to bankroll the project:

No, they say, who the hell's interested in George Washington? I heard one producer say that to [Capra]. I says, "I am, for one, and I know millions of other people are." He says, "Ah, that's dead fish, nobody's interested in the American Revolution." I said, "You ever read the *history* of the American

12.11
Arthur Rothstein, Farm Security Administration photograph of John Dudeck, an unemployed worker, taken in Dalton, New York, 1937

12.12
George Washington presiding over a German-American rally at Madison Square Garden, New York, 1939

Revolution?" He says, "Hell no, I had better things to do." I says, "They didn't teach you in the sixth grade, when you graduated?" He says, "What do you mean, I went through the *eighth* grade."[41]

Regardless of the defects in their schooling, the money-men were probably right to scorn a movie starring George Washington. In the realm of mass culture, a personality is popular because the significance of the figure is widely understood and the values embodied therein are generally endorsed. But because of such broad appeal, a popular idol is also susceptible to adoption by any number of attention-seeking causes, the nature and intentions of which often have little in common with the qualities originally attributed to and celebrated in the hero. When his fundamental meaning disappears under the crust of nuances added by the ad men, the novelists, the playwrights, and the politicians, Washington can no longer be said to be popular. He is familiar. He is, perhaps, a cultural cliché. But, since nobody knows exactly what he is good for anymore, he can also be confusing, tedious, even annoying—and a bad investment.

The front man for capitalists, Nazis, Reds, Republicans, the Constitution Sesquicentennial Commission, and at least one disillusioned cubist, Washington by 1939 had been too popular for too long. His popularity had finally blunted all sense of what that large and lonely figure really stood for. Worse still, from sheer overexposure, Washington had come to be a bore. The great white figure in the knee breeches towering over the 1939 World's Fair was, in fact, only his ghost. Although not quite moribund, as some feeble flutters of life and at least one forceable resuscitation in subsequent decades would show, George Washington had fallen into a deathlike slumber beneath the streamlined carapace of James Earle Fraser's statue.

A Postwar Pop Art Icon

World War II began during Washington's brief reign over the technological future at Flushing Meadow, a future finally defined, as it turned out, by the new technology of bombers and atomic bombs. When asked the traditional question, Generals George Marshall and Dwight Eisenhower both claimed Washington as their military exemplar, the latter calling him "the greatest man the English-speaking world ever produced."[42] But their troops had little use for bewigged gentlemen in short pants, except for comic relief. *This Is the Army* typifies the humorous approach to historical figures and values adopted by the media for the duration. A movie popular both in local theaters and in army camps in 1943, *This Is the Army* starred Ronald Reagan as a GI producer who entertains the boys with a musical review of the American heritage they are defending. Irving Berlin, playing a skinny doughboy from the First War, stands before his tent and croaks:

If George Washington were alive today
He'd pick up his sword,
    And then he'd say—
This is our country . . . [43]

Or perhaps Washington would simply have rolled over and gone back to sleep. In *George Washington Slept Here,* the 1942 Jack Benny comedy based on a none-too-successful Broadway play by Kaufman and Hart, chuckles arise from the local labor shortage, as a couple from Manhattan struggles to restore a run-down Bucks County farmhouse on a shoestring. The Fullers have bought the place because Washington is supposed to have spent the night there, but midway through the second reel they learn that Benedict Arnold was actually the famous Revolutionary houseguest.[44] The film ends with their demolition of the place, an act of wartime violence directed against Washington legends and tightfisted mortgage bankers alike.

In the Midwest in the 1940s, Washington's Birthday dinners were the kinds of affairs at which soldiers home on leave were shown off by their proud fathers (Figure 12.13). But despite such gatherings, which reinforced the old links between George Washington and the American home, he cannot be said to have been an important figure in the iconography of World War II. Only when the cold war made it vital for the custodians of popular culture to redefine the canon of traditional values that set Americans apart from their military and ideological adversaries did Washingtoniana figure again in Hollywood's symbolic vocabulary.

In his so-called Cavalry Trilogy—a group of Westerns starring John Wayne as an officer at a post isolated in the hostile landscape of Monument Valley—John Ford creates a strong, self-reliant American community out of Irishmen, Swedes, old-stock Yankees, and their families, who come together under the indulgent gaze of Gilbert Stuart's George Washington. In *She Wore A Yellow Ribbon* of 1949, the picture of George Washington hangs in the commandant's office:

12.13
Washington's Day dinner held in the St. Paul Hotel, St. Paul, Minnesota, February 22, 1943

12.14
Roy Lichtenstein, *Washington Crossing the Delaware,* ca. 1952, a lost painting

12.15
G. S. Stradling, superintendent of Washington Crossing State Park, ferrying youngsters across the Delaware; Lichtenstein was inspired by this picture.

it is a fixed element in the series of rituals whereby Wayne's Captain Brittles expresses the rightness of his world in clear distinction to the formless evils lurking outside the fort. *Fort Apache* of 1948 opens with a dance in honor of Washington's Birthday, a celebration of order and oneness interrupted by the arrival of the new superior officer, foredoomed by his own alienation from the mores of the group.[45]

In these manifestations, and in his appearance as a kind of historical mirage praying in the cold of Valley Forge on Norman Rockwell's 1950 Boy Scout calendar, George Washington was a holy picture. He manifested himself as a flat, two-dimensional thing meant for walls, a true icon, exuding the spiritual power of one-hundred-percent Americanism but lacking character, human interest, and all but the most rudimentary biography.[46] Paradoxically, however, Washington became appealing to practitioners of pop art because of his very banality. The young Roy Lichtenstein's *Washington Crossing the Delaware* (Figure 12.14), based on a *National Geographic* photograph of six little boys recreating the event in the sunshine of Washington Crossing State Park, anticipates his better-known Washingtons of the 1960s, comic-strip adaptations of the linecut adaptations of the Stuart portrait routinely printed in the newspapers.[47]

Although pop art eventually breathed new life into a nearly meaningless symbol, the genre also exposed the sorry state of contemporary Washingtoniana by revealing just how empty and formulaic the hero's treatment in the mass media really was. The *National Geographic* picture of the little boys was not an isolated reminder of the Washington-in-the-boat convention, for example (Figure 12.15). The same issue of the magazine reproduced a version of the definitive Leutze painting in the collection of the Metropolitan Museum (the original had been destroyed in 1942 in an Allied air raid on Bremen), then on loan to a church near the embarkation site and guarded by an encampment of Boy Scouts. Make-believe soldiers, the Scouts took up the role of an absent army, occupied in Korea. As Washington's strategic daring was being called to mind by the pantomimes of children, the military brass was fighting off McCarthyites at home.[48] In that atmosphere of muscular paranoia and aggressive patriotism, Washington icons began to multiply once more. They were signs of the true believer, emblems of orthodoxy.

Life devoted a number—and "17 pages of color"—to "the American Revolution: The Story as It Really Happened." George Washington graced the cover. Inside, there were maps of his campaigns that would have done Sol Bloom proud and a compendium of artwork noteworthy for showing the formerly businesslike, even passive hero as an active combatant, mounted on his horse, his sword at the ready.[49] The postwar craze for Americana-style kitchens, bedrooms, and "family rooms" in spool-turned maple (the cautious alternative to the modernism of turquoise Formica adorned with amoeboid or vaguely thermonuclear shapes) also encouraged *Life* and its competitors to chronicle such topics as "Early American Folk Art" with pictures of stiff Washingtons painted by unheralded geniuses on grainy barn-boards.[50]

In 1953, against that background of knotty-pine coziness, the painter Larry Rivers decided to do something "disgusting" to startle New York's abstractionists out of a stupor nearly as profound as Washington's. "So what could be dopier," he said, "than a painting dedicated to a national cliché—Washington Crossing the Delaware":

The only thing was that Washington Crossing the Delaware was always like the dopiest, funniest thing in American life. Year after year, as a kid in school, you see these amateurish plays that are completely absurd but you know they represent patriotism—love of country, so here I am choosing something that everybody has this funny duality about. It was also a way for me to stick out my thumb at other people.[51]

Once the work was under way, however, Rivers gave up the notion of doing a painting about the dopiness of a famous work of art (Figure 12.16). "I saw the moment as nerve-wracking and uncomfortable," he writes. "I couldn't picture anyone getting into a chilly river around Christmas time with anything resembling hand-on-chest heroics."[52] In Rivers's version of the familiar theme, a Washington frozen with tension and white with anxiety stands in the boat alone.

Although Alfred Leslie was inspired to do a Henry Ford with Model T and Harry Jackson tried a Custer's Last Stand, most of Rivers's friends laughed at the work. But as the art historian Helen Harrison remarks, "Within a few years Washington's image and other stereo-

12.16
Larry Rivers, *Washington Crossing the Delaware,* 1953

12.17
A bicentennial fireplug

typed trappings of Americana, often taken from mass-media sources, had become familiar devices in the Pop repertory."[53] Pop art and popular culture exchanged both form and subject content. In 1962 Otto Preminger's cast of venal senators paused at several points in their behind-the-scenes intrigues to recall George Washington's penchant for truthtelling: the duplicities of *Advise and Consent* flourished in the murky shadows cast by the Washington Monument. In 1962 and 1963 Jacqueline Kennedy revived the custom of holding elegant picnics on the lawn at Mount Vernon. In 1962 Edward Albee named the battling, childless, all-American couple of *Who's Afraid of Virginia Woolf?* George and Martha.[54]

Neither the renewed attentions of Hollywood and Broadway nor the ministrations of the avant-garde and the fashionable restored Washington's familiar image to its former place of honor among the most potent and communicative of all American emblems, however. A sparse exhibition of "Twentieth Century Images of George Washington" held in honor of the 250th anniversary of his birth at the Fraunces Tavern Museum in New York made it clear, in fact, that Washington was not a subject of abiding interest even to those painters most concerned throughout the 1960s with the visual cliché.[55]

The Gilbert Stuart portrait and its adaptation to the dollar bill did provide material for feeble pictorial witticisms, and at least one *Nixon Crossing the Delaware* was produced, but it took the celebration of the national bicentennial in 1976 to stimulate a genuine Washington revival, although a very modest one. While that celebration was in progress, painter Alex Katz added Washington to his gallery of big, bland portrait heads, alongside deadpan renderings of average American suburbanites, and sculptor Robert Arneson glazed ceramic busts of Washington in green and covered them in rows of stipples, lest his monetary significance be forgotten. But these isolated gestures from the enclaves of high art were overshadowed by the labors of Ruth von Karowsky, who organized a squad of four hundred citizen-artists, aged nine to seventy-nine, and painted the 4,800 fireplugs in South Bend, Indiana, to resemble General Washington, his contemporaries, and the soldiers of his army (Figure 12.17).[56]

"Mugs on Plugs" in '76

Ruth von Karowsky's project was copied first by Washington, D.C., later by communities in Tennessee, Wisconsin, Idaho, and West Virginia, and finally by most towns with hydrants. As a result, she may have done more for George Washington than any of the functionaries affiliated with the American Revolution Bicentennial Administration even though, as her idea spread, Betsy Ross, historic flags, and colorful ethnic garb came to dominate this new form of folk sculpture on the curb. That diffuseness, typical of the official observances of the two hundredth anniversary of the American Revolution, can be attributed in part to the political climate of the years after 1966, when the Eighty-ninth Congress mandated planning to start, and in part to events that unfolded after 1974, when the Ninety-third Congress directed a program of activities to begin in earnest.

The assassinations of the Kennedys and Martin Luther King, protests over the war in Vietnam, and radical unrest all encouraged a certain wariness about public ceremonial. In 1972, with the concurrence of his Bicentennial Commission, President Nixon announced that plans for an international fair in Philadelphia had been canceled. The "Expo" was to have been an updated revival of the great 1876 Centennial Exposition, stressing the theme of American progress. In its place, Nixon called for a "grassroots" celebration coordinated in Washington but created and executed at the local level, with the help of funds generated from the sale of official souvenirs.

Nixon's announcement provoked outrage in many quarters. Public ire was heightened by the *Washington Post*'s publication of confidential commission documents. Based on leaks from the commission's proceedings, charges of "politics, commercialism and jingoism" further dampened whatever residual zest for patriotic merrymaking remained abroad in the land. Existence of the damaging evidence eventually published by the *Post* had been made known by Jeremy Rifkin, leader of a Peoples Bicentennial Commission founded by the New Left to combat Nixon's "Tory celebration." "Allowing the giant corporations to participate in the Bicentennial," Rifkin told a hostile audience of business and advertising executives gathered at the Washington Hilton to learn how they could cash in on the festivities, "is as ludicrous as George Washington inviting Benedict Arnold to the victory celebration at Yorktown."[57]

At a recreation of the Boston Tea Party held on a snowy December afternoon in 1973, a contingent from the Peoples Bicentennial Commission dumped empty barrels into the harbor to protest inflated oil profits, a local militiaman in knickers heard his cry of "Down with King George" answered with shouts of "Down with King Richard," and disabled veterans dressed as Indians staged their own anti-ceremony over the noisy protests of the Boston Indian Council.[58] A year later, demonstrators opposing commercial sponsorship of bicentennial events marched on the White House carrying banners that read "John Hancock Didn't Sell Insurance" and "Impeach Nixon."[59]

Watergate, Agnew's resignation, and the eventual fall of Richard Nixon all helped to foster modest, homey bicentennial galas in the nation's libraries, town halls, state parks—places untainted by the corruption of the capital. But in the absence of federal guidance in the matter of pomp and circumstance, many local units of government had no clear idea of what symbols and ceremonies might contribute to a meaningful commemoration of the bicentennial. As a result, the character of such observances exhibited a very wide range of variables; sometimes the connection between a specific local project and the anniversay at hand was difficult to ascertain.

Lexington, Massachusetts, was able to draw upon a backlog of experience with patriotic rites in proposing to refight the first battle of the Revolutionary War and to erect a new flagpole on Battle Green, for instance, but the arrangements committee also decided to sponsor the participation of an eighty-seven piece all-girl band from New Orleans in the local Patriots' Day Parade. Lafayette, New Jersey, was determined to spruce up the civic tennis courts and add a replica of an old bandstand; to give the work a bicentennial flavor, the town fathers decided to crown the new recreational complex with a bust of Lafayette. In Norton, Kansas, however, two major bicentennial projects consisted of landscaping the cemetery and supervising a Scout troop that wanted to paint the picnic benches in two parks with red, white, and blue stripes.

The Kansans, it should be noted, also had a "Mugs on Plugs" project that lent their celebration a touch of 1776-ness woefully lacking in Rothsay, Minnesota, where the year's bicentennial activity consisted of fabricating a giant fiberglass prairie chicken—"the largest in the world"—to attract a little attention from tourists zipping past on the interstate. A similar sculptural enterprise occurred to the citizens of Sumner, Missouri, who put up "the world's largest statue of a Canadian snow goose."[60] The connection between these monstrous roadside birds and the American Revolution remained obscure to passers-by, although both sites were marked with replicas of the official bicentennial logo.

Unlike the memorabilia of earlier times that commemorated a place or a date through reference to historical specifics, bicentennial souvenirs also tended to be somewhat generic in character. In 1976 it sufficed to stamp the authorized trademark—concentric bands of red and blue (they were said to evoke "a feeling of festivity") that formed a sort of high-tech star "in keeping with the forward-looking goals of the . . . celebration"—on throw pillows, tote bags, coffee mugs, Frisbees, belt buckles, scarves, or T-shirts to produce a licensed bicentennial product with virtually no intrinsic or decorative ties to the past, the Revolution, or the concept of bicentennial remembrance.[61]

If there was a common quality tying one piece of authorized 1976 merchanise to another, it was the emphasis on items of apparel, things for personal use, that, by calling attention to the individual celebrant rather than the nature of the national rite in which he or she was taking part, only served to atomize the celebration further. Probably the single most popular *un*authorized memento of the year was the

12.18
The tricorn was the unofficial bicentennial headgear for 1976.

three-cornered hat, adopted in fancy versions by high school bands and in cheaper models by exuberant parade-goers, cynical protesters, and children everywhere (Figure 12.18). The faces that peeped out from under those thousands upon thousands of colonial brims made Washington's tired old features seem redundant to the proceedings; his was just another American face, no more or less interesting to contemplate than one of Alex Katz's ubiquitous and anonymous suburbanites.

George Washington got very little special treatment in 1976. Such tributes as were offered to the Father of His Country came erratically from unaccountable sources. Virginia, for example, used the patrician profile of her favorite son as the state bicentennial symbol, but since Illinois produced Abe Lincoln and Kentucky enlisted Daniel Boone for the same purpose, Washington evidently derived no privileged status from his firsthand connection with the events of 1776.[62] As its birthday gift to the rest of the country, Bedford, Indiana, at the urging of the Chamber of Commerce, hauled a thirty-ton, three-dimensional replica of Leutze's infamous composition made of local limestone to a site on the Pennsylvania side of the Delaware River and left it there on July 5, 1976. The Washington Crossing Foundation provided the land, local businesses financed the base, and the annual reenactments mounted by Philadelphians went on as usual, under the title of an "officially recognized Bicentennial project" (Figure 12.19).

In Pasadena, California, the annual Tournament of Roses Parade went off as scheduled, too, on New Year's Day, with a bicentennial theme: a large head of Washington in pink petals glided along on a float, flanked by Hancock and Franklin.[63] The nightly parades at Disneyland and Disney World, rechristened "America on Parade" for the duration of 1976, constituted one of the much-heralded "corporate-sponsored endeavors" of which the Nixon people had boasted; redesigned at a stated cost of $2 million, the floats featured a doll-like Betsy Ross and the trio of Donald Duck (fife), Goofy (drum), and Mickey Mouse (flag), but gave no prominent role to George Washington or to any other patriot without cartoon potential.[64]

Washington fared best in Texas, where bicentennial exercises had an old-fashioned flavor reminiscent of 1876 and 1889. The Midland Community Theatre of Midland, Texas, commissioned "an original drama on George Washington's genius," a quality to be made theatrically manifest through the representation of "some part of his challenging life." In Navasota, the Fourth of July bicentennial parade was routed down Washington Avenue, and the bicentennial ball held the following night in the Smith Hotel reverted to the ancient form of the Martha Washington tea. Guests came in Gilbert Stuart period costumes and danced "the minuet, waltz, square dance and Virginia Reel."[65]

12.19
The 1986 reenactment of Washington's passage of the Delaware; in 1976, this annual event had become a "recognized Bicentennial project."

But it was the French who did the most to rescue Washington from virtual oblivion, on the strength of his warm relationship with the young Marquis de Lafayette. France's bicentennial gift to the United States was a *son et lumière* spectacle called *The Father of Liberty,* using the Mount Vernon mansion as its backdrop. Valery Giscard d'Estaing presented the installation during a state visit. From Mount Vernon, he went on to Yorktown, Virginia, to honor the timely intervention of the French fleet in the Revolution, and to Philadelphia, to recall the accreditation of France's first representatives by Congress. At both stops George Washington, the hero all but forgotten on his own side of the Atlantic, was mentioned glowingly. Nor did the French president shrink from describing decisive events of eighteenth-century American history often reduced by nervous corporate sponsors of televised "Bicentennial Minutes" to upbeat entertainment.[66] Other French officials fanned out to Valley Forge; Hull, Massachusetts; Savannah, Georgia; Hartford, Connecticut; and Virginia Beach, Virginia: anywhere Washington had greeted Lafayette, met a French admiral, or planned a joint operation with his European ally became a hallowed site, resanctified in 1976 with Gallic appreciation for his acumen, his bravery, his esprit.[67]

It was the rare American who thought so highly of the Father of His Country or who knew so much about him, although New Englanders living in close quarters with Revolutionary haunts were better informed than most. Exclaimed one visitor to Boston's Old South Meeting House, when shown the historical treasures displayed there: "I have a piece of the tree where George Washington stood, when he commanded the army! A piece of the tree, Jesus!"[68] But asked to comment on the meaning of local history, a Bostonian dressed as a colonial militiaman drew some strange conclusions from the indigenous supply of historical half-truths:

George Washington was a real prick, he was a real son of a bitch. I don't doubt the man was gifted, he had some kind of gift to him. He had to be a gifted guy; because if you look at his coat in the Smithsonian Institute, he's got bullet-holes in his coat, seven different holes, and two of them are almost point-blank in his heart. Never once did one of those balls touch his skin. He always led his men in a battle, and never once was he even scratched.

Plus he's supposed to have seen the Indian, what's his name? Potomac? The Indian who predicted the Civil War, another war, would happen in a hundred years. He talked to the Indian the night before the march on Trenton, before they crossed the Delaware on Christmas eve, and the Indian told him to make this march. For a guy to predict that, almost a hundred years before, there's got to be something to him. Good old dirty George. I think there was more to Betsy Ross than her sewing.[69]

12.20
Tourists taking pictures at Washington's Tomb, Mount Vernon, 1984

The Georgian Revival in the Reagan Presidency

On stage, Washington was much less interesting. He barely appeared in *1776*, the Broadway musical (and movie spin-off) based on the antics of Adams, Franklin, and the more amusing of the Founding Fathers gathered at the Second Continental Congress. In any case, the 1972 film version disappeared from the screen long before the bicentennial arrived, despite its unflagging cuteness, gorgeous damasks and satins, and elegant furniture.[70] Among the very well-off, the very conservative, and aspirants to respectability through good taste, enthusiasm for the furniture and the neocolonial frou-frou had never really waned: throughout the 1970s, ads for the high-quality reproductions and decorative accessories sold under the auspices of the Colonial Williamsburg Foundation graced the pages of the better magazines.[71] But George Washington did not actually reappear in the settings his prestige had revived for the first time in the nineteenth century until 1982, the 250th anniversary of his birth and an occasion that could not decently be ignored.

Mount Vernon was refurbished for an expected onslaught of a million tourists (Figure 12.20). Although the white columns of the river façade still defined the image of the ideal home, the interior was in need of a major overhaul. A $10 million fundraising campaign headed by Robert Beck, chairman of Prudential Insurance, allowed the banquet hall to be redone in "pistachio-ice-cream green." The faux-bois graining was restored to the study, and more intense colors were added throughout in response to new chemical research and restoration techniques. As a result, the Sherwin Williams Company, which, since 1965, had paid a hefty royalty to market "the pale, chalky pastels that are the so-called Williamsburg shades," was said to be reconsidering its position.[72] What had been desirably colonial in the 1960s no longer suited the newer and richer definition of the term emerging in the 1980s.

The Washington memorial exhibition mounted by the Smithsonian's National Museum of American History added depth and luster to a revised neocolonial sensibility best described as Georgian—after George III, to be sure—in its emphasis on unadventurous good taste, refined lines, expensive materials, and a gentlemanly clubbishness common to the enclaves of the elite, whatever the date or locale. Entitled *George Washington: A Figure upon the Stage*, the show devoted the lion's share of attention to the physical environment through which Washington moved. Not since the Centennial Exposition of 1876 had so many Washington uniforms, camp chests, chairs, and bits of bric-a-brac been brought together under one roof.[73] Although the exhibit shied away from defining his personality or contributions in any substantive way, it showed that the acquisitive Washington first

12.21
Red Grooms's parade float/assemblage,
Philadelphia Cornucopia of 1982,
surrounded by tourists in the summer of
1984

12.22
"Collectible" Dolly Dingle George and
Martha paper dolls, on sale in 1982

presented through his artifactual remains in 1876 had come back into fashion. In 1982 George Washington was stylish. Just as the Art Deco, New Wave, and Country Casual "looks" were contemporary fashion statements of hard-to-explain but obvious appeal, upscale colonial had suddenly become chic.

Fully half of the exhibition dealt with what might legitimately be referred to as the "Mount Vernon look." George Washington's candlesticks, his plates, and his glassware were all presented in a glossy picture-catalogue that might have come from Neiman-Marcus. The manner of presentation, of course, did nothing to discourage interest in a fresh crop of posh Williamsburg advertisements, redesigned in fashionably inky blues and deepest russets.[74]

The other half of the Smithsonian show dealt with Washington's personal style. Promoters of Boy George and other entertainers with distinctive clothes and hairdos who would rise to fleeting superstardom in the early 1980s, along with the first president, might have called it "the Washington look." Political pundits referred to the combination of high style and low, conventionalized content as "image." Whatever the applicable term, the visitor to the exhibition was treated to glimpses of George Washington in a cowboy hat, a hardhat, and the altogether; with a hatchet, a horse, his sword, his wife; on the Delaware, on his knees, on a pedestal.[75] What each of these manifestations of the idol might signify was left to the imagination of the spectator. Like iconic photos of Elvis Presley in the army, Elvis with his little daughter or with Richard Nixon, Elvis on the comeback trail, and Elvis's tomb at Graceland; like photos of presidential candidates kissing babies, chopping wood, praying for guidance, and wearing cowboy hats, such pictures merely confirmed the well-deserved popularity of the hero and the good sense of the viewer who recognized an important American when he saw one.

Although still bereft of any real historical substance, this trendy George Washington was seen everywhere. Red Grooms's *Philadelphia Cornucopia* of 1982, an assemblage now on exhibit at the new Visitor's Center in the heart of that city, put him on the deck of the Ship of State, waving an enormous tricorn to his fans, with Martha as the figurehead below (Figure 12.21). "Dolly Dingle" collectors were treated to a reprint of Grace Drayton's coveted Washington's Birthday cutouts (Figure 12.22). Preteens caught up in the latest fad were tempted by George Washington stickers alluding to the cherry tree fable (Figure 12.23). In the pictures on the red-white-and-blue package, a "Spellbinder Tape" designed for eight-year-olds by Fisher-Price promised to explain the hatchet incident, the crossing of the Delaware, and the forbidding expression on Stuart's Washington.[76] Tourists at the Disney complex in Orlando could watch a robotic George Washington in the Hall of Presidents on Liberty Square bow sagely. On the opposite

12.23
A George Washington sticker made by Hallmark Cards, 1983

coast, Californians could be laid to rest in the Court of Liberty at Forest Lawn cemetery beneath a giant mosaic wall depicting Washington praying at Valley Forge, Washington crossing the Delaware, Washington and Lafayette at Valley Forge, and Washington with Betsy Ross.[77]

There were Washington ads—for an air conditioning system guaranteed to preserve his portrait in the National Gallery into the life times of the reader's grandchildren; for a trip to Rhode Island, where his wooden teeth might or might not have been made; for restrikes of the Gorham bust, last seen during Sol Bloom's 1932 gala; for an American-made television set displaying a color picture of the flag and operated by the ghosts of Betsy Ross and General Washington.[78] A writer of contemporary fiction thought it perfectly appropriate to start a fight among a group of "Modern Baptists" over a George Washington TV commercial:

"I was there, I heard them," Toinette's eyes sparkled. "There was this commercial with George Washington come on, and for no reason at all Burma says, 'Bobby doesn't like the way George Washington looks,' and Emmet says, 'Who the hell cares what George Washington looks like?' and the next thing you know, they're both getting all worked up— .... "[79]

Observed in most places with an orgy of Presidents' Day shopping, during the 1980s Washington's Birthday moved back onto the comic pages of the daily papers after a long absence. Seasonal cherry tree humor proved popular with *The Ryatts, Dunagin's People, The Family Circus, Shoe,* and *Peanuts.*[80] Syndicated pop psychologists, explaining social lies in the "Better Living" sections of the same newspapers, told moms not to worry about Junior's little fibs: "Even young George Washington, once he's put his hatchet down, must have broken form at least once for his mother—say, by telling her the cherry pie was terrific when in fact the crust was a bit soggy."[81] Apropos of nothing in particular, the *National Inquirer* reported that "while his soldiers were starving at Valley Forge, General Washington was enjoying sumptuous meals [of] chicken, mutton, oysters, pears, veal and cucumbers—and got Congress to pick up the tab!"[82]

In the pages of the alumnae magazine published by his daughter's college, a distinguished urologist speculated that the broad-hipped Washington might have suffered from Klinefelter's Syndrome: chromosomal abnormalities "would explain why the Father of our country was not a father."[83] In Wilmington, Delaware, a group of professional men formed a George Washington Club, with monthly dinner meetings—the dentist among them gave a talk on the false-teeth issue—and special excursions to Mount Vernon on which spouses were welcome.[84] Like the cover subjects of *People* magazine, who are of interest principally because they are so thoroughly "now," so "today"— people whose states of health, sexual preferences, possessions, and product endorsements are, accordingly, studied seriously by other trendsetters—George Washington had suddenly become a very eighties kind of guy.

Articles on the presidency took another look at the first of the line and praised his good clothes, his dignity, and something called "character," almost too elusive to be captured in print. The equivalent of what Emily Post had dubbed "personality" in the 1920s, the term carried with it an impression of solidity. Character signified a real presence, an embodiment of tradition, the antithesis of flashy glamour—and character was what the columnists admired most in George Washington.[85]

Garry Wills, who saw him as a charismatic leader and a cunning manipulator of the media of his day, was said to have "made George Washington interesting again" in his *Cincinnatus,* a 1984 book subtitled *Images of Power in Early America.*[86] Self-styled neoconservatives, who approved of Washington's alliance with Hamilton, openly admired his sensible marriage to a wealthy widow, and liked his military firmness, bemoaned the fact that "a larger-than-life figure to whom piety and reverence were naturally due" had been "radically diminished in size and virtually emptied of substance" over the years (probably by liberals).[87] Given George Washington's prominence in the public prints, however, editorial complaints about his lack of substance were really backhanded tributes to the substantial, avuncular, solid, militarily sound, and charismatic sitting president, who was about to celebrate the beginning of his second term with a round of televised balls, galas, parties, and other celebrity-packed functions that proved he was no more averse than Washington to money, expensive clothes, decent White House china, and the company of what passed for an American aristocracy in January of 1985.

The rest of America watched the spectacle in the privacy of formerly Danish-modern living rooms, into which new elements of home décor had recently crept: the posh comfort of velvet wing chairs; pseudo-Chippendale cabinetry with a richness of surface redolent of mellow maturity; and patterned wallpapers marked by a balance and restraint of design. If such artifactual nods to the eighteenth century should have looked incongruous amid the electronic litter of VCRs and PCs, they did not. Tradition was fashionable again. And through the magic of a live, coast-to-coast network hookup, Ronald Reagan, whose charm derived from a glowing patina of Americana not unlike the "heritage finish" applied to factory-fresh dining room sets, was about to toss the coin to begin Superbowl XIX.

George Washington Goes to the Superbowl

In a mannerly and politic gesture, Mr. Reagan had actually postponed his inauguration for a day so as not to compete with the key football game of the year. In a manly aside overheard by a TV audience of millions, the Gipper told the captains of the Miami Dolphins and the San Francisco Forty-Niners that he'd much rather be there at Stanford Stadium than sitting back in Washington in the White House. At half time, the giant scoreboard lit up in a patriotic tribute to America, the next day's inauguration, President Reagan, the National Football League, motherhood, the flag, and, of course the sponsors. And an electrified George Washington, with his frizzy hair and his puffy face, blinked down at late twentieth-century America in a sort of prim amazement.

The shot faded abruptly to a closeup of a cheerleader's cantilevered bosom—accounting, perhaps, for the startled expression on the face of the Father of His Country. Or maybe it was the next quick cut to a battery of commercials that disconcerted him. In any case, when the cars and the beer had been sold and the scoreboard loomed into sight once more, George Washington was gone.[88]

But he's never gone for long. Later that spring, Paul Harvey's noontime news made sport of a movie company headed overseas to shoot the final scenes of something called *Revolution 1776* on location in Norway because they don't have obtrusive telephones poles there.[89] As the international cast embarked for Scandinavia to reenact the decisive battle of the American Revolution, the only thing known with certainty about the production was that Natassya Kinsky had not been cast as Washington (although fates almost as strange had befallen the durable hero in the past two centuries). Now, several years later, the movie has been relegated to the home video market, where it competes with a network sequel that promised the return of "Barry Bostwick and Patty Duke . . . in their roles as George and Martha Washington." The underlying theme of the television miniseries was mature romance, with striking similarities to the plot of a real-life page-turner entitled *Ronnie and Nancy: A Very Special Love Story.*[90]

Part 2 in a discontinuous series with the potential for years of future episodes, *George Washington: The Forging of a Nation* was also promoted by its corporate sponsor in such a way as to take whatever advantage could be derived from association with tepid federal observances of the Constitution Bicentennial directed by former Chief Justice Warren Burger. "How to Create a Country Without a King," the mock headlines in the General Motors ads announced: "The Biggest Political Story of the Last 200 Years." So let's kick back in our tasteful neo–Mount Vernon recliners and thrill to a "human, dramatic" spectacle with genuine relevance to our daily lives:

History teaches us . . . that character survives, principles last. The government of the United States is now one of the oldest on Earth and, by any measure, surely one of the best. . . . [This program] shows how Washington proved that a country could have a head of state who was not a king. Personal and political currents swirled around him. . . . At the same time there was open rebellion in the countryside and bitter criticism in the press. *The principles of freedom were being tested by reality.* And through it all, Washington's moderate approach to the Presidency was defining the role of Chief Executive for generations to come.[91]

In the next installment George Washington probably won't pray in the snow: it has already been done. He might chop down the cherry tree during a flashback. But without question, he will continue to dance attendance at the most authentic, costliest Martha Washington tea ever mounted. Ah, the fabrics, the silver, the furniture! All of it perfect, of course, for the tasteful American home of tomorrow. And as the leading actor in the unending Colonial Revival, George Washington never strays far from home.

Notes

1. Two Prayers in the Snow

1. Garry Wills, "Reagan Redraws History," syndicated column, *Minnesota Daily,* 28 January 1985, 7.

2. *The Washington Centenary, Celebrated in New-York, April 29, 30–May 1, 1889* (New York: Tribune Association, 1889), 38.

3. Clarence Winthrop Bowen, ed., *The History of the Centennial Celebration of the Inauguration of George Washington as First President of the United States* (New York: D. Appleton, 1892), 45; *Washington Centenary,* 109; and "New York, April 30, 1789," *Harper's Weekly,* 4 May 1889, 343, which attributes the story to the eyewitness account of a Miss Elizabeth Quincy, who watched the ceremony from the roof of the first house up Broad Street, almost over the balcony of Federal Hall.

4. Souvenir pamphlets containing the actual stamp with a first-day cancellation are still sold in the gift shop of the National Park Service Visitors' Center at Valley Forge, Pennsylvania. On the cover of the *Saturday Evening Post,* 23 February 1935, the potent equation between Christmas and Washington had not yet been made. See Norman Rockwell, intro., *The J. C. Leyendecker Poster Book* (New York: Watson-Guptill Publications, 1975).

5. *United States Postage Stamps: An Illustrated Description of All United States Postage and Special Service Stamps* (Washington, D.C.: U.S. Postal Service, 1970), 56–57, and Ralph A. Kimble, *Commemorative Postage Stamps of the United States,* rev. ed. (New York: Grosset and Dunlap, 1936), 150 and 158–159.

6. For discussion of the mixed-media engraving by McRae, see Mark Edward Thistlethwaite, *The Image of George Washington: Studies in Mid-Nineteenth-Century History Painting* (New York: Garland, 1979), 101.

7. W. E. Woodward, *George Washington: The Image and the Man* (Garden City, N.Y.: Garden City Publishing, 1926), 342.

8. *New York Times,* 21 February 1932, sec. 7.

9. Charles B. Hosmer, Jr., *Presence of the Past: A History of the Preservation Movement in the United States Before Williamsburg* (New York: G. P. Putnam's Sons, 1965), 82–84. The Pennsylvania ladies were among the first to recognize that the Philadelphia celebration of the centennial of the Declaration of Independence was a prelude to a host of other anniversaries of the Revolutionary period, including that of the winter at Valley Forge.

10. Lewis Barrington, *Historic Restorations of the Daughters of the American Revolution* (New York: Richard R. Smith, 1941), caption accompanying plate 108. Although the structure was owned by the state of Pennsylvania, the care of the site was entrusted to the ladies' various organizations; the local DAR chapters of Valley Forge and Merion decorated the rooms of the Potts House.

11. On the origins of the Potts story, see Marcus Cunliffe's introduction to Mason L. Weems, *The Life of Washington,* ed. Marcus Cunliffe (Cambridge, Mass.: Harvard University Press, 1962), xxxvi.

12. Marshall W. Fishwick, *American Heroes: Myth and Reality* (Washington, D.C.: Public Affairs Press, 1954), 53; William Alfred Bryan, *George Washington in American Literature, 1775–1865* (New York: Columbia University Press, 1952), 93–94; and Dixon Wecter, *The Hero in America: A Chronicle of Hero-Worship* (Ann Arbor: University of Michigan Press, 1963), 110.

13. Mason Weems, *A History of the Life and Death Virtues and Exploits of General George Washington,* ed. Mark Van Doren ([New York]: Macy-Masius, 1927), 300–301.

14. Weems, *Life of Washington,* 182.

15. Bishop Meade, *Old Churches, Ministers, and Families of Virginia,* vol. 2 (Philadelphia: J. B. Lippincott, 1857), 238 and 246.

16. See Thomas A. Bailey, "The Mythmakers of American History," *Journal of American History,* 55 (June 1968), 6.

17. George Lippard, *Washington and His Generals; or, Legends of the Revolution* (Philadelphia: G. B. Zieber, 1847), 107–111. In a long footnote, Lippard calls the tale a "tradition" and alludes to other versions, placing the incident in a variety of Revolutionary settings, including the heights above Valley Forge (where a "mossy rock," like the boulder Christ often uses for a priedieu in representations of the prayer in the garden, conflicts with the image of snow almost always stressed in other accounts) and the Brandywine. He also notes that he told the story before as blatant fiction in his historical novel *Blanche of Brandywine.* According to Thistlethwaite, *Image of George Washington,* 101, in 1836 E. C. McGuire, in *Religious Opinions and Character of Washington,* also described the incident and provided two eyewitnesses, a Tory Quaker and General Knox.

18. A Peter Kramer lithograph of the painting was published in 1854. Among the earliest known representations of the scene is the engraving by Gilbert and Gihon published as an illustration in Horatio Hastings Weld's *Life of Washington* (1847). All of these works have been brought together in a permanent exhibit mounted by the Valley Forge Historical Society and opened on July 4, 1984; see "Society News," *Valley Forge Journal,* December 1984, 146–148, and a 1984 Valley Forge Historical Society pamphlet, "Valley Forge: The Reality and the Symbol."

19. Benson J. Lossing, *The Pictorial Field-Book of the Revolution; or, Illustrations, by Pen and Pencil, of the History, Biography, Scenery, Relics, and Traditions of the War for Independence,* vol. 2 (New York: Harper and Brothers, 1859), 126 and 130. Lossing states that Washington lived in the house of Isaac Potts, "a Quaker preacher," at Valley Forge and accepts the story of the prayer, witnessed by Potts, without comment or question, making him cry out, "If there is any one on this earth whom the Lord will listen to, it is George Washington; and I feel a presentiment that under such a commander there can be no doubt of our eventually establishing our independence, and that God in his providence has willed it so." Lossing also cites the following poem by J. L. Chester:

> Oh! who shall know the might
> Of the words he utter'd there?

> The fate of nations there was turn'd
> By the fervor of his prayer.

> But wouldst thou know his name,
> Who wandered there alone?
> Go, read enroll'd in Heaven's archives,
> *The prayer of* WASHINGTON!

20. Wesley Bradshaw, "General Washington's Vision," *National Tribune,* December 1880, currently reprinted and sold in pamphlet form (Minneapolis: Osterhus, n.d.). See Jon Kerr, "Mine Eyes Have Seen the Glory," [Minneapolis] *City Pages,* 13 February 1985, 3; employees quoted in the article call it "a steady seller."

21. Frances Davis Whittemore, *George Washington in Sculpture* (Boston: Marshall Jones, 1933), 97–98. Washington's grandnephew posed for the figure of the general that appears several times on the Monmouth Monument, and the young Thomas Edison, because he was clean-shaven in an age of beards, posed for the likeness of a wounded soldier.

22. "Clancy's Name off His New Tablet," *New York Times,* 14 February 1907, 3, col. 3.

23. Robert Bruce, *Art and Sculpture of James Edward Kelly, 1855–1933* (New York: George Hope Ryder, 1935), 35.

24. "Clancy's Name off His New Tablet," *New York Times.*

25. "Tablet Rejected by Mr. Roosevelt," *New York Times,* 19 February 1907, 6, col. 3. Clancy had planned a gala unveiling. The Hebrew Orphan Asylum Band was to have played while the Washington Guards marched about in full regalia.

26. "Clancy's Tablet Is in Its Place," *New York Times,* 23 February 1907, 5, col. 1.

27. The most famous of these prints is the etching by Evans, dated to 1913. Thanks to the good offices of Paul L. Holmer, Jr., I was able to examine a copy of this work in the collection of a dealer in New Haven in the spring of 1984. It bears several inscriptions, including J. E. Kelly's copyright (1904), the words "March, 1778," and these sentences: "George Washington's horse was tied to a sapling in a thicket. The General was on his knees praying most feverishly."

28. The prayer in the snow became an emblem of Cold War anxiety, too. In 1953 the DAR added a bell-tower to the Washington Memorial Chapel at Valley Forge that contained a rose window featuring the motif; see *In Washington: The National Society,*

Daughters of the American Revolution Diamond Anniversary, 1890–1965 (Washington, D.C.: Daughters of the American Revolution, 1965), 113. The society raised $500,000 for this purpose. In 1955 a second stained glass window picturing the praying Washington (see Figure 1.10) was donated anonymously to the Prayer Room adjacent to the rotunda of the U.S. Capitol, where, it was hoped, the image "might speak of that religious faith which has always been a part of the greatness of our Nation": see [Architect of the Capitol, under the direction of the Joint Committee on the Library,] *Compilation of Works of Art and Other Objects in the United States Capitol* (Washington, D.C.: Government Printing Office, 1965), 361.

29. Michael Kammen, *A Season of Youth: The American Revolution and the Historical Imagination* (New York: Alfred A. Knopf, 1978), 214–215 and passim.

30. Warren I. Susman, *Culture as History: The Transformation of American Society in the Twentieth Century* (New York: Pantheon, 1984), especially the discussion of Colonial Williamsburg, 189–191 and 207–208. Also pertinent is Barry Schwartz, *George Washington: The Making of an American Symbol* (New York: Free Press, 1987).

31. See Curtis Putnam Nettels, "The Washington Theme in American History," *Proceedings of the Massachusetts Historical Society,* 68 (October 1944–May 1947), 171–198.

32. *An Illustrated Handbook of Mount Vernon, the Home of Washington* (Mount Vernon, Va.: Mount Vernon Ladies' Association, 1932), 15, and Benson Lossing, "Arlington House, the Seat of G. W. P. Custis, Esq.," *Harper's New Monthly Magazine,* September 1853, 443.

33. Rev. E. B. Hillard, *The Last Men of the Revolution,* ed. Wendell D. Garrett (Barre, Mass.: Barre Publishers, 1968), 12. In February of 1864, the Pension Office had compiled a list of the oldest veterans with an eye toward increasing their stipends; the roster was made public in March in an effort to find the old gentlemen; and by July, when Hillard had tracked them all down for photographing, only seven remained to remember the spirit of '76. See Thomas H. Pauly, "In Search of 'The Spirit of '76,'" *American Quarterly,* 28, no. 4 (Fall 1976), 445–464, in regard to Archibald Willard's famous and blatantly nostalgic painting, first exhibited at the Philadelphia Centennial Exposition of 1876.

34. Hillard, *Last Men of the Revolution,* 13.

35. Ibid., 36–37.

36. E.g., W. S. Baker, *The Engraved Portraits of Washington* (Philadelphia: Lindsay and Baker, 1880).

37. John Neal, *Conversations on American Art: Selections from the Writings of John Neal,* ed. Harold Edward Dickson, Pennsylvania State College Studies, no. 12 (State College: Council on Research, Pennsylvania State College, 1943), 3 and 73. The Athenaeum Portrait by Stuart got its name from the fact that it once hung in the Boston Athenaeum, alongside Stuart's companion portrait of Martha Washington. At present the pictures are jointly owned by the Boston Museum of Fine Arts and the Smithsonian Institution's National Portrait Gallery.

38. Quoted in Morton Borden, ed., *George Washington* (Englewood Cliffs, N.J.: Prentice-Hall, 1969), 1. Hawthorne was complaining about Horatio Greenough's statue of Washington as a bare-chested Jove with a Gilbert Stuart head.

39. Quoted by Bryan, *Washington in American Literature,* 235. *The Virginians* was serialized over a two-year period beginning in November 1857.

40. Thistlethwaite, *Image of George Washington,* 5, has shown that the theme was introduced by Joseph Kyle in a lost canvas exhibited at the American Art Union in 1847 and 1848.

41. Martha is traditionally placed on the scene, as is a military aide to Washington. Jane Stuart, *The Stuart Portraits of Washington,* consisting of privately bound extracts from "The Stuart Portraits of Washington" and "Anecdotes of Gilbert Stuart" that appeared in *Scribner's Monthly Magazine* (July 1877), 372, puts Martha's granddaughter at the sittings. According to William T. Whitley, *Gilbert Stuart* (Cambridge, Mass.: Harvard University Press, 1932), 113–115, the historian Rufus Griswald added Harriet Chew to the company of observers. For the Schmolze portrait, see *The Artist's Studio in American Painting, 1840–1983* (Allentown, Pa.: Allentown Art Museum, 1983), text accompanying plate 1.

42. Thistlethwaite, *Image of George Washington,* 608. In addition to Leutze, the jibes at foreigners were directed at C. Brumidi, former restorer of the Vatican frescoes, who was in the process of adorning the Capitol in the manner of Raphael.

43. In my collection, for example, there is a framed magazine cover cropped to eliminate the headline that appeared above "Painter and President, 1795 [*sic*]—By

J. L. G. Ferris." Bits of text remaining identify this as a cover from *Literary Digest,* 6 February 1932. As the bicentennial of his birth approached, that journal ran a number of Washington covers based on Ferris paintings and several biographical sketches of the artist; see, e.g., "The Cover," *Literary Digest,* 10 October 1931, 17.

44. See "J. L. G. Ferris," *National Cyclopaedia of American Biography,* vol. 23 (New York: James T. White, 1933), 385, and "Jean Leon Gerome Ferris," in *Dictionary of American Biography,* ed. Allen Johnson and Dumas Malone (New York: Charles Scribner's Sons, 1958), 340–341. Many Ferris paintings were used as historical illustrations in the famous "Pageant of America" series issued by Yale. See vol. 1, Clark Wissler, Constance Lindsay Skinner, and William Wood, *Adventures in the Wilderness* (New Haven: Yale University Press, 1925), 202, 228, 239, and 251–252; vol. 6, William Wood and Ralph Henry Gabriel, *The Winning of Freedom* (1927), 55, 85, and 181; and vol. 8, Frederic Austin Ogg, *Builders of the Republic* (1927), 107 and 171. John Ward Dunsmore, Henry A. Ogden, Percy Moran, and Howard Pyle are among the other prominent painter-illustrators of the day who contributed to the series. The Ferris series is no longer on loan to the Smithsonian Institution: recalled by his heirs, the paintings are in private hands.

45. Among popular periodicals of the 1920s and 1930s, the *Saturday Evening Post* consistently devoted the most space to discussion of the antiques craze of the day and to redoing the middle-class home in the "colonial" manner. Ads reinforced the theme. See, e.g., Kenneth L. Roberts, "The Notes of an Antique Weevil," *Saturday Evening Post,* 21 January 1922, 8–9, 74, 77–78, and 81.

46. George Washington Nordham, *George Washington and Money* (Washington, D.C.: University Press of America, 1982), 102–103.

47. Kimble, *Commemorative Postage Stamps,* 66–70, and David Curtis Skaggs, "Postage Stamps as Icons," in *Icons of America*, ed. Ray B. Browne and Marshall Fishwick (Bowling Green, Ohio: Popular Press, Bowling Green State University, 1978), 198–208. The 1932 red two-cent stamp was, for its date, the most widely circulated stamp ever printed. Later in the year it became a three-cent issue when postal rates rose.

48. See Joseph C. Sindelar, ed., *Washington's Day Entertainments* (Chicago: Teacher's Supply Bureau,

1910), 14–15, and *History of the George Washington Bicentennial Celebration,* vol. 1 (Washington, D.C.: U.S. George Washington Bicentennial Commission, 1932), 421. Sindelar treats the poem as a play: "Make a big postage stamp (Washington design) from manilla paper; color and sketch to imitate the real article. Stamp should be large enough to almost hide the small speaker. Only his face and feet are to be seen, for he is a stamp, not a boy, you know. A real, live walking stamp." He also reprints the cherry tree and prayer-in-the-snow stories from Weems, 165–166.

49. Other similar manuals accept both stories, implicitly or explicitly. See Nellie Urner Wallington, ed., *American History by American Poets* (New York: Duffield, 1911), 187–188, reprinting Joachin Miller's "Washington on the Delaware," in which Washington

> . . . set his firm lips silently,
> Then turned aside to pray.
> And as he kneeled and prayed to God,
> God's finger spun the stars in space.

50. Clara J. Denton, "What Should Have Happened," in Sindelar, ed., *Washington's Day Entertainments,* 60–62.

51. Sindelar, ed., *Washington's Day Entertainments,* 28.

52. On the school festival cycle, see Theodore Caplow, Howard M. Bohr, Bruce A. Chadwick, Reuben Hill, and Margaret Holmes Williamson, *Middletown Families: Fifty Years of Change and Continuity* (Minneapolis: University of Minnesota Press, 1982), 225–226.

53. Weems, *Life of Washington,* 12. Contemporary humorists are the only writers who take Weems seriously on an annual basis. See, e.g., Russell Baker, "The Plausible Tree: Homage to the Truth on Washington's Birthday," *New York Times,* 22 February 1986, 15Y, cols. 1–6.

54. Clara J. Denton, "The Making of 'Old Glory,'" in Sindelar, ed., *Washington's Day Entertainments,* 63–66.

55. See Robert Haven Schauffler and A. P. Sanford, eds., *Plays for Our American Holidays* (New York: Dodd, Mead, 1928), 95, for MacKaye's abbreviated play. See also Percy MacKaye, *Washington, the Man Who Made Us: A Ballad Play* (New York: Alfred A. Knopf, 1919).

56. Rodris Roth, "The Colonial Revival and 'Centennial Furniture,'" *Art Quarterly,* 27, no. 1 (1964), 60 and 65–66.

57. Elinor Lander Horwitz, *The Bird, the Banner, and Uncle Sam: Images of America in Folk and Popular Art* (Philadelphia: J. B. Lippincott, 1976), 56–57, 109, and 112. Joseph Jackson, *Encyclopedia of Philadelphia*, vol. 1 (Harrisburg, Pa.: National Historical Association, 1931), 277, notes that Betsy Ross actually lived in a house that stood on the site of the present-day building at 233 Arch Street, and associates interest in the place where the flag may have been made with publication of the story in 1870.

58. George Canby and Lloyd Balderston, *The Evolution of the American Flag* (Philadelphia: Ferris and Leach, 1909), 10, 47–48, and 102.

59. Peleg D. Harrison, *The Stars and Stripes and Other American Flags* (Boston: Little, Brown, 1908), 61–63.

60. George Henry Preble, *History of the Flag of the United States of America*, 2d rev. ed. (Boston: Williams, 1880), 26–27.

61. Tristram Potter Coffin, *Uncertain Glory: Folklore and the American Revolution* (Detroit: Folklore Associates, 1971), 153 and 249.

62. Canby and Balderston, *Evolution of the American Flag*, 119–121. See also the photograph of the Betsy Ross House in Herbert C. Wise and H. Ferdinand Beidleman, *Colonial Architecture for Those About to Build* (Philadelphia: J. B. Lippincott, 1913), 181, with the Weisgerber print displayed in the front window.

63. See the listing for the Betsy Ross House in Laurence Vail Coleman, *Historic House Museums* (Washington, D.C.: American Association of Museums, 1933), 149. It was the association's original intention to turn the shrine over to the federal government, but as of 1933 this had proven impossible. The government did issue a Betsy Ross commemorative stamp in 1952, the bicentennial of her birth; and a flag always flies—day and night—over her grave, an honor also accorded to Francis Scott Key.

64. Just as Betsy Ross proved perennially popular, so the most tenacious of the Washington legends have survived sporadic outbursts of debunkery and intervals of neglect because their imagery is accommodating of multiple uses. The prayer-in-the-snow story suited the ministerial rhetoric of the Civil War, and the strong pictorial parallel between the suffering Christ and the general—and the humility of the suppliant hero in the face of catastrophe—made *that* Washington an appropriate symbol for the stricken 1930s, when the theme was revived for both adult and child audiences. The Brueckner version of the scene was redrawn and interest in it revived, for instance. Thus William Leverich Brower, ed., *Tributes to the Memory of George Washington by the Reformed Protestant Dutch Church of the City of New York* (New York: Consistory of the Collegiate Reformed Dutch Church, 1932), 19, lists the contents of a special collection of pictorial works from the collection of the editor installed in the Church House for the duration of the Washington bicentennial ceremonies. No. 130, in the fourth-floor corridor, is the 1866 McRae print after Henry Brueckner's *Prayer at Valley Forge*.

An illustrated biography of Washington for children distributed by a commercial firm as a premium in 1932 included a Valley Forge scene with troops who looked like the modern-day unemployed, shivering on a breadline. "They were half starved," said the accompanying text, "and their clothes were torn and ragged. One day, a friend saw the great General, with tears streaming down his face, as he knelt in the snow, praying to God to come to the aid of the American army." See Georgene Faulkner, *George Washington: The Father of His Country* (Chicago: Northwestern Yeast Co., 1931). Written and illustrated for children by recent immigrants to the United States, Ingri and Edgar Parrin D'Aulaire's *George Washington* (New York: Doubleday, 1936), 51, also shows the scene with all the necessary ingredients—starving troops around a fire, snow, a blasted tree with icicles, and Washington with his blue cloak and black hat—but Washington does not pray. The authors omit all the popular myths about Washington, preferring to allude to them by pictorial means alone; although the hatchet incident is not discussed, for example, little cherry trees are strewn throughout the illustrations.

65. Professor Michael H. Frisch, of the State University of New York at Buffalo, conducts an annual poll among his students that attests to the deathless popularity of Betsy Ross. I am grateful to him for discussing his ongoing research with me.

66. "'Washington' to cross Delaware December 25," *Capper's Weekly*, 18 December 1984, 1. "Ice Foils Delaware Crossing," [Rochester, New York] *Democrat and Chronicle*, 26 December 1983, 3, notes that Washington-impersonator John B. Kelly, Jr., and his band—Kelly had played "George Washington's role for several years"—were forced by the ice and cold to turn back that winter.

67. "Washington Crossing Assembly Supports Scholarship Program," *Main Line Times,* 8 November 1984, 6.

68. See special "television edition" of James Thomas Flexner, *Washington: The Indispensable Man* (New York: NAL/Signet, 1984), "with 8 pages of movie photos." Produced by David Gerber Co. in association with MGM/UA Entertainment Co., the original miniseries was screened on the CBS network on April 8, 10, and 11, 1984.

69. The miniseries won a 1984 George Foster Peabody Award for outstanding achievement in television programming; see "WCCO, 'St. Elsewhere' Among Peabody Award Winners," *Minneapolis Star and Tribune,* 15 April 1985, 2C. A sequel entitled *George Washington, the Forging of a Nation* was broadcast by CBS on September 21 and 22, 1986; *New Yorker,* 18 August 1986, 45.

70. "Money Matters" is the title of the financial segment on the *ABC World News Tonight* with Peter Jennings. Its graphic symbol is the center oval on the dollar bill, with Washington's face clearly visible.

71. The ad is one of a series of "Schumacher's Illustrated Notes on 20th Century Taste," *New Yorker,* 1 April 1985, 48–49.

72. J. S. Ingram, *The Centennial Exposition Described and Illustrated* (Philadelphia: Hubbard Brothers, 1876), 73; Edward C. Bruce, *The Century: Its Fruits and Its Festival* (Philadelphia: J. B. Lippincott, 1877), 222; and Theodore T. Belote, "Descriptive Catalogue of the Washington Relics in the United States National Museum," *Proceedings of the U.S. National Museum,* 19 October 1915, 14–15.

2. Teatime at Valley Forge

1. Edward C. Bruce, *The Century: Its Fruits and Its Festival* (Philadelphia: J. B. Lippincott, 1877), 22 and 222.

2. John Maass, *The Glorious Enterprise: The Centennial Exhibition of 1876 and H. J. Schwarzmann, Architect-in-Chief* (Watkins Glen, N.Y.: American Life Foundation, 1973), 89, is among those who argue for the lack of interest of the generation of 1876 in the past, except as a benchmark against which to measure modern progress.

3. Charles Moore, *The Family Life of George Washington* (Boston: Houghton Mifflin, 1926), 187. The far larger Lewis collection of Washington artifacts was purchased by Congress in 1878 from the heirs of Washington's adopted granddaughter. With the Custis material, the Lewis collection was transferred from the Patent Office to the U.S. National Museum in 1883.

4. See, e.g., Benson J. Lossing, "Arlington House, the Seat of G. W. P. Custis, Esq.," *Harper's New Monthly Magazine,* September 1853, 437 and 454.

5. Benson J. Lossing, *The Home of Washington; or, Mount Vernon and Its Associations, Historical, Biographical, and Pictorial* (Hartford: A. S. Hale, 1870), 133–134.

6. "The Centennial, Washington Relics," *Harper's Weekly,* 23 September 1876, 781.

7. The woodcuts depicting the Washington installation in Philadelphia do not agree in all particulars, although the intention seems plain enough. It is not entirely clear how these same items were customarily installed in their cases at the Patent Office. The old photograph of the uniform included in Theodore T. Belote, "Descriptive Catalogue of the Washington Relics in the United States National Museum," *Proceedings of the U.S. National Museum,* 19 October 1915, plate 20, shows the suit splayed flat on a surface, as Lossing shows it in 1870 but unlike the more "natural" disposition of the garments apparently attempted at Philadelphia.

8. "The Centennial, Washington Relics," *Harper's Weekly,* 781:

> They would hardly do for a gay cavalier, but the inimitable GEORGE gravely cut his bacon upon them, or laid his plate upon the coals to rewarm the meat, enjoying the sight, sound, and smell of the frizzle, and then mopping out his plate with the crumb of bread in solemn sort.
>
> Who have sat opposite to this grave gentleman—who carried his responsibilities like an Atlas—and divided with him his morsel, and brake bread, and dusted his bit of meat with the pepper, and then courteously passed it over? Which of the worthies in his confidence has not sat at the table and looked at his chief across these plain furnishings? Oh! but it is almost a history to look at and handle them!

9. Elizabeth Stillinger, *The Antiquers* (New York: Alfred A. Knopf, 1980), 149–150.

10. James D. McCabe, *The Illustrated History of the Centennial Exhibition* (Cincinnati: Jones Brothers, 1876), 429.

11. *Frank Leslie's Illustrated Historical Register of the Centennial Exposition, 1876* (New York: Frank Leslie's Publishing House, 1877), 107.

12. *Pennsylvania and the Centennial Exposition, Comprising the Preliminary and Final Reports of the Pennsylvania Board of Centennial Managers, Made to the Legislature at the Sessions of 1877–8*, vol. 1 (Philadelphia: Pennsylvania Board of Centennial Managers/Gillin & Nagle, 1878), 61.

13. J. S. Ingram, *The Centennial Exposition Described and Illustrated* (Philadelphia: Hubbard Bros., 1876), 379–380. Commercial and industrial displays routinely set up contrasts between past and present. Thus Ingram describes the booth of the American Button-Hole and Sewing Machine Company in which a working model of a sewing machine only one inch high was overshadowed by a glass showcase containing a pair of "life-size wax figures representing the different styles of dress worn in 1776 and 1876, showing such a marked contrast that they were much admired and excited considerable amusement." The ladies did not come to giggle at their *own* dresses, of course. The costume of 1776 produced the smiles and made them grateful to be alive in 1876, when the technology for stitching all manner of dressmaker's ruffles, pleats, ruches, and tucks into place in the twinkling of an eye had been perfected.

14. McCabe, *Illustrated History*, 617.

15. William Dean Howells, "A Sennight of the Centennial," *Atlantic Monthly*, July 1876, 103.

16. Josiah Allen's Wife [Marietta Holley], *Samantha at the Centennial* (Hartford: American Publishing, 1879), 535–536.

17. Ingram, *Centennial Exposition*, 730–731.

18. "Say It's Washington's Hair," *New York Times*, 15 May 1905, 7, sec. 1, col. 4. This article reports on a lock of hair deeded by a Miss Sarah Lawrence to her younger relations in 1873. Mourning rings containing Washington's hair are still the subject of comment in society columns. See, for instance, discussion of such a ring, dated to 1779 and valued at $100,000, shown at a recent fundraising event in the Midwest; Barbara Flanagan column, *Minneapolis Star and Tribune*, 25 August 1986, 17A, col. 6.

19. Neil Harris, *Humbug: The Art of P. T. Barnum* (Chicago: University of Chicago Press, 1981), 21–23, and Leslie Fiedler, *Freaks: Myths and Images of the Secret Self* (New York: Simon and Schuster, 1978), 15. Dixon Wecter, *The Hero in America: A Chronicle of Hero-Worship* (Ann Arbor: University of Michigan Press, 1963), 120, says that Barnum was still showing a nurse of Washington's in 1859.

20. For a parody on Washington nurses written in the centennial year, see Walter F. Brown, *Hail Columbia! Historical, Comical and Centennial* (Providence, R.I.: privately printed by the author, 1876), 32.

21. Stan Gores, *Presidential and Campaign Memorabilia* (Des Moines: Wallace-Homestead, 1982), 27–29.

22. McCabe, *Illustrated History*, 657. Iolanthe was the heroine of a popular play of the period. Mrs. Brooks was entirely self-taught and sometimes, as in the popular demonstration of October 14, worked before an admiring audience. See my article ". . . And She Brought Forth Butter in a Lordly Dish: The Origins of Minnesota Butter Sculpture," *Minnesota History*, 50, no. 6 (Summer 1987), 218–228.

23. *United States Centennial Commission International Exhibition 1876 Official Catalogue*, rev. ed. (Philadelphia: John R. Nagle, 1876), 88. Another lady, seventy-eight years old, also submitted mittens that attracted notice because she was the granddaughter of a Major Clapp who had served in the Revolution. Beside the mittens was hung a photograph of their creator, looking old in years but remarkably "young in health."

24. *Official Catalogue*, 109.

25. Ingram, *Centennial Exposition*, 382.

26. William B. Rhoads, *The Colonial Revival*, vol. 1 (New York: Garland Publishing, 1977), 14.

27. Bruce, *The Century*, 124.

28. Kenneth L. Ames, "Grand Rapids Furniture of the Time of the Centennial," in *Winterthur Portfolio 10*, ed. Ian M. Quimby (Charlottesville: University Press of Virginia/Winterthur Museum, 1975), 31–32.

29. The tree continued to stand until 1923; see Rodris Roth, "Pieces of History: Relic Furniture of the Nineteenth Century," *Antiques*, May 1972, 876–877.

30. Bruce, *The Century*, 79.

31. Ingram, *Centennial Exposition*, 604.

32. Thompson Wescott, *Centennial Portfolio: A Souvenir of the International Exhibition at Philadelphia* (Philadelphia: Thomas Hunter, 1876), 26.

33. "Exhibition of Relics at Salem, Massachusetts," *Frank Leslie's Illustrated Newspaper*, 22 January 1876, 324–325.

34. *Official Catalogue*, 125.

35. Wescott, *Centennial Portfolio*, 27, and Rhoads, *Colonial Revival*, vol. 1, 59. Mitchell, a bucolic humorist and author of *Reveries of a Bachelor* and

Dream Life, wrote under the pseudonym of "Ik Marvel."

36. McCabe, *Illustrated History,* 663–664.

37. Ingram, *Centennial Exposition,* 608 and 611.

38. [George D. Curtis,] *Souvenir of the Centennial Exhibition; or, Connecticut's Representation at Philadelphia, 1876* (Hartford: George D. Curtis, 1877), 72.

39. Robert F. Trent, "The Charter Oak Artifacts," *Connecticut Historical Society Bulletin,* 49, no. 3 (Summer 1984), 130–135.

40. See entry for Item #370; *Official Catalogue,* 111.

41. Curtis, *Souvenir of the Centennial,* 209 and 213–214. A genuine fragment of the oak is pasted into the book. Thanks to the apparent disbelief of typesetters, it is not uncommon to come across references to the lifelike "hands" (for "hams") made of the Charter Oak and displayed in the Connecticut building!

42. Ibid., 77–80.

43. Ingram, *Centennial Exposition,* 707. One of these stereo views is in the collection of the National Museum of American History, the Smithsonian Institution.

44. The Revolutionary historian Benson Lossing was among the few male members of the committee in charge of the Poughkeepsie Fair. See also Rodris Roth, "The New England, or 'Old Tyme,' Kitchen Exhibit at Nineteenth-Century Fairs," in *The Colonial Revival in America*, ed. Alan Axelrod (New York: W. W. Norton/ Winterthur Museum, 1985), 159 and 173–178. The Volkskuchen of Vienna, on which a utopian scheme for serving wholesome food to the working poor in American cities was based—it was called the New England Kitchen and opened in Boston in 1890—was also in evidence in 1873; see Dolores Hayden, *The Grand Domestic Revolution: A History of Feminist Designs for American Homes, Neighborhoods and Cities* (Cambridge, Mass.: MIT Press, 1981), 156.

The vignettes surrounding *Harper's* double-page illustration of the Brooklyn Sanitary Fair apparently show a series of theatrical "tableaux" performed in conjunction with it. These include "Washington and Mrs. Custis," "Spinning Wheel," and "Quilting Bee in '76." This suggests that the domestic scene William Dean Howells would admire at Philadelphia may have had its origin, too, in the Sanitary Fair; *Harper's Weekly,* 5 March 1864, 152–153.

45. J. C. Furnas, *The Americans: A Social History of the United States, 1587–1914* (New York: G. P. Putnam's Sons, 1969), 598–602.

46. Whittier's poem is included in Milton R. Stern and Seymour L. Gross, eds., *American Literature Survey,* vol. 2 (New York: Viking, 1968), 597.

47. Furnas, *The Americans,* 598.

48. Quoted in Marshall B. Davidson, ed., *The American Heritage History of Antiques from the Civil War to World War I* (n.p.: American Heritage, 1969), 196.

49. Ingram, *Centennial Exposition,* 107.

50. Harold R. Shurtleff, *The Log Cabin Myth: A Study of the Early Dwellings of the English Colonists in North America* (Cambridge, Mass.: Harvard University Press, 1939), 191.

51. *Visitor's Guide to the Centennial Exhibition* (Philadelphia: J. B. Lippincott, 1876), 21.

52. McCabe, *Illustrated History,* 723.

53. Howells, "Sennight of the Centennial," 100–101.

54. For *The Courtship of Miles Standish,* see *Longfellow Poems* (New York: Dutton/Everyman's Library, 1978), 178–180.

55. For "To a Child," see *Longfellow Poems,* 317.

56. Rhoads, *Colonial Revival,* vol. 2, 891.

57. In aid of the cause, Mary E. Taylor of Somerville, who claimed to be the Mary once followed by the famous nursery-rhyme lamb, sold scraps of authentic lamb fleece unraveled from an old stocking and mounted on cards bearing her spidery signature; she made $100. See Roger Butterfield, "Henry Ford, the Wayside Inn, and the Problem of 'History Is Bunk,'" *Proceedings of the Massachusetts Historical Society,* 77 (January–December 1965), 62–63.

58. Anne Hollingsworth Wharton, *Colonial Days and Dames* (Philadelphia: J. B. Lippincott, 1895), 93.

59. Alice Morse Earle, *Colonial Dames and Good Wives* (Boston: Houghton Mifflin, 1895), 311. Earle cites Whittier's *Snow Bound.*

60. See my articles "American Art and the American Woman," in Karal Ann Marling and Helen A. Harrison, *7 American Women: The Depression Decade* (New York: A.I.R. Gallery, 1976), 10–11, and "Portrait of the Artist as a Young Woman: Miss Dora Wheeler," *Bulletin of the Cleveland Museum of Art,* 65, no. 2 (February 1978), 49–50. Wheeler and her daughter later created a series of American "tapestries" in needlework adorned with heroines of literature and history, including several of Hawthorne's Puritan maidens.

The kind of Early American subject matter used in these pieces also came to the forefront of academic sculpture as the centennial approached. The Philadelphia sculptor Howard Roberts, for example, began a *Hester Prynne* in 1871; see David Sellin, *The First Pose* (New York: W. W. Norton, 1976), 39.

61. *New-York Tribune Guide to the Exhibition* (New York: New-York Tribune Co., 1876), 707–708.

62. Joseph Miller Wilson, "History, Mechanics, Science," in *The Masterpieces of the Centennial International Exhibition,* vol. 3 (Philadelphia: Gebbie and Barrie, 1878), clxiii.

63. Bruce, *The Century,* 78.

64. *Official Catalogue,* 150, under the heading "Special Buildings."

65. McCabe, *Illustrated History,* 723, and Bruce, *The Century,* 78.

66. Ingram, *Centennial Exposition,* 256–257. Unlike the Old Mill, several of the colonial buildings erected for the fair survived. The Connecticut Cottage was sold, dismantled, and moved to Long Branch, New Jersey, in 1877 as a summer cottage. Miss Southwick, who went on to open another New England Kitchen at the 1893 Columbian Exhibition in Chicago, ultimately donated her log cabin to Fairmount Park, where it may survive as a shed or comfort station. That was the fate of the U. S. Grant Log Cabin from the Centennial Exposition, which was also donated to the park commission: it became a women's retiring room and a men's lavatory on the footpath side of Wissahickon Creek, below Hermit Lane; see *Souvenir of Fairmount Park* (Philadelphia: Guard Pension Fund Association, 1913), 67 and 79.

67. Dorothy Ditter Gondos, "The Cultural Climate of the Centennial City: Philadelphia, 1875–1876," M.A. thesis (University of Pennsylvania, 1944), 97–98. The early history of the teas after 1873 is discussed in Wilson, *Masterpieces of the Centennial,* vol. 3, clvi–clxv.

68. "Mount Vernon," *Harper's Weekly,* 22 April 1876, 323. See also Susan Williams, *Savory Suppers and Fashionable Feasts: Dining in Victorian America* (New York: Pantheon, 1985), 187–189.

69. Quoted in Curtis, *Souvenir of the Centennial,* 58.

70. Ibid., 58–60. Miss Minnie Mitchell, who was fortunate enough to be assigned a part comparable to the dignity of the family heirlooms she wore, came decked out in "portions of a dress of her great-great-grandmother, Mrs. Rebecca Mott, of Revolutionary fame."

71. Ibid., 58.

72. Ibid., 60–61.

73. Ibid., 65.

74. Ibid., 65–67.

75. "Works of Art Now on Exhibition," *The Nation,* 12 October 1865, 472–474.

76. "Mr. Huntington's Republican Court," *New York Daily Tribune,* 21 October 1865, 9, sec. 1, cols. 1–2.

77. Rufus Wilmot Griswold, *The Republican Court; or, American Society in the Days of Washington* (New York: D. Appleton, 1868), especially 142 and 165 ff.

78. Mrs. Ellet, *The Queens of American Society,* 6th ed. (Philadelphia: Porter & Coates, 1873), 24 and 28–29. She also quotes Colonel Stone on the "celestial blue" gown.

79. "Mr. Huntington's Republican Court," *New York Daily Tribune.*

80. Quoted in Martha J. Lamb, "Washington as President, 1789—1790," *Magazine of American History,* February 1889, 93.

81. "Mr. Huntington's Republican Court," *New York Daily Tribune.*

82. "Lady Washington's Reception-Day," *Harper's Weekly,* 27 February 1875, 178, with a key identifying characters shown in the wood engraving by Ritchie (published by Emil Seitz) after the Daniel Huntington painting. At that date, the picture was owned by A. T. Stewart, the department-store magnate.

83. Ward McAllister, *Society as I Have Found It* (New York: Cassell, 1890), 323–324.

84. Ibid., 325.

85. Ibid., 326–327.

86. "The Martha Washington Reception," *Harper's Weekly,* 25 March 1876, 244 and 250.

87. "Martha Washington Reception and Centennial Tea Party in Aid of St. John's Guild," *Frank Leslie's Illustrated Newspaper,* 11 March 1876, 8–9, and 12–13.

88. Anne Wood Murray, "George Washington's Apparel," *Antiques,* July 1980, 121–122, discusses the exhibition of his clothes.

89. Edith Kermit Roosevelt, introduction to Moore, *Family Life of George Washington,* xvii.

3. Colonial History Domesticated

1. Charles Farrar Browne [Artemus Ward], "Fourth of July Oration," in *The Assault of Laughter: A Treasury of American Political Humor,* ed. Arthur P. Dudden (South Brunswick, N.J.: Thomas Yoseloff, 1962), 91–92.

2. "The Centennial," *Harper's Weekly*, 13 May 1876, 394.

3. James D. McCabe, *The Illustrated History of the Centennial Exhibition* (Cincinnati: Jones Brothers, 1876), 534.

4. Jennie J. Young, "Ceramic Art of the Exhibition," in Edward C. Bruce, *The Century: Its Fruits and Its Festival* (Philadelphia: J. B. Lippincott, 1977), 239 and 247. For the Gorham Vase, see McCabe, *Illustrated History of the Centennial Exhibition*, 370–371.

5. "Centennial," *Harper's Weekly*, 14 October 1876, 830 and 833, and "The Centennial," *Harper's Weekly*, 13 May 1876, 394.

6. Edward Strahan, *Illustrated Catalogue: The Masterpieces of the Centennial Exhibition, 1876, The Art Gallery* (Philadelphia: Gebbie & Barrie, n.d. [1876?]), 157. For reaction to the Guarnerio statue, see McCabe, *Illustrated History*, 584.

7. Quoted in J. S. Ingram, *The Centennial Exposition Described and Illustrated* (Philadelphia: Hubbard Bros., 1876), 82.

8. Phillip T. Sandhurst, *The Great Centennial Exhibition Critically Described and Illustrated* (Philadelphia: P. W. Ziegler, 1876), 25.

9. *New-York Tribune Guide to the Exhibition* (New York: New-York Tribune Co., 1876), 58.

10. Strahan, *Illustrated Catalogue*, 160.

11. William Dean Howells, "A Sennight of the Centennial," *Atlantic Monthly*, July 1876, 93. There were other novel and overblown tributes to Washington by foreign artists and industries, including a bronze bust two meters high from the French firm of Susse Frères, a statue by Baron Marochetti generally called "the largest work shown at this exhibition," and a three-dimensional marble version of Leutze's *Washington Crossing the Delaware* (with a twelve-foot Washington) from a Florentine company. This last work was often mistaken for a statue of Columbus discovering the New World. See, e.g., *United States Centennial Commission International Exhibition 1876 Official Catalogue*, rev. ed. (Philadelphia: John R. Nagle, 1876), 148.

12. *New-York Tribune Guide*, 61.

13. Quoted in McCabe, *Illustrated History*, 900.

14. Ingram, *Centennial Exposition*, 526.

15. *New-York Tribune Guide*, 61; McCabe, *Illustrated History*, 598; and *Official Catalogue*, 111–114. John Maass, *The Glorious Enterprise: The Centennial Exhibition of 1876 and H. J. Schwarzmann, Architect-in-Chief* (Watkins Glen, N.Y.: American Life Foundation, 1973), 80, says that Romanelli's *Franklin and His Whistle* (the parable accounting for his later interest in thrift) is in the collection of Crisconi Oldsmobile Co. of Philadelphia. In 1973 *Washington and His Hatchet* was seen by Maass in an unidentified antique shop in Philadelphia. These works are also mentioned in David Sellin, *The First Pose* (New York: W. W. Norton, 1976), 9.

16. Rodris Roth, "The Colonial Revival and 'Centennial Furniture,'" *Art Quarterly*, 27, no. 1 (1964), 64.

17. Charles Nordhoff, "Cape Cod, Nantucket, and the Vineyard," *Harper's New Monthly Magazine*, June 1875, 65.

18. "Lyme: A Chapter of American Genealogy," *Harper's New Monthly Magazine*, February 1876, 319 and 321.

19. Ibid., 318.

20. Walter F. Brown, *Hail Columbia! Historical, Comical and Centennial* (Providence, R.I.: privately printed by the author, 1876), 10.

21. *Official Catalogue*, 17, lists, as Entry #20 in the Department of American Painting, Boughton's picture, the property of R. L. Stuart. *New-York Tribune Guide*, 64, makes special note of "Boughton (half of whom we claim as American)" and his contributions to the British display. For the art displays at Philadelphia, see also Susan Hobbs, *1876: American Art of the Centennial* (Washington, D.C.: National Collection of Fine Arts, Smithsonian Institution, 1976).

22. Strahan, *Illustrated Catalogue*, 221.

23. Quoted in William B. Rhoads, *The Colonial Revival*, vol. 2 (New York: Garland, 1977), 849.

24. Deborah Fenton Shepherd and Kathleen Pyne, entries on Millet in *The Quest for Unity: American Art Between World's Fairs, 1876–1893* (Detroit: Detroit Institute of Arts, 1983), 121–124. H. Barbara Weinberg, "The Career of Francis Davis Millet," *Archives of American Art Journal*, 17, no. 1 (1977), 4, also discusses his neocolonial props.

25. Celia Betsky, "Inside the Past: The Interior and the Colonial Revival in American Art and Literature, 1860–1914," in *The Colonial Revival in America*, ed. Alan Axelrod (New York: W. W. Norton/Winterthur Museum, 1985), 256.

26. For Eakins's 1876 watercolors, see Donelson F. Hoopes, *Eakins Watercolors* (New York: Watson-Guptill, 1971), plate 10 and passim, and for Eakins's

activity at the Centennial, see Elizabeth Johns, *Thomas Eakins: The Heroism of Modern Life* (Princeton, N.J.: Princeton University Press, 1983), 76–77. The Hirshhorn Sculpture Garden (Smithsonian Institution) in Washington, D.C., exhibits two bronze reliefs by Eakins commissioned in 1892 (finished in 1893) for the west and south sides of the Trenton Battle Monument. One, presented by New York State, is called *The Opening of the Fight*. The other, *The Continental Army Crossing the Delaware*, is the gift of Pennsylvania and shows Washington in the lead boat. Eakins is said to have posed his models in authentic Revolutionary uniforms; in any case, his work was praised at the time for its historical accuracy.

27. *Official Catalogue*, 17–59. The history paintings cited were by Mrs. I. Robinson Morrell (she also exhibited a *First Battle of the Puritans*) and A. G. Heaton. Works entitled *One Hundred Years Ago* were shown by Whittredge, Saterlee, and W. H. Wilcox of Philadelphia.

28. Elizabeth McCausland, *The Life and Works of Edward Lamson Henry N.A.* (Albany: Museum of the State of New York, 1945), 29.

29. *Longfellow Poems* (New York: Dutton/Everyman's Library, 1978), 326.

30. Ibid., 327, the penultimate stanza. Betsky, "Inside the Past," 247, cites an article written by Mrs. M. E. W. Sherwood in 1881, entitled "The Influence of Aged People," in which these ideas of grandmotherliness are developed.

31. *The Complete Writings of Nathaniel Hawthorne*, vol. 12 (Boston: Houghton Mifflin, 1900), 228–236.

32. Quoted in Patricia Hills, *The Genre Painting of Eastman Johnson* (New York: Garland, 1977), 54.

33. Mark Edward Thistlethwaite, *The Image of George Washington: Studies in Mid-Nineteenth-Century American History Painting* (New York: Garland, 1979), 136–137.

34. Ibid., 196–200. For a discussion of Mount Vernon funerary keepsakes, see my "Minnesota Souvenirs: The Large and the Small of It," *Prospects*, 11 (1987), 285–286.

35. Harrison Howell Dodge, *Mount Vernon: Its Owner and Its Story* (Philadelphia: J. B. Lippincott, 1932), 99–100.

36. Ibid., 52 and 102. For the song, see "Whittier's Centennial Hymn," *Harper's Weekly*, 20 May 1876, 414.

37. "The Home of Washington," *Harper's Weekly*, 18 March 1876, 223.

38. Frederick L. Harvey, *History of the Washington National Monument and Washington National Monument Society* (Washington, D.C.: Government Printing Office, 1903), 14–18.

39. "Clark Mills's Statue of Washington," *Harper's Weekly*, 25 February 1860, 114.

40. "Monumental Celebrations," *New York Times*, 24 February 1860, 4, cols. 2–3.

41. "Washington's Birthday," *New York Times*, 23 February 1860, 1 and 8, cols. 1–5, 1–3.

42. Ibid., 1, col. 2, and "Monumental Celebrations," *New York Times*, 4, col. 3.

43. Harvey, *History of the Washington National Monument*, 39.

44. Ibid., Appendix, 129. Lack of funds had caused the cornerstone ceremony to be postponed from February 11 to July 4, 1848.

45. Ibid., 50.

46. Ibid., 82.

47. "The Home of Washington," *Harper's Weekly*, 223.

48. "Mount Vernon," *Harper's Weekly*, 22 April 1876, 323.

49. *Mount Vernon: An Illustrated Handbook* (Mount Vernon, Va.: Mount Vernon Ladies' Association of the Union, 1974), 106. John was responsible for squelching the last big push to translate the remains of George Washington to the District of Columbia on the occasion of the Washington centenary, in 1832.

50. Dodge, *Mount Vernon*, 185.

51. Brown, *Hail Columbia!*, 34.

52. Charles B. Hosmer, Jr., *Presence of the Past: A History of the Preservation Movement in the United States Before Williamsburg* (New York: G. P. Putnam's Sons, 1965), 81.

53. Michael Wallace, "Visiting the Past: History Museums in the United States," *Radical History Review*, 25 (October 1981), 64.

54. Mabel Lorenz Ives, *Washington's Headquarters* (Upper Montclair, N.J.: Lucy Fortune, 1932), 32.

55. Hosmer, *Presence of the Past*, 78.

56. [Morristown, N.J.] *Democratic Banner*, 5 June 1873, quoted in Hosmer, *Presence of the Past*, 79.

57. Edmund D. Halsey, *History of the Washington Association of New Jersey* (Morristown, N.J.: De Vinne, 1891), 5–7. The four competing bidders at first agreed to offer the house to New Jersey as "a historical place" if their alliance was successful.

58. Ibid., 10.

59. Ibid., 15–17.

60. Quoted in Marcus Cunliffe's foreword to Margaret Brown Klapthor and Howard Alexander Morrison, *George Washington: A Figure upon the Stage* (Washington, D.C.: Smithsonian Institution Press, 1982), 13.

61. Wallace, "Visiting the Past," 64, and Rhoads, *Colonial Revival,* vol. 1, 523. For discussion of the use of Washington as a principle of order, see also Frank Kingdom, *Architects of the Republic* (New York: Alliance, 1947), especially 80–84.

62. Presidential address of 1875, quoted in Halsey, *History of the Washington Association,* 11.

63. Gerald W. Johnson, *Mount Vernon: The Story of a Shrine, An Account of the Rescue and Rehabilitation of Washington's Home by the Mount Vernon Ladies' Association* (New York: Random House, 1953), 44.

64. *Historical Sketches of Ann Pamela Cunningham* (Jamaica, N.Y.: Mount Vernon Ladies' Association/ Marion Press, 1903), 48–49.

65. Ibid., 6.

66. Minnie Kendall Lowther, *Mount Vernon: Its Children and Its Romances, Its Allied Families and Mansions* (Philadelphia: John C. Winston, 1930), 40.

67. Benson J. Lossing, *The Pictorial Field-Book of the Revolution*; or, *Illustrations by Pen and Pencil, of the History, Biography, Scenery, Relics, and Traditions of the War for Independence*, vol. 2 (New York: Harper and Brothers, 1859), 209–211.

68. *Historical Sketches,* 8.

69. Paul Wilstach, *Mount Vernon: Washington's Home and the Nation's Shrine* (Garden City, N.Y.: Doubleday, Page, 1916), 260.

70. Ibid., vii.

71. Hosmer, *Presence of the Past,* 47–48 and 52.

72. Benson J. Lossing, *The Home of Washington; or, Mount Vernon and Its Associations, Historical, Biographical, and Pictorial* (Hartford: A. S. Hale, 1870), 9.

73. Quoted in Daniel J. Boorstin, *The Americans: The National Experience* (New York: Random House, 1965), 352.

74. Quoted in Thistlethwaite, *Image of George Washington,* 116. For the published call of "The Southern Matron" upon the women of the various sections of the country, with replies, see *An Appeal for the Preservation of the Home and Grave of Washington* (Philadelphia: T. K. and P. G. Collins, 1855), especially 5–6.

75. Lossing, *Home of Washington,* 429–430.

76. "Mount Vernon," *Harper's Weekly,* 323.

77. Lossing, *Home of Washington,* 338.

78. Johnson, *Mount Vernon,* 43.

79. Dodge, *Mount Vernon,* 55.

80. Hosmer, *Presence of the Past,* 5, and Elizabeth Stillinger, *The Antiquers* (New York: Alfred A. Knopf, 1980), 33–35. Mount Vernon purchased the spinning equipment from Mrs. Ben: Perley Poore. E. L. Henry, the Centennial Exposition painter of colonial interiors, also collected Americana and Washingtoniana. His loans to an 1872 relic show included several portraits of Washington, a clock, and a spinning wheel.

81. Dodge, *Mount Vernon,* 67.

82. Ruth Lawrence, *Colonial Verses (Mount Vernon)* (New York: Brentano's, 1897), 28.

83. Henry Adams, *Democracy* (New York: Harmony Books, 1981), 80 and 82–83. See also Bernard Mayo, *Myths and Men: Patrick Henry, George Washington, Thomas Jefferson* (Athens: University of Georgia Press, 1959), 40.

84. Dixon Wecter, *The Hero in America: A Chronicle of Hero-Worship* (Ann Arbor: University of Michigan Press, 1966), 122 and 131.

85. Henry Adams, *The Education of Henry Adams* (New York: Modern Library, 1946), 340–341 and 343.

86. Adams, *Democracy,* 85–86.

87. Johnson, *Mount Vernon,* 44.

88. Christopher D. Geist, "Historic Sites and Monuments as Icons," in *Icons of America,* ed. Ray B. Browne and Marshall Fishwick (Bowling Green, Ohio: Popular Press, Bowling Green State University, 1978), 58 and 61.

89. Daniel J. Boorstin, *America and the Image of Europe: Reflections on American Thought* (New York: Meridian, 1960), 83.

90. Quoted in Wilstach, *Mount Vernon* (1916), vii. Wister also wrote a popular biography of George Washington, reflecting his intimate knowledge of Mount Vernon; see Owen Wister, *The Seven Ages of Washington: A Biography* (New York: Macmillan, 1907).

4. Architecture, Ancestry, and High Society

1. *Nineteenth Annual Report of the American Scenic and Historic Preservation Society* (New York: American Scenic and Historic Preservation Society, 1914), 19–20.

2. William B. Rhoads, *The Colonial Revival,* vol. 1 (New York: Garland, 1977), 30–31, quoting an article published in 1868. Sloan also had a scheme for replacing the White House with an improved model farther away from the malarial Potomac.

3. William B. Rhoads, "The Colonial Revival and American Nationalism," *Journal of the Society of Architectural Historians,* 35 (December 1976), 239.

4. Roger Butterfield, "Henry Ford, the Wayside Inn, and the Problem of 'History Is Bunk,'" *Proceedings of the Massachusetts Historical Society,* 77 (January–December 1965), 62–63, quoting the *Boston Transcript,* 14 February 1878.

5. "Washington's Headquarters During the Revolution," *Magazine of American History,* February 1879, 157–60, and Charles B. Hosmer, Jr., *Presence of the Past: A History of the Preservation Movement in the United States Before Williamsburg* (New York: G. P. Putnam's Sons, 1965), 82–84.

6. Clarence Cook, *The House Beautiful* (New York: Charles Scribner's Sons, 1878), 188.

7. *United States Centennial Commission International Exhibition 1876 Official Catalogue,* rev. ed. (Philadelphia: John R. Nagle, 1876), 49. See also Eliza Greatorix, *Old New York from the Battery to Bloomingdale,* vol. 2 (New York: G. P. Putnam's Sons, 1875), 189.

8. Elizabeth Stillinger, *The Antiquers* (New York: Alfred A. Knopf, 1980), 49.

9. W. S. Baker, *The Engraved Portraits of Washington* (Philadelphia: Lindsay and Baker, 1880), v and 193. Under "fictitious portraits," the author mentions a print after a painting by Christian Schussele, *Washington at Valley Forge, 1777.* The James Sharples portraits of Washington that were shown in New York, Washington, Boston, Philadelphia, Chicago, St. Paul, and Cincinnati in 1882, under the auspices of such prominent business leaders as James J. Hill, excited great public response on the basis of their supposed correspondence to the actual, unaltered features of the great man. See James Walter, *Memorials of Washington and of Mary, His Mother, and Martha, His Wife, from Letters and Papers of Robert Cary and James Sharples* (New York: Charles Scribner's Sons, 1887), especially 25 and 45.

10. Mariana Griswold Van Rensselaer, "American Country Dwellings, I," *Century Magazine,* May 1886, 19.

11. Vincent Scully, *The Shingle Style* (New Haven: Yale University Press, 1955), 14–25.

12. Vincent Scully, *American Architecture and Urbanism* (New York: Praeger, 1969), 111–121.

13. Moses P. Handy, ed., *The Official Directory of the World's Columbian Exposition* (Chicago: W. B. Conkey, 1893), 76.

14. *The City of Palaces* (Chicago: W. B. Conkey, 1894), 51. The Liberty Bell was mounted on wheels so that it could be moved quickly in case of fire.

15. Quoted in Rhoads, *Colonial Revival,* vol. 1, 130.

16. Halsey C. Ives, *The Dream City: A Portfolio of Photographic Views of the World's Columbian Exposition* (St. Louis: N. D. Thompson, 1893), text accompanying unpaginated plate. The relics were enumerated as follows: "The portrait of the great Samuel Adams had a justly honorable and conspicuous place, and antique portraits of all the Yankee Revolutionary Fathers had been generously loaned to the Exposition. Copies of charters by King Charles, great seals and their bezels, autographs of the Boston poets and authors, the desk of George Washington, colonial furniture, a fire-screen painted by John Hancock, a remnant of the wedding-dress of Mrs. Governor Bradford, and ancient books brought in the Mayflower or printed by the Puritans, made a large and interesting museum."

17. *City of Palaces,* 136.

18. Ives, *Dream City,* unpaginated plate.

19. Major Ben C. Truman, *History of the World's Fair* (Chicago: E. C. Morse, 1893), 473–474.

20. Ibid., 474. Truman also reprints a woodcut of the Washington relics displayed by the government at the 1876 fair in his section on the Virginia building!

21. E.g., Wanda M. Corn, *Grant Wood: The Regionalist Vision* (New Haven: Yale University Press, 1983), 98 and 101.

22. Mary Mann Page Newton, "The Association for the Preservation of Virginia Antiquities," *American Historical Register,* September 1894, 9.

23. *The 350th Anniversary of Jamestown, 1607–1957: Final Report to the President and Congress of the Jamestown-Williamsburg-Yorktown Centennial Commission* (Washington, D.C.: Government Printing Office, 1958), 4.

24. See, e.g., Ella Bassett Washington, "The Mother and Birthplace of Washington," *Century Magazine,* April 1892, 830–842.

25. Newton, "The Association," 12.

26. Ibid., 11 and 15. Miss Irene Langhorne, leader of the "Saraband" at the 1892 gala, was described as "a daughter of the gods, divinely tall and most divinely fair," while Miss May Handy, dressed as Queen Anne (during whose reign the colony was founded), was eulogized thus: "What winning graces! What majestic mien! She moves like a goddess and looks like a Queen!"

27. *Register of the Empire State Society of the Sons of the American Revolution* (New York: Sons of the American Revolution, 1899), 10.

28. *Sons of the American Revolution: Minnesota Society Year Book, 1889–1895* (St. Paul: McGill Printing, 1895), 8–9.

29. Ibid., 8.

30. Martha Strayer, *The D.A.R.: An Informal History* (Washington, D.C.: Public Affairs Press, 1958), 1–12. Mrs. Harrison thought that the head of the organization would surely be called on to represent the First Lady and that anyone who might do so should have a certain social prominence and "a residence of some pretension in Washington." A husband of acceptable income and pedigree was also a social asset.

31. The source of the story is identified in "Hannah Arnett's Life," *Washington Post*, 21 July 1890, 5, sec. 1, col. 2.

32. [Mary S. Lockwood,] "Women Worthy of Honor," *Washington Post*, 13 July 1890, 12, sec. 2, cols. 1–2.

33. Ibid., col. 1.

34. Quoted in *In Washington: The National Society, Daughters of the American Revolution Diamond Anniversary, 1890–1965* (Washington, D.C.: Daughters of the American Revolution, 1965), 17.

35. John T. Goolrick, *Historic Fredericksburg: The Story of an Old Town* (Richmond: Whittet & Shepperson, 1922), 129–132.

36. Lewis Barrington, *Historic Restorations of the Daughters of the American Revolution* (New York: Richard R. Smith, 1941).

37. [Lockwood,] "Women Worthy of Honor," col. 1. The spinning wheel pictured on the DAR seal was one of the earliest and most popular commercial trademarks of the period. Chalmers Lowell Pancoast, *Trail Blazers of Advertising: Stories of the Romance and Adventure of the Old-Time Advertising Game* (New York: Frederick H. Hitchcock, 1926), 243–244, notes that in 1872 print ads featuring a spinning wheel symbol identified the firm of T. D. Whitney of Boston, retailers of cloth and sewing goods. When a real gilded spinning wheel above the exterior door was taken down for a period just prior to 1880, it was reinstated by popular demand. Ads for James McCutchen & Co., The Linen Store, on West Twenty-third Street in New York used a cut of a spinning wheel as a "registered trade-mark"; see the advertising pages of *Century Magazine,* July 1892, 66.

38. Clyde F. Trudell, *Colonial Yorktown* (Richmond: Dietz, 1938), 186 and 193–194. The Yorktown centenary of 1881 was celebrated by twenty thousand ladies and gentlemen who reached remote Temple Farm, on the site of the battlefield, aboard a specially constructed railroad. Ten thousand uniformed troops from the thirteen original states marched, as did the San Franciscans in the Revolutionary uniforms whose appearance in the order of march began the histories of the great ancestral societies of the late nineteenth century. The cornerstone of a commemorative column was also laid. For the speeches, see *350th Anniversary of Jamestown,* 5.

39. Light-Horse Harry Lee, quoted in Marshall W. Fishwick, *American Heroes: Myth and Reality* (Washington, D.C.: Public Affairs Press, 1954), 42.

40. "Promises of To-Morrow," *New York Times,* 25 November 1886, 1–2, sec. 1. The subject of the statue, the evacuation and Washington's triumphal entry, bringing nationhood and unity, was another that received special attention just before the Civil War, when the Duvals of Philadelphia did a print on the theme advertised as "the largest specimen of Chromolithography ever executed." See Peter C. Marzio, *The Democratic Art: Chromolithography 1840–1900* (Boston and Fort Worth: David R. Godine/Amon Carter Museum of Western Art, 1979), 27 and accompanying plates.

41. "Promises of To-Morrow," *New York Times,* 2, col. 1.

42. "Evacuation-Day," *Harper's Weekly,* 1 December 1883, 762.

43. "The Great Celebration," *New York Times,* 24 November 1883, 1, sec. 1, col. 7.

44. "Promises of To-Morrow," *New York Times,* 1, col. 7.

45. "Washington in Wall Street," *Harper's Weekly,* 8 December 1883, 783.

46. "A Great Day," *Harper's Weekly,* 8 December 1883, 778.

47. "Washington in Wall Street," *Harper's Weekly,* 783.

48. Agnes Miller, "Centenary of a New York Statue," *New York History,* 38, no. 2 (April 1957), 168 and 173–174.

49. James Lee, *The Equestrian Statue of Washington, New York* (New York: John T. Trow, 1864), 9. See also Frances Davis Whittemore, *George Washington in Sculpture* (Boston: Marshall Jones, 1933), 89.

50. Thomas Ball, *My Threescore Years and Ten: An Autobiography* (Boston: Roberts Brothers, 1891), 366–377.

51. Ibid., 370 and 374.

52. Thomas B. Brumbaugh, "The Evolution of Crawford's 'Washington,'" *Virginia Magazine,* 70, no. 1 (January 1962), 5.

53. Quoted in Brumbaugh, "The Evolution of Crawford's 'Washington,'" 24.

54. "Washington in Wall Street," *Harper's Weekly,* 783. Russell Sturgis, "The Work of J. Q. A. Ward," *Scribner's Magazine,* October 1904, 393, comments on this aspect of Ward's sculpture. Ward had already completed a similar Washington for Newburyport, Massachusetts, in 1879; when it was unveiled, on February 22 of that year, children built George Washington snowmen on front lawns all over town.

55. "Washington in Wall Street," *Harper's Weekly,* 783.

56. "Governor Cleveland in New York," *Harper's Weekly,* 8 December 1883, 778.

57. "Washington's Farewell," *Harper's Weekly,* 1 December 1883, 767.

58. Horace A. Scudder, "George Washington," *St. Nicholas,* January–October 1886, 65, 196, 591–593, 669, 758, and 839.

59. Ibid., 761, 763, and 909. See also Fridoff Jackson, ed., *Treasury of American Pen-and-Ink Illustrations, 1881 to 1938* (New York: Dover, 1982), 4, for the Henry Alexander Ogden (1856–1926) illustrations.

60. Julian Ralph, "The Centennial Celebration," *Harper's Weekly,* 11 May 1889, 375. There were, of course, earlier celebrations related to the centenary of the Constitution, including observances held in Philadelphia and elsewhere on September 15–17, 1887. Washington was not the primary focus of these celebrations.

61. Quoted in Martha J. Lamb, "The Inauguration of Washington, 1889," *Magazine of American History,* December 1888, 460.

62. Clarence Winthrop Bowen, ed., *The History of the Centennial Celebration of the Inauguration of George Washington as First President of the United States* (New York: D. Appleton, 1892), 95–96.

63. Lamb, "Inauguration of Washington," 446.

64. [New York Tribune,] *The Washington Centenary, Celebrated in New-York, April 29, 30–May 1, 1889* (New York: Tribune Association, 1889), 2–4.

65. "Our 'Happy Constitution,'" *Harper's Weekly,* 20 April 1889, 298.

66. "The Centennial Celebration," *Harper's Weekly,* 4 May 1889, 346.

67. "Presidential Hand-Shaking," *Harper's Weekly,* 27 April 1889, 327.

68. [New York Tribune,] *Washington Centenary,* 16.

69. "The Coming Centenary," *New York Times,* 10 April 1889, 1, sec. 1, cols. 5–6.

70. Bowen, ed., *History of the Centennial,* 254.

71. "McAllister Out Entirely," *New York Times,* 15 April 1889, 1, sec. 1, col. 5.

72. "Absent Ward McAllister," *New York Times,* 30 April 1889, 9, sec. 1, col. 5.

73. "The City Full of Visitors," *New York Times,* 29 April 1889, 1, sec. 1, col. 5.

74. "The Centennial Procession," *Life,* 18 April 1889, 232.

75. Editorial, *Life,* 25 April 1889, 238.

76. [New York Tribune,] *Washington Centenary,* 26.

77. Ibid., 29.

78. "The Ladies in the Quadrille," *New York Times,* 30 April 1889, 3, sec. 1, col. 7.

79. "Ladies of the Presidential Party," *New York Times,* 30 April 1889, 3, sec. 1, col. 7.

5. George Washington Humanized

1. "The Crush at the Ball," *New York Times,* 30 April 1889, 3, sec. 1, col. 5.

2. Julian Ralph, "The Centennial Celebration," *Harper's Weekly,* 11 May 1889, 378.

3. Ibid., 375.

4. "The President's Trip," *New York Times,* 30 April 1889, 1, sec. 1, col. 6.

5. "Washington's Historical Luncheon in Elizabeth," *Magazine of American History,* May 1889, 361–363.

6. Ralph, "Centennial Celebration," 375.

7. "The Centennial Celebration," *Harper's Weekly,* 4 May 1889, 346.

8. Clarence Winthrop Bowen, ed., *The History of the Centennial Celebration of the Inauguration of George*

Washington as First President of the United States
(New York: D. Appleton, 1892), 186.

9. "The Great Festival Begun," *New York Times,* 30 April 1889, 1, sec. 1, col. 7.

10. "Received by Friends," *New York Times,* 30 April 1889, 2, sec. 1, cols. 3–5. See also Ralph, "Centennial Celebration," 377–378.

11. "Received by Friends," *New York Times,* 2, sec. 1, col. 3.

12. *The Washington Centenary, Celebrated in New-York, April 29, 30–May 1, 1889* (New York: Tribune Association, 1889), 18.

13. Ibid., 19–20, and "Received by Friends," *New York Times,* 2, sec. 1, col. 5.

14. Ralph, "Centennial Celebration," 377.

15. Ibid., 379.

16. *Washington Centenary,* 78–79.

17. Advertisement in *Harper's Weekly,* 22 June 1889, 504.

18. Elizabeth Stillinger, *The Antiquers* (New York: Alfred A. Knopf, 1980), 48.

19. Bowen, ed., *History of the Centennial Celebration,* 138.

20. "The Centennial Loan Exhibition," *Harper's Weekly,* 27 April 1889, 331.

21. Bowen, ed., *History of the Centennial Celebration,* 135.

22. *Washington Centenary,* 31.

23. See Charles Henry Hart, "Original Portraits of Washington," *Century Magazine,* February 1892, 593–599; Moncure D. Conway, "The Disputed Picture in Sparks's 'Washington,'" *Century Magazine,* July 1892, 476–477; and Stan V. Henkels, *The Important Collection of Engraved Portraits of Washington Belonging to the Late Henry Wheeler, Jr., of Philadelphia . . .* (Philadelphia: Samuel T. Freeman, 1909), iii.

24. Paul Leicester Ford, "The Inauguration of Our Government," *Harper's Weekly,* 4 May 1889, 358.

25. Clarence Winthrop Bowen, "The Inauguration of Washington," *Century Magazine,* April 1889, 802–833. As secretary of the Committee on Literary Exercises, he read Whittier's centennial ode, "The Vow of Washington," beneath the outstretched hand of the J. Q. A. Ward Washington during the reenactment.

26. See Constance Cary Harrison, "Washington at Mount Vernon After the Revolution," *Century Magazine,* April 1889, especially 840, and "Washington in New York in 1789," *Century Magazine,* April 1889, especially 857.

27. Bowen, ed., *History of the Centennial Celebration,* 15, 45, and 146.

28. *Washington Centenary,* 31.

29. Ibid., 30–31.

30. *Harper's Weekly* for 27 April 1889, quoted in Stillinger, *The Antiquers,* 48–49.

31. "Centennial Loan Exhibition," *Harper's Weekly,* 27 April 1889, 331.

32. "Features of the Celebration," *New York Times,* 30 April 1889, 3, sec. 1, col. 2.

33. "The Civic Reception," *New York Times,* 30 April 1889, 2, sec. 1, col. 5.

34. Ibid., col. 6.

35. *Washington Centenary,* 23.

36. "The Civic Reception," *New York Times,* 2, sec. 1, col. 6.

37. *Washington Centenary,* 34.

38. Martha Strayer, *The D.A.R.: An Informal History* (Washington, D.C.: Public Affairs Press, 1958), 7.

39. *Washington Centenary,* 36.

40. "The Three Days," *Harper's Weekly,* 1 May 1889, 366.

41. *Washington Centenary,* 36.

42. Ralph, "Centennial Celebration," *Harper's Weekly,* 378.

43. Stan Gores, *Presidential and Campaign Memorabilia* (Des Moines: Wallace-Homestead, 1982), 12.

44. *Washington Centenary,* 38–47, and "Three Days," *Harper's Weekly,* 366.

45. "Three Days," *Harper's Weekly,* 366–367, and "Preparing for the March," *New York Times,* 30 April 1889, 3, sec. 1, cols. 3–4.

46. Many such wooden arches were erected, in addition to the official Washington Memorial Arch in Washington Square later recreated in permanent materials by Stanford White as a result of public subscription. Wall Street merchants and traders were particularly active, building one example at Wall and Front Streets and another at Wall and Pearl, the latter paid for by $700 subscriptions (Havemeyer's sugar concern was one of the sponsors). See Bowen, ed., *History of the Centennial Celebration,* 226 and 253.

47. *Washington Centenary,* 80.

48. Ibid., 75–76.

49. Ibid., 77.

50. Ibid., 85.

51. Ibid., 80 and 84–85.

52. Barbara S. Groseclose, *Emanuel Leutze, 1816–1868: Freedom Is the Only King* (Washington, D.C.: Smithsonian Institution Press/National Collection of

Fine Arts, 1975), 33. The work entered the collection of the Metropolitan Museum in New York in 1897. Leutze painted a number of other scenes from the life of Washington that fueled the Washington mania of the period just before the Civil War. Among these themes were: Washington rallying his troops at Monmouth, in several versions (1854); Washington at Princeton (1859); Washington at Dorchester Heights (ca. 1853); Braddock's Defeat (1858); and Washington as a young surveyor (ca. 1852).

53. *Washington Centenary,* 84.

54. See Constance Cary Harrison, "Washington at Mount Vernon After the Revolution," *Century Magazine,* April 1889, 834–850.

55. Marion Harland, *Some Colonial Homesteads and Their Stories* (New York: G. P. Putnam's Sons, 1897), 262–272.

56. Alice Morse Earle, *Colonial Dames and Good Wives* (Boston: Houghton Mifflin, 1895), 34–35.

57. Evert A. Duyckinck, *National Portrait Gallery of Eminent Americans . . . from Original Full Length Paintings by Alonzo Chappel,* vol. 1 (New York: Johnson, Fry, 1862), 66–67.

58. Benson J. Lossing, *Life of Washington: A Biography, Personal, Military, and Political,* vol. 1 (New York: Virtue, 1860), 199, and *The Home of Washington; or, Mount Vernon and Its Associations, Historical, Biographical, and Pictorial* (Hartford: A. S. Hale, 1870), 58–59.

59. Bishop Meade, *Old Churches, Ministers and Families of Virginia* (Philadelphia: J. B. Lippincott, 1857), 249.

60. Mrs. [Elizabeth F.] Ellet, *The Queens of American Society* (Philadelphia: Porter & Coates, 1873), 18–19. Mrs. Ellet also wrote popular etiquette manuals and at least one cookbook (1873).

61. Ibid., 21–27.

62. Constance Cary Harrison, "Washington in New York," *Century Magazine,* April 1889, 852, and Martha J. Lamb, "Washington and Some of His Contemporaries," *Magazine of American History,* April 1889, 280–281.

63. "George Washington as a Dancer," *Magazine of American History,* September 1888, 247.

64. Andrew D. Mellick, Jr., "The Scene of Washington's 'Pretty Little Frisk,'" *Magazine of American History,* October 1888, 325–327.

65. "Washington's Wooing of Mary Philipse," *Magazine of American History,* November 1889, 432.

66. [William S. Pelletreau,] reply to "Washington's Wooing of Mary Philipse," *Magazine of American History,* February 1890, 169–170.

67. Edward C. Towne, introduction to [John Frederick] Schroeder-[Benson J.] Lossing, *Life and Times of Washington,* rev. ed., vol. 1 (Albany: M. M. Belcher, 1903), iv–v. The revision comprises six volumes.

68. Worthington Chauncey Ford, ed., *The Writings of Washington,* vol. 2 (New York: G. P. Putnam's Sons, 1889), 95–96. There are fourteen volumes in all.

69. Paul Leicester Ford, *The True George Washington* (Philadelphia: J. B. Lippincott, 1897), 93.

70. [Edward C. Towne,] "Washington as Lover and Poet," *Harper's Weekly,* 4 May 1889, 343.

71. Ibid., 342.

72. Ibid., 342–343.

73. Lossing, *Home of Washington,* 68 and 78.

74. Woodrow Wilson, "Colonel Washington," *Harper's New Monthly Magazine,* March 1896, 553 and 573.

75. Garry Wills, *Cincinnatus: George Washington and the Enlightenment* (Garden City, N.Y.: Doubleday, 1984), 245.

76. Benson J. Lossing, "Arlington House, the Seat of G. W. P. Custis, Esq.," *Harper's New Monthly Magazine,* September 1853, 445.

77. Edith Tunis Sale, *Old Time Belles and Cavaliers* (Philadelphia: J. B. Lippincott, 1912), 53–54. See also Marion Harland, *The Story of Mary Washington* (Boston: Houghton Mifflin, 1892), and review in *Magazine of American History,* January 1893, 76.

78. Quoted in Bernard Mayo, *Myths and Men: Patrick Henry, George Washington, Thomas Jefferson* (Athens: University of Georgia Press, 1959), 40–41.

79. This passage is discussed in Marcus Cunliffe, *George Washington: Man and Monument,* rev. ed. (New York: New American Library, 1982), 150–151.

80. Henry Cabot Lodge, *George Washington,* vol. 1 (Boston: Houghton Mifflin, 1891), ii–x.

81. Quoted in Leonard Irving, "Do We Know Washington?" *Magazine of American History,* March 1893, 227–228.

82. Ibid., 222.

83. Ibid., 228–229.

84. "One of Washington's Sweethearts," *Magazine of American History,* February 1893, 178; in the same issue, see also James Grant Wilson, "Society in the Early Days of the Republic," 81–107, another inventory of luxurious food and dress in olden times centered on the figure of Washington.

85. Quoted in Charles Moore, *The Family Life of George Washington* (Boston: Houghton Mifflin, 1926), 79. Conway's pieces on aspects of Washington's private life and likenesses of him and his contemporaries were staples of the polite journals of the 1880s and 1890s.

86. General Bradley T. Johnson, *General Washington* (New York: D. Appleton, 1897), 6 and 69.

87. Elizabeth Eggleston Seelye, *The Story of Washington* (New York: D. Appleton, 1893), 366, and Irving, "Do We Know Washington?," 223.

88. Earle, *Colonial Dames,* 33–35, and Anne Hollingsworth Wharton, *Colonial Days and Dames* (Philadelphia: J. B. Lippincott, 1895), 159.

89. Wharton, *Colonial Days,* 162–163.

90. Samuel Blain Shirk, *The Character of George Washington in American Plays Since 1875* (Philadelphia: University of Pennsylvania, 1949), 34–35.

91. Thomas Allen Glenn, *Some Colonial Mansions and Those Who Lived in Them,* 2d ser. (Philadelphia: Henry T. Coates, 1900), 51 and 271.

92. Ibid., 272.

93. Towne, ed., *Life and Times of Washington,* 434 and v.

6. The Colonial Revival

1. Untitled article, *Life,* 16 May 1889, 282. Portland, Birmingham, Denver, and San Francisco celebrations received exhaustive coverage in the New York papers. In San Francisco's parade, the main attractions were twenty-eight sailors just rescued from an American warship that went down in a storm off Samoa, and floats showing forty-niners working their claims.

2. "A General Celebration," *New York Times,* 1 May 1889, 1, sec. 1, col. 1.

3. *Report of the Board of General Managers of the Exhibit of the State of New York at the World's Columbian Exposition* (Albany: James R. Lyon, 1894), 8–17.

4. *The City of Palaces* (Chicago: W. B. Conkey, 1894), 40–41.

5. Susan Prendergast Schoelwer, "Curious Relics and Quaint Scenes: The Colonial Revival at Chicago's Great Fair," in *The Colonial Revival in America*, ed. Alan Axelrod (New York: W. W. Norton/Winterthur Museum, 1985), 212–213.

6. See, e.g., Moses P. Handy, *The Official Directory of the World's Columbian Exposition* (Chicago: W. B. Conkey, 1893), 76, 85, 87, 91–92, 99–100, and passim.

7. *Report of the Board of General Managers,* 194–196. Much of the "colonial" detail of these buildings probably came from academic, Beaux-Arts sources: there was, in other words, no concerted effort to colonialize them in a "correct" manner.

8. Alice Morse Earle, *China Collecting in America* (New York: Charles Scribner's Sons, 1892), and Schoelwer, "Curious Relics," 203.

9. According to William B. Rhoads, *The Colonial Revival,* vol. 1 (New York: Garland, 1977), 314–328, few new buildings in the colonial style were erected in the Midwest before the 1893 fair. Thus the various state pavilions and commercial colonial displays were novel in that visual context.

10. *The Chicago Tribune Portfolio of Midway Types* (Chicago: American Engraving Co., 1893), parts 3 and 7.

11. Quoted and discussed by Howard N. Rabinowitz, "George Washington as Icon, 1865–1900," in *Icons of America*, ed. Ray B. Browne and Marshall Fishwick (Bowling Green, Ohio: Popular Press, Bowling Green State University, 1978), 78–79.

12. Handy, *Official Directory,* 101.

13. [Imre Kiralfy,] *Imre Kiralfy's Grand Historical Spectacle, America* (Chicago: Imre Kiralfy, 1893), 8.

14. For the ballet and the final scene, see ibid., 37 and 44.

15. Ibid., 31.

16. Quoted in Marshall Everett, *The Book of the Fair* ([St. Louis]: Henry Neil, 1904), 52–53.

17. David R. Francis, *The Universal Exposition of 1904,* vol. 1 (St. Louis: Louisiana Purchase Exposition Co., 1913), 277–278.

18. The seated Jefferson was by James Earle Fraser, who designed the colossal Washington, centerpiece of the 1939 World's Fair, and the Napoleon was by Daniel Chester French; see Robert A. Reid, *The Greatest of Expositions, Completely Illustrated* (St. Louis: Official Photographic Co., Louisiana Purchase Exposition, 1904), 131–139.

19. Walter B. Stevens, *The Forest City, Comprising the Official Photographic Views of the Universal Exposition Held in Saint Louis, 1904* (St. Louis: N. D. Thompson, 1904), unpaginated plate, "Arkansas."

20. Ibid., unpaginated plate, "The Birthplace of Daniel Webster."

21. Francis, *Universal Exposition,* 581–588.

22. Stevens, *Forest City,* unpaginated plate, "New Jersey."

23. Ibid., unpaginated plates, "Rhode Island's Colonial Mansion," "Heart of the Plateau of States," "Massachusetts," and "Connecticut." Katherine Cole Stevenson and H. Ward Jandl, *Houses by Mail: A Guide to Houses from Sears, Roebuck and Company* (Washington, D.C.: Preservation Press, 1986), 285, features a copy of the Longfellow House available in kit form in 1918. It was something of a novelty for the day. By 1926, the majority of the houses offered for sale were "colonials" (called "The Mount Vernon" and "The Betsy Ross"), although of a less elegant sort.

24. Francis, *Universal Exposition,* 292.

25. Stevens, *Forest City,* unpaginated plate, "Michigan."

26. Charles H. Carpenter, Jr., "The Tradition of the Old: Colonial Revival Silver for the American Home," in Axelrod, ed., *Colonial Revival in America,* 144–145.

27. See, e.g., *Century Magazine,* July 1892, ad section. The first mass-market instant coffee was the George Washington brand, which appeared in 1909; see *Time,* 16 June 1986, 64. The name of the product is an obvious attempt to make a newfangled idea seem traditional and unthreatening.

J. J. Johnson & Co. of Union Square, purveyors of a Columbus spoon that incorporated "1892" prominently into the design (the Chicago fair was delayed by a year), urged collectors to "send for complete illustrated price list of souvenir spoons," of which many other models were available by mail order.

28. Carpenter, "Tradition of the Old," 143. Irma Oredson, a spoon collector, mistakenly dates the beginning of the phenomenon to 1891 when a Salem jeweler created a spoon to recall the witch trials; see Barbara Flanagan column, *Minneapolis Star and Tribune,* 21 January 1986, 1B, col. 6.

29. Laurence Vail Coleman, *Historic House Museums* (Washington, D.C.: American Association of Museums, 1931), 102.

30. Wallace Nutting, *Massachusetts Beautiful* (Framingham, Mass.: Old America Company, 1923), 66. For the use of the past in general and Salem in particular as tourist attractions, see David Lowenthal, *The Past Is a Foreign Country* (New York: Cambridge University Press, 1985), 345–346.

31. Coleman, *Historic House Museums,* 18. For historical tourism, see a special section on souvenirs in *Prospects,* vol. 11, ed. Jack Salzman (New York: Cambridge University Press, 1987).

32. Coleman, *Historic House Museums,* 115, 125, and 133. The Old Stone House in Guilford, Connecticut, said to have been built in 1639, greeted its first tourists in 1903.

33. Lucia Ames Mead, "How the Old Wayside Inn Came Back," *Old-Time New England,* July 1931, 41–45.

34. *Longfellow Poems* (New York: Dutton/Everyman's Library, 1978), 393–395. Emerson's "Concord Hymn" had been written for the dedication of a monument at the "rude bridge" in Concord on April 19, 1836; it was sung during the ceremonies.

35. Roger Butterfield, "Henry Ford, the Wayside Inn, and the Problem of 'History Is Bunk,'" *Proceedings of the Massachusetts Historical Society,* 77 (January–December 1965), 59–61.

36. Quoted in William B. Rhoads, "The Colonial Revival and the Americanization of Immigrants," in Axelrod, ed., *Colonial Revival in America,* 359.

37. See Mrs. Joseph Rucker Lamar, *A History of the National Society of the Colonial Dames of America from 1891 to 1933* (Atlanta: Walter W. Brown, 1934), 30.

38. Lewis Barrington, *Historic Restorations of the Daughters of the American Revolution* (New York: Richard R. Smith, 1941), and *The National Society of the Colonial Dames of America Museum Houses Directory 11* (Washington, D.C.: National Historic Activities Committee, Colonial Dames of America, [1961–64]), 6, 16, 17, and passim.

39. *Official Robert Fulton Exhibition of the Hudson-Fulton Commission* (New York: New-York Historical Society, 1909), unpaginated ad section.

40. Alice Morse Earle, *Colonial Days in Old New York* (New York: Charles Scribner's Sons, 1896), iv. She also wrote poetry with colonial themes. See Alice Morse Earle and Emily Ellsworth Ford, *Early Prose and Verse* (New York: Harper & Brothers, 1893), a part of the "distaff series," a record of the accomplishments of the women of New York State published for the Chicago fair under the auspices of the New York Board of Lady Managers.

41. *Two Centuries of Costume in America* appeared in 1894; *Customs and Fashions in Old New England* in 1893; the volume on colonial children in 1899; and *Colonial Dames and Good Wives* in 1895.

42. Alice Morse Earle, *Home Life in Colonial Days* (New York: Macmillan, 1898), vi–viii.

43. Ibid., 37, 187, 197, 227, and 237.

44. Alice Morse Earle, *Colonial Dames and Good Wives* (Boston: Houghton Mifflin, 1895), 55–56.

45. Anne Hollingsworth Wharton, *Colonial Days and Dames* (Philadelphia: J. B. Lippincott, 1895), 27, 125, and 158–165, with illustrations by E. S. Holloway.

46. Marion Harland, *More Colonial Homesteads and Their Stories* (New York: G. P. Putnam's Sons, 1899), 1. Like Mrs. Ellet and Alice Morse Earle, she also wrote about domestic arrangements, including recipes and cookery. See, e.g., her *Breakfast, Luncheon and Tea* (New York: Charles Scribner's Sons, 1875) and *The Cottage Kitchen: A Collection of Practical and Inexpensive Receipts* (New York: Charles Scribner's Sons, 1883).

47. Marion Harland, *Some Colonial Homesteads and Their Stories* (New York: G. P. Putnam's Sons, 1897), v.

48. Ibid., 271 and 280.

49. Charles Arthur Higgins, "Mary Harrod Northend, Authority and Writer on Colonial Homes of New England," *Massachusetts Magazine,* January 1915, 23–24.

50. Ibid., 25.

51. Elizabeth Stillinger, *The Antiquers* (New York: Alfred A. Knopf, 1980), 149–151.

52. Melinda Young Frye, "The Beginnings of the Period Room in American Museums: Charles P. Wilcomb's Colonial Kitchens, 1896, 1906, 1910," in Axelrod, ed., *Colonial Revival in America,* 236–239. She links the notion of presenting a typical rather than a specific room to books of pictures of colonial interiors, such as Edwin Whitefield's *Homes of Our Forefathers in Massachusetts* of 1892 and Arthur Little's *Early New England Interiors* of 1878.

53. Higgins, "Mary Harrod Northend," 23.

54. Ibid., 25.

55. Mary H. Northend, *Colonial Homes and Their Furnishings* (Boston: Little, Brown, 1912), plates 34 and 48. The conventional name for this kind of chair apparently postdates the restoration of Mount Vernon, where the bedroom occupied by Martha Washington after the death of her husband was furnished, around the turn of the century, with several Chippendale chairs shrouded in fabric covers.

The obvious modernity of Northend's scenes incorporating both antiques and period reproductions recalls the deliberately quaint "New Englandisms" in the sets and manners of D. W. Griffith's *Way Down East,* a major silent movie of 1920 starring Lillian Gish.

56. Ibid., vii.

57. Mary H. Northend, *Historic Homes of New England* (Boston: Little, Brown, 1914), plate 7. Photos taken by and for Northend in the House of the Seven Gables were copyrighted by C. O. Emmerton, who operated the historic building as a guest house.

58. Ibid., vii.

59. Mary Harrod Northend, *The Art of Home Decoration* (New York: Dodd, Mead, 1921), i, ix, 1, and 10.

60. Ibid., 5 and 113.

61. Mary Harrod Northend, *Historic Doorways of Old Salem* (Boston: Houghton Mifflin, 1926), vii–viii, and *We Visit Old Inns* (Boston: Small, Maynard, 1925).

62. Northend, *We Visit Old Inns,* 28 and 34. In the parlor of an inn in Wayland, Massachusetts, she came upon a George Washington mourning sampler worked by one Elizabeth Thurston and pronounced it "depressing."

63. Northend, *Art of Home Decoration,* 10–11.

64. Both of these famous Nutting pictures of 1910 and 1911 were used as illustrations in his *Massachusetts Beautiful,* 112 and 122.

65. For a sample page from his 1912 catalogue, see William L. Dulaney, "Wallace Nutting, Collector and Entrepreneur," *Winterthur Portfolio,* 13 (1979), 55. For prints available during his early years of operation, see Joyce P. Barendsen, "Wallace Nutting, an American Tastemaker: The Pictures and Beyond," *Winterthur Portfolio,* 18, nos. 2–3 (Summer–Autumn 1983), 206.

66. Barbara M. and Gerald W. Ward, *The John Ward House* (Salem, Mass.: Essex Institute, 1976), 31.

67. The Northend negatives are now in the collection of the Society for the Protection of New England Antiquities in Boston; I consulted a set of prints on deposit in the Decorative Arts Library of the Henry Francis DuPont Winterthur Museum, Winterthur, Delaware.

68. Louis M. MacKeil, *Wallace Nutting* (Saugus, Mass.: Saugus Historical Society, 1982), 9, and William L. Dulaney, "Wallace Nutting," *Americana,* July–August 1978, 34.

69. John Freeman, "The Arts-Crafts Ideology of Wallace Nutting's Colonial Revival," in *Wallace Nutting Checklist of Early American Reproductions* (Watkins Glen, N.Y.: American Life Foundation and Study Institute, 1969). See also Edie Clark, "The Man Who Looked Back and Saw the Future," *Yankee,* September 1986, 110, 113, and 172–181, and David A. Hanks with

Jennifer Toher, "Tradition and Reform," in *High Styles: Twentieth-Century American Design* (New York: Whitney Museum of American Art, 1985), 14–15. The Nutting phase of the revival also produced other important pieces of decorative art, such as the 1912 Albert Herter tapestry, *George Washington Inaugurated President* (Metropolitan Museum of Art, New York), one of a series depicting the history of New York, 1613–1861, made for the mezzanine of the Hotel McAlpin.

70. Henry P. Maynard, "The Wadsworth Atheneum and Wallace Nutting," *Connecticut Antiquarian*, 13, no. 2 (December 1961), 16.

71. Wallace Nutting, *Wallace Nutting Pictures, Being Studies in America and Other Lands of the Aspects in the Life of the Fathers and the Country Life of To-day* (Framingham, Mass.: Wallace Nutting, 1912), 18 and 47.

72. A wide variety of fake Nuttings are on the market, including a piece of 1920s kitchen decor called "An Elaborate Dinner," a color lithograph of a colonial hearth posing as a hand-tinted Nutting "original."

73. Quoted in Freeman, "Arts-Crafts Ideology."

74. Nutting, *Massachusetts Beautiful*, 13.

75. Ibid., 133.

76. MacKeil, *Wallace Nutting*, 21.

77. Dulaney, "Wallace Nutting," 13, 53, and 58–59. For a summary of the elite and the popular impulses that fueled the revival, see Neil Harris, *Winterthur and America's Museum Age* (Winterthur, Del.: Henry Francis DuPont Winterthur Museum, 1981).

78. *Illustrated Catalogue of Rattan and Reed Furniture* (Boston: Wakefield Rattan Co., [ca. 1890]), 86–87. I consulted trade catalogues of the period in the extensive holdings of the Rare Book Room of the Winterthur Museum Library. Kenneth L. Ames suggested approximate dates for the many undated catalogues.

79. *Illustrated Catalogue: Hat Racks, Parlor and Music Cabinets . . .* (Chicago: Leo Austrian & Co., [ca. 1905]), 6, #446.

80. *Red Cedar Chests* (Statesville, N.C.: Piedmont Red-Cedar Chest Co., 1910), 8–9. See also Paul Leicester Ford, *Janice Meredith: A Story of the Revolution* (New York: Grosset & Dunlap, 1899), in which George Washington is a central character. The novel is dedicated to George W[ashington] Vanderbilt.

81. *Red Cedar Chests*, 12.

82. *Things Colonial, Being a Few Illustrations of the Reproductions Made and Sold by W. K. Cowan & Co.* (Chicago: W. K. Cowan & Co., [ca. 1915]), foreword and #253.

83. Francis B. Ellis, "Architectural Interiors of the U.S. Shipping Board S.S. 'Hawkeye State,'" *American Architect*, 13 April 1921, 446 and 449.

84. Dulaney, "Wallace Nutting," 59.

85. Olin Dows, *Franklin Roosevelt at Hyde Park* (New York: American Artists Group, 1949), 158–159, quoting from a memo by FDR describing his office furniture. See also my "Eleanor Roosevelt, the Arts of the 30s, and the Colonial Revival," address delivered at the Anna Eleanor Roosevelt Centennial Celebration, the National Museum of American History, Smithsonian Institution, Washington, D.C., October 20, 1984. A Danersk Co. ad for the Washington desk from *House and Garden* (1926) is illustrated in *High Styles: Twentieth-Century American Design*, 57.

86. *Furniture and Floor Coverings* (New York: Peck & Hills Furniture Co., [ca. 1916]), 3.

87. Ibid., 261–268.

88. Joseph J. Schroeder, Jr., ed., *1923 Sears, Roebuck Catalogue*, facsimile ed. (Northfield, Ill.: Digest Books, 1973), 626.

89. *Danersk Decorative Furniture: . . . Colonial Pieces in Solid Mahogany and Walnut for All Rooms* (New York: Erskine-Danforth Corp., 1917), 5 and 40–41.

90. *Authentic Hand Made Reproductions of Antiques* (Harrisonburg, Va.: Virginia Craftsmen, n.d.), 3–4 and 58, and *A Collection of Fine Period Furniture* (Boston: Old Colony Furniture Co., [ca. 1925]), 27 and 160.

91. *Furniture as Interpreted by the Century Furniture Company, Grand Rapids, Michigan*, 2d ed. (Grand Rapids: Century Furniture Co., 1927), 122–133.

92. H. Hudson Holly, *Modern Dwellings in Town and Country* (New York: Harper & Brothers, 1878), 191, recommends revival of the chimneypiece of "those good old colony days," on the strength of centennial spirit and revived interest in old colonial houses.

93. E. E. Holman, "Colonial Style in Bungalows," *International Studio*, July 1908, xxii–xxiii.

94. Mak Leroy Keith, *Keith's Book of Plans* (Minneapolis: M. L. Keith, [1911]), 3, 13, 16–17, 24, 26, 28, 38–39, 44, and 180, and *Keith's Bungalows and Cottages* (Minneapolis: M. L. Keith, 1912), 170 and 172. For 1950s tract colonials, see Thomas Hine, *Populuxe* (New York: Alfred A. Knopf, 1986), 41–47.

Witold Rybczynski, *Home: A Short History of an Idea* (New York: Viking, 1986), 175, distinguishes between historical and creative revivals of past styles and does not place the colonial revival in his creative category, but his arguments about the psychology of comfort suggest otherwise.

95. Henry H. Saylor, ed., *Inexpensive Homes of Individuality* (New York: McBride, Nast, 1912), 8–10.

96. Herbert C. Wise and H. Ferdinand Beidleman, *Colonial Architecture for Those About to Build* (Philadelphia: J. B. Lippincott, 1913), 1 and v.

97. Joseph Everett Chandler, *The Colonial House* (New York: Robert M. McBride, 1916), preface.

98. Ibid., 2–4, 33, and 52.

99. Ibid., 32 and Harold Donaldson Eberlein, *The Architecture of Colonial America* (Boston: Little, Brown, 1915), 190.

100. Eberlein, *The Architecture of Colonial America*, 1–2.

101. Joseph Jackson, *American Colonial Architecture: Its Origins and Development* (Philadelphia: David McKay, 1924), 5.

102. Ibid., 52–54.

7. Washingtoniana

1. R. T. H. Halsey and Elizabeth Tower, *The Homes of Our Ancestors Shown in the American Wing of the Metropolitan Museum of Art of New York, from the Beginnings of New England Through the Early Days of the Republic* (Garden City, N.Y.: Doubleday, Page, 1925), especially Plates II and XIII.

2. "Art of the American Home in New Wing of Museum," *New York Times,* 3 August 1924, 7, sec. 7, cols. 4–6.

3. Paul Leicester Ford, *The True George Washington* (Philadelphia: J. B. Lippincott, 1896), 17.

4. Ibid., 57.

5. Ibid., 91.

6. Ibid., 105–107. John C. Fitzpatrick, *The George Washington Scandals* (Alexandria, Va.: Washington Society of Alexandria, 1929), 2 and passim, takes up the Tory propaganda literature circulated as farces, pamphlets, and forged letters. See also William Alfred Bryan, *George Washington in American Literature, 1775–1865* (New York: Columbia University Press, 1952), 9.

7. Sally Nelson Robins, quoted in Dixon Wecter, *The Hero in America: A Chronicle of Hero-Worship* (Ann Arbor: University of Michigan Press, 1963), 122, and Rupert Hughes, *George Washington: The Human Being and the Hero, 1732–1762,* vol. 1 (New York: William Morrow, 1926), 411–412.

8. Wecter, *Hero in America,* 122.

9. Henry Van Dyke, *The Americanism of Washington* (New York: Harper Brothers, 1906), 3–4.

10. Ibid., 33–34.

11. Untitled editorial, *Life,* 20 February 1890, 104.

12. *American Architect* for 1907, quoted in William B. Rhoads, "The Colonial Revival and American Nationalism," *Journal of the Society of Architectural Historians,* 35, no. 4 (December 1976), 252.

13. Van Dyke, *Americanism of Washington,* 64–65.

14. Owen Wister, *The Seven Ages of Washington: A Biography* (New York: Macmillan, 1907), xi.

15. Ibid., 5 and 356.

16. Wister, quoted in Paul Wilstach, *Mount Vernon: Washington's Home and the Nation's Shrine* (Garden City, N.Y.: Doubleday, Page, 1916), vii.

17. Wister, *Seven Ages of Washington,* 85.

18. Ibid., 147–148.

19. Wilson Miles Cary, *Sally Cary, a Long Hidden Romance of Washington's Life, with Notes by Another Hand* (New York: privately printed, 1916); Wilstach, *Mount Vernon*; William J. Johnstone, *George Washington the Christian* (New York: Abington Press, 1919); Joseph F. Sabin, *George Washington as a Housekeeper with Glimpses of His Domestic Arrangements, Dining, Company, Etc.* (1924), cited in Margaret Brown Clapthor and Howard Alexander Morrison, *George Washington: A Figure Upon the Stage* (Washington, D.C.: Smithsonian Institution Press, 1982), 89; Paul Leland Haworth, *George Washington: Country Gentleman* (Indianapolis: Bobbs-Merrill, 1925); and Charles Moore, *The Family Life of George Washington* (Boston: Houghton Mifflin, 1926). See also Thomas J. Wertenbaker, *Planters of Colonial Virginia* (Princeton, N.J.: Princeton University Press, 1922).

20. Sinclair Lewis, *Babbitt* (New York: New American Library, 1961), 8 and 51.

21. Michael Kammen, *A Season of Youth: The American Revolution and the Historical Imagination* (New York: Alfred A. Knopf, 1978), 252.

22. *Address Delivered by Ex-Senator Albert J. Beveridge of Indiana on February 22, 1921, at the Second Washington's Birthday Celebration of the Sons*

of the Revolution and Other Patriotic Societies at Carnegie Hall, New York, and at the Thirty-Ninth Annual Banquet of the Sons of the Revolution at the Hotel Plaza, New York (New York: privately printed, 1921), 8.

23. Ibid., 7, quoting Lord Byron on the lesson of Washington.

24. Ibid., 9.

25. Ibid., 29.

26. Russell Lynes, *The Tastemakers: The Shaping of American Popular Taste* (New York: Dover, 1980), 240.

27. *Movie Week,* 10 June 1923, back cover. I am grateful to my colleague Rob Silberman for calling this ad to my attention.

28. Silas Weir Mitchell, *Red City: A Novel of the Second Administration of President Washington* (New York: Century, 1908), is about a French nobleman fleeing the Revolution in his own country and thus very much in the spirit of the American "Republican Court." *The Virginians* of 1859 (New York: Burt, 1923) had been before the public in dramatized versions almost continuously since its first appearance.

29. For dramatic treatments of *Janice Meredith,* see Kammen, *Season of Youth,* 130.

30. For *America* (1924), *Winners of the Wilderness* (1927), and *Janice Meredith* (1924), see Kenneth W. Munden, ed., *The American Film Institute Catalogue of Motion Pictures Produced in the United States,* vol. F2 [Feature Films, 1921–1930] (New York: R. R. Bowker, 1971), 17, 392, and 909.

31. See Munden, ed., *American Film Institute Catalogue,* 285–286. *George Washington Cohen* (December 1928) was based on Aaron Hoffman's *The Cherry Tree: A Comedy in One Act* (ca. 1915).

32. *Dodgeville* [Wisconsin] *Chronicle,* 22 January 1909, clipping in the collection of Vesterheim, the Norwegian-American Museum, Decorah, Iowa. I am grateful to Marion J. Nelson, director of Vesterheim, for calling this ad to my attention.

33. Arthur Preuss, *A Dictionary of Secret and Other Societies* (St. Louis: B. Herder, 1924), 275. I am grateful to Jeffrey P. Tordoff of the Minnesota Historical Society for calling the significance of this artifact to my attention.

34. Trudy Baltz, "Pageantry and Mural Painting: Community Rituals in Allegorical Form," *Winterthur Portfolio,* 15, no. 3 (Autumn 1980), 211–212, and David Glassberg, "From Jeremiad to Cultural Lag: The Transformation of American Popular Historical

Consciousness in the Early Twentieth Century," paper delivered at the annual meeting of the Organization of American Historians (April 1983), especially 12–25. I am grateful to Professor Glassberg for sharing his ideas and his fine paper with me.

35. Ralph Davol, *A Handbook of American Pageantry* (Taunton, Mass.: Davol, 1914), and Esther Willard Bates, *Pageants and Pageantry* (Boston: Ginn, 1912). From the 1920s onward, professional firms would, for a fee, swoop down upon a town bearing costumes and generic scripts and organize a pageant with local talent. See David Dempsey and Dan Herr, "Everybody Gets in the Act," *Saturday Evening Post,* 27 November 1948, 35 ff., in regard to the John B. Rogers Producing Company, the oldest and largest of the lot.

36. *Centennial of the Incorporation of Jamestown, 1827–1927* (Jamestown, N.Y.: Jamestown Centennial Commission, 1927), 27–38.

37. Virginia Tanner, *A Pageant of the State of Maine* ([Bath, Me.?]: privately printed, 1928), 118; *The Pageant of Portsmouth* ([Portsmouth, N.H.?]: privately printed, 1923), 62; and *The Founding of Albany* ([Albany, N.Y.?]: privately printed, 1924), 181.

38. Thomas Wood Stevens, *The Pageant of Newark* (Newark, N.J.: Committee of One Hundred, 1916), 7–8 and 102–103.

39. Michael Richman, *Daniel Chester French: An American Sculptor* (New York: National Trust for Historic Preservation, 1976), 29–47.

40. Stevens, *Pageant of Newark,* 106–108, includes a list of seamstresses that runs to three pages of very small type.

41. Davol, *Handbook of American Pageantry,* 85.

42. Edward Hagaman Hall, *The Hudson-Fulton Celebration 1909: The Fourth Annual Report of the Hudson-Fulton Celebration Commission to the Legislature,* vol. 1 (Albany: State of New York/J. B. Lyon, 1910), 282. For a different approach to the ideology of the parade, see Susan G. Davis, *Parades and Power: Street Theatre in Nineteenth-Century Philadelphia* (Philadelphia: Temple University Press, 1986).

43. Bates, *Pageants and Pageantry,* 4–5 and 15.

44. [Ellis Paxton Oberholtzer,] *Official Pictorial and Descriptive Book of the Historical Pageant* (Philadelphia: Historical Pageant Committee of Philadelphia, 1912), 2.

45. Hall, *Hudson-Fulton Celebration,* vol. 2, 756–763, 892–894, 906, 964, 1027, and 1052.

46. Gustav Kobbé, *The Hudson-Fulton Celebration* (New York: Society of Iconophiles, 1910), 26.

47. Ibid., 31–32.

48. Hall, *Hudson-Fulton Celebration,* vol. 1, 229–230. The replica, manned by Dutch sailors, was designed by C. C. Loder; see *New York Times,* 19 September 1909, 4, part 2, special Hudson-Fulton roto-gravure section.

49. Hall, *Hudson-Fulton Celebration,* vol. 1, 362–380.

50. Ibid., 283–286.

51. Kobbé, *Hudson-Fulton Celebration,* 44.

52. Ibid., 41.

53. "Tell City's History in Hudson Pageant," *New York Times,* 21 September 1909, 4, sec. 1, cols. 3–4.

54. Kobbé, *Hudson-Fulton Celebration,* 44–45.

55. Hall, *Hudson-Fulton Celebration,* vol. 1, 287.

56. Lary May, *Screening Out the Past: The Birth of Mass Culture and the Motion Picture Industry* (New York: Oxford University Press, 1980), 43.

57. Hall, *Hudson-Fulton Celebration,* vol. 1, 301.

58. Kobbé, *Hudson-Fulton Celebration,* 40.

59. Quoted in ibid., 46. For these Coney Island sculptures, see my *The Colossus of Roads: Myth and Symbol Along the American Highway* (Minneapolis: University of Minnesota Press, 1984), 97–100.

60. "Tell City's History," *New York Times,* 4, sec 1, col. 3.

61. Kobbé, *Hudson-Fulton Celebration,* 24–26 and 52-57.

62. Ibid., 42.

63. *Official Robert Fulton Exhibition of the Hudson-Fulton Commission* (New York: New-York Historical Society, 1909), 6, discusses recent colonial restorations in New York. This exhibition, featuring relics of Fulton and his era, was held in cooperation with the Colonial Dames and featured several subsidiary displays, one of them at the newly restored Fraunces' Tavern at 54 Pearl Street, and another in Washington's New York headquarters, the Jumel Mansion, once occupied by Mary Philipse. The latter was sponsored by the DAR. Although attitudes were changing rapidly, at this date it was still considered unseemly in some circles for women's organizations to engage in the kinds of public activities—marching in parades, holding public banquets, giving speeches—that their male brethren relished. They were more active in behind-the-scenes arrangements for the exhibitions held in conjunction with the Hudson-Fulton Celebration.

The status of Fraunces' Tavern, and the low estate into which it had sunk at points in its history, were subjects of frequent remark in the years before the restoration. Its use as a restaurant in 1883 and 1889 was deplored by some visitors, but a tourist from St. Paul who inspected the site in 1882 thought that free enterprise had saved the building, although he regretted the fact that a kitchen now occupied the place where Israel Putnam's office once stood. He was also pleased that there were no turnstiles or admission fees such as the pilgrim so often encountered in Europe. See "Historic Landmarks," *Saint Paul and Minneapolis Pioneer Press,* 5 March 1882, 9, sec. 1, cols. 1–3.

64. Hall, *Hudson-Fulton Celebration,* vol. 1, 298.

65. Ibid., 290–292.

66. *The 350th Anniversary of Jamestown, 1607–1957: Final Report to the President and Congress of the Jamestown-Williamsburg-Yorktown Celebration Commission* (Washington, D.C.: Government Printing Office, 1958), 6–7, and William B. Rhoads, *The Colonial Revival,* vol. 1 (New York: Garland, 1977), 137–138.

67. [Oberholtzer,] *Official Historical and Descriptive Book,* 52.

68. Ibid., 51.

69. Ibid., 99, 116, and 138.

70. Wecter, *Hero in America,* 9. In 1914, at a meeting of the British committee for celebrating the centenary of Anglo-American peace, held in London, a member donated a supposedly authentic portrait of Mary Ball Washington to Sulgrave Manor, the ancestral home of the British Washingtons. Restoration of that manor house—a tumbledown wreck, on the market in 1890—was an expression of the Anglophilia of the turn of the century. As an expression of the new realism, it was also widely reported that tradition cherished in the neighborhood of Sulgrave held Pastor Lawrence Washington, George's great-great-grandfather, a notorious public drunkard. See *Nineteenth Annual Report of the American Scenic and Historic Preservation Society* (New York: American Scenic and Historic Preservation Society, 1914), 268.

71. Quoted in Percy MacKaye, *Washington, the Man Who Made Us: A Ballad Play* (New York: Alfred A. Knopf, 1919), ix–x.

72. Ibid., 152.

73. Ibid., 284.

74. *Nineteenth Annual Report,* 255.

75. Ibid., 177.

76. Ibid., 1334 and 441, and plates 4, 7, and 8. The reason for the abortive parade in 1913 was practical: the committee did not get geared up in time to celebrate the tercentenary of the Dutch settlement of New York in 1913 properly and settled for the modest July 4 observances. They finally held the celebration of trade in 1914.

77. *New York Times*, 19 September 1909, 1, part 2, special Hudson-Fulton rotogravure section.

78. Hall, *Hudson-Fulton Celebration*, vol. 1, 453–456.

79. Ibid., 507–510. A founder of the Society of Mayflower Descendants and a member of the Colonial Dames, in 1907 Mrs. Sage had underwritten reconstruction of the Governor's Room in New York City Hall with colonial woodwork and furnishings.

80. Henry Watson Kent, quoted in Elizabeth Stillinger, *The Antiquers* (New York: Alfred A. Knopf, 1980), 132.

81. Henry Watson Kent, *What I Am Pleased to Call My Education* (New York: Grolier Club, 1949), 83–84. The critic Royal Cortissoz, in a *Scribner's* article reprinted as the introduction to the first catalogue of the American Wing, makes the same assertion; see Halsey and Tower, *Homes of Our Ancestors*, vii–viii.

82. Untitled article, *Bulletin of the Metropolitan Museum of Art*, 4, no. 5 (May 1909), 50.

83. [Robert deForest,] "The Hudson-Fulton Celebration Exhibition," *Bulletin of the Metropolitan Museum of Art*, 4, no. 5 (May 1909), 75.

84. Stillinger, *Antiquers*, 124–127.

85. [deForest], "Hudson-Fulton Celebration," 76. George S. Palmer was the other major lender to the silver show at the Met; in 1918 the museum acquired his collections of high-style eighteenth-century material. These pieces would form the nucleus of the silver collection of the American Wing. For the silver show, see also an untitled article, [F.N.L.,] *Bulletin of the Metropolitan Museum of Art*, 4, no. 8 (August 1909), 138.

86. [deForest,] "Hudson-Fulton Celebration," 76–77.

87. "The Bolles Collection of American Furniture and Decorative Arts," *Bulletin of the Metropolitan Museum of Art*, 4, no. 9 (September 1909), 219.

88. Illustrated in "Homes of Our Ancestors in the Metropolitan Museum," *New York Times Magazine*, 24 August 1924, 12; see also "A Household of Continuance," *New York Times*, 10 November 1924, 16, sec. 2, col. 5.

89. "Homes of Our Ancestors," *New York Times Magazine*, 12.

90. "Art of the American Home in New Wing of Museum," *New York Times*, 3 August 1924, 7, sec. 7, cols. 3–7.

91. "The World of Art," *New York Times Magazine*, 12 October 1924, 11.

92. "The New Wing at the Metropolitan Museum," *New York Times Magazine*, 9 November 1924, 11.

93. "The World of Art," *New York Times Magazine*, 11.

94. "Open American Wing at Museum of Art," *New York Times*, 11 November 1924, 25, sec. 2, cols. 3–4.

95. Ibid., col. 3.

96. "Household of Continuance," *New York Times*, 16. Henry Cabot Lodge's obituary appears on the same page.

97. M. L. Blumenthal, "Antiqueering," *Saturday Evening Post*, 16 February 1924, 18–19 ff., and James H. Collins, "Selling to a Crowd—The Auctioneer," *Saturday Evening Post*, 13 May 1922, 18 and 168–170.

98. Ruth Scott Miller, "Our Early American Builders," *Saturday Evening Post*, 20 September 1924, 16, 62, and 67; "The Junk Snupper," *Saturday Evening Post*, 19 April 1924, 25 and 150; "The Criminal Confessions of a Collector," *Saturday Evening Post*, 19 April 1924, 24 ff.; Sam Hellman, "Magoofus Glass," *Saturday Evening Post*, 5 January 1924, 10–11, 145 ff.; and Elizabeth Shackleton, "Fads and Fancies of Collectors," *Saturday Evening Post*, 9 August 1924, 126.

99. Cornelius Obenchain Van Loot, Milton Kilgallen, and Murgatroyd Elphinstone [Booth Tarkington, Kenneth Roberts, and Hugh Kahler], *The Curator's Whatnot: A Compendium, Manual, and Syllabus of Information on All Subjects Appertaining to the Collection of Antiques, Both Ancient and Not So Ancient* (Boston: Houghton Mifflin, 1923).

100. Kenneth L. Roberts, "Antiquamania," *Saturday Evening Post*, 14 March 1925, 12. See also his "The Notes of an Antique Weevil," *Saturday Evening Post*, 21 January 1922, 8.

101. Ethel Stanwood Bolton and Eva Johnson Coe, *American Samplers* (Boston: Massachusetts Society of the Colonial Dames of America, 1921), 115 and 255–256, and Elizabeth Shackleton, "Glass Mania," *Saturday Evening Post*, 8 December 1923, 97.

102. Shackleton, "Glass Mania," 92 and 97.

103. Wecter, *Hero in America*, 137.

8. Neocolonial Politics

1. Robert G. Ferris, ed., *The Presidents: From the Inauguration of George Washington to the Inauguration of Jimmy Carter,* rev. ed. (Washington, D.C.: U.S. Department of the Interior, National Park Service, 1977), 510–513.

2. For the minutiae of Harding's home life, furnishings, etc., see Francis Russell, *The Shadow of Blooming Grove: Warren G. Harding in His Times* (New York: McGraw-Hill, 1968), especially 108, 146, and 160.

3. Headley's book appeared in 1847. See William Allen White, *A Puritan in Babylon: The Story of Calvin Coolidge* (New York: Macmillan, 1938), 27.

4. Randolph C. Downes, *The Rise of Warren Gamaliel Harding* (Columbus: Ohio State University Press, 1970), 10. A representative of *Bookman,* sent to Marion in 1920 to write a feature on his literary tastes, discovered he had none, although he did have a respectable collection of Hamiltoniana. See Samuel Hopkins Adams, *Incredible Era: The Life and Times of Warren Gamaliel Harding* (Boston: Houghton Mifflin, 1939), 80–81.

5. Andrew Sinclair, *The Available Man: The Life Behind the Mask of Warren Gamaliel Harding* (New York: Macmillan, 1965), 65–66, quoting an address of May 18, 1922.

6. Ruth Miller Elson, *Guardians of Tradition: American Schoolbooks of the Nineteenth Century* (Lincoln: University of Nebraska Press, 1964), 228.

7. For Sparks on Washington's parental status, see Lawrence J. Friedman, *Inventors of the Promised Land* (New York: Alfred A. Knopf, 1975), 65.

8. This phrase is used by Bernard Mayo, *Myths and Men: Patrick Henry, George Washington, Thomas Jefferson* (Athens: University of Georgia Press, 1959), 38, and Dixon Wecter, *The Hero in America: A Chronicle of Hero-Worship* (Ann Arbor: University of Michigan Press, 1966), 108. See also John C. Fitzpatrick, "The George Washington Scandals," *Scribner's Monthly,* April 1927, 389–395. The contents of this article were widely discussed in the press during the previous year.

Eugene E. Prussing, *George Washington in Love and Otherwise* (Chicago: Pascal Covici, 1925), 32, documents revelation of the Fairfax letters by Constance Cary Harrison, writing in *Scribner's Monthly* in July 1876. A selection of these letters was printed in the *New York Herald* on March 30, 1877; see Rupert Hughes, *George Washington: The Human Being and the Hero, 1732–1762,* vol. 1 (New York: William Morrow, 1926), 406.

9. Paul Leicester Ford, *The True George Washington* (Philadelphia: J. B. Lippincott, 1896), 105. For the 1924 edition of the book, see introduction to James Morton Smith, ed., *George Washington: A Profile* (New York: Hill and Wang, 1969), xiv.

10. Cash Asher, ed., *He Was "Just Folks": The Life and Character of Warren Gamaliel Harding as Mirrored in the Tributes of the American Press* (Chicago: Laird & Lee, 1923), 199.

11. Frederick Lewis Allen, quoted in Mark Sullivan, *Our Time: The United States, 1900–1925,* vol. 6 (New York: Charles Scribner's Sons, 1935), 28. Harding's appearance as a senator is also noted favorably in "The Whole World Loves a Presidential Nominee," *Literary Digest,* 17 July 1920, 67.

12. Adams, *Incredible Era,* 89, and his "The Timely Death of President Harding," in *The Aspirin Age, 1919–1941,* ed. Isabel Leighton (New York: Simon and Schuster, 1949), 84.

13. Russell, *Shadow of Blooming Grove,* 438.

14. Henry Steele Commager, "The Search for a Usable Past," *American Heritage,* 16, no. 2 (February 1965), 6, argues that the ancestor cult of nineteenth-century Europe took different forms in America, especially before the Civil War, when a lengthy past was lacking and nationalists were therefore compelled to look forward in time, toward a Manifest Destiny. It is perhaps a mark of cultural maturity, or a sign of the demise of frontier self-reliance, that by the turn of the century American history had become spacious enough to accommodate an ancestor search on a broad scale.

15. Adams, *Incredible Era,* 179.

16. Frederick E. Schortemeier, *Rededicating America: Life and Recent Speeches of Warren G. Harding* (Indianapolis: Bobbs-Merrill, 1920), 136–144.

17. Wesley Frank Craven, *The Legend of the Founding Fathers* (New York: New York University Press, 1956), 134. Robert Coughlan, "Konklave in Kokomo," in Leighton, ed., *Aspirin Age,* 114, notes that the first Klan group established in Indiana in 1921 called itself the Nathan Hale Den. William Allen White, *The Autobiography of William Allen White* (New York: Macmillan, 1946), 633–634, discusses his own blacklisting by the DAR in 1928.

18. See especially texts of 1889 and 1879 cited by Howard N. Rabinowitz, "George Washington as Icon, 1865–1900," in *Icons of America*, ed. Ray B. Browne and Marshall Fishwick (Bowling Green: Popular Press, Bowling Green State University, 1978), 70.

19. Adams, "Timely Death of President Harding," 87, quoting "Colonel" George B. M. Harvey. See also Sinclair, *Available Man*, 144.

20. Letter from a supporter in Cambridge, quoted by Downes, *Rise of Warren Gamaliel Harding*, 556.

21. Adams, *Incredible Era*, 101.

22. Russell, *Shadow of Blooming Grove*, 347, traces the term to Davies and Peck's *Mathematical Dictionary* of 1857. The received wisdom holds that Harding merely mispronounced "normality" and the press covered his mistake by crediting him with the new coinage.

23. John Dos Passos, *1919* (New York: Washington Square Press, 1961), 495–496. The novel was originally published by Harcourt Brace in March 1932.

24. Ibid., 499 and 511.

25. Quoted by Russell, *Shadow of Blooming Grove*, 375.

26. White, *Autobiography*, 230–231.

27. Charles R. Hearn, *The American Dream in the Great Depression* (Westport, Conn.: Greenwood Press, 1977), 127. Barton's 1924 book led the nonfiction bestseller lists in 1925 and 1926.

28. Russell, *Shadow of Blooming Grove*, 406–407 and 410, and Downes, *Rise of Warren Gamaliel Harding*, 470–471 and 484.

29. Quoted in William B. Rhoads, *The Colonial Revival*, vol. 1 (New York: Garland, 1977), 399.

30. Downes, *Rise of Warren Gamaliel Harding*, 469.

31. G. B. Galbreath, writing in 1923 on the death of the president and quoted in Sinclair, *Available Man*, 24.

32. Quoted in Rhoads, *Colonial Revival*, vol. 1, 413. For nostalgia, see David Lowenthal, "Past Time, Present Place: Landscape and Memory," *Geographical Review*, 65, no. 1 (January 1975), especially 2–5.

33. Sullivan, *Our Time*, vol. 4, 131.

34. "Whole World Loves a Presidential Candidate," *Literary Digest*, 67.

35. Russell, *Shadow of Blooming Grove*, 410.

36. Robert P. Arner, "Plymouth Rock Revisited: The Landing of the Pilgrim Fathers," *Journal of American Culture*, 6, no. 4 (Winter 1983), 28–31.

37. See Francis Russell, "The Pilgrims and the Rock," *American Heritage*, 13, no. 6 (October 1962), 48 ff.

38. Downes, *Rise of Warren Gamaliel Harding*, 526–530.

39. Craven, *Legend of the Founding Fathers*, 152–153.

40. "The President's Day at Plymouth," *Boston Globe*, 1 August 1921, 1 and 6–7, sec. 1. For the new tercentenary portico designed by McKim, Mead and White to cover the reunited fragments of the Rock, see [Chester E. Rogers,] *Guide to Historic Plymouth*, rev. ed. (Plymouth: Rogers Print, 1956), 7.

41. "President Honors Plymouth Pilgrims," *Boston Globe*, 2 August 1921, 1 and 10–11, sec. 1.

42. "President's Day at Plymouth," *Boston Globe*, 7, col. 7.

43. Ibid., col. 5.

44. Curtis Putnam Nettels, "The Washington Theme in American History," *Proceedings of the Massachusetts Historical Society*, 68 (October 1944–May 1947), 175–176 and 184. I am grateful to Michael Kammen for calling this essay to my attention.

45. *Address Delivered by Ex-Senator Albert J. Beveridge of Indiana on February 22, 1921, at the Second Washington's Birthday Celebration of the Sons of the Revolution and Other Patriotic Societies at Carnegie Hall, New York, and at the Thirty-ninth Annual Banquet of the Sons of the Revolution at the Hotel Plaza, New York* (New York: privately printed, 1921), 8.

46. "Harding Hopes for Real World Brotherhood," *Boston Globe*, 2 August 1921, 10, sec. 1, cols. 1–4.

47. H. L. Mencken's March 7, 1921, column for the *Baltimore Evening Sun*, written on the occasion of Harding's inaugural address, in H. L. Mencken, *A Carnival of Buncombe*, ed. Malcolm Moos (Baltimore: Johns Hopkins University Press, 1956), 38–39.

48. "President Harding at Plymouth Today," *Boston Globe*, 1 August 1921, 12, sec. 1, cols. 2–3.

49. George P. Baker, *The Pilgrim Spirit* (Boston: Marshall Jones, 1921), 9. Virginia Tanner was in charge of the dancers and their routines.

50. Ibid., 95–98.

51. Ibid., 132–135. There were ads in the back of the pageant program for Wallace Nutting's *Furniture of the Pilgrim Century* and Della R. Prescott's *A Day in a Colonial House*.

52. For the Plymouth pageant in relation to overtly political examples of the genre, see Linda Nochlin, "The Paterson Strike Pageant of 1913," *Art in America,* 62, no. 3 (May–June 1974), 67. For the formal sources of historical tableaux in pageants, see Jack W. McCullough, "Edward Kilanyi and American Tableaux Vivants," *Theater Survey,* 16, no. 1 (May 1975), 27–28 and 31.

53. Downes, *Rise of Warren Gamaliel Harding,* 460.

54. Russell, *Shadow of Blooming Grove,* 539–544.

55. Quoted in Asher, ed., *He Was "Just Folks,"* 200.

56. Quoted in Sinclair, *Available Man,* 4.

57. Adams, "Timely Death of President Harding," 82. The novel in question was *Revelry,* published by Boni and Liveright. This thinly disguised portrait of the Harding presidency suggested that he died by his own hand and fueled rumors that—somehow—his demise was not natural. *Revelry* enjoyed added circulation as a play and a film. The self-styled investigator for the Department of Justice, Gaston B. Means, in *The Strange Death of President Harding* (New York: Guild, 1930), intimated that Florence Harding poisoned her husband to prevent his impeachment on charges arising from the Teapot Dome scandals. For comic commentary on these events, see Robert Plunket's novel, *My Search for Warren Harding* (New York: Alfred A. Knopf, 1983).

58. Adams, "Timely Death of President Harding," 81 and 84, quoting Harry Dougherty.

59. Geoffrey Perrett, *America in the Twenties: A History* (New York: Simon and Schuster, 1982), 420.

60. William Allen White, "Blood of the Conquerers," *Collier's,* 10 March 1923, 5–6, and "The Dawn of a Great Tomorrow," 17 March 1923, 11–12 and 27.

61. Sullivan, *Our Time,* vol. 4, 102.

62. Henry Van Dyke, *The Americanism of Washington* (New York: Harper and Brothers, 1906), 14, 33–34, and 64–65. The definitive treatment of the "society page" at the turn of the century is Dixon Wecter, *The Saga of American Society: A Record of Social Aspiration, 1607—1937* (New York: Charles Scribner's Sons, 1937), especially 348 ff.

63. Harold Stearns, "The Intellectual Life," in *Civilization in the United States: An Inquiry by Thirty Americans,* ed. Harold E. Stearns (New York: Harcourt, Brace, 1922), 146–147.

64. For an effort to correlate Lewis's fiction with American social history, see Leo Gurko, *The Angry Decade* (New York: Dodd, Mead, 1947), 20–27.

65. Sinclair Lewis, *Babbitt* (New York: New American Library, 1961), 145; Harcourt, Brace & World first published the novel in 1922.

66. Ibid., 77–78.

67. Ibid., 50, 140, and 259.

68. Ibid., 16.

69. Sinclair Lewis, *Main Street* (New York: New American Library, 1961), 129–130; the book was originally published by Harcourt, Brace & World in 1920.

70. Ibid., 136, 212, 288.

71. Ibid., 417.

72. The phrase comes from a title; see Paul Wilstach, *Mount Vernon: Washington's Home and the Nation's Shrine* (New York: Blue Ribbon, 1930). The first illustrated edition was published by Doubleday, Page, of Garden City, New York, in 1916.

73. Lloyd Lewis, *Myths After Lincoln* (New York: Harcourt Brace, 1940), 299. Lewis's book first appeared in 1929, with an introduction by Carl Sandburg. For wartime George Washington ceremonies and bond drives, see David M. Kennedy, *Over Here: The First World War and American Society* (New York: Oxford University Press, 1980), 65 and 105–106. Many of the big bond rallies of World War I were kicked off on Wall Street, at the foot of the George Washington statue.

74. The book was written by Joseph F. Sabin.

75. Wilstach, *Mount Vernon,* 276.

76. Grace King, quoted in Gerald W. Johnson, *Mount Vernon: The Story of a Shrine, An Account of the Rescue and Rehabilitation of Washington's Home by the Mount Vernon Ladies' Association* (New York: Random House, 1953), 50. Both Johnson and Wilstach cite King's *Mount Vernon on the Potomac* of 1929.

77. For Henry Ford's firetruck, see Johnson, *Mount Vernon,* 48.

78. Quoted in David Wallechinsky and Irving Wallace, *The People's Almanac* (Garden City, N.Y.: Doubleday, 1975), 275.

79. Quoted in Perrett, *America in the Twenties,* 149.

80. Harrison Howell Dodge, *Mount Vernon: Its Owners and Its Story* (Philadelphia: J. B. Lippincott, 1932), 124.

81. Mrs. Burton Kingsland, "Washington's Birthday Fetes," *Ladies' Home Journal,* February 1893, 10.

82. Elaine, "A Cheer-Up Party for Washington's or Lincoln's Birthday," *Good Housekeeping,* February 1932, 98. Souvenir pamphlets about "Dromedary Gingerbread Mix" prepared for the Chicago World's

Fair of 1933 stated that the recipe was owned by the Washington-Lewis Chapter of the DAR in Fredericksburg, Virginia, and was being used by the Hills Brothers Co. of New York with their permission. The same copy appeared in magazine ads during the Washington bicentennial period.

83. Alice Bradley, "Old Colonial Recipes, Including Mrs. Washington's fruit cake," *Woman's Home Companion,* February 1932, 74.

84. "In Honor of George Washington," *McCall's,* February 1932, 102: also available, for 20¢, was *Parties for Grown-Ups,* a booklet that included "A Lincoln Luncheon; Washington Party; Valentine's Affair; and others."

85. Rose O'Neill, "The Kewpies and Washington's Birthday," *Good Housekeeping*, February 1917, 44.

86. E.g., Joseph C. Sindelar, ed., *Washington Day Entertainments* (Chicago: Teachers' Supply Bureau, 1910).

87. Ibid., 31–32 and 60–62.

88. John T. Goolrick, *Historic Fredericksburg: The Story of an Old Town* (Richmond: Whittet & Shepperson, 1922), 195.

89. Quoted by Adams, "Timely Death of President Harding," 99.

90. Ibid., 81.

91. Friedman, *Inventors of the Promised Land,* 58, quoting contemporary accounts.

92. Quoted by Dixon Wecter, *The Hero in America: A Chronicle of Hero-Worship* (Ann Arbor: University of Michigan Press, 1963), 129.

93. Mason Weems, *A History of the Life and Death Virtues and Exploits of General George Washington,* ed. Mark Van Doren ([New York]: Macy-Masius, 1927), 279–280. See also Harold Kellock, *Parson Weems of the Cherry Tree; Being a Short Account of the Eventful Life of the Reverand* [sic] *M. L. Weems, Author of Many Books and Tracts, Itinerant Pedlar* [sic] *of Divers Volumes of Merit: Preacher of Vigour and Much Renown and First Biographer of G. Washington* (New York: Century, 1928), 96.

94. Fitzpatrick, "George Washington Scandals," 394.

95. Prussing, *George Washington in Love,* especially unpaginated preface, 4, and 16.

96. Fitzpatrick, "George Washington Scandals," 395, refers to the incident.

97. Paul Sann, *The Lawless Decade* (Cleveland: Crown, 1960), 71.

98. Quoted by Russell, *Shadow of Blooming Grove,* 632–633.

99. Roger Butterfield, "Henry Ford, the Wayside Inn, and the Problem of 'History Is Bunk,'" *Proceedings of the Massachusetts Historical Society,* 7 (January–December 1965), 56, notes that Ford was quoted in the *St. Louis Post-Dispatch* on July 15, 1919. The *New York Times* carried the phrase in an article published on May 20, 1919. Ford, apparently, tried the phrase out first in an interview with the *Chicago Tribune* on May 25, 1916. Garry Wills, *Reagan's America: Innocents at Home* (Garden City, N.Y.: Doubleday, 1987), 450, quotes Ford as adding, "I thought that a history which excluded harrows and all the rest of daily life is bunk, and I think so yet."

100. W. E. Woodward, *George Washington: The Image and the Man* (Garden City, N.Y.: Garden City Publishing, 1942), a reprint of the 1926 edition, especially 98–103, and Hughes, *George Washington,* vol. 1, 402–410 and 455.

101. Woodward, *George Washington,* 101 and 454, and Hughes, *George Washington,* especially chap. 12, "The Mystery of Sally Fairfax," 176–203, and chap. 27, "Sally Fairfax Again," 402–455.

102. See, e.g., Fitzpatrick, "George Washington Scandals," 390–391 and 393, and "Humanizing George Washington," *Literary Digest,* 6 November 1926, 24–25. John Corbin's "The Unknown Washington," *Scribner's Monthly,* September 1929, 255–264 and "Washington and Sally Fairfax," *Scribner's Monthly,* October 1929, 402–413 elaborate on the theme.

103. "Washington—Man or Waxwork," *The Nation,* 27 January 1926, 75.

104. Allan Nevins, "Washington à la Strachey," *Saturday Review of Literature,* 22 February 1930, 749.

105. Charles Phillips, "The Naked Washington," *Catholic World,* February 1927, 577–585.

106. Merrill D. Peterson, *The Jefferson Image in the American Mind* (New York: Oxford University Press, 1960), 347 and 349.

107. "Washington Dismounted from His High Horse," *Literary Digest,* 12 December 1925, 50 and 52.

108. Woodward, *George Washington,* 26. See also Lewis, *Babbitt,* 98.

109. Nettels, "The Washington Theme," 181.

110. William Roscoe Thayer, *George Washington* (Boston: Houghton Mifflin, 1922), 8–9, and 31–32.

111. Woodward, *George Washington,* 27.

112. Craven, *The Legend of the Founding Fathers,* 160–161, quoting Woodward's novel, *Bunk* (1923), and his autobiography.

113. See Charles Evans Hughes's comments on the subject, in "Not to Debunk Washington," *Literary Digest,* 16 March 1929, 24.

114. One of the most durable of the Coolidge anecdotes, the story is quoted in many places, including B. A. Botkin, ed., *A Treasury of American Anecdotes* (New York: Galahad, 1982), 153–154, and Cameron Rogers, *The Legend of Calvin Coolidge* (Garden City, N.Y.: Doubleday, Doran, 1928), 171.

115. Carl Sandburg, "Washington Monument by Night," from *Slabs of the Sunburnt West,* in Mildred P. Harrington, Josephine H. Thomas, and a Committee of the Carnegie Library School Association, eds., *Our Holidays in Poetry* (New York: H. W. Wilson, 1929), 70.

116. See *Handbook of the George Washington Appreciation Course for Teachers and Students for the Two Hundredth Anniversary Celebration* (Washington, D.C.: U.S. George Washington Bicentennial Commission, 1932), iv–v, for the text of the joint Congressional resolution of December 2, 1924.

117. For selection of the citizen commissioners and the duties of the group, see *Special News Releases Relating to the Life and Time of George Washington, as Prepared and Issued by the United States George Washington Bicentennial Commission,* vol. 1 (Washington, D.C.: U.S. George Washington Bicentennial Commission, 1932), 10.

118. Sinclair Lewis, *The Man Who Knew Coolidge: Being the Soul of Lowell Schmaltz, Constructive and Nordic Citizen* (New York: Harcourt Brace, 1928), 234 and 255.

119. Ibid., 271–272.

120. Quoted in Halsted L. Ritter, *Washington as a Business Man* (New York: Sears, 1931), 140.

121. "'Exposure' of Immortal George Makes Coolidge Laugh Out Loud," *Philadelphia Public Ledger,* 16 January 1926, 1, sec. 1, cols. 6–7.

9. Heroes, History, and Modern Celebrities

1. W. E. Woodward, *George Washington: The Image and the Man* (Garden City, N.Y.: Garden City Publishing, 1942), 453.

2. Lee Allen, quoted in Robert W. Creamer, "Revolution in Baseball: Ruth Reaches New York," in *Ain't We Got Fun? Essays, Lyrics, and Stories of the Twenties,* ed. Barbara H. Solomon (New York: New American Library, 1980), 133.

3. Quoted by Dixon Wecter, *The Hero in America: A Chronicle of Hero-Worship* (Ann Arbor: University of Michigan Press, 1966), 425 and 427. Similar analogies were drawn by the *New York Times,* 25 June 1927, and the *Literary Digest,* 1 October 1927, and 4 June 1927; see *American Folklore and Legend* (Pleasantville, N.Y.: Reader's Digest Association, 1978), 385.

4. Beverly Nichols, *The Star-Spangled Manner* (London: Jonathan Cape, 1928), 44.

5. John Lardner, "The Lindbergh Legend," in *The Aspirin Age, 1919–1941,* ed. Isabel Leighton (New York: Simon and Schuster, 1949), 190.

6. Grover Whalen, *Mr. New York* (New York: G. P. Putnam's Sons, 1955), 94–99. Whalen became a full-time "greeter" in 1922.

7. Quoted by Jules Abels, "Personality Craze," in Solomon, ed., *Ain't We Got Fun?,* 48.

8. See Orrin E. Klapp, *Symbolic Leaders: Public Dramas and Public Men* (Chicago: Aldine, 1964), 43; A. A. Brill, "The Way of the Fan," *North American Review,* October 1929, 429–434; and Richard Schickel, *Intimate Strangers: The Culture of Celebrity* (Garden City, N.Y.: Doubleday, 1985), 56–64.

9. Daniel J. Boorstin, *The Image: A Guide to Pseudo-Events in America* (New York: Atheneum, 1975), 68.

10. Charles A. Lindbergh, *The Spirit of St. Louis* (New York: Ballantine, 1971), 511–512, excuses the laconic tone of *We* on the basis of the rush to publish but is itself a very similar book, packed with tributes to carburetors and ignition systems. *The Spirit of St. Louis* was first published in 1953.

11. John B. Rae, *The American Automobile: A Brief History* (Chicago: University of Chicago Press, 1965), 99.

12. For the corporate component of celebrity in the period, see John W. Ward, "The Meaning of Lindbergh's Flight," *American Quarterly,* 10, no. 1 (Spring 1958), 3–16; Warren I. Susman, *Culture and History: The Transformation of American Society in the Twentieth Century* (New York: Pantheon, 1984), 122–149; and Kenneth S. Davis, *The Hero: Charles A. Lindbergh and the American Dream* (Garden City, N.Y.: Doubleday, 1959), especially 240–244.

13. Quoted in Wecter, *Hero in America,* 144.

14. Quoted in William E. Leuchtenberg, *The Perils of Prosperity, 1914–32* (Chicago: University of Chicago Press, 1958), 188. See also William Allen White, *Calvin Coolidge: The Man Who Is President* (New York: Macmillan, 1925), 218, and Robert J. Thompson,

ed., *Adequate Brevity: A Collation and Co-ordination of the Mental Processes and Reactions of Calvin Coolidge, as Expressed in his Addresses and Messages, and Constituting a Self-Delineation of His Character and Ideals* (Chicago: M. A. Donahue, 1924), 24.

15. David Curtis Skaggs, "Postage Stamps as Icons," in *Icons of America*, ed. Ray B. Browne and Marshall Fishwick (Bowling Green: Popular Press, Bowling Green State University, 1978), 206.

16. Quoted from an address entitled "Washington and Education," delivered before the National Education Association in 1926, in *Handbook of the George Washington Appreciation Course for Teachers and Students for the Two Hundredth Anniversary Celebration* (Washington, D.C.: U.S. George Washington Bicentennial Commission, 1932), 129.

17. Quoted in Thompson, ed., *Adequate Brevity*, 46.

18. Calvin Coolidge, *Foundations of the Republic: Speeches and Addresses* (Freeport, N.Y.: Books for Libraries Press, 1968), 265–285. The volume was first published in 1926.

19. Ibid., 177–178, 320, 337, and 378, for speeches of November 3, 1924, November 17 and December 7, 1925, and April 19, 1926. For the DAR address, see also Wesley Frank Craven, *The Legend of the Founding Fathers* (New York: New York University Press, 1956), 156.

20. Kenneth L. Roberts, *Concentrated New England: A Sketch of Calvin Coolidge* (Indianapolis: Bobbs-Merrill, 1924), 1–2, and Bruce Barton, "Back in Ward Four," in *Meet Calvin Coolidge: The Man Behind the Myth*, ed. Edward Connery Lathem (Brattleboro, Vt.: Stephen Greene, 1960), 188–190. Barton's article originally appeared in the *American Magazine* in March 1931.

21. Calvin Coolidge, *The Autobiography of Calvin Coolidge* (Rutland, Vt.: Academy Books, 1972), 243, originally published by the Cosmopolitan Book Corporation, New York, in 1929.

22. Mary Randolph, "Presidents and First Ladies," in Lathem, ed., *Meet Calvin Coolidge*, 97. Randolph's article originally appeared in the *Ladies' Home Journal* in 1936.

23. Charles Moore, *The Family Life of George Washington* (Boston: Houghton Mifflin, 1926), 13.

24. "Seeks to Buy Kenmore," *New York Times*, 10 May 1922, 7, sec. 1, col. 2.

25. "Coolidge Says We Must Live Up to Our Laws," *New York Times*, 7 July 1922, 7, sec. 1, col. 2.

26. Harrison Howell Dodge, *Mount Vernon: Its Owners and Its Story* (Philadelphia: J. B. Lippincott, 1932), 13. On November 8, 1925, they brought the visiting Prince and Princess of Japan to Mount Vernon also.

27. Moore, *Family Life of George Washington*, 26–27.

28. "Potomac Tide Plays Tricks on President," *New York Times*, 21 July 1924, 3, sec. 1, col. 4.

29. "Washington Farm a Model," *New York Times*, 6 September 1922, 14, sec. 2, col. 8.

30. Joseph Dillaway Sawyer, *Washington*, vol. 1 (New York: Macmillan, 1927), 90–91 and facing illustrations, and Ella Bassett Washington, "The Mother and Birthplace of Washington," *Century Magazine*, April 1892, 833.

31. M. H. Lowell's conjectural recreation is discussed and illustrated in Moore, *Family Life of George Washington*, vii, 27, and unpaginated plates.

32. Bernard M. Baruch, "His Silence and His Thrift," *Good Housekeeping*, February 1935, 181, discusses one such meeting of the commission.

33. Henry L. Mencken, *Selected Prejudices* (New York: Alfred A. Knopf, 1927), 120–121. See also the discussion of Mencken's view of the hero in Leo Gurko, *Heroes, Highbrows and the Popular Mind* (Indianapolis: Bobbs-Merrill, 1953), 67–68.

34. H. L. Mencken, "A Few Pages of Notes," *Smart Set*, January 1915, 435. For another version of this essay, see Alistair Cooke, ed., *The Vintage Mencken* (New York: Vintage, 1955), 67–68.

35. Mencken's 1920 update of his 1915 article, quoted in Douglas C. Stenerson, *H. L. Mencken: Iconoclast from Baltimore* (Chicago: University of Chicago Press, 1971), 183.

36. Quoted in Mark Sullivan, *Our Times: The United States, 1900–1925*, vol. 6 (New York: Charles Scribner's Sons, 1935), 416.

37. An article from *Collier's Weekly*, 21 February 1925, reprinted in the Muncie daily newspaper and quoted in Robert S. Lynd and Helen Merrill Lynd, *Middletown: A Study in Modern American Culture* (New York: Harcourt, Brace and World, 1956), 493. *Middletown* was originally published in 1929.

38. Walter Lippmann, "Puritanism de Luxe," in Lathem, ed., *Meet Calvin Coolidge*, 51–54; see also Jules Abels, "Personality Craze," in Solomon, ed., *Ain't We Got Fun?*, 39.

39. Coolidge, *Autobiography*, 176. Barton, "Back in Ward Four," 188, saw a reproduction of Keller's

painting over Coolidge's mantelpiece after he retired. For details of the inauguration, see Ernest C. Carpenter, *The Boyhood Days of President Calvin Coolidge; or, From the Green Mountains to the White House* (Rutland, Vt.: Tuttle, 1926), 29 and 43. One Guido Boer also painted a rendition of the scene circulated on the Associated Press wire. Along with a picture of the Presidential yacht *Mayflower,* it hung near Coolidge's coffin at his funeral. (According to some accounts, Coolidge had been putting together a picture-puzzle of George Washington moments before his death; see *Minneapolis Tribune,* 6 January 1933, 2, sec. 1, col. 1.)

40. Milton Plesur, ed., *The 1920's: Problems and Paradoxes* (Boston: Allyn and Bacon, 1969), 2; David Van Tassel, preface to Roderick Nash, *The Nervous Generation: American Thought, 1917–1930* (Chicago: Rand McNally, 1970), v; and William Allen White, *A Puritan in Babylon: The Story of Calvin Coolidge* (New York: Macmillan, 1938), v–vi.

41. George E. Mowry, ed., *The Twenties: Fords, Flappers and Fanatics* (Englewood Cliffs, N.J.: Prentice-Hall, 1963), 75.

42. Quoted in White, *A Puritan in Babylon,* 254. See also Gamaliel Bradford, "The Genius of the Average," in Lathem, ed., *Meet Calvin Coolidge,* 45. This article first appeared in the *Atlantic Monthly* in 1930.

43. Sullivan, *Our Times,* vol. 6, 246.

44. Grace Coolidge, ed., "The Real Calvin Coolidge," *Good Housekeeping,* February 1935, 184.

45. White, *Puritan in Babylon,* 237–238.

46. Geoffrey C. Upward, *A Home for Our Heritage: The Building and Growth of Greenfield Village and Henry Ford Museum, 1929–1979* (Dearborn, Mich.: Henry Ford Museum Press, 1979), 8.

47. Henry Ford, "President and Prince Autograph a Bucket," *Good Housekeeping,* March 1935, 218–219.

48. Nash, *Nervous Generation,* 77.

49. Ford, "President and Prince," 218.

50. Esther Singleton, "Restoring the Wayside Inn: Mr. Henry Ford Has Gathered Relics of the Past for This Old Tavern," *Antiquarian,* 4, no. 2 (March 1925), 5; *Longfellow Poems* (New York: Dutton/Everyman's Library, 1978), 389; Margaret Brown Klapthor and Howard Alexander Morrison, *George Washington: A Figure Upon the Stage* (Washington, D.C.: Smithsonian Institution Press, 1982), 56; and Paul Carter, *The Twenties in America,* 2d ed. (New York: Thomas Y. Crowell, 1975), 7.

51. Grace Coolidge, editorial commentary on Ford, "President and Prince Autograph a Bucket," *Good Housekeeping,* March 1935, 219.

52. White, *Puritan in Babylon,* 335. This, too, became a famous Coolidge story. Beverly Nichols, as quoted in Lathem, ed., *Meet Calvin Coolidge,* 112–116, claims to have asked the question and to have received a thoughtful, art-loving reply. Most other versions agree that Coolidge was indifferent to artists, if not openly contemptuous of them.

53. Sullivan, *Our Times,* vol. 6, 439.

54. Howard Chandler Christie, "Pies and Portraits," *Good Housekeeping,* May 1935, 249.

55. Mary B. Mullett, "The Biggest Thing That Lindbergh Has Done," in Mowry, ed., *The Twenties,* 81–82. Mullett's article was published in the *American Magazine* in October 1927.

56. Quoted in Russell Lynes, *The Tastemakers: The Shaping of American Popular Taste* (New York: Dover, 1980), 241. Emily Post's *Personality of a House* was published in 1930.

57. "Crazy Words, Crazy Tune," words by Jack Yellen, music by Milton Ager, published by Warner Brothers-Seven Arts, Inc., 1927. I am grateful to my friend and former student Henry Pisciotta for calling this song to my attention.

58. "The Romance of the Foshay Tower, a Washington Memorial," *Foshay Spot Light,* September 1929, 12.

59. See my *The Colossus of Roads: Myth and Symbol Along the American Highway* (Minneapolis: University of Minnesota Press, 1984), 89.

60. E. L. Austin and Odell Hauser, *The Sesqui-Centennial International Exposition* (Philadelphia: Current Publications, 1929), 51.

61. "Descendants at New Year Pageant Wear Genuine Costumes of 1776," *Philadelphia Public Ledger,* 1 January 1926, 2, sec. 1, cols. 3–5, and "Founders Sign Again," 1, cols. 4–5.

62. "Mummers Win Hearts of All in Vivid Parade," *Philadelphia Public Ledger,* 2 January 1926, 1, sec. 1, col. 1, and 2, cols. 3–6.

63. "Hibernian Pageant Depicts Signing of Declaration," *Philadelphia Public Ledger,* 26 January 1926, 2, sec. 1, col. 3, and "To Appear in Tableau Tonight," *Philadelphia Public Ledger,* 25 January 1926, 2, sec. 1, cols. 3–4.

64. "Not One Unethical Act in Life of Washington, Says Dr. Penniman," *Philadelphia Public Ledger,* 25 January 1926, 2, sec. 1, cols. 3–4.

65. "Woman Leader Champions Washington Against Slurs," *Philadelphia Public Ledger,* 30 January 1926, 14, sec. 2, cols. 6–7.

66. "Exposure of Immortal George Makes Coolidge Laugh Out Loud," *Philadelphia Public Ledger,* 16 January 1926, 1, sec. 1, cols. 6–7.

67. Ibid., 5, col. 1.

68. "Finds Washington Was Foe of Vices," *Philadelphia Public Ledger,* 31 January 1926, 16, sec. 2, cols. 4–6.

69. "Ford Snowed in at Wayside Inn Spends Day with Fiddlers Eight," *Philadelphia Public Ledger,* 10 January 1926, 2, sec. 1, cols. 4–5.

70. Photographs in *Philadelphia Public Ledger,* 17 January 1926, Pictorial Section, part 1, 1.

71. Austin and Hauser, *Sesqui-Centennial,* 67 and 73, and Esther M. Klein, *Fairmount Park: A History and a Guidebook* (Bryn Mawr, Pa.: Harcum Junior College Press, 1974), 39–40.

72. Marietta Minnigerode Andrews, *George Washington's Country* (New York: E. P. Dutton, 1930), 282–283.

73. Ibid., 284.

74. "Sesquicentennial Fair Shows Our Progress," *New York Times,* 4, sec. 9, cols. 4 and 7. "The Street" and the other recreated attractions on the fairgrounds were supplemented by walking tours of Philadelphia neighborhoods and by promotion of "the Chain," a group of restored colonial sites scattered through Fairmount Park; see *Colonial Walks in the Heart of Old Philadelphia* (Philadelphia: Historical Committee, Women's Division, Sesquicentennial, 1926), 16–17.

75. "Silks Swish Again Through Mt. Pleasant Hall," and "Arnold Mansion in Use Once More," *Philadelphia Public Ledger,* 4 July 1926, 6, sec. 1, cols. 3–6, and "Arnold Mansion Opens for Sesqui Visitors," *Philadelphia Public Ledger,* 3 July 1926, 24, sec. 2, photographs.

76. Austin and Hauser, *Sesqui-Centennial,* 22. See also *Greetings from the Sesqui-Centennial International Exposition: . . . A Pictorial Record of the Sesqui-Centennial* (Chicago: C. Teich, 1926), and *Official Daily Program,* 6 August 1926, 15 and 29.

77. Austin and Hauser, *Sesqui-Centennial,* 281, and George Morgan, *The City of Firsts: A Complete History of Philadelphia* (Philadelphia: Historical Publication Society, 1926), 25 and 118.

78. Austin and Hauser, *Sesqui-Centennial,* 22, 116, 155, and 244.

79. Wecter, *Hero in America,* 434.

80. *New York Times,* 20 May 1919, quoted in Keith Sward, *The Legend of Henry Ford* (New York: Rinehart, 1948), 110.

81. Leuchtenberg, *Perils of Prosperity,* 187–188.

82. John Dos Passos, *USA* (Boston: Houghton Mifflin, 1963), 48, a passage called "Tin Lizzie," from *The Big Money.*

83. Walter Karp, "Greenfield Village," *American Heritage,* 32, no. 1 (December 1980), 104.

84. [Homer Eaton Keyes,] "A Victorian Tavern," *Antiques,* 10, no. 6 (December 1926), 452. The advertising section of this journal provides the best possible commentary on the status of Americana in 1926. There are ads for boutiques located in big department stores, such as Lord & Taylor and Jordan Marsh, where both antique and reproduction furniture is to be had. Wallace Nutting offers a reproduction court cupboard for sale, while Israel Sack promises the genuine article. Several firms give notice that they can provide cut-paper silhouettes to "go with" the new colonial fashion in home decor or to spruce up an uncolonial interior.

85. Sward, *Legend of Henry Ford,* 100–104.

86. Geoffrey Perrett, *America in the Twenties: A History* (New York: Simon and Schuster, 1982), 257.

87. Warren Sloat, *1929: America Before the Crash* (New York: Macmillan, 1979), 90.

88. In an excellent paper on the modernization of colonial environments in the 1920s and 1930s, written under my supervision in 1982 at the University of Minnesota, Margaret Schwindler paid special attention to the "improvements" added to the Wayside Inn.

89. Karp, "Greenfield Village," 102. Ford cherished, promoted, and republished the McGuffey Readers of his youth. He began to collect them in 1914—the first such item he collected—and in 1926, he printed and distributed five thousand copies of *Old Favorites From the McGuffey Readers.*

90. David E. Nye, *Henry Ford: "Ignorant Idealist"* (Port Washington, N.Y.: Kennikat Press, 1979), 116–117.

91. Sward, *Legend of Henry Ford,* 259–260.

92. Ruth Kedzie Wood, "Henry Ford's Greatest Gift," *Mentor,* June 1929, 6; Upward, *Home for Our Heritage,* 50; and William Adams Simonds, *Henry Ford and Greenfield Village* (New York: Frederick A. Stokes, 1938), 208.

93. Quoted in Karp, "Greenfield Village," 105.

94. Quoted in Upward, *Home for Our Heritage,* 3.

95. Sloat, *1929*, 88–91.

96. Quoted in ibid., 248.

97. W. A. R. Godwin, "The Restoration of Colonial Williamsburg," *National Geographic,* April 1937, 410 and 426–427.

98. Reynold M. Wik, *Henry Ford and Grass-roots America* (Ann Arbor: University of Michigan Press, 1972), 209, and Upward, *Home for Our Heritage,* 209.

99. Sloat, *1929,* 3.

100. Quoted in Leuchtenberg, *Perils of Prosperity,* 176.

101. Van Wyck Brooks, "On Creating a Usable Past," *Dial,* 11 April 1918, 339.

102. William Peirce Randel, *The Evolution of American Taste* (New York: Crown, 1978), 184.

10. Herbert Hoover and the Cherry Tree

1. Will Rogers, "How to Escape a Lecture," *Good Housekeeping,* March 1935, 25 and 214. After he left office, Coolidge became a journalist. See, for example, Calvin Coolidge, "George Washington," *Minneapolis Journal,* 21 February 1932, 1, Editorial Section.

2. Ink Mendelson, "Ice Cream," *Minneapolis Star and Tribune,* 23 August 1982, 1B, col. 1.

3. Quoted in Richard Ketchum, *Will Rogers: His Life and Times* (New York: Simon and Schuster, 1973), 207–208.

4. See Warren I. Susman, "History and the American Intellectual: Uses of a Usable Past," *American Quarterly,* 16, no. 2 (Summer 1964), 257–259, and the version of that excellent essay included in Susman, *Culture as History: The Transformation of American Society in the Twentieth Century* (New York: Pantheon Books, 1984), 7 ff. See also T. J. Jackson Lears, *No Place of Grace: Antimodernism and the Transformation of American Culture, 1880–1920* (New York: Pantheon, 1981), 256.

5. Quoted in William E. Leuchtenberg, *The Perils of Prosperity, 1914–32* (Chicago: University of Chicago Press, 1958), 144.

6. Roger Dooley, *From Scarface to Scarlett: American Films in the 1930s* (New York: Harcourt Brace Jovanovich, 1981), 109–110.

7. See my "Thomas Hart Benton's *Boomtown*: Regionalism Redefined," in *Prospects: The Annual of American Cultural Studies,* ed. Jack Salzman, vol. 6 (New York: Burt Franklin, 1981), 92. Demuth's painting is now in the collection of the Metropolitan Museum of Art in New York.

8. Waldo Frank, *Our America* (New York: Boni and Liveright, 1919), 97–98; for Puritanism and the skyscraper culture of the period, see also 148 ff. See also the pervasive tone of the contributions by Van Wyck Brooks, Alfred Kreymborg, Lewis Mumford, and Paul Rosenfeld, eds., *The American Caravan* (New York: Literary Guild of America, 1927).

9. Geoffrey Perrett, *America in the Twenties: A History* (New York: Simon and Schuster, 1982), 343.

10. J. C. Furnas, *Great Times: An Informal Social History of the United States, 1914–1929* (New York: G. P. Putnam's Sons, 1974), 427.

11. Donald Robert Stolz, Marshall Louis Stolz, and William B. Earle, *The Advertising World of Norman Rockwell* (New York: Milton Square Press/Norman Rockwell Museum, 1985), 44, 52, 58, 118, and 134.

12. 12 Southerners [Donald Davidson, John Fletcher Gould, et al.], *I'll Take My Stand: The South and the Agrarian Tradition* (New York: Harper & Row, 1962), the manifesto of the agrarian movement, was published in 1930. The "Nashville Fugitives"—Davidson, John Crowe Ransom, Allen Tate, and Robert Penn Warren—had been publishing the poetry and criticism that led to the dramatic manifesto since the early 1920s.

13. The essay in question, entitled "The American Background," was written for a volume called *America and Alfred Stieglitz,* a collection of critical essays on American culture edited by Waldo Frank, Lewis Mumford, Dorothy Norman, Paul Rosenfeld, and Harold Rugg in 1934. The essay is included in *Selected Essays of William Carlos Williams* (New York: New Directions, 1969), 137–138 and 141–143. Williams's libretto is discussed in Paul Mariani, *William Carlos Williams: A New World Naked* (New York: McGraw-Hill, 1981), 139, 342, and 356–359.

14. William Carlos Williams, *In the American Grain* (New York: New Directions, 1956), 109, 180, and 188.

15. Ibid., 140 and 143.

16. Ibid., 141–142.

17. Ibid., 140–141.

18. Ibid., 143.

19. Ibid., 143–144.

20. E. L. Austin and Odell Hauser, *The Sesqui-Centennial International Exposition* (Philadelphia: Current Publications, 1929), 313, makes it clear that the celebration was an occasion for retailing. The

Chelsea Hooked Rug Knitter on display at the Philadelphia Sesqui-Centennial allowed hobbyists with time on their hands to eschew machine-made colonial fakery and produce their own authentic colonial carpets, artifacts fated to be prized for their "quaintness and character."

21. Irving Stone, "Calvin Coolidge: A Study in Inertia," in *The Aspirin Age, 1919–1941*, ed. Isabel Leighton (New York: Simon and Schuster, 1949), 131.

22. Pete Daniel, *Deep'n as It Come: The 1927 Mississippi River Flood* (New York: Oxford University Press, 1977), 10.

23. Williams, *In the American Grain*, 141.

24. Quoted in Paul A. Carter, *Another Part of the Twenties* (New York: Columbia University Press, 1977), 180. See also Elizabeth Stevenson, *The American 1920s: Babbitts and Bohemians* (New York: Collier, 1970), 209.

25. David Burner, *Herbert Hoover: A Public Life* (New York: Alfred A. Knopf, 1979), 14.

26. Quoted in Carter, *Another Part of the Twenties*, 180 and 182.

27. Mary R. Parkman, *Heroes of To-day* (New York: Century, 1928), vii and 304. The first edition was published in 1917.

28. Ibid., 309.

29. See Dilys Winn, ed., *Murder Ink: The Mystery Reader's Companion* (New York: Workman, 1977), 20. See also the discussion of the Victorian hero of enterprise and the professional man as hero in Jennie Calder, *Heroes, from Byron to Guevara* (London: Hamish Hamilton, 1977), especially 166–167 and 186–187.

30. Marling, "Thomas Hart Benton's *Boomtown*," 96 and 102.

31. Joseph Lewis French, *Pioneers All! Achievements in Adventure* (Springfield, Mass.: Milton Bradley, 1929), especially 292 and 323–324.

32. Parkman, *Heroes of To-day*, 313–14.

33. Alan Holder, "In the American Grain: William Carlos Williams on the American Past," *American Quarterly*, 19, no. 3 (Fall 1967), 501–503.

34. Eugene E. Prussing, *George Washington in Love and Otherwise* (Chicago: Pascal Covici, 1925), preface. See also Woodrow Wilson, *George Washington* (New York: Harper & Brothers, 1924), especially 313. Wilson's book, with illustrations by Howard Pyle, was originally published in serial form.

35. Prussing, *George Washington in Love*, preface.

36. Ibid., 70–73 and 35.

37. Ibid., preface.

38. Ibid., 156.

39. Ibid., 79–82 and preface.

40. Quoted in Lawrence C. Wroth, *Parson Weems: A Biographical and Critical Study* (Baltimore: Eichelberger, 1911), 69.

41. Owen Wister, *The Seven Ages of Washington: A Biography* (New York: Macmillan, 1907), 95.

42. Harold Kellock, *Parson Weems of the Cherry Tree* (New York: Century, 1928), 83–84. On the title page of M. L. Weems, *The Life of George Washington, with Curious Anecdotes Equally Honorable to Himself, and Exemplary to His Young Countrymen* (Philadelphia: Joseph Allen, 1847), the following verse sets forth the author's intention:

A life useful to his country led!
How loved! while living!—how revered! now dead!
Lisp! lisp! his name, ye children yet unborn!
And with like deeds you own great names adorn.

See also Emily Ellsworth Ford Skeel, ed., *Mason Locke Weems, His Works and Ways: A Bibliography Left-Unfinished by Paul Leicester Ford*, vol. 1 (New York: Privately printed, 1929), especially 91–96.

43. Mason Weems, *A History of the Life and Death Virtues and Exploits of General George Washington*, ed. Mark Van Doren (New York: Macy-Masius, 1927), 8–9. See also Lewis Leary, *The Book-Peddling Parson* (Chapel Hill, N.C.: Algonquin Books, 1984).

44. Wister, *Seven Ages of Washington*, 23–24 and 35.

45. Weems, *History of the Life and Death Virtues*, 19–20 and 25–26.

46. Ibid., 29.

47. Ibid., 19 and 24–25.

48. Quoted by Marshall Fishwick, *The Hero, American Style* (New York: David McKay, 1954), 38.

49. Ella Bassett Washington, "The Mother and Birthplace of Washington," *Century Magazine*, April 1892, 834.

50. Elizabeth Eggleston Seelye, *George Washington* (New York: D. Appleton, 1893), 6, 8–9, and 21.

51. Minnie Kennedy Lowther, *Mount Vernon: Its Children, Its Romance, Its Allied Families and Mansions* (Philadelphia: John C. Winston, 1930), 45.

52. William Roscoe Thayer, *George Washington* (Boston: Houghton Mifflin, 1922), vii.

53. Charles Moore, *The Family Life of George Washington* (Boston: Houghton Mifflin, 1926), 12.

54. Joseph Dillaway Sawyer, *Washington,* vol. 1 (New York: Macmillan, 1927), 90–91.

55. Lowther, *Mount Vernon,* 45–47.

56. W. E. Woodward, *George Washington: The Image and the Man* (Garden City, N.Y.: Garden City Publishing, Inc., 1942), 342. The book was originally published in 1926.

57. Debunking Washington was not solely a literary sport. In King Vidor's 1928 silent film *The Crowd,* the hero is brought up to believe he is special—another Washington or Lincoln, according to the title cards. The movie demonstrates that he is not. At one point he visits Coney Island and the camera stops to examine a tableau vivant of Washington Crossing the Delaware, presented inside a tunnel of love. The characters mock Washington's heroic gesture as they pass by and clearly disbelieve in the rugged individualism for which he stands.

58. Woodward, *George Washington,* 15, 21, and 16.

59. Rupert Hughes, *George Washington: The Human Being and the Hero, 1732–1762,* vol. 1 (New York: William Morrow, 1926), 14–15, 17, and 23–26.

60. See Prussing, *George Washington in Love,* preface, in which he notes that he had completed a draft of the study in 1918; Wilson Miles Cary called his privately printed 1916 study *Sally Cary: A Long Hidden Romance of Washington's Life, with Notes by Another Hand.* If Prussing's source is Cary, it also seems likely that Prussing was Cary's mysterious "hand."

61. Hughes, *George Washington,* 492, cites Cary, for instance.

62. "Grand Old Platform," *Time,* 25 June 1928, 11.

63. Quoted in Leuchtenburg, *Perils of Prosperity,* 238.

64. "The Beaver-Man," *Time,* 26 March 1928, 9.

65. Harris Gaylord Warren, *Herbert Hoover and the Great Depression* (New York: W. W. Norton, 1967), 30.

66. "In Topeka," and "Buses," *Time,* 27 August 1928, 9.

67. Warren, *Herbert Hoover,* 19, and Walter W. Liggett, *The Rise of Herbert Hoover* (New York: H. K. Fly, 1932), 3–8. Liggett's book is dedicated to "George Washington our first president and a great engineer whose works may still be seen." The adult Hoover first stopped in West Branch between trains in 1923.

68. Burner, *Herbert Hoover,* 6, and Will Irwin, *Herbert Hoover: A Reminiscent Biography* (New York: Century, 1928), 10–12, quoting Hoover's 1927 speech to the Iowa Society of Washington on local topography.

69. Quoted in Kent Michael Schofield, "The Figure of Herbert Hoover in the 1928 Campaign," Ph.D. dissertation (University of California, Riverside, 1966), 103.

70. Craig Lloyd, *Aggressive Introvert: A Study of Herbert Hoover and Public Relations Management, 1912–1932* (Columbus: Ohio State University Press, 1972), 79 and 131–132.

71. Claude H. Miller, *An Early American Home and the Fun We Had Building It* (New York: Thomas Y. Crowell, 1931), 232–234. The book was written ca. 1928–1930, as the author completed his dream house.

72. Samuel Eliot Morison, introduction, *Pathways of the Puritans,* ed. Mrs. N. S. Bell (Framingham, Mass.: Massachusetts Bay Colony Tercentenary Commission/ Old America Co., 1930), xi–xii. See plate opposite 182 for Wallace Nutting's photograph of the bar room at the Wayside Inn. See also George Francis Dow, "The Colonial Village Built at Salem, Massachusetts, in the Spring of 1930," *Old-Time New England,* 22, no. 1 (July 1931), 3–14. A floating replica of the ship *Arbella* was also built, and a highly realistic pageant of life in Salem was performed in the reconstructed village on June 12, 1930.

73. W. A. R. Godwin, "The Restoration of Colonial Williamsburg," *National Geographic,* April 1937, 443.

74. Alan Wellikoff, *The American Historical Supply Catalogue: A Nineteenth-Century Sourcebook* (New York: Schocken, 1984), 217.

75. Irwin, *Herbert Hoover,* 10. On the remembered imagery of boyhood, see also George H. Nash, *The Life of Herbert Hoover: The Engineer, 1874–1914* (New York: W. W. Norton, 1983), 4–5.

76. Herbert Hoover, *The New Day: Campaign Speeches of Herbert Hoover, 1928* (Palo Alto, Cal.: Stanford University Press, 1929), 46–60.

77. Herbert Hoover, *American Individualism* (Garden City, N.Y.: Doubleday, Page, 1922), 52; Irwin, *Herbert Hoover,* 23–24; and Herbert Hoover, *A Boyhood in Iowa* (New York: Aventine Press, 1931), 23, also refers to the same memories.

78. Burner, *Herbert Hoover,* 9.

79. William J. Marsh, Jr. (Age 11 Years), *Our President Herbert Hoover* (New Milford, Conn.: William J. and Charles Marsh, Pub., 1930), 9–10, 16, and 37.

80. Karal Ann Marling, "Of Cherry Trees and Ladies' Teas: Grant Wood Looks at Colonial America," in *The Colonial Revival in America,* ed. Alan Axelrod (New York: W. W. Norton, 1985), 309–311.

81. The sketch for the painting is reproduced in James M. Dennis, *Grant Wood: A Study in American Art and Culture* (Columbia: University of Missouri Press, 1986), 115.

82. Karal Ann Marling, "Don't Knock Wood," *ARTnews*, September 1983, 95.

83. Walter Friar Dexter, *Herbert Hoover and American Individualism: A Modern Interpretation of a National Ideal* (New York: Macmillan, 1932), 12–13 and 249, quotes extensively from Hoover's remarks in West Branch in a critique of his political values.

Many critics seem to sense that the same patterns can be discerned across a wide spectrum of American life—in politics, the presentation of myth and history, artifacts—although few have explored such phenomena as the Hoover-Washington-archaeology-house-antiques complex in a systematic way. Suggestive in this regard is Harvey Green, "Popular Science and Political Thought Converge: Colonial Survival Becomes Colonial Revival, 1830–1910," *Journal of Popular Culture,* 6, no. 4 (Winter 1983), 3–24. I am grateful to Harvey Green for calling this essay and a number of useful Washington artifacts to my attention.

84. Quoted in Leuchtenburg, *Perils of Prosperity,* 138.

85. *Address Delivered by Ex-Senator Albert J. Beveridge of Indiana on February 22, 1921, at the Second Washington's Birthday Celebration of the Sons of the Revolution and other Patriotic Societies at Carnegie Hall, New York, and at the Thirty-ninth Annual Banquet of the Sons of the Revolution at the Hotel Plaza, New York* (New York: privately printed, 1921), 8.

86. John Kenneth Galbraith, *The Great Crash: 1929* (Boston: Houghton Mifflin, 1972), 40–103.

87. Sloat, *1929,* 8 and passim.

88. See Frederick Lewis Allen, *Since Yesterday: 1929–1939* (New York: Bantam, 1965), 569.

89. Quoted in Robert Goldston, *The Great Depression: The United States in the Thirties* (Greenwich, Conn.: Fawcett, 1970), 478.

90. *Time Capsule/1929: A History of the Year Condensed from the Pages of Time* (New York: Time, Inc., 1967), 13, for March 25, 1929.

91. Quoted in Goldston, *Great Depression,* 48.

92. Quoted in Ketchum, *Will Rogers,* 288.

93. Quoted in *Handbook of the George Washington Appreciation Course for Teachers and Students, for the Two Hundredth Anniversary Celebration* (Washington, D.C.: U.S. George Washington Bicentennial Commission, 1932), 301.

94. *Time*'s 1931 opinion, quoted in *New York Times,* 20 October 1932, 14, sec. 2, col. 3.

95. William Starr Myers, ed., *The State Papers and Other Public Writings of Herbert Hoover* (New York: Doubleday, Doran, 1934), 570.

96. Henry Van Dyck, *The Americanism of Washington* (New York: Harper & Bros., 1906), 2.

97. See Alfred Haworth Jones, *Roosevelt's Image Brokers: Poets, Playwrights, and the Use of the Lincoln Symbol* (Port Washington, N.Y.: Kennikat Press/ National University Publications, 1974), 35–41, and Merrill D. Peterson, *The Jefferson Image in the American Mind* (New York: Oxford University Press, 1960), 420–432.

98. Ketchum, *Will Rogers,* photograph on 312.

99. Joseph J. Corn, *The Winged Gospel: America's Romance with Aviation, 1900–1950* (New York: Oxford University Press, 1983), 54–55.

100. Robert Bishop, ed., *Selected Treasures of Greenfield Village and Henry Ford Museum* (Dearborn: Edison Institute, 1969), 24–33 and 56.

101. Quoted in Schofield, *Figure of Herbert Hoover,* 147.

11. Popular History

1. Robert S. Allen, "'I Know My Washington,'" *New Yorker,* 20 February 1932, 26.

2. For the roster of commission membership in 1931, see *Special News Releases Relating to the Life and Time of George Washington, as Prepared and Issued by the United States George Washington Bicentennial Commission,* vol. 1 (Washington, D.C.: U.S. George Washington Bicentennial Commission, 1932), frontispiece; "Introduction," ix; and "The George Washington Bicentennial," 10. There were no other volumes published.

3. "Bloom's Boomerang, New York Congressman Gets Some Unwelcome Publicity," *Newsweek,* 17 January 1938, 15.

4. Sol Bloom, *The Autobiography of Sol Bloom* (New York: G. P. Putnam's Sons, 1948), 134–138.

5. "Portrait [of Sol Bloom]," *American Review of Reviews,* May 1924, 457.

6. "Inferior Pugilism in Congress," *Literary Digest,* 5 March 1927, 1011.

7. See the charge to the commission and its publicity goals, in *Special News Releases,* x.

8. Bloom, *Autobiography,* 219–220.

9. Ibid., 220–221, and "Bloom's Boomerang," *Newsweek,* 15.

10. Marshall Fishwick, *The Hero, American Style* (New York: David McKay, 1954), 50.

11. Dixon Wecter, *The Hero in America: A Chronicle of Hero-Worship* (Ann Arbor: University of Michigan Press, 1966), 145.

12. George M. Cohan, *Father of the Land We Love* (Washington, D.C.: U.S. George Washington Bicentennial Commission, 1931), 3–4, with a copyright assigned to Sol Bloom.

13. Wecter, *Hero in America,* 145. For the complete text of the Markham poem, see also *History of the George Washington Bicentennial Celebration,* vol. 1, Literature Series (Washington, D.C.: U.S. George Washington Bicentennial Commission, 1932), 648.

14. Marcus Cunliffe, foreword to Margaret Brown Klapthor and Howard Alexander Morrison, *George Washington: A Figure upon the Stage* (Washington, D.C.: Smithsonian Institution Press, 1982), 10. For the atlas, edited by Lawrence Martin, see *George Washington Bicentennial Celebration,* vol. 1, v.

15. Thomas S. Buechner, *Norman Rockwell: Artist and Illustrator* (New York: Harry N. Abrams, 1970), plate 611. In 1950, Rockwell used the same conceit for a calendar showing a Cub Scout and his older brother before a vision of Washington praying at Valley Forge.

A news photograph in the collection of the Minnesota Historical Society shows the planting of a Washington Memorial Grove at the north end of Lake Phelan in St. Paul (Maplewood) in May 1932. In attendance were "direct descendants of Augustin Washington, half brother of George Washington," and a great-granddaughter of Timothy Dwight, "who served as chaplain in Washington's army at Valley Forge."

16. See Allen, "'I Know My Washington,'" 25, for Bloom's interest in Mussolini. Bloom's only daughter also wrote several glowing articles in praise of Il Duce.

17. *George Washington Bicentennial Celebration,* vol. 4, 33, 93–94, 102–103, 155, 168, 209, 331, and 533.

18. Aristides Rojas, "Washington at the Centenary of Bolivar, Statue and Mementoes in Caracas," *Bulletin of the Pan-American Union,* 66, no. 7 (July 1932), especially 508, and, in the same publication, "The Americas Pay Homage to Washington," 457–459, 462, and 464–465.

19. Allen, "'I Know My Washington,'" 27.

20. Geoffrey Perrett, *America in the Twenties: A History* (New York: Simon and Schuster, 1982), 352.

21. *Special News Releases,* x.

22. Ibid., 5.

23. Ibid., 82. There is some reason to believe that Bloom and Grant had been chosen to head the Washington observances for reasons of economy: they were already on the federal payroll.

24. Michael Kammen, *A Machine That Would Go of Itself: The Constitution in American Culture* (New York: Alfred A. Knopf, 1986), 283–312, takes up the promotional career of Bloom, who went on to direct the Constitutional Sesquicentennial under FDR. In a chapter entitled "My God! Making a Racket Out of the Constitution," he cites Bloom's spirited defense of his catalogue of Washington bicentennial merchandise while under attack for similar marketing schemes in 1938. For Bloom, souvenirs, and historical celebrations in the 1930s, see also my "A 'New Historical Whopper': Creating the Art of the Constitutional Sesquicentennial," *This Constitution,* no. 14 (Spring 1987), 11–17.

25. *Special News Releases,* 5.

26. Ibid., 82 and 98.

27. Grover Whalen, *Mr. New York* (New York: G. P. Putnam's Sons, 1955), 174.

28. For a detailed description of the "Sky Ride," see *Official World's Fair Weekly,* 11 June 1933, 64.

29. See souvenir program, *Wings of a Century: The Romance of Transportation, 1833–1933, A Century of Progress International Exposition, Chicago* (Chicago: Neely Printing, 1933).

30. Promotional pamphlet, *Baltimore & Ohio Railroad, World's Fair Exhibit, Chicago* (ca. 1933–34), 16 and 1819.

31. Karal Ann Marling, "Don't Knock Wood," *ARTnews,* September 1983, 97.

32. James M. Dennis, *Grant Wood: A Study in American Art and Culture* (Columbia: University of Missouri Press, 1986), 110. See also my "Of Cherry Trees and Ladies' Teas: Grant Wood Looks at Colonial America," in *The Colonial Revival in America,* ed. Alan Axelrod (New York: W. W. Norton, 1985), 301.

33. Gertrude Stein, *Four in America* (New Haven: Yale University Press, 1947), 163.

34. Sol Bloom, "Questions and Answers Pertaining to the Life and Times of George Washington," in *George Washington Bicentennial Celebration,* vol. 3, 687, also published as a pamphlet in its own right.

35. Sol Bloom, "Washington the Everyday Man" (address delivered before the Kiwanis Club and other civic groups at Wilkes-Barre, Pa., June 30, 1932), quoted in "Selected Bicentennial Addresses Delivered by Hon. Sol Bloom," *George Washington Bicentennial Celebration,* vol. 2, 153–155.

36. Matthew Baigell, "Grant Wood Revisited," *Art Journal,* 26, no. 2 (Winter 1967), 120.

37. *Special News Releases,* 67.

38. Ibid., 14.

39. Harrison Howell Dodge, *Mount Vernon: Its Owners and Its Story* (Philadelphia: J. B. Lippincott, 1932), 215.

40. *George Washington, Jean Antoine Houdon, Sculptor: A Brief History of the Most Famous Sculpture Created of America's Immortal Patriot Issued to Commemorate the Bicentennial of His Birth, 1732–1932* (Providence, R.I.: Gorham Company, 1931), foreword.

41. John S. Hallam, "Houdon's *Washington* in Richmond: Some New Observations," *American Art Journal,* 10, no. 2 (November 1978), 80.

42. Alton Ketchum, *Uncle Sam: The Man and the Legend* (New York: Hill and Wang, 1959), 105–106.

43. *George Washington Bicentennial Celebration,* vol. 2, ii. For a consideration of 1932 souvenirs in relationship to the imagery of the 1939 Constitutional Sesquicentennial, see my "A 'New Historical Whopper.'"

44. Garry Wills, *Cincinnatus: George Washington and the Enlightenment* (Garden City, N.Y.: Doubleday, 1984), 237, takes Virginia to task for hoisting the Houdon bronze into the air on a lofty pedestal; the artist intended for the viewer to look the life-size figure right in the eye.

45. *Special News Releases,* 70–72. Directed and written by Donald Wrye, the controversial television miniseries *Amerika,* broadcast by ABC in February 1987, examined American institutions and the American heritage in the light of a fictional Soviet takeover of the nation in the 1990s. During the climactic episode, the occupying forces set fire to the U.S. Capitol. The camera watches a statue of Jefferson topple to the floor but returns symbolically several times to the bronze (Gorham) Houdon Washington, still standing behind a screen of flame.

46. Ibid., 73. The last new design for the quarter had been adopted in 1916.

47. Illustrated in Klapthor and Morrison, *George Washington,* 44–45. By the time the celebration began, the Bicentennial Commission staff had collected more than 650 reproductions of George Washington images, all of them more or less "authentic" in appearance; the collection included Currier and Ives prints, lithographic potboilers, and a lot of nineteenth-century academic history painting of a sentimental type. At any given moment, six thousand copies of these various images were on hand for distribution to publishers, editors, authors, and so on.

48. Bloom, *Autobiography,* 221.

49. *Handbook of the George Washington Appreciation Course for the Two Hundredth Anniversary Celebration of the Birth of George Washington* (Washington, D.C.: U.S. George Washington Bicentennial Commission, 1932), v.

50. Allen, "'I Know My Washington,'" 27.

51. *Special News Releases,* 78. For sour comments on the potential saturation of the market for Washingtoniana, see "In Honor of Greatness," *Antiques,* 21, no. 1 (January 1932), 12. For a novel use of bicentennial stamps as illustrations, see M. L. Weems, *An Anecdote from the Life of George Washington* (Madison, N.J.: Golden Hind Press, 1932), with notes by Frederick Lewis Allen. For portrait exhibitions, see also Charles F. McCombs, "The Washington Bicentennial Exhibition, 1732–1932," *Bulletin of the New York Public Library,* 36, no. 4 (April 1932), 206–217.

52. *Special News Releases,* 6.

53. See Wecter, *Hero in America,* 114.

54. See, e.g., the use of the official photograph of the Mount Vernon bust as the frontispiece to Louis Martin Sears, *George Washington* (New York: Thomas Y. Crowell, 1932).

55. See, e.g., Arene W. Burgess, *Souvenir Plates: A Collector's Guide* (n.p.: Arene Burgess, 1978), 42–43, for the Staffordshire earthenware made by Crown Ducal. In addition to a complete pictorial dinner set called "Colonial Time," issued in 1932–1933 to take advantage of the bicentennial, the firm also made two sets of a dozen George Washington Bicentennial Memorial plates each, in round and square shapes. Sosme subjects were also issued with Della Robbia–style borders.

56. Margaret E. Sangster, "Portrait of Washington," *Good Housekeeping,* February 1932, 33. Portraits of Washington were common prizes and premiums in 1932; my own collection includes, for example,

framed scenes from the life of Washington printed by Brown and Bigelow and distributed to newsboys by Minnesota newspapers as rewards for faithful service.

57. Marling, "Don't Knock Wood," *ARTnews,* 98.

58. Vachel Lindsay, *The Litany of Washington Street* (New York: Macmillan, 1929), 1.

59. Ibid., 22.

60. Ibid., 26.

61. Vachel Lindsay, "Thanksgiving for George Washington," *Christian Century,* 1 July 1931, 866.

62. *Special News Releases,* 107–109.

63. Ibid., 5.

64. Ibid., 87.

65. Ibid., 84 and 73, and any recent issue of *Scott Standard Postage Stamp Catalogue.*

66. For the use of the Kodak footage, see M. D. Holmes, *George Washington: The Soul of a Nation* (New York: John C. Winston, 1932), still photographs from "George Washington, His Life and Times," a film made by Eastman Kodak Teaching Films, Inc. An Associated Press still showing the Crossing of the Delaware from "a new movie film . . . produced by the Washington Bicentennial commission" appears in *Minneapolis Sunday Tribune,* 21 February 1932, 1, picture section.

67. *Special News Releases,* 12–13 and 132–133. See n. 24 above.

68. Lindsay, "Thanksgiving for George Washington," *Christian Century,* 866 and 868.

69. *Special News Releases,* 5–6.

70. Ibid., 321, 380, 390, 401–423, and 432–435.

71. Ibid., 240 and 294.

72. Ibid., 7.

73. Ibid., 30; see also John Corbin's comments on Fitzpatrick's bicentennial work in "Archivist's Washington," *Saturday Review of Literature,* 24 February 1934, 506–507.

74. Quoted in Charles A. Beard and Mary R. Beard, *America in Midpassage,* vol. 3 (New York: Macmillan, 1939), 124–125.

75. The myth of Hoover as a barefoot country boy with a little red hatchet was remarkably durable; see, e.g., Herman Hagedorn, *Americans: A Book of Lives* (New York: John Day, 1946), 313 and 325.

76. *Special News Releases,* 12.

77. "Address of Herbert Hoover, President of the United States, Delivered at a Joint Session of Congress, February 22, 1932," *George Washington Bicentennial Celebration,* vol. 2, 11–12.

78. Quoted in Michael Kammen, *A Season of Youth: The American Revolution and the Historical Imagination* (New York: Alfred A. Knopf, 1978), 287.

79. E. B. Crosswhite, "The Cherry Tree Incident—In the 1932 Manner," *Saturday Evening Post,* 27 February 1932, 26 and 74.

80. "February Junior Embroidery," *Woman's Home Companion,* February 1932, 97.

81. James Truslow Adams, "Our Heritage from Washington," *Woman's Home Companion,* February 1932, 13.

82. Alice Bradley, "Old Colonial Recipes," *Woman's Home Companion,* February 1932, 74, and "In Honor of George Washington Whose Bicentennial We Celebrate This Year," 103–106.

83. "A Large Little House in Colonial Design," *Good Housekeeping,* February 1932, 53 and 219, and Chesla C. Sherlock, "Forgotten Facts About Washington," *Ladies' Home Journal,* February 1932, 13.

84. Bernie Babcock, *The Heart of George Washington: A Simple Story of Great Love* (Philadelphia: J. B. Lippincott, 1932), 7. Babcock also wrote four romantic novels about Lincoln, including one on his love for Ann Rutledge (1919) and another called *Lincoln's Mary and the Babies* (1929); see Roy P. Basler, *The Lincoln Legend: A Study in Changing Conceptions* (Boston: Houghton Mifflin, 1935), 48.

85. Ralph Bradford, *The White Way: The Commander-in-Chief Tired from the Wars Rides Home on Christmas Eve to a Festive Mount Vernon, His Mind Full of Plans . . . and Memories* (Washington, D.C.: Judd & Detweiler, 1955), 5 and 35. The book was originally published by the same firm in 1931. See also a black romance with Washington as the central character: John H. Hill, *Princess Malah* (Washington, D.C.: Associated Publishers, 1972), a reprint of the 1933 edition. The author's grandmother, born before Washington's death, was a "mammy" at Mount Vernon, and he intimates that the story is based in part on her memories. The Washington family is at the center of a confused plot concerning colonial intermarriages between the black, white, and red races.

86. *Special News Releases,* 8, 57, and 152.

87. Olive M. Price, "The Redbud Tree: A George Washington Pageant-Play for Children," in *George Washington Bicentennial Celebration,* vol. 2, 642. "From Picture Book Towne," another play for grade-schoolers by the same author, p. 647, includes a tableau of "*George Washington* kneeling beside his

Mother," with her hand on his shoulder, a gesture derived from William H. Powell's 1864 painting, *Washington Receiving His Mother's Last Blessing* (now in the collection of the Senate House Historic Site, Palisades Parkway Commission, New York State Office of Parks and Recreation). Despite its much-publicized devotion to "fact," the Bicentennial Commission used this kind of potboiler to illustrate its own publications and to give to the press.

88. In the "Honor to George Washington" pamphlet series, see #14, Carl H. Claudy, "Washington's Home and Fraternal Life," in *George Washington Bicentennial Celebration*, vol. 1, 172, and especially part 2, "Freemasonry." For the 1932 Masonic knife, see Klapthor and Morrison, *George Washington*, 93. The George Washington National Masonic Association also commissioned an oil portrait, *George Washington in Masonic Apron*, painted by Hattie Burdette in 1932. The actor Tefft Jefferson, who had portrayed Washington many times on the stage, posed for the picture. The original is displayed in the George Washington Masonic Temple at Alexandria, Virginia; reproductions were made for every Masonic lodge in the United States. Apparently, the Bicentennial Commission subsidized production of ten thousand copies as an aid to the national promotional effort. See Elinor Lander Horwitz, *The Bird, the Banner, and Uncle Sam: Images of America in Folk and Popular Art* (Philadelphia: J. B. Lippincott, 1976), 22–23. Reproductions of a somewhat earlier painting by John Ward Dunsmore, *Washington as Master of Alexandria Lodge No. 22*, were also widely circulated during the bicentennial year.

89. Rex Alan Smith, *The Carving of Mount Rushmore* (New York: Abbeville, 1985), 201–219.

90. Rev. Fulton J. Sheen, "America's Calvary," *George Washington Bicentennial Celebration*, vol. 2, 479.

91. "Address of Herbert Hoover," *George Washington Bicentennial Celebration*, vol. 2, 11–12.

92. Ibid., 12–13.

93. Ibid., 12.

94. Ibid., 13.

95. "Listing Eighteenth-Century Businesses," *Special News Releases*, 122–124.

96. See George Morgan Knight, Jr., and Richard Harwood-Staderman, *What You Don't Know About George Washington* (Washington, D.C.: American Good Government Society, 1941), 208. Beard's

Economic Interpretation of the Constitution of the United States first appeared in 1913 and is often cited as a revisionist inspiration to the debunkers, particularly Woodward.

97. See also Hart's introduction to Halsted L. Ritter, *Washington as a Business Man* (New York: Sears, 1931), 9 and 16. The new businessman and engineer Washington, whom he describes in favorable terms, is diametrically opposed, says Hart, to "the boy who chopped down the cherry tree."

98. William B. Rhoads, *The Colonial Revival*, vol. 1 (New York: Garland, 1977), 523, numbers Hart among those members of the Harvard community of the 1920s who feared that the old Yankee stock was being crowded out (this faction favored neocolonial architecture at Harvard as a symbol of Old Americanism) and called for a quota on the admission of Jews. Samuel Eliot Morison, "A Memoir and Estimate of Albert Bushnell Hart," *Proceedings of the Massachusetts Historical Society*, 77 (January–December 1965), 31–48, notes that Hart took a dim view of Beard but otherwise stresses his enlightened attitudes. Hart advocated Negro advancement and served as a Howard University trustee; he also worked toward the establishment of a Jewish homeland in Palestine.

99. W. Lloyd Warner, *The Living and the Dead: A Study of the Symbolic Life of Americans* (New Haven: Yale University Press, 1959), 122.

100. David M. Matteson (four), James Hosmer Penniman (one), Col. Samuel Vestal (one), Professor Archibald Henderson (one), Carl H. Claudy (one), and a committee of the American Library Association (one) wrote the remainder. Matteson dealt with rather broad, abstract topics (e.g., #6, "Washington, the Colonial and National Statesman," and #7, "Washington and the Constitution") whereas the others dealt with areas of Washington's life in which they were particularly expert. See *George Washington Bicentennial Celebration*, vol. 1, 2, for an index to the "Honor to George Washington" series.

101. *Handbook of the George Washington Appreciation Course*, especially xi.

102. Ibid., xi–vii.

103. "Make Washington Your Ideal," *Special News Releases*, 49–50.

104. From Albert Bushnell Hart, pamphlet #2, "Washington the Man of Mind," part I ("Practical Education"), in *George Washington Bicentennial Celebration*, vol. 1, 17.

105. Ibid., 18–19.

106. Bloom, "Questions and Answers," *George Washington Bicentennial Celebration*, vol. 3, 687.

107. "Grant Wood Presents Parson Weems," *Art Digest*, 15 January 1940, 7.

108. Ritter, *Washington as a Business Man*, 12 and 17.

109. Ibid., 17–18 and 21.

110. Ibid., 22, 255, and 286–287.

111. Sol Bloom, pamphlet #2, "Washington the Business Man," in *George Washington Bicentennial Celebration*, vol. 1, 135.

112. Ibid., 135 and 145.

113. Ibid., 146.

114. Sol Bloom, "Washington the Every Day Man," address delivered before the Kiwanis Club and other civic groups, at Wilkes-Barre, Pennsylvania, June 30, 1932, in "Selected Bicentennial Addresses Delivered by Hon. Sol Bloom," *George Washington Bicentennial Celebration*, vol. 2, 153–155.

115. Sol Bloom, "American Farm Bureau Federation Independence Day Address," delivered on the American Farm Bureau Federation Nationwide Farmers' Bicentennial Program, National Broadcasting Company, July 4, 1932, in *George Washington Bicentennial Celebration*, vol. 2, 155–157.

12. A George Washington for All Occasions

1. Van Wyck Brooks, "On Creating a Usable Past," *Dial*, 11 April 1918, 339. See also Alfred Haworth Jones, "The Search for a Usable Past in the New Deal Era," *American Quarterly*, 23, no. 4 (December 1971), 710–724.

2. John Dos Passos, *The Ground We Stand On: Some Examples from the History of a Political Creed* (New York: Harcourt Brace Jovanovich, 1941), 3.

3. Alfred Kazin, "What Have the 30's Done to Our Literature?" *New York Herald Tribune Books*, 31 December 1939, 1.

4. T. S. Eliot, *After Strange Gods* of 1933, quoted in Michael Kammen, *A Season of Youth: The American Revolution and the Historical Imagination* (New York: Alfred A. Knopf, 1978), xxiii, posits that knowing "what in the past is worth preserving" will help create "the society we desire."

5. The Archives building was dedicated in 1937; the murals were completed in November of 1936. Michael Kammen, *A Machine That Would Go of Itself: The Constitution in American Culture* (New York: Alfred A. Knopf, 1986), 303, quotes Faulkner himself, speaking of a cocktail party held before a backdrop of the finished murals in the big room above Grand Central Station where he painted them: "As the crowd of guests moved between the life-sized figures of the murals, there was a slight alcoholic confusion in my mind as to which was which."

6. In 1941 Helen Lundeberg finished a petrochrome mural called *George Washington: Valley Forge, 1777* under the auspices of the government's WPA program, in the foyer of the auditorium at George Washington High School in Los Angeles; see Nancy Dustin Wall Moure, *Painting and Sculpture in Los Angeles, 1900–1945* (Los Angeles: Los Angeles County Museum of Art, 1980), 51. Lundeberg also did another Washington mural under the same auspices in 1943 in Patriotic Hall, Los Angeles. For a state sample of this kind of iconography, see Steven M. Gelber, "Guide to New Deal Art in California," in *New Deal Art: California* (Santa Clara: deSaisset Art Gallery and Museum, University of Santa Clara, 1976), 97. For the use of historical themes in New Deal mural painting, see my *Wall-to-Wall America: A Cultural History of Post-Office Murals in the Great Depression* (Minneapolis: University of Minnesota Press, 1982), 189–237, and "A Note on New Deal Iconography: Futurology and the Historical Myth," in *Prospects: An Annual of American Cultural Studies*, vol. 4 (New York: Burt Franklin, 1979), 420–440.

The major Washington artwork of the period is the "Life of Washington" series of stained glass windows created in 1936 by George Pearse Ennis under the auspices of the WPA's Federal Art Project for the cadets' mess at West Point; see *London Studio*, April 1936, 237.

7. Douglass Adair, "The New Thomas Jefferson" (1946), in *Fame and the Founding Fathers*, ed. H. Trevor Colbourn (New York: W. W. Norton, 1974), 239. The cover of *The Democratic Book, 1936* (Philadelphia: Democratic National Committee, 1936) features a medallion, superimposed on the dome of the U.S. Capitol, showing twin profiles of Jefferson and Roosevelt and the legend "1801–1936." In 1933, Sears built replicas of Mount Vernon and Federal Hall for ongoing Brooklyn observances of the Washington bicentennial; see Katherine Cole Stevenson and H. Ward Jandl, eds., *Houses by Mail: A Guide to Houses from Sears, Roebuck and Company* (Washington, D.C.: Preservation Press, 1986), 25. These replicas do not

seem out of place among the contemporary precut houses offered for sale by Sears in the 1930s.

8. The love story of Lincoln in New Salem dominated three important dramatic manifestations of the Lincoln legend in the 1930s. In 1938, the WPA's Federal Theatre Project opened *Prologue to Glory* on Broadway. Later that year, Raymond Massey brought Robert Sherwood's version of the story—*Abe Lincoln in Illinois*—to Broadway, too. Massey also starred in a film version of the Sherwood play, produced by RKO in the summer of 1939. John Ford's evocative film, *Young Mr. Lincoln,* with Henry Fonda in the title role and Pauline Moore as Ann Rutledge, opened the same year. See John O'Connor and Lorraine Brown, eds., *Free, Adult, Uncensored: The Living History of the Federal Theatre Project* (Washington, D.C.: New Republic Books, 1978), especially 15–16; Alfred Haworth Jones, *Roosevelt's Image Brokers: Poets, Playwrights, and the Use of the Lincoln Symbol* (Port Washington, N.Y.: Kennikat, 1974), 35–44, and 51; and Peter Bogdanovich, *John Ford,* rev. ed. (Berkeley: University of California Press, 1978), 72–73 and 134.

9. Rex Alan Smith, *The Carving of Mount Rushmore* (New York: Abbeville, 1985), 313.

10. For Jefferson iconography during the New Deal period, see Merrill D. Peterson, *The Jefferson Image in the American Mind* (New York: Oxford University Press, 1960), especially 420–432. For the poem "Thomas Jefferson," see Rosemary and Stephen Vincent Benét, *A Book of Americans* (New York: Rinehart, 1933), 39–41. The "George Washington" verse, 28–29, is a little dull:

> . . . The first in war, the first in peace,
> The goodly and the great.
> But when you think about him now,
> From here to Valley Forge,
> Remember this—he might have been
> A highly different specimen,
> And where on earth would we be,
>   then?
> I'm glad that George was George.

11. For Sherwood's Lincoln, see the ad, *New York Herald Tribune,* 30 April 1939, 58, sec. XI. A number of historical novels described in the same literary section and issue of the paper ("Gateway to the World's Fair") also dealt with the colonial period; these include Van Wyck Mason's *Three Harbors,* Kenneth Roberts's *Northwest Passage* (then in its twenty-fourth printing), and Bruce Lancaster's *Guns of Burgoyne.*

12. *Wall and Nassau: An Account of the Inauguration of George Washington in Federal Hall at Wall and Nassau Streets, April 30, 1789* (New York: Bankers Trust Company, 1939), 13, and Stanley Appelbaum, ed., *The New York World's Fair 1939/1940* (New York: Dover, 1977), xi.

13. Gilmore D. Clarke to Lee Lawrie, December 8, 1936, in Lee Lawrie Papers, Library of Congress, Box 36 (New York World's Fair Correspondence, November 30–December 31, 1936).

14. Sol Bloom, *The Autobiography of Sol Bloom* (New York: G. P. Putnam's Sons, 1948), 222–224, and [Sol Bloom,] *George Washington, the President: Triumphant Journey as President-Elect, First Term of the First President, 1789–1939* (Washington, D.C.: United States Sesquicentennial Commission, 1939). Four mystifying nudes by Leo Friedlander, purporting to represent the four freedoms, were erected on Constitution Mall behind the statue of George Washington, where they were quietly forgotten.

15. Helen A. Harrison, "The Fair Perceived: Color and Light as Elements in Design and Planning," in Helen A. Harrison et al., *Dawn of a New Day: The New York World's Fair, 1939/40* (New York: New York University Press, 1980), 46–47.

16. *New York World's Fair of 1939 Incorporated: Program for the Development of the Central Mall,* undated, filed with C. L. Lee to Lawrie, December 31, 1936; Lee Lawrie Papers, Library of Congress.

17. William Adams Delano to Lee Lawrie, May 25, 1937, Lee Lawrie Papers, Library of Congress. I am grateful to Professor Timothy Garvey of Illinois Wesleyan University for sharing this interesting body of documentation on the Washington statue with me.

18. For the painting entitled *George Washington and New York,* see Parker Tyler, *Florine Stettheimer: A Life in Art* (New York: Farrar, Straus, 1963), 170–172. See also Linda Nochlin, "Florine Stettheimer," in Ann Sutherland Harris and Linda Nochlin, *Woman Artists: 1550–1950* (New York: Alfred A. Knopf, 1976), 266–267. For Moran, see "Abe Lincoln: Frank Weston Moran's Kitchen Companion," *Heritage: The Magazine of the New York State Historical Association,* January-February 1985, unpaginated plate.

The standard presentation of Washington by folk artists is iconic and hieratic: see Douglas C. McGill, "A New Look at Folk Art," *New York Times,* 1 August 1986, C28, cols. 2–3, for a painting by the Rev. Howard Finster called *Vision of George Washington in the New World.* See also Didi Barrett, *Muffled Voices:*

Folk Artists in Contemporary America (New York: Museum of Folk Art, 1985). I am grateful to Nick De Marco and Adam Weinberg for calling this material to my attention.

19. Elizabeth McCausland, *A. H. Maurer* (New York: A. A. Wyn, 1951), 237.

20. Quoted in ibid., 244.

21. Ibid., 233. See also Sheldon Reich, *Alfred H. Maurer, 1868–1932* (Washington, D.C.: Smithsonian Institution, 1973), 105–109, and 113.

22. Grover Whalen, *Mr. New York* (New York: G. P. Putnam's Sons, 1955), 174.

23. Ibid., 175–176.

24. Henry Chase Hill, ed., *The New Wonder Book of Knowledge,* special World's Fair ed. (Philadelphia: John C. Winston, 1939), introduction, makes the function of Washington at the fair clear: "Here are exhibits that would have startled George Washington, showing how time and distance have been reduced to zero."

25. Quoted in *Official Guidebook of the New York World's Fair, 1939* (New York: Exposition Publications, 1939), 41.

26. Ibid., 40–41, quoting Whalen.

27. James Truslow Adams, "1789–1939: A Nation Rises," *New York Times,* 5 March 1939, 7, sec. 8.

28. See *New York Times,* 2 April 1939, 31, sec. 1, cols. 3–7. A number of giveaway color lithographs of the period depicting the inauguration of Washington in New York appear to have been produced for New York City's 1939 observances.

29. [Architect of the Capitol, under the direction of the Joint Committee on the Library], *Compilation of Works of Art and Other Objects in the United States Capitol* (Washington, D.C.: Government Printing Office, 1965), 138.

30. In 1940 American Potters also produced a matching Martha Washington toby jug in creamware along the same with modish lines.

31. Warren I. Susman, "The People's Fair: Cultural Contradictions of a Consumer Society," in *Dawn of a New Day,* 21.

32. For the Hollywood liberty bond drive in Wall Street, see Lary May, *Screening Out the Past: The Birth of Mass Culture and the Motion Picture Industry* (New York: Oxford University Press, 1980), 195.

33. Program notes for *Duck Soup,* Bijou Winter Film Series, University of Minnesota, January 13–14, 1984.

34. *The Depression Years as Photographed by Arthur Rothstein* (New York: Dover, 1978), frontispiece.

I am grateful to M. Sue Kendall for calling this picture to my attention.

35. "Washington," *New Yorker,* 24 February 1940, 12–13. E. M. Delafield, *The Provincial Lady in America* (Chicago: Academy Chicago Press, 1984), 186, describes that visitor's pilgrimage to Mount Vernon. She inquires "where the historical cherry tree can be seen" and is disappointed to learn that "the cherry-tree episode [is] now practically discredited." The "provincial lady" visited America to attend the Century of Progress Exposition in Chicago; the account of the trip was first published in 1934.

36. Robert Minor, quoted in Robert Bendiner, *Just Around the Corner: A Highly Selective History of the Thirties* (New York: Harper & Row, 1967), 98–99. David M. Oshinsky, *A Conspiracy So Immense: The World of Joe McCarthy* (New York: Free Press, 1983), 90, tells of the Young Communist League hiring a horse and rider to trot down Broadway one April morning in the 1930s when the DAR neglected its annual salute to the beginning of the Revolution. The rider carried a sign that read "The DAR Forgets but the YCL Remembers."

37. Quoted in *This Fabulous Century, 1930–1940,* vol. 4 (New York: Time-Life Books, 1969), 210–213.

38. Margaret Brown Klapthor and Howard Alexander Morrison, *George Washington: A Figure upon the Stage* (Washington, D.C.: Smithsonian Institution Press, 1982), 86, and Bendiner, *Just Around the Corner,* 213 and plate opposite 209.

39. *Wallace Nutting Final Edition Furniture Catalogue* (Farmington, Mass.: [Wallace Nutting,] 1937), unpaginated.

40. Maxwell Anderson, *Valley Forge: A Play in Three Acts* (New York: Samuel French, 1937), 3–4 and 108. This is the acting edition of a script written in 1934.

41. Quoted in Joseph McBride and Michael Wilmington, *John Ford* (New York: Da Capo Press, 1975), 42–43. I am grateful to Rob Silberman for calling Ford's remarks to my attention.

42. Quoted in William Bragg Ewald, Jr., *Who Killed Joe McCarthy?* (New York: Simon and Schuster, 1984), 29.

43. Program notes for *This Is the Army,* Bijou Film Series, "Popular Images of World War II in the Movies," University of Minnesota, April 20–21, 1984.

44. Scott Meredith, *George S. Kaufman and His Friends* (Garden City, N.Y.: Doubleday, 1974), 555, and Malcolm Goldstein, *George S. Kaufman: His Life and His Theater* (New York: Oxford University Press, 1979),

334–335. Henry F. Woods, *American Sayings* (New York: Duell, Sloan, & Pearce, 1945), 275, comments on the title of the 1940 production but cannot trace the origin of the familiar catch phrase: "The claim, 'Washington slept here,' made for so many places without supporting evidence, has become one which tourists and historians view skeptically," he notes. In 1936, George S. Kaufman and Katharine Dayton wrote *First Lady,* a Washington, D.C., drawing-room comedy. A publicity picture from the Broadway production showed the costars, Jane Cowl and Lily Cahill, snuggling up to one of Sol Bloom's authorized 1932 plaster George Washington busts; see *Vanity Fair,* February 1936, 44. The worshipful pose with a likeness of Washington had sometimes been used for children by nineteenth-century photographers.

45. Program notes, "The John Ford Barbecue," Walker Art Center, Minneapolis, Minnesota, July 28, 1984. Tom Russell and Ken Ellison, who attended the "barbecue" with me, confirmed these sightings of Washington.

46. Thomas S. Buechner, *Norman Rockwell: Artist and Illustrator* (New York: Harry N. Abrams, 1970), plate 609.

47. I am grateful to Ernst Busche, in 1984 a visiting professor at Cleveland State University, for sharing his research on "Roy Lichtenstein's Heroic America" with me. See also Diane Waldman, *Roy Lichtenstein* (New York: Solomon R. Guggenheim Museum, 1969), 25; John Coplans, ed., *Roy Lichtenstein* (New York: Praeger, 1972); and Sidra Stich, *Made in U.S.A.: An Americanization in Modern Art, The '50s and '60s* (Berkeley: University of California Press, 1987), 18.

48. Captions in *National Geographic,* July 1952, 14–15.

49. *Life,* 3 July 1950, especially 46–51. *National Geographic,* February 1951, 181–187, ran a similar feature.

50. "Early American Folk Art Records the 19th Century," *Life,* 2 July 1951, 69.

51. Larry Rivers, *Drawings and Digressions* (New York: Clarkson N. Potter, 1979), 59.

52. Ibid., 59; from the text of a radio lecture delivered in 1952.

53. Helen A. Harrison, *Larry Rivers* (New York: Harper & Row, 1984), 37. See also Suzanne Ferguson, "Crossing the Delaware with Larry Rivers and Frank O'Hara: The Post-Modern Hero of the Battle of Signifiers," *Word & Image,* 2, no. 1 (January–March 1986), 27–32. O'Hara's poem "On Seeing Larry Rivers' *Wash-ington Crossing the Delaware* at the Museum of Modern Art" was written in 1955.

54. *Advise and Consent* was screened by Channel 41 in Minneapolis/St. Paul on August 6, 1985; my friend and colleague Rob Silberman was kind enough to share with me his insights on that movie and his ongoing research into American political film. Jackie Kennedy's dinner at Mount Vernon for the president of Pakistan is discussed in Hugh Sidey, "Standing By Eight Presidents," *Time,* 27 January 1986, 22. Edward Albee's *Who's Afraid of Virginia Woolf?* (New York: Signet/New American Library, 1962) opened on Broadway in 1962; the film version with Richard Burton and Elizabeth Taylor appeared in 1966.

55. "Twentieth Century Images of George Washington," illustrated checklist of an exhibition held at the Fraunces Tavern Museum, New York, 1982. See especially #18, Bruce Hafley, *Washington Never Sleeps* (1969); #2, Alex Katz, *George Washington* (1961), a cutout figure made for a production of Kenneth Koch's *Washington Crossing the Delaware* and now in the collection of the National Museum of American Art (gift of Mr. and Mrs. David K. Anderson; Martha Jackson Memorial Collection) along with a cutout boat, a horse, ice floes, rowers, and so on; #8, George Deem, *George Washington Vermeer* (1974); and #12, Edward Sorel, *Nixon Crossing the Delaware* (1972). I am grateful to my colleague Sidney Simon for calling this exhibition and Robert Arneson's various Washington sculptures to my attention.

Pop artists in general, insofar as they were interested in the icons of commercial America, included oblique Washington references in their work; sculptor Claes Oldenburg's series of proposed replacements for existing public monuments included a giant functional scissors to be placed on the site of the Washington Monument, for example.

56. *The Bicentennial of the United States of America: A Final Report to the People,* vol. 1 (Washington, D.C.: American Revolution Bicentennial Administration, 1977), 96.

57. Quoted in Ted Howard, ed., *The P.B.C.: A History* (Washington, D.C.: Peoples Bicentennial Commission, 1976), 45.

58. *Bicentennial of the United States,* vol. 1, 106–107.

59. *The P.B.C.,* 4.

60. *Bicentennial of the United States,* vol. 4, IV, 20, 126, 207, and 381, and vol. 1, 172.

61. Ibid., vol. 1, introduction and 254–255, and vol. 2, 474–480.

62. Ibid., vol. 1, 72–75. See also such masterpieces of tie-in advertising as the Magnavox "Spirit of '76" stereo-in-a-dry-sink promotion, in Curtis F. Brown, *Star-Spangled Kitsch* (New York: Universe, 1975), 75 and 84.

63. *Bicentennial of the United States,* vol. 1, 126 and 165.

64. David Jacobs, *Disney's America on Parade* (New York: Harry N. Abrams, 1975), 49 and 73; it is important for understanding Washington's non-status in the bicentennial year to note that he was *not* the subject of a Disney parade float.

65. *Bicentennial of the United States,* vol. 5, 324–325.

66. For another perspective on the bicentennial and particularly on exhibitions connected with the anniversary, see Kammen, *Season of Youth,* 90–103.

67. *Bicentennial of the United States,* vol. 1, 222–223, and vol. 5, 399.

68. Quoted in Rosewell Angier and Norman Hurst, *The Patriot Game* (Boston: David R. Godine, 1975).

69. Quoted in ibid., opposite a photograph of a tourist photographing an old print of George Washington.

70. Pauline Kael, "Foundering Fathers," *New Yorker,* 25 November 1972, 180–181.

71. See, eg., a 1973 magazine ad for Stieff silver in a "Williamsburg Shell Pattern," in Walter C. Kidney, *The Architecture of Choice: Eclecticism in America, 1880–1930* (New York: George Braziller, 1974), plate 150. In the 1980s the Henry Francis duPont Winterthur Museum also began a vigorous campaign of marketing copies, adaptations, and furnishings "in the manner" of the objects in that superb collection.

72. For the Kennedy dinner, see Sidey, "Standing by Eight Presidents," *Time,* 27 January 1986, 22. For the redecoration, see Ben A. Franklin, "Mount Vernon Gets the Brighter Colors That Washington Preferred," *Minneapolis Tribune,* 28 February 1982, 3, sec. E, cols. 1–6.

73. Klapthor and Morrison, *George Washington,* part 2, 98 ff.

74. See, e.g., ad for Schumacher fabric, in *New Yorker,* 1 April 1985, 48–49.

75. Marcus Cunliffe, "The National Symbol Named George Washington," *Smithsonian,* February 1982, 74–81. A particularly nice example of recent Washingtoniana deliberately confusing the hero with modern media celebrities is the copyrighted Ken Brown postcard of 1984 showing Boy George and Martha Washington as "George and Martha."

76. See mail-order catalogue for Collector's Guild, Ltd. of New York, ca. 1982–83, offering a 10½″ copy of the Gorham Houdon bust, in an edition of 950, on sale: the item was reduced from $250 to $125. See also the ad of the Rhode Island Tourist Promotion Division, from *Americana,* 9, no. 1 (March–April 1981), known to the author from a clipping kindly provided by the staff of the Rare Book Room, Wilson Library, the University of Minnesota. The Fisher-Price tape, issued in 1983, is part of a series that includes others on Ben Franklin, the American Revolution, *The Wizard of Oz, The Three Little Pigs,* and *Tom Sawyer.*

77. *The Story of Walt Disney World* (n.p.: Walt Disney Productions, 1973), 32–33. See also "The Court of Liberty," an undated flier issued by Forest Lawn of Los Angeles, ca. 1984–85. There is also a very large reproduction of the J. Q. A. Ward Washington at Forest Lawn.

78. *Time,* 16 May 1983, advertising section between 42 and 47, and *Time,* 9 February 1987, after 12.

79. James Wilcox, *Modern Baptists* (New York: Penguin, 1984), 175.

80. I examined these syndicated cartoons in the *Minneapolis Star and Tribune:* Elrod and Alley, *The Ryatts* (July 18, 1985); Ralph Dunagin, *Dunagin's People* (February 10, 1984 and February 16, 1987); Bil Keane, *The Family Circus* (February 16, 1987); Jeff MacNelly, *Shoe* (November 13, 1984); and Charles Schulz, *Peanuts* (January 4, 1985).

81. Joyce Wackenhut and Arthur Weinberger, "It's the Truth: Everybody Lies at Least Some of the Time," *Minneapolis Star and Tribune,* 7 May 1984, 1, sec. C, cols. 1–5.

82. Paul F. Levy, "George Washington—First in War, Peace and Big Expense Accounts," clipping from *National Inquirer,* 20 February 1984.

83. Richard D. Amelar, M.D., letter to the editor, *Bryn Mawr Now,* Spring 1983, 13.

84. In February of 1985, one of the docents at the Winterthur Museum who heard of my interest in Washington was kind enough to tell me about her husband's club and some of its recent activities.

85. Hugh Sidey, "Above All, the Man Had Character," *Time,* 21 February 1983, 24–25.

86. From the dust jacket of Garry Wills, *Cincinnatus: George Washington and the Enlightenment* (Garden City, N.Y.: Doubleday, 1984).

87. Irving Kristol, quoted in Edwin M. Yoder, Jr., "George Washington: The Nation's Father Remains a Stranger," *Minneapolis Tribune,* 20 February 1984, 12, sec. A, cols. 1–6.

88. All the major networks repeated clips of the coin-toss and the half-time activities of January 20, 1985.

89. In Minneapolis, KSTP-AM carried the Paul Harvey broadcast at noon on August 8, 1985. The film with Al Pacino, Donald Sutherland, and Natassya Kinsky was released very briefly in 1985–86 to poor reviews; the video version has been more widely advertised.

90. See Bill Adler, *Ronnie and Nancy: A Very Special Love Story* (New York: Crown, 1985) for a geriatric romance pitched at an aging population; the TV series *The Love Boat,* now in syndication, aimed at the same audience. Debora Silverman, *Selling Culture: Bloomingdale's, Diana Vreeland, and the New Aristocracy of Taste in Reagan's America* (New York: Pantheon, 1986), decries the luxurious trappings of the Reagan presidency.

91. From an ad designed to resemble a news story and described as "Customer Information from General Motors," in *Time,* 22 September 1986, 11. The ad ran in all the major glossy weeklies and monthlies in the fall of 1986.

Credits

Frontispiece. Joe Bensen

1.1. Clarence Winthrop Bowen, ed., *The History of the Centennial Celebration of the Inauguration of George Washington as First President of the United States* (New York: D. Appleton, 1889), 45

1.2. Collection of the author

1.3. *Saturday Evening Post*, 23 February 1935, cover, © 1935 The Curtis Publishing Co.

1.4. Collection of the author

1.5. Library of Congress

1.6. Valley Forge Historical Society, Valley Forge, Pennsylvania

1.7. Valley Forge Historical Society; gift of John C. Countess

1.8. Library of Congress

1.9. Collection of the author

1.10. Architect of the Capitol

1.11. U.S. George Washington Bicentennial Commission reproduction in the collection of the author

1.12. Pennsylvania Academy of the Fine Arts, Philadelphia; John F. Lewis Memorial Collection, 1933

1.13. Collection of the author

1.14. Collection of the author

1.15. Library of Congress

1.16. *History of the United States George Washington Bicentennial Celebration*, vol. 1 (Washington, D.C.: U.S. George Washington Bicentennial Commission, 1932), 587

1.17. Collection of the author

1.18. © J. L. G. Ferris, Archives of '76, Bay Village, Ohio

1.19. Library of Congress

1.20. George Canby and Lloyd Balderston, *The Evolution of the American Flag* (Philadelphia: Ferris and Leach, 1909), unpaginated plate

1.21. Collection of the author

1.22. Carole Springer photo, *Main Line Times*

1.23. © 1985 American Broadcasting Companies, Inc., and Minneapolis–St. Paul affiliate, KSTP-TV

1.24. Donaldson's (Minneapolis), a division of Allied Stores

1.25. Republic Airlines

1.26. Collection of the author

2.1. *Frank Leslie's Illustrated Historical Register of the Centennial Exposition 1876* (New York: Frank Leslie's Publishing House, 1877), 113

2.2 *Harper's Weekly*, 23 September 1876, 781

2.3. Collection of the author

2.4. Margaret Woodbury Strong Museum, Rochester, New York

2.5. Margaret Woodbury Strong Museum

2.6. Margaret Woodbury Strong Museum

2.7. New-York Historical Society, New York City; Landauer Collection

2.8. National Museum of American History, Smithsonian Institution; gift of Leonard Carmichael

2.9. J. S. Ingram, *The Centennial Exposition Described and Illustrated* (Philadelphia: Hubbard Bros., 1876), 609

2.10. Society for the Preservation of New England Antiquities

2.11. *Harper's Weekly*, 16 September 1876, 752

2.12. Connecticut Historical Society

2.13. *Frank Leslie's Illustrated Historical Register*, 90

2.14. Missouri Historical Society

2.15. Mary Northend Collection, Society for the Preservation of New England Antiquities

2.16. Ingram, *Centennial Exposition*, 260

2.17. Brooklyn Museum; gift of the Crescent-Hamilton Athletic Club

2.18. *Harper's Weekly*, 25 March 1876, 244

441

3.1. New Jersey State Museum, Trenton

3.2. Schell and Hogan illustration, *Harper's Weekly*, 13 May 1876, 384

3.3. *Frank Leslie's Illustrated Historical Register*, 228

3.4. New-York Historical Society

3.5. Society for the Preservation of New England Antiquities

3.6. *Harper's Weekly*, 4 March 1876, cover

3.7. *Harper's Weekly*, 8 July 1876, 548

3.8. *Harper's New Monthly Magazine*, February 1876, 321

3.9. New-York Historical Society

3.10. Metropolitan Museum of Art; gift of George I. Seney, 1877. All rights reserved, The Metropolitan Museum

3.11. Corcoran Gallery of Art, Washington, D.C.; gift of the American Art Association

3.12. Shelburne Museum, Shelburne, Vermont

3.13. *The Writings of Nathaniel Hawthorne*, vol. 12 (Boston: Houghton Mifflin, 1900), frontispiece

3.14. Milwaukee Art Museum; Layton Art Collection

3.15. National Museum of American Art, Smithsonian Institution; bequest of Harriet Lane Johnston

3.16. *Harper's Weekly*, 25 February 1860, cover

3.17. Frederick L. Harvey, *History of the Washington National Monument and Washington National Monument Society* (Washington, D.C.: Government Printing Office, 1903), unpaginated plate

3.18. Corcoran Gallery of Art; gift of William Wilson Corcoran

3.19. Essex institute, Salem, Massachusetts; Frank Cousins Collection

3.20. Benson J. Lossing, *The Home of Washington; or, Mount Vernon and Its Associations, Historical, Biographical, and Pictorial* (Hartford: A. S. Hale, 1870), 338

4.1. Halsey C. Ives, *Photographic Views of the World's Columbian Exposition* (St. Louis: N. D. Thompson, 1893), unpaginated

4.2. Ives, *Photographic Views*, unpaginated

4.3. James W. Shepp and Daniel B. Shepp, *Shepp's World's Fair Photographs* (Chicago: Globe Bible, 1893), 435

4.4. *American Historical Register*, 1, no. 1 (September 1894), 15

4.5. Copyrighted by the White House Historical Association; photograph by the National Geographic Society

4.6. *Harper's Weekly*, 8 December 1883, cover

4.7. *Harper's Weekly*, 8 December 1883, 785

4.8. Collection of the author

4.9. *St. Nicholas*, August 1886, 758

4.10. *St. Nicholas*, September 1886, 839

4.11. *St. Nicholas*, July 1886, 669

4.12. *St. Nicholas*, October 1886, 909

4.13. *Magazine of American History*, 20, no. 6 (December 1888), 447

4.14. *Harper's Weekly*, 11 May 1889, cover

4.15. Clarence Winthrop Bowen, ed., *The History of the Centennial Celebration of the Inauguration of George Washington as First President of the United States* (New York: D. Appleton, 1892), facing 204

4.16. *Life*, 18 April 1889, 230–231

4.17. *Harper's Weekly*, 11 May 1889, 372

5.1 *Magazine of American History*, 21, no. 5 (May 1889), 363

5.2. *Harper's Weekly*, 27 April 1889, 336

5.3. Bowen, ed., *History of the Centennial Celebration*, 16

5.4. *Harper's Weekly*, 11 May 1889, 378

5.5. Bowen, ed., *History of the Centennial Celebration*, facing 234

5.6. *Harper's Weekly*, 11 May 1889, 375

5.7. Bowen, ed., *History of the Centennial Celebration*, facing 129

5.8 *Century Magazine*, April 1889, 840

5.9 *Harper's Weekly*, 27 April 1889, 333

5.10. Bowen, ed., *History of the Centennial Celebration*, facing 144

5.11. Collection of the author

5.12. *Harper's Weekly*, 4 May 1889, 359

5.13. *Harper's Weekly*, 11 May 1889, 375

5.14. *Harper's Weekly*, 11 May 1889, 369

5.15. *Harper's Weekly*, 4 May 1889, 353

5.16. *Harper's Weekly*, 11 May 1889, 379

5.17. Bowen, ed., *History of the Centennial Celebration*, 391

5.18. Bowen, ed., *History of the Centennial Celebration*, 396

5.19. *The Washington Centenary, Celebrated in New-York, April 29, 30–May 1, 1889* (New York: Tribune Association, 1889), frontispiece

5.20. *Harper's Weekly*, 11 May 1889, 376

5.21. Woodrow Wilson, "Colonel Washington," *Harper's New Monthly Magazine*, March 1896, 572

5.22. Woodrow Wilson, "First in Peace," *Harper's New Monthly Magazine*, September 1896, 496

5.23. Marion Harland, *Some Colonial Homesteads and Their Stories* (New York: G. P. Putnam's Sons, 1900), frontispiece

6.1. *Imre Kiralfy's Grand Historical Spectacle America* (Chicago: Imre Kiralfy, 1893), unpaginated plate
6.2. *Kiralfy's America*, cover
6.3. Walter B. Stevens, *The Forest City, Comprising the Official Photographic Views of the Universal Exposition Held in Saint Louis, 1904* (St. Louis: N. D. Thompson, 1904), unpaginated plate
6.4. Stevens, *Forest City*, unpaginated plate
6.5. Stevens, *Forest City*, unpaginated plate
6.6. Stevens, *Forest City*, unpaginated plate
6.7. *Life*, 2 February 1899, 97
6.8. Collection of the author
6.9. Alice Morse Earle, *Home Life in Colonial Days* (New York: Macmillan, 1898), 359
6.10. Earle, *Home Life in Colonial Days*, 147
6.11. Society for the Preservation of New England Antiquities; Mary Northend Collection
6.12. Society for the Preservation of New England Antiquities; Mary Northend Collection
6.13. Society for the Preservation of New England Antiquities; Mary Northend Collection
6.14. Collection of the author
6.15. Collection of the author
6.16. Collection of the author
6.17. *Red Cedar Chests* (Statesville, N.C.: Piedmont Red-Cedar Chest Company, 1910), 8–9; reproduced by permission of the Henry Francis duPont Winterthur Museum Library: Collection of Printed Books
6.18. Olin Dows, *Franklin Roosevelt at Hyde Park* (New York: American Artists Group, 1949), 158
6.19. *1923 Catalogue* (Chicago: Sears, Roebuck Company, 1923), 626
6.20. *Saturday Evening Post*, 27 March 1920, 144–145; used by permission of General Electric Company

7.1. *Movie Week*, 10 June 1923, back cover
7.2. Collection of the author
7.3. *Dodgeville* (Wisconsin) *Chronicle*, 22 January 1909, unpaginated
7.4. Collection of the author
7.5. Ralph Davol, *A Handbook of American Pageantry* (Taunton, Mass.: Davol Publishing Co., 1914), frontispiece
7.6. Davol, *Handbook of American Pageantry*, unpaginated plate

7.7. Davol, *Handbook of American Pageantry*, unpaginated plate
7.8. Davol, *Handbook of American Pageantry*, unpaginated plate
7.9. Davol, *Handbook of American Pageantry*, unpaginated plate
7.10. Davol, *Handbook of American Pageantry*, unpaginated plate
7.11. Edward Hagaman Hall, *The Hudson-Fulton Celebration 1909: The Fourth Annual Report of the Hudson-Fulton Celebration Commission to the Legislature*, vol. 1 (Albany: State of New York/J. B. Lyon, 1910), 1275
7.12. Hall, *Hudson-Fulton Celebration*, 665
7.13. Hall, *Hudson-Fulton Celebration*, 647
7.14. Hall, *Hudson-Fulton Celebration*, 655
7.15. Hall, *Hudson-Fulton Celebration*, 667
7.16. Davol, *Handbook of American Pageantry*, unpaginated plate
7.17. Metropolitan Museum of Art. All rights reserved
7.18. Metropolitan Museum of Art. All rights reserved
7.19. R. T. H. Halsey and Elizabeth Tower, *The Homes of Our Ancestors* (New York: Doubleday, Page, 1925), facing 41
7.20. *Saturday Evening Post*, 4 March 1922, 96
7.21. Collection of the author

8.1. National Park Service; photo by S. Sydney Bradford
8.2. *Life*, 20 February 1902, 149
8.3. Collection of the author
8.4. Collection of the author
8.5. Collection of the author
8.6. *Good Housekeeping*, February 1921, unpaginated ad; used by permission of General Foods Corporation (Jell-O is a registered trademark of General Foods Corporation)

9.1. Ernest C. Carpenter, *The Boyhood Days of President Calvin Coolidge; or, From the Green Mountains to the White House*, 2d ed. (Rutland, Vt.: Tuttle, 1926), 43
9.2. William Allen White, *Calvin Coolidge: The Man Who Is President* (New York: Macmillan, 1925), 243
9.3. Henry Ford Museum and Greenfield Village, Dearborn, Michigan
9.4. Henry Ford Museum and Greenfield Village
9.5. Henry Ford Museum and Greenfield Village
9.6. *Foshay Spot Light*, September 1929, cover

9.7. *Philadelphia Public Ledger*, 1 January 1926, 2, sec. 1, cols. 3–5

9.8. *Philadelphia Public Ledger*, 17 January 1926, 1, pictorial section, part 1

9.9. E. L. Austin and Odell Hauser, *The Sesqui-Centennial International Exposition* (Philadelphia: Current Publications, 1929), unpaginated plate

9.10. *Philadelphia Public Ledger*, 4 July 1926, 6, sec. 1, cols. 3–5

9.11. *Mentor*, June 1929, 1

9.12. *Saturday Evening Post*, 2 February 1929, 114; used by permission of PYA/Monarch, Inc.

10.1. Collection of the author

10.2. *Harper's Weekly*, 20 February 1904, 27

10.3. Minneapolis Institute of Arts and the Des Moines Art Center

11.1. Collection of the author

11.2. *History of the George Washington Bicentennial Celebration*, vol. 4, 102

11.3. *History of the George Washington Bicentennial Celebration*, vol. 4, 155

11.4. *History of the George Washington Bicentennial Celebration*, vol. 4, 168

11.5. Collection of the author

11.6. Collection of the author

11.7. Collection of the author

11.8. Cincinnati Art Museum; Edwin and Virginia Irwin Memorial Fund; © Estate of Grant Wood/ V.A.G.A., New York

11.9. Collection of the author

11.10. *History of the George Washington Bicentennial*, vol. 3, 691

11.11. Collection of the author

11.12. Collection of the author

11.13. *Handbook of the George Washington Appreciation Course for the Two Hundredth Anniversary Celebration of the Birth of George Washington* (Washington, D.C.: U.S. George Washington Bicentennial Commission, 1932), ii

11.14. Collection of the author

11.15. Collection of the author

11.16. Collection of the author

11.17. Collection of the author

11.18. Collection of the author

11.19. *Handbook of the George Washington Appreciation Course*, v

11.20. Collection of the author

11.21. Collection of the author

11.22. Collection of the author

11.23. Collection of the author

11.24. Amon Carter Museum, Fort Worth

11.25. Collection of the author

11.26. *Ladies' Home Journal*, February 1932, 13; collection of the author

11.27. Collection of the author

11.28. Collection of the author

11.29. Metropolitan Museum of Art; reproduced by permission of Associated American Artists

11.30. Collection of the author

12.1 University of Minnesota *Magazine of Art* Photo Archive

12.2. *New York Times*, 5 March 1939, sec. 8, cover.

12.3. New York State Historical Association, Cooperstown, New York

12.4. Portland Art Museum, Portland, Oregon; gift of Mr. and Mrs. Jan De Graaff

12.5. Sol Bloom, *The Story of the Constitution* (Washington, D.C.: U.S. Constitution Sesquicentennial Commission, 1937), cover

12.6. Bayart Reid photograph, University of Minnesota *Magazine of Art* Photo Archive

12.7. Collection of the author

12.8. Collection of the author

12.9. Collection of the author

12.10. Collection of the author

12.11. Library of Congress

12.12. UPI/Bettmann Newsphotos

12.13. Collection of the author

12.14. Professor Ernst Busche

12.15. *National Geographic*, July 1952, 14; © 1952 National Geographic Society

12.16. Museum of Modern Art; anonymous gift

12.17. *The Bicentennial of the United States of America: A Final Report to the People*, vol. 1 (Washington, D.C.: American Revolution Bicentennial Administration, 1977), 96

12.18. *Bicentennial of the United States*, vol. 4, 400

12.19. Joe Bensen

12.20. Joe Bensen

12.21. Joe Bensen

12.22. Collection of the author

12.23. © 1983, Hallmark Cards Inc., Kansas City, Missouri

Index